PLAYING THE OTHER

WOMEN IN CULTURE AND SOCIETY
A series edited by Catharine R. Stimpson

PLAYING THE OTHER

Gender and Society

in

Classical Greek Literature

FROMA I. ZEITLIN

THE UNIVERSITY OF CHICAGO PRESS

CHICAGO AND LONDON

Froma I. Zeitlin is the Charles Ewing Professor of Greek
Language and Literature at Princeton University.

The University of Chicago Press, Chicago 60637
The University of Chicago Press, Ltd., London
© 1996 by The University of Chicago
All rights reserved. Published 1996
Printed in the United States of America
05 04 03 02 01 00 99 98 97 96   5 4 3 2 1

ISBN (cloth): 0-226-97921-0
ISBN (paper): 0-226-97922-9

Library of Congress Cataloging-in-Publicaton Data

Zeitlin, Froma I.
    Playing the other : gender and society in classical
Greek literature / Froma I. Zeitlin
        p.   cm. — (Women in culture and society)
    Includes bibliographical references and index.
    ISBN 0-226-97921-0 — ISBN 0-226-97922-9 (pbk.)
    1. Greek literature—History and criticism.   2. Women
in literature.   3. Literature and society—Greece.
4. Gender identity in literature.   5. Women and
literature—Greece.   I. Title.
II. Series.
PA3016.W65Z44   1996
880.9′352042—dc20   95-2906
                                                        CIP

For Judith, Ariel, Claire, and Lida
dearly loved

CONTENTS

FOREWORD

Playing the Other: Gender and Society in Classical Greek Literature consists of essays that Froma I. Zeitlin has written from the late 1970s to the present. If published before, they have been revised for this book. Accessible to specialists and nonspecialists alike, the essays have a compelling subject: the literature of archaic and classical Greece, first the great figures of Homer and Hesiod, and next the equally monumental figures of the playwrights Aeschylus, Euripides, and Aristophanes, as well as the philosopher Plato, who died in 347 B.C., within two centuries of the birth of these playwrights. Using a multiplicity of methods, Zeitlin is anthropologist, linguist, historian, critic. She integrates these approaches to focus on a fundamental question: how did the Greeks use gender as an "organizing nucleus" of their literature and social imagination?

Zeitlin correctly refuses to label ancient Greek men simply as "patriarchs" and ancient Greek women simply as "oppressed." To be sure, Greek society was highly dimorphic. That is, it tended to act and think as if reality broke into two classes. Prime among these dualities is that of gender. Men and women are different, oppositional, and antagonistic. Men, moreover, exercise extensive powers that women cannot and must not touch. For the most part, Greek women were not allowed to appear in public as political or cultural figures—except on ritualistic occasions. Like that of Shakespeare, Greek theater had men play women's roles. Not surprisingly, the culture expressed a pervasive fear of the chaos and destruction that a role reversal, the "rule of women," might bring.

Despite this, Zeitlin knows that the phrase "powerful men/powerless women" inaccurately and inadequately captures Greek culture and society. Aware of the fluidity and dynamism of power, she shows how and why Greek literature and theater subvert rigid gender relations; how and why theater stages the encounter of "feminized males" and "masculinized women"; how and why Greek culture creates powerful women characters: a Clytemnestra, Hecuba, or Penelope; how and why a polytheistic system of divinities with potent female deities, for example the goddess Demeter, matters so much.

Codes also fascinate Zeitlin. They are systems in which things stand for something else again and again and again. The scholar/decoder shows how these systems operate to conceal and reveal meaning. Succinctly, Zeitlin calls Greece a "highly coded system of androcentric authority." The female was never simply a woman. Rather, she served a crucial cognitive, symbolic, and psychological function. She could represent the inside and internal, or nature, or, profoundly, the radical Other. In her commentary on the Greek theater, Zeitlin argues that the feminine was inseparable from the development of the genres of tragedy and comedy themselves.

Two essays on the theater are the last of the four sections of *Playing the Other*. The first, "Gender and Paradigm," explores master narratives of gender established in the works of Homer, Hesiod, and Aeschylus. These privileged models also serve as myths of origin for the state, society, and gender. Because Greece was a traditional society, it used and reused rather than neglecting these master narratives. The second section, "Gender and the Body," takes up the construction of womanhood and the several and significant consequences of essentializing woman as body. The third section, "Gender and Selfhood," then turns to the construction of manhood, what the boy must do to gain a self, especially if he is to be a citizen of a partially democratic Athens. Taken together, these sections embody Zeitlin's conviction that no one can study women without studying men; no one can study men without studying women; and no one can study history, culture, and society without studying gender.

I find a wonderful, indeed charismatic, mind at work in *Playing the Other*. Now a classicist of international reputation, Zeitlin was embarking upon her career when I first heard her lecture. Her topic was the Greek god Dionysos, commonly pictured as the god of wine, women, and song, an avatar of a contemporary rock star on tour. Her audience was a crop of undergraduates and junior faculty in a shabbily genteel college classroom, a site where few divinities rambled.

Zeitlin's lecture transfixed us. Her ideas were clear, original, supple, piercing. She asked us to see Dionysos as a figure of disruption, confusion, ambiguity, and tension. She conveyed her delight in first discovering the details of a myth, ritual, or text, in going further and further into these semantic fields in order to gather details; in then figuring out how a myriad of details cohered into a pattern; and finally, in showing how large patterns—aesthetic, social, ideological—fit together. She sought complexities, ironies, paradoxes, metamorphoses, and order. She thought structurally but never reductively. Within minutes, she routed the indifference to art and history that many students had lugged into the classroom.

We were spellbound by language, enthralled by recognizing both the otherness and the endurance of Greek culture.

A few years ago, wondering about the structure of this volume and the sequence that her essays might follow, Zeitlin spontaneously referred to them as "starbursts." Her introduction alludes to this figure of speech, as she writes that she wants "to see matters otherwise, to uncover what I called 'secrets' in the text, and [to search for] techniques for layering levels of analysis so as to draw them into the orbit of a broader cultural perspective—or, to use another metaphor, to fasten on a single essential nucleus from which other issues could radiate outward, sometimes unexpectedly, into a steady line of vision." Zeitlin's introduction explains her book better than any editor's foreword can, but I want to add another meaning to the starburst analogy. Zeitlin warmly and fully acknowledges the work of colleagues and other classicists. Even in this galaxy, her imaginative and scrupulous essays burn brightly. They are as tautly organized as a natural phenomenon, but they are fiery, glowing, and radiant with human creativity and intelligence.

Catharine R. Stimpson
Rutgers University (on leave)
Director, Fellows Program, MacArthur Foundation

ACKNOWLEDGMENTS

Reviewing these essays gave me the opportunity to recollect and record the many friends and colleagues who shared their thoughts and research with me, offered sound and invaluable advice, and proved a source of welcome (and needed) encouragement throughout these years. The individual essays acknowledge my many debts. Here I single out those good friends and congenial spirits who never fail to sustain me and whose work in turn has always enlightened me: Marylin Arthur (now Katz), Helene Foley, Page duBois, Georgia Nugent, and Nicole Loraux. I share with each a special and treasured bond of *homophrosunē*. I recall the late Jack Winkler, whose loss does not grow easier with time, and who taught me more than he ever knew. His vivid and engaging spirit lives on. Jean-Pierre Vernant occupies a position in my life and thought that can never adequately be described or appreciated. I shall not try.

I owe thanks to Marcel Detienne and to Pierre Vidal-Naquet for their illuminating work and enduring friendship, to François Lissarrague who has opened new windows for me in reading images and is an unfailing source of information and kindness, and to the Centre Louis Gernet and all its members for their affectionate hospitality over these many years. I mark my heartfelt appreciation also to Pierre Judet de la Combe, Philippe Borgeaud, and Claude Calame, whose work has always expanded my horizons and whose amicable company is a continuing source of pleasure. Gregory Nagy is an unending source of inspiration; James Redfield always knows how to turn a phrase or an idea into new and welcome perceptions. I have learned much from them both and count on their friendship. Piero Pucci possesses remarkable traits of integrity, creativity, and generosity; I have been fortunate in profiting from all three aspects, both at home and abroad. Likewise, I acknowledge the unstinting support and enthusiasm of Laura Slatkin, which, as many others can attest, she gives with such open-hearted abundance.

I make mention too of David Halperin for introducing new ways of thinking and reading and for all we shared in our collaboration; Eros will never look the same again. Neither will the body, as I have learned from Ann Hanson, whose responsiveness to others' work is more than noteworthy. Thanks also to David Quint for collegiality and sage advice. I have often imposed on him for both. Glenn Most remains an intellectual guidepost and an ebullient friend. His candor and acumen have rescued me more than once. Charles Segal's encouragement in earlier years is still vividly remembered. His prodigious accomplishments need no elaboration. Daniel Boyarin has provided fresh sources of revelation in enlarging my spheres of reference and in setting an example both for adventurous criticism and loyal trust. He has raised my sights, and I am grateful. I especially thank Simon Goldhill, an exacting critic and cherished comrade. His intellectual energy and keen perspicacity along with his willingness to engage in virtually unlimited discussion are gifts he has freely given and continues to give me. I do not take these for granted. His generosity of spirit and eagerness to share exemplify the communal rewards of the work we do.

I must also acknowledge my many students over the years who have contributed to my thinking in and out of seminar rooms, and who, to my joy, have gone on to find their own distinctive voices and do themselves proud. I cannot name them all, but I owe much to David Rosenbloom, Leslie Kurke, Rebecca Bushnell, Richard Goodkin, Patricia Rosenmeyer, Mark Padilla, Yopie Prins, Nancy Worman, Rafaël Newman, André Lardinois, Pavlos Sfyroeras, Deborah Lyons and Daniel Mendelsohn for instruction and continuing support.

My husband, George Zeitlin, has lived through these essays in more ways than one. That he has endured their (and my) vicissitudes is a tribute to his patience, love, and abiding faith in me. He is truly a man of valor. His worth is far above rubies.

I acknowledge my gratitude to the National Endowment for the Humanities in awarding me fellowships in 1975–76 and 1988–89, to the Guggenheim Foundation for a fellowship in 1984–85, and to Princeton University for supporting sabbatical leaves and funds for research. My thanks too to Kings College, Cambridge, which more than once has welcomed me for extended sojourns in its congenial environment and gave me the opportunity to share in full the intense intellectual and collegial life of the university.

Kate Stimpson has waited a long time for this project to come to fruition. She always believed in it, and her tactful encouragement and seemingly endless persistence always kept me going. She was my beacon. I can think of no greater honor or privilege than to be associated with her endeavors.

Earlier versions of chapters 3–9 have been previously published elsewhere. They have been revised for this volume, sometimes extensively. I owe special thanks to Ariel Zeitlin, whose critical acumen and practiced eye were of invaluable assistance in undertaking these revisions. My gratitude also to Nancy Worman for her help in preparing the manuscript, and, above all, heartfelt admiration for Lys Ann Shore, who edited it with skill, sensitivity, and tact. As far as limitations of space permitted, I have updated bibliographical references where I thought it essential or practical to do so.

Chapter 3 first appeared as "The Dynamics of Misogyny: Myth and Mythmaking in the *Oresteia* of Aeschylus" (*Arethusa* 11 [1978]: 149–84). It was later included in *Women in the Ancient World: The Arethusa Papers*, ed. John Peradotto and J. P. Sullivan (Albany: State University of New York Press, 1984), 159–94. Copyright © 1984 by State University of New York Press. Reprinted by permission.

Chapter 4 was first published as "The Politics of Eros in Aeschylus' Danaid Trilogy," in *Innovations in Antiquity*, ed. Ralph Hexter and Daniel Selden (London: Routledge, 1992), 203–52. It is reprinted here by permission of Routledge.

Chapter 5, "The Body's Revenge: Dionysos and Tragic Action in Euripides' *Hekabe*," originally appeared under the title "Euripides' Hekabe and the Somatics of Dionysiac Drama" (*Ramus* 20 [1991]: 53–94). It is reprinted by permission of Aureal Publications.

Chapter 6 first appeared as "The Power of Aphrodite: Eros and the Boundaries of the Self in the *Hippolytus*," in *Directions in Euripidean Criticism*, ed. Peter Burian (Durham, N.C.: Duke University Press, 1985), 52–111, 189–208. It is reprinted here by permission of Duke University Press.

Chapter 7, "Mysteries of Identity and Designs of the Self in Euripides' *Ion*," was first published in *Proceedings of the Cambridge Philological Society* 35 (1989): 144–97. It is reprinted here by permission of PCPS.

Chapter 8, "Playing the Other: Theater, Theatricality, and the Feminine in Greek Drama," first appeared in *Representations* 11 (1985): 63–94. A slightly revised version was later published in *Nothing to Do with Dionysos? Athenian Drama in Its Social Context*, ed. J. J. Winkler and F. I. Zeitlin (Princeton: Princeton University Press, 1990), 63–96. Copyright © 1985 by the Regents of the University of California. Reprinted here by permission of The University of California Press.

Chapter 9, "Travesties of Gender and Genre in Aristophanes' *Thes-*

mophoriazousae," was published in *Reflections of Women in Antiquity,* ed. Helene Foley (London: Gordon and Breach, 1981), 169–217. An abridged version appeared in *Critical Inquiry* 8 (1981): 301–28, and is included in *Writing and Sexual Difference,* ed. Elizabeth Abel (Chicago: University of Chicago Press, 1982), 131–57. Copyright © 1981 by Gordon and Breach Science Publishers. Reprinted here by permission of Gordon and Breach.

NOTE ON TRANSLITERATION AND TRANSLATION

Like others working with classical material and texts, I have confronted the problem of transliterating Greek names into English equivalents. Like them, I have found consistency difficult to maintain. I settled for a compromise that retained the Latinate spelling for the most familiar names and places but otherwise used the preferred Greek forms. To make this volume accessible to nonspecialists, I have provided English translations of all Greek passages. Citations of translators only refer to the editions of the Loeb Classical Library (Cambridge: Harvard University Press). I have also transliterated Greek words or phrases (except when it proved too cumbersome). In quoting the work of foreign scholars, I have made my own translations of the originals, if not otherwise available.

ABBREVIATIONS

AAntHung	*Acta antiqua Academiae Scientiarum Hungaricae*
AJP	*American Journal of Philology*
BAGB	*Bulletin de l'Association Guillaume Budé*
BICS	*Bulletin of the Institute of Classical Studies* (University of London)
BIFG	*Bolletina dell'Istituto di Filologia Greca*
CA	*Classical Antiquity*
C&M	*Classica et medievalia*
CGITA	*Cahiers du groupe interdisciplinaire du théâtre antique*
CJ	*Classical Journal*
CP	*Classical Philology*
CQ	*Classical Quarterly*
CR	*Classical Review*
CW	*Classical World*
D-K	H. Diels and W. Kranz, eds. *Die Fragmente der Vorsokratiker.* 3 vols. Oxford, 1945–56.
FGrHist	F. Jacoby, ed. *Die Fragmente der griechischen Historiker.* Berlin and Leiden, 1923–58.
GRBS	*Greek, Roman, and Byzantine Studies*
HSCP	*Harvard Studies in Classical Philology*
JHS	*Journal of Hellenic Studies*
LEC	*Les études classiques*
LfgrE	B. Snell, ed. *Lexikon des frühgriechischen Epos.* Göttingen, 1955–.
Loeb	Loeb Classical Library. Cambridge, Mass.
MH	*Museum Helveticum*

N²	A. Nauck, ed. *Tragicorum graecorum fragmenta*, 2d ed. Leipzig, 1889.
PCPS	*Proceedings of the Cambridge Philological Society*
Phil.	*Philologus*
Phil. Supp.	*Philologus* Supplementband
PP	*La parola del passato*
QS	*Quaderni di storia*
QUCC	*Quaderni urbinati di cultura classica*
Radt	S. Radt, ed. *Tragicorum graecorum fragmenta*. Vol. 3, *Aeschylus;* vol. 4, *Sophocles*. Göttingen, 1985, 1977.
RE	Georg Wissowa, ed. *Paulys Real-Encyclopädie*. Stuttgart, 1894–1963.
RGVV	*Religionsgeschichtliche Versuche und Vorarbeiten*
RhM	*Rheinisches Museum für Philologie*
SCO	*Studi classici e orientali*
SIFC	*Studi italiani di filologia classica*
SMSR	*Studi e materiali per la storia delle religioni*
SO	*Symbolae Osloenses*
TAPA	*Transactions of the American Philological Association*
WS	*Wiener Studien*
YCS	*Yale Classical Studies*

INTRODUCTION

The project of selecting and assembling a group of my essays of the last eighteen years into a single volume has been an enlightening as well as a sobering experience. Retrospection leads to introspection, and past and present engage in a curious dance, at times resulting in a strong sense of a linear advance, at others, of a spiraling circle where the last seems to rejoin the beginning. Divergence but also coherence, progression but also return as if by magnetic pull to a consistent set of problems that again and again were articulated and examined from different points of view. Above all, there is a reminder of an enduring desire to see matters otherwise, to uncover what I called "secrets" in the text, and of a search for techniques of layering levels of analysis so as to draw them into the orbit of a broader cultural perspective—or, to use another metaphor, to fasten on a single essential nucleus from which other issues could radiate outward, sometimes unexpectedly, into a steady line of vision.

That organizing center has most often been the category of gender and the dynamics of its manifold and varying uses as an integral structuring element of Greek literature and, more generally, of the social imagination. I was lucky. At a time when feminist criticism was in its infancy (at least, in the field of classics) a new adventure awaited those of us who sensed the possibility—and necessity—of embarking on a heuristic quest to probe the cognitive, symbolic, and psychological functions of the feminine in a highly coded system of androcentric authority, a system whose own quest for universal categories and success in making culture pass for nature have left its imprint on us even today.

It was no accident, I think, that feminist criticism was aided in its enterprise by the rise of other, more general theoretical developments and increasing demands for more rigorous techniques of analysis: for example, semiotics, which focused on codes of communication; narratology, in respect to mapping textual strategies; the new rhetoric and its interest in rehabilitating devices of persuasion and representation; and, above all,

1

structuralism in its encoding of mental operations and its ability to discern intelligible patterns behind a welter of disparate and often contradictory data. Other movements followed: notably, post-structuralism, which countered the hegemony of form with suppler and more subversive ways of reading. In the largest sense, however, it would be difficult to overestimate the value of a prevailing anthropological outlook that had long insisted on respecting the specifics of a given culture, bound to a certain time and place, but which now enforced a new self-consciousness about our own assumptions and preconceptions.

The idea of "otherness" is now a commonplace. It was not then, and if otherness could apply to the study of cultures not our own, it was also a fruitful concept for articulating the category of the female (and femininity) itself. This starting point led to new assessments and reevaluations of the female position in a hegemonic order that joined and divided female and male in the pairing of marked and unmarked terms. Probing the extent of that markedness, that otherness, that difference, that relationship of periphery to the center was the guiding aim of feminist explorations that shifted the angle of vision to look at matters the other way around. This was cultural study often through tactics of inversion, even subversion, sustained by the profound recognition that every text, every image, every cultural artifact necessarily participated in some type of ideological transaction that took its place in an ongoing debate with reference to other institutionalized forms of thought and practice. In such an anthropology of gendered relations, the aesthetic, the social, and the ethical inevitably assumed a political complexion, which brought new insights to bear on the workings of the polis and the making of civic identity. This sense of a fuller and more integrated network of diversified cultural meanings was founded in turn on the need for a dialectics of inclusion as the point of both departure and return. No men without women, no masculine self-presentation without consideration of the feminine as a major factor in the enterprise, and no exploration of the dominant discourse without developing convincing techniques of demystification.

This thumbnail sketch is not meant to describe or even to address a complex history, with so many different avenues of approach and so many internal debates about method, conceptualization, and aim. I can only speak for myself. Trained as I was originally in traditional modes of research and analytic techniques, my own "archaeology of knowledge" consists of different strata of consciousness, built up over time and experience. While my horizons expanded, I never abandoned the first interests that continued to exercise my curiosity: the workings of myth and ritual, questions of form and genre, the conventions of paradigms and plot patterns, and more generally speaking, the anatomy of a literary text, especially in the theatrical corpus. These concerns all came together through an overarching sense of their interlinking at different levels of discourse, representation, and performance.

In finding my own way, in searching for my own voice, the consideration of gender was a catalytic force, a driving source of energy and discovery. I wanted to find out how the "system" worked, what dynamic "logic" underlay these constructions and exercised such persuasive power. How did the mythmaking impulse in a traditional society operate, first to establish those durable paradigms and models (such as in Homer and Hesiod) and next to invest these time-honored stories with new resonances and cultural meanings, as in the theater of fifth-century Athens and beyond? How did these works elaborate the rules for the oppositions between male and female, both cognitive and social, and at the same time hold them up to question, even seditious scrutiny? How did the standard divisions between nature and culture, private and public, inside and outside, family and state, prove both useful and also too restrictive as a set of dichotomies? What motives led men in the texts they authored and in which they performed to bring women out of the house and onto the larger stage to play a determining role in men's affairs? As the women in Aristophanes' comedy, the *Thesmophoriazousae,* humorously put it: "If we are such a bane to men, why marry us? Why refuse to let us leave the house, if we are such a plague? And if a woman happens to look out of the window, why are the rest of you so eager to catch a glimpse of this pest?" (785–99). Why, furthermore, in a society that practiced a traditional form of marriage as an exchange between families, between the males on both sides (father and husband), do we find the issue of women's consent to be the decisive element in the outcome—whether, for example, in the case of Penelope in the *Odyssey* or the Danaid maidens in Aeschylus's dramatic trilogy?

In studying a culture that legislated a high degree of sexual dimorphism in the social division of labor—a dimorphism that also served to divide male from female as heading the list of binary oppositions in mapping the world, both above and below, both inside and outside—the first task was to establish the parameters of these divisions and the broader symbolic associations that trailed along in their wake. The second was to take cognizance of the drastic degree to which that initial division extended. It was not just a matter of a simple opposition between male and female, each category slotted into separate spheres of interest, but rather the notion of some more profound, even ineradicable difference between the sexes, as if they belonged to different species. There were men and then there appeared a "race of women," in Hesiod's words, which issued from their first exemplar, Pandora, once she was created by Zeus in punishment for Prometheus's theft of fire. Later, after the flood, only one human couple remained to repopulate the world, but the means of accomplishing this task, it seems, was not so obvious. Interpreting the oracle's injunction to use the "bones of their mother," Deucalion and Pyrrha each cast stones behind them: hers produced females, his engendered males. The same underlying concept recurs in the cultural demand that sons should resemble their fathers and daughters their mothers. Hence more than one scientific text, seeking to explain the secrets of embryology, felt obliged to offer a theory to account for the obvious cases of reversal in family likeness (as any observer could note) or, more radically, to speculate what conditions must prevail if male and female mix together in sexual union and produce a girl, not a boy.

Opposition and difference: to these we may add an important subcategory in emphasizing the typically Greek notion of an aggressive sexual antagonism, evident in myth as in cult, that situates males and females on adversarial sides, each bent on maintaining solidarity with their own kind. This sense of separate, incompatible attitudes, values, and domains of concern is often represented as generating some form of women's hostility and retributive action against men in a struggle for power that looks like a war between the sexes. Beyond anthropological explanations for such role inversions at certain times and for certain limited social or psychological effects, this combative stance strikes at the heart of the ways in which the Greeks not only articulated (and defended) the logic of sexual difference but also faced the illogic of such a radical split. Again I turn to Aristophanes' comic version of the dilemma, this time in his well-known play, the *Lysistrata*: the women, deprived of their husbands' sexual company due to the war between Athens and Sparta, stage a sex strike to compel the men to make peace and return to their respective homes. The goal is to rejoin the sexes in the pleasures of mutual conjugal love (an issue not usually addressed outside of comedy), but the route to accomplishing that desire is predicated on the women's prior withholding of their sexual favors from men and men's instigation of a war against them to resist that exercise of feminine power. To make love *not* war in effecting a peace treaty between hostile cities requires a preliminary war at home between the sexes, as though love *and* war were indissociable from one another on domestic terrain—as though, if women were to pose as subjects, they might easily pass from lustful wives to political tyrants. Joining forces with the militant virgin, Athena, the women take over the goddess's sacred Acropolis and defend its ramparts, but they also do so in the name of Aphrodite.

The motive may be to restore and uphold domestic norms, thus confirming and enforcing the role of wives in the social system, but the means the women choose also raise a specter that everywhere hovers over the Greek imagination: if women should gain power, they might institute a "rule by women" to substitute for a "rule by men." Feminine resistance to (or rebellion against) male hegemony over their women—the house as well as the broader spheres of politics, public space, and public discourse—may provide a perennial, if nervous, source of comic laughter. Inversion of roles to produce "virilized" women and "feminized" men may in the end be imagined to strengthen the clarity of sexual difference, but it may also undermine the lines between them to contemplate the varied uses of androgyny, effeminacy, and other permutations of gender along the way. At least, temporarily. Women, in these comic scenarios, rarely remain on top.

For some critics, this is the point: the threat of women's power requires reinforcement of masculine norms and predictable strategies of containing modes of feminine self-assertion, which so threaten demands for the orderly and rational (read, male) conduct of society. This challenge, as Greek texts represent it, also poses problems. Indeed, this is why it seems to furnish a never ending supply of recurrent themes and plot patterns. Rather than subscribing to the simplistic division of male and female into active and passive categories and taking issues of domination and subjugation as the necessary and inevitable outcome of any encounter, we may pose another set of questions. What do men do that requires, that instigates, female intervention? Why, in the face of a professed inferiority of woman, does the Greek imagination also continually confront the power of the feminine, each time with the need to find some resolution, some accommodation to female demands? What dilemmas, what contradictions, what issues are at stake in conceptualizing the world, whose territory includes not only the practice of politics and other typical male pursuits, but also those larger relations of nature and culture? Even more to the point, what of the relations between mortals and immortals, the foundation of the Greek world view that defines and yet continually challenges the boundary lines of human identity, capacity, and limit?

Hence the third, fundamental requirement in studying these gendered relations: consideration of the nature of the society that generated so many conflicts and so many attempts at resolution, conciliation, or incorporation of female forces. More precisely, what specific components, aspects, and issues constitute this culture's version of masculinity in social, political, and psychological terms and put it at risk? Masculine identity and the values at work in its construction are perennial issues. We find the problem in the *Iliad*, of course, where Achilles struggles with matters of warrior status and privilege in the heroic code, or in the *Odyssey* where Odysseus himself can fall under suspicion as the wily liar who consorts too much with women. We discern it more clearly still in Hesiod's *Theogony*, where the contrary holds true: men would like to dissociate themselves as far as possible from the female sex, a bane and a plague that brings only toil and woe to a previously edenic existence. The question is even more pronounced for fifth-century Athens in the context of a demo-cratic society that gave birth to the outrageously confident idea that "man is the measure of all things." What does it mean to be a man? What is manliness, the quality the Greeks call *andreia,* a word that is synonymous with virile courage, as even we understand it, and requires a willingness to face danger, to risk one's life, and to maintain control over self and over others? Continuing the epic values of heroic renown *(kleos)* and in pursuit of an everlasting name and glory in a city ruled by democratic principles as well as by protocols of honor and shame, the Athenian citizen male in this competitive, agonistic society faces problems of collective identity and responsibility along with a growing sense of individual selfhood that in later centuries will seek fuller articulation as a matter of urgent concern.

Others have addressed these same questions for a long time; they lie at the heart of traditional humanist inquiry. But with the present shift in approach, any new advances we have made in reviewing these terms stem from the hard-won recognition that masculinity too is a social construct. It is not given by nature, any more than are the social customs and rules of a particular society. The battle between *nomos* (convention, law) and *physis* (nature) for superior status arises precisely in this historical period and is vigorously debated on every side, for self as for society. Less overt (until Plato) seems to have been any systematic thinking about the rules of gender and what these may entail, although we may detect traces of such preoccupations and anxieties in earlier texts. This was our task, then, in our efforts to analyze these cultural documents that so often place femi-nine figures as the central point of conflict and so often use confrontations between male and female as the spur for confronting the larger political, existential, and moral dilemmas that spread outward from any and every local situation. The repetitive forms of these scenarios attest to their du-rable value and apparent necessity. The same is true of the unforgettable female paradigms created in Greek literature and myth, such as Penelope, Pandora, Helen, Hekabe, Clytemnestra, the Danaids, Phaedra, Electra (and their male counterparts), all of whom will appear in the chapters that follow.

The serious study of gender in a social context thus requires that we reach beyond the first level of analysis in identifying representative figures and the structures and forms of action or characterization specific to each sex. All these considerations also involve ideas about sexuality itself, in male or female form, the body and its parts: how constituted and how imagined in corporeal or noncorporeal terms. Furthermore, gender and sexuality operate on both a literal level of reference in family relations and a metaphorical one in those between male and female spaces, as between house and city. Speculations about parentage, kinship, or reproductive strategies affect not only social organization but also the constitution of the body politic and its modes of self-definition in relation to the land the polis occupies, the status of its various inhabitants, and the ties that bind or divide them. The reader will note that in speaking of the roles and functions of the feminine I have avoided such terms as *victimage* and *oppression*. I do not find them useful for studying a cultural system which, like so many others, was historically androcentric in the majority of its institutions. That an apparent symmetry appears in the pairing of male/female does not disguise the fundamental, even disabling, asymmetry in status, rank, and power or focus of interest and influence. No amount of wishful thinking, no strenuous efforts to recover an imagined feminine society, whether mythic or real, past or present, would, in my opinion, redress the serious imbalances. At the same time, power is not monolithic, either in concept or in exercise. It can and must be defined differentially, as official or unofficial, juridical or ritual, overt or covert, or at times, even jointly claimed and wielded.

If marriage in Greek society was organized, in Lévi-Strauss's famous formulation, as a semiotic system of communication in which women were put into circulation as signs to be exchanged between father and husband, it is certainly true that a wife's status as a "speaking sign" was undermined by social rules enjoining silence as the source of her virtue. This axiom is repeated on many occasions in the texts we read. Nevertheless, the bare outline of this theory, however useful it may be for identifying certain patterns and tactics, hardly addresses the psychological and social complexities of cohabitation and its reciprocity of obligations. Women are made to speak; indeed they are shown as demanding a voice that cannot be ignored with impunity. Neither can the values they express. Transaction, negotiation, compensation: these are the terms I prefer because they seem to me to give a more accurate account of what happens in varied situations, especially in a society so conscious of the dangers of unlimited power, the abuse of which, whether political or familial, may well redound upon the male self, in theory as in fact. The law of the talion is a highly operative principle in Greek thought and practice, in theogony as in philosophy, in the law courts as in the heroic code. It extends to vengeance in the execution of "justice," but it applies also to the principle of recompense, which levels out to some extent the potential for brutal domination of the strong over the weak and enforces a social and moral anxiety about overstepping the bounds in relations with others.

Another problematic term is *patriarchal*, a word I have learned to circumvent whenever I can. It now bears both too much and too little weight. Overuse has made it reductive, and in any case it is not particularly accurate as an anthropological tool of analysis. Yes, Greek society, like virtually every other, was oriented around the rule of men (in this sense I prefer the term *androcentric* in any case). But without further refinement or qualification with respect to cultural and historical specifics of political and family structures, the predictable label of 'patriarchy' now tends to produce more heat than light. Likewise, I make sparing use of the term *misogyny*, which I reserve for statements that, true to the word's etymology, openly express "hatred of women," such as Hippolytos's well-known tirade in Euripides' play, or for cases in which it is an implicit attitude, as, for example, in Hesiod's profoundly resentful indictment of the entire female sex. Even at the time when I was writing the essay on Aeschylus's *Oresteia*, which I entitled "The Dynamics of Misogyny," I hesitated before using this catchword, aware of its not quite precise application in this instance. I succumbed to its rhetorical appeal and have regretted it ever since, not least because it allowed some critics to take me at my word and to expend their energies in trying to refute the general concept rather than addressing the arguments of the essay. (I have retained the title in this volume, however, simply because that is how the essay is known.)

Finally, let me reiterate, my focus falls on the idea of inclusion, not exclusion in approaching the question of the feminine. Men's efforts to subordinate women's roles, functions, and influence, their efforts even to appropriate these for themselves, are only partially successful, even in the most ideologically driven documents, such as Plato's *Symposium* and *Phaedrus* or almost any of the tragedies or comedies. What interests me are the strategies used, the inventive nature of the fantasies at work, the range of imaginative "what ifs," and the underlying tensions and ambiguities these representations address in conducting their ever renewable negotiations with the feminine. What continually engages my interest is the opportunity to decipher unsuspected affinities and associations in the cultural codes, whose identification suggests greater coherence and logic in making sense of both familiar and unfamiliar materials. I find it illuminating to chart the interplay between the various elements that structure texts, such as forms of thought, semantic fields, narrative patterns and models, and the dynamic versatility with which they are used, generating each time a new and significant variation on a given set of themes. Formal conventions may offer predictable cues, but they also produce surprising differences. If we can claim that the feminine is *bonne à penser*—that is, a category good for "thinking with"—I, for my part, see the Greeks themselves as *bons à penser,* precisely because, despite their considerable differences from us, they furnish continual opportunities for thinking about issues that still engage and provoke us, whether as men or women or human beings at large.

What we gain from this confrontation with the past comes in part from studying another culture that is in the habit of thinking about the feminine as a category distinct from 'woman' or even 'female'. Greek culture is certainly not alone in this respect, although its propensity for theory and speculation supplies a particularly rich terrain for such explorations. Gender can always be used as a coded sign to stand for some more abstract category in organizing a specific world view and the means to its maintenance or transformation; gender can and does migrate across boundaries from private to public discourse, reframed as metaphor (and sometimes metonym) in broader spheres of reference that are concerned with hierarchies of priority and value. In the case of Greek culture, the language itself, in its grammatical system of gendered attribution, already encourages such extensions from words to concepts, from mythic narratives of genealogies to tenets of scientific and philosophical thought.

Of particular significance in considering the ancient Greek world is the conception of supernatural power that is attributed to a polytheistic system of gendered divinities. These are organized into a family structure of genealogies and relationships, and like the society they mirror, they are often engaged in competition with one another. Gods inhabit another realm of existence, but they also intervene in human affairs. The uncrossable boundary between mortal and immortal is an often reiterated principle. But the ground they share also gives rise to a certain productive tension between proximity and distance, resemblance and difference, model and antimodel—a tension that complicates and enriches the study of gender, particularly in respect to the feminine, where the gap in power and position is so marked between woman and goddess. In the hierarchy of a two-tiered system of values, femininity can be split between a primary role in the domain of the gods and a secondary, devalued one in the world of human affairs, as in the case of Hesiod's Pandora or Aeschylus's *Oresteia.* But the dialectical exchange between mortal and immortal also operates in more subtle ways, often aligning women on the side of the gods and their mysterious forces or, as in the case of Euripides' Phaedra in the *Hippolytos,* representing her as both victim and agent of Aphrodite. In the chapters that follow I return again and again to the figures of the major goddesses (Artemis, Aphrodite, Athena, Demeter, and Persephone) as they appear directly or indirectly, and to that of the male god Dionysos, lord of the theater, whose sexually ambiguous figure encourages role reversal and slippage of categories at all levels. The pairing of the mother and daughter in the myth of Demeter and Persephone (and the rites associated with them) deserves special mention as a principal model that addresses on the immortal level the experiences of feminine life as well as the differences in status between gods and mortals. As such, its narrative elements, along with the figures of the angry, mourning mother and the nubile maiden, are often profiled behind other dramatic scenarios. Its recall here will serve to round off this brief outline of theory, method, and principles with an instructive case in point.

First and foremost, this is a myth about marriage, about the separation of the daughter from the mother and the threat posed by their intimate bond that excludes men. By equating marriage with death (the husband is Hades, lord of the underworld) and configuring it along the lines of a forced seizure, the myth hovers over every instance of maiden sacrifice, voluntary or not, as behind every unwanted sexual union, whatever the circumstances. The topos of the bride of Hades is matched by the fearsome maternal figure, who resists male trespass on her prerogatives, whether in anger or in mourning or both. A single character may even be shown as playing the two roles: for example, Creousa in Euripides's *Ion*, who was raped by the god Apollo and in turn grieves over the loss of her child many years before. This mysterious joining of mother and maid that shifts between separation and reunion, between despair and joy, between female retaliation and male concession, gives rise to actual rites that empower women in festivals reserved for them alone (such as the Thesmophoria) to promote fertility in both human and agricultural spheres. On the other hand, the myth provides the sacred charter for the Eleusinian mysteries, open to all sexes, whose initiates acquire some secret knowledge from reenacting this myth of female experience that will promise them immortality after death.

The continuing integration of the various patterns and meanings of this myth and its rites into the texture of many of the works treated in this book demonstrates, as perhaps no other example might, the importance of studying the gendered categories of a given culture in its own context and in terms of its own analogical lines of thinking. The myth interweaves the categories of marriage and agriculture, establishing a parallel between the maiden and the seed corn. On the sociological and psychological level, it also suggests that marriage is a kind of death (a violent abduction from a former state), and on a religious level, that death may be assimilated to a mystic marriage. Questions of both sexuality and mortality are played off between the sacred and the mundane, between gods and mortals, all centered on the female predicament and the modes of female maturation as dictated in this society.

Greece was alone among Mediterranean cultures in imagining an agricultural scenario of death and rebirth that featured an exclusively female relationship, not one between a goddess and a young male consort (such as Aphrodite and Adonis, Cybele and Attis, Innana and Dumuzi, Ishtar and Tammuz, Isis and Osiris). The reasons for this reorientation are, no doubt, manifold and not easy to ascertain. But the mediating position of the myth of Demeter and Persephone as a means of communicating between different zones of experience and spheres of influence gives rise to a complex and elaborate model for thinking about the feminine. It is not the only one. Greek myth and literature as well as philosophical and scientific debate oscillate between ascribing too much power to the female and too little when it comes to thinking about matters of sexuality and reproduction or, more broadly, about the sources and guarantees of prosperity in the city. There are other, competing accounts that enter into play, and their different trajectories are traced in the following chapters.

In envisioning a shape to this volume that would lend some organizing themes to the disparate essays, written at different times and sometimes with very different aims, I have first of all restricted my purview to literary texts of the archaic and classical periods. I have organized the essays according to four rubrics: part 1, "Gender and Paradigm: The Privileged Models"; part 2, "Gender and the Body: The Woman's Story"; part 3, "Gender and Selfhood: The Boy's Story"; and part 4, "Gender and Mimesis: Theater and Identity." These headings do not reflect the order in which the essays were written or conceived. They are also misleading to some extent. The reader will find significant overlappings of theme and emphasis from one to the other, and in any case, none is restricted to treating these lines of inquiry alone. The headings are only meant to indicate a central focus or principal aim.

I have already pointed to my perception of the significance of paradigms or "master narratives" as the foundation of gendered identities and their lasting influence in shaping what came after. In a deeply traditional culture, whatever its propensities to innovate or rewrite, certain story patterns and role attributions regularly recur for rethinking or for profiling other stories. Story as exemplum has a vital function in techniques of rhetorical persuasion; the past is both separated from the present and reabsorbed into it, bearing the weight of authority and the familiar ring of recognition. If Herodotus could claim that Homer and Hesiod had given the Greeks their gods—that is, the concept of an Olympian system of a pantheon in organized form—we might add that the two authors also provided the most durable models of femininity, polarized at their two extremes—one positive and integrative, one negative and disjunctive—against which later ones were measured and judged.

Accordingly, in part 1 the first chapter, "Figuring Fidelity," addresses the figure of faithful Penelope in the *Odyssey,* and the second, "Signifying Difference," that of Pandora, the first exemplar of the "race of women," in Hesiod's versions of the story in his *Theogony* and *Works and Days.* Penelope wins eternal *kleos* for her fidelity and for "keeping everything safe and secure" in her husband's house (including herself) until Odysseus's return to Ithaca in quest of a legitimate status and identity only she can grant. Pandora, on the other hand, exemplifies the status of woman as outsider, an intrusive other brought into the man's house, a useless drone who does not work and only steals his substance—both nourishment and sex.

Chapter 3, "The Dynamics of Misogyny," turns to fifth-century theater in the public venue of democratic Athens to take up Aeschylus's
trilogy, the *Oresteia*. Aeschylus is, first of all, the founder of the dramatic
tradition, in fact if not in name. Moreover, this monumental work, his
last, immediately gained canonical status in the history of Greek drama,
and its prestige was used to support a political ideology of the city's claims
for its superior values in the wake of the Persian Wars. In the *Odyssey*
Clytemnestra, the "bad" wife, who with her lover prepared a bitter homecoming for her husband Agamemnon, had already been matched against
Penelope, the "good" one, as her foil and antitype, and also as a warning
to all men about trusting their wives. The dead Agamemnon in the underworld is given the last word. Assigning praise to Penelope and blame to
Clytemnestra for all time to come, he attaches a judgment that joins the
two: "a song of loathing will be Clytemnestra's among men, to make evil
the reputation of all womankind, even for one whose acts are virtuous"
(24.201–2). For all the later resonances of this verdict on the entire female
sex, the *Odyssey* mutes the role of Clytemnestra as the chief plotter
against Agamemnon and also the impact of Orestes' vengeance against his
mother. The *Oresteia*, however, shifts the focus to imagine a powerful
Clytemnestra in the roles of queen, wife, and mother. The second play of
the trilogy highlights the son's confrontation with his mother, and the
third one uses the juridical impasse created when a son is obliged to kill
his mother to avenge his father, making it the basis for founding a law
court at Athens. In the process the *Oresteia* challenges the notion of
maternity itself. Long regarded as the cornerstone of an evolution from
savagery to civilization, from the Furies' crude law of the vendetta against
those who have shed kindred blood to the reasoned debates of the impar-
tial law court, the *Oresteia* also stands as a new myth, a new paradigm,
in its own right to refound the law of the father for the interests of the
body politic.

The study of the *Oresteia* sets the stage for the rest of the volume,
which continues with the examination of individual dramatic texts and
ends with general theoretical considerations about the essential elements
of the tragic theater and their intimate connections with cultural definitions of the feminine. Part 2 includes essays on two dramatic works.
Chapter 4, "The Politics of Eros," takes up another trilogy of Aeschylus,
which, unlike the *Oresteia*, comes down to us with only the first play
(Suppliants) intact. Chapter 5, "The Body's Revenge," examines a rela-
tively early play of Euripides on the fate of the Trojan women after the fall
of their city *(Hekabe)*. Aeschylus dramatizes the proverbial story of the
Danaids who, to escape their violent suitors, their Egyptian cousins, flee
to Argos in company with their father, seeking refuge and protection
from the local king and his people. When ultimately forced to marry their

cousins, as the subsequent play must have shown, they slay the bride-grooms on the wedding night at their father's injunction—all except one daughter who disobeys and spares her partner's life. In the *Hekabe* the spotlight falls on a single feminine character, the Trojan queen and mother, now a Greek captive. In the course of one day she sees her daughter sacrificed by the Greek army and discovers the body of her son murdered at the hands of the local king to whom she had previously entrusted him. Goaded into action by this double blow, she retaliates in a bloody revenge. In both scenarios, women are shown as ready to kill men in return for bodily violence done to them and their own. I argue in both cases, although from different perspectives, for the significance of the body in configuring the female world and psyche, whether in its virgin state that invites male violation through sacrifice or rape, or in the mother's bonding with children, particularly the daughter, whom she carried within her body and brought to birth.

It may seem too one-sided, even tendentious, to emphasize these corporeal aspects above other considerations. Theater in particular demands attention to the body and its condition on stage in the person of the actor. Even more, the nature of the body, male or female, its subjection to the gaze of others, and its need for identification (or recognition) are also significant issues at stake. So are sexual and procreative roles and the body's management of outside surface and interior depth; this is true in respect to both genders from Homer on. The female is not reduced to a body, nor, to be wholly fair, is her "story," whether she is a virgin, wife, or mother (or a combination of the three). Still, cultural insistence on defining the unfamiliar body of the *other*—on defining the other as *body*—particularly in sex, childbirth, and loving or lethal embrace, leads me to distinguish the female's story from the male's in these terms.

All these women may be said to possess 'selves,' even if their actions and reactions are all used finally to serve masculine ends, as I argue in chapter 8. Selfhood in the Greek sense may apply in the most general terms to persistent problems of identity and its maintenance, even if in a negative form of unhappy self-discovery. To be a character, to be represented as a figure who acts and speaks, suffers or triumphs, is in some sense to propose a version of what we think of as a 'self'. But for purposes of specific cultural emphasis, I have reserved this concept for the "boy's story" in identifying selfhood and the self's definition as the primary problem that preoccupies the two Euripidean plays I treat in part 3, both of which chart a youth's difficult passage to adulthood. Chapter 6, "The Power of Aphrodite," focuses on Euripides' *Hippolytos;* chapter 7, "Mysteries of Identity and Designs of the Self," on his *Ion.* Creousa, Ion's unknown mother in the *Ion,* has a 'self', and so does Phaedra in the *Hippolytos*. Both of them are complex figures, who share their conflicted feelings with the audience and whose psychology is of considerable, even dominant, interest. Their attacks upon the young male are undertaken to sustain an outraged sense of self, and there are important, even unsuspected, affinities as well between masculine and feminine characters that command our attention. I take 'self' in this context not only as a teleological result of these plays' actions, but also and primarily as social identity, as the route to inscription in the social and political structures of the city. Hippolytos, the bastard Amazon's son, is tested in his fidelity to himself and his ideals; Ion, the unknown orphan (in reality the son of Creousa and the god Apollo, through rape), starts out as a cipher who needs to find and come to understand and accept who he is. In both cases, fathers end by claiming their sons. At the same time, the route to obtaining 'selfhood' is predicated on encounters with significant maternal (or quasi-maternal) figures, who either set the terms or propel these young masculine characters into forms of self-knowledge, whether for disaster or success.

Part 4 includes two essays that address more theoretically the significance of the cultural category of the feminine in aesthetic, literary, and cognitive terms. Chapter 8, "Playing the Other," reviews the phenomenon of women's puzzling predominance in the theater and speculates on the uses that feminine intervention and characterization might serve in this all-male theater, in which male actors by convention are necessarily called upon to impersonate women. Chapter 9, "Travesties of Gender and Genre," takes up the question from the comic side. From the outset, Aristophanes' lampoon of Euripides and his dramas in the *Thesmophoriazousae* advertises its metatheatrical intent, giving us the first known exposition, in comic guise, of some formal theories about mimesis: imitation, impersonation, and mimicry. Using both transvestism (intersexuality) and parody (intertextuality) as the means of trespassing on sacred female space forbidden to men, the play uses the feminine to cross a series of boundaries: between gender and genre, myth and ritual, theater and festival, sacred and secular, and finally, life and art. In the spirit of comic license under the auspices of Dionysiac revelry, this lively piece exposes a whole range of hidden analogies and the shifting relations between them to unsettle the foundations of representation itself. By revealing women's "secrets" as the ground of the plot (and of the accusation against Euripides), Aristophanes also reveals the feminine as both source and object of mimesis, forever poised, as men imagine, on the boundary between fiction and truth.

Comic vision in this last essay teases all these hidden relations into the open as a telling source of productive laughter. It serves me too as a convenient place to join the end to the beginning by distinguishing some of the various strands that, with differing outlook and degree of emphasis, are interwoven throughout the essays in this collection. While "Playing the Other" was concerned with theater and with questions of theatricality, I have used the phrase as the title for this volume, taking it in a more extended sense to signify two related principles in the study of the social imagination: representation as the key element in all these male-authored texts and the continual play with gender categories that often elide any confident definition or opposition.

PART ONE

Gender and Paradigm:
The Privileged Models

· ONE ·

Figuring Fidelity in Homer's *Odyssey*

The *Odyssey* has an extraordinary capacity for creating memorable visual
objects, signs, and symbols as focusing elements of a highly complex narrative structure. In a world ruled by uncertainty, suspension, disguise, and
dimmed perception, such apparent tokens of a tangible reality emerge at
critical interpretative junctures in the plot, often serving as means of prediction, identification, or proof.[1] Generally speaking, all material objects
in both the *Iliad* and the *Odyssey* are invested with psychological and
cognitive resonances that go far beyond the details of their mere description to exemplify a typical and indispensable mode of charting social and
mental experience. As M. I. Finley remarks, the "heroic world is unable
to visualize any achievement or relationship except in concrete terms. The
gods are anthropomorphized, emotions and feelings are located in specific
organs of body, even the soul was materialized. Every quality or state," he
concludes, "had to be translated into some specific symbol, marriage into
gifts of cattle, honor into a trophy, friendship into treasure."[2] Jasper
Griffin takes another view of this well-known epic feature, judging it "not
as just a matter of literary style, but [one that] arises from the way the
Homeric poet sees the world itself." "Symbolic and significant objects
and gestures," he suggests, "developed out of those which were originally
conceived as magical and charged with supernatural power," even if such
distinctions are not always clear.[3] What accounts in part for this sense

Many thanks to Daniel Mendelsohn and Deirdre von Dornum, who offered sage advice and
excellent editorial suggestions. A preliminary version of this essay was presented at a conference on female figures in the *Odyssey*, held at Bard College in 1992. This essay also appears
in *The Distaff Side: Representing the Female in Homer's Odyssey*, ed. Beth Cohen (Oxford:
Oxford University Press, 1995).

1. These cover a range of categories: cosmic phenomena, bodily marks, elements of a
landscape, or some specimen of artisanal handiwork.
2. Finley 1954, 122. See also Gernet (1981) on "pre-monetary signs."
3. Griffin 1980, 24.

of compelling presence is an aesthetic quality that heightens the value of articles primarily designed for practical use. Homeric epic, observes Kenneth Atchity, is "a treasure house of beautiful objects of art: swords, cups, robes, bows, beds, shields,"[4] outstanding specimens of craftmanship that elicit the amazed awe of the spectators *(thauma idesthai)* in an experience that often comes close to an epiphanic viewing.[5]

The result is that such objects are often talismans of power: they can be circulated and exchanged, transmitted as precious heirlooms, endowed with certain active values that inhere in the genealogy of their ownership as well as in the beauty of their manufacture. In some instances, like the shield and spear of Achilles, they may belong wholly to particular individuals, functioning as personal attributes or as inalienable signs of identity that no one else *(oude tis allos)* can appropriate. An item can also belong to several categories. Odysseus's bow, for example, although ultimately reserved for his use alone, was originally a gift from a guest-friend. Like many such items, it constitutes a tangible link of memory that connects the hero to the world of other heroes, and its evocation in the text provides the occasion for a tale that integrates it fully into its epic setting.

Of all these signifying objects, however, the most famous by far is the bed in Book 23 of the *Odyssey* whose owner and maker are one and the same. This is the sign by which Penelope comes to test Odysseus's identity following the slaying of the suitors, and the revelation of its existence is the necessary prelude that leads directly to their long-awaited reunion. Situated between the identifying signs in Book 19 (the mantle and brooch described to Penelope, the scar recognized by Eurykleia) and Book 24 (Odysseus's identification of the trees in the orchard), the scene of the bed is the centerpiece in the unfolding drama of recognition at home—so much so that already in antiquity, we may recall, Alexandrian scholars promoted the idea that the poem actually ended, not with the close of the work as we have it, but with the immediate aftermath of this striking moment.[6] Anything else would seem to some to be an anticlimax—a disappointing follow-up to that most satisfying of all romantic closures: "and so to bed."

And so to bed—after twenty years of waiting—not just any bed, but one that is sui generis, a single and unique artifact, since we know of no other like it in all of Greek tradition. Some have looked for affinities with

---

4. Atchity 1978, 1.

5. On the phenomenology of these objects, signs, and symbols and how they are viewed and received in archaic poetry, see Prier 1989.

6. For documentation and discussion of the relevant sources, see, most recently, Heubeck 1992, *ad* xxiii, 297.

a species of world tree or *axis mundi* or have suggested mythic or ritual parallels, whether of Indo-European or Near Eastern provenance.[7] But the power of its significance lies (if you will pardon the pun) in its embeddedness within the narrative, a sign-symbol made to order only for the purposes of this poem, its manufacture assigned to the only one who could have made it.

The bed is an object of value, artfully crafted with remarkable skill, as we are told in the combined description and narrative, when Odysseus in his own words recalls its special properties and retraces the steps of its making:

> ... What man
> has put my bed in another place? But it would be difficult
> for even a very expert one, unless a god, coming
> to help in person, were easily to put it in another place ...
> but of men there is no other living mortal, not even in the full
> strength of his youth,
> who could have easily moved it away, since a great mark *[mega sēma]* is wrought
> into the artfully fashioned bed. It is I who made it and nobody
> else *[oude tis allos]*.
> There was the bole of an olive tree with long leaves growing
> in full flowering in the courtyard, and it was thick, like a
> column.
> I laid down my chamber around this, and built it, until I
> finished it, with close-set stones, and roofed it well over,
> and added the compacted doors, fitting closely together.
> Then I cut away the foliage of the long-leaved olive,
> and trimmed the trunk from the roots up, planing it with a
> brazen
> adze, well and expertly, and trued it straight to a chalkline,
> making a bed post of it, and bored all holes with an auger.
> I began with this and built my bed, until it was finished,
> and skillfully embellished it with gold and silver and ivory.
> Then I lashed it with thongs of oxhide, dyed bright with purple.
> In this way I proclaim and make manifest the sign/token *[sēma piphauskomai]*.
> But I do not know now whether the bed is still firmly in place
> *[empedon]*, O woman/wife *[gunai]*

7. For example, see Germain 1954, 211; de Vries 1956, 2:385; Eisler 1910, 2:596–99; and Dietz 1971.

or if some man has cut underneath the stump of the olive and
moved it elsewhere.

$$(23.184-204)^8$$

The bed is an integral part of the bedchamber itself, which Odysseus
had built at the time of his marriage. But unlike other such constructions,
as we know, for example, from the reference to Paris's house in Troy (*Iliad*
6.314–17), the most distinctive feature of this particular bed is its immobility. Oddly fixed in place for all time, it is located at the center of a widening set of circles that constitutes a social topography of habitation in
accord with fixed conventions of property and propriety, a focal point that
dictates its privileged position in the architecture of the house. If the bed
is curiously stationary, however, it is hardly a static symbol. Rather, in the
circumstances in which its "discovery" is staged, it is the site of a dynamic
and two-sided operation, one that involves a complex interplay between
two characters, whose knowledge of one another is made to inhere both
in the shared secret of its existence and in the surprising reversal of roles
that brings it into the light of day. Above all, the bed is a *sēma,* and this in
the two senses of the word: first, some exceptional mark or aspect in its
own right—in this instance, the *mega sēma* that is wrought into this unusual bed (188–89); second, as a sign or token of something else—that is,
of the stranger's true identity.[9]

The tempting allure of a sign, any sign, is its implicit invitation to be
deciphered, and its message interpreted, even appropriated, by those who
can discern its meaning. Like a wonder or *thauma,* as Raymond Prier suggests, a symbol-sign is "a phenomenon made to be seen or recognized." It
is something wrought or "created" *(teuchomai)* which produces a quality
"of affective signification" in the eye and the mind.[10] This is especially the

8. Translations throughout are, for the most part, by Lattimore (1965) with occasional
modifications.

9. On the two meanings of *sēma,* see Stanford 1961, *ad* 188–89. See also Heubeck
1992, *ad* 187–89: "Odysseus obviously means by *sēma* the special distinguishing mark, the
unique feature involved in his construction of bed rather than the token of identity which P.
seeks (cf. *sēmata,* 110; cf. also 202) for he is quite unaware that his response to his wife's
orders to the maid (177–80) supplies the very *sēma* which Penelope presumably had in mind
at 108–10." See also Besslich 1966, 96; and Eisenberger 1973, 310n.21.

10. On *sēma* in connection with interpretation and the faculty of "mind" or *noos/
noēsis,* see Nagy 1983. On its place in archaic thought, see Prier 1976, 27: "The term for
symbol in Greek is *sēma.* It may indicate any apparition of exceeding beauty or terror. It is
always surrounded by an aura of the cosmic, supernatural, affective, or we should say, I
think, 'metaphysical' or 'otherworldly.'" See the further development in Prier 1989, especially 110, explaining the *sēmata* in Homer: "*Sēma* is more or less a synonym for *teras*
(marvel, portent) and is intimately and often linked with the verb *phainesthai* (to appear for
oneself and another . . .). It also stands with *phasthai* (to speak immediately for oneself and

case when the suggestiveness of a *sēma* expands in so many symbolic and psychological directions and so far exceeds the express reactions of the actors within the text. The bed belongs to both Penelope and Odysseus: the divulgence of its concrete reality, unchanged and unmoved through all these years, is enough to overcome the last impediment to their reunion. As a double-sided sign—of identity for him, fidelity for her—it is meant to be the visual proof of a private and unique relationship.[11] The bed is there, we might say, because it is made to be there; it needs to be located in this place and at this time. We want more. The urge to enter the sacrosanct *thalamos* once more is irresistible, and many others before me have ventured there.

Much has been written and continues to be written on the many possible implications (and satisfactions) of this scene of *anagnōrisis*. It is taken to exemplify the complementary relation between Odysseus and Penelope—the sign of their *homophrosunē*, "like-mindedness," by which she shows herself a match for her husband in cleverness when she pretends at first that the bed has been moved. As the mark of Odysseus's identity, the bed he made matches him to his characteristic skill as an artisan. Through the sharing of a marital secret recalled from the distant past, it is an especially appropriate means to reclaim his role as a husband, which he "reconstructs" in the process of recalling how he first "constructed" it.[12] Hence, the delay in Penelope's recognition is her need to "adjust past to present" in the demand that "Odysseus prove himself her husband now as he was then."[13] Or, beyond the personal story of this notorious couple, the bed, in its allegiance to both nature (living tree) and culture (its craftsmanship), is an emblem of the desired solidity of the house and the place

---

another), *piphauskomenos* (to make manifest for oneself and another, to tell of for oneself and another), and *teuchesthai* (to make or fashion for oneself and another)." In his description of the *mega sēma* of the bed, Odysseus uses *teuchesthai* at the outset, before proceeding to *describe* its actual making, and ends with *piphauskomai* in precisely the two meanings suggested by Prier.

11. See Newton 1987, 17; Murnaghan 1987, 116.

12. See, for example, Beye 1968, 178 ("The live olive tree is still rooted in earth like their sexual knowledge of each other, personal and immutable"); Clarke 1967, 78 ("the marriage of Odysseus and Penelope has a primal strength—it is secure, fixed in time and place, yet alive, natural, capable of further growth"); Thornton 1970, 105 ("This is the 'sign' that Odysseus has for Penelope, a 'sign' which is also a beautiful symbol of the deep rootedness of their mutual loyalty"). On the "nature/culture" symbiosis of the bed, see Vidal-Naquet 1986a, "Land and Sacrifice"; Bonnafé 1985; and Starobinski 1975. On the reunion at "the dark of the moon" that brings the couple "into phase with the courtship of sun and moon," see Austin 1975, 252. More generally, see Emlyn-Jones 1984; Murnaghan 1987, 140–41; and Katz 1991, 177–82.

13. Suzuki 1989, 76.

of marriage within it. As Marylin Katz has put it most recently, "the bed . . . retains a connection with the natural world from which it came, and thus represents the institution of marriage itself, which, centered on the biological realities of sexuality and procreation, nevertheless is configured in space and time as a social artifact." [14] In particular, the fixed position of the bed is understood as a figure of marriage itself: permanent, durable, stable, and inalienable. Even the ancient scholiast on this passage underscores this point in observing that the bed's "immovable" *(akinēton)* quality is a riddling way of stating that the nuptial couch (the conjugal bond) is "indestructible," "indissoluble" *(adialuton)*. [15]

I am not going to controvert these interpretations. Indeed, I am generally in accord with them. But I want to drive a small wedge between text and interpretation to open a space for exploring the nature and uses of this singular bed as the master sign in the *Odyssey's* emplotment, and to do so, I aim to ground the scene more fully in the cultural context as well as in the narrative, semantic, and symbolic structures of the poem itself.

At first glance, it should not perhaps seem strange that masculine identity should be intertwined with feminine fidelity in the dynamics of this scene or that the idea of marriage between a man and a woman should rely on two such unequal modalities of self-definition. Even beyond the obvious social disparities in the institution of marriage, the configurations resemble each other in one important sense: each is ultimately open to doubt. After all, he may not be who he says he is. And she, in not conducting herself as the rules prescribe, may not be what she appears to be. Only if these two quite disparate "truths" are made to converge, we might say, as two divided halves of a *sumbolon,* only if husband and wife match their knowledge of the secret *sēmata* (23.107–9) in the one artifact they both share (and agree to recall), can this marriage be recreated, reconstructed, and finally resumed.

Yet a certain paradox remains in the unequal symmetry between identity and fidelity that dictates to each sex its defining terms—a relation first challenged in the reversal of roles and an apparent shift of power between male and female before the scene reaches its expected conclusion in reaffirming the social norms. That challenge gives rise to certain questions I would like to explore further: What is at stake in this elaborate backhanded game? Why, for example, should moving the bed be instantly construed as a sign of infidelity? What more may be implied by Penelope's action in initiating the test of the bed, or, more precisely, how does her ruse address the inherent dilemma of the poem, which assures us of

14. Katz 1991, 181.
15. Scholiast, *ad* 23.288, ed. Dindorf.

Penelope's fidelity, while also keeping it in doubt? The further unraveling of these various strands in what follows will, I hope, help us to decipher the underlying logic of this scene that requires (and reinforces) the ideological need to resort to the external and externalizing sign of the bed as the requisite "foreplay" to the "real thing."

Penelope is the first to set the terms of an *anagnōrisis* as a testing of her husband. Refusing the evidence of the scar and the assurances of Eurykleia and Telemachos in her initial encounter with him after the slaughter of the suitors, she maintains that

> . . . If he is truly Odysseus,
> and he has come home, then we shall find other ways, and
> better,
> to recognize each other, for we have signs *[sēmata]* that we
> know of
> between the two of us only, but they are secret *[kekrummena]*
> from the others.
>
> (23.107–8)

Odysseus, however, is the one who actually gives the cue. Freshly bathed and marvelously restored by Athena's handiwork, he again takes his place opposite an unyielding Penelope, and as if resigned to her stony attitude, he orders the nurse to make him up a bed (23.171–72). Now it is her turn, and although not denying she knows what he looked like long ago when he sailed for Troy, she takes him at his word and instructs Eurykleia to set up a bed outside the well-built chamber. Not just any bed, such as the kind regularly offered to guests in the house, but "that very bed he himself had made," she adds, and the text forewarns us that this is the means she has chosen to "test her husband" (23.181). It is a clever ruse, for it catches Odysseus off guard, and by eliciting his spontaneous indignation, her trick succeeds far better than any direct interrogation [16] to guarantee the authenticity of his knowledge and hence of his identity.

But the ruse works in two directions, because in raising the awful possibility that his bed has been moved, her testing of *his* identity raises the far more important question of *her* sexual fidelity to him. This is the principal anxiety that hovers over the whole poem. It conditions Odysseus's entire strategy once he has returned to Ithaca and accounts for Penelope's belated position in the sequence of his several self-revelations to others at home. At this, the moment of reckoning, the crucial issue is never directly stated. Yet its presence is instantaneously grasped through a series of

---

16. This is what Telemachos expects her to do: "Why do you withdraw so from my father, and do not sit beside him and ask him questions and find out about him?" (23.98–99).

oblique and symbolic moves. The secret existence of this particular bed, which only the two of them (and a trusted maidservant) are permitted to know, suggests the intimacy shared by the couple and the husband's sexual monopoly of his wife, whereby it is understood that mere divulgence of the bed's existence would be equivalent to an irrevocable betrayal. To move it, however, would be to undermine the entire cultural ideology that supports the bed in its "natural" grounding of the house in the institution of marriage. Immobility is equated with the desired permanence of the conjugal bond, which would be fatally undermined by the blow of the ax. So much is clear. The symbolic values hold.

But does representation fully replace reality? After all, in principle, Penelope could have made love with another man in the very same bed or, for that matter, anywhere else she chose.[17] Yet the fact of not moving the bed becomes a decisive and incontrovertible proof. Why should this be so? She could not, of course, have moved it by herself. The effort, says Odysseus, would have required the strength of some remarkable man (with a god's help) to accomplish it. Moving the bed is represented as a heroic feat, a task beyond the capacity of most mortal men. It requires exceptional physical prowess, such as only a worthy virile rival might display. Hence the man who moved the bed will have done more than violate the idea of a stable marriage. In unmaking what Odysseus had previously made, he will have proved himself Odysseus's sexual equal, even superior, who could rightly claim the title of "best of the Achaeans" in his stead (16.74–77; 19.525–29). To displace the bed, therefore, suggests another male's entitlement to displace him, an entitlement exercised by the first encroachment into the bedchamber that is followed now by this permanent and irreversible sign of mastery.[18]

Merely to enter the bedroom is to gain access to the innermost region of the house, its protected core. This is the domain the woman inhabits, once she has been brought into the household as the lawfully wedded wife, and the benefits of which she enjoys because of her relationship with her husband, which is symbolized, above all, in her sharing of his bed.[19] On the other hand, if the marital bed cannot be alienated from its maker with-

---

17. Germain 1954, 212; Murnaghan 1987, 141.

18. Menelaos, when told of the suitors, had waxed indignant that, although being unwarlike *(analkides)*, they should wish to lie in the bed of a strong-hearted man *(kraterophronos andros*, 4.331–34), but the lover's feat would give the lie to this contention.

19. As Vernant (1980, "Marriage," 62–63) remarks, "it is as if the conjugal bed in which the king sleeps with the queen held powers which qualify the king's house to provide his kingdom with sovereigns who will make it bear fruit. To take the king's place at the heart of his house, in his bed, by becoming united with his wife, is to acquire a claim to reign after him over the land which his wife, in a way, symbolizes."

out destroying its integrity (and his), its place of honor in the spatial arrangement of the house signifies that the woman, for her part, has ceased to be an object of exchange among men in the protocols of betrothal and matrimony. She, too, like the bed, is expected to be fixed in place from then on, and her continuing fidelity to him finds its direct correlative in the object that has remained in place through all these years as a secret no one else knows. Its lasting condition then must depend on a corresponding steadfastness of mind in the wife, who, in her husband's absence, agrees to guard the privacy (and exclusivity) of both her body and their bed.

In her role as the custodian of his rights to exclusive possession of her and hence as the mainstay of the social system in which both spouses are awarded their respective positions, Penelope is faced with a situation that gives her unaccustomed power in the right to determine what man will finally share that bed, and in so doing, to grant or withhold from her errant husband the stability of a safe anchorage at home. As Mihoko Suzuki puts it, "refusing to become an object of exchange between the suitors and either her son Telemachus or her father Icarius [in remarriage]," Penelope is more than "a sign that is exchanged among men; instead, she insists upon her status as a [speaking] subject, a generator of signs," a role that reaches its climax in the sign of the bed.[20]

II

A bed, of course, is the place for sleeping;[21] it is also the place for sex, and hence the central and virtually indispensable feature of any description of sexual activity in Homeric narrative. In Hera's deception of Zeus in *Iliad* 14, he is so overwhelmed by desire that although he utters the conventional formula, "let us go to bed and turn to love-making," *(en philotēti trapeiomen eunēthente),* he cannot wait to return to their well-fitted

20. Suzuki 1989, 88, borrowing from Lévi-Strauss's well-known formulation (1967, 496): "Women, like words, are signs to be communicated and exchanged among men, but women too, as persons, are generators of signs. . . . In the matrimonial dialogue of men, woman is never purely what is spoken about; for if women in general represent a certain category of signs, destined to a certain kind of communication, each woman preserves a particular value arising from her talent, before and after marriage, for taking her part in a duet. In contrast to words, which have become wholly signs, woman has remained at once a sign and a value."

21. These homely moments of bedding down at night and arising in the morning, which align human activity with the world of nature in its predictable passages of alternating days, seasons, and years, make up one of the consistent strands in that web of symbolic associations, which invest day and night with those more metaphysical values adhering to light and darkness, seen and unseen, wakefulness and sleeping, mobility and rest, conscious and unconscious mental functions, and finally, life and death—or even death and rebirth.

bedchamber, as propriety demands. But a bed is needed, and the god therefore creates its equivalent in a grassy meadow he magically causes to grow on the mountain, as thick *(puknon)* and soft *(malakon)* as any cosy boudoir, and he ensures their privacy from prying eyes in the golden cloud he lowers around them (*Il.* 14.312–53).

An invitation to lovemaking may or may not begin with a formal move to the bedchamber *(es thalamon t'ienai)*, but a constant feature of such scenes is an explicit mention of mounting a bed *(eunē:* e.g., 10.333–34, νῶι δ' ἔπειτα εὐνῆς ἡμετέρης ἐπιβήσομεν) followed by some version of the formulaic expression, "they mingled together in *eunē* and *philotēs*": (ὄφρα μιγέντε ἐυνῇ καὶ φιλότητι, 10.340, 334–35).[22] Claude Calame translates this phrase to mean "unite in amorous exchange in a bed" and suggests that each term is properly placed to designate the three components of a sexual act: a bed *(eunē)*, commerce or interchange *(meignumi)*, and a fiduciary aspect *(philotēs)* that signifies the reciprocal nature of the erotic relationship.[23] *Eunē*, however, has a richer valence. In its lexical range, the word corresponds most closely to the English verbal noun "bedding," in that it literally refers to the bedcoverings as well as the act of bedding down. From these two meanings the term may extend to indicate the actual bed itself or the activity conducted there, whether sex or sometimes just sleep. But when it comes to designating the bed as a material object, an article of furniture, then *lechos* (or sometimes *lektron*) is the standard word,[24] just as in the case of the bedstead Odysseus has fashioned in his chamber (23.171, 177, 179, 184, 189, 199, 203).[25]

Unlike *eunē*, the word *lechos* has an institutional meaning. The *lechos* is the basis of a woman's legitimate status as a wife, signified by their "mingling together in *eunē* and *philotēs*." She is her husband's *alochos*, one who shares the same bed, and the adjectives that sometimes accompany the word (*mnēstē, kouridiē* [lawfully wedded]) confirm that she has been brought into the household under the proper social and ritual protocols.[26] It is only one short step further from bed to marriage, and *lechos*

22. Cf. *Iliad* 3.441, 445; 6.25; 9.133=9.275=19.176; 14.207, 209, 295–96, 306, 314, 331, 360; 15.32. Also *Odyssey* 5.126; 15.420–21; 23.219.

23. Calame 1992, 30–33, and see his entire analysis of epic scenes of lovemaking. For an excellent discussion of erotic terminology, see also Luca 1981.

24. Hence the formula *lechos kai eunēn* (*Od.* 3.403, 7.347, 8.269; cf. 23.179), which comprises both the bed and its coverings.

25. Note that when Penelope takes Odysseus's description of the bed as the clear proof (*sēmata ariphradea*) she had demanded, she shifts from *lechos* to *eunē* (23.226), naming it for the first time as "ours," and using the more erotic term.

26. Another word is *akoitis*, which has a similar meaning to *alochos* (as one who shares the same resting place, *koitos*), although corresponding more nearly to "spouse" (*LfgrE*, s.v.). *Akoitis* (or *parakoitis*) is always used alone, unlike *alochos*, which may be included in the larger social scene of children, parents, and household possessions. A man may be called a

can stand in for the institution of matrimony itself (*Il.* 8.291), as it does more regularly in later, especially tragic, texts, where it may even be taken as a synonym for the wife herself. Thus, while *lechos,* strictly speaking, remains a visual and concrete artifact, a practical necessity in the house, it also means something more. Both object and idea, both artifact and symbol, the bed stands for itself and also for something larger than itself that Homeric idiom can fully put into play.[27]

There are no precise terms in Homer either for sexual adultery or for marital fidelity. True, women may deceive their husbands and elicit Agamemnon's pessimistic remark that there is nothing trustworthy *(pista)* among women (11.456). But *pistos* as a qualifying adjective refers only to comrades *(hetairoi),* and the negative form *apistos,* used both of Odysseus and Penelope, points rather to a quality of suspicious caution that both of them exhibit (14.150, 391; 23.72). In traditional diction, terms for adultery and fidelity focus on the state of the marital bed, defined between the two poles of "shaming" *(aischunein,* 8.269) or "respecting " *(aidomenē)* its sacrosanct qualities. Yet marital fidelity assumes still another dimension, expressed in the phrase, "to stay in place by one's child and keep everything safe" *(menei para paidi kai empeda panta phulassei).* This is how Odysseus's mother, Antikleia, describes Penelope's behavior to him in the underworld (11.178) and how first Telemachos and then Penelope herself characterize one of the two alternatives facing her: "either to remain beside her child and keep everything *empeda,* her possessions, maidservants, and high roofed house, respecting the bed of her husband *[eunēn t'aidomenē posios]* and the opinion of the people *[dēmoio te phēmin]*— or to follow after that one, the best of the Achaeans who is wooing her in the halls, and offering her gifts" (16.74–77; 19.525–29).

Empeda is the key word. Translated as "steadfastly," "with firm stand" or "fixedly," even "safe and secure," it literally means to be grounded in the earth *(en pedōi),* precisely the issue at stake for Odysseus in regard to his bed: "I do not know whether the *lechos* is still *empedon* or whether some man has put it elsewhere, having cut under the stump of the olive tree" (23.203). *Empedos* as an adjective is a highly prized trait of human

---

parakoitēs, but there is no such equivalent for *alochos.* The two words share some of the same adjectives, but we may observe their different nuances in *Iliad* 9.396–99, where Achilles, rejecting Agamemnon's offer of his daughter in marriage, states that he will take an *akoitis* for his own at home, "where his desire stirs him to wed a wife he has wooed *(gēmanta mnēstēn alochon),* a fitting bedmate *(eikuïan akoitin)* to delight in the possessions the old man Peleus has acquired for him." Loraux (1981b, 32–34) correctly argues for the relation between *lechos* and *lochos* (of childbed), as signifiying the connection between sex and reproduction in legitimating the status of the wife *(alochos).* See also Calame 1992, 98–99.

27. As, for example, when Hera, to mollify Zeus's anger at his deception in their improvised bed, swears a holy oath on his head and on their *kouridion lechos* (*Il.* 15.37).

behavior. In the world of warriors, it characterizes a man's strength *(bia)*, vigor *(menos)*, wits *(phrenes)*, heart *(ētor)*, mind *(noos)*, feet *(podes)*, limbs *(guia)*, as well as his shield *(sakos)* and spear *(egchos)*, and denotes any purposeful activity. Often *menō* (remain) and *empedos/on* are coupled in literal fashion to describe troops on the plain firmly awaiting the onslaught of battle *(Il.* 5.526; 15.405, 622) or horses that wait patiently for their master's return *(Il.* 13.37). The obverse is a man who is past the flowering of his youth and can no longer count on such steadfast strength, and its negation is fear and timidity opposed to courage. Helen in the *Iliad* resigns herself to the fact that Paris will never conform to the proprieties, since he is a man whose *phrenes* will never be *empedoi (Il.* 6.352–53), always preferring bed to battle and taking his pleasures as he can with charming insouciance.

In the *Odyssey*, *empedos* recurs, typically again as a masculine trait, and it covers the same spectrum of meaning that includes physical valor as well as mental resolve. The minds of Odysseus's men remain *empedoi*, as they always were, even though Circe has changed their human forms into swine (10.240). In the underworld Teiresias is granted the special capacity to keep his mind *empedos* (10.493), unlike the strengthless dead, such as Agamemnon, who mourns the fact that his power and strength *(is, kikus)* are no longer *empedos* (11.393). Most often the word describes Odysseus himself. In the underworld, he is twice depicted as waiting *empedos*, in hope of conversing first with his mother and then with some of the shades of his Iliadic comrades (11.152, 628). When passing the island of the Sirens, he needs to be bound to the mast so that he may hear their seductive song but still remain *empedos* (12.161), and in facing the dangers of Skylla and Charybdis, he searches in vain for a foothold to brace himself *empedos* on the rock (12.434). When one of the suitors pelts him with a footstool, now he is the rock that faces the attack *empedos* (17.464), and in stringing the bow, he rejoices that his *menos* is still *empedon*, as it once was in the past (21.426; cf. 14.468, 503; 22.226). Only once does *empedos* apply directly to a woman: Eurykleia, who, when enjoined on pain of death to keep his identity a secret, assures her master of a *menos* that is likewise *empedon*, unyielding *(oud' epieikton)*, and promises she "will hold as stubborn as stone or iron" (19.493–94).

Penelope too has just such a resolve, but it is initially a cause for reproach in this scene, when she refuses to accept her husband, although others have assured her of his identity and he sits in her presence. Telemachos speaks of her "hard heart" *(apēnea thumon*, 23.97) and her "stubborn" or "steadfast" spirit *(tetlēoti thumōi*, 23.100), more firmly fixed than stone (23.103). Odysseus echoes his son's sentiments in almost the same terms *(kēr ateramnon*, 23.167–68). But all through these years, precisely because of her "stubborn heart" (cf. 11.181, 16.37)—a phrase characteristic too of Odysseus (9.435, 18.135, 24.163)[28]—Penelope has "remained by her child and kept everything *empeda*." To be literally *empedos* is to be fixed in the earth—like the wall the Achaeans built (*Il.* 11.9, 12) or a funeral stele that remains planted in the ground (*Il.* 17.434), a *sēma* that will endure, just like the bed of Odysseus. The fixity of the marriage bed may enact the principle of fidelity itself, which, like the trunk of the olive, sustains the institution on which it is founded. But this steadfastness must be matched reciprocally by a psychic correlative in the characters and actions of the partners who share it, each of them marked by the same quality of endurance, the capacity to *be* (Odysseus) or to *keep* (Penelope) everything *empedos*.

Yet the relative symmetry between the couple in this respect may be more apparent than real. Penelope's position, as she outlines it to Odysseus in disguise when they first exchange confidences in the firelight in book 19, exemplifies the dilemma in which she is placed by the circumstances of the poem: either wait steadfastly for Odysseus, who may be no longer be among the living, or go off with one of the suitors as his wife and leave her husband's house forever. Indeed, the latter is continually presented as a legitimate choice. Her son has come of age, and is impatient now for her to make a decision so that he can assume his rightful place and resolve his own ambiguous status as heir to his father's title and possessions. She has exhausted her own strategies of delay in the ruse of the loom, and time has brought her custodial function to an end. The suitors have become still more dangerous, plotting to kill Telemachos on his return from his voyage, and the impoverishment of the household's resources through the suitors' insolent feasting increases day by day. She is ready to initiate a bride contest in the trial of the bow to find a replacement for Odysseus, someone who may openly replace him by duplicating his special feat with his own weapon. Yet her perfectly legitimate choice, urged upon her from every side—to go home to her father or accept one of the suitors—is continually undermined by the intimation that to do so would constitute a betrayal of Odysseus, whose fate is still unknown. She would have failed to "reverence" both the bed of her husband and the public opinion of the townsfolk.[29]

But if the bed has been moved (we know not when or by whom), then an entirely different issue is raised. To accept a second marriage is not,

---

28. On the positive valence of *tetlēoti thumōi* for Odysseus and its more ambivalent use for Penelope, see Emlyn-Jones 1984, 13–14; Katz 1991, 164–65.

29. Katz (1991, 170–73) suggests that the innovation of the poem is the maintenance of an ideal of "exclusivity," so that for the first time courtship by suitors is considered a crime.

after all, equivalent to adultery, despite the wanton conduct of her suitors. There is a distinction between acquiescence to courtship, no matter how unwelcome, and actually sleeping with the enemy—between public consideration of the choice of another mate and a furtive coupling with some unknown partner.

III

The *Odyssey* is noticeably reticent about addressing acts of adultery. The question of Helen's infidelity is raised only obliquely in Book 4 when she and Menelaos offer their respective tales about Helen's behavior at Troy (4.242–89). Both stories avoid any direct mention of their marital relationship, focusing instead on the larger matter of her allegiance to or betrayal of the Greeks. In any case, the primary motive for telling these tales is to recall the cunning feats of Odysseus, with the aim of reviving memories of a lost friend and of edifying his son, Telemachos, who, coming to Sparta to find news of his father, learns instead about Odysseus's heroic past at Troy. We may take the cues of these two stories as offering possible alternatives for Penelope herself. Will she, as in Helen's version, receive Odysseus as a stranger in disguise and give him welcome? Or conversely, following Menelaos's tale, will she behave with the suitors in a way that resembles Helen's provocative temptation of the Greeks hidden inside the wooden horse? But for now, everything is pure innuendo. The erotic undertones at the banquet in Sparta run deep and strong, to be sure, but even so, they resonate only as whispers of seduction—the foreplay, perhaps, but not the "real thing." [30]

Avoidance is one strategy; euphemism is another. The adulterous act is called an *ergon aeikes,* an unseemly act. This is how Penelope, after the scene of *anagnōrisis* in Book 23, describes Helen's action in going off with Paris (23.222). Clytemnestra too is charged with performing an *ergon aeikes,* which may refer both to her sexual misdeed and to its outcome in the murder of Agamemnon (3.265; 11.429). There is one scene, however, that tells a tale of adultery, complete with a guilty couple and an outraged husband. It is the only one, in fact, that does not hesitate to speak plainly (8.332).[31]

30. On these stories, see Schmiel 1972; Dupont-Roc and Le Boulluec 1976; Bergren 1981; Goldhill 1991, 62–64; see also this volume, chapter 9, 409–11. On their relevance as alternative paradigms for Penelope, see Anderson 1977; Katz 1991, 77–80 and *passim;* and this volume, chapter 9. Olson (1990) is largely derivative, but his claim that Menelaos's story is the "right" one and Helen's the "wrong" one, on the basis of his understanding of the "sexual dynamics" of the poem, is both naive and misguided.

31. The technical term for adultery is *moicheia.* It appears only here in the *Odyssey,* under the compound *moichagri[a],* "a fine imposed on someone taken in adultery."

This scene is the song of Ares and Aphrodite, performed in Book 8 by the bard Demodokos at the Phaeacian court (8.266–366), a song that so scandalized ancient commentators that, along with some of their modern counterparts, they wanted to athetize it from the text.[32] But the tale has its virtues, not the least of which is that it provides some important parallels and contrasts with our scene in Book 23, for their mutual elucidation. Its significance is enhanced through its presentation by Demodokos in the very episode of the *Odyssey* that, as we shall see, is carefully framed to foreshadow and ultimately validate the dramatic reunion of Odysseus and Penelope.

The song of Ares and Aphrodite occupies the central position in the triad of the bard's recitations at the court of Alkinoos, between two others that refer to Odysseus at Troy: a quarrel between Odysseus and Achilles (8.75–82) and Odysseus's role in the sack of Troy through the ruse of the wooden horse (8.493–520). The contrasts are striking: a tale about gods, not mortals; about sex, not war; and about relations between men and women, not those between men. While all three tales are constructed around themes of antagonism and conflict, the lay of Ares and Aphrodite also differs markedly from the others in its ribald tone and comic outcome.

A bed, the marital bed, plays the starring role in this erotic triangle that recounts the *philotēs* between Ares and Aphrodite, how "they first mingled *[migēsan]* secretly in the house of Hephaistos," when he "shamed the *lechos . . . kai eunēn* of the lord Hephaistos" (8.266–70). This bed too is an unusual exemplar of its kind—not in its unusual mode of manufacture or position in the bedroom, but in what its owner devises for it after Helios observes the guilty couple "mingling in *philotēs*" and tattles to the cuckolded spouse (8.270–73). The craftsman god is not at a loss for skillful tricks. The stratagem he chooses is to construct an invisible net, finer than a spider's web, which he suspends over the bed to catch and hold fast the adulterous pair, so they may be exhibited in all their shame to the prurient and ridiculing gaze of the assembly of gods (except for the virginal goddesses). His plan was to "hammer out unbreakable bonds that cannot be loosed," so that when the lovers next indulged in *philotēs,* they would remain there *empedon*—fixed fast (*menoien empedon,* 8.275)— with no hope of escape. Hephaistos indeed succeeds in this literal version of entrapment: "neither of them could stir a limb or get up and now they saw the truth and they could not escape" (8.298–99). By his clever device, Hephaistos reverses the balance of power between his all too virile rival and himself, one he could maintain in perpetuity, if he so wished, as he ironically remarks:

32. Burkert 1960, 137n.16.

But you shall see how the two of them have gone into my bed
    and lie there
making love. I am sickened when I look at them, and yet
I suppose they would not like to lie this way even a moment
    more
much though they are in love. Nor will they soon want to
sleep, but my ruse and my bonds will contain them. . . .
                                            (8.313–17)[33]

In the private chamber of Odysseus and Penelope, the bed remains
fixed in the interplay between husband and wife as the private site and
condition of their marital reunion and the enduring permanence of their
conjugal bond. Adultery, on the other hand, answers to these same principles but is configured in their parodic and sinister inversion. Here the
issue at stake is not the status of an immovable bed but rather the lovers
themselves, who remain locked in a perpetual embrace, neither able to
separate from one another nor together enjoy the pleasures of sex and
sleep. In an erotic context, the quality of steadfastness is represented as
shifting between a positive and a negative pole: between a virtuous ideal
and an unimpeachable emblem of shame, between stability and constancy
on the one hand, and detainment, even imprisonment, on the other. It
signifies the difference between a licit and an illicit sexuality, the latter
threatening to become an unbearably permanent state of being, if Hephaistos were not persuaded finally to let the errant couple go.[34]

Once viewed mainly as an embarrassing if not interpolated digression,
which reflects well on neither the gods nor the poet, the tale of Ares and
Aphrodite has more recently undergone a satisfying rehabilitation at the
hands of critics. The effect of this renewed interest extends from situating
the song in the immediate context of the framing events in Phaeacia to
considering its implications for the sexual ideology of the poem, with particular emphasis on the situation of Odysseus himself. The distancing effects of "a poem within a poem," along with its tone of bawdy humor and
shift to the realm of the gods, may seem to divide it sharply from the two
other songs, which directly address the exploits of Odysseus at Troy. But
these same features also enhance the symbolic values of the story as a suggestive and complex sign—a *sēma* in its own right, we might say—which,
accordingly, solicits efforts to determine what and how it might mean.
The immediate setting furnishes one parallel in both content and form:
the ultimate reconciliation between the two erotic rivals is matched by

33. Translation of Lattimore (1965) modified.
34. One might justly compare their permanent state of attachment to Aristophanes'
myth in Plato's *Symposium* (192c–e), where Hephaistos offers to reunite the two halves of
the original spherical beings into their former love-locked existence.

the amicable settlement of the strife between Odysseus and Euryalos in the matter of athletic competition, whereby Odysseus is exonerated and his burly opponent shamed.[35] At the same time, the air of comic burlesque also works to the same effect: male rivalry on the playing fields is recoded into sexual joking, and the shared laughter of the male audience, including Odysseus, at the laughter of the gods, repairs the previous tensions for all concerned. Yet, as already observed by ancient commentators,[36] the pertinence of a theme of sexual infidelity extends beyond the context of the present performance to address the central concern of the poem itself in advance of Odysseus's return to Ithaca to reclaim his wife and his bed.

The objective of this pivotal book of the poem is precisely to reestablish Odysseus's identity through his own active participation in events as well as in the songs of the bard. The narrative is cunningly fashioned to construct that identity through a complex layering of past, present, and future with the aim of merging the Iliadic and Odyssean facets of his character into a composite and convincing portrait of this uncommon hero. Only when the current deeds and reactions of the unknown stranger are matched up with the past of Odysseus through the two tales of the hero's experiences at Troy[37] is he finally empowered to take the last step toward self-revelation, when he finally launches the first-person narration of his own story under his own name. In this dense texture of reenactment and recall, the love song of Ares and Aphrodite moves to another plane of relevance in the forging of that identity by staging a conflict between two wholly other adversaries and by supplying an erotic context that obliquely looks to future events while also recasting them in a more problematic way.

True, the defense of a husband against adultery conducted in his own bed and the resort to trickery in outwitting a male rival hint at the theme of the entire poem (if not its facts) and at the characteristic quality of *mētis* that Odysseus shares with Hephaistos, the master builder.[38] This is the salient point of identification, to which we will return. On the other hand, if Hephaistos's honor is restored through his exposure of the lovers and his successful demand for retribution, the rest of the tale implies that the model does not fully hold. Beyond the universal embarrassment of a cuck-

35. The song in its context: on Ares and Aphrodite in Book 8, see Bliss 1968; Edinger 1980; Braswell 1982.

36. Cf. Athenaeus, 5.192d–e.

37. On the Trojan songs of the bard, see especially the fine analysis of Pucci 1987, 214–27. For the poet's "invention" of the unknown theme of the quarrel between Achilles and Odysseus, see Marg 1956, 20–21; for its "traditionality," Nagy 1979, 43.

38. For the definitive study of *mētis*, including craft, craftsmanship, and binding/unbinding, see Detienne and Vernant 1978. On Hephaistos in particular, see also Delcourt 1957.

olded husband is the singular unattractiveness of this lame and ugly spouse, as Hephaistos himself acknowledges. As a result, he cannot claim a full virility, according to the prevailing epic standards. More significant still, he never actually reclaims his wife, since once released from his trap, she conveniently finds refuge in her distant sanctuary at Cyprus where she may restore her sexual allure for another occasion of (illicit?) lovemaking. The erotic mismatch between this married couple therefore compromises the analogy, which is further undermined by a quasi-exoneration of Ares, when Hermes declares that he too would desire "to sleep by the side of Aphrodite the golden" even if "there could be three times this number of endless bonds, and all you gods could be looking on and all the goddesses" (8.339–41). Manliness is measured by a fine male body and evidence of physical prowess, as even here, when Athena magically transforms Odysseus at the beginning of the episode "so that he might be loved by all the Phaeacians, and to them might be wonderful and respected, and might accomplish many trials of strength by which the Phaeacians tested Odysseus" (8.17–23). For the situation on Ithaca, Odysseus will need all his strength; he must exercise *bia*, after all, as well as his resourceful *mētis* to overcome the suitors, even if the cunning of *mētis* is essential to prepare the way for his retributive victory over them.[39]

Nevertheless, the ostensible triumph of Hephaistos in the tale offers significant parallels for the future. These not only align Odysseus with his Hephaestean attributes but also keep the narrative context of the song in mind at the reunion of Odysseus and Penelope in Book 23. In an illuminating essay, Rick Newton focuses on the correspondences between these two masters of ruse and practical skills, who both possess the qualities of *mētis* and *technē*. He notes that allusions to Hephaistos increase toward the latter part of the poem, until they culminate finally in echoes from the scene at the Phaeacian court in the *anagnōrisis* of Odysseus and Penelope.[40] The first clues pertain to physical appearance. Hephaistos is, of course, noted for his limping gait. Odysseus, for his part, when extolling his various competitive skills to the Phaeacian men, specifically excludes any strength of foot, claiming that life at sea has put him out of practice (8.230–33).[41] On Ithaca, too, we note that in his beggar's disguise

---

39. Edwards (1985) argues for the *lochos* or ambush through *mētis* as defining the *kleos* of Odysseus. But *bia*, the quality relevant to both Achilles and Ares, is also fully deployed in the Iliadic-style battle against the suitors, as will be further argued below.

40. Newton 1987.

41. See Braswell 1982, 134; and Newton 1987, 13. Note, however, that in the funeral games in *Iliad* 23 (echoed in the games in Phaeacia), Odysseus actually won in the footrace (significantly, against Ajax: *Il.* 23.740–83). Demodokos's first song tells of a quarrel between Achilles and Odysseus—a first move, I suggest, to establish Odysseus's identity by posing his

he requires a staff to assist him in walking (17.196, 203, 338), and like Hephaistos he seems to be continually at risk of being hurled out of doors by his foot (17.478–80; 18.10; cf. *Il.* 1.590–91; 15.18–24; 18.395).

More notable are the interests the two share in carpentry and metallurgy. Odysseus's credentials as a craftsman are established elsewhere in the poem before he arrives among the Phaeacians: first when he builds his raft on the island of Calypso (5.228–61), and then in the simile of the blacksmith's art that he chooses to describe his blinding of the Cyclops with the heated point of the sharpened log (9.391). Newton cites the parallel between Hephaistos's departure for his forge to devise his means of entrapment (8.273) and its later echo in Ithaca in the jeering suggestion made to Odysseus that he get out of the house and find a smithy somewhere as lodging for the night (18.328).[42] The figures are also associated through their house-building skills. In *Iliad* 1, when the gods disperse for the night, we are told that "strong-handed Hephaistos had built a house [for each] by means of his craftsmanship and cunning" (*Il.* 1.607–8), and it is not an otiose detail that Odysseus's first glimpse of his house leads to an approving assessment of its excellent handiwork.

> . . . Surely this is the handsome house of Odysseus
> Easily it is singled out and seen among many,
> for one part is joined on to another, and the courtyard is worked on
> with wall and copings, and the doors have been well made, with double
> panels. Nobody could belittle this house.
>
> (17.264–68)[43]

Finally, and above all, is the shared emphasis on marital beds as the site of lovemaking—beds that each had made and that prove to have special devices for testing wifely fidelity. Newton looks back still earlier in the poem for a "possible analogy between Hephaistos's net and Odysseus' actual bed." The scene is Telemachos's return from his journey in Book 16, where he "wonders whether his mother is still at home or whether she has

---

difference (dissent) from that other Homeric hero. Achilles, of course, is best known for his swiftness of foot, and if Odysseus wins the footrace in *Iliad* 23, it is because Achilles presides over the games but does not himself compete. Here Odysseus explicitly renounces the footrace, so as to emphasize instead his skill in archery, the trait for which he is best known (8.215–28).

42. Newton 1987, 13.

43. Note too that when Odysseus first enters the house, he sits on the threshold, "leaning against a pillar of cypress wood which a carpenter had once smoothed and made straight by the rule" (17.340–41).

married one of the suitors, and Odysseus' bed lies in want of bedclothes
or occupants *[eneunaiōn]*, collecting foul spider webs" (16.33–35). It was
Athena, as Newton observes, who had first "plant[ed] the suspicion in his
mind" when he was tarrying at the court of Menelaos, with the precise
intention of stirring him to return home (15.4–20):

> For you know what the mind is like in the breast of a woman.
> She wants to build up the household of the man who marries
>   her,
> and of her former children, and of her beloved and wedded
>   husband,
> she has no remembrance, when he is dead, nor does she ask after
>   him.

Newton wants to compare the image of the neglected bed at home to "Hephaistos' net that is said to resemble fine spider webs" (8.280), on the
grounds that the context in each case indicates a suspicion of adultery.[44]
But, in truth, the parallel is far from exact. The spider webs in Ithaca
merely signify that the wife may have abandoned her husband's bed to
make a marriage elsewhere; it is not an act of adulterous defilement.
Moreover, the two references perform different, contrary functions that
revolve around the two extremes of excessive use and disuse, presence and
absence. For Odysseus's bed, the spider webs are a *visible* sign of a wife's
flight from the marital bed, while in Hephaistos's case, the simile describes
the *invisibility* of the bonds he has designed to detain his spouse and to
prevent her and her lover from escaping. Fragility marks the literal gossa-
mer threads of the first, tensile strength the figurative properties of the
second. If Hephaistos's ruse is recalled once more on Ithaca, it is surely in
the other simile, which describes Telemachos's uncommon punishment of
the unfaithful maidservants by stringing them up from a ship's cable that
he fastened to the pillar of the house:

> and like thrushes, who spread their wings, or pigeons, who have
> flown into a snare set up for them in a thicket, trying
> to find a resting place, but the sleep given them was hateful;
> so their heads were all in a line, and each had her neck caught
> fast in a noose, so that their death would be most pitiful.
>   (22.465–71)

We note the same sarcastic humor about bed and sleep as in Hephaistos's
ironic comments on the effects of his handiwork and the same resort to
entrapment in bonds as a fitting retribution for sexual transgressions.

44. Newton 1987, 18n.22.

More portentous, however, are the extended echoes of Demodokos's song as the moment of *anagnōrisis* draws ever closer. The first instance is Penelope's appearance before the suitors in Book 18. To prepare her entrance, Athena has attended to her physical enhancement while she was sleeping, renewing the beauty of her face with an ambrosial salve, "such as fair-garlanded Kythereia uses, whenever she joins the lovely dances of the Graces" (18.192–94). Both the language and the context recall certain details of the bard's tale. Only in these two passages is Aphrodite named as "fair-garlanded Kythereia," and after her flight to Cyprus, the Graces were named as the ones, who, to restore the goddess's beauty in the aftermath of her misadventure, bathed and anointed her (8.364–66). Additionally, this is the first time Penelope has explicitly exposed herself publicly to the suitors with a seductive aim, and as Newton rightly points out, she arouses much the same response from them as did the spectacle of Aphrodite among the other gods ("Their knees gave way, and the hearts in them were bemused with passion, and each one prayed for the privilege of lying beside her," 18.212–14; cf. 18.245–49).[45] It is precisely after this scene that Odysseus is most closely identified with Hephaistos. He offers to tend the fires in the house and is cruelly advised to take up lodgings instead in the smithy. The old and ugly beggar likewise arouses laughter from the group, and it is perhaps no accident that his chief tormentor is the ungrateful maidservant who, we are told, has been sleeping with one of the suitors (18.306–29).[46]

Finally, we can point to the significant recall of the Phaeacian festivities in their pretended counterpart in Odysseus's house. For in the interval between Penelope's refusal to recognize Odysseus and the later *anagnōrisis*, Odysseus orders a celebration replete with dancers and bards as a way of gaining time, to hold off news of the suitors' massacre. In this way, he says, "anyone who is outside, some one of the neighbors, or a person going along the street, who hears us, will think we are having a wedding" (23.130–40). For Newton, the general analogy between the two scenes holds, however they may differ in purpose.[47] But the marriage theme itself

45. Newton 1987, 16. This temptation scene might also recall Menelaos's story about Helen in her efforts to seduce the Greek chieftains at Troy (4.266–89). See Katz 1991, 133.

46. Her behavior prompts Odysseus's threat to tell Telemachos, who, he claims, will savagely punish her (18.338–39)—an exact preview of events when, after the massacre of the suitors, the father will bid his son to "cleanse" the house of its sexual "pollution" by the unfaithful maidservants.

47. Newton (1987, 17) suggests that the echo serves to distract the audience's attention from the darker side of Odysseus's revenge. Many critics have noted the "truth" in the pretended wedding feast as heralding that the reunion of Odysseus and Penelope is to be a (re)marriage. See, for example, Besslich 1966, 89; Segal 1983, 44–45; Pucci 1987, 91; Katz 1991, 166–71.

may be far more exact. Although the song of Ares and Aphrodite is performed for a male audience, with male dancers miming all the parts,[48] the submerged idea of a wedding celebration as its motivation may not be far removed.

Marriage is uppermost in the minds of the Phaeacians. Nausikaa is of the right age to find a husband, and from her first meeting with Odysseus on the seashore, his possible role as her bridegroom is a complicating theme that runs uneasily throughout his sojourn on Scheria. Indeed, some critics had proposed an earlier version in which Odysseus was intended to wed Nausikaa, and folklorists have pointed to the widespread pattern of a handsome stranger meeting a young girl at a source of water and eventually becoming her husband.[49] If this paradigm were operating silently behind Odysseus's reception at the court of Alkinoos, it might explain some of the ambiguities that critics have noted about the Phaeacians' brand of hospitality, particularly among the other would-be suitors, who are hostile at first, yet end up showering him with gifts, once Odysseus has shown his mettle. In this context, as Steve Reece has lately suggested, the song of Ares and Aphrodite may do more than safely articulate some of the erotic tensions aroused by Odysseus's presence among the Phaeacian men, especially after his victory in the games: it might itself be an actual wedding song.[50] There is no certain evidence that such songs were performed during (or before) Greek wedding ceremonies. Nevertheless, ribald burlesques were no doubt a common feature of symposiast joking, and the idea of a prenuptial context for such rude "male talk" (as in other cultures) might well account for the bard's choice of this particular theme. A backhanded compliment for the bride, to be sure, and an obscene teasing of male virility, represented as a precise (and temporary) inversion of accepted social norms that are soon to be reaffirmed in the proper conduct of marriage.[51] A disguised wedding song in Book 8, a feigned wedding

48. Critics do not agree as to whether the dancers mime the song or dance independently. It is worth mentioning that later tradition (Lucian, *De saltatione* 62–63) knows just such a mime: "He danced the amours of Aphrodite and Ares, Helios tattling, Hephaistos laying his plot and trapping both of them with his entangling bonds, the gods who came in on them, portrayed individually, Aphrodite ashamed, Ares seeking cover and begging for mercy, and everything that belongs to this story, in such wise that Demetrius was delighted beyond measure with what was taking place and paid the highest possible tribute to the dancer; he raised his voice and shouted: I hear the story that you are acting, I do not just see it; you seem to me to be talking with your very hands."
49. Woodhouse 1930, 54–65; and see Reece 1993, 104–21, for fuller discussion and bibliography.
50. Reece 1993, 115–16.
51. Olson (1989) pompously claims that the song exposes the "hypocrisy" of the *Odyssey's* "double standard" in order to debunk the absurdly high moral expectations of the poem

feast in Book 23: it is a tempting hypothesis that aligns the echoes of one in the other with still richer resonance for the reunion of Odysseus and Penelope in the allusive style of a (re)marriage.

The implicit reference to Hephaistos in the ruse of the bed, however, leads to another, even more vital point. Just before the recognition scene, Odysseus is bathed and dressed, and the goddess makes certain he will look his best:

> And over his head Athena suffused great beauty, to make him
> taller
> to behold and thicker, and on his head she arranged
> the curling locks that hung down like hyacinthine petals.
> And as when a master craftsman overlays gold on silver,
> and he is one who was taught by Hephaistos and Pallas Athena
> in art complete, and grace is on every work he finishes;
> so Athena gilded with grace his head and his shoulders.
>
> (23.159–62)

A surprising number of critics have been disturbed by the fact that this simile is repeated almost verbatim from an earlier episode, when Athena transformed Odysseus's appearance to present him before the eyes of Nausikaa (6.157–62), and some go so far as to insist that it is a late interpolation into the text.[52] It would be difficult to register the degree of my dissent from this opinion. In the first place, the simile is especially appropriate as a recall of an earlier would-be bride just at the moment when Odysseus and Penelope are to be reunited. In the second, the explicit mention of Hephaistos gives the cue to the further echoes of his role in the stratagem of the bed. But there is an additional value to be gained from the description of Hephaistos's handiwork. It will establish another set of relations that, I suggest, are designed to strengthen the sense of stable enclosure that the bed represents and thus to offer further conclusive proof of Odysseus's identity.

Odysseus is likened to an art object that is overlaid with gold and silver by the hands of one endowed with the gifts of both Athena and Hephaistos. The description of this craftsman might well apply to Odysseus himself, specifically in the case of the bed that he himself has made, which he decorates in precisely the same way by embellishing it with gold

---

that run counter to any notion of believable "reality" in the fallen world in which they (we?) all live. By contrast, Peradotto (1993), who characterizes the song as an alternate and uncensored view of unlawful sexual desire in a spirit of exuberant and life-giving comic license, properly respects the conventions of archaic Greek culture and poetry.

52. For discussion, see Heubeck 1992, *ad* xxiii, 157–62.

and silver (and ivory). In identifying person with object, body with artifact, and in tracing the shift from a passive to an active role as essential
steps to a process of transfiguration, a powerful link is created that suggests a parallel between the bed and its maker, between the article of ownership and the physical figure of the one who constructed it. Others have
pointed out how the construction of the entire bedchamber recapitulates
and condenses the essence of Odysseus himself: the secret of a secret self
that now may be revealed, the interplay between inside and outside, by
which the external can now bring to light the truth of that hidden part and
give proof of a dissimulated identity.[53] And so it does, not only, as Starobinski observes, by replacing the assertion of "I am" with the active force
of "I made it," but also through a set of semantic coincidences and trans-
ferrals, by which words of double meaning now coalesce into a powerful
unity of reference.

The two key terms are *sēma* and *empedon,* each available for wordplay at this critical moment. Penelope had first adverted to the "hidden
signs that are only known to the two of us and no one else" (23.110). But
it is left to Odysseus to join the two ideas of a *sēma* into one, when
through the device of ring composition he first invokes its other, more
literal use as a distinguishing mark *(mega sēma),* before he can claim at
the end that this *sēma* of the bed is also a *sēma* of proof. And what, in
fact, is the final verification, if not the query as to whether the bed is still
empedon (23.203)—that is, whether it remains still fixed in the earth?
Only then is Penelope persuaded to acknowledge the the bed as the *sēmata*
she had required to ratify Odysseus's identity, and this because she takes
the sign as *empeda*—as a solid and secure proof of who he is (23.205,
250; 24.346).[54] In other words, the *sēma* that is *empedon* (i.e., the bed
rooted in the earth) emerges as a *sēma empedon* (a valid sign). In these
two junctures—the maker with his object, the words with their literal and
figurative meanings—the system of reference gains a deeper coherence
and closes in upon itself as securely as the chamber that Odysseus "built
around the tree trunk, finished it, with close-set stones, and roofed it well
over, adding the compacted doors, and fitting them closely together"
(23.190–94).[55]

---

53. Above all, see Starobinksi's remarkable essay (1975) on the "inside" and the "outside," and see further Katz's use of his work (1991, 179–81).

54. *Sēmata* that are *empeda* are matched by the clarity and visibility *(ariphradēs)* of the
sēma (11.126; 21.217; 23.73, 225, 273; 24.329).

55. From this point of view, we may also distinguish between the two craftsmen, Odysseus and Hephaistos. The latter, by means of his art, is uniquely the agent of transformation,
but is not himself subject to physical change. The ugly artist remains forever as he is, bound
to his forge and deploying his skills of beautiful embellishment. Odysseus, on the other hand,

IV

These are extraordinary measures, and rightly so, if we consider both the nature of the defensive system and what it aims to protect. If we return now to the quotation from M. I. Finley at the beginning of this essay, on the habit in the heroic world "of translating every quality or state into some specific symbol, some concrete and material object," we might then instance the bed and its construction as a proof text of this principle. But I believe there is more. The impulse to turn a social bond into a visible emblem and to represent the intimacy of feeling in external form has the power in this case not just to signify the stability of the marriage relationship but to serve as the stabilizing factor itself of a quality, idea, or proposition that finally remains beyond the reach of all definitive proof. It is an attempt to master a fundamentally unmasterable situation.

First and foremost is the radical unknowability of the unexpressed secrets of a woman's desire. She might be pure of hands but not of heart, even if only for a brief moment, then or now. How is one to guarantee the constancy, the steadfastness, of that heart, especially under the present circumstances? The precondition, after all, that regulates the entire situation at Ithaca is the apparent freedom given to Penelope to *choose* the man for her husband whom her heart desires. If she is to choose "the best of the Achaeans," what would this title mean in designating the man whom she might desire? The contest of the bow, a traditional means for selecting a victorious suitor from among his rivals, might indicate that a heroic feat of physical prowess is to be the deciding factor. Yet since the poet structures his entire plot around Penelope's imagined state(s) of mind, we cannot exclude some cultural notion of feminine desire as an internalized emotion, hidden from view and maintained as a private and undivulged secret. And if this is the case, how is that desire to be manifested, investigated, or controlled?

Second and more substantive is the nagging possibility of a real adul-

---

enjoys the benefits of both aspects: an aesthetically enhanced persona (signifying his erotic status) merges with the artistry of what he has made. At the same time, embedded in the verb *piphauskomai* (related to the root for *phaos*) is an enduring relation between Hephaistos and Odysseus in the matter of fire and light. Aithon (the blazing one) is what Odysseus names himself in his lying tale to Penelope (19.183) when they sit by the fire at the hearth in their first intimate conversation, and in Book 23 the hearth again is prominent as the site of their two-phased reunion. In his arrival on Scheria, the transitional point of his journey from the fabulous world of his adventures to the realities of life on Ithaca, Odysseus is significantly linked to fire in the simile that compares his burrowing under a pile of heaped-up leaves in a dense thicket to a spark buried in the embers (5.490). Here too, as in Book 23, he plays true to form by making a bed in a place of private and hidden enclosure. See further Bonnafé 1985; and on Odysseus and fire (light), see especially Bremer 1976 and Flaumenhaft 1982.

terous tryst that would simply have escaped the husband's notice. As a god, Hephaistos has the unusual advantage of Helios the Sun, the All-Seeing, as his reliable informer. He also has magical skills that can expose the errant couple and put them on potentially permanent display in the presence of eyewitnesses. This twofold scenario might be the wish-fulfillment fantasy of more than one suspicious husband.

The case at Ithaca is perhaps an extreme example of the same problematic. Its more complex turns are predicated, first of all, on the figure of Penelope herself. The poem presents her in such a way as to assure us of her fidelity.[56] At the same time, it endows her actions with sufficient ambiguity to arouse the need for interpretation, often with diametrically different readings, if we chart the range of opinions that swirl around the evaluation of three especially significant moments: her decision to appear before the suitors, the dream of the geese, and the setting up of the contest of the bow. As Suzuki observes, "unlike Odysseus, Penelope is portrayed from without, and the poet, while according her subjectivity, does not seek to represent it; he sees her through the eyes of the male characters around her—Odysseus, Telemachos, and the suitors, and he conveys their uncertainty about her."[57] Sheila Murnaghan goes further in outlining the dilemma. "Penelope's motives are difficult to assess," she remarks, "because the poet is generally uncommunicative about her thoughts, but not about Odysseus', leaving us to deduce her state of mind from outward gestures and speeches." She continues, "Because Penelope has been shown to be capable of duplicity, in particular through her trick with the shroud, it is not clear whether those speeches are to be taken at face value." Closely bound to these concerns is the asymmetrical quality of their knowledge. Hence, Penelope "is responding to the presence of the apparent stranger who is actually the returned Odysseus in disguise, so what seems to be a meeting of strangers is actually the reunion of husband and wife." Moreover, since Odysseus intends that she remain in this state of ignorance, his deception of her "is not the byproduct of the plot against the suitors, but a major element in his strategy."[58]

---

56. Aside from explicit statements (e.g., Odysseus's mother in the underworld in response to his query, 11.177–83), fidelity is figured by Penelope's immobility in the house and her continuous weeping—another sign that she has not forgotten her husband. Fidelity is less an affair of the heart than the mind (*noos*), and infidelity is equated as much with changing that *noos* or failing to remember as with engaging in conscious and active deception. Hence, Penelope's epithet, *echephrōn* (keeping good sense), not only attests to her intelligence and perspicacity but also includes a capacity to remain steadfast in that *noos,* keeping her husband always in mind. *Sōphrōn* (and the noun *sōphrosunē*), the literal meaning of which is "to keep the mind safe," is unknown in Homeric diction but later becomes the standard word for chastity.

57. Suzuki 1989, 91.

58. Murnaghan 1986, 105.

Athena, after all, had bidden Odysseus not to declare himself to Penelope "until you test your wife even more." The first reason given is that a premature reunion might divert him from his obligation to punish the suitors' infractions of social rules and reveal his identity too soon. But underlying the goddess's advice is the unspoken possibility that his wife might yet betray him (13.190–93). This apparently clever narrative strategy, which maintains suspense about her fidelity until the very end, is based culturally on a profound mistrust of women. This mistrust is exemplified, above all, in the foil story of Clytemnestra, but it is also intimated in the two tales told by Helen and Menelaos. As Murnaghan puts it, "the *Odyssey's* unusually sympathetic portrait of the exemplary wife is placed in a wider context of suspicion towards women from which even she cannot altogether escape. Through the presentation of Penelope as an exception to the general rule, the poem self-consciously depicts the formation and authorization of a tradition of misogyny even as it places the counterexample at the center of its story." [59]

Furthermore, as often noted, every female figure in the poem—including Calypso, Circe, Arete, and even Nausikaa—contributes some element to the complex and composite portrait of Penelope. On the sinister side, Penelope most resembles Circe. Does not she too have the charms to enchant men and turn them into swine—creatures, who, like the suitors, are perpetually at the mercy of their bellies? Like Circe, she too might lure an unsuspecting man to her bed and, having persuaded him to lie in *philotēs* with her, take advantage of his nakedness and even unman him. Homeric epic categorically defines a woman's role in the household as divided equally between the two material poles of loom and bed (e.g., *Il.* 1.31). Are not these the same two symbolic objects that Penelope's guile puts into play: the ruse of her web in the first instance, and the trick of the bed in the second? Who then could be certain from the start that her gift for duplicity against the suitors in the matter of the loom might not this time be turned against her husband, precisely with regard to the marital bed?

At the same time, the configuration of male sexual desire, as delineated in this poem and elsewhere in Greek literature, itself creates the circumstances for the idea of such a betrayal. This psychological construct is evident in the timing of Penelope's appearance before the suitors, since it also serves as the occasion when Odysseus catches his first glimpse of the wife he left long ago. The motives given for Penelope's sudden desire to exhibit herself to them are revealing. The fact that Athena and not she is the agent of this unexpected turn of affairs sustains a certain ambiguity in her choice of action. On the one hand, the goddess's intervention relieves Penelope of responsibility and might seem to guarantee the alienation of this desire from Penelope's "true" thoughts. Yet who can vouch for the troubled and complex sources of human desire? In the lover's discourse, the irresistible impulse is often attributed to divine agency as an outward projection. All the same, resort to this erotic psychology might also be a way of veiling (and hence expressing) what the person cannot recognize or acknowledge as internal to, or at least compatible with, the desiring self. Hence Penelope can laugh nervously at the idea that Athena put into her mind and express her wonderment that "my heart [thumos] desires, though before it did not, to show myself to the suitors, although I still hate them" (18.163–65). And who can exclude the possibility of a merely convenient pretext, when she adds that she will use the same occasion to reproach her son for consorting with these insolent men (18.166–68)?

A further and essential point is the paradox that the disclosure of these motives only increases the uncertainties about what she has in mind. The poet tells us that Athena conceived this plan "so that Penelope might all the more open up the desiring hearts [thumos] of the suitors, and so that she might seem all the more precious in the eyes of her husband and son even than she had been before" (18.158–62). The tangible results of this encounter are the gifts she beguiles from the suitors to add to Odysseus's household wealth, and in this way it might be said that she indeed proves more "precious" than before in Odysseus's eyes: he applauds her accomplishment and praises her too in that "she enchanted their spirits with blandishing words, while her own mind had other intentions" (18.281–83). He voices his approval of what he takes to be her deception of the suitors, but he profits too from their voiced appreciation of her beauty, which Athena has just now restored with this express idea in mind (18.191). The twin ideas—to stir the hearts of the suitors *and* to make herself more precious in the eyes of her husband—are framed in the proper order. They are not just an instance of parataxis but should also be construed in a relation of cause and effect. Odysseus may be permitted to test the behavior of this Aphroditean Penelope in front of the suitors— a test that, the poet assures us, he is convinced she has passed. But Odysseus gains yet a further satisfaction. The suitors' lovestruck reaction to her beauty renews the ardor of their desire for her and impels them to offer her still more bountiful gifts. Yet this response, witnessed by Odysseus, as he gazes on them gazing on her, validates *his* own desire in turn and renews it, in the flesh, we might say. Athena knows what she is doing.

This doubly voyeuristic scene is a classic instantiation of triangular or "mimetic" desire. This mechanism postulates the major spur to masculine desire as deriving not from some intrinsic quality of the beautiful object herself, but rather from a mimetic rivalry among men, whereby male subjects are led to desire the same woman precisely because she is the object of others' desire.[60] Hence the double bind of Penelope's position in the symbiotic interdependence of Odysseus and the suitors: in order for her husband to desire her, she needs to prove her desirability to others, but by the same move, she also falls under the shadow of suspicion with respect to the state of her own desire. This same double bind requires that she continue her teasing of the suitors, even to the extent of staging the contest of the bow, while at the same time ostensibly pining for Odysseus—a strategy whose underlying reasons she does not yet understand, or so we think. For that same device of maintaining her ignorance also leads up to the kind of *anagnōrisis* the Greeks like best: the affective sympathy between persons and an affinity they reveal to one another as a precondition of mutual recognition. It is predicated in this instance on his identity and her fidelity, both of which will attain full acknowledgment in Penelope's ruse of the bed. If the *Odyssey* is justly admired for playing out this narrative strategy in its most extended and developed form, is it not because the erotic setting heightens the thrill of each obstacle to recognition, each detour and deferral on the way? Does not this ploy raise the stakes of the game by requiring men to try and chart the meandering and conflicting paths of what they imagine as a woman's desire?

In commenting on the pervasive appeal of the recognition scene in literature, Terence Cave probes some of its more troubling aspects. The "regime of anagnorisis invites us compellingly, seductively, violently to assent to its simulacrum of order," he argues, " but also to discover in the process that the means by which we define ourselves as individuals in relation to social and legal authority may be no less contrived and trivial than birthmark and casket."[61] A further point he makes is equally relevant—namely, that the power given to female characters in assenting to recognition of a male could also be construed as a "challenging of a male order, represented here by the desire to impose an anagnorisis which would leave the male firmly on top. Women [as men represent them] undo recognitions, or perform it in another way, disquietingly and always scandalously. . . . Only women know, in private, what is really going on. And they may not always care to say," especially when it comes to the "scandal of impossible or incomprehensible sexual knowledge."[62] The mystification continues. What man (even as astute a critic as Cave) is allowed to claim that he knows for sure what a woman thinks or feels?

Penelope's ruse of the bed might seem to follow Cave's proposition.

60. On the concept of mimetic or mediated desire (the male subject desires the object because the rival desires it), see Girard 1977, 145.

61. Cave 1988, 464.

62. Cave 1988, 494–95.

For the first time, she is permitted to take the upper hand. All finally rests in her choice to award or refuse acknowledgment of Odysseus's identity and to set the terms, those "secret signs" they share, as a test of who he is. Yet if she reverses their roles to test the one who has tested her for so long, by the nature of the stratagem she selects, she inevitably puts herself to the test as well. Her tears and her instant and spontaneous acceptance of the *sēma* may well offer satisfactory proof that Odysseus's fears are truly ungrounded. In this way, the reunion can take place through the "specially crafted object," which, unlike the opposite case of Aphrodite, as Newton observes, proves "to be the touchstone of the wife's faithfulness."[63] But Penelope's ruse operates in the present tense as well as attesting to the fidelity she has maintained for so long in the past. For in tricking Odysseus into revealing the secret of the bed, she proves herself to be his match in the same qualities that characterize him (and that therefore identify her as a suitable wife for him, his "other half"). Conversely, in the mode of her testing, she herself is also being tested again by what might prove a too swift capitulation to a potential impostor. This is, in fact, what she herself claims in defending her initial resistance:

> Do not be angry with me nor be resentful, because
> I did not at first, when I saw you, embrace you as I do now.
> For always the *thumos* in my breast trembled
> lest some one of mortals would come my way and deceive me
>   with words.
>
> (23.213–17)

Paradoxically, perhaps, the very trait of a *thumos* that was always *apistos*, mistrustful, as the nurse charges, redeems her from Agamemnon's generic accusation that there is nothing "trustworthy [*ouketi pista gynaixi*] in women" (11.456). At the same time, as Marylin Katz points out, the "coldness of Penelope's welcome upon Odysseus' homecoming provides the associative link with her negative exemplar [Clytemnestra] and this association, like the celebration of the fictional wedding and the trick of bed, configures *anagnōrismos* in the text as if a betrayal." Thus, "the transformation of duplicity into complementarity for Penelope is then configured in part around the duplicity that characterizes Odysseus, but incorporates also those aspects of *dolos, mētis*, and inflexibility associated with Clytemnestra and consequently with the alternative of Penelope's betrayal."[64]

Interestingly enough, Penelope knows nothing of Clytemnestra. Telemachos, in relating to his mother the tale of his own adventures, never

63. Newton 1987, 18.
64. Katz 1991, 164.

mentions the name or the story of Agamemnon's wife (which he now knows in detail), and Odysseus, warned to keep Clytemnestra's example in mind when approaching his own wife, is not about to impart this dangerous information to Penelope. This serious gap in information is hardly an oversight. The only story of an errant wife in present time that Penelope is permitted to know (and this from Telemachos) is that of Helen, whose conduct she now curiously defends, just after explaining that her own reluctance to acknowledge her husband straight off was due to her fear of impostors, since experience had taught her that "there are many who scheme for wicked advantage" (23.217).

> For neither would the daughter born to Zeus, Helen of Argos
> have lain in love with an outlander from another country *[emigē*
>   *philotēti kai eunēi]*,
> if she had known that the warlike sons of the Achaians would
>   bring her
> home again to the beloved land of her fathers.
> It was a god who stirred her to do the shameful thing *[ergon*
>   *aeikes]* she
> did, and never before had she had in heart *[thumos]* this terrible
> folly *[atē]*, out of which came suffering to us also.
>   (23.218–24)

A strange and disconcerting prelude indeed to her final affirmation that Odysseus has passed her test:

> But now, since you have given me accurate proof *[sēmata*
>   *ariphradea]* describing
> our bed, which no other mortal man beside has ever seen,
> but only you and I, and there is one serving woman. . . .
> So you persuade my heart *[thumos]*, though it has been very
>   stubborn.
>   (23.225–27, 230)

Without resorting to the desperate expedient, as many critics have done, of excising the previous embarrassing passage altogether, one must admit that Penelope's speech remains disturbing. While it is true that the mention of Helen's departure recalls the reason why her husband left so many years ago, the way it is framed seems at best a kind of non sequitur—either a loose association following her claim of wicked schemers (seducers) or a conscious dissociation of herself from Helen's infidelity. At worst, in going so far as to excuse Helen's offense on two very different and potentially incompatible grounds (someone would bring her back, *atē* sent by the god made her do it), it might sound like an unconscious vindication of what we do not know (will never know) with regard to

Penelope herself. In this seeming collusion between one woman and another under the guise of self-differentiation, is this a way of giving and taking back at the same time? And in the use of a divinely sent *atē* to explain what Penelope sees as contradicting the hitherto unblemished character of Helen, can she then exempt herself from the possibility of the same helpless capitulation in the face of desire? Above all, does Helen's undesired lapse fatally undermine the principles of steadfast mind and stubborn resolve that have guided Penelope's own actions, and hence, in some way, undermine the fixed proof of the bed, which she immediately reconfirms?

No resolution to every facet of this problem is fully satisfactory.[65] There are, however, some further interesting points to consider, which may provide a context by linking the passage to other episodes in the poem. Penelope's reference to the fact that the Achaeans brought Helen back might be one last allusion to the scene in Phaeacia. Recall that after the love song of Ares and Aphrodite, the bard tells another tale, this time at Odysseus's behest, of the starring role he played in the taking of Troy. This tale ends with "Odysseus went, with godlike Menelaos, like Ares, to find Helen at the house of Deiphobos, and there endured the grimmest fighting that ever he had, but won it there too, with great-hearted Athena aiding" (8.517–19). If the previous song of Ares and Aphrodite had aligned Odysseus with Hephaistos, this one now leaves no doubt that Ares too is his model. If the story of the wooden horse looks forward, and even more directly, to future events on Ithaca, it also seems to align Helen and Penelope, whom Odysseus may reclaim for his own after his slaughter of the suitors. Yet there is a crucial and obvious difference: Helen went away, Penelope did not. One left her husband's bed, the other remained where she was. Why then is it of such concern to Penelope that Helen would not have gone, had she known that the Achaeans would bring her back? Yet if Helen went away, we might add, so did Odysseus. Does Penelope's version hint at a reversal of genders and thus obliquely refer to Odysseus as well? This suggestion might seem oversubtle, except that to clinch the moment

65. For a recent and thoughtful discussion of the passage, see Murnaghan (1987, 141–43), who concludes that "Penelope cannot believe that she might herself be an exception, a wife who in no sense betrays her husband even after so long a separation," while shrewdly comparing Penelope's "attention to the example of Helen" with Odysseus's "attention to the example of Agamemon," both leading to hesitation in recognition/identification. Katz (1991, 184–87) takes a more extreme position. Reviewing the multitude of other opinions on this passage, she claims that "Penelope both consolidates her own *kleos* by differentiating herself from Helen and undermines the fixity of its meaning at the same time. In this way she incorporates into the narrative as a self-conscious statement about herself the indeterminacy of meaning that has characterized her throughout the poem." Morgan (1991), on the other hand, favors the situation over character and emphasizes the purely conventional rhetoric of Penelope's diction.

of their final reunion, the text immediately resorts to the last instance of those "reverse sex similes" that are such an important and recurrent stylistic feature in the *Odyssey*.[66]

> He wept as he held his lovely wife, whose thoughts were
>   virtuous *[kedn'eiduian]*.
> And as when the land appears welcome to men who are
>   swimming,
> after Poseidon has smashed their strong-built ship on the open
> water, pounding it with the weight of wind and and the heavy
> seas, and only a few escape the gray water landward
> by swimming, with a thick scurf of salt coated upon them,
> and gladly they set foot on the shore, escaping the evil;
> so welcome was her husband to her as she looked upon him.
>   (23.231–39)

Even as a specimen of a reverse simile, this one comes with a surprising twist, since only at the last line are we informed that it applies to her, not to him, and to confuse matters further, Odysseus, not Penelope, is the one who is moved to tears. Moreover, the content of the simile returns us directly to Odysseus's experience on the open seas in Book 5 that ended with his arrival, battered and bruised, on the shores of Scheria (5.394–95). Yet the theme of gender inversion recalls in turn the striking simile that described Odysseus's reaction to the bard's tale, when he wept like a woman "lying over the body of her dear husband, who fell fighting for her city and people," a woman who is shortly to be "led away into slavery, to have hard work and sorrow" (8.522–30). The effect of his weeping, we may recall, leads directly to his self-revelation at the court of Alkinoos and the first full resumption of his true identity.

Odysseus goes to the house of Deiphobos to fetch Helen. He is compared to a woman who will shortly be led away to undergo hardship and grief. In this cross-referencing between Phaeacia and Ithaca, between experience and simile, between male and female, Penelope may be said to share in Odysseus's past in advance of his own recitation of his experiences that she is shortly to hear. And if Helen is the figure whose name elicits these interchanges, she is also the one, as always, upon whom charges of infidelity can be conveniently displaced, even as her motives (and hence culpability) are always open to interpretation.[67] Penelope may be the first to launch this long literary and rhetorical tradition, but in context, she raises these questions before returning to the all too visible *sēmata* of the

66. On reverse sex similes in the poem, see the now classic essay of Foley 1978.
67. See Suzuki 1989, 90, who comments that the poet makes the Iliadic Helen a scapegoat for Penelope, "in order to exorcize anxiety-producing qualities from his own heroine."

bed and accepting Odysseus who, in identifying them, has "persuaded her *thumos*" of his identity.

The entire scene of recognition that revolves around the ruse of the bed continually loops back upon itself, like the infinite turnings of a Moebius strip, as it plays off the entwined but also divergent issues of Odysseus's identity and Penelope's fidelity. It does so, as we have seen, through the device of an object that can be minutely described, located in space, and recalled to its functions and emblematic status through the opportunity given Odysseus to reclaim it in the act of narrating how he first made it. This is an ekphrasis, after all, that describes a work of art. Its function is to transform representation into narration, and it stands in an intermediate space "between the outward force of perceived events and the inner ability to perceive them," so that it may finally turn into a convincing sign-symbol of recognition.[68]

But there is one last paradox. The conditions of its representational function ensure its unrepresentability. No blueprint can be extracted from the details of the bed's manufacture, and in the long tradition from antiquity to the present day, no artist seems to have taken up the challenge to translate its presence into a visual reality that we may view with our own eyes. It is precisely the vivid and concrete reality of its material existence that ensures its efficacy as the double-sided sign it was meant to be, but to retain its powers of persuasion, it must remain what it always was: a mental construct, an image in the mind's eye.

68. Prier 1989, 114, on the general properties of *sēmata*.

· TWO ·

Signifying Difference:
The Case of Hesiod's Pandora

The myth of Pandora is a variant of a well-known theme in myths of origins the world over. The story of how and why woman came into the world accounts for the fact that there are not one but two sexes. Logically, both male and female should come into existence at the same time as the human species is created. Each is the complement of the other, each indispensable to the other's identity. As a pair, they attest to the universal fact of gender in nature and assure reproduction of one's own kind.

The mythic imagination does not view matters this way. More often than not, woman is an afterthought, created as a secondary category following the emergence of man. Her ontological status is therefore not a self-evident or spontaneous fact. To account for her supplementary presence requires a motive, a reason, a purpose—in short, a myth. Two of the best-known examples of this type are the story of Eve in the Book of Genesis and the Greek myth of Pandora, as recounted by the archaic poet Hesiod. Each in its own way conforms to this pattern: Eve is created from Adam's rib as a companion to ease his loneliness; Pandora is fashioned at Zeus's orders in retaliation for the Titan Prometheus's theft of fire. Whether created by the supreme male deity out of compassion or anger, woman makes her entry onto the scene and thereby provides the occasion for an aetiological narrative that tells how through her agency the world was transformed into its present state. Her secondary status operates as a signifier of difference and disruption that brings about the so-called "human condition." That is, she introduces death, woe, and evil into the world, along with the laborious toil of human existence.

Hesiod tells the myth of Pandora in two versions, the first in the

A version of this essay was presented as the Heller lecture at the University of California— Berkeley (1991), the Jane Ellen Harrison lecture at Cambridge University (1991), the George Walsh Memorial lecture at the University of Chicago (1992), and the Humanities Council lecture at Princeton University (1992).

Theogony, a cosmogonic poem, and the second in the *Works and Days,* a didactic work of wisdom literature. In each case, she figures as the outcome of a game of wits between Prometheus and Zeus that revolves around a series of deceptions and counter-deceptions in connection with the exchange of gifts. Zeus wins, of course, and in return for the theft of fire, he has Hephaistos, the artisan god, fabricate the first woman as a molded creature, who astounds men by her god-given beauty and ruins them by her thievish nature.

In recent years these two Hesiodic versions have attracted a great deal of attention, which can be ascribed both to the development of more sophisticated techniques for interpreting the discourses of myth and to the current interest in the cultural construction of gender categories. These newer methods address the underlying logic and coherence that govern the structure, language, and content of mythic narrative, and aim to situate a given myth in its literary and sociocultural contexts in order to take account of its wider ideological resonances in the processes of cultural formation. Despite important differences in detail and purpose, the two versions have been read together as two halves of a single extended narrative that mutually illuminate the double-sided question of the origin of woman and woman as the origin. Let me first recall the outlines of these two accounts.

The version in the *Theogony* begins with Prometheus's fraudulent division of the portions of the sacrificed ox allotted respectively to gods and men. Zeus chooses the inedible bones concealed beneath a covering of gleaming fat. For men is reserved the meat hidden under the unappetizing casing of the animal's belly. In angry retaliation, Zeus refuses to give (i.e., hides) celestial fire, whereupon Prometheus steals it, hides it in a hollow stalk, and brings it to men without being seen by the gods. When Zeus perceives "the gleam of fire," he counters by creating woman as a "beautiful evil" *(kalon kakon),* an "anti-fire" *(anti puros)*—an exchange "instead of" or "in recompense for" fire. Hephaistos fashions her of earth in the likeness of a young virgin, and Athena robes her as a bride in silvery garments, with a veil, garlands of flowers, and a golden crown. Thus adorned, she is a wonder to behold *(thauma idesthai)* but also a dangerous trap *(aipus dolos).* Brought to men, she is a continual source of woe to mortals *(pēma mega thnētoisi),* an unwelcome supplement to those with whom she dwells (*Th.* 561–91).

Like a drone she sits within the house and reaps the fruits of others' toil to fill her belly. And a second evil is added to the first, for if a man avoids marriage he looks forward to an old age without anyone to care for him and after his death his estate is divided among his kinsmen. But even for a man who relents and takes a good wife—that is, one whose heart is in agreement with his—Hesiod still maintains that "all through life, in her and by her, misfortune will come to balance out the good" (*Th.* 594–609).

The other version in the *Works and Days* omits the scene of sacrifice but adds a second unhappy consequence of Prometheus's deception in that now the gods also keep hidden from men the source of their livelihood (i.e., the grain that must be seeded in the earth). Again in his anger at the theft of fire, Zeus determines to create a great woe *(mega pēma)* for men to bring them delight while also encompassing their destruction (*WD* 46–58). But this time the creation of Pandora is recounted in more detail.

Hephaistos molds the lovely shape of a maiden out of water and earth, with a face resembling the immortal goddesses but endowed with the "voice and strength of humankind." Athena is to teach her weaving, Aphrodite to pour grace *(charis)* over her head and "cruel longing and cares that weary the limbs." Hermes adds a shameless (doglike) mind and a thievish nature. Athena now dresses her like a virginal bride, while Aphrodite's representatives, the Graces (Charites) and Persuasion (Peitho), give her golden necklaces and the Hours (Horai) crown her with spring flowers. At the end Hermes names her Pandora because, as the text says, "all *[pantes]* the gods gave her a gift *[dōron],* a sorrow *[pēma]* to men who live on bread" (*WD* 59–82).

Now follows the familiar story of how Pandora was sent as a bride to Epimetheus, who had been warned by his brother Prometheus (Foresight) to accept no gifts from the gods. In true fulfillment of his name (Afterthought), he takes her in and regrets it later. For Pandora's first act is to remove the lid of the jar she brought with her, releasing all the evils and diseases that now wander silent and invisible over the earth. By Zeus's will, only Hope or Elpis is left behind in the jar (*WD* 83–104), an ambiguous quality to whose meaning we shall return.

The most influential analysis of this myth is that of Jean-Pierre Vernant[1] (with further elaborations and refinements/correctives by Nicole Loraux and Marylin Arthur [Katz]).[2] Vernant demonstrates a series of homologies, inversions, and correspondences between all the different elements in these narratives: the various animal parts of the sacrifice apportioned by Prometheus *(Theogony);* the fire first hidden, then stolen, then hidden again *(Theogony, Works and Days);* the grain now hidden in the earth *(Works and Days);* the jar that conceals all evils *(Works and Days);* and the first woman, lovely to look at but defined as a belly *(Theogony).* Taken together, these now define the new and permanent quality of human life, its ambiguity and deceitfulness—a mixture of evils concealed under beautiful exteriors and virtues under ugly ones.

1. Vernant 1980, "Prometheus"; 1979, 21–86, 224–37.
2. Loraux 1981a, "Race"; Arthur [Katz] 1982, 1983. See also Pucci 1977.

In one or another of her aspects, Pandora herself corresponds to each term of these several transactions that always operate under the seemingly opposite modes of giving or not giving (hiding) gifts, but that on closer inspection prove to be variations on the single theme of giving through concealment and trickery. Like the sacrificial portion of food offered to the gods, Pandora has a beautiful exterior and a worthless interior. Like the portion offered to men, concealed in the belly (or paunch) of the ox *(gastēr)*, she is a hungry belly, insatiable of food. Above all, in direct and inverse return for the celestial fire stolen by Prometheus, Pandora comes equipped with a thievish nature and is later likened to a fire that consumes and withers man by her appetites for both food and sex (cf. *WD* 704–6). Seed, on the other hand, applies to the germ of technological fire, which unlike its celestial parent, must now be engendered and stored in a hollow container (the narthex stalk): it applies, too, both to the seed the farmer must plant within the earth and to the one he deposits in his wife's belly to produce children.

Pandora therefore emerges as none other than the symbol of ambiguous human life. In her appearance, her gifts given by the gods, she echoes the divine. By her bitchlike mind and the primacy of her bodily requirements she approaches the bestial. By her human voice and status as wife she is human. But, as Vernant concludes, she is also the reverse of man, forming another and fundamentally different breed. Man and woman cannot converse with one another because she conceals the truth in order to deceive. At the same time, the conditions of her creation establish the fundamental triad of activities that are central to Greek views of culture: sacrifice (relations of men and gods), agriculture (men and nature), and marriage (men and women). The last two categories are especially linked in Vernant's discussion by the analogy, so familiar in Greek thought, that likens the woman to the earth and gives men the task of seeding both the womb and the earth.

Every detail contributes to the logical coherence of the whole. Woman has her designated place and aetiological function in this mythic account of the foundations of human culture that accords well with consistent Greek values, preoccupations, and priorities. The view from a cross-cultural perspective, however, casts some intriguing shadows over this instantiation of a widely diffused mythic archetype, which goes so far in its negativity as to unbalance any tidy scheme of a universe that consists of mixed goods and evils. In particular, the Greek version is conspicuous in creating woman as a separate and alien being, the first exemplar of a race or species, the *genos gunaikōn,* who as the agent of separation between gods and mortal men remains estranged, never achieving a mediated partnership with man.

In the first place, we note that this radical disparity between the genders is founded on the absence of any general myth of anthropogony. Woman is created on her own without any parallel or preceding account of how the category of man came into existence.[3] A further sign of woman's uniqueness is her mode of production, differentiated from all the other acts of begetting recorded in the *Theogony*. "Woman is anything but a natural being."[4] She is a gift, a technical invention, an artisanal product, a work of art, an artifice. Finally, in contrast to man, who evolves in stages over time—as, for example, in the parallel tale of the Five Ages in the *Works and Days*—woman's nature is static and unchanging. The sum of her attributes is fixed from the beginning, defined by the circumstances that brought her into being, a material sign that crystallizes the essence of these previous transactions into a permanent, tangible form. She is a hybrid mixture of qualities drawn from different elements and different spheres that combine into a blend, at once an original product and an imitation, whose purpose and nature are to deceive.[5]

Two additional factors support this gloomy picture. Woman is not created as a companion to remedy man's solitude—as we are told, for example, in the biblical account of Adam and Eve (Gen. 2:21)[6]—but rather as a punishment (not even merited through human fault). Second, there is no reconciliation after the fact, since even if Hesiod can broach the possibility of a companionable wife (*Th.* 608), male and female roles maintain a drastic asymmetry. There is no basis for a division of labor between the sexes that would ultimately make them partners, albeit unequal ones, in the conduct of mortal existence. Thus, while Vernant's reading of the cultural implications of the myth of Pandora remains valid in more general terms, it cannot explain the special features of Hesiod's economy: his insistence on the fact that only men work while women re-

---

3. For these issues, which many have observed, see in particular the acute analyses of Loraux 1981a, "Race," with relevant bibliography. For Greek creation myths in a comparative perspective, see Guarducci 1927.

4. Loraux 1981a, "Race," 83.

5. I am persuaded by Saintillan (1995) and Vernant (1995) that the concept of an "imitation of a model" cannot wholly be applied to the making of the first woman, since the artisanal gods also imbue this fabricated object with the life energy of *charis* (charm, glamor). Nevertheless, in designating Pandora as an inescapable trap *(dolos)* and as a *kalon kakon*, the text suggests a fundamental gap between appearance and reality that implies more than her status as a gift or *agalma*.

6. I acknowledge but do not discuss here the problem of the two accounts in Genesis of human creation, the first of which suggests that male and female came into being at virtually the same time: "And God created man in his own image, in the image of God created he him; male and female created he them" (1.27). Both versions, however, insist on the parity of one male and one female, destined to form the first couple.

main perpetually idle, useless drones who sit within the house, "filling their bellies up with the products of the toils of others" (*Th.* 599) and providing a source of endless disaffection, which leads to the conclusion that even in the case of a worthy wife, "evil still continually contends with the good" (*Th.* 608–10).

Women could contribute to the household, for example, with their typically feminine skills of weaving, already given by Athena to Pandora at her creation (*WD* 63–64). Male and female could be active in their respective domains, as Xenophon's *Oeconomicus* prescribes, the man working outside to increase his household's wealth and the woman managing the stored-up goods. Above all, as wife and mother, woman herself is also a giver, not just a taker, of gifts, because she produces children from her belly and gives them nurture *(trophē)*. Hesiod only elliptically acknowledges that woman is needed to produce offspring, viewing this reliance as a second source of evil that follows upon the first complaint that had characterized women as drones: "Whoever avoids marriage *[gamos]* and the baneful works of women *[mermera erga gunaikōn]*, and is not willing to wed, reaches deadly old age without anyone to tend his years *[gērokomos]*, and though he at least has no lack of livelihood while he lives, yet, when he is dead, his kinsfolk divide his possessions amongst them" (*Th.* 602–6).

All is inference. Nothing is stated directly—neither sex nor procreation. There is only *gamos* (marriage), the allusive *mermera erga gunaikōn* (what are these *erga*? cf. 595), the equally vague *gērokomos* (who is this?) and the emphasis on man's old age, his death, and its aftermath.[7] We typically take this passage to mean that if the creation of woman interrupted the presumed commensality of men and gods, when they feasted together and shared the same food, it also confronted man with a mortality that she alone can remediate in the compromise of providing progeny to take care of him in his old age, who will live on after his death and, as his substitute(s), maintain (and increase) the fruits of his labor. But in extracting this reading, we also fail to take the full measure of the evasions and ambiguities that complicate both this text and that of the account in the *Works and Days,* where, in the context of agricultural labor, woman's sexual and reproductive roles remain still more discreetly obscured. Let us take a closer look.

First is the problem of sexuality itself: a natural instinct, fueled by the mysteries of desire and accompanied by pleasure in physical contact, yet also fraught with ambivalence. In Hesiod, woman's lovely exterior, enhanced by those adornments of sexual allure, proves only a snare and delusion, a "hopeless trap" (*Th.* 589; *WD* 83). The *Theogony* dwells on the

7. See further note 18 below.

effects of her appearance, the stupefied wonder *(thauma)* of those who gaze at her, both gods and mortals alike *(Th.* 575, 581, 582, 584, 588), and the seductive charm *(charis)* that radiates from everything she wears. But in the *Works and Days* we learn further that this *charis* is inseparable from "painful longing" *(pothon argaleon)* and "cares that devour the limbs," all equally gifts of Aphrodite (*WD* 66).

We note too that in both texts, far from "cleaving together and becoming one flesh" as the biblical account tells us (Genesis 3:24–25), or even "mingling in love" *(philotēs),* as the canonical euphemism in Greek texts (and elsewhere in the *Theogony*) would have it, man and woman remain distinct and disjoined entities. Pandora may be arrayed as a bride in a proto-version of marriage and given as a wife to her foolish husband Epimetheus in the *Works and Days* (cf. *Th.* 511–14), but oddly enough, nowhere are we told of any carnal activity between them or again, as the parity of the biblical story suggests, of a mutual awareness of themselves as genitalized beings once they have come into their fallen state (cf. Genesis 2:25 and 3:7).

The dangers of sexuality as encroachment on the autonomous male body and the potential imbalance of its humors, the limitations or qualifications set to its unrestricted enjoyment, its separation from a specified love object, and the attribution of unbridled (extravagant) sexual appetites to women are characteristic and recurrent features of Greek attitudes. Later medical and philosophical texts will spell out the dangers to men's health in taking sexual pleasure, as Foucault's astute analysis reminds us,[8] but the framework in its most negative form is already in place in Hesiod, particularly in the context of woman's creation as an *anti puros,* a "fire" that takes the place of the one that was stolen. Sex is treated as an unequal transaction by which woman steals man's substance, both alimentary and sexual, and by her appetites even "roasts man alive and brings him to a premature old age" (*WD* 705). Thus in the *Works and Days* men are later warned to beware of making love in the summertime, because this is the time when "women are most wanton, but men are feeblest, since Sirius, the Dog Star, parches the head and the knees and the skin is dry through heat" (*WD* 586–89). No wonder then that sexuality is viewed as a less than mixed blessing, since men and women do not share the same rhythms or seasons of desire, and woman's desire, in any case, consumes the man and robs him of what is his own.

But the second and corollary point may be more essential. This is the ambivalence about women's reproductive capacities, which may account even more strongly for the notable imbalances we find in Hesiod's economic system. As Loraux points out, in the *Theogony* woman is not even

8. Foucault 1985.

modeled in "the canonical image of the reproductive good wife. If the text implies that with the woman, marriage appears and therefore reproduction, the function of fecundity is hidden. Nothing indicates that the woman is expected to 'imitate the earth' as the standard Greek representations of fertility suggest."[9] Hesiod in fact explicitly separates woman from the bountiful earth by inverting the usual etymology of her name from an active to a passive construction, from the one who gives to the one who is given. Not "the giver of all gifts," as a related epithet of Gaia (Earth) indicates, "Pandora" is here glossed as "the one to whom the gods have given all gifts" (*WD* 80–82).[10]

Additionally, the suppression of woman's fertility means ignoring the value of her experience in childbirth, the *ponoi* of her suffering and travail. In other Greek contexts these are sometimes made equivalent to the trials and labors *(ponoi)* of men engaged in battle and other heroic endeavors, exemplified in Medea's famous statement that she would rather stand three times in the forefront of battle than bear a single child.[11] Here, by contrast, only man is burdened with *ponoi,* the doleful exertions of daily life, attributed in fact to woman herself who has imported them into his present existence (*WD* 90–92).

The significance of these two omissions is again reinforced by comparison with the parallel story in Genesis of Adam and Eve: expelled from the garden of Eden, the male is condemned to bring forth his daily bread by the sweat of his brow (i.e., agriculture) and the female to bring forth children in pain and travail (Genesis 3:16–19). Their mutual dependency is further emphasized by God's earlier injunction that they be fruitful and multiply, populating the earth with their numberless progeny (Genesis 2:28).

In short, the biblical story reflects a shared existence and responsibility, once woman has been created; it also suggests an economy of abundance, proliferation, and expansiveness. The Hesiodic tale, in contrast, is rooted in an economy of scarcity, parsimony, and anxious surveillance over what man has patiently accumulated by and for himself.[12] To cap it all, far from being characterized in the *Theogony* as the "mother of all

9. Loraux 1981a, "Race," 88–89.

10. With Loraux (1981a, "Race," 89n.73), I too insist on the significance of Hesiod's etymology as a deliberate "counterstatement" to the standard meaning.

11. See Loraux 1981b on childbirth and Loraux 1982 on the meanings of *ponos*.

12. For the earlier abundance and prodigality associated with the Charites that belong to the world of the gods and the Golden Age, see Saintillan 1995. The economy of scarcity and parsimony is best summarized in *WD* 354–69. On the biblical world view see, for example, Eilberg-Schwartz 1990, chap. 6; and Cohen 1989, chap. 1. I hope to amplify these differences elsewhere.

mankind," as Eve is described in the biblical account (hence the etymology of her name, Hava, Genesis 3:20), Pandora is named instead as the origin only of the *genos gunaikōn,* the "race of women," as though to deny, or at least to elide, the drastic notion that men are from women born.

What factors might account for this harsh outlook on life? What issues are at stake in Hesiod's version that might lead to the view that woman is only a rapacious and famished belly, a "companion to Plenty but not to Poverty," a creature who takes everything without giving in return? Various socioeconomic explanations have been suggested: (1) a change in methods of agriculture, particularly the plow, better suited for men, that devalues women's contribution to subsistence; (2) a disembedded social organization of the Greek polis in this archaic period (eighth century), in which the private *oikos* or household is separated from communal, public life; (3) a growing scarcity of land and resources relevant to this age of colonization; and (4) class distinctions between aristocratic and so-called peasant attitudes.[13]

All these hypotheses may have merit to greater or lesser degrees, with respect to the proposed time and place of composition, but they cannot account for Hesiod's enduring prestige. These texts become canonical in Greek thought, both as the major account of the creation of the present world order under the hegemony of Zeus (over against competing versions) and as the authoritative statement of Greek values that revolve around the polarization of justice *(dikē)* and injustice *(hubris).* Hesiod's extreme rancor toward woman, while open to compromise and mitigation in other texts and other spheres of interest, still remains the touchstone of an underlying attitude concerning this intrusive and ambivalent "other," who is brought into a strange man's household and forever remains under suspicion as introducing a dangerous mixture into the desired purity of male identity and lineage, whether in sexual relations or in the production of children.[14]

A further difficulty with these "practical" rather than ideological considerations, as enumerated above, is the tendency to separate the creation of Pandora from its context instead of treating it as an integrated (and inserted) episode in a longer and more complex narrative.[15] Pandora is not an independent entity in her own right, nor is her story in Hesiod a random digression. In both senses, she is a means to other—another's—ends, entering into the world at a critical moment of its formation. In each nar-

13. See, for example, Sussman 1984.
14. On woman's "otherness" and man's attempts to overcome or master her difference, see especially Pucci 1977, 111–13.
15. Arthur [Katz] 1982 is a notable exception.

rative, the creation of woman is introduced as the outcome of a quarrel between two males over the apportionment of rightful shares. In the *Theogony*, her story is a part of the larger struggle for power among divine forces, the result of the strife between Prometheus and Zeus. In the *Works and Days*, Hesiod's dispute with his brother Perses over the division of their inheritance is the situation that frames the Pandora myth, where it is used both as explanation and admonition. It accounts for the current conditions of our postlapsarian existence and warns what men must do to survive in the harsh environment of the Iron Age.[16] Yet in both versions, Pandora's creation marks a conclusive rupture between men and gods. This means that Pandora not only defines the categories of male and female in the human sphere but also stands at the intersection of relations between gods and mortals. Given the anthropomorphic nature of Greek divinity, mythic discourse habitually dramatizes the issues of gender, sexuality, and reproduction from a double perspective, and perhaps nowhere more pointedly than in the confrontation between divine and human worlds underlying the two Hesiodic accounts. We must, therefore, approach the question of Pandora while bearing in mind both these sets of relations, with the twofold aim of placing Pandora in her Hesiodic context and Hesiod in the context of more extensive Greek attitudes about the female.

Let us turn then first to the human world, to the status of children and questions of reproduction in the household, before expanding the analysis to encompass the inevitable distinctions between mortal and immortal modes of existence. These, as I shall suggest, are founded on a two-tiered system of values, whereby femininity can be split between a primary role in the domain of the gods and a secondary, devalued role in the world of human affairs. This principle holds true in addressing the mode of Pandora's creation (the origin of woman) and also in appraising the limits on the roles and functions assigned her (woman as the origin).

Household Economy

There is a persistent strain of ambivalence in Greek thought about the nature and value of children. Although treasured as bearers of the family line, they are also a potential source of disappointment and sorrow. They may turn out well, of course, but, like the woman herself, they may eventually bring trouble to a man's household. A reference to just such an idea may be implied in an ambiguous passage in the *Theogony* that concludes Hesiod's remarks about marriage and its discontents:

16. On the parallels between the two quarrels, see Vernant 1979b, 54–57.

For a man who chooses to marry and gets an agreeable wife,
evil still continually contends with the good,
but he who meets up with an *atartēroio genethlēs*
(ἀταρτηροῖο γενέθλης)
lives always with unceasing grief in his heart,
and this is an evil that cannot be healed.

(*Th.* 607–12)

The crux of the problem lies in how we interpret the word *genethlē*. Does it mean "race" (i.e., of women) or "progeny" (children)? If *genethlē* refers to woman, then the passage contrasts two kinds of wives: a good one (in which case, the negative still vies with the positive), and a bad one, whose effect is unrelieved misery and woe. On the other hand, if we ask *why*, even in the case of an agreeable wife, evil is still said to contend with the good, then we may prefer to read *genethlē* as "progeny," since even under the best of circumstances, children may well prove a mischievous bane to their parents. Each reading has its merits, and with no definitive way to resolve the dilemma (for the word appears nowhere else in Hesiod), scholarly opinion remains divided.[17] But this uncertainty of reference may well be the essential point,[18] as reflecting the double ambivalence about women and about the necessity of having children, the latter most fully expressed in the famous choral ode in Euripides' *Medea* (1090–1110):

. . . those who have never had children, who know nothing of
    them,
surpass in happiness those who are parents.
The childless, who never discover
whether children turn out as a good thing

17. Many scholars prefer "wife," including West (1966, *ad loc.*) and *LfgrE* (s.v.), along with Loraux (1981a, "Race," 95n.103), but the arguments for excluding alternate readings are not supported by the diction.

18. Woman and child can often be conflated, as, for example, in the parable of the lion cub in Aeschylus, *Agamemnon* 681–749. The problem of *genethlē* in Hesiod is heightened by yet another ambiguity in that the preceding passage never mentions the word *child* at all. What we hear instead is that "the man who does not marry . . . reaches baneful old age without anyone to look after him" (605). This caretaker or *gērokomos* is a word invented for the occasion (and found only here in archaic and classical literature). It is sufficiently obscure that West (1966, *ad loc.*) feels obliged to make clear that the text refers to "the son, not the wife," a claim he bases (not without reason) on the well-known rule that the son is expected to provide *gērotrophia* for his parents in return for his own nurture. So too, in the sentence that follows, the son as heir to his father's possessions is not named but merely implied; his identity is inferred from the alternative, that in his absence, distant kinsmen (*chērōstai*) will later divide the man's estate (605–7). There are other, more suggestive reasons, as I will later propose, why the text refuses to name either father or child.

Or as something to cause pain, are spared
many troubles in lacking this knowledge.
And those who have in their homes
the sweet growth of children, I see them always
worn down by worry.
First how to bring them up well and leave them something to
live on.
And then whether all their toil is for progeny
who may turn out well or not remains unclear.

Finally (I paraphrase here), even under the best of circumstances, death may still carry them off.

Even more decisive for this argument, however, is the fact that the vexed passage in the *Theogony* concerning *genethlē* occupies virtually the same structural position as the mention in the *Works and Days* of the Elpis or Hope that remains in Pandora's jar. Each text marks the conclusion of the episode, and each is followed by a similar tag line: "So it is not possible to deceive or go beyond the mind of Zeus" (ὣς οὐκ ἔστι Διὸς κλέψαι νόον οὐδὲ παρελθεῖν, *Th*. 613) and "So there is no way to escape the mind of Zeus" (οὕτως οὔ τί πη ἔστι Διὸς νόον ἐξαλέασθαι, *WD* 105). In the context, Elpis functions as yet another ambiguous quality of mixed good and evil, a sign of the uncertainties of the future to which human life is now consigned. Hope is good if it inspires men to work and assure their livelihood, to fill their *pithos* with grain, and bad if it lulls an idle man into illusory expectations for the future.[19]

For Vernant, the image of the jar represents the house or *oikos*, and woman is the ambiguous figure of Elpis, who resides within. In this reading, the jar replicates the domestic space of the household to which woman is consigned. She can therefore be correlated with Elpis because, like any wife, she may turn out well or badly. Other textual echoes support this idea of an enclosure in which the woman resides (cf. *Th*. 598 and *WD* 96–97), but the equation of woman and Elpis is more problematic. In the *Theogony*, even in the case of a companionable wife, evil still contends with the good, and in the present context of the *Works and Days*, woman is unequivocally named as an evil and a plague.

But taken as an image that embodies an idea, the Elpis that is left in the jar corresponds most closely to the child (or the hope of a child) who resides inside its mother's womb. In this reading, Pandora's *pithos* can be

---

19. Much has been written about whether Elpis is a good or an evil, or both. For convenient summary of the many views, see especially Verdenius 1985, 66–71; Saïd 1985, 123–30; and for extensive bibliography, Noica 1984. To be brief, I concur for the most part with Vernant that Elpis is an ambiguous quality with both negative and positive aspects (like Eris, Zēlos, Aidōs, and Nemesis). See his judicious discussion (1979b, 121–32).

correlated with the *gastēr*, her defining feature in the *Theogony*, and like the *gastēr* of the sacrificial portion that contained the edible portions of the ox, the *pithos* too is an independent repository that conceals something within.

References in other texts to the child as the Elpis, or hope, of the household provide a strong argument for this identification.[20] But a more precise indication is the fact that later medical and philosophical texts associate and even correlate the womb with a container or jar. Throughout the Hippocratic corpus and the works of the later, more sophisticated anatomists, the woman's uterus is likened to an upside-down jar, furnished with two ears or handles. The *stathmos* or *puthmēn* (Latin *fundus*) is the base or bottom of the jar, located now on top; the *stoma* (Latin *os*), or mouth, lies at the bottom; and the neck (the *auchēn, trachēlos,* or Latin *cervix*) opens in a downward direction. The jar/uterus is modeled on features of human anatomy. It too has a mouth and neck. This nomenclature is also pertinent to the widespread idea of a correlation between woman's sexual and oral appetites, emphasized in the Hesiodic text as located below in the rapacious belly *(gastēr)* that fills up on man's substance. Popular and medical notions insist on a symmetry between a woman's two orifices, the mouth and the belly, reflected in prescriptions for gynecological therapy. A jar, as in Hesiod, has "lips" (*cheilē*, WD 97), and so does a womb (e.g., Aristotle, *Historia animalium* 7.3.583a16). The analogy continues in the notion of a seal or stopper that is needed to prevent entry, with the aim of preserving virginity or, conversely, of retaining the seed deposited in it to allow a successful pregnancy to occur.[21]

What does it mean, then, that Pandora comes equipped with her own jar, and that she removes the lid to open it, releasing a swarm of ills that now wander silent and invisible all over the world, leaving only Hope

20. Significantly mentioned in funereal epigrams (e.g, *Anthologia Palatina* 7.389, 453) and grave inscriptions (Peek 1955, nos. 661, 720).

21. For the medical texts, see Hanson 1990, and further discussion in Hanson 1992. See also Sissa 1987, 76–93 (on mouth and uterus), and 181–85 (on closure: "The closed body of the maiden corresponds to the body of the mother who, surfeited with children, has experienced the *symmysis* of her womb" [185]). On the idea of a seal or stopper for the uterus, see Hanson 1990, 324–30. Hanson disagrees with Sissa on how this closure was perceived, distinguishing between the mouth of the uterus and that of the labia. Sissa (178) understands the *pithos* in Hesiod as the belly of the woman ("a faithful and fertile wife") but does not discuss the status of Elpis.

For the equation of the child and Elpis, see also Hoffmann (1986, 72–76), who notes the correspondence between marriage (*WD* 800) and the opening of a jar (*WD* 819) in Hesiod's agricultural calendar. Her arguments, however, take a different and nontextual direction, focusing on the connection with agriculture and on the abstract notion of the child as a signifier of mortality.

Might one understand the *mega pōma* that Pandora removes from the jar as a play on words with her own characterization as a *mega pēma* (e.g., *Th.* 592)?

within? This sequence of acts is what now determines man's condition: that he will suffer "ills, hard toil, and heavy sicknesses which bring the fates of Death upon him" (*WD* 90–92) with only Hope to deceive or console him. Elpis, of course, is a general, even abstract concept. Yet we may understand its import better if we take the measure of Pandora's actions. If the implicit analogy between Pandora and the jar holds true, then it is difficult to escape the conclusion that to open the *pithos* is equivalent to breaching her virginity, while to close the jar upon the Elpis that remains within marks the beginning of pregnancy, not yet brought to term. Under these circumstances, it is also difficult to resist the idea, even though it is nowhere directly stated, that what escapes from the jar equally escapes from the vagina in the most negative encoding of female sexuality,[22] and that the child (or Hope), uncertainly placed between evil and good, is the single best, if still unsatisfactory, result.

The idea of the uterus as a jar or container is based on more positive associations. In its literal meaning, the *pithos* (or *aggos*) is a storage container for grain, oil, and wine, carefully sealed up with its contents and broached at the appropriate time and with the appropriate precautions for the prudent use of what it holds (*WD* 368, 815, 819; also 475, 600, 613). In ordinary social practice, it would be the woman's task to take care of these provisions, protecting them from pilferage and untimely opening, even as she safeguards the contents of her own *pithos*. The proprieties of household management support the analogy between the storage jar and the woman's belly, both of them sources of *bios* (life and livelihood) entrusted to the wife for safekeeping to assure the maintenance of her husband's estate. But in Hesiod, these two functions sharply diverge. Ownership is divided between the man's *pithoi* in which he has stored his goods and Pandora's jar filled with the evils it first contained. The jars, like the house in which they are kept, belong to the man, who has stored his provender in them for his exclusive use (*WD* 365–69, cf. 597–603). He alone negotiates the boundary between inside and outside ("Better to have your stuff at home *[oikoi]*, for whatever is out of doors *[thurēphin]* may be subject to harm," *WD* 365). The reason, Hesiod says, is that "it is good to take from what is present, but a *pēma* for the heart to desire what is absent," *WD* 366–67. The same principle applies to the broaching of

22. This is a hypothesis I cannot prove. One example comes close: the myth of the Lemnian women, who were shunned by their husbands for unpleasant odors. The story has been related convincingly to myths of renewal of fire on the volcanic island of Lemnos with its sulfurous odors (closely associated with Hephaistos, we might add), but the point of Pandora's jar is that the evils it releases are silent and invisible, not ill smelling. From a medical standpoint, the opening of the jar-womb also releases menstrual blood, but again the analogy cannot hold, since blood is, of course, a highly visible substance outside the body.

the jar itself: "Take your fill *[koresesthai]* when the jar is first opened and then again when it is nearly spent" (368).[23] By contrast, the woman, that *mega pēma* sent to dwell with men and take what is theirs, is "no companion of Koros [satiety] but rather of Penia [poverty]." Whether taking his goods or dispensing her woes, she remains on the side of prodigality, as a signifier of both excess and lack.[24] In this economy of plenitude and emptiness, storage and loss, the woman's *pithos* thus stands in antithesis to the other one in his care. It is kept separate, as she is from him, in the conduct of the *oikos*, as though her reproductive potential (Elpis) were also contrasted with his parallel functions of conserving and increasing the household's resources (e.g., WD 376–77).[25]

The logic of this contrast may be clarified by what follows in the *Works and Days* directly after the mention of the farmer's *pithos*. This is the preference, explicitly stated, for a family consisting of a single child: "There should be an only son *[mounogenēs pais]* to feed his father's house, for so wealth will increase in the home" (WD 376, cf. 271). The prospect of a second son *(heteron paida)* elicits the ominous remark that in that case, better to die old—or as the text is often read, the only son in turn should have another only son (WD 378).[26] We find this attitude ex-

23. Also instructive is a little-known myth, preserved in several late texts (Parthenius, *Erotica Pathemata* 28; Nicolas Damascius, frag. 19; Scholiast *ad* Apollonius Rhodius 1.1063; Eustathius, *Iliad* 357, 43f.; and cf. Strabo, 13.621c). Piasos, a ruler of the Pelasgians, conceived a passionate desire for his daughter, Larissa, and secretly raped her without revealing his identity. Learning the truth, she plotted the following revenge: as Piasos was leaning over a huge *pithos* filled with wine, she seized him by the legs and plunged him headfirst into the cask where he drowned. See Rudhardt (1981, 739), who is mystified by the tale, but the correlations are not difficult to find. Her action both parodies his plunge into her *pithos* and fittingly repays him in kind, since the use of wine was typically restricted to men, who had access to the containers *(pithoi;* cf. WD 359–69, "Take your fill when the jar is first opened and then again when it is nearly spent"; and also 597–603). Sexual and alimentary appetites are neatly joined, with the added element that wine encourages sexual desire. "Drunk" with passion, she drowns him in a surfeit of his own lust.

24. Pucci (1977, 86) also emphasizes Pandora's dual association with excess and lack (or loss), but in a different way: "She is an excess because she introduces toil as the way of producing what the earth once provided spontaneously, and a loss because toil does not fully restore the goodness of the preceding life." She thus corresponds, as he argues, to the Derridean "supplement," which is both an addition and a replacement.

25. For a discussion of the full and empty jar, see Vernant (1979b, 115–21), who notes the correlation between the two kinds of *pithoi*, but without reference to the continuing exclusion of woman from participating in the household.

26. West 1966, *ad loc.;* and, among others, Pucci 1977, 111. I prefer the first interpretation, which gives a straight progression: one, two, or many sons, but best to have only one. In the case of a second son, you should die old (presumably after having acquired sufficient wealth to divide it), and if you have many, then you need Zeus's assistance, since he can "easily bestow prosperity." As West remarks, this is "a typical Hesiodic provision for exceptions to the general rules at the discretion of the gods."

pressed elsewhere,[27] but in the Hesiodic economy in which women and offspring are viewed only instrumentally and in relation to the dynamics of masculine acquisition and retention, the potential proliferation of children poses a significant threat.

Woman is therefore defined as an economic liability. If her reproductive capacity is only to be tapped once, thereafter she is a surplus who does not increase the household wealth but rather diminishes the resources of both house and husband with her gluttonous appetite for both food and sex. She thus resembles neither the fields that are worked outside nor the bountiful Earth of the Golden Age (which, in Hesiod's version, at any rate, is populated only by men). Marriage and agriculture may be understood as two related spheres in which men toil and deposit their seed, but they are also disjoined in the case of Pandora. If man once took freely from the unstinting produce of earth, woman now takes from the abundant stores accumulated by man who, since her creation, has had to become the sole author of his own sources of nurturance.

Finally, the emphasis on raising an only child has a more pointed significance if we consider its thematic relevance to Hesiod's personal status as represented in the *Works and Days*. He is certainly *not* an only son: the entire poem is framed as a protreptic exhortation to his good-for-nothing brother Perses. We cannot recover the full details of Hesiod's complaints, but two issues seem to be evident. First, Hesiod has been in some kind of litigation with his brother over the division of their father's estate. Perses has somehow acquired more than his share by stirring up quarrels and has bribed the judges to sanction this unfair division. He has encroached on property that is not his, that rightfully belongs to Hesiod. If brothers must share, the portions at least ought to be equal, thereby satisfying the demands of Dikē (justice). But having only one heir to the patrimonial estate would do more than forestall the possibility of a fraudulent division leading to destructive *eris* (strife)—it would obviate the need for any division at all.[28]

At one level, as Vernant has observed, the dispute between Hesiod and his brother concerning the fair division of their inheritance parallels the

---

27. Whatever the particular economic conditions of Hesiod's day might have been, the continuation of this attitude in the tradition is already mentioned by the various scholia *(vetera, ad loc.)* following Plutarch's commentary. See, e.g., Xenocrates, frag. 97; Aristotle, *Politics* 1274b19ff.; and Plato, *Laws* 740b–d, 923c–d, in the context of optimal family size and population control in the Greek polis. For a treatment of this complex topic, see, for example, Golden and Golden 1975, 345–58. Space does not permit a fuller discussion that would have to include, among other issues, exposure of the newborn.

28. The Scholiast, *ad* 376–78, already notes the possible relevance for Hesiod of the preference for a *mounogenēs*.

inequitable sharing of the sacrificial meal in the *Theogony* between Zeus and Prometheus.[29] But the characterization of Perses in the *Works and Days* also gives rise to a second analogy, for this Perses is an idler who must be persuaded to accept the divine necessity of labor so that he does not end up as a burden on others or even as a beggar. "If he had filled himself up with a year's supply of grain in reserve," says Hesiod, "then he could turn to the quarrels and strife in the agora to lay his hands on another's goods" (*WD* 33). It is after this first address to his brother that Hesiod tells the story of Prometheus and Pandora as the founding myth of why men are obliged to work and to accumulate the means of life through agricultural toil. This account is followed by the myth of the Five Ages with its emphasis on the relation between material prosperity and the pursuit of justice in the evolution from the Golden Age to the conditions of the present day.

In the *Theogony*, as we have seen, Pandora is compared to a useless drone, "no companion to Poverty but only to Plenty," who sits within and consumes another's goods. In the *Works and Days*, we learn that the gods gave her a shameless mind and a thievish nature. Perses, we may note, combines both her qualities in his unregenerate state. Like Pandora, he is deceitful and thievish (*WD* 322). Like her, he intends to acquire for himself what belongs to another. Like woman, he is an idler who does not work and belongs with Hunger (Limos) rather than Satiety (Koros), and he too is "like the stingless drones who waste the labor of the bees, eating without working" (*WD* 303–4). Pandora is the opposite of the "bee wife," who, as the archaic poet Semonides tells us, is the single and only paradigm of the virtuous wife. Perses, in turn, is a bee with no sting in him, a drone, like the woman, within the hive that is the house, assimilated now to her earlier identification as a drone in the *Theogony*.

Two inversions therefore come into play. First is the opposition between animal and human worlds, in which the bee community inverts the usual division of roles to assign the active part to the female and the passive to the male.[30] Although the woman-drone may seem to be occupying a position reserved for males, the analogy is operative only with regard to the management of the household, which, like a hive, consists of bees and drones. The industrious woman may well be compared to a bee, if she

29. See above, note 16.
30. On the problem of bees, drones, and gender inversion, see Loraux 1981a, "Race," 82; and Vernant 1979b, 107–14. Roscalla (1988) dissents from this interpretation to argue on the basis of ancient evidence that drones are not viewed as males, per se, but rather as an alien *genos*, the members of which, like the woman, enter into another's dwelling. Yet, given that *drone* is a masculine noun and *bee* a feminine one, there is no reason to limit the terms of the analogy, as Roscalla does.

fulfills her domestic functions; if not, she can be called, as here, a lazy drone who fills her belly with the fruit of another's work. For the man, however, whose place is out of doors and in the fields, the image of the drone in the hive can apply only if he loses his masculine dignity by refusing to work *(aergos)* and, like a woman, by living off the toil of others. Thus despite the proper alignment of male and drone, the indictment of Perses only attains its full resonance as an allusion to the Pandora of the *Theogony*—Pandora, whose story is told to Perses yet again, now in the context of the god-given necessity that decrees that men must earn their living by tilling the fields. In short, if Perses is a drone, it is because this woman, in negation of her positive image as the bee wife, provides a pertinent analogue to Perses himself.

The result is that Pandora occupies a double position in Hesiod's system of the household. She is, first of all, the potential overproducer of progeny, who in bearing more than one child introduces the risk of a fraternal rivalry that is exemplified in the *eris* between Hesiod and Perses. Yet she also serves as the model for Perses himself: a drone, a supplemental and unwelcome addition who takes what does not belong to her rather than working or giving in return.

Perses, however, may be persuaded to assume his proper masculine role and to enter into the economy of labor by which he may rightfully prosper as well as share in the generalized social rules for exchange and reciprocity ("Give to the one who gives, but do not give to the one who does not give . . . Give *[dōs]* is a 'good girl,' but Seize *[harpax]* is a bad one, the giver of death," WD 354–56).[31] Pandora, by contrast, remains an ambiguous and untrustworthy entity, excluded from participation in the household economy. She is defined as an outsider, unwillingly brought by the man inside his house and carrying within her belly the equally ambiguous Elpis, who even if turning out well for man's future, is nevertheless restricted to the grammatical category of the singular *(mounē)*, not the plural.

Several important consequences attend this Greek view of woman's origin and functions. We note first by contrast that the myth of Adam and Eve justifies both the social, even organic, dependency of wife upon husband and her subordination to his authority. She is born from Adam's rib as a creation secondary to his, and God later decrees a separate punishment for her in his injunction that along with suffering travail in childbirth, she will be ruled by her husband (Genesis 3:16). Yet in Hesiod, oddly enough, although woman's inferior status is strongly implied, the

---

31. Some critics have proposed that the second half of the *Works and Days* implicitly "corrects" Perses' vexing behavior in the first, whether in respect to Dikē or to good Eris. For the first, see Nagy 1982, 59; for the second, Hamilton 1989, 53–66.

husband's control over his wife is not unequivocally established as a "natural" social rule. In fact, woman seems to retain an intrinsic power over man. She can, by her appetites, enfeeble and impoverish him, seduce him and rob him. ("Do not let a flaunting woman coax and cozen and deceive you: she is after your barn," *WD* 374). Man has no effective means of retaliation, no sure way of exercising his authority. He can perhaps only minimize her inherent danger by taking a young wife, as Hesiod later advises, hoping thus to train her in his ways (*WD* 700). But in essence, his only options are to avoid woman by shunning marriage altogether, thereby losing his patriline and irrevocably fragmenting his substance, or to suffer the miseries she inflicts upon him. On the other hand, by undermining the woman's maternal functions of both nature and nurture, the myth separates her from the true underlying sources of her power. The story thereby ratifies woman's secondary and derivative status in man's household, emphasized by the mode of Pandora's own creation, since as an artisanal product accompanied by another artisanal product (the jar), she is also separated at the outset from the natural processes of generation by which the entire universe came into being.

Yet in his turn man has claimed neither his paternal role directly nor a potent virility. As Daniel Boyarin comments, "If the opening of the jar represents the breaching of Pandora's virginity, then she is made wholly responsible, as it were, for this act as well. The text refuses to record the first sexual act between a man and a woman, because by doing so it would have to reveal that which it seems determined to suppress, the simple fact that men are also agents in the performance of sex and thus responsible, at least equally with women, for whatever baneful effects it is held to have."[32] Adam and Eve both eat of the fruit of the tree; both become aware of their identity as genitalized beings; both cover their nakedness, and they leave together when expelled from the garden of Eden. Hesiod's reticence on the topic of human sexuality and reproduction is all the more striking and significant, considering the broader aim of the *Theogony*, which is to recount the creation of the universe through the birth of the gods.

The creation of Pandora marks the definitive rupture between gods and mortals, forever separating them into different categories. Until now, we have focused on the import of this separation that determines the nature of relations between the sexes in the human realm, affecting men's lives for all time to come. But what of the other side? The creation of Pandora is only a single element in the larger creative project of the *Theogony* that constructs an extended evolutionary design in which gods play the central roles. Here the *Theogony* differs from Genesis in two striking

---

32. Boyarin 1993, 85, commenting on an earlier draft of this essay.

respects: first, as noted earlier, woman is created on her own without any parallel and preceding account of how the category of man came into existence; second, if Pandora is meant to stand for all humankind, as some critics have suggested, the text does not situate her creation as the final and culminating display of divine generative power. It occurs, rather, at a very different juncture, during the unfolding of a cosmogonic drama in which, unlike in Genesis, there is a multitude of gods—gods who themselves come into being by various means and at different moments of time. In these struggles at the divine level for differentiation, self-definition, and superior power, the place reserved in the text for Pandora's creation deserves detailed consideration in further assessing her roles and functions.

Mortals and Immortals

The essential aim of the *Theogony* is to establish Zeus's claims to supreme power over the universe and to chart the steps that lead to the eventual consolidation of his reign. These claims depend, in the first instance, on his gaining hegemony over the other gods and, in the second, on the decisive separation of gods from mortals. The two themes combine in the circumstances of Pandora's manufacture, since, with Prometheus as advocate of human interests, the quarrel between two generations of gods (Olympian and Titan) is also staged as a contest between gods and mortals.

Given the vast scope of this topic, I will focus on Zeus's rise to power in the frame of a succession myth that requires both the replacement of a father by a son (Ouranos by Kronos and Kronos by Zeus) and the eventual triumph of male over female, particularly with respect to rights over reproduction and matters of engendering and parentage—even, we might say, over the creative principle itself. The struggle begins with the castration of Ouranos (Sky) by his youngest son, Kronos, at the instigation of Gaia (Earth), the first maternal principle. In the face of the primordial father's refusal to uncouple from Gaia, castration is the drastic means she devises to allow their children to emerge from the mother's depths and see the light of day. But in his defeat, Ouranos initiates the first challenge to female fecundity, since his castration results in the birth of Aphrodite from his semen and in the engendering of the female Erinyes from the drops of his blood that fell to the earth from his severed phallus (*Th.* 184–200). In the second stage, Kronos may be said to imitate pregnancy itself by swallowing his children once they are born and, when forced to disgorge his progeny, "giving birth" to them through his mouth (*Th* 453–500). In the last stage, Zeus absorbs the female into himself, swallowing the pregnant

Metis, principle of resourceful intelligence, and producing a female off-spring—his daughter, Athena—from his head (*Th.* 886–95). Only in this way can he ensure the permanence of his rule, putting an end to the generational evolution of the male gods, and appropriating both the physical and mental creative capacities of the female in the interests of paternal—or, more accurately, patriarchal—power.[33]

Before the narrative reaches this momentous event (*Th.* 886–900, 924–96), Zeus has already accomplished his first creative act in producing the first mortal female, Pandora. In so doing, he ratifies the definitive split between gods and men. Two questions therefore arise: Why is the story of Pandora placed where it is, and which dilemmas is the mode of her creation designed to resolve? Logically, Zeus ought to have instituted his sovereignty over the universe before turning his attention to the condition of mortals. But the text takes a curious turn and situates the quarrel with Prometheus and the subsequent division between gods and men just *after* the narrative of Zeus's own birth but *before* the narrative of the mighty battle against the Titans. The last challenge follows in Zeus's solo combat with Typhoeus, Gaia's last child, a monstrous offspring of her mating with the primal depths of Tartaros. Only after this victory are we are told that the "blessed gods finished their toil *[ponon]*" and in the wake of their struggle for honors *(timai)* with the Titans, "urged Zeus to rule and be king over them, by the counsels of Gaia. And he divided their *timai* in turn among them" (*Th.* 881–85). The story of the birth of Zeus and his rescue from his devouring father, Kronos, is itself preceded by another apparent interlude, introducing a remarkable female goddess, Hekate. Her appearance constitutes another kind of *hysteron proteron,* in that she is especially honored by Zeus, even though Zeus has yet to be born, and she presides over human activities in a world of men that is not yet constituted.[34]

Why should this be so? Why should the "hymn" to Hekate *precede* the birth of Zeus, the centerpiece of the entire *Theogony,* and why should the story of Pandora *follow* directly after?[35] What logic insists on framing the birth of Zeus by the accounts of two female personages, who, taken together, form a complementary pair sharply divided into positive and

33. See this volume, chapter 3, 108–9, for a preliminary outline of this progression; for a full discussion, see Arthur [Katz] 1982. Bergren (1983) follows the same scheme. For the role and significance of Metis, see Detienne and Vernant 1978, chaps. 3 and 4.

34. Zeus's victory is, of course, forecast in the proem and alluded to at strategic intervals, including in the narrative of his birth, where it is mentioned just after Kronos swallows the stone (*Th.* 488–91).

35. Arthur [Katz] (1982) emphasizes this triadic structure. See also Boedeker 1983 and Clay 1984.

negative poles? Situated as two points on a continuum of feminine characters that leads from Gaia to Athena, including especially Aphrodite and
Styx, the figures of Hekate and Pandora are distinguished from all the
others, not least because each is defined in a significant relationship to
both mortals and gods, particularly Zeus.[36]

On the principle that the sequence of the narrative is itself a determining factor in the production of meaning, I propose in advance that Zeus's
own ontological status is indeed predicated on this intersection between
immortal and mortal realms, as he evolves from the first instantiation of a
divine child to the figure of sovereign ruler under the title of "father of
gods and men." Thus, while Hekate and Pandora have been rightly interpreted as important factors in together defining the ambiguities of the
"human condition," they are also essential in constructing the definition
of Zeus himself. Let us therefore take a closer look, starting with the passage about the goddess Hekate (long a puzzle to critics for its unusual
length and content),[37] before turning to review the question of Pandora
herself.

The Goddess Hekate

Hekate crosses the generational line that divides Titan from Olympian
divinity. Zeus honors her above all the gods, and she is honored in turn
by men and gods alike. She retains all the powers allotted as her share "at
the first time, from the beginning," and she retains these privileges on
earth, in the heavens, and in the sea, wielding her influence over all domains. The prestige of these prerogatives is underlined by her receiving
them twice, once at the outset and then again from Zeus (411–12, 421–
27). Moreover, these are formidable powers, far less restricted than those
of other divinities to whom Zeus apportions their respective *timai* after
the consolidation of his rule.[38] In her allotted role as intercessor between
men and gods, Hekate is highly responsive to petition, bestowing her favor

36. Arthur [Katz] (1982, 69) proposes that "Hekate is . . . a sign . . . of the positive pole
of female potency, a precursor to Athena and the other kindly daughters of Zeus, and the
antitype to Gaia who struggles for supremacy with the male, to Aphrodite who subdues him
through *philotēs* and *apatē,* and to Pandora 'the incurable curse' (612; cf. 588)." See also
her interpretation of Styx (80–81).

37. On the role of Hekate in the *Theogony,* see the extensive study of Kraus 1960. More
recently, see Marquardt 1981; and for more contextual readings, see Arthur [Katz] 1982;
Boedeker 1983; Clay 1984; and Griffith 1983, 51–55.

38. It is true, as Clay (1984) observes, that Hekate acts in concert with other gods (such
as Poseidon and Hermes), but the text stresses the universality, not the limitation, of her
powers in all domains.

as she wills.[39] She is called upon by all men in in all their diversified pursuits: war, athletics, horsemanship, navigation, law courts, and assemblies, as well as the work of tending herds and flocks. Her most important epithet is fittingly reserved for last; it is hers through the offices of Zeus, but it was so, it seems, from the beginning (450–52). This is her function as *kourotrophos*, "nurse of the young," a role that assures the continuation and well-being of life from its inception. Hekate is dedicated to fosterage but creates no new genealogical line of her own, for she remains forever a virgin.

What is more, she is called a *mounogenēs*, "a single-born child." She has no siblings, and oddly enough her father bears the name of Perses, which in the *Works and Days* is also the name of Hesiod's rival brother, whose lazy and thievish conduct occasions the admonitory tale of Pandora's creation.[40] Unlike that brother, she is a daughter, and unlike him, of course, she has no one with whom she must share. Quite the contrary. She receives more than her share; in fact, she gets it all—not once but twice.[41] Her social position in Zeus's family circle is unclear. As a *mounogenēs* from her mother, Hekate seems to remain inside the maternal sphere. As a daughter without brothers, she is also like an *epiklēros* (heiress) of her father's line and hence comes under the special paternal protection of Zeus.[42]

---

39. Note that Hekate's assistance is reserved for men, in marked contrast to her later associations, which are restricted to women and feminine spheres of activity. Clay (1984, 34), following Bollack (1971), insists on the ambivalence of the goddess's mode of intervention: Her "essential character . . . resides in the easy exercise of arbitrary power over success or failure in every human enterprise." Clay thus agrees with earlier scholars who glossed Hekate's name as "the willing goddess" *(hekōn, hekēti)*, "the one *by whose will* prayer is accomplished and fulfilled" (34n.32). Judet de la Combe (1995) also subscribes to this view and goes even further in equating chance with disorder. The question of Hekate's volition is important, I agree, in defining her power. She can, as the text says, give and take away, as she wishes *(Th.* 442–46), but volition is not the same as caprice. The general tone of the passage is one of goodwill and kindliness, as befits her genealogy from Phoebe, who bore both Hekate's mother, Asteria *euōnumos* (happily named), and the gentle Leto (406–8). On Leto and Hekate, see note 43 below.

40. Walcot (1958, 13–14) and Nagy (1982, 65) note this connection.

41. Marquardt (1981, 245), who views Hekate as belonging to another (Carian) religious tradition, proposes that "the absence of siblings . . . might also suggest an original genealogy outside the Olympian family." Nagy (1982, 65) offers the explanation that if Hekate were *not* a *mounogenēs*, she might split into two, like Eris (or Discord) in *Works and Days* (cf. 11–26). If she were divisible into a "primary positive and secondary negative pair," she would lose her beneficent status. He further argues that Hekate's all-encompassing powers make her an "ideal paradigm for the Panhellenic nature of Hesiodic poetry. . . . Accordingly, the invocation of Hekate at a sacrifice is tantamount to a blanket invocation of all the other gods as well."

42. See Arthur [Katz] 1982, 69. Arthur further equates Hekate's "social isolation" with "the universality of her powers," arguing that "Zeus' overvaluation of this goddess" is "a

Yet, however we understand her status,[43] she is unique, both because of the archaic plenitude of her power in a world to be defined by the distribution of *timai*, and because Zeus reconfirms her power, thus in a sense recreating her. Pandora, as Zeus's own invention, represents a new mode of creation through which a singular being can be made, not born, and needs no generational antecedents. Hekate's status is the result of another kind of innovative act. This time, Zeus's creativity consists in redoubling the nature of an already existing entity under a second dispensation. If his renewal of privilege does not exactly give Hekate a "second birth," it does award her a twofold status and thereby combines the categories of the old and the new, the first and the last.[44]

As an intermediary in human affairs between gods and men, honored by all alike, Hekate may be said to neutralize or at least mitigate in advance the negative effects for mortals of Prometheus's guileful mediation that motivates the anger of Zeus and the creation of Pandora. Hekate also compensates in advance for the negative presence of Pandora herself, who henceforth will become an integral dimension of human existence and re-

---

compensation for her undervaluation in the patriarchal social order, and as an indication that the beneficence as well as the honor of the female are conceived in inverse proportion to female autonomy."

43. There have been many other efforts to explain *mounogenēs;* here are two further thoughts, based on the text itself.

First, Asterie, the mother of Hekate, is also the sister of Leto, who heads the list of progeny born from Phoebe and Koios. Leto possesses two major attributes: her sweet nature and her status as the mother of *two* children, Artemis and Apollo. The text suggests that Leto, like Hekate, has originary powers and receives universal honor from mortals and immortals alike: "always gentle, kindly to humans and the deathless gods, mild from the beginning" (*Th.* 406–8). While the text here makes no mention of Artemis and Apollo (postponed until line 919), the extended emphasis on Asterie's single offspring may answer to Leto's famous double progeny, cousins of Hekate.

Second, the category of singleness relates to calculation of quantity: the one and the many, the one and the all, the more and the less. Because Hekate is a *mounogenēs*, Zeus gives her not less but more (426, 427), and this "more" turns out in the end to be "all" ("although a *mounogenēs*, she is honored with *all* privileges," *Th.* 448–49). Hekate herself has the power to increase and decrease, *Th.* 447). The categories of the one and the two also enter into the game, but at a different level. Aside from the relation between Leto's two children and Hekate, mentioned above, the *single*-born receives her powers *twice*, once from the beginning and again from Zeus, and this double bestowal is repeated *twice* in the narrative. This point is discussed further below.

44. The strategy of Zeus in making alliances with members of the older generation is crucial to his eventual success, whether with the Cyclopes or Hundred-Handers or with another feminine figure, Styx, who directly precedes Hekate in the narrative (383–401). Styx, however, has no previous role before she makes her compact with Zeus, and her function is here confined to the world of the gods. For Styx's place in the larger scheme, primarily as the mother who gives her children to Zeus, see Arthur [Katz] 1982, 80n.16; and Boedeker 1983, 90.

main its perennial burden. Thus these two female figures may be viewed as an antithetical pair: the first represents an economy of abundance, the second one of scarcity, and both are drawn into the essential game of reciprocity and exchange. Pandora is a baneful gift, who takes and does not give, herself given in exchange for something else that was taken away. Hekate, by contrast, is one from whom nothing is taken away, one who in fact receives more privileges than she had before. She gets these honors as gifts from Zeus and continues his beneficence by bestowing honors on mortals in turn, if she so wishes.

Convincing parallels have been noted between Zeus and Hekate. In the range and extent of her powers, she looks like a "small-scale reflection" of Zeus himself, and given Zeus's sponsorship, she prefigures the beneficent quality of his own rule in feminine form.[45] This is an important observation. Yet in highlighting her role as *kourotrophos,* Zeus also introduces a new form of feminine activity that shifts the emphasis from female fecundity and generative power to a maternal nurturance that is independent of the act of childbirth and that, additionally, is placed under the auspices of the major male deity.[46] *Kourotrophos,* it is true, was mentioned once before in passing as an attribute (and etymology) of the Kourai (daughters of Tethys and Oceanus), "who with Apollo and the Rivers, nurture *[kourizousi]* men on earth, a portion they received from Zeus." But Hekate's function extends to both gods and mortals, and its import is further underlined by its placement in the text as the last named of her attributes—enunciated not once but twice in the space of three lines (*WD* 450–52). Naming is a creative act that brings a figure, epithet, or concept into existence. It founds a reality that until then is not available for use in the world. Hekate's role as *kourotrophos* anticipates the innovations of Zeus's birth and also of Pandora's creation, leading to several significant consequences in both human and divine realms. The nurturant function is transferred from the mother of human offspring to a kindly feminine deity (sponsored by Zeus) in advance of the creation of woman, to whom, as we have seen, no such role is ever assigned. But the general principle of detaching nurse from mother may equally apply to the realm of the gods

45. Boedeker (1983, 90–91) discusses the resemblances and suggests that the reason may be Hekate's role as a transfunctional goddess in the Indo-European tradition.

46. As Arthur [Katz] (1982, 70) puts it: "The . . . redefinition of Hekate includes a revaluation of female generative potency to mean, in a more abstract and generalized way, the willing sponsorship of activities of human life. Life-giving has become life-sustaining" (i.e., *kourotrophos*). She further argues that "Hekate . . . is the first female whose pre-eminence derives from the patriarchal father. And she embodies female fecundity in a transmuted form . . . *in abstracto*—as nurturance, tendance, fosterage, and not as the direct expression of the child from her womb."

and especially to Zeus himself, whose emergence into the world is beset
with unusual difficulties. Let us examine the matter more closely.

If progress and evolution are to end in the establishment of a permanent world system, then the first imperative is to put an end to the inevitable replacement of father by son in the sequence of generations (which
Zeus does by swallowing Metis and giving birth to Athena, a daughter).
Before this eventual outcome, Zeus's birth story introduces two new elements into the system of generation that also come into play. The first is
the father's threat to reabsorb his young once they are born, the second is
the postponement of Zeus's retaliation upon his father until he himself has
grown to adulthood. Two potential difficulties attend this new dispensation. Zeus is the first instance of an infant god. This means that, like any
child, he requires nurture until he comes of age. It means too that he must
undergo a maturational process that brings him perilously close to the
realities of the mortal condition and the exigencies of human development.[47] Second, although the last-born child enjoys a symbolic advantage
in that he closes a genealogical series and embodies principles of higher
evolution, there is also an undeniable value in being first, already present
"from the beginning." Zeus's claim to hegemony over the cosmos resides
in his status as the last and most developed of the Olympian gods. Yet he
must somehow attain the prestige of origins that will connect him to the
first foundations of the world[48]—that is, to Gaia, from whom Zeus is ge-
nealogically twice removed.

By reason of her status and her functions, the figure of Hekate is indispensable for resolving these two predicaments. Having received her
honors twice, both from the beginning and now again from Zeus, she
exemplifies in advance a solution to the ontological paradox of being both
first and last. But in her role as *kourotrophos,* she offers yet another service to Zeus, since, as an infant separated at birth from his mother, he also
requires nurturance from a surrogate female figure. This figure is none
other than Gaia herself, to whose care he is entrusted in order to save him
from his father's greedy appetite. The order of the narrative is revealing.
The naming of Hekate as *kourotrophos* ends the "hymn" to the goddess
(452). It also furnishes the point of transition to the account of how Rhea,
in sexual conjunction with Kronos, "gave birth to glorious children"
(453) in a sequence of begettings that ends with Zeus. No sooner is the
category of *kourotrophos* "invented" for general use[49] than it is immedi-

---

47. His maturation is swift, of course, as befits a god, taking only one year (*Th.*
492–93).

48. For the general principle, see Eliade 1958.

49. The category of *kourotrophos* was not needed until now in the recitation of divine
genealogies and births, all of which stopped short with parturition and only incidentally
mentioned the rearing or *trophē* of offspring (*Th.* 313, 323).

ately represented in the divine sphere in the relation of Gaia as nurse to Zeus.[50]

The goddess's initial association with the infant Zeus is an essential step in the process that leads to his eventual triumph. Gaia is the primordial principle of earth, the locus of origin for the entire cosmos. The nurture she gives him in her function as foster mother thus establishes a primary and enduring bond between the first and the last. Her dual identity as active agent (divinity) and receptive element (earth) has still further import: *Gaia* takes the child from Rhea "to nurse and rear" (480); *gaia* is the place she puts him, "taking him in her arms and hiding him in a remote cave beneath the secret places of the holy *earth*" (482–84). When Zeus emerges from her care, we might say that he too undergoes a "second birth," this time as a kind of autochthon, a child of earth in his own right. In this way, he too, like mortal men, can circumvent or pass beyond the natural facts of maternity to claim the kind of engendering Greek males like best: born (or reborn) from the female principle of earth and not from the womb of a mother.[51]

If the question of maternal affiliation is settled in Zeus's separation from his true mother and his secondary status as a nursling of earth, he still remains in the circle of women, whose presence is needed to safeguard his right to exist despite his father's hostility. But what about the paternal principle? Is it thereby also put into question? Kronos presents a curious case. His actions, as we have seen, imitate feminine functions in respect to pregnancy and birth, yet he also remains a male and a father who strives to suppress the next generation in order to assure the permanence of his kingship. When Zeus compels Kronos to disgorge his progeny, he in effect "forces him to yield up his *timē*," since "the right to rule is identified with control over procreation."[52] But there is more. Born once from their mother, the other Olympians are replaced in their father's belly only to undergo a "second birth," this time from the paternal source. Thus, if

50. On a frieze of a late Hellenistic temple in Lagina, Hekate is depicted as presenting the stone to Kronos, in imitation of Gaia's role. The Hekate of Hesiod remains a *kourotrophos* in actual cult (unlike the other roles attributed to her). See Marquardt 1981, 244n.2; and Boedeker 1983, 83–84nn.21–22. On the rupture of the relationship between mother and son (Zeus and Rhea) and the role of Gaia as *kourotrophos*, see Arthur [Katz] 1982, 71.

51. Gaia also takes a primary role (along with Ouranos) in the entire affair. Kronos learns from the two of them that his son is destined to overcome him (*Th.* 463–65), and in turn they suggest the ruse to Rhea (*Th.* 467–73), but Gaia acts alone in tricking Kronos to give up his offspring (*Th.* 494–95). Arthur [Katz] (1982, 70–71) argues that Rhea's "diminished potency" is a further sign of "the weakening of female primacy" in favor of "the elevation of the male (Kronos and Zeus) into the role of *genitor*." Loraux deserves full credit for emphasizing the significance of autochthony in Greek mythical thought, a concept she has elaborated in much of her work.

52. Arthur [Katz] 1982, 72.

Zeus's triumph over Kronos represents the victory of the son over the father, it also signifies the triumph of the father over the mother as a higher
form of reproduction. Whether on the side of the female (autochthony) or
on the side of the male (disgorgement), both strategies promote the idea
of a second birth as a way of eliding the obvious and natural fact that man
is from woman born.[53]

A further consequence of Kronos's obstetrical adventure provides another means of establishing the requisite connection between first and last,
since, as the text is careful to note, the stone representing Zeus that
Kronos ingested *last* is necessarily brought up *first* (πρῶτον δ' ἐξήμησε
λίθον. πύματον καταπίνων, 497).[54] On the maternal side, the last generation was aligned with the first through the nurturing function of Gaia,
who substitutes for the real mother. On the paternal side, however, another kind of substitution also plays a role in joining first to last, starting
from Rhea's original sugstitution of the stone for the child and ending with
the reversal of the order of birth when Kronos disgorges his progeny.[55]
Masculine and feminine tactics combine in the final disposition of the
stone. Sign *(sēma)* of its birth from the father, it is fixed in place by Zeus
himself "in the broad-wayed *earth* in holy Pytho, under the hollows of
Parnassus,"[56] a prodigy from heaven *(sēma)* destined to be a *thauma*

53. In the last stage of the succession myth, Zeus will take one more step to complete
the inversion of gender roles and ratify the primacy of the father, first by absorbing the
mother (Metis) into himself and then by giving the first, original birth to the daughter
(Athena). Arthur [Katz] (1982, 77) observes that "Zeus' swallowing of Metis . . . is an act of
synthesis . . . [that] closes the pattern in upon itself. For like Ouranos, Zeus suppresses the
child in the mother's womb, and like Kronos, he swallows the child itself, by consuming
Metis when she is pregnant with Athena and about to give birth (cf. 468f. with 888f.)."

54. West (1966, *ad Th.* 454) mentions this point and adds that Zeus would have been
the first to attain maturity, since the other offspring remained in their father's belly.

55. Bergren (1983, 74) offers a compelling interpretation of the stone from another
viewpoint: "Here is the primary *mētis,* the first imitation, one that seems to symbolize a
supposititious child. For Kronos is baffled by the disguise, as any man would be, when his
wife presents him with what she says is his child, for who except his wife can vouch for his
true child, the legitimate heir to his property and his proper name? Only the female has the
knowledge necessary to tell the true from the false heir, but it is this very knowledge that also
makes her able to substitute for the truth, a false thing that resembles it. Her knowledge
gives her the power of falsification in the domain of sexual reproduction, just as on the level
of language the knowledge of the Muses [in the proem] makes it possible for them to utter
either *alētheia* or *pseudea homoia etumoisin.*"

56. See also the elegant analysis of Mezzadri (1987), who adds that Hestia, the oldest
of Kronos's children and hence the last to be born, also combines the principle that applies
to the stone-Zeus (but in reverse). His further remarks on the correlation between temporal
and spatial structures at Delphi (with respect to the stone and the *omphalos*) are also pertinent. I quote his summary (302): "A same conception of the center and a same logical structure inform both the episode of the birth of Kronos' children in Hesiod and the famous

(marvel) for mortals (*Th.* 498–500).[57] Sky and earth, male and female, father and mother: Zeus's act of setting up the *sēma* in the world proclaims his sovereignty. It converts his birth story into a visible emblem and also ratifies the principle of substitution in the form of a material sign that will stand at Delphi alongside another *sēma* of birth, the omphalos stone that marks the site as the navel or center of the earth.

The Woman Pandora

Once the stone has fulfilled its function in the divine realm, it is destined for mortals, both a sign and a wonder. The stone also links human and divine realms, this time through verbal echoes and in the matter of procreation. The stone, disguised as a baby, was a substitute for Zeus, and he was left behind "in place of the stone" (*anti lithou, Th.* 489). Now in power, Zeus introduces another substitute, Pandora, "in place of the stolen fire" (*anti puros, Th.* 570). Like the stone, she too is a *thauma* to behold (*Th.* 500). The two have been justly taken as evidence of a higher level of social relations in a context of exchange and reciprocity.[58] Both were duplicitous gifts, given in response to an offense of unlawful appropriation. In semiotic terms both *sēmata* function as second-order signifiers. The first prepares for the second. "Zeus sets up the stone to be a sign of his control of signification, to be a sign to all who come to learn the mind of the father through the oracle of his son, that Zeus's regime is built upon the knowledge necessary to disguise, imitate, substitute—knowledge now securely embodied by father of men and gods." This capacity is put to immediate use, first in the contest of wits with Prometheus, and then in the fashioning of the first woman, by his plan and his own devising.[59] Zeus also redeploys another element from the story of Kronos in the transfer of the belly from its mark of his father's voracious appetite into the permanent and defining attribute of woman (her *gastēr*-belly) through the *gastēr*-paunch of the fraudulent division of sacrifice that led to her creation.

---

aetiological story of the *omphalos* [or navel stone]. But the first is a temporal articulation of what the other expresses spatially: Zeus last and first, Hestia first and last, conjoin opposites just as the two eagles bind the two extremes together" [i.e., when they set off from either end of the world to meet at Delphi].

57. *Sēma* has the two meanings of "sign" and "distinctive mark" or "prodigy" (cf., e.g., *Od.* 23.110, 188, 205, on the *sēma* of the bed as both a special object and a sign of recognition). See this volume, chapter 1.

58. Arthur [Katz] (1982, 72–73) sees the fixing of the stone as "the symbolic resolution of the father/son struggle in the form of the *sēma,* and the introduction of a cycle of reciprocity (in the form of gift exchange)."

59. Bergren 1983, 75.

At one level, Pandora is only a byproduct of a contest between males. She is a secondary, even tertiary effect, in that she comes in the third stage of that contest, as a retaliation for Prometheus's theft of the celestial fire that Zeus had just received from the Cyclopes. Zeus's control over this cosmic fire, in fact, will later determine his decisive victories in the cosmos, first over the Titans and then over the monstrous Typhoeus, the last of Gaia's progeny.[60] But coming just after the narrative of Zeus's birth and his subsequent triumph over his father, the creation of the first mortal woman mediates between past and present by renewing the question of male control over procreation (to be finally resolved in Zeus's mating with Metis) and also by reflecting upon Zeus's own status in the cycle of divine generations.

As a creation of the ruling masculine god, Pandora can be linked to the figure of Aphrodite and even to that of Athena.[61] Yet she also stands as a unique product, not only in reference to man and his estate but also with regard to the biological principles of creation that regulate the *Theogony*, whether through parthenogenesis or sexual reproduction. She also does not participate, except in a secondary and self-conscious way, in the basic genealogical scheme by which the *Theogony* suggests the natural unity of the world as it evolves from the moment that Chaos comes into being and Gaia, or Earth, emerges immediately afterwards. Genealogy is an effective means by which myth can posit a coherent scheme of relations and affinities. By tracing out family ties through successive generations, the generational scheme may sort out like from unlike, modify and distinguish categories and concepts, and establish temporal priorities and hierarchies of value.[62] Zeus is Pandora's author, not her natural sire, and she has no mother. By contrast, Athena's birth follows a heterosexual union

60. Zeus has just used fire in striking Prometheus's brother, Menoitios (*Th.* 514–16). While many have discussed the connections of Pandora and fire (sexuality, technology, cooked food, and so forth), no one, to my knowledge, has asked the obvious question of why Zeus should retaliate by withholding celestial fire in the first place. The division of the parts of the ox ends with the aetiological explanation that this is why men burn the white bones on the redolent altars (in sacrifice), and it is followed directly by (1) Zeus's punishment of refusal to give fire; (2) Prometheus's theft of fire; and (3) the creation of Pandora, *anti puros*. The sacrificial context may be sufficient to justify the logic of this narrative sequence (and the connection of woman and fire is a widespread mythic motif). But the implied logic of the *story* suggests that Zeus acts to forestall any future challenge to his authority, not just in a game of wits, as here, but in a full-scale struggle of opposing forces. He punishes Prometheus, of course, but by withholding fire, he safeguards the true source of his power, his chief weapon in later combats.

61. Schwabl (1966, 80) notes the parallels with Aphrodite. For fuller exposition, see Arthur [Katz] (1982, 75), although I cannot follow her further observation that Pandora is also a kind of Gaia reborn.

62. See Philippson 1936.

(with the goddess Metis) and, in a sense, follows the laws of organic pro-creation, despite the inversion of head for loins and father for mother. Pandora's nature, on the other hand, is determined by the gods' seemingly arbitrary bestowal of gifts, which makes her only a composite imitation of the "real thing," and because she is detached from natural modes of repro-duction, she is descended from no family line.

The result is that the introduction of the female sex as a *genos gunai-kōn,* a race of women apart, does not coincide with the creation of gender as it does in the Genesis myth. Once Gaia emerges independently after the neuter entity of Chaos, the female principle is established once and for all, and indeed is the source of the male principle (Ouranos) derived from it. From that time on, the idea of biological (genealogical) reproduction had coincided with the grammatical distinctions between male and female, so that all the various entities that came into being were automatically en-dowed with a gendered identity, enhanced, of course, by a polytheistic system of gods, who follow anthropomorphic lines in their relations with one another and in their modes of begetting. Zeus's invention of Pandora and her subsequent status as a gift indicate, therefore, that she is far re-moved from femininity as an original category. This is a strategic move, with two important implications for the separation of gods and mortals.

First comes the rupture of continuity with the principles of both ge-nealogical relationship and natural procreation. However these categories have been manipulated in the divine realm, the actual workings of nature remain the same.[63] With the manufacture of Pandora, on the other hand, mortals and immortals are henceforth divided between nature and cul-ture, or perhaps between the natural and the "nonnatural."

The second implication pertains directly to the split between woman and goddess. This strategy displaces the undeniable powers of the female upward to the gods, allows for the "deification" of the female and femi-nine attributes, while repressing any validating alternatives to the mortal woman.[64] Zeus adopts and empowers an original femininity in the person

63. See Judet de la Combe 1995, who also observes the significance of this "rupture in this continual process of physical engendering" as essential to the "history of gods and men." But it is a species of circular reasoning to argue first that "this [event] has perhaps more to do with the particular status of men faced with the gods than with the specific essence of woman." It is not the woman but what she represents, he claims. But what does she repre-sent, if not a woman?

64. Rudhardt (1986) also notes that femininity arises at the beginning with Gaia, but he makes no clear distinction between the two levels. For the value of a two-tiered system of goddesses and women, see this volume, chapter 3, 112–15, on the *Oresteia,* where the prob-lem of woman (Clytemnestra) is displaced upward to the level of the Erinyes. The resolution in the *Eumenides* is also organized according to a theogonic model of a struggle between chthonic and Olympian forces, and the dilemma is solved by a new distribution of *timai.*

of the goddess Hekate, who assists men in all their undertakings and sustains generational continuity among mortals by sponsoring the growth of children apart from actual maternity.

Thus, in the complex interplay between immortal and human realms, in which the dilemma remains how to separate the two categories while retaining their underlying kinship, the role of Hekate works in two directions. Maternal concern has been continuously present in the *Theogony*, not only in the proliferation of children in the divine realm, but also in the mother's insistence on securing her children's right to exist and in her alliance with them against a hostile father, as in the case of Gaia (vs. Ouranos) and Rhea (vs. Kronos). But Hekate, above all, represents this principle in its most disinterested form. A virgin and not a wife, a virgin and not a mother, a goddess and not a woman, only distantly related to Zeus but of an older generation, Hekate attests to Zeus's patronage of a femininity among both mortals and gods just before he is about to negotiate his own birth, nurture, and subsequent validation of paternal procreative powers.[65] In the creation of Pandora (and later when she puts put the lid back on the jar by his command), Zeus exercises this paternal power in a new dimension. Yet in so doing, he contributes a new and supplemental category, which is that of woman.

This woman, as argued earlier, is hardly represented as a "bringer of fertility" and the "principle of reproduction," as most interpreters like to insist—or, put another way, to the extent that she is, the text suppresses these functions as much as possible. It avoids any direct mention of sexual congress and only grudgingly acknowledges the need for a child, who is never mentioned as such but must be deduced from the context. In this sense, woman is deprived of those feminine powers that only goddesses and nature possess. But by her unwelcome presence and the necessities she imposes upon man's existence, she is empowered in another way. Her creation implies, as we know, that man can never be independent of woman because he requires children to remedy the facts of both aging and mortality. But since he is burdened by these limitations, it also means that man, through woman, can never successfully challenge the rule of Zeus, who has now earned his title of "father of gods and men" as the sign of an elevated masculinity and paternal hegemony.

Yet a serious paradox remains. Whether in the divine or human

65. Hekate and the monstrous Typhoeus may also make up an antithetical pair. If Hekate is the beneficent double of Zeus, promoted in advance of his birth, then, following Blaise's hypothesis (1992), Typhoeus is his negative antitype. Hekate is the transvalued and nurturant maternal principle, not born of Gaia. Conversely, Typhoeus is the offspring of the negative, chthonic aspect of Earth; her last parthenogenetic challenge to the Olympian order, which Zeus must overcome.

realms, whether by nature or by artifice, whether man or god is the subject, whether an abstract opposition can be maintained between a principle of unlimited growth (female) vs. the limits of order (male), an underlying theme of the entire *Theogony* concerns the anxiety of the male
confronted with fear of a "natural" female superiority, best expressed in
the deployment of a series of reproductive strategies. These run the gamut
from the realistic norm in the natural union of male and female to parthenogenesis, autochthony, fictions of nurture, second birth, and, in the case
of mortals, the alienation of woman from the species of man.

If the world of the gods aims to establish the paternal principle through
inventive (and mimetic) tactics that harness the forces of nature and kinship in both sex and procreation, the case of Pandora must, of necessity,
address the same problem in another way. As we have seen, once Pandora
is represented as the sole agent who will forever inscribe man in his mortal
condition, the fact of man's role as the father of his children cannot be
acknowledged directly. To do so would admit the male's joint responsibility for sex and procreation, which before the creation of Pandora, he
presumably did not need. Rather, the insistence that she is an artificial
creation, imposed on man as an unwelcome supplement, only creates a
further distance between them. If the text cannot name her as mother, it
follows that it cannot empower him as father. The relationship between
man and woman is rather an economic one, framed in the disparity between producer (he) and consumer (she), ownership and appropriation,
abundance and lack, self and intrusive other. As a result, paternity too is
commodified by being translated elliptically into economic terms as requirements of the male ego: man needs the support of a caretaker in his
old age who will also keep intact the assets that he and only he owns, once
he is gone. The father continues after the end through the preservation of
his property in the hands of his heir.[66] The triumph of paternity is projected into the world of the immortal gods, gods who can accomplish
what men desire and dream of, in order to assure a perennial existence
in time.

The double problem of the origin of woman and woman as the origin
is thus deeply embedded in the structures and strategies of the *Theogony*.
Neither god nor mortal is exempt from it, although it is woman who is
the signifier of their difference. Why this persistent concern with control
over reproduction, with the desire either to imitate or deny what women
do? One speculation is that it is, as Mieke Bal has noted, "the control of
time, directly related to reproduction, that is so desirable. The sense of
time is itself a sense of the end. Reproduction is a way to overcome the

---

66. Money lent out at interest is envisioned as breeding further money like offspring,
and the "product" is called *tokos* (progeny).

tragic feeling of contingency which is the result of mortality. It makes history, that is, continuity." If this is so, it is fair to conclude that "the fear of the end is compensated by the obsession with beginnings. Myth is in itself an utterance of that obsession."[67] And nowhere more so than in Hesiod's *Theogony*, where if the price for mortals is high, it is probably woman, in the final analysis, who must pay the greater share.

Nevertheless, if Pandora is made to embody the separation between mortal and immortal realms of existence, she also continues to blur the lines between them. Fashioned by the gods to resemble them in the beauty of her allure, she is both an imitation and an original production, both a copy and a model. How to tell the difference? Once woman is invented, the story has just begun.

67. Bal 1983, 118–19.

· THREE ·

The Dynamics of Misogyny: Myth and Mythmaking in Aeschylus's *Oresteia*

The *Oresteia* occupies a privileged position in any examination of the Greek mind and spirit. It stands as one of those monumental works of art that transcend their aesthetic values, for it gives voice and form to the social and political ideology of the period at the same time as it actively shapes the collective fantasies of its audience with its own authoritative vision. By taking as his subject a dynastic myth known to us from the beginning of Greek literature and transforming it into a wide-ranging myth of origins, Aeschylus draws upon his mythopoetic powers in the service of world building. The last play in the trilogy leads us back to a re-enactment of the cosmic struggle between Olympian and chthonic forces, ending with two social but divinely sanctioned acts of creation: the first human court to judge cases of homicide and the new religious cult of the Eumenides. The program of the *Oresteia* is to trace the evolution of civilization by placing the polis at the center of its vision and endowing it with the creative power to coordinate human, natural, and divine forces.

For Aeschylus, civilization is the ultimate product of conflict between opposing forces, achieved not through a *coincidentia oppositorum* but through a hierarchization of values. The solution, therefore, places Olympian over chthonic on the divine level, Greek over barbarian on the cultural level, and male over female on the social level. But the male-female conflict subsumes the other two by providing the central metaphor that "sexualizes" the other issues and attracts them into its magnetic field, even while it maintains its own emotive function in the dramatization of human concerns, This schematization is especially marked in the confrontation between Apollo and the Erinyes in the *Eumenides,* where juridical and theological concerns are fully identified with male-female dichotomies. Moreover, the basic issue in the trilogy is the establishment, in the face of female resistance, of the binding nature of patriarchal marriage in which wifely subordination and patrilineal succession are reaffirmed. In the course of the drama every permutation of the feminine is exhibited: goddess, queen, wife, mother, daughter, sister, bride, virgin, adulteress, nurse, witch, Fury, priestess. Every issue, every action stems from the female, so that she serves as the catalyst of events even as she is the main object of inquiry.[1]

Viewed as a gynecocentric document, the *Oresteia* holds an equally privileged position in any exploration of the Greek image of the female, the definition of her social role and status, her functions and meanings. If Aeschylus is concerned with world building, the cornerstone of his architecture is the control of woman, the social and cultural prerequisite for the construction of civilization. The *Oresteia* stands squarely within the misogynistic tradition that pervades Greek thought, a bias that projects a combative dialogue in male-female interactions and also relates the mastery of the female to higher social goals.

In the breadth of its scope and in the complexity of its treatment, however, the *Oresteia* moves out beyond the other exemplars. The diachronic sweep of the trilogic form creates a broad field in space and time for amplifying patterns and themes, while mythopoetic stratagems lend authority to dramatic enactment. The *Oresteia* expands the paradigm by incorporating other myths and mythic elements into a comprehensive frame of reference and transforms it by an imaginative synthesis that culminates in the creation of a definitive new myth. The trilogy looks both ways. It stands as the fullest realization of an attitude that from its first literary expression in the *Odyssey* is already associated with Clytemnestra (*Od.* 24.199–202).[2] But by integrating the issue into a coherent system of new values, by formulating it in abstract terms, and by shifting to a new

1. "The infidelity of Helen was the cause of a vengeance that brought disastrous results; it was a goddess, Artemis, who blocked the fleet at Aulis and demanded a virgin as the price of the expedition. The hatred left by the memory of this daughter sacrificed to paternal ambition and the jealousy aroused by the concubine in the service of his royal pleasure excited the hatred of a mother and wife. Electra armed Orestes, and his persecuting divinities were female, guardians of mother right. Finally, it was a woman, the daughter of Zeus, to whom the judgment fell" (Green 1969, 59).

2. "An overwhelming misogyny accompanies the appearance of Clytemnestra everywhere. Agamemnon only names her in the *Iliad* in order to reject her. In the *Nekyia* (11.400), he hardly mentions Aegisthus and he burdens all women in general with the example of Clytemnestra: Odysseus should be careful of making too many concessions to his own wife! In the second *Nekyia* (24.201), he finds some comfort in the certainty that the transgression of Clytemnestra will weigh on the reputation of all women, even the most irreproachable. . . . It is neither possible nor useful to distinguish the different layers of interpolation here. The sentiment that inspired the first poet satisfied those who later enriched the diatribe, thanks to two favorite themes of popular misogyny, that which never accuses a woman of anything without immediately extending the grievance to all the others, and that which concludes in recommending to husbands to keep watch over their authority" (Delcourt 1959, 84).

mode of argumentation, it provides the decisive model for the future legitimation of this attitude in Western thought.

The Myth of Matriarchy

The progression of events in the *Oresteia* is straightforward. Woman rises
up against male authority in a patriarchal society. By slaying her husband
and by choosing her own sexual partner, she shatters the social norms and
brings social functioning to a standstill. Portrayed as a monstrous andro-
gyne, she demands and usurps male power and prerogatives. Son then
slays mother in open alliance with the cause of father and husband, and
mother's Erinyes, in turn, pursue him in retribution.

The dynamics of the process, however, are noteworthy. Clytemnestra,
the female principle, in the first play is a shrewd, intelligent rebel against
the masculine regime. By the last play, through her representatives, the
Erinyes, the female principle is now allied with the archaic, primitive, and
regressive, while the male, in the person of the young god Apollo, champions conjugality, society, and progress. His interests are ratified by the
androgynous goddess Athena, who sides with the male and confirms his
primacy. Through gradual and subtle transformations, social evolution is
posed as a movement from female dominance to male dominance, or, as
it is often figuratively phrased, from "matriarchy" to "patriarchy." [3]

For J. J. Bachofen in the mid-nineteenth century, as for many who
followed him, this evolution represented a true historical development. It
was no accident that for the verification of his general theories of the
origins of society he drew heavily on ancient classical sources, including
the *Oresteia*, and gave his different phases names drawn from Greek
mythology. [4] For the Greek mythic imagination is rich in projections of
female autonomy, and Greek religion is amply populated with powerful
female deities who seem to antedate their male counterparts in the pantheon. The great Greek cultural heroes, Herakles and Theseus, are aggres-
sively involved with women, and each counts among his founding acts of
civilization the confrontation and defeat of those woman warriors, the
Amazons. [5] Iconographically, the Amazonomachy figures on the same

3. E.g., Lattimore 1953, 30; and in more general terms, Thomson 1966, 45–46; Neumann 1954, 168.

4. Bachofen (1967 [1861]) insisted on the primacy of matriarchy, or more correctly,
Mutterrecht (the law of women) in the early stages of a universal cultural development. He
designated his two main phases at this period as Aphroditic (hetairic) and Demetrian (matrimonial) with an aberrational stage of Amazonism. *Mutterrecht* represented the telluric, the
material, and the feminine that gives way gradually to the higher Ouranian, spiritual (Apollonian), and masculine values. See also Delcourt 1959, 78–79.

5. Slater 1968, 393.

level of significance as those other two great victories over the giants and the centaurs. The female, the earthborn elements, and the hybrid beast share the same associative sphere.[6]

But matriarchy in the literal meaning of the term is not provable as a historical reality, whatever the differences in social structure may have been between the inhabitants of the Aegean basin and the invading Indo-Europeans.[7] Far more compelling is Joan Bamberger's theory of the myth of matriarchy as myth, not "a memory of history, but a social charter," which "may be part of social history in providing justification for a present and perhaps permanent reality by giving an invented 'historical' explanation of how this reality was created."[8]

From a cross-cultural perspective, the *Oresteia* can be characterized as an intricate and fascinating variant of a widely distributed myth of matriarchy, the so-called Rule of Women, whose details differ but whose general scenario conforms to a consistent pattern. Such myths are normally found in "societies where there also exist a set of cultural rules and procedures for determining sexual dimorphism in social and cultural tasks." Women once had power, but they abused it through "trickery and unbridled sexuality," thus fostering "chaos and misrule." the men, therefore, rebelled. They assumed control and took steps to institutionalize the subordination of women. The point of the myth is not the recording of some historical or prehistorical state of affairs, but rather the demonstration that women are not fit to rule, only to be ruled.[9]

While the simpler myth of matriarchy reads as a definitive masculine triumph that establishes the pattern for all time, the variations, repetitions, and frequency of occurrence of the pattern in Greek myths attest to the continuing renewability of the battle between the sexes in many areas and circumstances. The conflictual nature of the encounter is consonant with the generally agonistic outlook of the Greek world, while the consistency of the portrayal of woman may reflect the deep-seated conviction that the female is basically unruly. The vigorous denial of power to woman overtly asserts her inferiority while at the same time expressing anxiety about her persistent but normally dormant power that may always erupt into open violence. But the eruption of that force is not perceived as un-

6. See duBois 1982.

7. By "matriarchy" is meant the actual political and economic supremacy of women in a given culture, not matriliny or matrifocality. See Delcourt 1959, 15, 77; also Thomson 1965, who has much interesting material but whose conclusions are not generally accepted. See further Pembroke 1965, 1967, 1970; Vidal-Naquet 1986a, "Black Hunter," and 1986b; and especially, Arthur [Katz] 1976, 383–87.

8. Bamberger 1974, 267.

9. Bamberger 1974, 276, 280.

predictable; rather, it follows a discernible linear pattern that proceeds in conformity to its own particular "logic," its own dynamics, which arises directly out of this fundamental ambivalence toward woman.

The central role played in mythology by male-female encounters attests to the significance and complexity of the problem, even as the proliferation of versions may indicate the impossibility of finding a satisfactory conclusion. In turning to Aeschylus to outline the version of this "logic" of misogyny operative in his drama—the dramatic sequence of events and the hidden assumptions that regulate it—we find that the poet must in effect invent his own solution.

The conjugal relationship is the focus of the struggle. Already assumed as the preexisting norm, it is not accepted in its current form by the female as an absolute imperative. In the *Oresteia,* wife and mother Clytemnestra repudiates it from inside the society, although it may equally be rejected from the outside, as the Danaids, militant young virgins, do in another trilogy. The goal of both trilogies is the female's full acceptance of the marital bond as necessary, natural, and just. In each case, the prior rejection of marriage leads to the massacre of the male, the corollary of which is the threat of extinction to human society as a whole. Clytemnestra slays her husband. The Danaids slay their bridegrooms on their wedding night. The polarizing imagination of Greek mythic thought not only establishes a strong dichotomy between male and female, it also posits predictable behavior responses at either end of the spectrum where female self-assertion on her own behalf comes only at the cost of annihilating the Other. We might perhaps speak of an "Amazon" complex that envisions that woman's refusal of her required subordinate role must, by an inevitable sequence, lead to its opposite: total domination, gynecocracy, whose extreme form projects the enslavement or murder of men. That same polarizing imagination can conceive of only two hierarchic alternatives: Rule by Men or Rule by Women. (Cf. Euripides, *Orestes* 933–37).

The portrait of Clytemnestra in the *Agamemnon* specifically links her independence of thought and action with a desire to rule,[10] an emphasis that transforms a personal vendetta into a gynecocratic issue, which presents the first motive as synchronic, not diachronic with the other. Husband is also king, an economy that conflates the two social statuses, erases political and domestic distinctions, and permits the merger of personal revenge and political ambition. Clytemnestra begins, in fact, as woman in charge; as the chorus remarks, she is entitled to rule in the absence of the husband-king (*Ag.* 258–60, cf. 84). She seems intent, however, on making that regency permanent, so she is made to assume the stance

10. Winnington-Ingram 1948, 130–47.

of political *tyrannos,* an impression that is explicitly confirmed by both the choruses in the first two plays.[11] She does not rule alone, in a full gynecocracy, but the principle is maintained by the delineation of her lover and later coregent Aegisthus. He is the male who has already succumbed to female domination. He occupies the female interior space (*oikouros, Ag.* 1225, 1626) and renounces masculine heroic pursuits of war and glory (*Ag.* 1625). He is only an adjunct to, not an initiator of, the plot against Agamemnon (*Ag.* 1633–37, 1643–45). In his erotic susceptibilities, he is not unlike his barbarian counterpart Paris, who also commits adultery with a daughter of Tyndareus. The subordinate male, the strengthless lion (*Ag.* 1224–25), is the only possible partner for the dominant female, and the chorus contemptuously marks this reversal of rules by calling him "woman" (*Ag.* 1625; cf. *Choe.* 304).[12] When he does assert himself by baring his own motives and flexing his new-found power, he himself conforms to the stereotypical male model of *tyrannos.*

Note too that Agamemnon must also be assimilated to the pattern of reduced masculinity before his murder at the hands of a woman. The prelude to his death is his defeat in the verbal exchange between himself and Clytemnestra, a debate that is specifically posed as a power struggle between male and female in which male eventually yields (*Ag.* 940–43). The cause of that dispute, the walking on the tapestries, is itself concerned with a clash in values, and Agamemnon's objections are based on his correct perception of the gesture as one appropriate only to women and barbarians. But he has already revealed his sensuous weakness by bringing back Cassandra as his concubine from Troy, while his yielding to Clytemnestra's temptation marks his secret affinity with the Trojan king Priam and with barbarian values of luxury and gratification of desires (*Ag.* 918–21, 935–39). This antithetical barbarian world is portrayed in the Greek imagination as one of effeminacy and sensual delights, even as it is the world where, logically enough, female domination is perceived as a cultural reality and where the myths of matriarchy are most often located.

Clytemnestra fully understands this cultural dichotomy and reveals it in an oblique and subtle way. After Agamemnon has yielded to her persuasion and has entered the palace, she urges Cassandra now to come into the house and to accept her fate of slavery, and she supports her argument by allusion to a mythological precedent: even the son of Alkmene, when sold into servitude, endured his life of bondage (*Ag.* 1040–41). Herakles is identified not by name but only through his maternal genealogy, and his enslavement, of course, was to the Lydian queen Omphale who is everywhere in the tradition associated with the Rule of Women. In fact, one of the prominent features of the relationship between Herakles and Omphale is the terms of his enslavement at her hands, which required him to take on a female role, to wear women's dress and do women's work, and also appropriately to serve as the male sexual object to satisfy the needs of the queen.[13]

If Omphale is an archetypal exemplar of the Rule of Women, two other paradigms point even more directly to the same mythological construct. In the *Choephoroi*, the series of monstrous women recited by the chorus culminates in a reference to the famous myth of the Lemnian women, so notorious that their deed need not be recorded, but only the judgment passed upon it as proverbial for the epitome of evil (*Choe.* 631–36). The crimes of single women come first; Althaea (mother), Scylla (daughter), and Clytemnestra (wife). The Lemnian allusion completes the misogynistic progression by moving from one to all, from individual transgression to a collective menace that wipes out an entire race. Moreover, by redoubling the example of husband murder that immediately precedes, the ode places Clytemnestra's offense (which itself has already passed into paradigm) within the larger frame of the Rule of Women where female aims to annihilate male.

If the Lemnian women serve a programmatic function in the *Choephoroi* as a justification for the murder of Clytemnestra, the Amazons assume that role in the third play, where Aeschylus shifts the aetiological explanation for the name of the Areopagus from Ares's trial on that site to the battle between Theseus's Athens and the Amazons, worshippers of Ares. There the Amazons, the open rivals of men, had built their own city, had asserted their will in rival architectural and ritual structures (*Eum.* 685–90). If in the *Choephoroi* the mythological emphasis falls both on the murderous aspect of the female in domestic relations and on her victory over the male with its predictable results, the other exemplar shows the Rule of Women as a political issue and celebrates its decisive defeat at the hands of Theseus, champion of male public interests. Clytemnestra is no longer the point of reference, as Apollo points out, since she did not confront the male in open combat (*Eum.* 625–28), and she is the threat from within the system, not from without. The Amazonomachy in this context rather serves to demarcate the major substantive issue of Orestes' trial as a battle between the sexes. Moreover, the prior victory over the Amazons not only foreshadows the outcome of the trial but also, by as-

13. For ancient testimony on Omphale, see Ps.-Apollodorus, 2.6.3; Diodorus, 4.31; Ovid, *Heroides* 9.55ff.; Sophocles, *Trachiniae* 247ff.; Lucian, *Dialogue of Gods* 13.2; Plutarch, *Greek Questions* 45; Scholiast, *ad Od.* 21.22; Hyginus, 32. See also Bachofen 1967 [1861], 142, 216–27, who makes interesting comparisons with Tanaquil, Dido, Cleopatra, and others. The importance of Omphale's name is obvious (i.e., "navel"); cf. Slater 1968, 379; Fontenrose 1959, 108–10.

sociation, invests the new defeat with the same symbolic significance and prestige as the earlier one. In the synchronic perspective, then, past is paradigm, but if we shift to a diachronic view, the substitution of tribunal for warfare, of law for violence, indicates an evolutionary development and offers a new paradigm in the present for the pacification of hostilities.

These three gynecocratic allusions, each allotted to a different play of the trilogy, and together forming a series of increasing elaboration and emphasis, mark out different aspects of the general pattern of the Rule of Women. Omphale implies role reversal and sexual bondage, while the Lemnian women point to the potential outcome of feminine desire as the destruction of the male by the female, and the Amazons indicate the predictable conclusion to such a myth of matriarchy: the drawing of open battle lines and the ultimate, inevitable triumph of male over female.[14]

In the Aeschylean version of the myth, the woman does not initiate the hostilities; she is spurred to retaliation by an outrage inflicted upon her by a male.[15] Clytemnestra, outraged by the treatment of her daughter as a sacrificial animal, plots revenge and is reinforced in her resolve to kill her husband by Agamemnon's intention to introduce his concubine into the domestic space of the legitimate wife.[16] For their part, the Danaids are fleeing their suitors who view marriage as acquisition, rape, and enslavement.

But the female response invariably exceeds the provocation offered by the male and creates a still more violent disequilibrium that brings society to a standstill. The havoc caused by the female in the first play of the *Oresteia* requires two sequels to alleviate it, and the shock waves ripple out first to the city of Argos and then to the universe at large. In the *rhetorical* progression of the drama, the crimes of the males of the house— Thyestes, Atreus, and Agamemnon—first fade into lesser significance and finally are mentioned no more.

In the *Choephoroi* the uncanny power of the monumental androgynous figure of the *Agamemnon* has receded.[17] Clytemnestra rules with Ae-

14. On Amazons, see further duBois 1982; and now the magisterial study of Blok 1995. For Athenian mythmaking, see Tyrrell 1984, who expanded on the themes of this essay. Bachofen uses all three myths as important testimony to his scheme of cultural evolution.

15. Clearchos proposes this principle in speaking of the Lycian "matriarchy" initiated by Omphale: Athenaeus, 5153–56c = Wehrli 1969, frag. 43a. Cf. Hesiod, *Theogony* 154– 72, on Gaia's response to Ouranos. See also Bachofen 1967 [1861], 104–5, 141–42, whose views are consonant with his idealization of pre-Hellenic womanhood. Shaw (1975, 255– 56) suggests a similar scenario for Greek drama, without considering either the social imbalances between the sexes or the extent of the threat created by woman's "intrusion."

16. Cf. Sophocles's *Trachiniae* and Euripides' *Medea* for similar scenarios.

17. Vickers 1973, 382–88, 393–94.

gisthus over Argos, but she is now back in the interior of the house, not visible in the world of men and politics. She sends libations to the tomb of Agamemnon, but her action creates a ritual impasse since the wife who owes this duty to her husband is also his murderer (*Choe.* 84–100). This impasse is emblematic of the dysfunction of the social order under her regime, and she herself poses the problem that must be resolved if the social order is to be repaired and restored. The impasse is also manifested in the social status of the legitimate children: Electra, unwed, arrested in maidenhood, bound to the paternal hearth,[18] and Orestes, an exile, as yet unable to cross the boundary to adulthood, a status contingent upon his assumption of his father's name and space. The house is shrouded in darkness, literal and metaphorical, the blood is frozen in the earth (*Choe.* 51–53, 66–67), and the children have a past but no future. That past, in fact, must be recalled and recreated in the long *kommos,* even as the free flowing of pent-up libations, tears, and verbal laments is the first symbolic step toward liberation from the suffocating spiritual and social deadlock of the current regime.

The only solution envisioned by the myth is the retaliatory defeat of this self-willed female principle whose potency is still a living and malignant force. And the myth proposes only one candidate for the task, because the rules of blood vendetta exclude any other. Son must slay mother, father must be avenged; but in so doing, son's alliance with paternal power and interests must simultaneously be seen as repudiation of the mother. Mother must therefore be shown as hostile both to father and to son. In Clytemnestra's dream of the serpent at the breast and in his encounter with his mother, Orestes represents both himself and his father, acting on behalf of both.[19] For Orestes interprets his exile from the palace as rejection by the mother (*Choe.* 912), and mother's hostility to her children is confirmed by her treatment of Electra (*Choe.* 189–91, 418–19, 444–46), by her call for a man-slaying ax at the moment of recognition (*Choe.* 889–90), and, above all, by the nurse who exposes Clytemnestra's hypocritical grief at the report of her son's death and who herself lays claim to responsibility for having nurtured him as a child (*Choe.* 737–65).

But in the *Agamemnon* the queen's primary motive was maternal vengeance for her child, Iphigenia; her second one was the sexual alliance she contracted with Aegisthus in her husband's absence. There the two traits of mother love and conjugal chastity diverge—are, in fact, contradictory. Here in the *Choephoroi* adulterous wife is now fully equated with hostile mother. The woman who betrayed her husband and took his usurper into

18. Vernant 1969, 110–12.
19. Green 1969, 68–69n.41.

her bed has now betrayed her other children to gratify her own sexual desire (*Choe.* 915–17, cf. 599–601).[20] The confrontation between Clytemnestra and Orestes is remarkable for the queen's mingled appeal of maternity and sexual seductiveness; the breast she bares to him (*Choe.* 894–98) has both erotic and nurturant significance. The gesture that momentarily stops him in his tracks is the source of her power over him, the source of all female power. It is the emblem of the basic dilemma posed by the female: the indispensable role of women in fertility for the continuity of the group by reason of her mysterious sexual nature, and the potential disruption of that group by its free exercise.

It is significant that the maternal role should be exemplified in the first place by the mother-daughter dyad, for this is a relationship from which the male is excluded, a closed circle in which his interference can only be construed as an invasion, as the myth of Kore and Demeter demonstrates so well. It is essential too that the mother-daughter bond be attenuated as it is in the second play, where Electra is her mother's antagonist and her father's ally, and that the mother-child bond in the *Choephoroi* include both male and female offspring, although the emphasis now falls on mother and son.

The dramatic sequence of events in the trilogy suggests a linear chain of cause and effect. If the female overvalues the mother-child bond, her own unique relationship, she will undervalue the marriage bond, which in turn will lead to or be accompanied by an assertion of sexual independence (free replacement of one sexual partner by another) and will be manifested politically by a desire to rule. The next step, paradoxically, will be her undervaluation, even rejection, of the mother-child bond, as in the case of Electra and Orestes. Child, in response, will undervalue and reject mother.

Orestes' victory over Clytemnestra does not, however, result in the defeat of the female and in the curtailment of her power, as in the more typical myth of matriarchy. Far from it. The murder of the mother evokes a renewed and redoubled power, exemplified now in a proliferation of negative female imagoes of supernatural origin. The chorus in the *Choephoroi* had resorted to another mythological paradigm to exhort Orestes to action: he is to be another Perseus who will slay the Gorgon (*Choe.* 835–37), the archetypal myth, on another level, of masculine triumph over the female.[21] But the projected model is not fully applicable, first,

20. The ode on monstrous women makes universal the force of *eros* that is *thēlukratēs*, a phrase that can be read in two ways: "the female mastered by *eros*," or conversely, "female power to master men through *eros*." See also Winnington-Ingram 1948, 138n.76.

21. For the general psychological import of dragon combat with a maternal figure, see Neumann 1954, 152–69. For him, Orestes' victory over the mother and the psychological

because Orestes himself is given ophidian attributes, and second, because the serpent dead is deadlier still. The chorus's exulting allusion, after the deed, to Orestes's liberation of Argos by lopping off the heads of the two serpents (*Choe.* 1046–47) is instead an ironic cue for Orestes' first glimpse of the serpentine Furies. In this play, the Erinyes by their appearance terrorize him into frenzy and flight. In the next, they would annihilate him by absorption into themselves in an exact and retaliatory inversion of the symbolism of Clytemnestra's dream.

This final stage in the developmental progression, in fact, links the perversion of both relationships—mother-child and female-male. For the devouring voracity of the Furies, the vengeful incarnations of Clytemnestra, who would pursue and suck the blood from their living victim, represents both oral aggression against the child they should nourish and sexual predation against the male to whom they should submit.[22] Clytemnestra has banished both legitimate males from the house, and blood guilt infects the earth. In the case of the Erinyes, as transmutations of Clytemnestra, the result of hypersexuality is sterility and death. The virginal Erinyes are barren and sterile, and create sterility in all of nature.

In the primitive portrayal of the Furies there is a regression to the deepest fantasies of buried masculine terrors. They are *paides apaides,* "children who are no children," because they are old and also because they are children who have no children of their own. They are shunned and rejected by men and gods (*Eum.* 1033, 68–73). Daughters of Night, they inhabit the depths of the earth. Repulsive in physical appearance, they drip and ooze from every orifice; even their breath, their words, their thoughts leak poison (*Eum.* 478–79). Their virginity is negative virginity, as Clytemnestra's sexuality is negative sexuality, and in each case the fertility of the land is threatened (cf. *Ag.* 1390–92).

The pacification of the Erinyes becomes the ideological effort to solve the dilemma of the inextricable connection between female fertility and female sexuality, between female beneficence and female malevolence, for the equation of the female with sterility and death creates a new impasse that spells an end to society and to life itself. The solution moves to repair the female archetype that has been polarized at its extreme negative limit

"matriarchate" of female domination "has gone a stage further. . . . Here, the identification with the father is so complete that the maternal principle can be killed even when it appears, not in the symbolic form of the dragon, but as the real mother—and killed precisely because this principle has sinned against the father principle" (168). But at the end of the *Choephoroi,* this liberation has not been achieved.

22. Green 1969, 74; Slater 1968, 189–90. The female's appetites for both food and sex are already important features of the Prometheus-Pandora myth in Hesiod. See Vernant 1980, "Prometheus," and 1979b. See also this volume, chapter 2, 65, 81.

in response to its rejection and denigration. The solution also establishes marriage as the institution that controls sexuality and ensures fertility even as it serves to assert the inherent subordination of female to male. For female dominance is expressed paradigmatically by the mother-child relationship: concretely in the *Oresteia* by Iphigenia's death as the motive for the female's attack upon the male and generically by the natural dependency of the male child upon the female adult. Patriarchal marriage is paradigmatic of male dominance, including the primacy of the father-son bond in patrilineal succession and the primacy of the male in political power.

Separation from the Mother and the General Pattern of Puberty Rites

In speaking of the myth of matriarchy and the general function of myth and ritual as educational tools in preliterate or traditional societies, Bamberger draws a parallel between the myth of matriarchy and puberty initiation rites that aim at detaching the boy from his natal household and maternal associations and retraining him for his social and political roles in the domestic and public spheres. She points out that "this regrouping of adolescent boys with adult males is prefigured in some societies in myths foretelling the demise of female power and in the concomitant rise of male privilege. The myth of the Rule of Women in its many variants may be regarded as a replay of these crucial transitional stages in the life cycle of the individual male."[23] Myth and ritual are indeed closely correlated: In the myth men often seize sovereignty from women by stealing their sources of power, the sacred objects (e.g., masks and trumpets), and taking exclusive possession of them; in the initiation rituals, one of the important events involves revealing these same sacred objects to the boys and explaining their meaning. But in these cases myth is prior to ritual, so that an event of the past supports and justifies the ritual and its message.

What we find instead in the *Oresteia* is the sophisticated interweaving and transposition of traditional motifs from both a myth of matriarchy and a ritual initiation scenario. Orestes, specifically characterized in the *Choephoroi* (6) as standing on the threshold of maturity, lives out the myth in terms that bear a remarkable resemblance to generalized and widely diffused initiatory patterns, but his own special situation now determines and directs the final outcome of the myth. Rather than following out a well-trodden path to adulthood, as countless others would have done before him, and as we would expect of an actual cult experience,

23. Bamberger 1974, 277.

Orestes must make his own way through an unprecedented set of procedures created expressly for him, and he himself must act as the catalyst to bring a secular, noncultic institution into being. Likewise, the myth of matriarchy reaches its predictable conclusion through a series of stratagems that combines the old and the new.

Orestes in the second play is the anomalous male, the logical counterpart of the anomalous female, Clytemnestra. Male activity is normally directed outward, away from the hearth, for external validation of prowess in the hunt and in war, but the domain that Orestes must enter is feminine space. If Pierre Vidal-Naquet is correct, as I believe, in suggesting that Orestes is of ephebic status, the inversion is still more precise. The boy, before entering adulthood, must be separated from the attachments of home and childhood to serve out his military term on the wild frontiers, where he is situated temporarily in a savage state, in a liminal space as befits his liminal position.[24] But Orestes, the exile banished in childhood by his mother, *returns* at puberty to his home, that space made savage and undomesticated by his mother's action, in order to undertake the most savage act of all.[25]

24. Van Gennep (1960 [1909]) was the first to identify and formulate the three main stages in rites of passage: separation, liminality (or *marge*), and incorporation (or aggregation). Turner (1967, 1969, 1974) has powerfully elaborated the sociocultural values of liminality.

25. Vidal-Naquet 1981a; 1986a, "Black Hunter"; 1986a, "Recipes"; and 1986b. The *ephēbeia* seems to have been in origin the equivalent of male puberty initiations attached to the tribal phratry and modified later to make boys into hoplite citizens. Our evidence is late, scanty, and transmitted by a secular source (Aristotle, *Athenian Constitution*). The Spartan *krypteia* (to which the *ephēbeia* bears certain marked resemblances) and the Cretan *agelai* conform even more closely to traditional tribal initiations. Vidal-Naquet (1986a, "Recipes," 147) suggests that in the historical period "what was true of the Athenian ephebe *at the level of myth* is true of the Spartan *kryptos* in practice." See also Eliade 1958, 108–9. Vidal-Naquet (1981b) argues also for the ephebic status of Neoptolemos in Sophocles's *Philoctetes*. See Jeanmaire (1939, 227–375) for the initiatory motifs in the myth of Theseus. For the most recent survey and discussion of these Greek mythic motifs, see Versnel 1994.

Orestes' role in Euripides' *Iphigenia in Tauris* also displays some initiatory features. See Brelich 1969, 242–44. Fortes (1959, 9–10), alluding to another variant in the Orestean myth, recognizes the frame of reference. "What is significant for us in the Orestes story is that he murdered a kinswoman, that this kinswoman was his mother, and that his expiation was to mutilate himself by cutting off a finger. . . . The parallels that leap to mind, for an anthropologist today, are other apparently irrational mutilations of the body carried out in the context of an overt or suppressed conflict between successive generations. We think . . . of the very widespread association of circumcision and other forms of mutilation with the initiation of youths and maidens into adulthood."

Thomson (1966, 46–47) and Tierney (1937) find initiatory patterns in the trilogy but refer them respectively to the Eleusinian and Orphic mysteries. The ephebes, we might note, played an important public role in the preliminaries to the Eleusinian mysteries. But their participation might have been due to their status as civic representatives (since they were separated from their families) or to their own initiatory status in another sphere. What can

To effect that separation Orestes must commit a crime, the crime of matricide, and far from releasing him from his mother and her influence, the Erinyes now sing a binding song over him to draw him into their domain and keep him there. Orestes' true initiatory experience begins only after his *second* expulsion from the palace in Argos and ends when—reincorporated into society in the third stage of the rite of passage—he returns to Argos as lawful ruler and successor to his father. The overt mission of the *Eumenides* is to effect the salvation of Orestes. That salvation is contingent upon his successful separation from his mother—in other words, upon completion of the enterprise undertaken by Orestes himself in the second play. The task now ascends to a higher level, that of both gods and city, even as the myth of matriarchy can reach its prosperous conclusion in this new setting only through a similar upward revision of its traditional terms. That is, the *Eumenides* must now once and for all establish and justify in abstract, scientific, and mythopoetic terms the principles upon which the predictable sequence of the myth of matriarchy is based.

This shift to a more inclusive level of discourse is necessitated by the terms of the main preoccupation of the trilogy, which reaches its fullest articulation in this third and final play. The primary issue in the *Oresteia* is, of course, justice and how it should be defined. In the proper execution of justice under all circumstances, matricide—the extreme transgression and here the insoluble case—serves only as the means, the irresistible catalyst. Richard Kuhns shrewdly observes, "Orestes cannot know that he is directed to act on behalf of a further purpose; he does not know that the crime is committed in order that it may be judged."[26]

But by posing the son's action in separating himself from his mother as a crime, the issue of justice and the issue of the female are inextricably blended. For in first offering the justification for matricide and then exonerating it, mother is also judged. And she is judged on two levels. First, the woman is judged as wife. The crime of Clytemnestra (mariticide) is measured against Orestes' (matricide) and found to be more opprobrious: "For it is not the same thing that a noble man die, a man honored with god-given sovereignty, and at the hands of a woman at that" (*Eum.* 625–27). Second, the Erinyes themselves, the first judges of Orestes, are also judged. Mother has been turned into vindictive and archetypal female. In the new genealogy invented by Aeschylus for the Erinyes, they

---

be said is that the general cluster of details (to be discussed further below) was familiar to the Greek world through the scenario of the Eleusinian mysteries, and that for ethnology, mystery initiations everywhere are secondary elaborations of tribal initiation. Sabbatucci (1965, 153n.30, 177–79) suggests the derivation of the mysteries from Athenian tribal initiations.

26. Kuhns 1962, 35.

are now daughters of Night—that is to say, they are wholly identified with the primordial negative female principle. And they champion a justice that is judged blind, archaic, barbaric, and regressive, a justice that is to be superseded by the new institution of the law court in which they will in the future play a supporting rather than a starring role.

The problem of the female is posed in a new set of terms, and the victory that is won is predicated on a social transformation of a higher degree. The *Eumenides* is therefore everywhere concerned with change and transformation on every level, both for the son Orestes and for the mother. For the archaic mind, as Mircea Eliade points out, it is a characteristic belief that "a state cannot be changed without first being annihilated" and then regenerated. "Life cannot be repaired. It can only be recreated by a return to sources."[27]

The first word of the last play of the trilogy is *prōton*, "first": as Kenneth Burke puts it, "the final oracular beginning."[28] The *Eumenides* is preoccupied with beginnings, with origins. Its *mythos* is itself a myth of origins, of aetiologies, on both secular and cultic levels, and it supports and redeems itself by reference to the ultimate beginnings. To quote Eliade again:

> Every mythical account of the origin of anything presupposes and continues the cosmogony. From the structural point of view, origin myths can be homologized with the cosmogonic myth. The creation of the World being *the* preeminent instance of creation, the cosmogony becomes the exemplary model for 'creation' of every kind. This does not mean that the origin myth imitates or copies the cosmogonic model. . . . But every new appearance— an animal, a plant, an institution—implies the existence of a World. . . . Every origin myth narrates and justifies a 'new situation'—new in the sense that it did not exist *from the beginning of the World*. Origin myths continue and complete the cosmogonic myth; they tell how the world was changed, made richer or poorer. . . . This is why some origin myths begin by outlining a cosmogony.[29]

And this is precisely how the *Eumenides* begins.

The opening scene, as many critics have noted, is both paradigmatic and anticipatory of the ending of the play. The Delphic succession myth (a parallel to the evolution of power in Hesiod's *Theogony*) provides a direct

27. Eliade 1958, xiii; 1963, 30.
28. Burke 1966, 133.
29. Eliade 1963, 21.

mythological model for the transference of power from female to male.[30] Although it would not have been inappropriate, in view of the prevalence of serpent imagery in the trilogy, to cite the traditional Delphic version of Apollo's acquisition of the shrine by dragon combat with the Pytho (as in the *Homeric Hymn to Apollo*), Aeschylus has substituted an orderly and peaceful version of the succession myth in order to foreshadow the peaceful and consensual ending of the trilogy: "For a thing to be well done, it must be done as it was *the first time*."[31] Here is true mythopoesis and a reversal of terms: a new civic order is in the process of creation and therefore requires as its model an alternate cosmogony, a new myth of origins.

By the terms of the revised myth, Aeschylus provides a paradigm of positive matriarchy that acknowledges the principle but relegates it to a primordial past that has been superseded. But by his other act of mythopoesis, he presents the Erinyes as daughters of Night, representatives of a negative matriarchy or "mother right" that must be overcome. In the Hesiodic attribution of their origin to the blood of Ouranos's severed phallos, they were also associated with vengeance and retribution. This, the first crime—the son's castration of his father—automatically generated its own (feminine) agents of retaliation. In their new genealogy, however, as parthenogenetic offspring of Night, the principle of vengeance is posed as arising from a purely female source, female too in its blackest and most negative manifestation.[32] The new genealogy anchors them to a stage antecedent to Ouranos's creative powers, manifested in bisexual reproduction with Gaia and the generation of regular, nonmonstrous forms.

In this juxtaposition of two matriarchal representations, the Erinyes are invested with the symbolism of dragon-combat mythology that was displaced from the Delphic myth. The Erinyes' desire to suck Orestes' blood, to engulf him, paralyze him, and draw him down into the darkness of Hades, is consonant with the general pattern of the archetype. Earlier I remarked on the failure of the Gorgon-Perseus paradigm for Orestes in the *Choephoroi*, but that failure resides not in the misnaming of the monstrous serpent female but only in Orestes's inability to play Perseus. Here in the transpersonalization of the female dragon (*Eum.* 128), the archetypal encounter recurs, but its outcome will be changed. For Apollo cannot reenact his previous victory over the Pytho, and Orestes himself will not play out the part of the typical hero and slay the serpent. The dragon

---

30. On the *Theogony* see Brown 1953, 17. On the paradigmatic function of the prologue in the *Eumenides,* see, e.g., Solmsen 1949, 21, 23, 64, 157–66; Clay 1969; Finley 1955, 277; and Ramnoux 1959, 139–43.
    31. Eliade 1958, xiii.
    32. Ramnoux 1959, 138–39.

will not, in fact, be slain: it must rather be tamed, and this act of domestication will be presented in collective, social, nonheroic terms, with violence yielding to open persuasion, Peitho.[33] Yet with the gods as agents, the struggle is also represented as a mythic conflict between chthonic and Olympian forces, between regress and progress, that resonates with the emotive power of theogony and gigantomachy (*Eum.* 295–96) as well as with dragon combat. The defeat of the Erinyes is already prefigured in the prologue by their temporary pacified sleep at the shrine (*Eum.* 47, 68) and by their subsequent expulsion from it by Apollo (179).

From the perspective of the myth of matriarchy, the Erinyes and their characterization conform even more closely to the generalized pattern we have been following. For they are now a collective of females rather than a single figure, and their quarrel with Apollo turns precisely on the issue of his attempted usurpation of prior female power and privilege. But it is the conflation of the myth of dragon combat with the myth of matriarchy that gives the *Oresteia* its most persuasive rhetorical weapon. The Erinyes on stage embody the metaphorical allusions to them in the earlier plays and also, as true primordial dragon figures, make visible the metaphors of serpentine female monstrosity that have been associated with Clytemnestra from the beginning of the trilogy (cf. *Ag.* 1233–36; *Choe.* 249, 835, 994). The two strands meet in the ode on monstrous women, in which the women of myth who slay men are likened from the first strophe to monstrous eruptions in nature on sea, on land, and in air, and in which the human Scylla, daughter of Minos, recalls her homonymous counterpart in the monstrous bitch of Cassandra's accusation (*Choe.* 612–22).[34]

Already in the first play this rhetoric provides the yeast that transforms the shrewd political rebel into an archaic *daimōn* who menaces the world with a renewed cosmogonic threat of total disorder. It also marks the male-female conflict as not a feminine revolution but a struggle between the new (male) and the old (female). Female is allied with the forces and values of the past both on the mythological level and, as the combat shifts from husband and wife to mother and son, on the personal and human level. In the generational code, mother is anterior in time to son. In the juridical code, the ancient principle of the blood vendetta becomes fully identified with mother. It was her championship of the priority of blood ties that led her first to slay the male to avenge her daughter's death. Now she is the one who pursues the slayer, the kinsman who has shed kindred blood, and the one who refuses her son the normal passage into adulthood.

33. For the details of the combat myth, see Fontenrose 1959.
34. See Zeitlin 1966, especially 653; and Rabinowitz 1981.

If the recitation of Delphic genealogy is a myth of beginnings, the second part of the prologue—Orestes himself at the shrine—represents another modality of beginnings directly consequent upon the first one. Orestes is seated at the *omphalos,* the navel of the world, holding suppliant emblems of white wool and covered with the purifying blood of a pig. Since he is a matricide, his condition symbolically represents his status of moral ambiguity—guilty and not guilty, polluted and purified.[35] If he is regarded as a neophyte, however, his ambiguous status is emblematic of puberty rites everywhere. In a state of liminality, betwixt and between, he is separated from the world and not yet reincorporated into it. In the process of transition and change, he must go back again to beginnings, a process that, this time, is marked in the biological domain by the imagery of parturition. In fact, "neophytes are [commonly] likened to or treated as embryos, newborn infants, or sucklings by symbolic means that vary from culture to culture."[36] All initiations employ some nexus of death-and-rebirth symbolism as a mark of transition to a new state, but the imagery in puberty rites has special relevance because the essential aim of the rite is to dramatize the biological life cycle by indicating the demise of childhood and a concurrent rebirth into adulthood—a symbolism supported, for example, by the dual use of the cutting of hair to serve both rites of puberty and those of mourning (*Choe.* 6–7).

Marie Delcourt, in her *Oreste et Alcméon,* poses the question of why the blood of a pig is used in rites of purification. She suggests that its value lies in neither the sacrificial nor the lustratory functions of the animal, but rather in its close association with female genitalia. The pig, as artistic representations make clear, was held over the head of the subject who sits "like a new-born under the blood organ that gave him birth. The blood of the piglet was only symbolically purificatory. The guilty was supposed reborn, and reborn innocent, from the mystic *choiriskos.*" Varro informs us that the same treatment was applied alike to homicides and to those who had been mad and were now restored to reason (*De re rustica* 2.4).[37]

35. Jones 1962, 105–6.

36. Turner 1967, 96. In the same discussion, Turner states that "the symbolism attached to and surrounding the liminal *persona* is complex and bizarre. Much of it is modeled on human biological processes. . . . They give an outward and visible form to an inward and conceptual process. The structural 'invisibility' of liminal *personae* has a twofold character. They are at once no longer classified and not yet classified. Insofar as they are no longer classified, the symbols that represent them are, in many societies, drawn from the biology of death, decomposition, catabolism, and other physical processes that have a negative tinge. . . . The other aspect that they are not yet classified, is often expressed in symbols modeled on processes of gestation and parturition."

37. According to Delcourt (1959, 97), "all the words which in Greek and Latin designate the piglet also designate the feminine organ, *porculus* as well as *choiros* and its diminutives, *choiriskos, choiridion,* all equivalents of *kteis.* Baubo on the back of a pig holds a

"Just as pollution is disease and disease is death, so purification is a renewal of life."[38]

Orestes, then, is ritually reborn at the *omphalos* of Delphi, the female symbol at the center of a place whose name itself means womb. But this symbol has been appropriated by the male hegemony of the shrine that Apollo himself received as a *birthday* gift (*Eum.* 7). The implication of the scene is a second birth, this time from the male—a necessary condition both for Orestes' redemption from the guilt of matricide and for his passage into adulthood as the son of his father. Cross-cultural ethnographical data confirm that one of the most consistent themes of puberty rites is, in fact, the notion that the first birth from the female is superseded by a second one, this time from the male. The initiate is born again into the social world of the fathers and is thereby definitively separated from the world of his childhood and his maternal dependence.[39]

---

loom comb *(kteis)*. *Orthagoriskos* and *orthagoras*, other names for piglet, signify *to aidoion* [pudenda] . . . (scholiast *ad* Aristophanes, *Ecclesiazousae* 915; cf., e.g., *Wasps* 1364). The womb is called a *delphys;* the suckling pig is called a *delphax*, probably the same word as *vulva*. The Latins call *porca* the projecting part of a ploughed furrow, and the tracer of the furrow in the list of the twelve gods of the *Sacrum Cereale* is called an *imporcitor*." See also Henderson 1991, 130–32.

Delcourt (1959, 97–98) also points to analogous rites of palingenesis. Men believed dead were not reintegrated into the community until after a simulated rebirth (washing, swaddling, nursing), on account of which they were called *Deuteropotmoi* or *Hysteropotmoi*. A Roman rite obliged those thought dead in a foreign land to reenter their houses through the chimney in the roof, not through the door (Plutarch, *Roman Questions* 5).

The most famous account of a man's return home after a long absence when it was not known whether he was alive or dead is, of course, the *Odyssey*. Others have pointed to general themes of death and rebirth. But Odysseus's reentry into his palace in Book 19 recapitulates the stages of the life cycle in a scene that Eric Auerbach (1953) in his well-known study treated merely as a digression. To reclaim adult status on Ithaca, Odysseus begins again from birth and reconstitutes his youth: (1) Eurycleia, his nurse, who "took him in her own hands when his mother first bore him" (19.355), washes his feet and through her recognition of his scar recalls (2) his naming on the knees of his maternal grandfather when an infant (19.399–409) and (3) his killing the boar at the age of puberty, which left a permanent mark (scar) on his body, a common initiatory feature.

38. Thomson 1946, 93.

39. "One of the most important purposes of the puberty rites is to loosen the tie between boys and their mothers and to bind the novices to the society of men. This part of primitive education . . . is accomplished by drastic means. The strongest tie binding the child to the mother is, of course, the fact that she gave birth to him and his dependence resulting from that. To break it, the male child is supposed to die, to be killed and to be born by man again, by his father or a father-representative. This new or newborn being begins a fresh existence as an adult and as a member of his tribe . . . [thus] undoing birth from the mother" (Reik 1960, 123–24). Cf. Eliade 1958, 7–10. Often the women are, in fact, duped into thinking their sons have died. Often they are required to mourn for their sons who have been taken away from them by ritually aggressive means and to pretend not to recognize them when they return. *(Note that Orestes reports himself dead and that Clytemnestra does not*

What is remarkable in the compressed symbolism of rebirth in this opening tableau is its double reference. If Orestes' ambiguous appearance is attributable first to his liminal status as neophyte, it also refers to the nexus of guilt and innocence that proclaims him still attached to his mother (that is, guilty) or separated from her (that is, innocent). He can hardly negotiate the second set of terms until he has resolved the first. This second issue—which is the primary focus of the trilogy—will be determined by the new Apollonian argument in the new juridical sphere that his mother is no kin to him, that he is born from the father and only from the father.

Apollo's argument, then, is a restatement in another mode of discourse of what has already been represented here at Delphi. Orestes himself is drawn into the Apollonian milieu and is assimilated, if obliquely, to the pattern of Apollo's own development that brought the god from Delos where he was born to the shrine at Delphi—that is, from the mother's domain to the one where his father Zeus has control.[40] But Orestes' position still lacks the conclusive ratification of society and its gods. It is only a beginning. For full authorization he must be removed from Delphi to Athens, from isolation to community, and from the exclusively religious world to the political arena. And the process that is to define his identity will be linked to the process by which society will define itself. In this double task that the drama poses for itself as a simultaneous and reciprocal development, the action veers away from the sphere of myth and ritual even as it continues the impulse in a new and different way.

Orestes' experience continues to conform to the constellation of symbols and events that cluster about the pubertal initiation scenario. In addition to the liminal situation of ambiguity and the recurrent imagery of

---

recognize him.) In extreme cases, "the initiate is allowed to insult and even manhandle his mother in token of his emancipation from her tutelage" (Hottentot), or he "walks over his mother's body, deliberately stepping on her belly, and this gesture confirms his definitive separation from her (Papua)" (Eliade 1958, 30).

On rebirth from the male or attested to by male sponsors, see also Bettelheim 1954, 113–21; Turner 1962, an account of Ndembu circumcision ritual; and Eliade 1958, 27, on the importance of blood symbolism. Vidal-Naquet's remark (1986a, "Recipes," 145) is eminently relevant: "The Athenian polis was founded upon the exclusion of women, just as, in other respects, it was founded upon the exclusion of strangers and slaves. The sole civic role of women was to give birth to citizens." We should not, however, overlook the importance of autochthony (substitution of Earth as mother) in Athenian political ideology.

40. Delcourt (1959, 104) remarks that "the Greeks unanimously saw in Apollo the natural defender of the avenging son. . . . Even earlier than Aeschylus is the image of the young god assisting the young man, his double . . . Apollo of Delphi is a symbol. Apollo of Delos, tenderly associated with images of birth, has a totally different value. Delphi ignores Leto and represents maternal power in its most terrible aspects [Pytho]."

birth, death, and rebirth, other typical features include: (1) ordeal, wakefulness, suffering, silence, isolation, wandering, and terror produced by encounters with the monstrous and supernatural; (2) close connection with the ruling deities of the group; (3) the presence of a male authority figure as guide, who dispenses the "arcane wisdom" or "gnosis" pertaining to social and political realities couched in mythic and symbolic form (with reference especially to theogony and cosmogony), as well as "instruction in ethical and social obligations, in law and kinship"; and (4) the passive submission and obedience to that authority.[41] The main event of initiation rites is, of course, the revelation of the hallowed traditions and secret lore of the group. Here in the *Eumenides* this revelation combines old and new elements to formulate the future tradition, the foundation of which is the judgment by law and the definitive hierarchical disposition of male and female statuses.

In the *Eumenides* the power of the mother is first drastically undercut and even denied by Apollo who, as representative of male interests, logically champions the cause of patriarchal marriage. But the denial is then mitigated by a limited restoration of that power through Athena's intervention and the transformation of the Erinyes into Eumenides (Gracious Ones). Apollo must come first, however, to be superseded in the course of events, but not fully suppressed.

Apollonian Strategies

In the short view, Apollo's argument can be regarded as a sophisticated legal maneuver designed to get his client off on a technicality or, in a more ameliorative reading, to break the impasse caused by the disparity between the Erinyes' absolutist and rigid formulation of the issue (guilty or not guilty) and the Apollonian defense of extenuating circumstances. In the wider view, the Apollonian argument is actually the hub of the drama: mother right vs. father right, old justice vs. new.

On the one hand, Apollo's method of argumentation is fully consonant with archaic modes of thought that can express change in status and attitude only through total repudiation or negation of a previous position. The god had already maintained the superiority of male over female on the sociological level by proclaiming that husband-king-male is more important than wife-queen-female and by pressing the cause of conjugality over blood kinship (*Eum.* 625–26). Now he moves back still further to the beginning to assert the primacy of the male through appeal to the primacy, even exclusivity, of the father. This he can achieve only by first de-

41. Turner 1967, *passim*. The brief quotations are from pages 102–3.

nying the mother's role in procreation on the biological level and then, resorting to the mythological level, denying the mother altogether. The mother is only necessary conditionally in the case of a uterine association. Where that bond is lacking, mother need not exist at all. The denial of *matriarchy* is accomplished by the denial of *mater*. The tables are decisively turned.

On the other hand, however, this archaic mode of argument is presented in the service of a new synthesis in a new environment. To break the binding force of the symbiotic link between mother and child (best expressed by the circular image of serpent symbolism that applies to them both), Apollo needs a new forum, namely, the law court, the city's mechanism that admits the use of logical argument and debate even as it establishes the right of nonkin to decide disputes among kin.

In this context of a founding act, a new creation, the content of the argument is concerned with beginning again, expressed biologically as embryology, mythically as theogony. The rebirth of Orestes into innocence and the birth of the law court and civic justice are confirmed by resort to the archetypal paradigm of beginnings. But the argument itself is of a new kind. In proposing that the father, the one who mounts the female, is the only true parent of the child, while the mother is merely the stranger host to the embryo, the passive vessel during its gestation, the argument draws upon the new scientific theories of the day. But even as the argument looks forward in its advancement of new intellectual trends, it looks backward in relying for proof of this contention on the mythic idea of Athena's birth from the head of Zeus.

The appeal to this myth is not just an exercise in logical absurdity that takes the anomaly for general paradigm. Its deployment is a sound strategy within the rules of mythic thinking—and not only as a species of archaic argument, as mentioned above. Athena's birth is of founding significance in the creation of the world. By the terms of Hesiod's theogonic myth of succession, Zeus's act puts an end to any threat to his sovereignty by incorporating the principle of intelligence through his swallowing of Metis and by making that principle manifest in the world through the birth of a child whose sex indicates that she will be no political threat to her father and even more, whose filial relationship proclaims her eternal dependence on the male. The mythic form his act of creation assumes completes the trend of the *Theogony* that began with Earth's natural parthenogenetic capacity and ends with the male's imitation of her. The seal is set on the finality of the transition from female dominance to male dominance by conscious male usurpation of her procreative functions, the basic source of her mystery and power. That usurpation is consummated in the reversal from female as begetter of male to male as begetter of female.[42] But in the course of this transition, male generative creativity is displaced from phallos to head—or rather, put somewhat differently, phallos and head are brought into alignment with one another.

This connection is precisely the basis that underlines the "scientific" argument. Already in some of the pre-Socratic philosophers as well as later in Plato and Aristotle, seminal fluid is associated with spinal and cerebral fluids. The hypothesis is that semen is transmitted from the brain and the spinal column through the genitals to the womb. There is more: the major component of semen is *pneuma,* a foamlike airy substance that contains the seed of the divine. Originating in the brain, semen is responsible for endowing the offspring with the distinctive human capacity for reason, for *logos.* Seed of generation, of intellectual ability, and of the divine element in the human species, semen confirms the innate superiority of male over female. For Aristotle, "the male provides the form and the principle of the movement; the female provides the body, in other words, the material. . . . the male provides that which fashions the material into shape. . . . Thus the physical part, the body *[sōma],* comes from the female and the soul *[psuchē]* from the male since the soul is the essence *[ousia]* of a particular body" (*De generatione animalium* 1.20.729a, 2.4.738b).[43]

Here in the *Oresteia, logos* and *mythos,* most often posed in two different and even antithetical modes, become allies and combine to support one another. This alliance is, in fact, a microcosmic reflection of the larger connection being constructed in this last play between male and female, new and old, secular and sacred, on which the trilogy relies for its conclusion. Through the myth of Athena's birth, theogony is now recapitulated in the new embryology, championed by the new generation of gods in the interests of a new kind of justice. If theogony supports embryology, its

42. See Reik (1960, 128–31) on the creation of Eve and his remarks on the analogous but different myth of the birth of Athena. The struggle of the male to control or usurp the female reproductive function is a repeated motif in Greek myth. Zeus himself gives birth to Dionysos, the "twice born," from his thigh. In the preceding episodes in the *Theogony,* Ouranos attempts to control creation or begrudges female productivity by refusing to allow his children to be born; more important, the blood and semen of his severed genitals prove to have generative power. In particular, Aphrodite, the principle of bisexual reproduction, is born from the essence (semen) of the male. Kronos swallows his children in imitation of pregnancy, but is forced to disgorge them, while Zeus goes one step further and swallows the mother and successfully gives birth to the daughter. As Vernant (1969, 106) remarks in general, "this dream of a purely paternal heredity never ceased to haunt the Greek imagination."

43. Trans. A. L. Peck. See Kuhns 1962, 45–49; Delcourt 1959, 85n.1; Vickers 1973, 414–15; Peretti 1956, 241, on the theory of patrilineal generation in Aeschylus. Kuhns cites Onians (1954, 108–9) on the likely connection of *engkephalos* and semen in the *Iliad* as evidence of an earlier Greek belief in the primacy of the male role in procreation, but such a belief does not deny the female's role, nor does it promulgate a scientific doctrine.

own prestige is reaffirmed through the authority of the other. Through this union of *mythos* and *logos,* a new mythos is engendered, one that mounts a final assault on the power of the female and brings a novel ending to the myth of matriarchy. Bamberger points out that "from [her] cursory study . . . women frequently are subjected to harsh outside controls because of their putative immorality. . . . And so it seems from myth that less tangible forces than biology [her unique ability and her important contribution to group survival normally celebrated in female puberty ritual but overlooked in myth] were brought to bear on the subversion of the female sex role. . . . The case against her was made out to be a moral one, divorced from the biology that might have given her sex priority under other circumstances."[44] Here in the *Oresteia* the attack is a double one—against *both* the adulterous wife *and* the reproductive function of the female.

As James Hillman astutely remarks, since "embryology is a *logos* of beginnings, it will be influenced by creation mythemes," and "because theories of generation reflect the differences and union of opposites, these theories will be influenced by *coniunctio* fantasies. Perhaps still more fundamental are the fantasies which afflict the male in regard to the female when the male is observer and the female the datum." He continues: "We encounter a long and incredible history of theoretical misadventures and observational errors in male science regarding the physiology of reproduction. These fantastic theories and fantastic observations are not misapprehensions, the usual and necessary mistakes on the road of scientific progress: they are recurrent deprecations of the feminine phrased in the unimpeachable, objective language of the science of the period. The mythic factor recurs disguised in the sophisticated new evidence of the age."[45] Apollo is the first to initiate this trend: "The Apollonic fantasy of reproduction and female inferiority recurs faithfully in the Western scientific tradition."[46]

---

44. Bamberger 1974, 279. Embryological speculation is not, of course, limited to the Western tradition. For some examples see, e.g., Barnes 1973, 65; Leach 1966, 13–14; and Vickers 1973, 637–39. Nor are beliefs pertaining to procreation necessarily linked to kinship systems (e.g., matriliny, patriliny). The denial of maternity, however, is unusual, as it is for other Greek embryological speculations that follow a less drastic course. See Lesky 1951 for the range of such theories; also Lloyd 1983, 86–111.

45. Hillman 1972, 224–25. In the same discussion, he states that "the Apollonic view of the feminine appears to be inherent in the same structure of consciousness as the methods by which the fantasies are supposedly proven." For instance, van Leeuwenhoek, inventor of the microscope, insisted he saw homunculi in the spermatozoa he viewed, and Leonardo, the founder of modern embryology, drew, on the basis of data from anatomical dissections, two urethral passages, one of the seminal fluid and a second one for the *pneuma* or *aura seminalis* (222). See also Barnes 1973, 61–87.

46. Hillman 1972, 225.

Here at its inception *mythos* still plays a determining role, and the *logos* of scientific argument is still rudimentary: copulation is equated with gestation in a misleading analogy. But for *mythos* and for *logos* the true model is social relations, and woman's new reduced biological function is a sophisticated translation of her social function, ratified by both god and science. It is the patent absurdity of Apollo's argument that offends our own fully developed scientific sensibilities (leading critics to sometimes desperate measures to minimize or even deny its significance),[47] not the principle itself of biology (false or true) as a justification of ideology. The issue of whether anatomy is destiny is still very much alive.

The terms of Apollo's argument bring together phallos and head in yet another way, for the ending of the trilogy is also concerned with a shift in modes and behavior, as it charts a progression from darkness to light, from obscurity to clarity. Representation of symbolic signs perceived as a form of female activity gives way to the triumph of the male *logos*. Repetition and lyric incantation yield to dialectic and speech, and magic to science.[48] Even more, "this turning away from the mother to the father," as Freud observed, "signifies a victory of intellectuality over the senses . . . since maternity is proved by the evidence of the senses while paternity is a hypothesis based on inferences and premises."[49] A whole series of antitheses takes form around the polarization of male and female roles; it can be tabulated as follows (although not all of them are treated in this essay):

47. Hence the tendency to discount the argument as "rhetorical," "meaningless," "frigid," "absurd," "tongue-in-cheek," "unproven speculation," and "parody." See Kuhns 1962, 45–46; and Vickers 1973, 414, 435n.47.

48. Faraone (1985, 150) argues that the Furies' binding song is "closely related to a specific kind of curse tablet used to affect the outcome of law cases in Athens as early as the 5th century B.C." and hence is "important to the dramatic context of a tragedy which depicts the mythical foundation of Athens' first homicide court."

49. Freud 1958 [1939], 145. Freud's view of the female as a mutilated male lies squarely within the Aristotelian doctrine of the woman as a "deformity in nature." Moreover, his debt to Bachofen seems evident in the following passage from *Civilization and Its Discontents* (1961 [1930], 50): "Women soon come into opposition to civilization and display their retarding and restraining influence—those very women who, in the beginning laid the foundations of civilization by the claims of their love. Women represent the interests of the family and of sexual life. The work of civilization has become increasingly the business of men, it confronts them with ever more difficult tasks and compels them to carry out instinctual sublimations of which women are little capable. Since a man does not have unlimited quantities of psychical energy at his disposal, he has to accomplish his tasks by making an expedient distribution of his libido. What he employs for cultural aims he to a great extent withdraws from women and sexual life. His constant association with men, and his dependence on his relations with them, even estrange him from his duties as a husband and father. Thus the woman finds herself forced into the background by the claims of civilization and she adopts a hostile attitude towards it."

Male	Female
Apollo	Erinyes
Olympian	Chthonic
Unbind (will, salvation)	Bind ("Fate," binding song)
Marriage (nonkin)	Kinship
Father	Mother
Law (court)	Ritual (altar)
Intention	Act
Odd (three, trilogy)	Even (two, tie, *lex talionis*)
Center	Limit (frontier, interior)
Greek	Barbarian
City	House
CULTURE	NATURE
Future (young)	Past (old)
Order	Chaos
Rule	Unruly (misrule)
Above	Below
Head-Phallos	Belly-Womb
Active	Passive
Creativity	Fertility
Reason	Unreason (sexuality, passion)
Light	Dark
Life	Death
Clarity (plain speaking)	Obscurity (riddle, metaphor)
Intellect (paternity, inference)	Senses (maternity, representation)
Positive	Negative

Goddesses, Not Wives or Mothers

If the birth of Athena is necessary for Apollo's synthesis and Orestes' re-incorporation into community, her pedigree and status are necessary for reaching any workable solution to the problem of the female who resists the encroachment on her prerogatives. Androgynous compromise, Athena is the benevolent answer to her opposite and doublet, Clytemnestra. Female born of male, she can ally herself with male interests and still display positive nurturant behavior. As female divinity, child of Zeus, she can initiate authoritative religious and social change. As female herself, she can also serve as model of the female—but not alone. For Athena and the Erinyes whom she has placated are not separate entities but complements of one another, both virgins, both now charged with the fostering of group welfare, and together representing the reconciliation of the positive and negative aspects of the female archetype on the transpersonal level. Both agree that female will be subordinate to male within the family in patriarchal marriage and that the family itself will be subordinate to the city. Both in turn shower the city with blessings of prosperity and fertility. Each is content with daughter status, for the father-daughter relationship is the purest paradigm of female dependence, while the oxymoron of virginal maternity promises fertility without its dangerous corollary of sexuality. Mother is denied but not denied.

Orestes had denied his own mother by the act of matricide and sought a new birth at the male-centered *omphalos* of Delphi. That new birth was just a beginning that sent him further to another altar, this time at Athena's shrine, upon which he sat, embraced her image, and held on tight. In providing him first with her protection as the necessary preliminary to the court proceedings, she also exonerated him and therefore supplied the ultimate salvation he had sought. The positive maternal figure, in fact, restored him to his father and his patrimony and freed him to claim his social and political identity based on the terms of a new embryology and a traditional theogony. Like Athena, Orestes now belongs wholly to his father.

In the double movement of this last play of the trilogy, Aeschylus modifies and diminishes the role of Delphic Apollo as the sole arbiter of the Orestean dilemma in favor of a larger, more expansive transaction[50] that includes the allotment of prerogatives to the Erinyes—their old sinister ones of vengeance that are now defined and limited for the city's interest, and their new constructive ones of benison and fosterage. The Hesiodic model of theogony is still operative, since Athena is both spokesperson of Zeus and the living embodiment of the *character* of his sovereignty and how he came to secure it for all time. When she allots specific roles and functions to the Erinyes, she therefore directly continues her father's work, which was not to create the world *ab initio* but rather to organize and classify its many components (Hesiod, *Theogony* 885) and to make accommodations between different generations. If the *Oresteia* can be viewed, as I suggested at the start, as a gynecocentric document, an inquiry into the nature and limits of feminine power, this last act completes the transference of the *political* power (along the lines of the myth of matriarchy), which Clytemnestra had brazenly claimed in the first play, to the *ritual* power of the female, exemplified by the role now assigned to the Erinyes in Athens.

50. It is generally agreed that the connection of Orestes with the founding of the Areopagus is Aeschylus's own invention. Delcourt (1959, 27–30, 103–13) also insists that he originates the link between Delphi and Orestes, although others posit another and earlier "Delphic" version against which Aeschylus is reacting.

From the anthropological perspective, the solution is perfectly consistent with the observable principle of patrilineality in which the male "transmits membership in the corporate descent group," while the female transmits "mystic potentialities, powers, or attributes" through the uterine tie.[51] From this same outlook, the complementarity of positive and negative femininity is readily understandable. As Grace Harris observes, "the double association of women as mothers with life and nurturance on the one hand and with death and destructiveness on the other is certainly widespread and may well nigh be universal. . . . The mother-child nexus and other ties through women always and everywhere appear both bad and good precisely because they are at the opposite end of the scale from the authority of society."[52] For Harris, this double association is confined to the two poles of Erinyes-Eumenides, but I would include Athena, the other and chief custodian of Athens, as the main representative of the positive side, the one who persuades the Erinyes to modify their malevolence and accept the city's terms for permanent residence there. But Harris's perspective enables us to understand why it falls to Athena to pacify the Erinyes, for if she represents a fully positive femininity, it is precisely because she has no uterine tie of her own and does not herself create one. Free from any but symbolic maternal associations, she thus forswears any matriarchal projects. In this sense, the *Oresteia* also judges and justifies Athena.

Oddly enough, the androgynous woman in power does not disappear but is reasserted and reaffirmed in her divine counterpart. The displacement of the issue upward in this last play avoids the specifically human dilemma of the female in her dual role of mother (power) and wife (deference). It also effectively removes the psychological dimension from the

51. Harris 1973, 157. Ortner's remarks are even more precise (1974, 85–86): "The psychic mode associated with women seems to stand both at the bottom and the top of the scale of human modes of relating. The tendency in that mode is to get involved more directly with people and individuals and not as representatives of one social category or another; this mode can be seen as either 'ignoring' (and thus subverting) or 'transcending' (and thus achieving a higher synthesis of) those social categories, depending upon the cultural view for any given purpose. Thus we can account easily for both the subversive feminine symbols (witches, evil eye, menstrual pollution, castrating mothers) and the feminine symbols of transcendence (mother goddesses, merciful dispensers of salvation, female symbols of justice, and the strong presence of feminine symbolism in the realms of art, religion, ritual, and law). Feminine symbolism, far more often than masculine symbolism, manifests this propensity toward polarized ambiguity—sometimes utterly exalted, sometimes utterly debased, rarely within the normal range of human possibilities."

52. Harris 1973, 157, 158. A special value is attached to the Greek word for sibling, *adelphos* (of the same womb). According to Athenian law, marriage is permitted between brother and sister, if they are not of the same mother.

human dilemma of a son who has killed his own mother by redefining it as a social and cosmic problem and quite literally putting it in the lap of the gods. Only they can free him (as far as it is intellectually possible) from the irrefutable and often anguished fact of human existence that man is from woman born.

Closer to Home: Athena on Trial

But beyond these general, even abstract, principles, this closure to the myth of matriarchy has another, more local aspect that aligns it more directly with the city of Athens—home of Athena, its patron goddess—and reinforces the ideological validity of the part the polis takes in the resolution of Orestes' case.[53] For however Athens may glory in Athena's prestige, a certain paradox resides in the fact that this city of patrilineal kinship is named for and belongs to a female divinity. More than one mythic tradition attempts to account for this disturbing anomaly.[54] One myth in particular is especially relevant to the construction of events in this last play of the trilogy. I will go so far as to suggest that it constitutes a kind of silent obbligato that underlies what we take to be Aeschylus's "inventive" solutions regarding Athena's successful mediation in the dilemma of Orestes and the affairs of Argos.

In the history of the city, Athena did not at first gain clear title to her preeminence in Athens without a prior struggle with another divinity for the right to claim it as her own and call it by her name. The myth relates that Athena and Poseidon were disputing the ownership of the city in the time of Cecrops, the primordial king and ancestor of the Athenians. The matter was ultimately resolved by soliciting the votes of the city's citizens, including its women, who at that time had the right to vote. The men voted for Poseidon, the women for Athena. The judgment would have been a tie if the number of women had not exceeded the number of men by exactly one, and if the women had not voted unanimously for the goddess. Athena therefore won the victory, but the women, it seems, did not. Quite the contrary: as a result (of Poseidon's wrath), the king Cecrops not only took away forever women's right to vote (that is, their political status) but also made certain drastic changes in the social organization of the city in which until then children did not know their father but were called after their mother's name. Henceforth, the system of patrilineal kinship was put into effect, and sexual promiscuity was replaced by the insti-

53. The discussion that follows concerning the Athenian version of a "myth of matriarchy" is an addition to the original essay.
54. Loraux 1981a, "Autochtonie," 60–61; 1981a, "Nom," 119–52.

tution of marriage in which husbands held the right to rule over their wives.[55]

Bachofen himself invoked this myth in support of his theory of matriarchy, as indeed he did with the *Eumenides,* but he only juxtaposed the two on the basis of "mother right" without noting the more extensive resemblances between them.[56] The myth of Cecrops and the *Oresteia* both relate how women once enjoyed parity with men in the civic domain, but in exercising power, they lost it along with their superior position in the household.[57] Both share the setting of a juridical dispute between competing male and female claims, as well as the logic that insists on the vital connections between political and domestic hegemony. Both clearly identify the basic source of women's power as maternal dominance. Hence, the solution is to attenuate (or deny) that power, while at the same time reserving honor for a virginal goddess (Athena). She is finally the key figure in both contests, whether as adjudicated or adjudicator.

In Aeschylus the jury that is to decide the case of Orestes is made up of Athenian citizens (male) who, as in the quarrel between Athena and Poseidon, are summoned to arbitrate a dispute between opposing divinities (Apollo and the Erinyes). But as in the earlier story, there is a risk that the matter might not reach a definitive outcome, as indeed would have been the case in the Athens of Cecrops, had there not been an extra vote to tip the balance in favor of Athena. Our play anticipates the dilemma of

55. Varro cited in St. Augustine, *De civitate dei* 18.9: "The women must lose the vote, no child shall take the mother's name, and they themselves cannot be called Athenian women." On Cecrops as the inventor of marriage, one of the sources (Scholiast *ad* Aristophanes, *Ploutos* 773) claims: "Some say he found men and women having intercourse quite casually, so that no son could tell who was his father, no father who was his son. Cecrops accordingly drew up the law making them cohabit openly and in pairs." Other sources: Clearchos quoted by Athenaeus, 13.555d (=*FGrH* 2, p. 319, F 49); Justin 2.6; Charax of Pergamum (*FGrH* 103 F 38); John of Antioch in *FGrH* 4, p. 547, F 13.5; Nonnus, *Dionysiaca* 41.383. For discussion (and other relevant sources), see Pembroke 1967, 26–27, 29–32; and Vidal-Naquet 1986a, "Slavery," 216–17. The evidence is late, but the themes and typology are familiar. As Pembroke (27) remarks on assessing the provenance of the tale: "What is certain is that variations and combinations of these stories were circulating over a period of centuries. It makes no difference whether the process was predominantly oral, or literary, and [there is] no reason why the story in Varro, or an earlier version of it, should not be taken as [the] model rather than the copy."

56. Bachòfen 1967 [1954], 158.

57. Clytemnestra's bid for political power would be the correlative of this "right to vote," since in the first play the chorus honors her as regent in her husband's absence (*Ag.* 258–60) and in the second Orestes includes her when he proclaims his victory over the "tyrants" (*Choe.* 973). The "domestication" of the Erinyes in Athenian cult functions to reduce their juridical power over men's affairs, and they are defeated, of course, in their defense of a mother's rights.

such a judicial impasse. It establishes in advance a means of resolving a tie vote and, in the face of its actuality in the jurors' evenly distributed votes, promptly puts it into operation. Athena, we note, is the one who takes the lead on both accounts and for her own interests. It is she who makes the rule in reserving the right to cast a vote, if the other votes are equal, and she who exercises it, when the situation arises, in favor of Orestes, claiming as her justification that "but for marriage [that is, for herself], I am always for the male with all my heart, and strongly on my father's side" (*Eum.* 737–38).

From the juridical perspective, the provision for breaking a tie vote might seem a necessary precaution to ensure the proper functioning of a jury in a law court.[58] But viewed through the lens of the myth of Cecrops, both the provision itself and Athena's reasons for putting it into practice take on a different cast. Underlying the explanation for Athena's victory over Poseidon is the assumption that males and females pursue their own separate interests, each group bound to maintain solidarity by siding automatically with their own kind.[59] Only on this basis, in fact, can the myth of Cecrops resolve the paradox of how a female divinity came to hold power in a city of men. But in the *Oresteia,* it seems, Athena returns the favor. She repudiates any allegiance to a feminine cause (since she has no mother) and explicitly declares her partisanship of men and masculine institutions. While the goddess had initially profited from the women's loyalty to gain possession of the city, she now both upholds (and extends) the law of Cecrops that had decreed the primacy of the paternal bond and uses her tie-breaking vote to side with the men. Athena thereby ratifies again, as it were, the reorganization of the city's structure that followed her original victory for control over Athens, a victory that put an end to women's signficance in procreation and politics and brought that particu-

58. The status of Athena's vote is a source of continuing debate, along with the question about the number of jurors. Were the votes of the jury equal and her vote the tie-breaker, as I outlined above? Or did her vote create the tie, and she then decreed the rule that a tie equals acquittal? For the most recent discussion of both sides of this debate, see Sommerstein 1989, 221–22. Whatever the solution (and neither, in my opinion, is definitive), it does not affect my argument, since the parallels between the two stories are not exact. My point is simply that the emphasis on setting the rules in case of a tied vote denotes, and perhaps hints at, the same preoccupation we find in the earlier myth.

59. The Danaids, for example, in Aeschylus's *Suppliants,* praise the citizens of Argos for voting to grant their supplication and give them sanctuary: "For they pitied us and cast a vote of kindness *(euphrōn);* they respected *(aidountai)* Zeus' suppliants . . . nor did they cast their vote on the side of the males *(met'arsenōn),* dishonoring women's dispute *(atimōsantes erin gunaikōn)*" (640–45). In Aristophanes's *Thesmophoriazousae,* Euripides' kinsman, who has infiltrated the women's rites in female disguise, is unmasked by the fact that he behaves as a traitor to his "sex," since he speaks ill of women and betrays their secrets (520–26). See this volume, chapter 9, 380.

lar version of a myth of matriarchy to an end.[60] Aeschylus's version of the
same dilemma is framed for different ends (the foundation of the law court
and the cult of the Eumenides). At the same time, because it recalls, and
partially reverses, the terms of this earlier myth of origins, it gains additional authority by placing a distinctive Athenian stamp on the strategy of
mythmaking that appealed for its prestige, as we have seen, to more general cosmogonic and theogonic motifs.[61] If the outcome of the *Oresteia*
also judges and justifies Athena, as I earlier suggested, it also justifies the
male citizens' endorsement of her hegemony over their affairs from the
time of Cecrops up to the present day.

In the end, this new Aeschylean myth, like all myths, as Claude Lévi-
Strauss says, "perhaps explains nothing and does no more than displace
the difficulty, but by displacing it, it appears at least to mitigate any logical
scandal."[62] But Lévi-Strauss is interested in defining the objective functions of myth and mythmaking in a society, not in confronting the poten-

60. St. Augustine's remarks (*De Civitate dei* 18.9 [trans. E. M. Sanford and W. M.
Green]) about the justice of the ultimate outcome are illuminating: "And when Athens was
struck by the conquered male, it was compelled to avenge the victory of the victorious female, being more in awe of the waters of Neptune [Poseidon] than of the weapons of Minerva
[Athena]. Nor did she defend the women who had voted for her; when they lost the right of
suffrage for the future, and their sons were cut off from their mothers' names, she might at
least have seen to it that they had the privilege of being called Athenians and of bearing the
name of the goddess, since they had given her the victory over the male god by their votes.
What comments, and how lengthy, might be offered on this subject, if only my discourse
were not hurrying on to other themes."

61. Another comedy of Aristophanes, the *Ecclesiazousae*, also replays a "myth of matriarchy" along the lines of the same Athenian myth (a point critics seem to have entirely
overlooked). In this play, women determine to take over the rule of the city, which has been
badly mismanaged by men, claiming their superior virtue as custodians of archaic values
(214–32). They disguise themselves as men, go to the assembly, and exercising their vote
win the right to put their plans of "reform" into effect. Henceforth, the city will abolish all
families, and private property will be held in common. In reply to the men's query of "how
will each of us be able to recognize his own children?" they reply that "children will regard
all older men as their fathers" (635–37). The women add a further clause to the law: no
young man can have sex with a woman of his own age, until he has first serviced the older
ones (689–709, 1014–20). What this plan implies, I suggest, is a return to the days of Cecrops, when children did not know the names of their fathers and sexual promiscuity was the
order of the day. Note, too, how well Aristophanes's plot conforms to the predictable plot of
the "myth of matriarchy." Women get power to rule (here claimed as a radical innovation,
455–57), but they abuse it by their unruly sexual appetite, which undermines the value of
their utopian schemes and raises the specter of regression to pre-Olympian times. As the play
expresses it in representing the figure of a young man in the grip of a lusty old woman, "If
you put this law into effect, you'll fill the land with Oedipuses" (1038–42). The key issue, as
always, is maternity. I have treated these issues elsewhere ("Myth and Utopia in Aristophanes' *Ecclesiazousae*," forthcoming).

62. Lévi-Strauss 1969, 13.

tially distorting properties of myth for legitimating social and political ideology whose mythic basis is neither recognized nor acknowledged. Psychic impulses compel the creation of the myth, but once objectified and projected outward, the myth reinforces, legitimates, and even influences the formation of those impulses by the authoritative power of that projection, especially when it is embedded in a magisterial work of art. There is a continuing reciprocity between external and internal, between individual psyche and collective ideology, which gives myth its dynamic life far beyond the static intellectual dimension. By uncovering the apparent "logic" that informs the myth, we can acknowledge the indispensable role of myth and mythmaking for human cognition and at the same time lay bare the operations by which it organizes and manipulates reality.

PART TWO

Gender and the Body:
The Woman's Story

·FOUR·

The Politics of Eros in the Danaid Trilogy of Aeschylus

Conflict between the sexes is the governing theme of two Aeschylean trilogies, both set in the city of Argos and both focused on the disturbing problem of women who kill their husbands. Clytemnestra in the *Oresteia* slays Agamemnon to avenge the daughter he had sacrificed at his departure for Troy; the virginal maidens of the Danaid trilogy, forced to marry against their wishes, slay their unwanted mates on their wedding night. In retaliating upon their male partners, the women, whether mothers or virgins, rebel against the institution of marriage itself, which in this androcentric society legitimates sexuality and procreation within the family and dictates that husbands rule over wives for the orderly conduct of domestic and civic affairs. As a social transaction of regulated exchange and reciprocity in the giving and taking of wives, marriage also necessarily involves questions of nonkin relations between one *oikos* (household) and another. In the process it therefore also provides a cardinal point of negotiation between *oikos* and polis, between private and public interests. Finally, like all Greek institutions, it comes to include relations between divine and human realms. Thus the essential role of marriage in maintaining the body politic must be further supported by a powerful ideological construct that considers wedlock a major prerequisite of civilized life, one that, along with sacrifice and agriculture, defines the boundaries between nature and culture and establishes a mediate position for men between

Earlier versions of this study were completed in 1976 and 1981, and an abbreviated French version, based on a lecture given at the Collège de France in 1981, appeared as "La politique d'Eros: Féminin et masculin dans les *Suppliantes* d'Eschyle," in *Mètis* 3 (1989). I have since treated aspects of the Danaid trilogy elsewhere, in connection with myths about rape (Zeitlin 1986) and with the representation of the masculine in Aeschylus (Zeitlin 1989a). I thank Charles Segal for his encouragement many years ago. My profound gratitude to Marylin B. Arthur (Katz), the late Jack Winkler, Anne Carson, and James Zetzel for their astute comments and criticisms of previous drafts. I have revised the essay extensively yet again for this volume, and I rededicate it to Jean-Pierre Vernant, from whom I have learned so much.

beasts and gods.[1] It is no wonder then that when wives murder husbands, their actions shake the entire social system to its foundations, finally provoking the gods' intervention to settle the seismic effects of women's resistance to men's claims to power over them.

Because the *Oresteia* has survived in complete form and because it enjoys an unquestioned prestige in the study of fifth-century Athens, it has monopolized debate about the issues of masculine and feminine in the theater of Aeschylus. But the Danaid trilogy, even in the one remaining play (the *Suppliants*), along with some tantalizing fragments and testimonia, extends and seems to challenge the terms of that debate as it confronts the most primary questions about relations between the sexes and the roles assigned to each in the social imagination. When a band of virgins sets foot on the shores of Argos to escape from their violent suitors, their predicament takes us back to the beginning—to the inaugural moments of courtship and the disquieting potential for sexual violence that lies behind the taking of wives. In so doing it confronts more starkly the normative position both of women in marriage and of marriage in society as the designated means to "domesticate" the nubile young girl, bringing her from a condition of wildness to accept the "civilizing" yoke of matrimony.[2] The Danaids' twofold status as nubile maidens and suppliants at the city's altars also more starkly represents the problems of eros as inextricable from a political context in which family business immediately becomes an affair of state, and the state in turn is confronted with competing claims between sacred and secular interests. At the same time, the dilemmas posed by the women also serve to explore the wider network of social relations in which matrimony itself occupies a premier position but has ramifications that also serve, as we shall see, as paradigm and even metaphor for other forms of alliance and modes of exchange.[3]

The issues of courtship and marriage are already framed in a larger perspective from the moment the first play opens, when the Danaids, with their father, arrive from Egypt on the shores of a Greek city and plead their cause before the Argive king as suppliants seeking sanctuary from their detested barbarian cousins. They appeal to the rights of suppliants as well as to their genealogical ties with Argos through their distant ancestress, Io, who in the form of a heifer mated with Zeus on the banks of the Nile and founded their lineage through her offspring Epaphos.[4] The

---

1. See, in particular, Detienne 1977; and Vernant 1980, "Beasts and Gods" and "Prometheus."

2. On the virgin as heifer (*damalis*, cf. 351) or filly (*polos*), see Calame 1977, especially 411–20.

3. See, e.g., Seaford 1987, 107–11.

4. Textual references to the *Suppliants* are cited from the edition of Friis Johansen and Whittle 1980, hereafter FJW.

Danaids are thus curious hybrids. By reason of their unusual lineage *(genos)*, they are related to two different cultures (Egypt and Argos), and since Zeus, god of suppliants, is also their forefather, they are associated too with divinity. Yet, like all suppliants, the Danaids represent a potential source of conflict for the city, since supplication is a dramatic means for staging a clash between sacred and practical claims, between the opposing demands of religion and politics: either refuse the suppliants and risk violating their sacred status, or receive them and risk the city's welfare in armed conflict with their pursuers. But beyond the standard triangle of suppliant, rescuer, and pursuer, the Danaids' situation takes a still more radical turn, for the primary motive at work is a fundamental and seemingly intractable conflict between the sexes.

The Danaids, after all, are female. The history of these exotic virgins makes them a unique anomaly and yet also a typical, if extreme, example of feminine behavior and attitudes. They object to *this* marriage, both because they detest their brutal suitors and because they consider union with cousins a form of incest. Yet their language of protest is sufficiently ambiguous to suggest a more general maidenly aversion to the idea of marriage itself as a form of violence and subjugation that, starting with defloration, delivers them against their will to the power of men (e.g., 392–93).[5] In their flight from Egypt to Argos, the suppliants' intermediate position also corresponds to the position of virgins, who are situated on the margins of society, betwixt and between, both "other" to the culture and a part of it, above and below it at the intersection of the worlds where beast (Io) and god (Zeus) may meet. As insiders and outsiders, the Danaids are both Greek and barbarian. They belong in the city yet remain foreign to it. The king Pelasgos calls them *astoxenoi*, "citizen-strangers/ guests" (356), referring to their ambiguous status. But the term can also serve more broadly as an excellent metaphor for the ambiguities of women's social status in the community.[6]

Moreover, the Danaids' multiple involvement in questions of *genos* (to Argos, Egypt, and Zeus) reflects a distinctively female association with kinship ties that, in tragedy, often contrasts and even conflicts with the broader theater of operations belonging to the polis. In their attachment to the myth of Io, these women seem also to be identified with the past rather than with the historical present, with the world of gods and the sacred rather than with the secular political concerns of men,[7] and with

5. On the much debated subject of the possible reasons for the Danaids' refusal, see, e.g., Lévy 1985; and Sicherl 1986. On their characteristics as brides, see Seaford 1987.

6. On the term, see FJW *ad loc.* See also Petre 1980.

7. Antigone, in Sophocles' play, conforms in many respects to the same pattern: upholding of sacred over secular claims, refusal of marriage in a loyal attachment to *genos* and the past.

the value of *mythos,* often ascribed to the feminine, rather than with the discursive uses of *logos* or reason claimed by men. But if the Danaids represent a range of issues that will require mediation by men, the reverse is also true. As females in transition, they are equally mediating figures, who can communicate between opposing worlds and different spheres of interests.

Vernant has remarked on the interlinking relations in the play and justly characterizes the Danaid trilogy as an "interrogation of the true nature of *kratos* [power]. What is authority, that of man over woman, of husband over wife, of chief of State over his citizens, of the city over stranger and metic, of gods over mortals? Does *kratos* reside in law, i.e., mutual accord, sweet persuasion, *peithō?* Or does it reside in domination, pure force, brutal violence, *bia?* The play of words . . . allows the enigmatic expression of the problematic character of the bases of power as it is exercised over someone else." [8] But if the language of power and authority (e.g., *kratos, archē, anax*) establishes distinctions among various domains, all these strands intersect in the figures of the Danaids themselves, whose arrival in Argos dominates the dramatic action. For this reason, we must also privilege the problems of relations between the sexes in eros and marriage, and above all, the dilemmas posed to society by the Danaids' refusal of their violent suitors. These are the elements that constitute the core of the action, providing the points of both departure and return. Because the manifest question revolves around the rules for exchanging women, the idea of marriage itself also works as a powerful means of exchange on which Aeschylus focuses the dynamic energies of his drama. Its effects expand to include the wider, more comprehensive world he constructs as an intricate network of interdependent relationships, conflictual forces, shifting alliances, and finally, organized hierarchies of value and power.

What, then, does it mean when the Danaids, suppliants and virgins, daughters and future wives, kin and strangers, ask for entry into the polis? It is the purpose of this essay to examine the highly patterned, even schematic nature of a theatrical world in which dramatic figures are also highly codified types, endowed with certain clusters of attributes and interests, and who at times function almost as abstract ideas. The cast of major characters is small: a female group, the Danaids, who play a double role as both chorus and protagonists; a father, Danaos; an Argive king, Pelasgos; an unnamed Egyptian herald; and screened behind them all, the figures of Zeus and Io. [9] Through the various encounters between male and

---

8. Vernant 1981a, 15.
9. Female handmaidens and male bodyguards may also be present at times. Offstage, there are two other masculine groups: a body of Argive citizens convoked in an assembly,

female, male and male, mortal and immortal, we can explore a further set of relations: between Greek and barbarian, polis (city) and *genos* (family), secular (politics) and sacred (ritual), public (politics) and private (erotics). What can we infer from the Danaids' preoccupation with myth (in the story of Io), theology (in their attachment to Zeus), family structures (in their attachment to their father), and the relationships of all these to the physical body (in matters of sexuality and reproduction)? What finally brings eros out of the bedroom and onto the shores of Argos? Or, more accurately, what are the necessary preludes to bringing eros into the bedroom, marriage, and society?[10]

Femininity: Virgins and Suppliants

Despite the particular legal and social intricacies of the Danaids' position, their gestures and language reflect the constellation of images and ideas surrounding the virginal bride in a scenario of flight and pursuit. Like her, they view marriage as rape and enslavement (839, 918, 924), a predatory assault upon a tender animal, a brutal invasion of an untouched meadow, and an occasion for fear and resistance.[11] At its worst, marriage is imagined as an enforced union with death (Hades); conversely, the bride may long for death as her only escape from the socially ordained "fulfillment" of femininity (154–60, 465, 788–91, 804–7). Love *or* death, love *and*

---

and later, it is presumed, the Egyptian host following upon the herald, although the edition of FJW *ad* 851–52 assumes an actual chorus of Egyptians.

10. Interpretation of the trilogy must, of course, remain conjecture: only the first play is extant, and its text contains many serious corruptions. Otherwise, we are left with fragments and other relevant testimonia concerning the myth. I concur with many of Winnington-Ingram's sensible suggestions (1960), later updated (1983). See also Garvie 1969, 163–233, the most complete repertory; also Podlecki 1975; and FJW, 40–55.

Mainly, I accept the following: Danaos assumed the kingship but became a *tyrannos* (for the evidence, see the sources in FJW, 48). The Danaids' action somehow posed a threat to the state, complicated by the *miasma* of kin murder and violation of *xenia* obligations. In the sequel, altars played an important part, and the polluted Danaids may well have had to return to them as suppliants of a different sort. In addition, there was probably some legal procedure, and the union of Hypermestra and Lynkeus inaugurated a new dynasty for Argos. I agree with the hypothesis that the drama ended with the establishment of the festival of the Thesmophoria, as I shall argue below. I am not certain about Seaford's suggestion (1987, 112–17) that the last play staged the remarriage of the Danaids and provided the aetiology of the *hymenaios* or wedding song. Rösler's radical thesis (1992), based on Sicherl's argument (1986), is that our play was the second drama in the trilogy. See below, note 13.

11. See, e.g., Porzig 1926, 150–51; Hiltbrunner 1950, 36–37; Bogner 1947, 125–27; and Seaford 1987. Their suitors are hawks (223–24, cf. 510), ravens (751), wolves (351), serpents (511, 889), dogs (758), spiders (887). The Danaids are doves (223–24, cf. 62) or heifers (351).

death. These pairings are two sides of the same notion that marriage is a violent rupture with a former state of life and mind. But another set of related ideas—love *or* war, love *and* war—reaches still deeper into a psychology of eros that senses the potential conflict, even paradox, in a union of contraries (male and female) and yet strives, if it can, to maintain the boundary between sexual violence and the pleasures of love. Thus, if men are supposed to be made for war and women for marriage, the two institutions determining the requisite passage to adulthood, then feminine resistance may, as with the Danaids, turn to a war between the sexes. Militant virginity can indeed resort to masculine weapons and in a striking reversal, work retaliatory violence upon men.[12]

The special situation of the Danaids may, as some have thought, undermine their value as a typical, if drastic, representation of virginal attitudes. But it is the apparently exceptional features of their story—the brutality of the Egyptian suitors, the claims of incestuous kinship, and the resort to supplication at an altar—that heighten the symbolic implications of maidenly aversion ordinarily represented in myth and rite. The field of reference thus expands to encompass the full range of the tensions and ambiguities appropriate to the tragic idiom. In particular, the plot's emphasis on the kinship between Egyptians and Danaids, which is essential to a substantive concern with *genos,* contributes two other significant elements to the cluster of associations and implications surrounding the maiden's condition.

In the first instance, the taboo the Danaids insist upon in marriage with their cousins as those of the "same blood" introduces the idea of sexual encroachment upon the feminine body as a form of pollution, or *miasma* (225–29), a concept that cannot otherwise legitimately be invoked.[13] It sets up a powerful contrast to the "purity" *(hagneia)* of the virginal state.

---

12. See Vernant's now canonical formulation (1980, "Warfare," 23–24): "Marriage is for the girl what war is for the boy: for each of them these mark the fulfillment of their respective natures as they emerge from a state in which each still shared in the nature of the other. Thus a girl who refuses marriage, thereby also renouncing her 'femininity' finds herself to some extent forced towards warfare and paradoxically becomes the equivalent of a warrior. This is the situation in myth of females like the Amazons and, in a religious context, of goddesses such as Athena: their status as warrior is linked to their condition as a *parthenos* who has sworn everlasting virginity. It could even be said that this deviation both from the normal state of women, who are destined for marriage, not warfare, and from the normal state of warriors who are men, not women, gives a special intensity to warrior values when these are embodied in a girl. They cease, in a way, to be merely relative or confined to a single sex and become 'total.' In this situation, the virgin turned warrior not only fights alongside men but against men, as indeed the Amazons do."

13. Since marriage was the accepted norm, it is true, as Vernant observes (in Detienne 1977, xxxiii), that generally, "purity consists not in the rejection of marriage but in the re-

Second, although the Danaids' numerous references to kinship as "blood" relations underline the fact of consanguinity, they also link up with the image of kindred blood that will later be spilled when the women avenge themselves for the violation of their virginity. But of immediate concern in this first play is the war that must take place between Egyptians and Argives in which kindred blood *(homaimon haima)* will be shed on both sides, all "for the sake of women" (473–77; cf. 449, 662, 1044). When the suppliant Danaids give their grateful blessings to Argos for respecting them as blood kin *(homaimous, 652)*, they pray that Ares not "harvest mortals in fields plowed by others" (636–37), that the land never be bloodied with the fall of its native sons (662), that the "blossom of its youth not be plucked," and that Ares not "shear off its tenderest bloom" (664–66). Their language reinforces the links between war and sex: Ares is described as *machlos* ("lewd" or "wanton," 636), and his role of destroyer *(brotoloigos)* is paired with the epithet "bedfellow of Aphrodite" *(eunatōr, 664–65)*. The "blossom of youth," which applies to both contexts (cf. 78, 73)[14] as does the broader agricultural notion of reaping and plowing, assimilates the death of warriors and the defloration of virgins into the same negative sphere.[15] Human blood will drench the earth in destructive conflict, and the timid Danaids, who now claim they have "no Ares in them" (749), will later take up deadly arms. But, as the king tells the Danaids, the Argive earth had in an earlier time brought forth a destructive brood of man-killing monsters in response to its "defilement by the pollution of ancient bloodshed" (260–67). The allusion to the past is surely an ominous model for the future. But for the moment, its significance lies in the fact that it combines the key terms—blood, pollution, earth—and situates them in a context of antifertility and malignant reproduction.

In this first play, questions of pollution and purity are mobilized

---

jection in the name of marriage, of illegitimate sexual relationships." These include male prostitution, adultery, and incest, the last of which constitutes the substance of the Danaids' aversion to their suitors. This factor accounts, in part, for their use of the vocabulary of purity and pollution in sexual conduct (225–28, which here also includes the idea of coercion, and cf. the vexed *enagea telea* of 122). More generally, see Parker 1983, 74–103. Sicherl (1986) claims that the mentions of pollution refer to the undisclosed reason for the Danaids' flight, which is an oracle given to Danaos that he would be killed by one of his sons-in-law, and hence if the daughters married, they would be guilty of pollution in ensuring a father's death.

14. For the reading *hēban* at line 78, see Friis Johansen 1966; on the connection of flower imagery, Io, and the Danaids, see Whittle 1964a. On notions of *hēbē* and warrior death, see Loraux 1975. On flowers, virginity, and defloration, see Caldwell 1974, 59 and n. 64; cf. Gantz 1978.

15. See FJW *ad* 663–66.

around the sacred space of the altar and the suppliant condition of the Danaids. Almost from their first lines, the Danaids explain that they are not fleeing for sanctuary from a charge of bloodshed (*eph' haimati,* 6; cf. *anaimaktous phugas,* 196) and are thus not guilty of pollution. Yet it is the Danaids' despairing threat to hang themselves from the sacred images at the city's altars, if their supplication should fail, that finally motivates the king to accept their suit and plead their cause before his assembly (473, 619). Even without the defiling intrusion of death in the sacred precinct, to refuse supplication, in general, entails the dangers of pollution and dishonor to the gods, a special affront to Zeus Hikesios, who oversees suppliant rights.[16] It is a central irony of the drama that to protect their purity (*hagnos,* 225–28) from an unholy alliance, the Danaids incur the pollution of kindred bloodshed (cf. 449, 662) and thereby also threaten the welfare of the entire city,[17] which accepted them in the first place in order to avoid the baneful effects of *miasma* (375, 473, 619; cf. 649–51, 995).[18]

The concept of chastity is part of a semantic complex that includes virginity, ritual purity, modesty, moderation, wisdom, respect, honor, and reverence toward gods and men: *aidoios, hagnos, sebas, eusebeia, semnos, timē,* and *sōphrosunē* (with their cognates).[19] Danaos combines several of these terms when he instructs his daughters to "honor chastity [*sōphrosunē*] more than life." But whose "life" does he mean? Is he exhorting them to choose death rather than endure the violation of their chastity? Or conversely, do his words hint at those lives the Danaids will take in reprisal for that same violation?[20] Matters are not yet clear, but in Danaos's emphasis on the supreme value of physical virtue, a further warning note is sounded because, paradoxically, such an exclusive devotion to *sōphrosunē* (chastity) hints at a dangerous lack of *sōphrosunē*

16. On pollution and failed supplication in connection with sacrilege in shrines, see Parker 1983, 144–51.

17. The irony is precise, since *hagnos* refers not only to those who are chaste but also to those who have *not* shed blood or who have been purified from it (Sophocles, *Antigone* 889, *Trachiniae* 258; Euripides, *Electra* 975, *Hippolytos* 316–17, *Orestes* 1604; Plato, *Laws* 759c).

18. On *miasma,* the violation of the laws of Zeus Xenios, and the possible importance of altars in the sequel, see Winnington-Ingram 1960b, 145–46, 150; cf. Murray 1958, 80–81.

19. In general, see von Erffa 1937; North 1966, especially 36–38; Fehrle 1910, 42–51; Hiltbrunner 1950, 37; Rudhardt 1958, 38–43; and Parker 1983, 147–50.

20. In the thesis of Sicherl (1986), followed by Rösler (1992), "life" here refers to Danaos's life, pursuant to an oracle that predicted that Danaos would be slain by one of his sons-in-law, but this reading, if true, does not preclude the others. See note 10 above.

(moderation),[21] which in the end will compromise his daughters' purity as both suppliants and virgins.

But beyond questions of tragic irony and the predictable reversals in tragic plots, there are some powerful reasons for linking the virgin with the sacred, by which she retains mysterious but ambivalent associations with the immortal and higher aspects of life. The virgin body, untouched and untouchable (790), is whole unto itself, a sign of the self's integrity that resists any enroachment upon its boundaries, any admixture or compromise to contaminate its pure state of being. Permanent virginity is an attribute of goddesses, in whose domain it assumes an absolute value, undisturbed by the vagaries of time and change.[22] Cultic chastity, prescribed under certain circumstances, is a way of entering into this domain in the service of the gods. Whether a state of actual virginity or sexual abstinence after marriage, chastity bears a "heightened charge of power," precisely because it temporarily exempts female worshippers from the mortal exigencies of death and generation.[23] But this exemption from mortality in the sacred sphere is matched by its exact opposite, and herein lies the ontological problem of the virgin condition. For in suspending the maiden outside of time and process, virginity removes her from life on earth and places her between two equally unviable alternatives: the world above or the world below.

When the Danaids long to escape to Zeus on high, to sit beside him, or to join the ether as smoke, the neighbor of Zeus's clouds (208, 779–82, 792–93; cf. 381, 595–97), they seem to express a tragic desire for

21. The double meaning is already present in Danaos's injunction, which implies both prudent behavior and chastity, and is consonant with his continual references to proper comportment and strategic planning (e.g., 198, 710, 724, 992). *Sōphrosunē*, in its multiple meanings, is the semantic focus of conflict in Euripides' *Hippolytos* for its virginal hero (730–31, 1034–35). See below, chapter 6, 222, 252–53.

22. This is especially true for the three virginal goddesses, Artemis, Athena, and Hestia, who have no part in the "works of Aphrodite" (*Homeric Hymn to Aphrodite* 7–33). It is true to some extent of Kore, and certain cult practices attested for Hera and perhaps for Demeter "renewed" their virginity each year.

23. See Fehrle (1910) for the uses of various kinds of sexual abstention in cult for both sacerdotal officiants and laity. Rudhardt's definition of *hagnos* (1958, 41) clarifies the links between virginity and the sacred: "*Hagnos* means a solemn quality. It is perceivable in divinity to the extent that it remains above humans, that it is not confused with the happening, and is correlative rather, we might say, with transcendence; a quality that human beings possess or can experience temporarily to the extent that they avoid generation or death: to the extent, as a result, that they are abstracted from real life; a quality preserved in sanctuaries and sacred places through attentive protection against pollutions; in short, an extratemporal purity possessed by *hiereis* [sacred officiants] and *hiera* [sacred offerings], persons and objects called upon to bear a heightened charge of power." See also Parker 1983, 90–94. See further chapter 6, 232–35, below.

self-effacement, for death. Yet these fugitive desires also signify a wish to find an enduring place in the world of the gods, which, if fulfilled, would violate the boundaries between mortal and immortal domains.[24] More broadly, the Danaids long for a life without labor or pain, a wish that bears the same ambivalence—either an exclusive prerogative of the gods (ascribed to Zeus in this play, invoked as *pan aponon daimonion,* 100; cf. 576) or the lot of mortals only after death (802–3).

But in the social world the Danaids must come to inhabit, the virgin's association with the sacred is founded on the ritual of supplication. From one point of view, the virgin and the suppliant are isomorphic categories. Both are inviolable and untouchable like the altar itself. Both are situated in the same semantic field of purity and reverence, and both are expected to refrain from immodest or impudent display (197–203, cf. 994ff.).[25] It is in this sacred place *(en hagnōi)* that the Danaids seek protection from their suitors, who are both "blood kin and enemies, pollutors of their race" *(ekhthrōn homaimōn kai miainontōn genos),* seeking a marriage that cannot be *hagnos* (222–28). Thus when the Egyptian herald attempts to tear the Danaids away from the altar by force, he doubly transgresses the rules of sanctity, giving graphic demonstration of the close links between the virgin and the sacred.[26]

Those who sit at the altars are, by religious conventions, sacred to the god. Virgin and suppliant in this case are still more closely linked, since the children of Io belong to Zeus both through the tie of kinship and

24. The seat beside Zeus's throne is the privileged place of his daughter, Dikē. Cf. Aeschylus, frag. 281a Radt; and Hesiod, *Works and Days* 259–60. Their threat of suicide by hanging (from the images of the gods, 465; cf. 160, 789) can also symbolize their longing for elevation and ascent. Note the opposite but equivalent desire to join the other Zeus in the underworld (757–61). This second death wish also continues the idea of vertical movement, for the Danaids long to find a steep and lonely crag from which they can plunge to their death (794–99, and note the context of 792–93). Sabbatucci (1965, 66 and n. 17) remarks that suicide through drowning or hanging connotes not just an end to life but also a passage into the realm of alterity (water and air as other than earth). The sexual connotations will be further discussed below.

25. *Aidoios:* 28, 192, 194, 345, 362, 455, 478, 491, 641; *hagnos:* 214, 223, 228, 254, 653, 696; for the analogies see further Hiltbrunner 1950, 37. In Homer, *aidoios* refers to both *parthenos* (*Il.* 2.514) and suppliant (*Od.* 7.165). *Dusagnos* for suitors: 751. *Aidōs* and *hagnos* in connection with *parthenoi:* see Aesch. frag. 242 Radt. *Sebas* and *parthenos:* see Aesch. frag. 99.12 Radt. The Danaids like to refer to gods as *hagnoi:* Artemis (145, 1030), Apollo (214), and Zeus (653).

26. Virgins and altars are well suited, since the altar is also the place for sacrifice to the god of suitably pure victims. If virgins are the victims of choice for human sacrifice (especially in tragedy), it is also because the bloody violence of the sacrificial knife is seen as analogous to defloration. On the correlation between sacrifice and defloration, see Loraux 1987, 31–48, 61; on the connection between sacrifice and marriage, Foley 1985, 68–102; and in general, Burkert 1983, 58–71.

through the rules that make every suppliant a ritual possession of the gods, *hieros* like the altar itself, and *hagnos*.[27] Moreover, both suppliant and virgin stand outside the social system, on its threshold. When the Danaids emerge from their sheltering ship (134–35) at the edge of the sea (31), in the liminal space between sea and city, they cling to the altar as testimony of their identity in their kinship to Zeus. But as soon as they claim the ritual role of suppliants, they have entered the world of politics, for the god and his altar act only as intermediaries in the transaction between suppliant and polis. Supplication at the altar is a prelude to entry into the polis. In tragic drama it serves to procure the promise of protection from the authorities, who, in accepting the obligation to safeguard suppliants from their persecutors, have agreed in a sense to invest the public space of the city with the same inviolable sanctity as the altar.[28]

For the polis, the myth of Zeus and Io also proves compelling, when the Danaids voice their double appeal to piety and to kinship with Argos through their ancestral connection. These claims, however, challenge the political integrity and principles of the state, because sheltering suppliants requires the city to defend them against their inevitable pursuers.[29] Here the suppliants test the king, who is caught between his obligations to the Danaids and his practical concern for the welfare of the city (342, 377–80, 410–11, 449, 474–77). Safety for these virgins means the danger of war for the Argives. To complicate the decision further, the Danaids' case is not as straightforward as it might seem.

In the first instance, their appeal to kinship stems from a remote pedigree. It is discontinuous with the present dynasty in Argos, which derives its origins from an autochthonous ancestor, Palaechthon (250–51, 348). Second, Pelasgos is asked to defend virgins whose motives for flight run counter to the social expectation of matrimony as their destiny (cf. 1050–51). Lastly, the Danaids' rejection of cousin marriage may not even contravene Egyptian law (390–91). But regardless of the details, suppliants, as a general category, have the god on their side. The transaction at the altar is a power game (207) conducted between the powerless (the suppliants) and the powerful (the city) through an appeal to the most powerful of all (the god). In this sense, the suppliants perform a mediating function between gods and men, between sacred and political concerns. They appeal to one to test the other.

Suppliants also mediate between different sorts of men, since every rescue in tragedy entails a pursuit and a confrontation between two po-

27. Schlesinger 1933, 33.
28. On the mechanics of supplication, see Schlesinger 1933; Kopperschmidt 1967, 11–34; and Gould 1973.
29. On the tragic pattern, see Kopperschmidt 1967, 46–48.

litical powers. Here, the confrontation is found in its purest form, staged not only between males but also, more precisely, between Greek and barbarian.[30] On the other hand, historically, the suppliant transaction is one of the earliest forms of foreign relations (the herald is another). It is a means of mediating between two cultures, a way to import or adopt alien others into one's own society. The Danaids personify this latter function, since by genealogy they are already half barbarian and half Greek, related to both Egyptians and Argives.[31] Yet they are also kin to Zeus, the third element of the suppliant triangle (Argos–Egypt–Zeus), so that the figures of the Danaids are literally related to all sides. They thus condense and synthesize the oppositions that the act of supplication aims to mediate. In other words, the Danaids at all levels embody in their persons what is represented by the generic act of supplication.

On the other hand, as I have suggested, by virtue of these same ambiguities, the Danaids also represent a schematic paradigm of the feminine. Consequently, if these suppliants build bridges between men as between men and gods, social rules will require that a way be found to resolve the typical "feminine" contradictions women are thought to embody. In other words, the mediator too requires mediation. The preliminary means of mediating the contradictions of the suppliant virginal female is precisely the dialectic of supplication, which itself looks in two directions, as both an archaic ritual and a contemporary political institution. Thus the whole system is interlocked in a powerful economy of symbols.

The opening dialogue with the polis, in which the Danaids finally persuade the king to adhere to immutable values of altar and kinship, marks the first stage of their education about the rules of this "civilized" society into which they will be incorporated, while the procedure adopted by Pelasgos reflects in turn how the archaic ritual can be translated into the newer idiom of the city. Yet, less abstractly, the question remains: how will the city "socialize" its virgin suppliants and persuade them to marry? What means will bring them within the city and give them a permanent home?

Because of their particular history, the Danaids know only two male models. Both are autocratic in nature, but they are sharply contrasted in role and function: on the one side, the barbarian suitors, who view marriage as conquest, acquisition, and enslavement, and on the other, authori-

---

30. The conflict between Greek and barbarian over a woman echoes the archetypal *aition* (cause) for armed conflict (see 477). Helen is the paradigm and is so treated in the *Oresteia*. See also Herodotus, 1.1–5, who begins his history of the Persian Wars with a catalogue of such mythic rivalries, starting with Europa. On Helen and the Danaids, see Finley 1955, 200.

31. In a certain illogical split, the Egyptians remain foreign, but their female cousins, nurtured in that same environment, are also considered Greek.

tarian paternal figures in the person of Danaos and, more remotely, of Zeus. The middle term of the masculine is already present in the person of the Greek king and his citizens who are summoned to a democratic debate in the assembly. This image of the Greek male as a citizen of a polis is made to justify in advance, by his political, social, and moral behavior, the marriage of male and female as an institution that does not sanction patterns of excessive domination or submission. In short, the Greek male will prove to occupy the position of the proper mean between beast and god.

If marriage is designed to tame and "civilize" the female partner, it is also envisioned as an institution of a "civilized" society. To socialize the female, then, requires a male counterpart, who is socialized too in his approach to her. The later events of the trilogy will fulfill this prerequisite on the erotic level (in the relationship of Hypermestra and Lynkeus), an outcome already adumbrated in the positive view of marriage proposed at the end of this drama (1034–42). But the first play anticipates this possibility, when the Danaids encounter the political world of Argos in the figures of its representative king and his citizens.

The king Pelasgos is the pivotal figure, who confronts female in the Danaids and male in the forms of Zeus, Danaos, his citizen body, and the Egyptian herald. At first, the Danaids situate the king at the positive pole of the masculine archetype in order to complete a predictable triad of father/king/god: [32]

> You are the city, you are the people. A leader subject to no
>   judge,
> you rule the altar, the heart of the land,
> by your will that casts the single vote,
> and on your throne of a single scepter,
> you determine all matters.
> Beware of pollution.
>
>   (370–75; cf. 425)

But Pelasgos rejects the autocratic rule they attribute to him. He insists on the collective power of the *dēmos* (365–69) whose decrees, reached through public debate, will have binding authority (600–625, 942–49).[33] Although male, the king will defend feminine rights: he will persuade his assembly to grant sanctuary to the Danaids. He will be true to his promise, when the Egyptian herald tries to drag the women forcibly from the altars before their suitors arrive, and at the end of the play, he will bring them courteously into the city according to the prescribed rules

---

32. E.g., the Danaids' lyric address to Pelasgos in 348–49, *kluthi mou/prophroni kardiai*, "hear me with a propitious heart," uses terms addressed normally to a god. See FJW *ad loc.*

33. On contemporary echoes of democratic decrees, see Petre 1986.

of hospitality. Having proved himself *hagnos* with respect to obligations toward suppliants (cf. 364), Pelasgos, as well as his citizens, is rightly called reverent (*eusebēs*, 340; cf. 419), respectful (*aidoios*, 362; cf. 491, 641), well minded (*euphrōn*, 378, 640; cf. 19, 971, 1034), and gracious (*eumenēs*, 488, 518; cf. 1067). The *telos* (rite, completion) of marriage is preceded by and perhaps modeled after the political *telos* of the assembly's decision (603, cf. 601), a *telos* that, like the imperative to marry, is ratified by Zeus (624, cf. 1048–52). Correct conduct in one sphere (politics) will reflect correct conduct in the other (erotics).

This first stage of incorporating the suppliant into society, which brings her inside the polis, seems to function like an initial phase of that other ceremony, which will incorporate the virgin into marriage and bring her inside her husband's house. The incorporation of the suppliant into the city is therefore analogous to the incorporation of the virgin into married life. Our play makes the first (supplication) a necessary preliminary to the second (marriage), but the metaphorical connections between the two make one rite of passage the emblem of the other. Just as husbands take on the role of guardians, the *kurioi* of their wives, the king and his citizens assure the Danaids that none are *kuriōteroi* (of higher authority) than they to guarantee them protection (965). We are reminded here of the Pythagorean injunction that instructed husbands to be faithful to their wives and to beware of mistreating them by neglect or base conduct and advised that "they should also consider that a man has brought his wife into his home after having taken her, to the accompaniment of libations, *from the hearth, like a suppliant,* in the presence of the gods."[34] At the end of the first play, the king offers the Danaids a choice of residence in the city: in his private quarters or in designated public dwellings (954–65). This magnanimous gesture leads directly to a last choral song, in which the Danaids renew their implacable resistance to marriage. But for the first time, other antiphonal voices are now heard, voices that speak for the other, the seductive side of eros. The stage is set for the future.

Courtship and Supplication: The Politics of Persuasion

King and Suitors

Eros and politics are inseparable. Courtship is the transaction in each case and may be conducted in two ways: through *peithō* (persuasion) or *bia*

---

34. Iamblichus, *Life of Pythagoras* 9.48, cf. 18.84. Cf. Ps.-Aristotle, 1.4.1, 1344a10–13. For discussion of this and other testimony relevant to Pythagoras's ideas about matrimony, see de Vogel 1966, 110–11. On the woman as *metoikos* at her husband's hearth, see Vernant 1969, 103–5; and Gould 1973, 97–98.

(force).[35] The women reject the violent courtship of their suitors *(bia)*, but as suppliants, they themselves must become suitors for acceptance into Argos and resort to the protocols and rhetoric of persuasion.[36] This they do in their appeals to the king, although perhaps paradoxically, it takes a final threat of violence—self-inflicted at the altars (465)—to bring him to their side. At the same time, as suppliants, they must become suitors of Zeus *(pithou,* 527), to whose previous "courtship" of Io they refer again and again. But despite the parallels between virgin and suppliant, the two are also antithetically opposed: the virgin is courted by suitors, while the suppliant must, like the Danaids, court the goodwill of their host and press their suit for formal acceptance into the city.[37]

The act of supplication introduces the Danaids into a wider network of social relations. Their father is their first mentor. He instructs them each time in the rules for the three spheres of ritual, politics, and finally, social life (176–209, 710–75, 980). But their task is to find their own means of persuasion. Pelasgos, in turn, must become a suitor himself and persuade the assembly *(eupeithēs . . . dēmos)* to vote in favor of suppliant rights, trusting in the persuasive *thelxis* (charm) of his political oratory *(dēmō-gorou . . . strophēs,* 623–24).[38] In this way he validates the principle of courtship *(peithō)* as the mode of communication on which his democratic society is based, and in this way, too, he provides a pattern for an erotic persuasion that will succeed, at least in the case of one Danaid, Hypermestra. Pelasgos already adumbrates his support for this principle of

35. Buxton (1982, 67) notes the importance of "the place of *peithō* and *bia* in personal (particularly sexual) and political relationships," but not their interrelation, concluding only that "both in sexual relations between individuals and in the handling of a city's political affairs, persuasion is preferable to violence." For the sharp increase in the importance of *peithō* in Athens, connected with political rhetoric (sophists) and with erotic themes, see Shapiro 1993, 186–207, on the iconography of the period.

36. Danaos coaches them in the proper form of address for their status as newcomers and strangers. They should speak reverently, without arrogance or impudence, and above all, they should be flexible and remember to yield where they must *(memnēso eikein)* (194–203, cf. 207, 231–32).

37. As Kenneth Burke suggests (1969, 174–80, 208–44), "sexual courtship is really an analogue of social courtship, and is closely allied with questions of both hierarchy and the rhetoric of persuasion. By the 'principle of courtship' in rhetoric we mean the use of suasive devices for the transcending of social estrangement. There is the 'mystery' of courtship when 'different kinds of beings' communicate with each other" (208). Gorgias's *Helen* is an excellent example of the relations between rhetoric and erotics, as Plato demonstrates in his critique of this position in, e.g., *Phaedrus* and *Gorgias.* See also the general principles for successful persuasion throughout Aristotle's *Rhetoric.*

38. In the prelude to seduction the lover sends a *thelktērion* (bewitching) arrow from his eye (1104, cf. 447). *Thelxis* and *peithō* apply frequently to the spheres of eros, politics, and religion *(thelxis:* 386, 447, 571–72, 1004, 1040, 1055; *peithō:* 523, 527, 615, 623, 941, 1040). On the other hand, Zeus is implacable, and his anger cannot be charmed away *(dusparathelktos,* 386), as the Danaids argue to persuade their host.

courtship in confronting the Egyptian herald, when the Argive king affirms the validity of the people's vote and says the herald may lead the Danaids away only if the women are willing, only if the herald first gains their goodwill *(eunoia)*—as the Danaids in their turn have had to win the *eunoia* of the assembly (489)—and only if his "reverent word can persuade them" (*eiper eusebēs pithoi logos,* 940–41).

It is striking that *peithō* was a powerful sign of political principles in Athens. *Peithō* was already worshipped as a goddess of persuasion in the city to whom public officials (the Prytaneis) sacrificed, and her priest was assigned a special seat in the theater of Dionysos itself.[39] Yet the drama's correlation of the two types of *peithō* (erotic and political) may well have reflected and poetically expanded upon this formal connection. For, as Pausanias tells us (1.22.3), there was a temple near the Agora consecrated to Aphrodite Pandemos and Peitho, alleged to have been founded by Theseus himself. *Pandēmos* is an ambiguous epithet. It may refer to a vulgar Aphrodite of prostitutes or, alternatively, and more likely in this context, to an Aphrodite "of all the people," whose proximity to the Agora spells her relevance to a public place of assembly.[40]

If this twofold use of Peitho (cf. *pandēmiai,* 607) held a special resonance for Athenian spectators, Argive tradition supports these same associations even more directly in a context relating to the Danaids themselves. Pausanias reports a temple of Artemis in Argos, "surnamed Peitho, which was also dedicated by Hypermestra [a Danaid], after her acquittal at the trial to which she had been brought by her father on account of Lynkeus" (2.21.1)—that is, after her dissenting action in refusing to murder her husband.[41] The last play of the trilogy may well have staged such a trial, a possibility supported by the numerous references to legal language and procedure in this first play. It is a tempting hypothesis, at any rate, for in this way the conclusion would encompass the entire range of the uses of *peithō,* which extend from erotic courtship to supplication and prayer, from the political milieu of the assembly to the juridical scene of the law court. At this point, however, the *peithō* of sexual desire remains a latent

---

39. Demosthenes, *Prooemion* 54, *IG* 3.351; see also Buxton 1982, 34.

40. See Buxton 1982, 33–34.

41. The scholiast on Euripides, *Orestes* 872, reports that according to Phrynichus's dramatic version of the Danaid myth, "Aigyptos came to Argos to avenge the murder of his sons, but Danaos found out about it and was calling the Argives to arms when Lynkeus *persuaded* them to settle their hostility by arguments, and he established jurymen for them, the best of the Egyptians and Argives." Lynkeus's art of persuasion would then apply to both juridical and erotic domains, and the former adversaries shared the responsibility for judgment. See Podlecki 1975, 7, although his theory that Aeschylus also used this version can only remain speculative.

motif, only affirmed at the end by the hemichorus (1039–42) but as yet
still denied by the Danaids themselves, who adamantly resist the charms
of persuasion (*thelgoi an athelkton,* 1055).[42]

For their part, the Egyptians, represented by their spokesman, the herald, are equally consistent in word and deed as emblems of a brutal masculinity: violence, desire for mastery and possession, lewdness, impiety,
and unheeding self-interest. If, through their herald, they seize suppliant
women whose petition for asylum has been honored, they are *dusagnoi*
(impure, 751), and as in their former assault upon the Danaids in Egypt,
they are *dustheoi* (impious, 421–42). Now they trespass upon both virginity and altars (750–52, 755–56, 850–53; cf. 921–22), dishonoring
these sanctities as they dishonor the land in its sovereign autonomy (911–
12). The Egyptians' violence at the altar reflects and parallels their desa-
cralized concept of marriage that ironically inverts that same Pythagorean
injunction; at the same time it indicates improper forms of courtship in
religious and political affairs. As strangers *(xenoi)* they refuse to court
the hosts of a foreign land in the correct procedures (917); they insist
sarcastically that Hermes, the god who seeks and recovers lost or stolen
property, is their legal representative in the city, their *proxenos* (920, cf.
220–21), and they do not hesitate to threaten armed combat *(bia)* as the
preferred method to arbitrate the dispute (935–37). The term *margos*
(lustful) is identical in love and war (741–58) for those who are always
insatiable of battle. In the Egyptians' vocabulary, lordship and rule apply
to both marriage and politics, as the herald indicates in his jeering reply to
the Danaids' piteous invocation of the *anax* of the land: "Lords *[anaktas]*
in great numbers you will soon see: the sons of Aegyptos! Don't worry, you
will have no reason to complain of a lack of rule *[anarchian]*" (906–8).

Refusal to court in the proper manner also implies an active desire for
conflict. Whether verbal, political, or sexual, warfare is always the medium. The arrival of the Danaids and their demands for protection necessarily involve the threat of war against those who receive them (Argos),
those who put *peithō* above *bia.* The crisis is instigated by those who treat
courtship as warfare—that is, as seizure and rape (Egypt). The paradoxical result is that men (Argives and Egyptians) must engage in violence
(war) for the sake of women, who reject suitors because of their violence.
Greek and barbarian may supply different cultural definitions of mascu-

---

42. Opinion is divided on the identity of this hemichorus at the end. The best candidates
are either the Danaids themselves, who split off into two groups (perhaps representing themselves in their dual role as protagonists, external to the city, and as choral voices of the
community), or the Argive bodyguards, who raise male voices to praise a positive eros
against continued female resistance. For recent discussions, see Lévy 1985; and Seaford
1987. The problem defies solution, but either alternative supports my point.

linity, but both insist on a contest of phallic pride. Egyptian taunts Greek with effeminacy for championing the cause of women and breaching male solidarity (950–51, cf. 643–45). The Greek proclaims his virility, his superior fighting ability (746–47, 913, 952–53). The fruit of the papyrus cannot master the ear of wheat (761), they claim, nor are drinkers of barley beer a match for those who drink wine (953).[43] Danaos's injunctions to his daughters at the end of the play concerning the modesty of their comportment (991–1013) intimate that these Greeks are just like all men. The force of desire is universal; the Greeks are no more exempt from lust than the barbarians, but they are expected to regulate erotic desire through courtship, using the weapons of charm and persuasion (1004), even as, in their role as citizens in the assembly, they themselves have been persuaded to endorse an ethically correct course of action.

In the alliance of the Danaids and Argives against the barbarian Egyptians, the lines of opposition are clear. Yet refusal of love and desire, rejection of courtship, engenders its opposite—martial resolve—and the Danaids declare war, as it were, on their suitors. Physically helpless in the first play ("a woman alone is nothing; there is no Ares in her," 749), in the second the maidens take up swords, the male weapons, except for Hypermestra who has evidently been persuaded by "the charm of desire" (cf. *Prometheus Bound* 865).

The Danaids thus resemble the Egyptians in that they think in terms of antitheses. On the positive side, their claims for the unwritten laws of supplication and kinship are not, at least in tragedy, finally open to contravention. On the negative side, the Danaids' conflict with their suitors, despite the special circumstances, easily escalates into a permanent antagonism between male and female. The race of women, the *genos gunaikōn*, is inalterably and starkly opposed to the race of males, the *genos arsenōn* (cf. 29, 393, 487, 818, 951), as both the Egyptians and Danaids would have it. The Danaids' tendency to think in binary opposition explains, in part, the strange shifts they seem to make from specific to general misandry, an oddity that has puzzled many critics.[44] Put somewhat differently, war is the only possible interaction between the two extremes, since

---

43. Male potency is reduced by the consumption of these foods. See scholiast, *ad* 761, who explains the proverb by remarking that the Egyptians are eaters of papyrus. See also Zenobius, 2.72, and the Suda, s.v. *bublos*, who claim that the maxim refers to virility. Wheat is "stronger" than papyrus, which does not produce a good crop.

On the Egyptian habit of drinking barley beer, see Herodotus, 2.77, and Diodorus, 1.34. On the enervating effects of this drink, see also Aeschylus, frag. 124 Radt = Athen. 10.477c, although the text is not wholly certain. The Hippocratic *Regime* (40.1 Littré) claims that wheat is more nourishing than barley. Artemidoros, *Oneirocritica* 1.51, states that to dream of a field of wheat signifies sons and to dream of barley signifies daughters.

44. See, e.g., Garvie 1969, 220–23; and Lévy 1985.

the Danaids "oversacralize" the female and insist on her untouchability, while the Egyptians "undersacralize" her as an object of rape and violent seizure.

Pelasgos accepts the validity of supplication and kinship. Yet although he yields to the coercive constraint of these principles, he adapts and modifies them to fit his political outlook. In the matter of supplication, he transfers to the *dēmos* the archaic sovereignty of the king in ritual affairs, for the altars belong not to him but to the polis. His primary reason for acknowledging the power of suppliants is the threat of *miasma* for the entire city, were their petition to be denied.[45] The claims of kinship are more complex, because the archaic priority of the clan is at odds with the new democratic emphasis on civic obligations between nonkin. Kinship itself has both literal and figurative uses. The Danaids base their appeal for acceptance on the immutable law of kinship, but the model of a fictive kinship is also the city's means for incorporating suppliants or any other outsiders into the group.[46] Pelasgos's solution accepts the Danaids' terms but translates them into the political idiom. He limits claims to a citizenship based only on genealogical ties but not on *sunoikia* (cohabitation) by resorting to the hybrid term of citizen-stranger (*astoxenos*, 356, 618; but cf. 401),[47] and he confers upon the Danaids the more normal status of *metoikoi* (resident aliens, 609), with their legally defined privileges and restrictions.[48] The numerous juridical references throughout the play suggest, over and above the specific legal problems of cousin-marriage in Egypt or Argos, the broader significance of a polity guided by law and institutional procedures.

Yet if Pelasgos modifies these categories of kinship and supplication, he upholds other principles that operate within a secular context. The king is not accustomed to women insisting on their *eleutheria* (freedom, 221, 609).[49] For him, as for all Greeks, women are legally defined in terms of their male guardians (*kuros*, 387–91). Nevertheless, it is morally con-

---

45. See further Diamantopoulos 1957, 225. Note also that the *miasma*, which the king fears in the Danaids' threat of suicide at the altar, is here translated into the double *miasma* the city would incur by dishonoring guests and citizens (474, cf. 366, 616–20). In both cases, the anger *(kotos)* of Zeus Hikesios is the compelling factor (478–79, 616).

46. See Gould 1973, 93. On kinship and the clan, see Diamantopoulos 1957, 225.

47. The term is later defined specifically as "a blood relation, though a foreigner by birth." See FJW *ad* 356.

48. See Gould 1973, 90: "All this, of course, is a fifth-century Athenian vision of the progress of supplication and its interest lies in the way in which it presents a sophisticated 'political' version of a primitive and ancient social institution." See also the bibliography cited at 90n.32, for the suggestion that "*hiketeia* was the source of the Athenian system of metic rights." For a study of metics and the development of this institution, see Gauthier 1972, especially part 2; and the more general study of Baslez 1984.

49. On *eleutheria*, see Finley 1955, 198–200. Cf. Snell 1928, 69.

sistent that democratic Argos, devoted to the concept of *eleutheria* (948), should support those who flee despotism and enslavement, even in the domestic sphere. The same idealism that views sovereignty in enlightened terms compels the protection of the weak, for the proper exercise of power is revealed in the treatment of the powerless:

> It may well be that someone will feel pity at the sight of you [the
>   suppliants]
> and become hostile against the insolence *[hubris]* of the
>   company of males,
> and that the people will be better disposed toward you.
> For every one acts favorably [with *eunoia*] towards the weaker.
>   (486–89)

For Pelasgos, this means the male must side with the female even when that partisanship constitutes a challenge to masculine interests, as the Danaids themselves say:

> For they pitied us
> and cast a vote of kindness *[euphrōn]*;
> they respected *[aidountai]* Zeus's suppliants
> . . . nor did they cast their vote
> on the side of the males *[met'arsenōn]*,
> dishonoring women's dispute *[atimōsantes erin gunaikōn]*.
>   (640–45)

Persuasion is ultimately the mediator between two opposing groups or points of view. It implies an effort made by one to identify with the other, whether involving political parties, different classes or nationalities—or relations between the sexes. Above all, persuasion admits the dynamic principle of compromise that accepts negotiation, arbitration, and dialogue between two sides. In other words, Greek democratic ideology insists on excluding absolutism from the political process, or indeed from any social relations, and recognizes the power of public opinion. This is why Pelasgos himself is open to persuasion, why his city respects the act of supplication, both as a proper ritual and as a legal-political procedure. Supplication acknowledges the possibility of incorporation through persuasion, even though admitting the Danaids into the city also implies the risk of admitting other values represented by the suppliants that may challenge civic definitions of the body politic.

The city rests on the dialogue between fixed values and the dynamic power of persuasion and mediation. The city is indeed a city of men *(andres)*, as Pelasgos declares, not of women (911–13), and the test of its manliness *(andreia)* will give a civic definition of masculinity: the political man who is master of the *logos* in debate. The possibility of changing one's mind (446–47, cf. 1055) implies also the possibility of transformation on a larger scale. The Danaids' inflexibility is based on their experience with their violent suitors. But their refusal also stems from their relationship with their autocratic father. Danaos guides and leads them, keeping them under his surveillance. Like the other figures in the play, he functions not only as a dramatic character but also as a masculine construct that extends to the broader spheres of politics and religion.

Father and King

As the two major masculine figures on stage, Danaos and Pelasgos present an interesting set of contrasts. They spell out different styles of leadership and authority with larger implications for the sequel, when, it is presumed, Danaos will replace Pelasgos as ruler in the city. For now, these differences revolve around ideas of rational political conduct and the uses of intelligence. Danaos is shrewd, practical, confident, and decisive; his prudence is born of experience (492–99). He has a kind of wisdom that Pelasgos disclaims when he says: "I am at a loss about this quarrel; I prefer to be ignorant [aidris] rather than wise in misfortune [sophos kakōn]" (453–54). Danaos's intelligence (phronēsis, 176; sophia, 516) is instrumental, oriented toward technē (skill) and mēchanē (devising). He gives instructions in imagery drawn from the technē of writing (991–92), while Pelasgos rejects the contractual procedure of written ratification in favor of the oral consensual authority of the dēmos (944–49, cf. 607–8).[50]

Above all, Danaos is an expert in navigation and seamanship (764–70), the trusty nauklēros of his ship (177).[51] But Pelasgos, who in metaphor is the captain of his ship of state (e.g., 470–71), finds himself out of his element. Like the territory of Argos, which marks its boundary at the sea (258–59), and like his autochthonous ancestor Palaechthon, who sprang from the earth (150–53), he is inexperienced in the ways of the unbounded and shifting deep. He feels at a loss (amēchanos, 379); he founders in an "unfathomable sea of disaster" with no easy passage and no "harbor against distress" (438–42).[52] For Danaos the expanse of the ocean presents a practical challenge for the clever pilot (769–70); for Pe-

50. On the significance of scriptural metaphors in the play in respect to writing and inscribing the woman's body, see duBois 1988, 140–46. In the tradition of the Danaid story, Danaos is the protégé of Athena, who counsels him and under whose auspices he builds the first ship.

51. On the tradition that Danaos was the archetypal naval architect, who built the ship Danais and/or the Argo, see Lindsay 1965, 80–81, and 410n.20 with relevant sources. On the possible etymological relationship between pansophon onoma (all wise name) and Danaos (daēnai, "to know," 320–21), see Würtheim 1928, 182; and FJW ad 320.

52. On the vocabulary of the sea and navigation, along with the metaphorical connotations of pontos (the deep) and poros (path, ways and means) and its opposite, aporia, see Detienne and Vernant 1978, 133–74 and 215–16.

lasgos the sea is a metaphor for the storms that may shipwreck his state and a symbol of profound moral perplexity. There is need of "deep thought to win salvation," and "the eye, steady and undimmed by wine, must dive into the depths in order to avert disaster for the polis"—and for himself as well (407–10).

Pelasgos and Danaos are defined, of course, by their respective circumstances in the play: one is the head of state, the other is leader of his daughters. Both may be judged, however, as figures of masculine authority to the Danaids. The thoughtful king, who tends to take counsel, "makes suggestions [to the Danaids]," as one critic remarks, "and solicits their understanding, whereas Danaos dictates."[53] As their chief (boularchos, 10; stasiarchos, 11; cf. 969), Danaos makes the major decisions; when it comes to choose their lodging place in the city, they defer without question to his judgment (967–71). There is no dialogue between father and daughters, only paternal instruction and filial acquiescence.

In the Danaids' benediction of Argos, they praise the ancestral worship of gods in the land and emphasize the honors reserved for both gods and city, concluding with the particular reverence owed to parents (tekontōn sebas, 704–9).[54] The Danaids, it has been suggested, identify father with god and even confuse the two,[55] and Danaos encourages this comparison. He "even seems to identify himself with Zeus. He speaks of his own gazing eye (713) with the . . . word used elsewhere for the deity's vigilant gaze (381, 647, 768)."[56] In a further confusion of categories, he goes so far as to bid the suppliants to both pray to their Argive saviors in gratitude and offer them sacrifice and libations as to the Olympian gods (980–82, cf. 967). His instructions may well reflect an Egyptian idea of the god-king, but they also reflect his unquestioned control over his daughters, whom he instructs at the end, on his own authority, "to honor chastity [to sōphronein] more than life" (1012–13).

In Danaos, the power of the father[57] is exposed as consonant with a

53. Lembke 1975, 16.
54. Von Erffa (1937, 88–89) comments on 707–9 that reverence for parents, earlier expressed in terms of aidōs, is now drawn into the field of dikē and sebas (and see further, 90–91). Note also that the Danaids, who attribute their success in supplication to archaic principles (672), also support the prestige of the older generation, as manifested in family, cult, and political power (666–68, cf. 673, 704–6). In their conservative attitudes, the Danaids perhaps also reflect some typical Egyptian patterns. Cf. Herodotus, 2.77–80: "The Egyptians . . . among all men, are those who are most concerned to preserve the memory of the past."
55. On the significance of patēr applied to Zeus and Danaos, see Caldwell 1974, 53–54; also FJW ad 810.
56. Lembke 1975, 14–15. Cf. Hiltbrunner 1950, 29, but the image of the eye is more complex, associated with guardianship, desire, and knowledge.
57. Pelasgos too shows a paternal concern for the Danaids, and like Danaos, soothes and pacifies their fears. Yet his masculine persona is, in some sense, defined (and refined) by

monarch's political rule[58] and even with the divine prestige of a god. The titles coined to describe his role as leader of his little group, however, may also convey other, sinister undertones: *boularchos* may mean "the one who desires to rule," and *stasiarchos,* "he who begins civil strife."[59] The bodyguard he obtains at the end (985–88) also has disturbing political aspects. If, as some have suggested, Danaos becomes a *tyrannos* in the next play, then father and king will become one. If, as father and king, he presses his daughters to kill their bridegrooms through guile, his talent for shrewd plotting *(mētis)* will cast his technical mastery in an unattractive light. Above all, he will have transgressed against the laws of Zeus Xenios and the political ideals of Argos.[60] If Hypermestra defies her father to save her husband, then some limits must have been imposed on paternal prerogatives in the final outcome of the trilogy. The social rules of marriage dictate that the father must give up his daughters and that they trade the parental household for that of their husbands. When Danaos, at the end, emphasizes the care his daughters must take to preserve their virginity, he does so ostensibly to warn them against a premature sexual consummation that would disgrace him (and them) in Argos and bring joy to his enemies (995–1009). He never speaks of a time when they might marry and leave the monopoly of his protection. In practice, when daughters remain eternally dependent at the father's hearth, they are blocked from assuming adult roles as wives and mothers in other men's households, thus cutting off the dynamics of exchange that regulate the association of households under the sanction of the state. Already in this first play, the trilogy indirectly addresses a contemporary problem in democratic Athens, which "for more than a century tried to work out a family law and to find forms of a political regulation of marriage and of relations between *oikos* and *polis.*"[61] In this case, the relationship of authority between father and daughter bears still further implications. The potential conflation of father and *tyrannos* suggests a negative paradigm for political rule, re-

---

his initial similarity to the women. Both are concerned with the question, *ti draō,* "what am I to do?" (94, 806–7; cf. 469–70, 126, 397). Unlike the confident Danaos (498), both are fearful (e.g., 734, cf. 346, 379–80). Both consider life unfathomable, and despite their different outlooks, they share the same imagery (407–9, 470 and 95, 1057–58; cf. 1048–49). Yet once Pelasgos makes his political decision, he no longer falters (cf. 440 and 945), while their anxiety persists.

58. Aristotle *(Politics* 1259b11–15) describes a father's authority over his children as kingly *(archē basilikē),* because of his *philia* and *presbeia* (superiority of age). See also Petre 1980, 177.

59. See Sommerstein 1977, 67. FJW contra.

60. On Danaos as probable *tyrannos,* see Winnington-Ingram 1960b, 142n.9; Sommerstein 1977, 74; and FJW *ad* 985–88.

61. Petre 1980, 181; see Broadbent 1968, 113–20; and Humphreys 1978, 201–2.

lying both on an exclusive control of power *(tyrannos)* and on an excessive emphasis on kinship (father).

Yet Danaos's domination of his daughters suggests, above all, what Zeus represents to them on the divine level. Politics and social life take second place to the god, and the myth that connects the Danaids to divinity is the focal point around which they organize reality.[62] This, in turn, raises two other, interrelated questions concerning, first, the general nature of Zeus's power and, second, the meaning of his ancestral role as lover of Io and author of their race.

Divinity, Power, and Hierarchy

Through the myth of Io, the Danaids approach Zeus as god, sovereign, father, and the lover who mates with mortals. With Zeus as their touchstone of value, they can insist on the widest hierarchical distance between partners in any given relationship. Hence, although the maidens' aversion to their suitors and their deference to figures of authority may seem contradictory, both reactions accord with the logic of extremes that characterizes their world view. On the other hand, in assigning all the roles to Zeus, they collapse distinctions between the varying relationships that exist in different domains. Thus the monopoly of power they attribute to Zeus produces an excessive asymmetry that confuses the limits between sacred and secular, immortal and mortal, thereby also reducing the possibilities for human action.

The Zeus of the Danaids is a blend of Greek, barbarian, and universal attributes, apprehended in the full range of his various powers and epithets. His is the all-embracing omnipotence of which the Danaids sing again and again (e.g., *pankrates,* 816), his the vast reservoir of all potentiality, a container and catalyst of all that occurs.[63] Associated with Zeus both as descendants and suppliants, the Danaids can assent to their feminine roles as human actors only if some way is found to refine the concept of Zeus and along with it the more general role of the gods in human affairs and even the impulse to mythopoetic thought. There is a kind of "theogonic" problem raised in this first play, suggesting that the resolution of the trilogy must somehow qualify Zeus's unlimited omnipotence in favor of a sovereign rule that defines levels of hierarchy and distributes

62. Zeus is named as the first word in the play and is mentioned a total of fifty-five times. See FJW *ad* 1. He is invoked as ancestor (162–63, 167–75, 295, 300, 302, 312, 313, 524–37, 595–96), as god of suppliants and strangers (1, 346, 385, 479, 616, 627, 641, 653, 670–71), and as omnipotent ruler (306, 403, 437, 524, 527, 646, 651, 816). See also Petre 1980, 176n.35.

63. On the omnipotence of Zeus, see Kiefner 1965, 94–99, 108–28, 133–34. In this play, Zeus encompasses the entire universe: sky, water, land, and underworld.

roles and powers, among gods and humans alike. In the Hesiodic model, this evolutionary process takes place as the universe comes into being and assumes the authority of a *hieros logos* in the epic voice. Aeschylean drama, on the other hand, as in the *Oresteia*, enacts such a process, but it entails the reciprocal participation of gods and mortals, who evolve together under the pressure of dramatic events in the present world of the polis, and finds its *telos* or completion only by the end of the trilogy.[64] Zeus may be all encompassing in his powers, but that "all" is affirmed through the polis's ratification of a new order, which redefines the powers and privileges of both gods and men, and which is represented, above all, in the founding of new institutions in the city. At this point, then, the Danaids may be said to "overvalue" Zeus, the supreme divine principle, on all levels. In so doing, they introduce a serious disequilibrium that sets the tragic action in motion.[65]

In the *Suppliants,* unlike other Aeschylean plays we know, the genealogy of Zeus is never mentioned. He has no patronymics and therefore no history of becoming, no temporal dimension. He is fixed forever in time (574), just as he sits unmoving on his throne of power (101–3, 595–96). It is rather Io who moves dynamically in space and time, like the suppliant Danaids themselves, who claim to follow in her footsteps (538, 1017). Io founds the Danaids' pedigree, but they view her existence as fixed at two single points between Egypt, her destination, and Argos, her place of origin to which they wish to return. In their great hymn to Zeus, the Danaids distinguish between the "unending lifetime" of Zeus (*di'aiōnos . . . apaustou,* 574) and the merely "long lifetime" of their ancestor Epaphos (*di'aiōnos makrou).* But Epaphos, Io's "blameless child," is called *panolbos* (all-fortunate, 581–82), a term that links him to the brilliant past that created him and defines their own hopes and aspirations with regard to divinity.

The altars of the gods stand both outside the city and within it (222, 501). Pelasgos already understands that Zeus, in one sense, stands outside the pragmatic concerns of the city.[66] *Telos* (end or fulfillment) is the pivotal term. As the true *telos* (i.e., marriage) of the Danaids' lives unfolds, the nature of Zeus Teleios will also become clear to those figures who claim to apprehend the meaning of *telos.*[67] This point is already antici-

64. On the influence of Hesiod's *Theogony* on the *Oresteia,* see Solmsen 1949, 21, 23, 64, 157–66; Clay 1969; and chapter 3, 101–3, 108–9, 113 above.

65. The same imbalance can result from the converse, "overvaluing the human." This attitude is more typical in tragedy, but is mostly reserved for men, especially kings and rulers, whose misplaced confidence in their cognitive powers leads to their downfall: Eteocles in Aeschylus's *Septem,* Oedipus in Sophocles' *Oedipus Tyrannus,* and Pentheus in Euripides' *Bacchae.*

66. For example, Pelasgos, in contrast to the Danaids, invokes no gods. See Bogner 1947, 109; and also Finley 1955, 201–2.

67. See especially Hiltbrunner 1950, 10, 26, 35; Fischer 1965, 120–21, 124.

pated in Zeus's ratification of the political *telos* of the assembly's vote in Argos to accept the suppliants (625), when the citizens raised their hands in assent, in contrast to both the violent hands of the Egyptian suitors and the miraculous touch of Zeus.[68]

Aphrodite's presence in the third play (frag. 44 Radt) suggests that the will of Zeus requires other divinities to intervene in the cosmic process (even as he delegates power to Apollo, Athena, and also the Erinyes in the *Oresteia*). The monolithic authority of Zeus, expressed by the Danaids in their orientalizing superlatives and accumulated epithets,[69] must therefore be modified to accommodate the complexities of a pantheon of gods in their shifting alliances and oppositions and in their various modes of intervention in human affairs. The suppliants restrict Aphrodite, who is also a child of Zeus, to her role as the bedpartner of Ares (664–66, cf. 636), although the second chorus corrects the insult by surrounding the goddess with other, more benign, companions:

> Yet our gracious group does not neglect Cypris;
> for she together with Hera, is next to Zeus in power,
> and the goddess of shifting wiles
> is honored in solemn rites.
> And Desire *[Pothos]*, and she to whom nothing
> is denied, seductive Persuasion *[Peithō]*,
> follow their mother as her companions;
> and to Harmony *[Harmonia]* has been given
> the whispering share of Aphrodite's work and the paths of
> lovemaking.
>
> (1036–42)

The Danaids persist until the end in calling upon a "virginal" Artemis (*hagna*, 1030), just as they had done earlier when invoking the protection

68. A small but telling point is the Danaids' consent to "submit" to the words, the *logos,* of Pelasgos (507), expressed somewhat oddly as *cheiria* (to come under the hands of). This term, as FJW indicates, directly echoes (and contrasts with) their earlier wish concerning their suitors that they "never be subordinate to (under the hands of) the power of males" (*hupocheirios/kratesi g'arsenōn,* 392–93). The use of *cheir,* "hand," is an important motif. It refers to the violent hands the Egyptians will lay upon the Danaids (756) and also to the gentle touch of Zeus, who with "his own hand" was the planter and architect of their race (592–93; cf. 313, 1063, and the pun in 568), and it is repeated in describing the action of the Argive assembly, whose citizens voted with their "right hands" (604, 607, 621) to signify their decision. The Danaids, as instructed by their father, use their left hands for holding the suppliant boughs (195) that earlier are oddly called *encheiridia* (21). The word is normally used for hand-held daggers, and the ambiguity obviously forecasts the murder of their bridegrooms, already adumbrated perhaps in the lyrical allusion to Procne's murder of her child with her own hand (*autophonēs . . . pros cheiros,* 73).

69. On the oriental liturgical style, see Schäfer 1974; on affinities with Egyptian hymns, see Kranz 1933, 101–8. Froidefond 1971, 96n.173, contra. See also FJW *ad* 524ff.

of this *hagna* goddess who, like them, is "untamed" (*admētos admēta*, 144–50). Yet, for a brief moment during their official blessings on Argos, the Danaids refer to Artemis Hekate, acknowledging her role as one who watches over women in childbirth. The hostility of Hera, named only as the wife of Zeus (164), may prove significant to a larger design in which Io had already figured as her priestess (291–92). Seated next to Zeus, as Hera already is in the words of the second chorus at the end of the play (1035), the goddess may yet play a role as patron deity of Argos and, in her cult title, Teleia, join up with Zeus Teleios to represent the wedded couple who are protectors of marriage.[70] In fact, the conflict between the archetypal married couple is itself the sign of a more general conjugal disorder, which is the dominant theme of the trilogy and source of the problems it must resolve.

The image of Zeus as autonomous sovereign may serve as the improper paradigm for relations between ruler and state, and in a manner of speaking, even for relations among gods in the cosmic hierarchy. Here it is not only the Danaids' legacy as Io's offspring that shapes the maidens' image of both king and divinity, but also their Egyptian heritage and the pattern of the god-king of Egyptian monarchy.[71] In the context of relations between male and female, however, Egypt is also a crucial locus for particular ideas about masculine powers of procreation, which are implied both through the miracle of Io's conceiving through Zeus's touch and breath and through the syncretism of Zeus and the Nile. Both features are contributing factors to the Danaids' attitudes about sexuality and its role in reproduction.

Body Politics

Reproduction

Although the *Prometheus Bound* mentions only touch, the *Suppliants* emphasizes both hand and breath as agents of conception (16), an idea that is not found in Greek myth at this period but rather comes from Egyptian tradition. Later sources insist on the equivalence of Zeus and *pneuma*, or the breath of life, which accounts for his role as the father of all things

70. Kraus (1933, 180) and Hiltbrunner (1950, 17) point to the importance of Hera's Argive connections (which the Danaids elide, since they invoke only Zeus as protector of Argos). Hera Teleia holds the keys to marriage (Aristophanes, *Thesmophoriazousae* 973), and in this play (as opposed to the *Prometheus Bound*), Io is named as the keeper of the keys to Hera's temple (291–92). On the Danaids, marriage, Hera, and Argos, see further Detienne 1989b.

71. On the Egyptian elements in the play, see Kranz 1933, 98–107. For the Egyptian god-king, his religio-political paternalism, and his associations with the sun and the Nile, see Wilson's convenient summary (1946, 39–102, especially 80–96).

(Diodorus, 1.12.2), but "breath" is the etymology of the name of an Egyptian divinity, Atum, "whose creative power lies in his inspiration of life" (Plutarch, *Numa* 44).[72]

In addition, while rivers are generally associated in Greek thought with male fertility, the waters of the Nile were especially so renowned. Strabo, quoting Aristotle, claimed the Nile's procreative energy *(gonimos)* far surpassed the power attributed to other rivers (15.1.22).[73] The Egyptians, famed for their piety, worshipped the Nile as the source of life, the dispenser of both purity and fertility. In the *Suppliants* Zeus too is both healer and genitor. Aeschylus juxtaposes the two motifs of the Nile and Zeus by locating the scene of the god's mating with Io in the "snow-fed meadow by the banks of the Nile." By his epithet *physizoos* (384), Zeus may well be assimilated to the Egyptian Amon-Re,[74] and in the economy of the play, as one critic rightly observes, "Zeus is to the action what the Nile is to the poetic climate. The fecundating and healing powers are united in their sovereign sanctity."[75] By linking Zeus to procreative power, the Danaids exalt their own genealogy. Yet they also thereby overestimate the sexual and reproductive value of the male. The *kratos* the Danaids crave would give them victory over their male suitors in resisting the constraints of marriage. But there is another kind of *kratos* that may be included as a factor in this struggle between the sexes: the issue of procreative power. Conditioned by Io's myth, this is the *kratos* they do not yet recognize as one they may claim from men, a *kratos* promoted by the position allotted them in nature and society, which grants them an indispensable role in matters of fertility and reproduction.

From this point of view, the problem of the Danaid trilogy seems precisely the reverse of that in the *Oresteia*. There the female figure (Clytemnestra) asserts her sexuality by taking Aegisthus as her lover, but more significantly, she may be said to overvalue maternity when she avenges the death of her daughter Iphigenia by killing the male. To resolve the issue of Orestes' legal culpability for matricide in the third play, Apollo must, in turn, overvalue the male role in procreation, by denying the role of the mother altogether. To support his claims for the primacy of the male, he appeals to a "scientific" argument that the father and only the father is the parent of the child.[76] For the Danaids, who resist marriage as an unacceptable exercise of power by the strong over the weak in the violent sei-

---

72. Cf. Plutarch, *Quaestiones conviviales* 718b. See also Vürtheim 1928, 47–48; Kranz 1933, 105; and Norden 1924, 76–77.

73. Cf. Diodorus, 1.10.1: *polugonon;* and cf. scholiast, *ad Supp.* 854–56.

74. See Kranz 1933, 106; Froidefond 1971, 81, contra.

75. See Froidefond 1971, 81. Nature and supernature (miracle) converge in the figure of Zeus in Egypt. See also Wilkens 1974, 179.

76. For the "logic" of this argument, see chapter 3, 107–11, above.

zure and control of women's bodies, the opposite solution seems to be indicated, one that would validate their essential part in reproduction and enhance the position of wives by making them mothers.

There are no goddesses of fertility in the pantheon of the Danaids. Io passes by (or bypasses) the domain of the Great Goddess in Asia Minor (547–48) to arrive in Egypt, the locus of male fertility. Apollo's arguments in the *Eumenides,* in truth, owe more to Egyptian thinking than to Greek,[77] and as Diodorus, for example, observes: "The Egyptians hold the father alone to be the author of generation and the mother to supply the fetus with nourishment *[trophē]* and a place to live *[chōra]*, and they call the trees which bear fruit 'male' and those which do not, 'female'" (1.80.3–4). At the birth of Epaphos, say the Danaids, the land cries out at the miracle, "This is in truth the offspring of life-giving *[physizou]* Zeus" (583–85), a claim that reverses the usual connection between earth and fertility, transferring to the male the standard Homeric epithet for earth.[78]

The Danaids adore the Nile, whose "cattle-nourishing *[alphesiboion]* water makes life-giving *[zōphuton]* blood grow forth and bloom for mortals" (855–57, cf. 281).[79] The Nile in its purity is *athikton nosois*, "untouched by diseases," and in the meadow by its banks Zeus put an end *(katepausen)* to the *nosoi epibouloi* (the disease of madness Hera devised for Io, 585–87). In the Danaids' new land, then, it is not surprising that they will transfer their allegiance to the rivers of Argos and bestow upon them the epithet *poluteknoi* (1028), "producers of many children" (or, as the scholiast also suggests, "with many tributaries"). In their benediction, they call upon Zeus alone "to bring the fruits to perfection with crops in every season" (687–89). Zeus is the first begetter (*gennētōr,* 206), the father lord and planter by his own hand *(autocheir anax, patēr phutourgos)*, the great ancient artificer of their race (*genous palaiophrōn megas tektōn,* 592–94; cf. 313, 172).

By contrast, the Danaids elide mention of their own mother, and if they stress Io's maternal role as founder of their lineage, they do not address its physical aspects in either sex or childbirth.[80] Pelasgos speaks

77. See Pestalozza 1964; and Peretti 1956.
78. All editors accept the emendation of *physizoou* from *physizoon* (the latter would modify Epaphos, not Zeus), and cf. 313. *Physizoos* as epithet of earth: *Il.* 3.243, 21.63; *Od.* 11.301. On the etymology of *Zēnos* as *zēn* (life), see FJW *ad* 470–72.
79. In Homeric usage (*Il.* 8. 593; *Homeric Hymn to Aphrodite* 119), *alphesiboion* is a feminine epithet modifying *parthenos,* and the phrase is generally understood as "maidens who yield many oxen as presents from their suitors, i.e., much courted" (LSJ s.v.).
80. This is why *tiktō* and its cognates (give birth, beget) are not used of Io, but only *gen*- words (in keeping with her genealogical function: *progonou,* 44, 533). Even so, only in line 581 does *egeinato* refer unequivocally to Io (cf. *egennasen,* 46, a more ambiguous construction, which may have a different subject). The Danaids use *tiktō* only once in passive

more plainly of the *mixis,* the sexual merger of Io and Zeus (295), to which the Danaids respond with an obscure euphemism (*empalagmata,* 296), glossed by the scholiast to mean "embraces."[81] Later they ask: "Who was it who charmed *[thelxas]* poor much-wandering Io who was stung by the gadfly? It was he who rules through an unending lifetime *[aionos kreōn apaustou],* and by his force of painless power *[biai apēmatosthenei]* and by his divine breath, her wanderings and sufferings were ended *[pauetai].* Then she with her tears washed away her sorrowful *aidōs,* her virginal shame. And taking up the burden which may truly be called that of Zeus, she bore *[geinato]* a blameless child" (571–81).

Io's experience seems to promise both sexuality and childbirth without *ponos,* without pain. Even more, the god releases her from all her previous anguish, since *ponoi atimoi* (undeserved suffering), *odunai* (labor pains), and *nosos* (sickness) are the terms that describe her earlier presexual state, when she suffered under the sting of the gadfly and was called the maenad of Hera (562–63). The *ponoi* associated with the feminine condition—here merging desire, sexuality, and childbirth—thus links up with the more general condition of *ponoi,* the condition of all mortals in their life here on earth.[82] Zeus is named here as the cause not of Io's misery but of her cure beside the pure waters of the Nile. In this curious rewriting of the story, the Danaids' exclusive emphasis on the benign

---

voice, when they pray that new *ephoroi,* "overseers," be born for the city (673), referring, as the edition of FJW observes, not to "the condition of the successive generations of children at birth but their role when they have attained maturity." Danaos uses *tiktō* twice, each time as metaphor and in a pejorative context (498, 770). On the other hand, the Danaids refer to themselves three times as the seed or *sperma* of the mother (141, 151), of "the cow with the fair child" (*euteknou,* 275).

81. FJW contra.

82. The text conflates terms for sexuality and parturition; cf. Loraux 1981b, 52. See also FJW on *ponoi ad* 126. *Ponos* for women in childbirth matches men's *ponos* in agricultural labor. The assimilation of Zeus to the Nile is again instructive. As Herodotus (2.14) observes: "These people get their harvests with less labor than anyone else in the world, the rest of the Egyptians included; they have no need to work with the plough or hoe, nor to use any of ordinary methods of cultivating their land; they merely wait for river of its own accord to flood their fields; then, when the water has receded, each farmer sows his plot, turns pigs into it to tread in seed and then waits for the harvest." *Ponos* in all its uses is even more significant in Sophocles' *Trachiniae,* since it also includes Herakles' famous labors, or *ponoi,* and interpreting the meaning of *ponos* in an oracle is critical to the outcome of the plot. In the *Oaristus* (Love Talk), a little Hellenistic bucolic poem, Daphnis, the shepherd, attempts to overcome the resistance of the girl (Kore), who swears to remain a *parthenos* forever because she views marriage as filled with pain *(ania).* He replies that marriage has no *odunē,* no *algos,* but rather the joys of the dance *(choreia).* She rejoins that she trembles at the pangs of birth *(ōdinein),* for "harsh is the dart of Eileithuia" (goddess of childbirth); she fears to give birth *(tekein)* lest she spoil her beautiful body (25–31; text in Legrand 1927, vol. 2).

sexuality of Zeus raises yet another question. What do these women desire?

Sexuality

The Danaids refuse marriage with their suitors because the Egyptians represent a savage form of human male sexuality. By contrast, the mythological precedent of Zeus's miraculous mating with Io offers another pattern of desire and its fulfillment. Zeus is both the ancestral father of the Danaids and the lover of Io. The virgin's dramatic rejection of eros may be attributed to an overdependence on the father, but it may also be predicated on an erotic yearning for the divine. Danaos, for his part, as the human father, resists separation from his daughters, while they in turn appeal to the original paternal figure (Zeus) in terms that may also suggest the sexual lover.

The Danaids, as representative virgins, are poised at the critical moment when they are objects both desirable and yet taboo in men's eyes. As Danaos puts it in his final counsel to them (996–1013), they are in their "prime of youth that makes men's eyes turn to them; they are a tender summer fruit that is in no way easy to guard from predatory beasts or men" (977–99). Fleeing a detested marriage and hostile to the race of men, they might yet be subjected to a premature and shameful eros. They may even harbor other erotic desires of their own. Pelasgos himself articulates this virginal tension in an interesting way when, in querying their exotic appearance, he asks whether the "Cyprian stamp" is impressed on their female forms by male artisans (282–83) or whether they are Amazons who shun men *(anandroi)* and eat flesh *(kreoboroi)* (287–89).

The comparison of Danaids to Amazons, those savage females who excel in hunt and war, needs little explication. This convenient analogy is already intimated in a fragment of the seventh-century epic, *Danaïs* (frag. 1 Kinkel). The reference to Cypriot women, however, is more intriguing, especially since the meaning of the phrase is not entirely clear. Whether as daughters or wives, they belong to the milieu of Aphrodite in their sensuous appeal. As artifacts fashioned according to male specifications, they are subject to fabrication by men.[83] If the presence of Danaos suggests daughters, the image of striking a stamp *(charaktēr)* is a sexual metaphor (as even the scholiast noted), particularly when mentioned in the context of Cyprus, Aphrodite's most sacred site. At any rate, the very idea of the male as the *tektōn* or artificer, who in "constructing" the female impresses his mark on her body, far exceeds any notion of filial or erotic dependency, and ascribes to men the same creative power that the

---

83. See further Sommerstein 1977, 69–71; and FJW *ad loc.* For further implications, cf. duBois 1988, 140–47.

Danaids themselves later attribute to the *tektōn* Zeus, whom they call the "artificer of their *genos*" (593).

The Danaids tell us again and again what they do *not* want. They never express, however, what they *do* want, aside from their immediate goal of acceptance into Argos and protection from their pursuers in the present contest between male and female. The ambiguity of their reasons for refusing their suitors and the vagueness of their hopes for the future open the way to innuendo and double entendre. But certainly the one wish the Danaids may not directly express is an erotic desire for Zeus.[84]

The model of Io's myth is the device that promotes the necessary mystification.[85] The major motif of the play, stated from first to last, is the wish that as Zeus redeemed Io from her sufferings, so may he release the Danaids from theirs (62–74, 1072–73). The Danaids, like Io, have arrived on a foreign shore in flight from a persecution instigated by eros. Io's story, far better than theirs, exemplifies the precarious situation that attends the scenario of a virgin's transition into matrimony. She is driven forth from her father's house, turned into a heifer, watched over by an all-seeing herdsman who guards her virginity. Afterward she is stung into maddened flight by a gadfly *(oistros)* and compelled to wander like a maenad over a vast geographical expanse. Io's experience seems to capture the strange contradictions of the critical moment when the maiden, like a young animal, is yet untamed. Placed under strict surveillance, she escapes custody, and goaded by desire, she flees in panic, unable as yet to find the settled resting place of a domestic haven. Detached already from her father, she is subject to the conflicting claims of the adult world in the figures of Zeus and Hera—his desire, her interdiction of it. Yet the gadfly, sent by Hera to separate her from Zeus, must also be the masked agent of Io's own unknown desire, which drives her mad with an unbearable and restless torment. Caught cruelly between the extremes of excessive constraint and excessive freedom inflicted on her by the censorious agency of another (a female), she is represented as the victim of a disease that only a male's sexual touch can cure. Io's scenario reads suspiciously like a mythologized version of a syndrome described in an all too brief Hippocratic treatise called the "Diseases of Virgins" (Littré 8.466–81), which relates how young girls may suffer an attack of madness (*paraphrosunē* and *mania*) that causes them to roam about aimlessly and, if left untreated, may even

84. Others have observed the erotic attachment to Zeus, but without close attention to the text: Murray 1958, 19; Caldwell 1974, 57–61. Note the Danaids' numerous allusions, explicit or veiled, to Zeus as the lover of Io, especially 15–17, 40–46, 291–315, 524–37, 575–89, and 1062–67.

85. See Murray's extensive analysis (1958, 18–76); and on lines 556–73, see Sommerstein 1977, 73.

lead to suicide. The only cure, as the doctor advises, is to marry off the virgin as soon as possible and hope for a quick pregnancy.

For the Danaids, however, Io's story points up the drastic difference between their situation at the mercy of lustful suitors, who would seize and subdue their brides, and the benign outcome in Io's remarkable sexual initiation that brings instead a welcome and painless release. By assigning the persecution of Io to Hera and her redemption to Zeus,[86] the Danaids succeed in further separating violence from pleasure in the sexual act. Indeed, their version of events rewrites any equation between the two and, in its finale, even elides the dolorous aspects of childbirth. If pressed to its fullest extent, the analogy between Io and the Danaids implies not just the saving power of Zeus but also the correlation of all the relevant terms. Thus *neōson euphron' ainon,* "renew the tale of kindness" (534), seems to resonate between the two poles of piety and sexual desire, between filial and erotic emotion, and thus their appeal further underlines the ambiguity of their various positions as fugitives, suppliants, and virgins.

It has been observed that the Danaids' *genos* from Zeus leads them to believe *gamos* (marriage) is not their *telos,*[87] that in appropriating the "allegory" of Io, they do not yet understand the meaning of the "happy ending" to her story, which dictates that Io's release from her suffering also must imply "submission to the male and to motherhood."[88] In this reading, which merely replicates without analysis a masculine point of view, Io and Zeus are taken to represent the typical roles assigned to male and female in the social system, and their encounter may thus signify the normal *mixis* (sexual union) of matrimony. But it can plausibly be argued that the Danaids understand that same encounter as exemplifying a unique relation of god to mortal: a different *telos* in a different *gamos.* They already imitate the details of Io's story in many respects. Like her, they roam about in flight *(phugada peridromon)* and compare themselves to a heifer pursued by a wolf (350–52). They cull flowers of grief (73) as Io gathered flowers while browsing in the meadow (43, 539), and they view their persecution as an extension of Hera's wrath against Io (162–67). The motif of Argus with his multiple eyes, who kept watch over Io, returns but is transferred now to Zeus, the all-seeing god *(panoptēs,* 304), and to Danaos, the scout and lookout, both entrusted with safeguarding the Danaids' virginity. The Egyptians are a new reincarnation of the gadfly. Incited now by their own masculine desire, they sting the Danaids into

---

86. The Danaids' version of the myth incriminates Hera and not Zeus (as in the *Prometheus Bound*) for Io's sufferings. See FJW *ad* 299.

87. Hiltbrunner 1950, 10, 26–27, 35. Garvie 1969, 223, contra.

88. Murray 1958, 69–70.

flight and continue to torment them with the prick of their "inescapable goad" (*kentron aphukton*, 109–10; cf. 540–42, 556–57, 563–64). In a literal repetition of the myth, therefore, Zeus must deliver the Danaids exactly as he delivered Io.

Already in the parodos, when describing their virginal state (their "tender cheeks," "their heart inexperienced in tears," "the flowers of lament they gather," 69–73), they speak in terms rife with ambiguous meanings. "Zeus's desire [*Dios himeros*]," they say, is "difficult to hunt down [*ouk euthēratos*, 86; cf. *Prometheus Bound* 858–59], "for in shadowy thickets stretch the ways of his mind, unperceivable to the sight." *Himeros* bears both erotic and nonerotic connotations (desire/will),[89] and the genitive, *Dios*, may be of the subjective or objective kind, referring either to desire *for* Zeus or to the desire *of* Zeus.[90] The erotic undertone is heightened by the hunting metaphor, a well-known trope in the semantics of amorous pursuit, and the idea is further supported by the reference to a dense and tangled underbrush in language that implies the bearded appearance of a virile male (93–95; cf. Sophocles, *Trachiniae* 9, 13). In their desire *not* to be hunted down by their suitors as doves by hawks (223–24; cf. *Prometheus Bound* 857–59), the suppliants may be offering themselves instead as objects of Zeus's desire.[91] Or the reverse may be implied, with equal significance, since the syntax of *Dios himeros* allows for the alternative reading: the Danaids "with difficulty hunt down the desire of Zeus."

Even their wishes for death are veiled in expressions that do not exclude the erotic. They desire to join a Zeus in the underworld if they cannot reach the one on high (157–61). They contemplate death by hanging (160, 465, 789) or a plunge from a steep rock (794–99, cf. 96–100). These longings for escape from misery in the here and now are conventional tragic utterances. Yet in these circumstances they can also be read as evidence of erotic tension and longing for sexual relief.[92] The opposite wish, yearning to fly upward to Zeus (208, 779–82, 792–93), is also significant, as soaring flight in an erotic setting is also a well-attested sign of sexual desire.[93] On the simplest level, their sense of intimacy with the god stems from the rite of supplication at his altar, which puts the Danaids in

89. Hiltbrunner 1950, 13. See also Kraus 1948, 126; and Rode 1965, 91n.4. FJW *ad* 87 contra.

90. See Wilkens 1974, 122–31. FJW contra.

91. See Booth 1955 for punctuation and interpretation of this vexed passage.

92. See Nagy 1973, 145–48. On analogies between suicide and rape as signs of entry upon puberty, see Calame 1977, 261. Cf. the Hippocratic treatise, "The Diseases of Virgins," mentioned above, on self-inflicted hanging and drowning. See too Loraux 1987, 11, 15; Loraux 1984; and below, note 95.

93. For evidence, see Arrowsmith 1973, 165–67.

closest proximity to Zeus, enhanced by the two-way identification of suppliant and supplicated.[94] Earlier I proposed that the maidens' desire to
hang themselves from the divine images implied a wish to dissolve the
boundary between mortal and divine—to reach up to the level of the gods.
But it is significant that to do so, they intend to use their belts (zōnai),
which are normally only loosened for a girl at the moment when she sur-
renders her virginity.[95]

The first stasimon is still more suggestive. Pelasgos, on his way to persuade (peithein) the assembly to accept the suppliants' suit, urges the
Danaids to pray to the local gods of the country for assistance in obtaining
what they desire (erōs, 521). They ignore his counsel, turning instead to
Zeus alone, whom they beseech to be persuaded by their plea (pithou,
527). The basis of their appeal is his courtship of Io, which they now recount in detail, and here is the moment when Zeus is implored to "renew
the ancient tale of kindness" (534). As ephaptōr of Io, the one who
touched her with touch and breath (producing the child etymologically
called Epaphos), he is asked to be polumnēstōr, "much remembering," a
double entendre that also means "much courting" (535; cf. Prometheus
Bound 740).[96]

Obviously the unusual mating of Io and Zeus stands outside the physiological and social norms of human society. But it should be added that
the union of a god and a mortal runs counter to Greek popular wisdom,
which counsels that spouses be social equals. The response of the chorus
of Oceanids to Io's plight in the Prometheus Bound is retrospectively an
appropriate warning against the Danaids' implied aspirations:

> A wise man indeed he was
> that first in judgment weighed this word
> and gave it utterance [diemuthologēsen]:
> the best by far is to marry in one's rank and station [to kēdeusai
>   kath'heauton]:
> let no one who works with her hands desire a marriage
> [erasteusai gamōn] with those pampered by wealth or lifted
> high in pride because of ancestral glory.

---

94. Vürtheim (1928, 163) speaks of the unio mystica between the Danaids and Zeus in
the suppliant relationship (aphiktōr: 1, 241, cf. 243; hikesios-hiketēs: 343, 360, 616, 22, 28,
346, 528, 641, 814; aidoios: 192, 194, 455).

95. E.g., Od. 11.245; Pindar, Olympians 7.45; Euripides, Alcestis 177. Cf. Euripides,
Troades 501. For an anecdote about a virgin hanging herself with her belt (zōnē) to avoid
rape, see Plutarch, Moralia 253c–d. On the cultic significance of such zōnai in virginity and
nuptial rites, see Schmitt-Pantel 1977, 1059–73; and Detienne 1979a, 32–33. On hanging
(and asphyxiation) as the counterpart to the bloodshed of defloration, see King 1983; Loraux
1987, 34–35, 42–45, 105n.15; and cf. Seaford 1987, 113.

96. On the pun, see Ellis 1893, 30; and Murray 1958, 36.

Never, never may you see me, O Fates, a bed-mate drawing
near the couch of Zeus
nor ever may I wed a heavenly bridegroom *[gamēta]*.
I tremble when I look upon the maidenhood of Io, unloved by
any man *[asterganora parthenian]*[97]
consumed by the ill-straying
wanderings of the sufferings *[ponōn]* given by Hera.

But for me, when a match has equal partners *[homalos ho
gamos],*
it brings no fear. Never may the eye
inescapable of the mightier gods look with desire on me *[mē
kreissonōn theōn erōs aphukton omma prosdrakoi me]*.
(887–904)[98]

The Egyptians would lay brutal hands on the Danaids as a prelude to
rapacious sex; Zeus laid a gentle generative hand upon Io. What is the
solution to the Danaids' dilemma, caught as they are between the harsh
physical facts represented by the violent suitors and the marvelous promise of the myth of Io? The answer must lie in a consummated eros that
combines both *peithō* and *bia,* whereby the female through *peithō* and
thelxis tolerates the *bia* inherent in the sexual connection.[99] Proper courtship will lead to the joining of two opposites *(mixis),* engendering a third.
This principle of sexual reproduction also functions as the middle term
between two other extremes: the spiritual union of Zeus and Io, accomplished through touch and breath, is countered by the tradition in Argos
of an autochthonous founder, Palaechthon, a *gēgenēs* (250), who fathered
Pelasgos. Both modes are asexual, one from below (chthonic, birth from
the mother earth) and the other from above (celestial, impregnation by an
Olympian father).[100]

Persuasion, we know, is the key term—that of the political king and
later of the bridegroom—which substitutes courtship behavior for rapacious force. This shift is already anticipated in the Danaids' ambiguous
reference to the "painless power" *(biai apēmatosthenei)* of Zeus, who
through his divine grace put an end to Io's sufferings and engendered a

97. Griffith 1983 reads the adjective in an active sense and translates it as "this virgin
who dislikes her (would-be) husband."

98. Translation by Grene with my adaptations. For similar sentiments see Euripides,
Electra 936–977; frag. 214, 502, 775 Nauck²; *Rhesos* 168.

99. On *bia* in connection with the ambiguous imagery of touch and seizure, see Hiltbrunner 1950, 34; Murray 1958, 32, 56–63, 68; and Whittle 1964b.

100. Paradoxically, both incidents take place through the intermediate term of bestial-
ity. In Egypt Io, the object of divine desire, is turned into an animal and is viewed as a
monstrous prodigy (565–70). In Argos the Earth, responding to ancient blood pollutions,
spawned an "ill-willed band of serpents" in a negative version of autochthony (260–67).

child (576–81). As the text puts it, Zeus "made violence into kindness" (*eumenē bian ktisas*, 1067), an expression that might also be read as an oxymoron to suggest the paradoxical idea of a "kindly violence." Given the weight, however, of the mythic prototype of Zeus and Io, persuasion must also work through recourse to the still greater prestige of another, more universal, mythic paradigm, as an important fragment of the last play seems to confirm:

> Now the pure Heaven desires [*erāi*] to pierce or wound [*trōsai*]
>   the Earth.
> Now desire [*erōs*] grips the earth for her marriage [*gamou*].
> The rains showering from the mating sky
> impregnates her [*ekuse*], and for mortals
> she gives birth [*tiktetai*] to flocks of sheep and to the life-giving
>   wheat of Demeter.
> And from this moist wedding [*gamou*], the season of trees'
>   blooming
> comes to fulfillment [*teleios*]; of these things I am an immanent
>   cause [*paraitios*].
>
> (Frag. 44 Radt)

Aphrodite is probably the speaker, and in her role as goddess of carnal love, she authorizes the norms of sexuality and reproduction in the primal couple, Heaven and Earth, whose mating is impelled by erotic desire. Sexual difference is acknowledged in the two forms this desire takes: for the male, a desire to "wound" the female, and for the female, a desire for sexual union in the interests of procreation. Superseding Io's misleading model of human sexuality, the sacred marriage *(hieros gamos)* of Heaven and Earth recalls the union that originally brought the world into being. In representing relations between the sexes as elemental forces of nature, it also "naturalizes" the socially prescribed causes of human desire, assigning phallic energy to the masculine side and receptive fertility to the feminine. The persuasiveness of this cultural model is difficult to resist, for it suggests to the woman that she may imitate the earth and compensates her for her grievance by emphasizing her reproductive powers.[101] This is the ideological strategy designed finally to mitigate the scandal of sexual violence and thereby win the woman's consent.

The repetitive seasonal rhythm of sacralized nature also replaces a paradigm of reproduction that occurs in a single event of the mythical past, represented by spontaneous autochthony in Argos and by miraculous conception in Egypt. Instead we are given a set of analogies proceed-

---

101. In what follows, see also Zeitlin 1986b.

ing through a hierarchical series of sexual relations, each in its approved position and with the proper marital partner: the primal couple (Heaven and Earth), Olympian Zeus and Hera, and finally a man and a woman in the social institution of marriage.

Mythos and Logos

In this first play of the trilogy, the myth of Zeus and Io assumes a function beyond its value as a paradigm for the Danaids. The story works rather like a living allegory, which directs their actions, colors their responses, and defines their mode of thought. The Danaids not only retell their *hieros logos,* they also long to relive it and call upon the powers of Zeus to reactualize the myth. Thus, if this myth serves to raise questions about the gods, the workings of the human body, and social relations, its extraordinary status in the play also addresses the cognitive implications of a mythic conception of reality. Embedded in the drama of the Danaids, the story of Zeus and Io provides a forum in which myth can reflect upon itself as a mode of apprehending experience and of rewriting the present in terms of the past.

The Danaids represent the past in their obsession with the *genos* of origins and in their singular reliance on *mythos.* The first poses a political problem to the democratic polis, the second an intellectual one. The question of the asymmetrical relations of power between the sexes is parallel to the question of *logos* and *mythos,* in which female is identified with *mythos* and both, it seems, must be integrated into a society that gives priority to male and to *logos,* that is, to reasoned argument and decision making in the frame of present time.[102]

In its literal rendering as the union of god and mortal, the story of Io is discontinuous with human experience. Yet it can also symbolize the union of male and female, which is necessary to the process of generation and the legacy of family lineage. The past founds and supports the present, anchoring it in the prestigious account of origins. As such, a myth can be retold again and again, and the act of retelling is a perennial source of renewal for the society that consents to its validity. Greek foundation stories often propose such unions of gods and mortals as a way of legitimating family dynasties and enhancing the political prestige of cities through

102. *Logos* involves two kinds of thinking. First, it introduces principles of hierarchy—that is, it divides and discriminates between different orders and kinds (e.g., Plato, *Sophist*). Second, it applies to practices of deliberation and decision making. The exercise of *logos* in this play takes several forms: Pelasgos's mode of cross-examining the Danaids, his debate with himself over what course to follow, and the account of the proceedings in the assembly.

the power that accrues from the divine. Yet the primordial time when gods mated with mortals is past and gone, and to repeat its patterns in the present can only trace a circle of eternal return that would foreclose a linear model of history in its dynamic and evolutionary dimensions.

Tragedy, in general, acts out these two models of time when it places its age-old myths within a contemporary setting. It dramatizes the contradictions between old and new in its dialogue between the authority of the exemplifying patterns of myth and the attempt to overcome or deny the power of myth over the present, a process that if taken to extremes, most often leads to a compulsory and tragic repetition. Tragedy is a complex retelling of a traditional story and works its deformations or "interferences" upon mythic plots in its own distinctive ways.[103] Myth remains the *mythos,* the primary story and the plot of the action, but it is also coded to speak about the present. In this role, it works as a secondary signifying system that draws attention to its status as symbolic re-presentation.

Argos too has its founding myth, which will surely be relevant again in the future. Apis, the seer and healer, son of Apollo (although clearly of mortal status) long ago effected a cure for the monsters whom the earth spawned in retaliation for ancient blood pollutions (260–70), and he gave his name to the country of Pelasgos. A god released Io from her misery; a wise man did the same for the land of Argos (268, cf. 1065). Each new story is framed in the light of some preceding paradigm, which may be replaced or augmented by another, more powerful model to obtain (and justify) a different outcome of events. The *hieros gamos* of Earth and Heaven supersedes the myth of Zeus and Io as the model of sexual union. It may also have been invoked to counter the maleficent image of Earth who, without a male partner, produced a crop of monsters in a negative autochthony. In this way, the myth may function as yet another common ground of mediation between the suppliants and their hosts.

For now, however, Pelasgos only alludes in passing to myths of the past, in notable contrast to the Danaids' insistent focus upon their story of origins and to their reliance on mythic and ritual modes of thought, which determines everything they do and say. Myth and ritual converge as the Danaids' appeal to the one (the story of Io) to effect the success of the other (supplication). Their hymnic and incantatory style likewise corresponds to their mythic view of the world. If the blending of chorus and protagonists leads to certain contradictions at times,[104] the lyric frame matches the cultural belief in women's special access to a more transcendent vision, but it also imprisons them in the poetry of their myth.

---

103. See, for example, Vernant 1981a; and Loraux 1973.
104. See Ireland 1974.

A chorus in tragedy ordinarily speaks with a collective social voice, drawing upon the common store of accepted values and public myths. The Danaids, however, are called a band, swarm, or flock in implicit contrast to the masculine community *(koinon)* of the polis, whose members, persuaded by *logos,* act unanimously in the political arena of the assembly (605–8).[105] Although in their benediction of Argos the Danaids pray that internal discord *(stasis)* not come to the city (677–83), in the sequel they probably brought about just that, breaching the solidarity of the citizen body. But the same merging of chorus and protagonists also may look ahead to the time when this collective of women will be integrated into the city and, once persuaded to assent to its social values, will become a true source of blessings for those who took them in.

Once again the example of the *Oresteia* is instructive. The events that unfold in the course of the Oresteian trilogy are condensed into the third and last play, the *Eumenides,* which ends by converting its feminine collective of Erinyes (likewise unwed) from a stance that threatens the city's welfare to one that endorses it. Once they are pacified and promised a permanent place in the city, they close with a similar benediction of Athens. By contrast, the Danaids, whose maidenly reserve still veils their future menace to the city, sing their song of blessing in gratitude for their initial acceptance into the polis, a song whose promise must be postponed until the end of their trilogy. The route that leads them to the city follows another *ichnos,* the track of Io's journey, which they adopt as the fixed *ichnos* of their virginal resolve (538–39, 1017)—that is, "unless something novel *[neon]* has been devised by the gods." Thus they leave the way open for a new outcome in the future, although one still left in the hands of the gods. The outcome must be different, at any rate, for the Danaids have already reversed the direction of Io's journey (538), and the Argos they seek is changed from the one she had left.[106] Unlike her, they have chosen their destination, and their task, as we have seen, is to sue for acceptance through the courtship protocols of supplication.

If the Danaids brought with them a claim to Argive ancestry, these *astoxenoi* also were bearers of a barbarian heritage. Their flight instigated

---

105. Danaids as a band, swarm, or flock: *stolos,* 2, 30, 187, 234, 324, 461, 933, 944, 1031; *hesmos,* 223, 1034 [emended]; *poimnē,* 642. The primary meaning of *stolos* is a military expedition, and its initial use (2) may ironically anticipate the Danaids' future belligerence. On the contrast between the maidens and the *kosmos* (order) of the city, see Porzig 1926, 151–62. The male suitors are also called a band or swarm (30, 487, cf. 683). Hence, both Danaids and Egyptians stand at the opposite pole from the political community *(koinon)* of Argos (325, 366, 369, 518).

106. Io wandered ignorant of her destiny, mystified by the geographical expanse that the Danaids know and name (if in brief). See Froidefond 1971, 83–85.

pursuit in the persons of their rapacious suitors, who invaded the land of Argos, and they showed their Amazonian affinities in their violent retaliation against their violent cousins. To support the prestige of one myth (Zeus and Io), they may well revive the Argive myth of Apis, themselves a new throng of monsters dwelling in Argive homes *(xunoikian)* and eliciting the same urgent need for a healing medicine (260–67, cf. 415).[107] The "cure" must depend on the parts played by Hypermestra and Lynkeus. If the trilogy ended, as suggested, with the couple founding a new dynasty in Argos, the emphasis on *genos* must assume a positive dynamic role within the city, one that includes both Argive and Egyptian elements (mediated perhaps by the fact that the land of Apis has both Egyptian and Greek provenance; 117–28, 260). Some resolution must be found too for the apparent conflict between endogamous and exogamous marriage, which was a major source of the conflict and which, aside from the legalities of the case, must have complicated matters further in combining murder of husbands with the shedding of kindred blood. The Danaids, who have crossed the sea that both divides and connects the two cultures, may also have incorporated beneficent Egyptian elements into the Greek polis. Perhaps they will bring water to thirsty Argos from their association with the Nile and its fluvial fertility, as intimated in their song of blessing (1019–29) and supported by the plot of the accompanying satyr play, the *Amymone*.[108] Or, as may be more likely, the Danaids may import from Egypt a new ritual that they will introduce into Argos.

If the trilogy unfolded in this way, the staging of the Danaids' story would serve as the aetiology of this new ritual, now established in Argos for all time. In addition to the *telos* of marriage, it would institute another *telos* in the ritual the Danaids will found. In this way, the modes of myth

107. A new pollution will come: see Winnington-Ingram 1960b, 149; Murray 1958, 81; cf. FJW *ad* 249–73. *Knōdala* (beasts) is used of the Egyptians (762), and they are also described as serpents (511), but the *knōdala* in the next play may well be the women (cf. *Choephoroi* 587, on monstrous women).

108. Amymone was another Danaid. Sent to find a source of water for arid Argos, she was first rescued by Poseidon from a satyr's attempted rape. The god, however, took her himself and in recompense showed her a spring that would ultimately bear her name. On the Danaids' connections with rivers and springs, see Hesiod, frag. 24; Strabo, 1.23.5; Ps.-Apollodorus, *Bibliotheca* 2.14; Pausanias, 2.15.4; Hyginus, *Fabulae* 31.24ff. See further Vürtheim 1928, 29; Lindsay 1965, 32; Garvie 1969, 172–73; Fowler 1967, 18–19; and Detienne 1989b. There are numerous allusions to water in the play, but sea and river each have their own associations. Although still subject to debate as to origins and interpretation, the tradition that the Danaids carried water in a sieve in the underworld as punishment for slaying their husbands is a relevant motif; see further below, note 114. For recent discussion, see Detienne 1989b; and especially Sissa 1987, 147–79. On women's bodies and leakage, see also Carson 1990, 153–58.

and ritual that bound the Danaids to an unrepeatable past would be oriented to the future for the benefit of the city's collective interests. The move would follow some typical rhythms of Aeschylean drama, which, as in the *Oresteia,* proceeds from conflict to reconciliation, from antithesis to compromise.

Ritual and Reparation: The Thesmophoria

Herodotus mentions in another context that the Danaids brought the festival of the Thesmophoria, a fertility rite reserved for women alone, from Egypt to Argos (2.171). Others have already suggested that like the *Oresteia,* which concludes with the establishment of the new cult of the Eumenides in Athens, the Danaid trilogy ended with the institution of this festival, which likewise both verified and limited the extent of female power.[109] It is an appealing hypothesis: the details of the ritual reply to many of the issues raised by the Danaids' story, and its foundation would grant them cultic powers that specifically depend on their assuming the status of married women.

Aphrodite in her speech that praised eros in the name of fertility referred to the "life-giving wheat of Demeter." Why mention Demeter, the only goddess so named, and in the course of praising the earth for her fecundity? Could this be a sign pointing to the festival of the Thesmophoria, which is founded on the myth of Demeter and her daughter, Kore-Persephone? This myth, beyond any others, supplies the cultural paradigm of marriage as forcible abduction. Its scenario also includes a drastic feminine protest in the person of the mother, Demeter, whose grief and anger at the loss of her daughter to Hades, god of the underworld, provokes a universal crisis when she withdraws from the earth and the crops cease to grow.

In representing marriage as seizure and rape and even as a form of death, the two myths portray the brides' passage to their new status as a forcible severance from parental ties, whether from Danaos the father or Demeter the mother. But the myth of Demeter and Kore also dramatizes the quasi-mystical unity of mother and daughter that seems to defy full separation.[110] The connection of the Danaids to the Thesmophoria would therefore represent a compensatory shift from the father-daughter bond to that of mother and daughter, which is sacralized in the special relationship between Demeter and Kore. Constructed around the deep and inalienable affection, even identity, between the two women, the myth of the Thesmophoria dramatizes rape, grief, and loss. But since one aspect

109. See Garvie 1969, 227–28; Robertson 1924; and Thomson 1966, 308.
110. See Kerényi 1963; Arthur 1977; and Zeitlin 1982b, 149–50.

of the compromise to which Zeus must accede grants a periodic reunion of mother and daughter, the myth also promises recovery and partial restitution of their primary bond. If this arrangement in a sense contravenes the irreversible pattern of matrimony in human life, its terms also admit, at least symbolically, the need to renew consent to marriage. It sanctions a reunion between mother and daughter aligned with the cycle of agricultural seasons and the beneficent powers of nature. Thus the shared relations between them also affirm the mysteries of fecundity in which both maid and mother have a part.[111] The father-daughter relationship brings no such rewards. On the contrary, it is consistently associated with the blocking of fertility, either demanding a permanent virginity or leading to hopeless sterility and premature death.[112]

I cannot explore here the many and varied uses of the myth of Kore and Demeter. My aim is only to suggest the dramatic logic that may link the Danaids to the founding of a Demetrian festival commemorated annually by the women of the city.[113] The Danaids' violent protest in reaction

111. On its own, the Danaids' story conforms to a discernible pattern of a fertility myth and ritual that emphasizes a hostile separation of the sexes. Its closest parallel is the myth of the Lemnian women, the paradigm of male-female antagonism (e.g., Aeschylus, *Choephoroi* 631–34), which the available evidence explicitly links to a seasonal ritual that took place on Lemnos. That ritual in turn resembles the Thesmophoria, and Burkert (1970, 12) observes that "the similarity of the myths of the Danaids and Lemnians and the similarity of the rituals of the Thesmophoria and the Lemnian fire-festival is finally confirmed by Herodotus who connects myth and ritual."

112. For the implications of a father-daughter pair as evidence of a social crisis (i.e., refusal to exchange women), see Massenzio 1969, especially 94–95. Ovid (*Metamorphoses* 10.431–71) recounts the story of Myrrha (later mother of Adonis), who rejected marriage and refused the law of Aphrodite, and was punished by the goddess with desire for her own father. Ovid specifies that their incestuous consummation took place at the time of the annual festival of Ceres (Demeter), which like the Thesmophoria excluded men and even forbade the use of the words *pater* and *filia* (Servius *ad* Vergil, *Aeneid* 4.58). Myrhha's offense is thereby redoubled. As Detienne (1977, 77) remarks: "In a ritual which served to emphasize the intimacy between Demeter and Persephone, the privileged nature of the relations between mother and daughter were strengthened by the censure directed against all links between father and daughter." In Euripides' *Phoenissae*, Antigone chooses exile with her aged father over marriage with Haimon, and defying Creon's insistence, she threatens to become a Danaid on the bridal night, swearing an oath by an iron sword (1675–79). On this point, see further note 113 below.

113. Later poetic allusions (especially Euripides) are also useful in reconstructing an Aeschylean trilogy. In this case, the *Phoenissae* may be an unsuspected source: the chorus of Phoenician maidens owe their ancestry to their *promētōr* Io (*Phoe.* 626, 828; cf. 246, the only occurrence in Euripides); they invoke Persephone and Demeter (along with Ge, the nurse, *trophos*, of all) when they call upon Epaphos and pray to the goddesses to protect the city (676–89). Like the Danaids, these maidens come from a barbarian land (Phoenicia), claiming kinship with Thebes through a common ancestry (*suggeneia*, 291) stemming from Agenor, father of Cadmus (291). Like the Danaids, they are devoted to a male deity (Apollo) in whose service they will actually be enrolled (214–15). Above all, even if the Phoenician

to prior male violence joins up with Demeter's resistance to release an energy that can be channeled back into the ritual sphere for the public welfare. Women's potential for violence against men remains, but only if they trespass on this now ritually forbidden feminine domain. All males are excluded from the Thesmophoria, and sexual abstinence is required for the women, but it is paradoxically this separation of the sexes and the ritual powers of temporary chastity that testify to women's unquestioned authority in matters of fertility. Thus, the Thesmophoria circumscribes but validates the Danaids' defense of their virginity and sanctions their avoidance of men in the interest of intensifying the value of their feminine functions. The reunion of mother and daughter in the setting of the festival also offers women a temporary distance from marriage, their husbands, and sexual relations, and it further affirms the importance of social bonds within the female collective.[114] At the same time, participation in the rite supports the desire to associate with divinity, for the sacred time and place of the festival return the women to the atemporal world of myth, where they may identify with Demeter and Persephone by reenacting their story. The relentless advance of historical time is temporarily suspended, and human existence is once again allied with the transcendent aspects of life.[115] For the duration of the three days of the festival, then, the Danaids can satisfy the aspirations that earlier had threatened to keep them virgins in perpetuity. Through the exemplum of the myth of Demeter and Kore, they

---

maidens frequently refer to maternity and children, their presence suggests the Danaid pattern (1674, 1690) to the principal kore of the play (Antigone).

114. On the Thesmophoria, best known in its Athenian form, see especially Deubner 1932, 50–60; Farnell 1896–1909, 3:83–112; Nilsson 1906, 313–25; Nilsson 1955, 1: 461–66; Fehrle 1910, 137–54; Harrison 1922; Harrison 1966, 120–34; Arbesmann 1937, cols. 15–28; Burkert 1977, 365–70; Detienne 1977, 78–83, 129–30, and passim; Detienne 1979, 183–214; Sfameni-Gasparro 1986, 223–83; Scarpi 1976, 151–59, and passim; and Zeitlin 1982b, 129–58. On its agricultural ideology, see, e.g., Chirassi-Columbo 1975. Dahl (1976) collects all the ancient sources. The festival lasted three days, named respectively the Anodos (the way up), Nesteia (fasting), and Kalligeneia (fair birth). Among other activities, it included special fertility sacrifices, ritual obscenity, and a final feast, presumably to celebrate Persephone's return and to assure the prosperity of the crops and the birth of children.

The logic of the Danaids' connection with the Thesmophoria is enhanced by their contrary association with the Eleusinian mysteries. Both rites celebrate the myth of Demeter and Kore. In the first, the Danaids are figures of marriage (or remarriage) aligned with the fertility motifs of the women's festival. In the second, they are figures of antimarriage. Sentenced to carry water in a leaky sieve forever, they come to represent the noninitiates into the mysteries.

115. "The function of myth is to translate the real into terms of the ideal, the punctual into terms of the durative and transcendental. This it does by projecting procedures of ritual to the plane of ideal situations which they are then taken to objectify and reproduce" (Gaster 1961, 24).

must yield anew to the necessity of marriage in this society of men, but through the rite they can also mourn what they have lost.[116] Yet the myth and rite equally imply that marriage is not a radical rupture with the past and previous family bonds, because it assures them of a periodic reunion with those they left behind.

Above all, marriage itself as an institution is given a place of honor in the city's ideology and elevated from a relationship the Danaids had viewed as a form of enslavement and degradation to a microcosmic reflection of the *hieros gamos*. Aphrodite's paradigm in the fragment of the last play sacralizes the act of sexual penetration, the prelude to fertility, and teaches the female to imitate the earth. The Thesmophoria sacralizes female fertility to suggest conversely that the earth imitates the woman. Each model is a counterpart to the other. Together they affirm the symbiosis of human and divine spheres as a dependable law of nature in a hierarchical system that allots to each a socially designated place and role but which, through analogy, coordinates the terms into a coherent ideological whole.

The Danaids, as I have suggested, seem to overvalue the male procreative role by comparison with their own. If this hypothesis is correct, the aim of the trilogy is not only to "teach" the Danaids to accept a subordinate feminine role in marriage but also to proclaim the significance of their maternal functions and their primary role in the reproductive process. This is the *kratos* that makes them powerful—indeed, sometimes too powerful—in the eyes of men. How better to validate the Danaids' acceptance of that *kratos* than to credit them with the founding of a festival that honors feminine prestige and confirms women's essential contribution to the prosperity of the community? Demeter is the third term in the trio of goddesses concerned with feminine life. Aphrodite and Artemis, in their opposite roles, may represent the conflicting demands placed on the virginal daughter, but Demeter certifies her status as an adult and anchors her, as male ideology would have it, in family and society.

In this solution to the Danaids' dilemma, myth is also allotted its place as the story of primordial events that can be renewed by human actors, but only when it operates according to a symbolic logic and within a ritual frame. The myth of the Danaids, as performed on stage in the theater, is first and foremost a drama, a *mise en scène* that unfolds according to the aesthetic conventions and demands of the genre. In the end, it reverts again to the status of a myth, the retelling of a story already known. The

116. The Danaids also might be able to act on their aggressive instincts, since there is evidence of secret blood sacrifices at the festival and some ritual called a *diōgma,* or "pursuit." On the former, see Detienne 1979b. Burkert (1970, 15) suggests the function of ritual here as "'cathartic' discharge" in the "never-dying tensions . . . between the sexes."

Danaids, who had viewed their lives through the myth of Io, now contribute this dramatic version of their own myth as the aetiological explanation for the advent of the rite of the Thesmophoria in Greece—a ritual itself based on yet another myth, that of Kore and Demeter. At the close of the trilogy, the performance of ritual extends beyond the bounds of theater and myth into the social time of the community to serve as a promise of enduring reenactment for the city's wives and mothers, who meet annually to celebrate the festival of the Thesmophoria.

At the same time, the ritual, which is forecast from within the trilogy, would compensate the female for her assent to traditional roles in the family and community. Power *(kratos)*, as we know, is the dominant issue in the *Suppliants,* and any ideational solution to the power struggle between the sexes must be based, as in all such struggles in Greek thinking, not on unqualified domination and submission but on redistribution of rights and powers. Ritual compensation, therefore, is a way of acknowledging female power but also of limiting it to the ritual sphere, which does not encroach upon the domain of political life and action from which women are excluded. The ritual power the Danaids exercised as suppliants at the beginning of the trilogy was necessarily a political strategy, directed by their father, a male. That rite symbolically expressed the liminal status of the virginal female in society. Now, however, its power would be transferred to another ritual that is the symbolic token of woman's incorporation into the community, in her changed status of wife and mother. In political terms, the woman is first an *astoxenos* (resident alien), then a *metoikos,* and finally a citizen-wife of the Thesmophoria.

The *Oresteia* also resorts to the principle of compensatory ritual to pacify and integrate the hostile female element into the city. As personifications of outraged maternal power, the Erinyes had opposed the masculine structures of city and family, threatening the existence of the polis through their powers of malediction. Athena courts the Erinyes on behalf of the city through good persuasion *(peithō, Eumenides* 885–86) and includes an element of force *(bia)* in her appeal to the paternal authority of Zeus's thunderbolts (826–28). But in drama every transaction must be reciprocal and every loss to one side must be balanced out by some gain. In return for the limitations placed upon the Erinyes' autonomy, they are given a broader sphere of influence in a civic context, including even the protection of marriage and fertility. They are transformed from Erinyes to Eumenides and given the new civic status of *metoikoi (Eumenides* 1011). Here too the permanent sign of the alliance of the Erinyes with the city is the new cult through which the citizens will render them honor.[117]

---

117. Note, however, that the *Oresteia* displaces the problem of the wife to a higher level of reference. The cult "domesticates" the Erinyes by giving these surrogates of Clytem-

That the *Oresteia* and the Danaid trilogy (if I am correct in my surmise) end with the establishment of ritual is a poetic resolution consistent
with the fact that ritual is the typical mode of public action allowed to the
feminine in the city. Ritual has performative value in the real world, but
its larger value lies in its status of perennial repetition, which assures those
calendrical punctuations essential to ordering and defining seasonal time.
Through her social and ritual roles, the woman is associated with two
kinds of time: the linear trajectory of the life cycle between birth and
death, and the circular repetition of time renewed. By contrast, the male
may participate increasingly in a linear historical time. In his androcentric
world the present takes on the urgency of a *kairos,* the moment that determines the appropriate action for each contingency in the flux and uncertainty of both individual and collective life. The establishment of the
law court in the city of men, which will judge each case on its own terms,
and the permanent installation of the cult of the Eumenides on the Areopagus attest to these different dispositions of sexual roles in a patriarchal
society. Given the prominence of legal vocabulary in the *Suppliants,* the
Danaid trilogy too must have concluded with the institution of a law court
(although it is not entirely certain who was tried there) in which the acts
of pursuit and flight *(diōkein, pheugein)* might be transformed into the
specialized meanings of prosecution and defense (cf., e.g., 390, 395). But
the course of the trilogy determines the entrance of the Danaids into the
current of biological time, which was doubly impeded by their adherence
to their father and to the myth of Zeus and Io. It places this imperative
under the rules of a social order that dignifies the institution of marriage.
Paradoxically, the ritual of the Thesmophoria proposes a new paradigm
that signifies the Danaids' transformation into bearers of children and
hence of mortality, but as ritual it fixes their transformation forever and
signifies that the story men have told about them is truly over.

Conclusion

The two trilogies, the *Oresteia* and that of the Danaids, complement one
other as variations on a single theme, involving the institution of marriage
in Argos and the slaying of husbands in response to the dismissal of woman's concerns and rights. I have underlined the affinities between Clytemnestra and the Danaids, both of whom demand *kratos* for the female.
Their motives are also linked, for in both cases an attachment to bonds of
primary kinship devalues the husband. Clytemnestra avenges the outrage

---

nestra a "home" in the city, although they always remain *metoikoi* (*Eumenides* 1011,
1017). The institution of a cult for the Erinyes in the last play corresponds in a sense to
Clytemnestra's first action on stage, which also involves a performance of ritual.

to her daughter Iphigenia by killing her husband Agamemnon, while Danaos's daughters are motivated by their exclusive allegiance to the paternal figure. On the other hand, as we have seen, the Danaids can also be compared to the Erinyes. Both groups constitute a collective of women at odds with the city, who will be integrated into the city's norms only through the persuasive force of a *peithō* that pertains to gender and politics alike.

Between Clytemnestra and the Erinyes, who frame the beginning and end of the action of the *Oresteia,* a parade of other female figures passes before audience, each making a momentary point of contact with the Danaids. It is as though a femininity that is dispersed and distributed in the *Oresteia* had first been assembled and condensed in this earlier group of maidens. These figures are Iphigenia, Cassandra, and Electra, all potential brides. The first is sacrificed by her father at an altar; the second refuses sexual union with a god—becomes indeed the captive and bride of a mortal man—and is sacrificed for it; the third, wholly devoted to the paternal cause, cannot wed in the fatherless house of Atreus.

The most telling point of comparison between the two trilogies, however, is one that crosses gender lines and yet finally seals the differences between the roles of male and female in Aeschylean theater. Orestes, like the Danaids, is at the liminal moment of his life in the crossing from childhood to adulthood. Like them, his criminal act will require divine intervention and the establishment of new civic and ritual institutions in the city. If he too is a suppliant at an altar (in both Delphi and Athens), his reasons are precisely opposite to those of the Danaids in the first play, who insist on the fact that they are not fleeing a charge of bloodshed (although his model may serve them in the future, when they will sit again at the altars, polluted with kindred blood). Yet the contrast is best taken between Orestes, bidden to *destroy* the feminine, turned angry and vengeful, and Hypermestra, who alone of all her sisters *defends* the masculine principle when it has proved benign—actions for which Orestes and most probably Hypermestra were later tried in a court of law.

In another parallel, both adolescent figures must separate from the parent of the other sex, but without proposing a permanent breach between male and female that would lead to a lasting and untenable separation of the sexes into a race of women and a race of men. The asymmetries remain, to be sure, and are integral to the allotment of socially prescribed roles in the male-centered polis. Nevertheless, in both cases, Aeschylus stages a drama around the dire consequences of a drastic inequality between male and female that opens a dialogue between eros and politics, one that inevitably raises still more pressing questions about the mysteries of sex, parentage, and the processes of generation in the polis. In this respect, the *Oresteia* and the Danaid trilogy face one another from opposite sides, for Apollo's argument in the *Eumenides* suppresses the role of maternity in determining the parentage of the child, while the Danaid trilogy, as I have argued, seems to operates in reverse, muting paternal claims in favor of the female reproductive power that is essential to the institution of marriage and the prosperity of the land.

Through its dramatic techniques, Aeschylean tragedy aims to represent a world in process that requires means to address evolving changes in the world of the city. In the *Oresteia* and presumably in the Danaid trilogy, the project is to lay the female to rest, at least temporarily, and to define the parameters of male hegemony. But in the course of its enactment, the dynamic impulse belongs to the female. The male is landlocked like Pelasgos, unmoving even as Zeus upon his throne in the *Suppliants*, as Orestes at the altars of Delphi and Athens, goaded into movement by the female Erinyes. In the intricate rhythms of Aeschylean theater, the choreography of male and female categories defies simple notation.

· FIVE ·

The Body's Revenge: Dionysos and Tragic Action in Euripides' *Hekabe*

The stage setting of Euripides' *Hekabe,* set in Thrace, is a sinister place. Its denizen is an ogrelike king, Polymestor, who masquerades as an ally of the Greeks and a friend of the Trojans. He is a host who has taken in a *xenos* (guest friend) along with his golden hoard, both of which he had promised to keep safe within his house. Site of death, site of thesaurization, Polymestor's locale bears an uncanny and parodic resemblance to the house of Hades, and he himself resembles the form of that death god called Pluto. Paradoxically, the names of the victims who die there—the one he killed, Poly*doros,* and the one whom others sacrificed, Poly*xena*—sound like those ironic and euphemistic epithets of that underworld deity, who both gives and receives.[1] This place also is haunted by ghosts. One, Polydoros, appears on stage and speaks the prologue; the other, Achilles, transmits his demand for the sacrificial gift of a "bride of death" (Polyxena). In the end, there is a "house of Hades," but it is a secluded tent that belongs to Hekabe and it is Polymestor and his children who are lured into it, following a path, as the chorus says, that leads to *thanasimon . . . Haidan* (1031–32, cf. 1021–22).[2] The maimed king will later call the avengers (Hekabe and her women) bacchants of Hades (1077), alerting us to the growing influence of a deadly Dionysos that will rule this play.

Strictly speaking, this setting is not, of course, an underworld. In the first lines of the play the ghost of Polydoros announces that he has left the "hiding-place *[keuthmona]* of corpses and the gates of darkness where Hades far from the other gods has made his dwelling" (1–2). The ghosts

This essay is a revised version of the original, which bore the title, "Euripides' *Hekabe* and the Somatics of Dionysiac Drama." In the first instance, I owe grateful thanks to S. Georgia Nugent, Simon Goldhill, and David Quint who, as always, have proven to be discerning and exacting readers.

1. Polydoros as euphemistic title of Hades: Sophocles, *Antigone* 1200; Polyxenos for underworld Zeus: Aeschylus, *Suppliants* 157–58. See further Schlesier 1989, 113n.2.
2. All textual references are cited from the Oxford Classical Text, ed. J. Diggle.

rise up from the "real" domain of Hades, and the darkness of the night gives way to the light of day (32). Polyxena, in freely embracing her sacrificial fate, prefers to give over her body to Hades (368, cf. 208, 418) rather than endure her present life and the one that awaits her. Much later, Polymestor too can wish to go there as one way to escape his tormentors (1105). And if Hekabe in her grief speaks of herself as no longer among the living, of having died before she is dead, she uses a hyperbole we know well from the traditional idiom of suffering and lament (cf. 431, 668, 683).

Let us say, then, that the setting serves as a mediate or transitional space between the world of the living and the world of the dead, a home to dreams and visitations from those who have already died. It is the site of two deaths that converge when Hekabe discovers the body of her son (Polydoros) while fetching the funeral lustrations for her daughter (Polyxena), and later the site of still others when the children of Polymestor are killed under the nurturing hands of women in the dark interior of the captives' tent. And death will soon come to those who are left, as Polymestor predicts—a strange doom for Hekabe still in the vicinity of Thrace and a more distant preview of what awaits Agamemnon and Cassandra across the sea at the hands of an outraged wife.

The stage locale is also a transitional point between the world of the past and the world of the future. The Greek host and their captives have already left Troy and are only stopping here. This was not their destination, and its position on the coast of Thrace in the Chersonese just across from the Troad even occasions some confusion in the text itself as to whether the play's action takes place here or still at Troy.[3] Euripides wants it both ways: a ghost of one logically buried at Troy (Achilles), a ghost of one yet unburied in Thrace (Polydoros). In any case, before Euripides, was there any such "Thrace" as a way station for the Greeks in accounts of their return home? Was there even a story of Polydoros, son of Hekabe and Priam, and a Thracian king named Polymestor?[4] The scholiasts are silent on this point, and we have few clues to guide us. Euripides may have invented it; it would not be the first or last time that he took his authorial prerogatives to startling extremes.

This setting called "Thrace," however, is more than is usual an imaginary theatrical space. Despite the reality of its geographical location and even the mythic and cultic associations that surround it (a point to which we will return), the place comes into being only for the duration of the play. It seems to have only one inhabitant—a man, Polymestor, together

3. This confusion is already noted by the scholiast *ad* 521. See, e.g., Méridier 1965, 173–74; and Conacher 1967, 151n.14.
4. For the evidence, see Meridor 1983, 13–14.

with his children (who is their mother?)⁵—and by the end there will be
none. He is dispatched from this now deserted spot to some other nameless deserted island (1284–86). Two landmarks will remain, called (or
recalled) into existence by the action of the play. The first is the temporary
(and anomalous) trace of Achilles' tomb; the other, more permanent, is
Hekabe's cenotaph, identified not by her name but by the emblem of her
fate: Kynossema, "sign of the dog," the marker that henceforth will guide
sailors on their way (1271, 1273).

This Thrace is depicted, then, as a border zone, betwixt and between,
a frontier territory where barbarians dwell. The sea is all around; it provides the passage from Troy and a route to Hellas, infusing the play with
its presence in both image and fact. If the place has a king, it has no citizens in evidence and no city. Polymestor moves only from one dwelling to
another (his house, Hekabe's tent) or else absents himself in the interior of
the land (963). A city, *the* city, was there across the straits. It fell that one
night and is now destroyed—its walls, its houses, and its inhabitants—its
fate in that last nocturnal scene relived, detail by detail, in choral memory
(905–42). The rising smoke of its burning can still be seen from this new
lookout (823, cf. 476, 1215).

Otherwise there is only the transient community that consists of the
Greek army and its Trojan captives. Both groups are called an *ochlos,*
"crowd" or "mass" (521, 533, 605, 607, 868, 880), and they inhabit a
cluster of temporary dwellings by the seashore—the encampment of the
Greek men, the tents of the Trojan women. Even so, the play maintains
the usual contrast between private and public zones in the demarcation of
male and female spaces. Apart from Agamemnon's tent, which he shares
with Cassandra and from which Hekabe first emerges (53–54), the two
worlds are separated into the secluded residences of the women (981,
1015–16)⁶ and the open territory by the shore where men gather for
political action, to hear rhetoricians speak, to cast votes and make public decisions (107–9, 116–40), or to assemble by Achilles' tomb where
Polyxena's sacrifice is enacted, as Talthybios reports, before the eyes of all
the host.⁷

There are no sacred precincts here. The chorus refers to the altars at
Troy, where Priam was slain (23) and the Trojan women were torn away
from sanctuary (290, cf. 935). Troy had a temple of Athena (1008) and a
cult of Artemis (935), as does Greece, so the chorus reminds us (Artemis

5. His cavalry host is nowhere in evidence even though he will call upon it for help
(9, 1088–90).

6. These tents are called *domoi* and *dōma* (59, 665, 980, 1038, 1049, 1053, 1149);
oikoi (174, 178, 1019, 1040); and *stegai* (1014, 1179). The standard term for tents is *skēnē*
(53, 99, 733, 1289, 1293) or *skēnēma* (616).

7. On public and private spaces in the play, see Chalkia 1986, 198, 200.

at Delos, 464–65; Athena at Athens, 466–78). Here there is only the tomb of Achilles as the altar for sacrifice and a demand from his ghost that his comrades offer a maiden as a fitting tribute, a *charis* to honor their dead hero (321). His son will officiate as priest (224). The chorus bids Polyxena flee to the temples and altars, cry aloud to the celestial and chthonic gods (144, 146–67). But where are these altars and temples? All the supplications in the play, regardless of their outcome, are direct human appeals made by one person to another.

In fact, where are the gods in this play? They seem to be absent. A spectral child speaks the prologue; a blinded king foretells the future. A woman requites wrongdoing and will later undergo a mysterious supernatural transformation, we do not know how or by whose agency. Many general references are made to divinities, many conventional appeals to the usual pieties. Certainly Zeus might belong here in his dual capacity as god of suppliants and of guests and strangers. He is mentioned once as Hikesios in regard to Polyxena, but precisely as the one to whom appeal will *not* be made (345). And instead of some normative allusion to Zeus Xenios, we get Hekabe's unusual and provocative call to the authority of Nomos (convention or law), which she claims is deemed to be stronger than the gods (799–800). Talthybios, the herald, reporting the sacrifice of Polyxena, wonders whether Zeus even looks upon the affairs of men. Is he just an empty illusion, since it is only the power of an aimless *tuchē* (fortune) that oversees all (488–89, cf. 786)? Above all, there seem to be no local gods in this place—that is, until the end of the play, when for the first time we hear the name of Dionysos in Thrace, a god with prophetic powers (*mantis*, 1267), who authorizes the divinatory role that the king of his land now assumes.

Dionysos's oracle could not alert Polymestor in advance as to what he was about to suffer (1267). Its value for him lies only in the future as the prospective means of his revenge—on Hekabe, Agamemnon, and Hekabe's daughter Cassandra (1259–81). But for the audience, the small but telltale clues have been there from the beginning, and the mention of the god works retroactively to give shape and meaning to all that has occurred, from the first description of Cassandra as the bacchant seer (*mantipolos Bakchē*, 121; cf. 676–77), passing through the sacrifice of Polyxena and the discovery of the dead Polydoros, until the fully Dionysiac revenge of Hekabe and her women, bacchants of Hades, when they blind Polymestor and slay his children inside the tent.[8]

The utterance of the god's name does more than orchestrate the de-

8. See also the excellent article of Schlesier 1989, which was published during the course of writing this essay. We agree on the significance of Dionysiac language and action in the play.

tails of Dionysiac language, myth, and practice that I will review below. It puts the seal on the dramatic structure of the play and the concatenation of events, on the logic of the locale and the underlying scenarios, as well as on the allotment, reversal, interchange, and even confusion of roles between one character and another. With this allusion we know we are fully in the theater of Dionysos that is constructed in this land called Thrace where, as Herodotus tells us (7.111), Dionysos indeed had an oracle,[9] a place that is neither Troy nor Athens, neither on the fields of honor nor in a city's precincts. Here there are no gods and no polis to mitigate or avert the Dionysiac effect of women who are made to take over the power and the plot when men abdicate their roles of moral authority and the most sacred cultural taboos are transgressed. What we have here, after all, is the exemplary Dionysiac plot, the one that arouses men's deepest fears, when mothers who love children and hold them close turn in anger against them—their own or those of others—and in a reversal of roles do injury to the bodies of men.

This is the frame of reference I have chosen to explore the nature and complexities of Hekabe's revenge. My concern is how and why it works as it does—under what auspices, what constraints, what underlying assumptions. What theatrical forms and conventions shape its unusual double plot? On first inspection, the plot seems to consist of two separate and distinct actions, united under the figure of this aged queen who on a single day will view the lifeless bodies of her two children, with the prediction of death for the one (Cassandra) who remains. The play is a staging ground for many familiar Euripidean themes and techniques: the oppositions between virgin and mother, slave and free, Greek and barbarian, public and private, enemy and friend, male and female, beast and human; the contrapuntal ironies of shifting roles and relationships that involve forms of doubling, identification, and exchange among all the characters. Yet if the play is also a staging ground for a case study in the extremes of human behavior, it is not, I will argue, primarily intended to "permit us to examine areas of human experience that might otherwise remain hidden" in any general sense.[10] Rather, it attempts an experiment in displacing the conditions and dynamics of a Dionysiac drama to a temporary and barbarian locale, where it can operate without the safety net of political or sacred institutions that would cushion, even if only at the end, its potentially unhappy and regressive aspects. The play may protect its audience in that the crucial encounter takes place between one non-Greek (Hekabe) and another (Polymestor). Perhaps this is why there is no *deus ex machina*, however ironically introduced, no establishment of cult, no

9. See also [Euripides], *Rhesos* 970–73.
10. Michelini 1987, 113.

conciliatory gesture, no haven of refuge elsewhere. The only transcendence here is in the prophecy of overcoming the limits of the human form. Metamorphosis is the event that finally condenses and caps the remarkable fixation of the play from beginning to end on the physical aspects of the body in life as in death, in contact and disjunction, in devotion and enmity—a somatic preoccupation that reaches its climax in Hekabe's Bacchic revenge and concludes in the prediction of her fate. Is not this prediction, after all, the consummate Dionysiac gesture that both transforms the shape and nature of Hekabe's body and raises her to a dizzying lookout, like Pentheus, from which she similarly will take a fatal downward plunge?[11] As Renate Schlesier astutely remarks, only in this play is Hekabe named (and from the start) as the daughter of Kisseus, Dionysiac "man of ivy,"[12] who also, strangely enough, is a native of Thrace.

In addition to linking Dionysos with the factual condition of the human body and its component parts, gestures, and attitudes, there is a further advantage in taking a "Dionysiac" approach to the play: to shift the focus away from the judgmental type of criticism that so dominates the interpretation of this, the least consoling of Euripides' dramas. This popular approach, with varying degrees of fidelity to the text, treats character, language, and action with the single aim of repudiating the moral world represented by the play and, above all, of registering dismay at Hekabe's so-called "fall from nobility and decency"[13] when she turns from victim to avenger and brutally repays the violence done to her and her kin. It is true that Euripides has constructed a plot in which the execution of revenge puts maximum pressure on our moral sensibilities, exposing the psychological tensions between a secret universal desire and its equally strong prohibition by civilized norms.[14] But aside from the perhaps discomfiting fact that ancient opinions strongly supported the justice of Hek-

11. The term *karchēsia* (1261), to designate the height of the ship's mast, is rarely used (cf. Pindar, *Nemeans* 5.51). This lexical meaning is secondary and derived from its shape, which resembles a certain kind of drinking vessel narrower at the waist than at the top or bottom. The word may therefore carry a faint Dionysiac allusion. The comic poet Epicrates puns on the two meanings (frag. 10 Kock).

12. Kisseus as Hekabe's father occurs probably first in Euripides and is used as an epithet of Apollo in connection with Bacchant seercraft in Aeschylus, frag. 341 Radt. See Schlesier 1989, 112n.3. For problems of Hekabe's patronymic, see Méridier 1965, 172n.1. In *Iliad* 16.718, Dymas is her father who lived in Phrygia, while Kisseus is the father of Theano, wife of Antenor (*Il.* 11.221). Theano nursed the bastard son of Antenor with the same care she gave her own children (*Il.* 5.69–71), and she is the priestess of Athena who greets Hekabe and her women when they come to the temple with their offering of the peplos (*Il.* 6.297–300). Paradoxically, the possible echoes of this Iliadic scene later in the play (discussed further below) may have motivated Euripides' choice of Kisseus.

13. Reckford 1985, 114 and n. 1 (bibliography).

14. See Burnett 1973, 1. Reckford 1985, 118: "We cannot help conniving at this victory. It is (let us admit it) exhilarating as well as horrifying."

abe's revenge,[15] Euripides has constructed a plot that puts maximum pressure on the tension between the stability (and autonomy) of a singular self and the network of reciprocal relations, both manifest and hidden, into which a character is inexorably drawn. These tensions, so typical of the dynamic operations of tragedy in the name of Dionysos, whether explicitly stated or not, are heightened by the density of allusion in this play. These echoes create hidden correspondences between characters in the first and second parts of the action between Greek and barbarian as between male and female. They also draw upon mythic, epic, and dramatic associations that are screened behind the figures we see on stage, associations that combine to bring the Dionysiac aspects of the plot into fuller resonance—in character as in action, in body as in name.

Dionysos in Thrace

Let us return to Thrace, our point of departure, the site of transition between two events so familiar to epic and theater: the fall of Troy and Agamemnon's return to Argos. If Euripides' innovation was to refashion this moment of transition in a new locale, Thrace itself was a well-known geographical space, situated between Greece and Asia. It was a strange and remote territory, fabled for its wintry winds and its gold,[16] home to certain distinctive, even aboriginal, forms of Dionysiac myth and cult.[17] One well-known myth involved a king named Lycurgus, whose story bears a suspicious resemblance, as we shall see, to this other Thracian king, Polymestor. It is attested first in Homer and was later elaborated in a lost Dionysiac trilogy of Aeschylus (the *Lykourgeia*) in addition to other sources.[18] As a figure bridging both epic and theater, Lycurgus is especially pertinent to a Dionysiac drama set in the aftermath of Troy, the first half

15. As Heath (1987) shows in his study of the play's reception in later antiquity and beyond, the inculpation of Hekabe and the focus on moral degradation are modern preoccupations.

16. Wintry: Aeschylus, *Persians* 494–97, 501ff.; Euripides, *Alcestis* 67. Snowy: Euripides, *Andromache* 215; *Hekabe* 81, 710; *Cyclops* 329. Winds: Euripides, *Rhesos* 440; *Cyclops* 329. Gold: Euripides, *Alcestis* 498; *Hekabe* 25–27; *Rhesos* 303, 305, 382–85, 439, 921–22. See further Chalkia 1986, 196–97.

17. For the evidence see Chalkia 1986, 197. Earlier scholars maintained the theory, now outdated, that Dionysiac worship originated in Thrace and migrated to Greece. See, e.g., Rohde 1925, 253–81; and Farnell 1909, 5:85–133.

18. *Il.* 6.130–41 with scholiast; Eumelos, frag. 10 Kinkel; Sophocles, *Antigone* 955–65; Ps.-Apollodorus, *Bibliotheca* 3.5.1; Hyginus, *Fabulae* 132, 242; Servius *ad* Vergil, *Aeneid* 3.14; Diodorus, 3.65.5–6; Nonnus, *Dionysiaka* 21.166. Hall (1989, 107) notes that Lycurgus is not specifically named as a king of Thrace in Homer and suggests that Aeschylus supplied this geographical detail.

of which concerns Achilles, the Greeks' most distinguished hero, whose status in death his comrades would now honor with the gift of a maiden sacrifice.

In the *Iliad* the tale of Lycurgus is recounted as an embedded story in the encounter between a Greek (Diomedes) and a Trojan ally (Glaukos) who, discovering their relations of guest friendship *(xenia)* from the days of their fathers, agree to honor that bond and refrain from hostility to one another. Indeed, it is then that they make their famous exchange in which Glaukos, to the poet's astonishment, exchanges gold armor for bronze (*Il.* 6.119–236). Beyond the fact that Polymestor's crime was precisely to violate his bond of *xenia* with Polydoros's father, Priam, we note too that greed for gold was the motive for slaying the boy who had brought with him the treasures of Troy for safekeeping.[19] But there are further grounds to suspect that these Homeric echoes extend to the broader context of the Glaukos-Diomedes scene, which in the *Iliad* is the central panel of a triptych, framed by two other significant episodes, the first on the Greek side, the other on the Trojan. The parallels are not explicit in either case, but we may detect a field of suggestive Iliadic associations that involve certain similar themes, situations, and figures, screened behind the present actions in Thrace.

The preceding Homeric scene is one of supplication on the battlefield, in which a Trojan (Adrestos) offers his father's treasure of bronze and gold to a Greek (Menelaos). The ransom is almost accepted until Agamemnon persuades his brother not to spare a single Trojan, "not even the young man child that the mother carries still in her body . . . but let all of Ilion's people perish, utterly blotted out and unmourned for" (*Il.* 6.37–60). In a sense, the young Adrestos combines the figures of both of Hekabe's last remaining children. In the first instance, a mother's supplication for her daughter's life (Polyxena) is refused by the Greek army; in the second, a young son (Polydoros) at first is saved along with his father's gold, but is later killed because of it and his body cast out unburied.

The Iliadic scene that follows the story of Glaukos and Diomedes is Hekabe's first entrance into the epic. She has been bidden by Hector to bring a propitiatory offering of the fairest and costliest peplos to lay on the knees of Athena and to offer prayers to the goddess "in the hopes that she might have pity on the city of Troy, the Trojan wives, and their innocent children."[20] We may compare in the present context not only Heka-

---

19. Achilles' golden armor (110) may perhaps also perhaps allude to the Iliadic Glaukos-Diomedes episode.

20. The details of Hekabe's visit to Athena's temple are repeated three times for emphasis: *Il.* 6.86–95, 269–76, 286–310.

be's leading role and the plight of these same women and children, but also several other, more subtle references in the staging of the women's revenge: First, Hekabe lures Polymestor with a promise of the Trojan treasure that she claims had once been secreted in the temple of Athena (1008) but is now kept safe in her tent (not in the folds of her peploi as Polymestor first imagines, 1113–14). Second, Polymestor enters the tent also clad in peploi, which, in their intricate workmanship so admired by the women, may well recall their Homeric counterpart that in its beauty "shone like a star" (*Il.* 6.295).[21]

To return, however, to the major figure of Lycurgus himself, the story of his fate seems to echo in Polymestor's account of his misfortunes, shaping his language and perceptions in Dionysiac terms. Diomedes tells how Lycurgus, in his impiety against the gods, once pursued the nurses of maddened *(mainomenoio)* Dionysos. They scattered and fled in disarray, while Dionysos in terror dived into the sea, where Thetis received him into her bosom. The gods were angered, and Zeus punished Lycurgus with blindness, "nor did he live long afterwards, since he was hated by all the immortals" (*Il.* 6.130–40).[22]

The immediate parallels are obvious. Lycurgus and Polymestor are both persecutors of children; their victims, Dionysos and Polydoros, are both consigned to the sea. Hekabe's role is more complex. In the *Iliad,* the myth of Lycurgus is a story of divine retribution against a man who failed to recognize the power of the gods. In this play, however, where the gods are conspicuously absent, vengeance falls to Hekabe, who, in the role of Zeus, herself exacts the penalty of blindness on the misdoer. At the same time, in the enactment of an additional revenge on Polymestor's children, Hekabe's maternal role (and that of the other Trojan women) now shifts to the other, Dionysiac, side of the equation in a double-edged encounter between persecuted and persecutor. In this new scenario, Hekabe and the Trojan women play the part of Dionysos's nurses: they are both tender mothers who lovingly pass Polymestor's children from hand to hand and "murderous bacchants of Hades," as Polymestor calls them, in his own state of Dionysiac madness, after they have drawn their daggers from their

21. Cf. too the earlier choral allusion to the weaving of the peplos for Athena in Athens (466–74), a first clue perhaps to alert us to this later reference. In the *Iliad,* the peplos is of Sidonian manufacture (6.289–91); here the robes are admired as examples of Edonian skill (1154–56). Recall too (note 12, above) that Kisseus in *Iliad* 6 was the father not of Hekabe, as in this play, but of the priestess of Athena, Theano, who received the peplos. Later, I shall adduce another, closer parallel (from the *Odyssey*) to this reported admiration of the women for the peploi. One reference does not preclude the other.

22. It is significant, too, that Diomedes tells this story. It is his murderous *aristeia* that occasions Helenos's instructions to Hector to go into the city with the express purpose of bidding the women to offer the peplos to Athena. In Achilles' absence, Diomedes has become "the strongest of all the Achaians," mad for battle (*mainetai, Il.* 6.96–101).

peploi and slain the children. Only now does Polymestor pursue the women, as Lycurgus had earlier pursued the nurses of Dionysos.[23]

Beyond Lycurgus, Dionysiac echoes expand still further when Polymestor, searching in vain for the women in his first maddened exit from the tent, calls upon Helios with the wish that the sun might restore the light of his blinded eyes (*tuphlon . . . phengos*, 1068–69). The allusion is clarified at the end of the scene, when the king, in a despairing wish to escape his woes, cries out his desire to soar up to the heavens, to the constellation of Orion, the mighty hunter, and Sirius, the hound who accompanies him in the heavens (1100–1105). Orion, we may recall, was blinded by Oinopion, son of Dionysos and Ariadne, for raping Oinopion's daughter, but was cured finally of his blindness by Helios when he traveled eastward to meet the rays of the sun.[24] I will have occasion to return to the importance of Sirius. What is notable here is the aptness of Polymestor's allusion to the blinded hunter and his dog as the climax to his scene of madness. This is the moment when he has rushed out of the women's tent like a wild mountain beast, to track down and catch the "manslaying Trojan women" (*androphonous . . . Iliadas*, 1062–63), a *thēr* (wild beast) pursuing hounds, hunting them down like a leader of hounds (*kunēgetēs*, 1172–75).[25]

The story of Lycurgus may provide the implicit pattern for Polymestor's fate. But it is the starry hunter together with his dog who provides the transition to the familiar Dionysiac imagery of the tragic stage, promoting the curious mixture of beast, hunter, and hound that will later materialize into a concrete reality when Polymestor predicts Hekabe's metamorphosis into a dog. He may call the women bacchants of Hades, but if he turns hunter like Orion, he does so as a bacchant himself, the beast who tracks the hounds instead of being tracked by them. Eager to sate himself on the women's flesh, making a banquet like a wild animal in revenge for the outrage he has suffered, he imagines these bacchants, for their part, will carve up his children and cast them out on the mountains as a bloody repast for dogs (1072–79).

Schlesier reads this scene as an exchange of gender roles: the women are not typical bacchants because they are not mad and do not kill with their bare hands; the man abandons his role to become a female bacchant. But if Polymestor is converted to bacchant status, other non-Homeric traditions recount how Lycurgus himself was driven mad and in this

---

23. See Schlesier (1989) for a fuller comparison between Lycurgus and Polymestor. I have omitted from this version of the essay a closer enumeration of her points.

24. This version of Orion's story is known from Hesiod 148a M–W (= Ps.-Eratosthenes, *Caterisms* 32). See Fontenrose 1981, 5–32; and Massenzio 1969, 27–113, especially 42–49; and further, Schlesier 1989, 132nn.59–61.

25. Diggle obelizes *kunēgetēs*.

condition killed his own son by mistake and later mutilated himself.[26] With the story of Lycurgus as an implicit guide, a man too may go mad, become a bacchant, and kill children—his own (like Herakles in Euripides' play)[27] or the child Dionysos himself.

In any case, the myth of Lycurgus, Homeric or otherwise, is only one Dionysiac element among others. A Dionysiac contest in the hunting milieu, as the *Bacchae* demonstrates, depends far more on the fluid and reversible exchange of roles or even their merger.[28] Above all, we should not take Polymestor's killing of Polydoros as a kind of real Dionysiac ritual, as Schlesier argues, in which an actual *sparagmos* took place to which the women reply in kind.[29] For it is precisely in the theatrical setting that literal elements of Dionysiac myth and ritual can be converted to image and metaphor, encoded into the tragic process ruled over by Dionysos, when preceded by telltale cues and grounded in prior ritual references, such as supplication and sacrifice. All these elements—the myth of Lycurgus and Dionysos in Thrace, Polymestor's confusion of categories (beast, hunter, and hound), and the reciprocal conversions between Polymestor and Hekabe—are theatrical indications of Attic tragedy's general conventions, which come to the fore when directly bound to

26. Servius *ad* Vergil, *Aeneid* 3.14, relates that "Lycurgus began to cut off Dionysos' vines and driven mad by the gods, cut off his own legs." Ps.-Apollodorus, *Bibliotheca* 3.5.4: "Lycurgus in his madness thinking his son was a vineshoot, struck him with an axe and killed him, and when he had cut off his son's extremities, he was restored to sanity." In Hyginus, *Fabulae* 132, Lycurgus denies that Dionysos is a god, gets drunk, wants to rape his own mother, and tries to cut down the grapevines; alternatively, he is driven mad and kills his own wife and son. In *Fabulae* 242 he is included among other mythic figures who kill themselves. Blind, mad, or inebriated: all three are states of altered perception, and the context each time is the introduction of viniculture. On this Dionysiac resistance myth, see Massenzio 1969, 60–82. For the Homeric myth, see Privitera 1970, 53–84. In addition to the typical motive of sexual transgression that accounts for blindness as a punishment, the mythic variants suggest other reasons that are germane to the case of Polymestor. I will return to this point later.

27. Athamas is another example. In a lost post-Euripidean drama, the basis of Pacuvius's tragedy *Iliona*, Polymestor did not kill Polydoros but his own child, Deipylos, by mistake. See further, Schlesier 1989, 113n.8.

28. On hunting in the *Bacchae* and Dionysiac images of beast, hunter, and hound, see, e.g., Segal 1982, 32–33.

29. Schlesier (1989, 117–19) argues for a real Dionysiac sacrifice, based on (1) Hekabe's words upon discovering her son's body ("unspeakable, not to be named, beyond all wonder, unholy and unbearable") and (2) her suggestion of a ritual slaying and mutilation ("how you divided his flesh, cutting the limbs of this child with an iron sword," 716–20). This *sparagmos*, in her view (125–26), can be deduced from the mode of Hekabe's vengeance. The language indeed has a Dionysiac coloring, but a literal reading (unmarked in the text) would actually undermine the case against Polymestor, who is condemned precisely because he has not respected the rights of *xenoi* (715) and has killed a child entrusted to his care, for the vilest of reasons, and not because he has carried out some Dionysiac rite.

a Dionysiac context.[30] This dynamic movement across boundaries is the defining characteristic of the god, accounting for his role as patron of the theater and for the typical devices of his stage. What especially marks this play, however, is how it several times crosses the boundary between word and deed, metaphor and fact, and reverses the process that turns act into metaphor by making metaphor itself the agent of a real metamorphosis when Polymestor pronounces his prophecy of Hekabe's fate.

The capacity to shift from trope to tangible fact is embedded in Polymestor's remarkable borrowing of bacchant imagery when he refers to hunting and omophagy (eating raw) and transforms the scene into the wild mountainous setting appropriate to Dionysos and his maenads. Under the effects of his mad passion (*thumos*, 1055), Polymestor puts on a show in which he mimes the role of the beast, going on all fours, sniffing his quarry, preparing to pounce and devour the women, but eager too to rush back into the tent, "the lair of the beast," to stand guard over the bodies of his own. Thus he is both the blind hunter (Orion) and the prey *(thēr)*. He names the women as bacchants of Hades whom he fears will cast out his children for the dogs to devour, but in his report to Agamemnon, he names them too as murderous hounds (1173). All these are *his* gestures, *his* words, *his* interpretation, and in a final reversal, his Dionysiac experience of pain and suffering in the hunting milieu will transform him into a seer with actual power to predict the future. His temporary metamorphosis in a state of madness enrolls him on the side of Dionysos and enables him, in his blindness, to speak as a prophet in the god's name, whereby he can convert metaphor into actuality and image into permanent identity under the sign of the dog.

The Sign of the Dog

What might this prophecy signify? What are the implications of Hekabe's ascent and fall and her metamorphosis into animal shape? For the first, I have already noted the Dionysiac parallel between Hekabe's fall from a height and that of Pentheus in the *Bacchae*. In terms of the plot, however, the descent of Hekabe is made to spell out the final fall of the house of Priam and the city of Troy (with all that a human community represents). Although no reason is given for her climb to the top of the mast, the motive that suggests itself is a last backward look at Troy. The chorus has already expressed this idea (*polin t'aposkopous[a]*, 938) just before the entrance of Polymestor, in reviewing the night of Troy's destruction. Aga-

---

30. Dionysos and Pentheus, both enemies and doubles, provide the model in the *Bacchae*, but the case holds true for the *Herakles* in the symbiosis between Lykos and Herakles.

memnon renews it later when he comes in response to the shouts rever-
berating by Hekabe's tent and exclaims that the noise would have given
great cause for fear "if we did not know that the Phrygian towers had
already fallen by the Greek spear" (1109–13).

The play is filled with allusions to falls of different sorts: the fall of
Troy (5, 11, 1112), the suppliant's posture at the knees of the other (339,
737, 787), the fall of the victims (Polyxena, 569; Polydoros, 699), the
warning to Hekabe of a violent push to the ground if she does not submit
to those in power (405). To these we may add the fall of the young wife
upon her bed on the night Troy fell, of which the chorus sings (927), and
finally the wish of an observer (the Greek herald Talthybios) to die before
he "falls in with some disgraceful misfortune" (498; cf. 374, 846).[31]

One last passage is particularly revealing because it pertains to Polymestor himself and seems to anticipate exactly what will happen to
Hekabe. Just as the Thracian king leaves to enter the tent on the "deceptive path into that deadly Hades to which his hopes have led him,"
the chorus predicts he will pay the penalty for his deeds, robbed of life
"like one fallen sideways into a foul flood from which there is no escape into harbor" (1025–27). The curious nautical wording of this vexed
passage has puzzled many critics, but beyond a possible Homeric echo
with special relevance for Polymestor,[32] it uses a metaphor for him that

31. I have only charted the actual uses of the verb *piptō-pitnō* (fall) and its cognates.
Obviously, the change in status from high to low, royalty to slavery, pride to humiliation
is a recurrent theme, enacted physically in the attention given to shifts in bodily position.
Hekabe's entrance as a tottering old woman dramatizes the queen's fallen and helpless state
(59–67). Talthybios's later exhortation that she rise up from her prone position to hear his
news of Polyxena's death repeats the theme in miniature, momentarily reversing Hekabe's
prostrate attitude of grief to celebrate the noble heroism of her daughter (486–500). Polyxena's refusal to lower herself to supplicate Odysseus belongs to the same register of symbolic values (cf. 339–41), where *piptō* would be countered by other words used, such as
hairō (raise), *anistēmi* (get up), and *orthos* (upright). On the other hand, the same gestures
of raising and lowering echo again in the women's actions against Polymestor in the tent,
when to help his children he keeps on trying to lift up his face, and they grip him by the hair
and forcibly restrain him (1162–67). I will return to this scene.

32. Translation by Tierney 1946, 119. *Antlos* is the questionable word. Normally
it means "bilge water" in the ship and not the sea itself; *alimenon,* "without a harbor,"
is a more appropriate adjective for the sea than for bilge water. *Antlos* as "bilge," however, is a good Homeric word (as elsewhere). In one case in the *Odyssey,* the mast and
the tackle break off and fall into the *antlos* (*Od.* 12.410), and in another a woman, struck
by Artemis's arrow, actually meets her death by falling into it (*Od.* 15.479). The difficulty may stem from the concept of combining the idea of a sea journey (which needs a
harbor) with a fall into water (which might be of either kind). The difference is not essential
for my point, but it is worth recalling that in the *Odyssey* the woman was the perfidious
nurse of Eumaios who stole him away from his royal family to be sold into slavery, when
sailing off with Phoenician sailors, and was thus punished by Artemis in this peculiar way.
Note again the reversal of gender roles, but the fact that both the nurse and Polymestor failed

the terms of his prophecy will later reverse by turning it into fact for the other.[33]

Hekabe's metamorphosis, as noted above, can likewise be interpreted as a reversal of the self's experience onto the other, a transferred epithet turned into fact. But why a dog? Critical comment has focused for the most part on the dog as a negative cultural symbol, taken to confirm Hekabe's moral conversion to bestial status.[34] But let us look more closely at the text. Polymestor's prediction makes no reference to her howling or snapping (as in Ovid, *Metamorphoses* 13.545–75) or to her bitch-like qualities. He gives one single detail: she will be turned into a dog with a "burning gaze" (*pursa . . . dergmata,* 1265). Some have claimed a hidden allusion to Hekate, the quasi-namesake of Hekabe, and the case is strengthened by another Euripidean text (possibly from the *Alexandros* [frag. 968 N²]) in which Cassandra prophesies to her mother: "you will become a dog, the image *[agalma]* of torchbearing Hekate *[Hekatēs phōs-phorou].*" The gloss is useful and locates the "burning gaze" in an appropriate cultic context that can also include Dionysos. But the ellipsis is equally significant.[35] The absence of any explicit divine agent or identifi-

---

in their duty as *trophoi* and did so because of motives of personal gain might well justify a Homeric echo in this passage.

33. He first takes the nautical metaphor for himself when in the midst of his mad scene, he compares the girding up of his robes to a ship's unfurling its sails with the help of hoist and tackle (1080–82).

34. Almost all commentators stress this point to varying degrees. See most recently Conacher 1967, 152–54; Luschnig 1976, 232; Daitz 1971, 222; Michelini 1987, 172; and above all, Nussbaum 1986, 414–17. Some resist on more technical grounds: Gellie 1980, 41–43; Meridor 1978, 33–34; and Adkins 1966.

35. For relations between Dionysos and Hekate, see Jeanmaire 1970, 271. Dio Chrysostom reports a possibly earlier lyric tradition (*Orations* 33.59 [= *PMG* frag. 965.1]) that "as a climax to all her terrible misfortunes, the Erinyes made Hekabe into a dog with blazing eyes. And when she poured her brazen cry from hoary jaws, Ida gave ear and sea-girt Tenedos and all the wind-swept crags of Thrace." Nicander (cited by scholiast, *ad* 5) claims that it was in seeing her city in flames and her husband dying that Hekabe threw herself into the sea and was changed into a dog. According to the scholiast on Lycophron, *Alexandra* 1181 (where the Hekabe-Hekate connection is explicit, 1174–88), she was stoned after the sack of Troy by the Greeks, who were irritated with her laments. Saintillan (1987, 193 and n. 37) argues for an implicit identification with an Erinys, who is often represented in the form of a dog with a gorgon eye (e.g., Euripides, *Orestes* 260–62; Sophocles, *Oedipus at Colonus* 84). He relies on the lyric fragment cited above but ignores Cassandra's prophecy in the *Alexandros* that associates Hekabe with Hekate, although I agree with his basic point. Loraux (1990, 76 and n. 122) refers to Semonides's characterization of the dog as *autometor* to account for the maternal element of Hekabe's transformation. "The bereaved mother," she says, "has fulfilled her destiny."

The one powerful Homeric referent for a "burning gaze" is the anger *(cholos)* that Agamemnon in the play immmediately takes to be the motive of Polymestor's as yet unidentified attacker (1118). In the *Iliad* one can be possessed of *mēnis,* but more generally anger

cation with a supernatural doublet directs us instead to look for the clue in the text—in its dominant themes and images, especially the recurrent motif of eyes and vision that culminates in the enduring contrast between Polymestor's blinding and Hekabe's acquisition of a more-than-human gaze. Earlier, as we know, Polymestor had declared his wish to escape up to the heavens—to Orion, the blind hunter, and Orion's companion Sirius, the dog star. Orion is invoked merely by name, but Sirius is described as "casting the flaming rays of fire from his eyes" (1104–5). Escape on high is one alternative for Polymestor; the other is the wish to "plunge into the black passage that leads to Hades" (1105–6), a spatial opposition that also traces an arc of ascent and fall. But where Polymestor and Hekabe match up is in the matter of vision and sight, joined through Orion the blind hunter and the heavenly dog with the burning eyes who accompanies him. The one is deprived of the light of his eyes, the other is all gaze, the fiery look transferred from the celestial star to the mysterious dog who plunges into the sea from the lookout high up on the ship's mast.

Fields of Vision

Fire, sun, golden gleams, shining rays, light, day, life, eyes, vision, and modes of seeing: all these elements are traditionally associated in Greek thought and poetry. They recur in this drama with a remarkable frequency and variety, preparing the way for the twofold surprise of Hekabe's revenge when she blinds Polymestor and slays his children instead of merely requiting her son's death with that of the king, as we (and Agamemnon) are led to expect (e.g., 876–88).[36] Eyes have light (368, 1035, 1069); they shine (1049); they have power, beauty, and erotic appeal. Helen "ruined prosperous Troy most shamefully through her beautiful eyes" (442). "She was the fairest upon whom the golden-gleaming Sun cast its rays" (636–37). Eyes look upon the light of day and gaze at the rays of the sun (248, 412, 435). There are also the encircling rays of golden mirrors in which

---

is called *cholos* and sometimes *menos:* one would like to quench anger (*Il.* 9.678); it makes the eyes blaze as with a gleam of fire (*selas, Il.* 19.16; cf. 1.104); a serpent's fiery gaze (*drakōn . . . dedorken*) is due to its terrible anger (*Il.* 22.93–96). It is worth remarking that for the Romans, the dog was the proverbial symbol for anger (cf. Cicero, *Tusculan Disputations* 3.26.63, where Hekabe is mentioned by name, and also 4.21). Interestingly enough, Stoic sources (Seneca, *De ira* 1.2.3–4; and especially Lactantius, *De ira dei* 17) understand anger as motivated by the desire to repay wrong unjustly suffered *(ad nocendum ei qui nocuit aut nocere voluit),* an appropriate analysis of what happens to Hekabe in our play. For Ovid's version of Hekabe's fate, see Néraudau 1981.

36. Nussbaum (1986, 411–14) discusses the motif of eyes and vision in ways very different from mine.

the young Trojan wife gazes at herself (*leussous[a]*, 926) while combing her hair, and the rays of light in the tent under which the Trojan women gaze at (*leussousai*) the fine embroidery of Polymestor's peploi (1154), observing (*theōmenai*) the skill with which they were made (1155). To look at the light of the sun or of day is to have life (415, 668, 706); not to have it is to die, although in the extremes of misery one can look at the light but claim no longer to exist (668, cf. 1214, 168). For the living to close a parent's eye in death is an obligatory act of piety (430). Sweet sleep is scattered on the eyes, but it prevents the sleeper from seeing the host's advance into Troy on the night of destruction (915, 921). People look at one another; they direct others to look or not look at them; they exhibit their persons to view as figural aesthetic compositions, whether in Polyxena's careful staging of her death on the altar (560–62, 569–70, cf. 355) or when Hekabe demands that she be observed as by a painter, who steps back and regards his handiwork from afar (807–8). People can confront or refuse to confront the gaze of the other. They may be seen to turn their face aside to avoid being supplicated (Odysseus, 342–44) or cast down their eyes out of shame or modesty (Hekabe, 968–75). Women's private things need to be hidden from the eyes of men (570, cf. 1017).

All this visual play in the dramatic setting focuses the theme of sight, but not with the aim, as often in tragedy, of bringing truth to light and revealing what has been hidden from human perception in order to attain a deeper *anagnōrisis* of the workings of the world and the self. The emphasis falls rather on the uses, both metaphorical and literal, of vision, light, and eyes. These converge in the motives for Hekabe's act, which will result in blindness for Polymestor and the intensification of her gaze. Revelation is restricted to the discovery of Polydoros's body and the knowledge of the cause of his death, anticipated from the outset of a play that begins with the "third light of day" after his death, the morning that followed the night when he appeared to his mother as a ghostly dream. His *phasma,* apparition, makes him visible to the audience as the speaker of the prologue;[37] his body is now to be brought on stage for viewing, its identity to be revealed.

This is the central visual event, the turning point of the play at its Dionysiac core in the carefully orchestrated scene that proceeds from identifying the victim to divining the name of his slayer, and it is filled with words for sight and seeing. The body is revealed in stages. Muffled in robes, it seems at first to Hekabe to be the corpse of Polyxena or perhaps that of her other daughter, the bacchant seer Cassandra (676–77). When the body is bared *(gumnōthen),* she is bidden to gaze at its form *(athrē-*

---

37. See Jouanna 1982 for the theatricality of Polydoros's dream visitation in the prologue and its relationship to traditional Homeric representations of dream experience.

son); it is then she beholds (blepō) her dead child whom she names Polydoros, and beginning her wild lament, "having just learned the bacchic
tune of the avenger" (685–87), she takes in with her eyes the shocking
new sight (derkomai) of her child's ruin (679–90). When informed that
his body had been cast up on the shore, Hekabe realizes the truth: "Now
I understand [emathon] the nocturnal sight [ennuchos opsis, 72, 702–4]
that appeared to my eyes [ommatōn] . . . which I saw [eiseidon] of you,
my child, no longer being in the light of Zeus [ouket' onta Dios en
phaei]," (702–6). "It was the accursed Thracian xenos, who rent the flesh
of my child, stabbing his limbs with an iron sword" (716–20). Polymestor's children, as we know, will be stabbed and killed with the same kind
of instrument (1161–62); their maddened father will fear he is abandoning them to bacchants of Hades who will rend their bodies and cast them
out, just as he had done to Hekabe's child.

More interesting, however, is how the drama inside Hekabe's tent will
replay these same gestures of identification and revelation, with Polymestor now as the body in question. This scene will also include echoes of
Agamemnon's reaction to his first sight of Polydoros's unknown body
when he remarks upon its foreign peploi, the clue that marks the motion-
less figure as a Trojan, not an Argive (733–35). Matching this detail is the
women's curious inspection of Polymestor's peploi in the tent, when they
gather around him to admire the Edonian craftsmanship of his robes,
which they examine closely under the light (ὑπ' αὐγὰς τούσδε λεύσσου-
σαι πέπλους, 1153–54). In the first scene, the maidservant bared the
body of Polydoros (gumnōthen) to reveal its identity; the women now
strip Polymestor (gumnon) of both peploi and weapons, so they may com-
mence their revenge (1166).

This first scene of discovery also suggests why Hekabe chooses a revenge that includes the double and simultaneous acts of blinding Polymestor and killing his offspring. One antiphonal cue is sufficient. When the
maidservant arrives bearing the body, she prefaces her awful news by exclaiming to Hekabe: "You are done for; and you no longer exist [ouket'
ei] although you look upon the light [blepousa phōs]; without a child, a
husband, and city, you are utterly destroyed" (668–69). Once her eye falls
on the body, Hekabe too will reply: "I see [blepō] my child now dead . . .
I am ruined . . . I no longer exist [ouket' eimi]" (681, 683). Light is therefore equivalent to child, and one depends upon the other. Without living
children, one may look at the light but yet no longer exist: to look at a
dead child negates one's existence, both present and future, for the child
is often imagined as the light or eye of one's life and also of one's house.[38]

38. See, e.g., Euripides, Andromache 406, and cf. 418 (the child is the psuchē). With
the recovery of Ion, Kreousa exclaims that "the house no longer looks upon the night but

In the women's revenge both these terms are fulfilled and reversed at the same time. The ghost of Polydoros had predicted that on a single day Hekabe would behold *(katopsetai)* the two corpses of her children (45–46). To Polymestor, however, Hekabe declares: "you will never replace the shining light *[omma lampron]* in the pupils of your eyes (1045, cf. 1035, 1067–68) nor will you ever see your children alive since I have killed them" (1045–46). What she means, of course, is "you will not see your children, since you are blind: nor alive for they are dead,"[39] but the curious fusion of terms suggests the symmetry between eyes and children, between one's blindness that is an absence of light and one's children no longer alive. Blind, Polymestor will be seen by others, as will the bodies of his two children (1049–53), but he is henceforth barred from a reciprocity of gaze.

If Polymestor, as I observed earlier, turns his metaphor into reality and his imagery into identity when he prophesies Hekabe's metamorphosis into a dog, Hekabe too in her own way turns the figurative into a literal truth. In so doing, she precisely reverses the paradoxical idea that one could look at the light and yet not exist. Now you will no longer see the light, and yet you still live, not seeing your children, either alive or dead. To the terrible spectacle of having to gaze upon one's dead child, as she did, Hekabe opposes a double penalty: seeing his children killed before his eyes, and becoming a spectacle, to be seen but not to see in return.

Vision, we must recall, is always reciprocal in common Greek notions about optics, which hold that light emanates from the eye as well as from the source of light.[40] It is reciprocal too in social terms, in the relations between one self and another, because each party both sees and is seen by the other in the mutuality of vision. From the moment that Hekabe beholds the body of her dead child, she positions herself in this interplay between seeing and being seen. Indeed, she can be said to take control over vision, spectacle, and revelation in the ensuing scene with Agamemnon. Here again the body is revealed to one who does not know, and the drama of disclosure is emphasized by the long delay between the moment when Agamemnon first catches sight of the body *(horō*, 733) and Hekabe's final consent, after much deliberation with herself, to reveal the mystery of who he is ("Do you see this corpse?" she asks, and "I see it," he replies, 760–61; cf. 766, 833). Hekabe knows too that pity is born from the eyes. When Agamemnon first beholds the body of the unknown Trojan, the

gazes up at the light of the sun" (Euripides, *Ion* 1466–67). A corrupt line of Aeschylus's *Septem* seems to equate two eyes with two children (782); and cf. Euripides, *Phoenissae* 1613. Already in Homer (*Od.* 16.23, 17.41) Telemachos is described as a "sweet light."

39. See Hadley 1904, *ad loc.*

40. See, most recently, Simon 1988.

queen's back is turned and he cannot see her face, but once she has determined to be his suppliant, she asks not just that he look at her but that he
see her in her entire self as a figure of sorrow: "pity me, behold me *[idou]*,
and like a painter, standing at a distance, gaze at me *[athrēson]* in my
sufferings" (807–9). In her last appeal, she will invoke the power of vision
again but now as a metaphor of honor and salvation in aid of her cause,
addressing the king as the *megiston phaos*, "the greatest light" among the
Greeks (841).

This emphasis on vision is highlighted in the choral ode that directly
intervenes between Agamemnon's exit and Polymestor's entrance on the
scene, which looks back to relive the sequence of events on the fateful
night when Troy fell. The second strophe of the song provides a startling
vignette of an interior scene. In the bedroom lies the man on whose eyes
sleep has fallen and who, all unsuspecting, does not see the approaching
doom, while the girl, the young bride, is all eyes, we might say, gazing at
herself in the rays of the golden mirror that returns to her, as in a circle,
the image of that gaze (924–25). This intimate glimpse into a woman's
chamber with its typical object, the mirror, that is the sign of her private
world (so often depicted upon vase paintings) is matched with the equally
feminine gesture of the women in the tent gazing in the light at the fine
embroideries of Polymestor's robes. In both cases, these apparently domestic details direct us to observe how women at home are attentive to
the aesthetic gaze, whether self-regarding or directed to other objects of
beauty. Yet the social rules also dictate that women concern themselves
with the proprieties of vision when confronted with others: whom they
may regard and how in turn they may be viewed.

This shift from private to public, from self to other, directly follows
upon the ode of the girl with her golden mirror once Polymestor arrives
on stage in response to Hekabe's initial summons. The first moment of
their encounter is a brilliant *coup de théâtre*: she has sent for him, he
comes, they converse, but she refuses to look at him. More precisely,
Hekabe refuses him the power of vision over her. She will neither look at
him nor let herself be seen by him. There are two reasons, she says: first,
in her state of misery, she is ashamed to be seen by one who had seen her
in her former good fortune, so she cannot look at him *(prosblepein)* directly (with upright eyes, *orthais korais*); second, custom prescribes that a
woman not look at *(blepein)* a man face to face (968–75). With Polymestor she maintains the proprieties of etiquette or *nomos* (custom) in the face
of one who has transgressed the most serious *nomoi* (laws); she will lull
him into a false sense of security so she can lure him into her tent according to plan. Yet a certain reversibility is implicit in her words, since by
rights it is he who should be ashamed to look her in the eye. In this sense,
she projects onto him the reticence of vision, the *aidōs* (shame/reverence)

he rightly owes to her. In mythic narratives the lack of *aidōs,* best exemplified in the transgression of a visual taboo, is often the underlying cause for the gods' punishment of blindness.[41] When explained, however, in the idiom of human relations, as it is explained by Oedipus, the motive given is the shame he would feel to look upon those he had harmed (Sophocles, *Oedipus Tyrannos* 1371–85).[42] This initial interchange between Hekabe and Polymestor, in which she interrupts the normal flow of vision, thus establishes the cultural norms for the condition of sight. In this play those norms also rely on the mythic exemplars of divine retribution (Lycurgus, Orion) as well as on the semantic play with metaphors of vision, life, and light—all of which are soon acted out, when Hekabe deprives Polymestor of his two eyes and his two children in the Dionysiac way.

Reckoning by Numbers: Two by Two

Two eyes and two children, equivalents of one another in the economy of the family. But in the economics of a matched revenge that requires an exact accounting, point for point, is there not one death too many? Polymestor killed only one of her children. He will later make up the difference, we know, by predicting the death of her last remaining daughter. For now, this is the day on which Hekabe has seen the bodies of two children, the death of one (Polyxena) a necessary preliminary to Hekabe's discovery of the death of the other (Polydoros). Yet if a contrived coincidence brings brother and sister together, each has met a different death and by different hands: one in a ritual sacrifice in full public view, the other in secrecy and stealth. The first, while a gruesome deed, arouses resistance and despair but no thoughts (or power) of retaliation. Although human sacrifice may be an ugly act and demanded in a spirit that corrupts the heroic values of epic,[43] Polyxena, by her mode of dying, turns sacrifice into victory and

41. See Buxton 1980; and for this play, Meridor 1978, 35n.24, on the apt parallel in Nebuchadnezzar's blinding of the mutinous Zedekiah who, like Polymestor, was compelled to witness the killing of his children (2 Kings 25:6–7). For an instructive summary of cases of blinding in mythic and historical contexts, see Collard 1991, 185–86, who concludes that its general purpose was both "to incapacitate and stigmatize."

42. Oedipus does not use the terms *aidōs* and *aischunē,* although his sense of shame is clear enough. Mythically speaking, blinding would have been an appropriate penalty for incest with his mother, in that he saw what he was forbidden to see. Indeed, the fact that he uses her brooches as the instruments of his blinding suggests that she would have been the more likely agent of the deed, as the *Hekabe* also attests; cf. Antoninus Liberalis, *Metamorphoses* 5. (Cf. also the historical case reported by Herodotus, 5.88, of the Athenian women's use of their brooches to stab the single survivor of a battle against the Argives and Aeginetans.) Oedipus, however, extends the range of what he can no longer look upon to include his father, children, city, images of the gods, and the citizens of Thebes, in keeping with the civic issues of that play and the representation of his character.

43. See, e.g., King 1985, although I cannot follow her in all her conclusions.

even steals the show, we might say, from the real hero to whom her death
was consecrated (cf. 315, 348). While Hekabe wonders what clever subtlety *(sophisma)* was involved in voting a sentence of death for her daughter and asks what necessity impelled the Greeks to make a human sacrifice
(anthrōposphagein) over the tomb, where the immolation of an ox would
be more fitting *(bouthoutein, 260–61)*, it is never openly suggested that
the killing of Polyxena is an impious crime. Rather, the cruelty of the deed
is stressed in the refusal of supplication and in the forcible separation of
mother and daughter. Hekabe may appeal to *aidōs* and to pity, to the
invidiousness of the act, and even to its violation of Greek *nomos* regarding the treatment of slaves (286–92), but she cannot claim any more than
this.[44] In Polymestor's case, on the other hand, there is no question as to
the atrocious nature of his deeds. Beyond his violation of the cardinal
moral rules in the treatment of a *xenos*,[45] his act would be judged as murder in a law court and would even oblige the family to prosecute for vengeance on the wrongdoer.[46] These are the legitimate grounds on which
Hekabe can appeal to Agamemnon for the right to vengeance, a right he
never denies, even when first refusing direct assistance, and one he is eventually compelled to confirm when Polymestor demands that the Argive
king adjudicate his case against Hekabe. Polyxena's death cannot be
openly requited in this way, yet her fate is still linked with that of the other
in the dramatic structure of the play, and her funeral rites are deferred at

44. Odysseus offers the counterexample of another Greek *nomos*, that of giving honor
to heroes, which he concedes may involve a charge of *amathia* (crudity). But while Hekabe
demands her rights under Greek (Athenian) law as a *slave*, Odysseus reframes the argument
as a distinction between Greek and *barbarian* usage (326–31).

45. Polymestor is called the "most impious host" *(anosiōtatou xenou)*, who did the
most impious deed *(ergon anosiōtaton, 790, 792)*; he is not *eusebēs* (pious), not *pistos*
(loyal), not *hosios* (pure of heart), and not *dikaios* (just) as a *xenos* (1233–35). There is
irony, of course, in Hekabe's earlier questioning of the Greeks' resort to human sacrifice
(anthrōposphagein, 260) and Agamemnon's indignant remark to Polymestor that "guest-
killing *[xenoktonein]* may be an easy thing for you but is deemed a disgrace *[aischron]*
among Hellenes" (1246–47). But, as we know, Agamemnon argued against the sacrifice of
Polyxena in the public debate, even though he was motivated by his liaison with Cassandra
rather than by higher moral principles (120–28).

46. See Meridor 1978, on the legal merits (and language) of Hekabe's actions as a
necessary corrective to the popular idea that her actions are "impious" and "unjust," judgments that the text never substantiates. Strictly speaking, repayment of two for one is an old
Greek notion (cf. Hesiod, *Works and Days* 709–11) that is codified in laws about theft in
Athens (cf. Demosthenes, 24.114f.) and elsewhere. See further Fraenkel 1962, 2:273–75,
on Aeschylus, *Agamemnon 537 (dipla eteisan)*. The issues of the play concern the principle
of *dikēn didonai* and the crime of murder (rather than theft), not the number of Polymestor's
children. Blinding in any case obviously requires the loss of two eyes. I have raised the question more rhetorically than literally so as to explore the implications of Euripides' double
plot, which has Hekabe lose not one but two children, each by a different hand and for a
different motive.

Hekabe's request until the queen can perform the ceremonies for both her offspring together.

To pose the problem again: two eyes and two children. Polymestor is deprived of both in the symmetry their pairing represents (e.g., 1117–18, 1255: "woe for my children and my eyes"). But if one child answers to Polydoros and the other to Polyxena, does this mean that the vengeance against Polymestor is also designed to perform a double function, one that implicitly responds to two different victims and the two different agents of their deaths?

The most unusual feature of the play is its double plot that seems to consist of "two unrelated events." If the drama is judged as a "unity," this status is generally granted on the grounds of a convenient coincidence, the thematic repetition of certain key moral terms and rhetorical techniques, and above all, the "unifying force of Hekabe's role" as a woman subjected to increasing levels of unbearable suffering.[47] Other studies stress the idea of contrast, especially between Polyxena and Hekabe, in their "roles, nature, fate, and character"[48] or between certain strategic interchanges. The formal conventions of tragic drama call for the second part to reply in kind to the first. Is the *Hekabe* anomalous in this regard? Or is the break of the play into two apparently distinct actions more problematic than previously supposed—and far more provocative—if we can detect how the first half exerts a subtle but profound influence on the second? If this is indeed the case, then Hekabe's plan will assume a fuller shape, serving as a more inclusive rationale for what happens in the tent and afterward, both with respect to the cast of characters and in the enactment and general import of her revenge.[49]

It may be argued that in taking the siblings as a pair, I may be eliding a critical difference between them: one is a daughter, the other a son, the last remaining heir of Priam's house. He might have yet lived to raise up the ramparts of Troy and resettle the city, as Polymestor slyly claims before Agamemnon as his pretext for killing the boy (1139–40). His fate, therefore, is of greater social and ideological weight than that of Polyxena, whose destiny would have been marriage and incorporation into another family circle. Hence it is the failure of the last hope of Troy that spells the finality of the doom of the city and the house and provides the compelling motive for Hekabe's revenge that deprives Polymestor in turn of any continuation of his family line in the reigning paternal order. But Polydoros, both as the ghost who speaks the prologue and as the lifeless corpse brought back onstage, is in a sense only the catalyst for the action, the

---

47. See, e.g., Michelini's summary 1987, 132 and n. 3.
48. Michelini 1987, 134; see also Conacher 1967; and Reckford 1985.
49. The following two paragraphs are added from the original version of this essay.

emotional intensity of which is founded on the daughter's sacrifice, the
event that is fully dramatized before the spectators' eyes and engages their
full attention in the first part of the play. The power of these scenes provides the dynamic energy that fuels the next sequence of events, not just
as the first of two terrible blows to the economy of family relations, but,
in its hidden return in the second, as both the affective and formal basis of
what that economy might mean in terms of the self, the body, and the
civilized community, whether Trojan or Greek.

Polymestor forecasts the metamorphosis of Hekabe and the death of
her remaining daughter, Cassandra. But more important, he also predicts
the death of Agamemnon on his return home and by a woman, his wife,
whose vengeance upon him is motivated by his sacrifice of their daughter,
Iphigenia, at the start of the Trojan war. The curious structure of the play
does not merely displace the moral opprobrium from the Greek army to
the barbarian king, from Polyxena to Polydoros, with a final goal of turning Hekabe from victim to victimizer. No, in displacing the focus from
Odysseus to Agamemnon, it also links up the sacrifice of one daughter to
another (as last to first) and ensures the eventual recoil upon the Greeks
of a retribution that Hekabe's revenge upon a man's killing of her son sets
into motion for the future.

Odysseus, however, is the pivotal figure, paired with Agamemnon as
one Greek to another, each linked with Hekabe as a result of some private
obligation and confronted by her in a scene of supplication. Yet Odysseus
is also in a sense the partner of Polymestor: each is entertained by Hekabe
in a prior relationship of *xenia,* and each, in one way or another, is responsible for the death of her child. Strictly speaking, Neoptolemos, the
officiant at the sacrifice, is the true agent of Polyxena's death, but he never
appears on stage and is never implicated in any way in the dramatic action. Although it was Odysseus who persuaded the Greek assembly to
assent to Polyxena's sacrifice (131–39), he commits no act of violence,
and he arrives on stage only to carry out the Greek army's orders, a fact
that may well account for his disappearance from the scene (and the text).
After all, Polymestor has no reason to vent his anger against any Greek
except Agamemnon, who is directly involved in his affairs. Yet is Odysseus
entirely effaced, or does his figure continue to shape the course of the
action?

The Double Return

Two mythic paradigms are screened behind the figure of Polymestor:
Lycurgus, king of the Edonians in Thrace, an appropriate model for a
Dionysiac play in an Iliadic setting, and Orion the hunter, who with

his dog Sirius matches the two Dionysiac antagonists, Polymestor and Hekabe. But there is yet another relevant figure, the most obvious prototype of all, the one whose shadowy presence would best refer to the first part of this drama and to whom Polymestor is in fact most closely related. This figure, of course, is none other than the Cyclops of the *Odyssey*. It is he who actually fits each of the significant attributes assigned to Polymestor: violator of *xenia*, blinded in revenge, threat of anthropophagy, parting curse. He too inhabits a remote territory by the shores of the sea at which Greeks stop, to their peril, on their journey home from Troy. His name, Polyphemos, most directly evokes the king's name, Polymestor, which, as critics agree, seems to have been invented by Euripides for the express purposes of his plot. Furthermore, the dramatic depiction of a blind character, mad with pain, groping to find his tormentors and destroy them, finds its closest model in the parallel scene in the *Odyssey*. Certainly, as others have observed, Hekabe imitates Odysseus to the extent that, having learned from him the use of rhetorical skills in debate, she reverses her failed supplication with him into her later success with Agamemnon.[50] But perhaps she is imitating Odysseus in more ways than just his political Iliadic role as "counsellor and speaker of words": by taking over his most famous exploit in the *Odyssey*, exchanging the Cyclops, his traditional enemy, for one who looks, sounds, and acts just like him. Once Hekabe has persuaded Agamemnon and embarked upon the machinations of her plot, have we moved from an Iliadic context of warrior community and heroic glory to the Odyssean one of *mētis*, deception, and masquerade?

The resemblances go even further. Oddly enough, if Polymestor recalls Polyphemos, he also recalls Odysseus himself in two ways: first, in details of the scene that subtly suggest another epic moment in the *Odyssey* and second, in allusion to an episode recounted about him in the first part of the play. While these two references differ radically in their contributions to the composite scene before us, both involve settings in which Odysseus responds with some degree of deception to a woman's offer of hospitality. The first instance takes place in *Odyssey*, Book 19, where in his first conversation with his wife, the disguised Odysseus claims to have seen the "real" Odysseus when he landed at Crete on his way to Troy. His proof is the clothing Odysseus was wearing: a magnificent cloak of purple, of such remarkable workmanship that "many of the women were gazing at it in admiration" (πολλαί γ'αὐτὸν ἐθηήσαντο γυναῖκες, 19.235), just as Hekabe and her women do here. Furthermore, this cloak was fastened with a brooch, depicting a fawn struggling in the grip of a dog (19.226–

31), both of which echo in the present scene: the brooches used by the women to blind Polymestor and the proto-Dionysiac depiction of dog and prey acted out in Polymestor's maddened exit from the house.[51]

The second instance is the earlier mention in the play of Hekabe's and Odysseus's encounter in Troy, when Odysseus came as a spy in filthy disguise and supplicated Hekabe, who yielded to his entreaties and saved his life. This is the basis of Hekabe's personal appeal to Odysseus for the life of her child in the name of the *charis*, the gratitude, he owes to her, a claim whose validity he freely admits, "through which he met with good fortune" (301–2). In the *Odyssey,* it was Helen alone whom Odysseus approached on his secret errand, a tale that Helen herself tells in the company of Menelaos and Telemachos (*Od.* 4.240–65). Only in this Euripidean play do we learn the curious fact that Helen then passed him on to Hekabe. In the *Odyssey,* Helen's ulterior motive for recounting the story was to demonstrate her continued fidelity to the Greek cause (and to Menelaos), but why would Hekabe ever have taken this enemy into her house? And once she had him in her power, why would she ever have let him go free?[52] For the purposes of the play, Hekabe's prior contact with Odysseus in Troy in a similar context of supplication reinforces the moral power of her appeal and complicates the neat polarity of enemy and friend. But attention to three significant details will, I think, support the idea that Polymestor also recalls Odysseus himself (especially since two of these were sufficiently odd to attract the scholiasts' attention).

First, when Odysseus came to Hekabe's house in Troy, we hear that he was "unsightly in his filthy clothes" and that "drops of blood dripped down from his eyes onto his chin" (240–41). This strange disfigurement has been explained as alluding to the Homeric version in which Odysseus lacerated himself as part of his beggar's disguise so as to gain entry to Helen's chambers. But the Homeric text only says that he had flogged himself with blows of the lash (*Od.* 4.244). There is no mention at all about eyes or even blood. Second, when Hekabe here reminds Odysseus that in her presence he "sank down and grasped her knees," Odysseus agrees and adds the remark that his "hand 'died' in the folds of her peploi" (245–46). *Enthanein* is the word in question, and the scholiasts gloss its unfamiliar lexical use as *nekrōthēnai,* "to grow numb," meaning, I surmise, that he supplicated her for a long time. The idea of death, implicit in the word *enthanein,* is carried over in Odysseus's reply to Hekabe's further

51. This paragraph represents an addition to the first version of this essay.

52. Scholiast M, *ad* 241, expresses the same puzzlement: "This fiction is incredible and not Homeric: Hekabe would not have kept quiet if she saw an enemy spying upon the Trojans' circumstances, but Helen would naturally have done so because she was repenting of Aphrodite's folly." See also Collard 1991, *ad* 239–50.

inquiry as to what he said when it was he who was her slave: "I invented many things so I would not die *[hōste mē thanein].*" When Hekabe continues to press him ("Did I save you then and send you forth from the land?"), he answers still more directly: "yes, so that even today I look upon this light of the sun" (247–48). Odysseus, with blood running from his eyes, his hand grown dead in Hekabe's peploi, saved by her from death so that he still looks upon the light of the sun: these elements are all repeated when Polymestor, like Odysseus, gains access to the private intimacy of Hekabe's dwelling and, unlike the Greek hero, leaves it with eyes literally dripping with blood, which can no longer look upon the light of the sun. It seems then that the Thracian king, while bearing a strong resemblance to Polyphemos the Cyclops, is also a stand-in for Odysseus himself. Hekabe may herself have "changed places" with Odysseus, yet he is also the hidden target behind Polymestor upon whom she also symbolically (and silently) takes her revenge.

It has been suggested that the satyr play to the *Hekabe* was none other than our one extant example, the *Cyclops*. The date of the play is contested, with the majority of scholars relying on metrical evidence to opt for a later date (412) and one emphatic dissenting voice favoring pairing it with the *Hekabe* (424), precisely on the grounds of parallels between the two plays. Neither side, however, has addressed the context of the *Hekabe* itself—the importance of Odysseus to the first part of the play, the doubling of both Polyphemos and Odysseus behind the figure of the Thracian king—or even the commonality of Dionysiac reference within the two dramas, typical for a satyr play but strongly contrived for the *Hekabe*.[53] It is a tempting hypothesis. The return of Odysseus in the satyr play would answer to his apparent disappearance from the second half of our play, which still keeps traces of his presence in the invented dramatic figure who replaces both himself and his epic opponent, but which defers any direct retaliation until the dramatic sequel. In such a reading, the Polymestor scene can be said to imitate the *Odyssey,* but in turn the *Cyclops* parodically imitates and continues what has already happened in the *Hekabe.*

Despite the obvious virtues of such a Cyclopean coda, it is not an essential factor to support the contention that Odysseus's part in the first half of the play is cunningly refracted in the second. There is another and more obviously absent figure to consider: Odysseus's victim, Polyxena, the other child of Hekabe. Is she just a foil to Hekabe, as so many have ar-

---

53. For the most recent round in the debate, see Seaford 1982, who rejects Sutton's arguments (summarized 1980) that would link the *Cyclops* with the *Hekabe*. He proposes instead a pairing with the *Orestes* of 408.

gued, or is Hekabe's deed also meant to pay back her death in kind? There are some direct continuities: animal imagery is also used of Polyxena,[54] and the same weapon (the sword) and means of death link her sacrifice with both the killing of Polydoros and the revenge on Polymestor's children. Formal criteria are also relevant. By the rules of tragic drama, a Dionysiac scenario of metaphorical sacrifice (here both the death of Polydoros and Hekabe's revenge) requires prior grounding in actual ritual cues or actions (e.g., supplication and sacrifice).[55] Yet the particulars of the text seem to suggest more extensive connections among all these acts. Three times Polyxena speaks of "looking at the light," far beyond what might be expected in a maiden's farewell to life. Each instance occurs at a significant moment in the drama of her sacrifice: her decision to die a voluntary death ("I cast forth this light of liberty from my eyes and dedicate my body to Hades," 366–67); her parting embrace of her mother ("Now for the last time I behold the rays and circle of the sun," 411–12); and her final words of direct address to the light (phōs) as she leaves the stage (435–37). These are traditional utterances, but their reiteration emphasizes the degree to which Polyxena identifies light as life and shows too the value she attaches to the "free light" of her eyes in heroically choosing to die. Hekabe picks up the cue after her daughter departs, returning to the idea of vision, this time her own, as she voices the bitter desire to look upon (idoimi) Helen, for it was "Helen's beautiful eyes which had visited shameful destruction on the prosperous city of Troy" (441–43). Polymestor will wish to escape to the heavens, to Orion and to Sirius, the dog star that "casts forth a fiery glance from his eyes," which I earlier argued was the direct antecedent of Hekabe's "fiery look." With a shift from day to night and from sun to star, however, the Thracian king also echoes the words of Hekabe's daughter.

The thematic of light and eyes is one important strand linking Polyxena to Polymestor. Another is the matching of narrative descriptions that in length and detail contraposes Polymestor's fate with the circumstances of Polyxena's death. Although Polydoros tells us in the prologue that Polymestor has killed him, the ghost is noticeably reticent on how the deed was done. Hekabe, when examining his lifeless form, can only refer to the visible signs on the body, the wounds she sees as evidence of the violence—the Dionysiac violence—he suffered and which she repays in kind on Polymestor's children as well as on their father. But in truth, the symmetries of reversal inside the tent answer more fully and more for-

54. Cf. 142, 205–6, 526, and 90–91 (if genuine).
55. The *Herakles* is the best case in point: supplication, followed by preparation for a purificatory sacrifice, which turns into a Dionysiac scene when Herakles becomes himself a "bacchant of Hades" and slays his wife and children.

mally to three important moments in the first part of the play: Hekabe's separation from Polyxena, the conditions of the maiden's acceptance of her role, and the description of the scene at Achilles' pyre.

First, the setting: on the one hand, a public viewing place with a spectacle staged before an audience of the entire Greek army; on the other, an intimate private space isolated from the prying eyes of men. A second contrast is drawn between robing and disrobing, which links up with the thematic opposition between freedom and constraint. When standing on the pyre, Polyxena, in a remarkable gesture, tears her peploi from the top of the shoulder to the center of her belly to reveal her breasts and bosom *(mastoi kai sterna)*, like those of a beautiful statue. Dropping to one knee, she presents her body to the sacrificer, offering him his choice of striking either her bosom or neck. Yet when she drops under the knife, she takes care *(pronoian)* to fall with grace *(euschēmōn)*, hiding what must be hidden from male eyes (558–70). Earlier I suggested how the women's act in baring Polymestor's body corresponded to the initial unveiling of Polydoros's corpse (1155–56). But it also recalls, and even more strongly, the moment when Polyxena exposes her body by tearing her peploi. This display has other connotations to which I will return, but it also serves as the visible sign of how the girl translates her passion for freedom into a refusal to be touched, already anticipated when she renounced the idea of touching Odysseus in the required suppliant gesture, as her mother had earlier bade her do (342–44). At the altar Neoptolemos first takes Polyxena "by the hand" and the young men hold her down "with their hands" to restrain her from movement (526), but she resists: no man should lay a hand on her, no one should touch her flesh (548), either during the ceremony or, as her mother demands, even afterward when it comes to paying her funeral honors (605, cf. 728–29). Polyxena controls both the display and the concealment of her body in the spectacle she stages before the enemy host. If after her death the men want to cover her with leaves in a gesture of respect and to bring suitable adornment, they may do so only from afar (573, 578).

In Hekabe's tent, however, bodies are pressed together, and the emphasis is on touch—the direct and forceful laying on of hands. Polymestor, seated with bended knee in the tent, is surrounded by the women "on either hand" (1151). They dandle the children "in their hands," they "pass them in turn from hand to hand" (1157–59)[56] before drawing their swords from their peploi, and striking the young bodies with a mortal

---

56. Cf. Hekabe's response to Talthybios's report of her daughter's death: "I know not where to *look [blepō]* amid my ills . . . if I grasp *[hapsomai]* one of them, another stops me, and then another grief summons me, in a relay of ills piled upon ills *[diadochos]*" (585–88). Once again, the metaphorical language of an emotional state is translated into an active reality.

blow. They seize Polymestor, holding down his hands and legs and over-powering him when he tries to aid his children: "If I tried to lift up my face, they held me back by the hair, if I tried to move my hands, I was defeated by their numbers." Then "they bloodied the pupils of his eyes," the text tells us, "striking them with their brooches," as they had struck his children with their swords (*kentousi*, 1171, 1162; cf. 387). Blood is what Agamemnon sees when he enters and asks Polymestor, "Who made you blind and bloodied your eyes *[koras]*?"(1117). Blood is what Poly-mestor desires in his wish to seize Hekabe "with his hands and bloody her flesh" in turn (1125–26). Blood for blood. But blood in the first instance is the essence of Polyxena's sacrifice, required as a drink offering to honor the tomb of Achilles (127, 151, 392, 537), duly reported by Talthybios as the climactic moment when her throat was cut and the blood gushed forth (567–68). A further link between the two scenes may be the pun on *korai* as "pupils of the eye" (1045, 1117, 1170) and *korai* as "maidens." Again and again Polymestor cries out that it is women *(gunaikes)* who have ru-ined him (1071, 1095–96, 1120, 1178), mothers *(tokades)* who fondled his children, but at times he also strangely calls them *korai* (1064, 1152, cf. 485). Why should this be so?

There are two motivations, I believe, for this double confusion, be-tween *korai* as pupils and *korai* as maidens, and between *korai* and *gun-aikes*. The first hints at the significant theme of the erotic body that emerges at strategic intervals in the plot's unfolding; the second attests to the close, even symbiotic bond between mother and daughter that domi-nates the first part of the play and sustains the marked emphasis we find throughout on the physical aspects of human relations and the later move to a maternal Dionysiac revenge.

The Body and Eros

First, the erotic body.

Both mothers and maidens, both women and brides. A man and his children who pay the price for a mother's two children: a son who lies an outcast on the shores of the sea and a daughter who is sacrificed as a bride of death. One body is bared to reveal its identity, another is exposed in a provocative gesture that combines erotic display with a show of untouch-ability, and a third is the unclothed body of Polymestor, constrained by hands that also slew his children. We cannot appreciate the full resonances of these overlapping images unless we consider the significance of the erotic motif in the play. It defines Polyxena in the contradiction of a bride who is no bride, a virgin who is no virgin (612), a condition exemplified in the gesture of baring her untouchable body, which enacts the terms of her former nubile status among the *parthenoi* of Troy as the object of a cherished gaze *(apobleptos,* 355).[57] The passion of eros also motivates Agamemnon in the person of Cassandra, for whose sake he would have saved Polyxena and in whose name he finally consents to accept Hekabe's supplication and allow the queen to take her revenge.

The choral ode on the fall of Troy that intervenes between Agamemnon's exit and Polymestor's first appearance refocuses our attention on this erotic body. I earlier noted the parallels between the young wife in her bedroom at Troy gazing into the mirror and the women's inspection of Polymestor's peploi in the tent.[58] The girl had earlier left her marital bed and rushed forth, like a Dorian maiden *(kora),* she says, clad only in a single garment *(monopeplos),* but she failed to reach the safe haven of Artemis's altar (933–36). Led away in exile, she curses the cause of it all, that other Dorian girl—Helen—whose marriage was not a marriage but "some avenger's woe" (943–51).

Blaming Helen is standard practice in the theater. Everyone does it, starting with Aeschylus's *Agamemnon,* to whose famous Helen ode this passage tellingly alludes, just before Polymestor enters. Helen's maligned figure is so conventional that we are in danger of passing over it as the obligatory nod to the topos shared by Greeks and Trojans alike. But Helen is a significant if shadowy presence that hovers in the background of the *Hekabe,* summoned forth at strategic moments of the plot and involved throughout in a network of significant themes and ideas.

Three times her name recurs in the first part of the play. She is mentioned first in connection with Odysseus's previous supplication of Hekabe at Troy (243) and second when Hekabe suggests that the Greeks sacrifice Helen instead of Polyxena over Achilles' tomb (265–69). The third mention occurs in Hekabe's last words after Polyxena's departure, how she wished she could look upon Helen, whose "beautiful eyes" caused the destruction of Troy (441–43). The choral allusion to Helen as an avenging *alastōr* and to her marriage as a nuptial of woe occurs just before the start of the peripeteia, in the interval between Agamemnon's exit and Polymestor's entrance. But her story had already furnished the theme of the earlier choral ode that divides the first part of the play from the second, coming between the funeral preparations for Polyxena and the discovery of Polydoros's corpse.

This ode has a curious structure that shuttles back and forth in time

---

57. On the associations between defloration and sacrifice, see Loraux 1987, 31–65; on those between sacrifice and marriage, see Foley 1985, 68–102. See also Burkert 1983, 58–71. Polyxena as *korē*: 46, 222, 394, 522, 537, 566; as *parthenos*: 151, 355, 545, 554, 612; as *numphē*: 352, 416, 612.

58. The ode offers a further parallel between the body of the bride's young spouse, whom she sees finally lying unburied on the shores of Troy, and the corpse of Polydoros, equally unburied on the sands of Thrace.

and space, between past and present, Greece and Troy. The strophe recalls the circumstances of Paris's sailing *from* Troy to Helen's bed; she was "the fairest upon whom golden gleaming Helios shines with its rays" (633– 36). The antistrophe reverses direction to look back at the first event, the judgment of Paris, which brought the present disaster *to* Troy. The conclusion spans the distance between Greece and Troy, the first line enjambed with the preceding stanza in spelling the details of Trojan misery (sword, bloodshed, and ruin of their homes), and the remaining verses devoted to women's mourning in Greece. Anticipating a Trojan mother's lament in discovering the body of her child, we hear of a Greek maiden in the house, *poluklautos,* "both weeping and bewept," and a mother too, striking her gray head and "rending her face with bloody nails" in sorrow for her dead children (654–55). Not wives but maidens and mothers, not husbands lost but children dead, the anguish of maternal bereavement shared by all women, an exact preview of what is to follow, as in a mirror image. *Sparagmoi* (rendings), the very last word in the ode, describes the typical mimetic gestures of mourning. It also gives the significant cue for Hekabe's transformation into the Dionysiac mode, the moment when she finds Polydoros's torn body, and cries: "O child, o child, alas, I lead off the Bacchic tune, learned just now from the avenger of woes (*ex alastoros . . . kakōn,* 687).

We detect a kind of mosaic of references in all these allusions to Helen, each different image bearing on the dramatic situation: sacrifice, eros, beauty, eyes, sun, *alastōr,* and grief for children that is turned into bacchic action. Together they furnish a running motif that links the sacrifice of Polyxena with Hekabe's Dionysiac revenge, passing through the transitional moment of the erotic ode on the golden mirror in Troy that both looks ahead to the scene inside the women's tent and answers to Hekabe's previous appeal to Agamemnon "in the name of Cypris, for the sake of Cassandra who sleeps by your side in your bed, entwined in the embraces of love" (825–30).

Hekabe calls Helen by her patronymic, Tyndaris, when she proposes that Odysseus substitute her for Polyxena as a more fitting victim. This is the title by which Polymestor alludes to Helen's sister Clytemnestra at the end of the play, when he forecasts the fate that awaits Agamemnon and Hekabe's other daughter, Cassandra, in Argos. The retribution is exact. "Hekabe's means of persuasion, the sexual relation between her surviving child and the king, will cause the death of them both." [59] But Polymestor's Dionysiac gift of prophecy suggests a more dynamic role for Cassandra, who, as Schlesier observes, is named from the beginning as the authentic source of both mantic and bacchic powers, which are transferred first to

59. Michelini 1987, 172–73.

Hekabe and then to Polymestor. When Hekabe identifies the body on the shore as Polydoros (and not her bacchant daughter, as she had first suspected, 676), she becomes a *mantis*, correctly interpreting the dream she had seen during the night (702–9), although she had initially looked to Cassandra, the expert, to divine its meaning (88–89). Now the queen, turned bacchant herself, prepares her Dionysiac revenge upon Polymestor, who will at the end assume the prophetic gift that traditionally belongs to Cassandra.[60] Through these connections we understand why "once the thought of Cassandra's bacchic madness and the body of Polydoros had driven Hekabe to bacchic lament and led her to undertake bacchic actions, she enlists the help of the lover of the prophesying bacchant."[61]

Cassandra is Hekabe's last resort, when she seems to have failed in her plea to Agamemnon to uphold the laws of justice and the ethical norms of human conduct. *Peithō* (persuasion) is what is called for, some glamorous means by which to win mastery over her hearer and gain her desire. Only then does she appeal to the power of Kypris in the name of Cassandra (825–27). "How then will you show that the nights are dear to you? Or what *charis* will my child receive from the embraces of love in bed, and I of her? For the greatest *charis* comes to mortals from darkness and the charms of the night" (828–32).[62]

No other lines have occasioned more wrathful indignation from critics, who generally point to them as the sign of Hekabe's utter debasement: a woman who would traffic in sex and abandon her moral standards for the sake of revenge. But this double *charis* is an essential concept for interpreting both the scene and the play. Hekabe herself is concerned that this argument may be *kenon*, but the word is ambiguous, encompassing both the idea that her appeal is morally "empty" (persuading the other to do the right thing for the wrong reasons) and the likelihood that this appeal too is "fruitless," destined to fail.[63] More consequential is the question of what *charis* signifies in this passage. Why should it be shared, and on what basis?

At one level, *charis* might simply mean gratitude, favors received for favors given. This is the reading that provokes the charges of vulgar debasement. Sex should not be made into a commodity, not for the girl and certainly not for her mother. But *charis* is also an erotic term (cf. 855),

60. Polymestor foretells the future (and is not believed) just as Cassandra will do in Euripides' later drama, the *Troades*, when she emerges as a raving bacchant and bride of death. See Schlesier 1989, 113–19, 135.

61. Schlesier 1989, 119.

62. I retain these last two lines with Daitz 1971 and Michelini 1987. Diggle contra, and also Collard 1991.

63. On no account should *kenon*, the manuscript reading, be changed to *xenon*, as Nauck and Diggle have it.

suitably used to describe the pleasures of the night. Gratification and gratitude here coincide in this network of human relations, complicated further
by two other such instances. The first is the overlapping between the se-
ductions of sophistic and erotic persuasion, *peithō,* named here as *tyrannos,* an epithet that more usually belongs to Eros (cf., e.g., Euripides, *Hippolytus* 538 and frag. 136N²). The second is a corollary of the first: the
transference of *charis* between mother and daughter (she has a *charis*
from him, and I from her). We have already seen how Hekabe acquires
Cassandra's mantic and bacchic powers in a more generic sense. Here in
demanding the *charis* her daughter should receive from her lover, Hekabe
both attaches herself to Cassandra and appeals to Agamemnon, as she
further argues, to honor that bond by considering the dead boy lying before him as an in-law (833–36). Striving to turn this enemy into a *philos,*
her argument strives to cross the boundary between nonkin and kin but
also attests to the solidarity of the family unit and the reciprocal current
that runs between all its members.[64] I will return to these points. For now,
let us observe that Hekabe's merging of expression and content (her seductive rhetoric, Cassandra's eros) occurs in the suppliant context, in the
physical contact between herself and Agamemnon that reaches its peak in
the lines that immediately follow, when the queen concludes her passionate appeal with a strange and desperate wish: "If only," Hekabe cries,
"there might be a voice in my arms, my hands, my hair, and the step of
my foot, either through the arts of Daidalos or one of the gods, so that
weeping in unison, they might grasp your knees and launch [or enjoin]
words at you of every kind" (836–40). The coherence of the body's form
dissolves and yet reunites, gathering force and intensity along the way. To
divide is also to multiply, and the singular would become a plural in order

64. Tarkow (1984, 134) too views Hekabe's argument as the sign of her belief "in the
transference of obligation from generation to generation" and "the equivalence of value of
any family member for any responsibility or duty." But he judges it self-serving exploita-
tion, claiming that Hekabe suffers such anguish because "such beliefs are at odds with the
way in which the world operates." Tarkow is correct in observing the obsessively numerous
references to children and lineage in the play (*pais, teknon,* and the use of patronymics). But
like so many others, he focuses mainly on the contrast between Hekabe's "moral collapse"
and Polyxena's "moral purity," which he takes as an ironic invalidation on Hekabe's part of
the significance of bonds between parents and children (or between generations), without
specifying either Greek notions about the reciprocal nature of these relations or the values
attributed to the maternal role. He thus reads the theme of children in terms of what they are
supposed to represent (innocence, hope, and progress) and reduces the moral tensions and
dramatic intricacies of the play into a sentimental homily, a "sad lesson" that teaches us that
in hard and inconstant times, the continuity of familial relations fails to serve as a measure
of "constancy and permanence" or to sustain the idea of a "hereditary nobility." On the
contrary, it seems that the "lesson of the play," if any, is that men ignore or destroy these
bonds to their peril, a typically tragic pattern.

to put irresistible pressure on the other's body—the knees she would grasp, the hand she hopes he will offer her (842, 851). He succumbs to the pity evoked by the suppliant's clinging touch, to the *charis* of Cassandra's erotic embraces (850–56, cf. 855, 874). If the body is here parceled out and enumerated in its component parts, the better to engulf Agamemnon with the power of her touch and voice, Hekabe's suppliant appeal begins by presenting the opposite image of the body, one that centers on distance and vision in the perception of its form: "Pity me, behold me [*idou*], and like a painter, standing at a distance, gaze at me [*athrēson*] in my sufferings" (807–9).

I earlier quoted this passage in the context of eyes and sight. I invoke it again for comparison with the stance of the other daughter, Polyxena, when she stood at the altar like a beautiful statue, with breasts and bosom bared, one knee dropped to the ground (558–61). Hekabe takes up the pictured image of her daughter's body and applies it to her own visible form. Yet, although baring her breasts and bosom can be construed as an erotic gesture, a visible sign of Polyxena's contradictory status as a bride who is no bride, the gesture indicates her intrinsic identification with her mother's body, the nourishing *mastoi* and *sterna* (cf. 142), which she directly apostrophizes in her maiden's farewell (424). Both maternal and erotic, the breast and bosom are shared in the physical intimacy of mother and daughter, emphasized at the moment of their separation, repeated (and enacted) mimetically at the moment of Polyxena's death.

Somatic Economies

Cassandra and Polyxena, two daughters of Hekabe: one replaces the other in determining the postures and attitudes of the mother's body, and both are recalled in the presence of that other body, Polydoros's corpse, which lies at Hekabe's feet and to which the queen explicitly gestures as she persuades Agamemnon to help her cause. Cassandra was essential to Hekabe's revenge, essential too for Polymestor, as spelling out Hekabe's loss of her last remaining child. But this daughter belongs to Agamemnon as much as or more than to Hekabe. She is destined to be his partner even in death after the end of the play. Polyxena, by contrast, is Hekabe's very own, the support of her self, her other self, to whom she is inextricably bound; "she gladdens me," says Hekabe, "and I forget my ills; she is my consolation, my city, my nurse, my staff, and guide of my way" (280–81).

It was Polyxena's burial rites that brought Agamemnon on the scene and that led in the first place to the discovery of Polydoros's body, the event that motivates the desire for vengeance that governs the rest of the drama. But Hekabe's revenge is also predicated, as we have seen, on

elements borrowed from the first part of the play, both in the veiled
references to Odysseus and in the replay in reverse of Polyxena's sacrifice.
Hekabe's successful supplication of Agamemnon was the necessary preliminary to that retaliation, but her failed supplication of Odysseus established the conditions, I will argue, for the mode of its enactment. These
two scenes in which Hekabe strives to make contact with her enemies
serve as foil and antithesis to one another in their antiphonal echoes. From
Hekabe's experience with Odysseus, she learns much about the seductive
arts of persuasion, lessons she can put to use once she fails to persuade
Agamemnon (and Odysseus before him) with appeals to *nomos* and justice, to pity and *aidōs*. The question, above all, revolves around the various implications of *charis* and the kinds of transaction the term may
imply. Hekabe's resort to the argument of *charis* with Agamemnon combines the power of rhetoric with that of eros; as such, it links up with the
women's earlier characterization of Odysseus as the demagogue, "the
sweet speaker who gratifies the people to win their favor" (*hēdulogos
dēmocharistēs,* 131–40, 254–57) and so to persuade the Greeks to sacrifice Polyxena. In this sense Hekabe may be said to "change places" with
Odysseus and to adopt the tactics she had formerly decried, transferring
to the private domain the principles that were said to be operating in the
public sphere. But the primary issue at stake involves the *charis,* "gratitude," owed to Achilles, "the best of the Danaans," and the *charis* owed
by Odysseus to Hekabe. How and on what basis are favors to be given
and repaid? [65]

Odysseus had been Hekabe's suppliant in Troy. On his knees, he had
touched her hand and cheek. She wants him to return the favor (*anta-
dounai,* 272) now that the roles are reversed, now that it is she who
touches him (*anthaptomai,* 275). The *charis* she wants is that he not tear
Polyxena from her hands, that he not kill her child (276–78). Sufficient
numbers have already died (278), she pleads. In acknowledging his debt,
Odysseus reckons precisely by the law of the talion, one in return for one.
She saved him, so he is ready to save her body *(sōma),* and hers alone
(301–2). Another *charis* takes precedence, the one owed to the hero

---

65. Polymestor will later plead speciously that he killed Polydoros to give *charis* to the
Greeks as his allies (1175), a point that Hekabe refutes (1201, 1211) and in which Agamemnon concurs (1243). For the theme of *charis* in the play as it pertains to the management of
tragic drama, see Saintillan 1987, who emphasizes (1) the double meaning of *charis* as both
eunoia (benevolent attitude with its corollary, gratitude) and *hēdonē* (the attraction of pleasure) and (2) the absence of a "good" *peithō* (such as Athena's in the *Oresteia*) to mediate
between *charis* and *timōria* (revenge). See also Conacher 1967; for a political analysis of
charis in an Athenian context (and with reference to this play and the *Oresteia*), see Oliver
1960, 92–117.

Achilles as his share of honor for his exploits. This is the *charis* that lasts, the sort Odysseus would want for himself after his death, and the one needed to justify the risks men take in war (309–24).

One body and no more. Hers and not that of Polyxena. She makes yet another appeal, once Polyxena has determined on her sacrificial death. Take me instead, Hekabe says, if a *charis* for Achilles is needed (383–88). Again Odysseus refuses, saying that "the ghost did not ask for you but for her" (389–90). Mother and daughter are not interchangeable but exist as separate and distinct entities, one life given in requital for the *charis* of supplication, one death given in requital for the *charis* of heroic valor. "Then kill me along with my daughter; the corpse and the earth will thereby receive a double drink-offering of blood" (391–93). No, the death of the maiden is enough. No need to add one to the other (394–95). His arithmetic remains precise: two are too many, either to save Polyxena in addition to Hekabe, or to double the sacrificial offering made to Achilles.

For Odysseus, the self is a single unit. It cannot be substituted or added to another's, but within these autonomous limits, the self is nothing more than a body and objectified as such. The question of innocence or guilt that involves the whole of a human actor is beside the point. Its relationship to other selves is transactional and also revolves around the uses of the body: the *sōma* of Hekabe is granted in return for Odysseus's through the medium of suppliant contact; the same is refused for Polyxena and signified by "hiding his hand under his robe and turning his face away, lest the girl touch his chin" in the protocols of appeal (342–44).

Hekabe views matters differently. For her, it is a "necessity" *(anankē)* to die together with her daughter, but for Odysseus, with his politics of force and his distinction between victor and vanquished, her talk of necessity is a sign of a slave's insubordination. Odysseus treats her as a single self; for Hekabe to be singular is also to be solitary. She resists: she will cling to Polyxena like ivy to an oak, she will not let her go. Mother and daughter are fused in somatic interdependence: their hearts melt at each other's grief (433); each shrouds her head or body in peploi (432, 487). Polyxena accepts their separation at the last, the cruel tearing away she earlier deplored (207–8). She is ready for her fate, to lie apart from her mother in Hades (418), and ready too for a last embrace: "Give me your hand and press your cheek to mine," she says (409). At the end Hekabe begs for the same: "O daughter, touch your mother, stretch forth your hand" (439–40). Hekabe's strength leaves with her daughter (438–40). The form of her body dissolves, and "her limbs are loosened [*luetai melē]*" (438).

The woman, it seems, relies on the power of touch, of contact with other bodies, whether in supplication or in erotic embrace. Above all, she relies on the corporeal unity between children and parents that attests to their shared identity and their mutual self-definition,[66] for each without the other can equally be called an orphan (149), and in the inexorable march of time, the *trophē* granted by the nurturant mother is returned in kind by the daughter as nurse (*tithēnē*, 281). This is the originary symbiotic economy Hekabe reinstitutes in her revenge on Polymestor: baring his body, piercing his children and his eyes, waging a war against him in a parody of heroic valor with the "best" of the Trojan women (1052, cf. 134). The enforcement of this economy puts him in the feminine condition as bacchant and stages his losses to correspond to her own. Hekabe repeats upon him in miniature the violent rupture she herself had endured, for the women's seizure *(sunharpasai)* of his children in forcible separation replays the earlier seizure of her daughter, "snatched *[anarpastan]*, like a young mountain animal, from her mother's hands" (207–8), as Polyxena cries first and Hekabe does later after her daughter's death (513). At the end of the play, Polymestor too will be dragged off stage, thus changing places with Hekabe, who previously had yielded to her daughter's persuasion to give up her resistance, "so as not to be dragged away" and subject her aged body to further humiliation (405–8). In Polymestor's Cyclopean aspects, he may recall his counterpart in the *Odyssey* with the implications we have already discussed, but in this context, his name joins up with that of Polydoros and Polyxena in a unity of semantic reference that ironically replicates a triadic family of secret sharers, indissociable finally from one another, and all tended by a mother's hands.

Dionysos and the Body's Revenge

Like all tragedies, the *Hekabe* is a drama of human relations, involving friend and enemy, kin and nonkin. Like most, it is structured around distinctions between the world of women and the world of men. It goes further, however, in several ways. First, gender relations are radically polarized in the distribution of power. The play initially assigns all the power to men and none to women in the circumstances of war. It takes as the foundation of its plot the violence inflicted by men, not once but twice, upon women and upon their young, a violence that is more than matched in the counterturning of the drama and the staging of a woman's revenge. Second, there is an increased complexity in the dynamics of these relations. Three different interests (Greek, Trojan, and Thracian) are involved, and the shifting alliances and mediations among them are charted each time through some transaction that concerns the body of a child of Hekabe: a sacrifice for Achilles, a bedmate for Agamemnon, a fosterling for

---

66. See Loraux 1990, 79, for the physical intimacy between a mother and her children, especially her daughter.

Polymestor. Third, most notably, all human relations in the play are expressed and determined by the body, whether in contact or disjunction, supplication or slaughter, embrace or lament. No other play forces upon us so insistently the sheer physicality of the self and its component parts: the head, face, cheek, neck, throat, eyes, breasts and bosom, hands, arms, flanks, knees, feet, flesh and blood.[67] Our attention is drawn to the body upright or prone, vigorous or weak, alone or assisted, naked or clothed, free or constrained, alive or dead.

Suffering and death, of course, are the usual circumstances in tragedy for spotlighting the corporeal status of the self. This is never truer than in the treatment of the body after death, when it is no more than an inert and defenseless object and for this reason requires cultural intervention to certify the new status of the self in relation to the living and its former life. On these grounds alone, the focus of the play, signaled at the beginning by the ghostly double of the dead and the subsequent display of its inanimate body on stage, might account for the relentless interest throughout in the somatics of human relations. This is especially the case because the cause of death is violent murder and betrayal and the corpse has been cast out, unburied and alone. Its dishonoring is contrasted ironically with the honors to be paid to another corpse, which is made the occasion for discovery of the first one. The irony is sharpened further by the motive for this second death, because the sacrifice of Polyxena is an excess of honor paid to the heroic dead in the name of a masculine military code that demands another death as its right. Between excess and deficiency, overvaluation

---

67. Most of these have already been discussed. In addition to eyes and hands, the many references to knees occur within the suppliant context, as might be expected. The foot, however, is also prominently featured as a formal framing device at the beginning, climax, and end, and as a special motif that links Hekabe with Polymestor in reverse. At the end of his prologue, the ghost of Polydoros prepares us for the entrance of his mother by announcing his intention to withdraw, "to get out from underfoot," as he says (*ekpodōn chōrēsomai*, 52–54). At the climax of the play, Hekabe comes forth again, and echoing his words and gestures *(ekpodōn apeimi kapostēsomai)*, she prepares us this time for the exit of blind and furious Polymestor from the interior of her tent (1054–55). Both exits emphasize the gait, the placement of the foot. There we saw Hekabe, crossing the threshold, struggling to remain upright, trying to hasten her "slow-footed steps" and needing support (53, 65–66; cf. 169, "o wretched foot"; and 812, 837). Here Polymestor comes out in front of the audience, "blind and with blind foot," and goes before us with "four-footed gait, putting a hand in the foot's track" (1057–58), listening for the "stealthy footfall" of the women so he can find and catch them (1070–71; cf. 1039, "you will not flee with swift foot"). Earlier he had claimed to Hekabe: "I was just leaving, raising my foot and your servant fell in with me" (965). He later inquires: "Why did you send for my foot from the house?" (977). In the closing lines of the play, his turn too will come to be *ekpodōn*, but only now as taken by force at Agamemnon's orders and removed permanently from the scene (1282). This will happen, however, only after his prediction of Hekabe's climb "with her foot" to the top of the ship's mast, herself transformed now into a dog "with fiery gaze" (1264–65).

and undervaluation of the dead, there is yet a third term. This is the metaphorical condition of death as the privation of the living, which in breaking the bond that binds one self to another will cancel out and negate a
living existence. This dependency on another self is heightened by the circumstances of the vanquished, which have eliminated any other mode of
being and have frozen the members of a nuclear family into a closed circularity of affective relations. In the wake of a destroyed city, the individual, particularly the child, assumes an increased charge of meaning and
is called upon to embody all that has been lost—city, hearth and home,
social status, and the fabric of communal life. For the victors, on the other
hand, the inverse is true. Now is the time when a person can most easily
be reduced to the status of a mere body, a *sōma,* and nothing more. The
action and reaction of the play are staged in the face of this radical difference between victor and vanquished, producing what I have called the
"pure" Dionysiac effect that reaches its climax in the familiar theatrical
idiom of a maenadic scene.

This Dionysiac scenario is governed by standard rules of operation in
the theater. Men instigate the original offense, women retaliate, and the
violence of the first is more than outdone by the savagery of their later
reprisals. Women play true to form, passing through three predictable
stages: from grief to wrath and then to revenge,[68] which plots a deception
that ends in an assault on the body of the other, expressed in the form that
parodies the usual feminine, especially maternal, role. Characteristically,
competing claims conflict: public vs. private concerns, calculation vs.
emotion, power politics vs. moral principles. These issues divide according to gender lines and are dramatized in the disposition of outside and
inside spaces. Hekabe is the only standard-bearer in the play for an objective moral order: the norms of justice and fair treatment, the sanctions of
respect and pity for the weak, the rules pertaining to *xenia,* and, of course,
the proper treatment of the dead.

At the same time, Hekabe is also the most closely connected to the
syntax of the body—its intimate physical relations with others, its expressive gestures and attitudes, and its overwhelming intensity of feeling, as
exemplified in the somatics of supplication and mourning. Hekabe therefore stands both above and below the operative politics of force and expediency in which the body of the other is depersonalized, made a spectacle for others' eyes or discarded as no longer useful. The standards of
manly excellence insist first on the value of an individual life and second
on the fact that a hero's peers must recognize his valor after death to justify his dying. The test of manliness *(andreia)* is therefore the transvalua-
tion of the physical body, which in its heroic context is defined by the risks

68. See also Loraux's discussion (1990, 76) for this threefold progression.

(kindunos) it takes, all the better to transcend its corporeal limits in the end. The uses of this male body are therefore public and are opposed to its physical satisfactions or desires in the private sphere. In this respect, although Odysseus and Agamemnon both pursue the course of self-interest, their actions situate them at either end of the spectrum of masculine conduct. Odysseus austerely shuns any physical contact with the other by refusing a suppliant touch, but by the same token, Agamemnon shows that a man may be touched if he has already proved susceptible to a body's allure. In the public arena, Agamemnon's first espousal of Polyxena's cause is scorned by his peers: war is stronger than love, and the claims of Cassandra's *lektra* (bed) must give way to those of Achilles' *logchos* (spear, 128–29). The public self wins out over the private one, but it is on these precise grounds that Hekabe can make common cause (and contact) with her daughter's lover (providing it remains private) and so clear the path to the direct physical enactment of her revenge.

However the theater stages its dramas of embodiment and charts the physical states of its characters as they occupy the stage, its closures will continually move toward some transcendence of these brute corporeal facts of human existence and the literal (and temporal) boundedness of the self. Closure may come about through some kind of divine intervention, through the uses of ritual that will symbolically transform the experience for future generations, or through a civic institution established in response to the dilemmas posed by the action of the play. Closure may also come about through an encounter between two or more persons that looks to reconciliation, but it is always available through the public acknowledgment of death itself and the ritual forms of funeral rites. The performance of these rites underlies the action of the *Hekabe;* they begin after the announcement of Polyxena's death, are interrupted by the discovery of Polydoros's body, and are then deferred to allow the brother and sister to be buried together, only to be dispatched summarily at the end in Agamemnon's order to Hekabe to bury her children before they must all depart (1287–88). No ceremony takes place on stage, no formal mourning—in marked contrast, for example, to that other Euripidean drama, the *Troades,* which in situation and cast of characters most closely resembles the *Hekabe.*

In the *Troades,* Hekabe suffers the same losses (replace Polydoros with Astyanax); she is the same wasted and grieving mother and is charged too with the task of burial rites for children. Her one act of resistance (against Helen) remains in the sphere of words, not deeds, and if the queen ostensibly wins her case on its judicial merits, she (and the myth) know that she ultimately fails. The two play diverge most sharply in the role of the gods. They are absent from the *Hekabe* (with the exception of Dionysos's oracle at the end) but all too present in the *Troades,* where gods speak the prologue, condemn what they see as impiety, and forecast disaster for the homeward-bound fleet. They have been intimately involved in the fate of the city: Poseidon as the local god who is now to take his leave and Athena, who once championed the Greeks until they violated her altars, precisely in the matter of a girl seized from sanctuary by force (*Tro.* 69–71). Here too, although the play celebrates the glory that was Troy, the city is no more. The final fall of its burning towers coincides with the end of the play, but divine agency, through the appearance of the gods as well as through Cassandra's divinely inspired prophecies for the future, obviates the need for a human avenger on stage.

Most notable of all, the *Troades* too has a powerful Dionysiac referent. It comes early in the play rather than at its end, in the mad scene of Cassandra, the doomed bacchant bride of Agamemnon (*Tro.* 306–461), and concerns dire predictions, although the drama never delivers to its audience the full resonance of this opening cue. Rather, the Dionysiac import is muted, returning only in muffled and diminished form in Hekabe's arrangement of Astyanax's mutilated corpse for burial, during which, by addressing each part of the body in turn, she restages a kind of Dionysiac *compositio membrorum* (*Tro.* 1156–1250), such as we later find in more explicit form at the end of the *Bacchae*. Even more muted is a fleeting gesture that might be construed as a Dionysiac allusion: after the burial Hekabe evinces a sudden, mad desire to cast herself into the flames of the dying city. This is a likely interpretation, both because the desire is framed in the language of bacchic *enthousiasmos* (*Tro.* 1284) and because the flames correspond to those that first issued from the captive women's tents, heralding Cassandra's maenadic entrance on stage with her nuptial torches (*Tro.* 298–303). But it is only a brief and transitory impulse, which the old queen is not permitted to fulfill in a play that emphatically turns away from enacting a Dionysiac scenario and that focuses its energies instead on the funerary ritual that closes both the play and the history of Troy with a last, extended lament for the city itself.[69] Two factors, therefore, seem to be essential for deflecting the full force of the negative Dionysiac paradigm when a city itself no longer exists: the presence of the gods and the performance of funeral ceremonies for the body, which dignify the dead and the community to which the individual once belonged. The end of the *Hekabe,* however, even as it gives us a juridical decision in favor of Hekabe, remains throughout at the somatic level of the body. Polymestor is dragged away by force; he predicts the grotesque corporeal

---

69. In her last dirge, Hekabe in the *Troades* bewails the fact that Priam was cast out unburied and, as the chorus adds, "dark holy [*hosios*] death covered his eyes in unholy slaughter [*anosiais sphagaisin*]" (1313, 1315–16). Priam is a symbol of Troy itself, but his burial does not become an issue in this play (or in the *Hekabe* either, where his sacrificial death is mentioned only in the prologue, 21–24).

change in form for Hekabe and, in another reference to *mania,* foretells Agamemnon's and Cassandra's bloody deaths to come. The *loutra* (lustral waters) that were sought in Thrace for the tending of Polyxena's body will turn into the *phoinia loutra* of Agamemnon's bloody bath in Argos (1275–81), and the cycle of physical violence will continue, as we already know, in what is to happen far from Troy and even farther from Thrace.[70]

Hekabe's revenge on Polymestor and his children has shocked critics who construe her calculated cruelty as the sign of the erosion of her character, even if justice is on her side because her sufferings are so undeserved and Polymestor's offenses so unredeemable. But the play has its own internal logic, unrelated to these pious and probably anachronistic scruples. The problem, as Ann Michelini well states it, resides in the change from a drama of suffering to a drama of revenge in which the reversal of roles also entails a hidden identification: "The perfect revenge demands reciprocity between the wronged and the wronger, so that comparable wounds are suffered by each, and each becomes the image of the other."[71] Retaliation is a form of repetition that binds both parties together in a relationship of equivalent exchange that, by demanding the matching of term for term, also retains the symmetrical balance between the self and the other, regardless of the ethical differences between the two sides. The problem of vengeance in Greek drama is further complicated by the conflicting emotions of satisfaction and terror it arouses in the spectator.

But Hekabe's revenge strikes an even deeper note of anxiety because its chosen form entails a full and final reversion to the unsublimated (or desublimated) body against which, or in suppression of which, we usually mobilize defenses of all sorts—in art as in life. These defenses are mounted precisely against the power and will of the mother who is physically bound to her children by the fact of having carried them within her body and who, having given birth to them, continues to nourish them from her own physical substance. The bond of maternity is never stronger than when it involves the relation of mother and daughter, a unity composed of same to same, which is encoded at the very heart of Greek belief in the paradigmatic myth of Demeter and Persephone and the resistance engendered by

---

70. Space does not permit discussion of the play as the "prehistory" or "aetiology" of Aeschylus's *Oresteia.* For some parallels, see Tarkow 1984; and for Agamemnon's role, see Meridor 1983. Note, however, that the fate predicted for Agamemnon and Cassandra is based on their sexual bond, which here leads Agamemnon to give this Trojan mother her freedom to act (in ironic counterpoint to his own previous sacrifice of his daughter). In the *Oresteia,* Clytemnestra will react as a wife to Agamemnon's return with his new love, Cassandra, but above all she will react with an avenging anger as the mother who has lost her daughter. The Aeschylean echoes begin in earnest from the second stasimon, which precedes the king's entry onto the stage (659–66) and recalls the Helen ode in the *Agamemnon.*

71. Michelini 1987, 170; see also Burnett 1973.

their separation.[72] Although in this play it is the son's body that elicits the mother's devastating revenge, the revenge itself replies even more directly to the forced disunion of mother and daughter and the mimetic circularity of being that defines them—cheek to cheek, hand to hand, and breast to breast.

At the same time, Polymestor's offense not only violated the strict codes of *xenia* but also specifically rejected a foster parent's role of nourishing and rearing *(trophē)* another's child as his own (20, 1134, 1212). "If you had reared *[trephōn]* the child as you ought to have reared him *[echrēn trephein]* and thus saved his life," Hekabe declares to Polymestor, "you would have won a fair renown *[kleos]*" (1224–25). "And if you lacked for money and my child had prospered, he would have been a great treasure *[thēsauros . . . megas]* for you" (1228–29). Now Polymestor has lost this *philos* along with the benefits of gold and the lives of his own children (1230–31).

The continuity between mother and daughter is marked in this play not so much through the attachment of birth as in the sharing of "breast and bosom" and in the reciprocity of nurture (281, 424). Nurture or breeding again is the quality invoked by Hekabe in evaluating the heroic death of her daughter when she debates whether Polyxena's conduct derived from the hereditary influence of her begetters *(hoi tekontes)* or the manner of her nurture *(trophai, 599)*. In this Dionysiac scenario, Polymestor may play the part of Lycurgus who persecutes the child, but he is also, as we have seen, a failed *trophos*. Although men cannot bear children, they can join up with maternal interests in giving nurture. In this sense, the Dionysiac child is signified not only in the intimate relation between mother and child (as in the *Bacchae)* but also in the theme of fosterage by which the child may also be reared by others, as in this play (and the *Ion*), where male and female each have a part to play in the physical and moral nurturing of a child.[73] Polydoros will never live to serve as a substitute for the lost Polyxena, nor, as his sister promises, will he ever close his mother's eyes in death in the required ritual gesture (430). He

72. See also Loraux 1990, 57–65, 75–76, on the dangers that mourning mothers pose to the body politic and the significance of their maternal ties.

73. Critics have uniformly overlooked Polymestor's responsibility for rearing the child (note the emphasis in the text of *trephein* and *trophē*: 20, 232, 424, 599, 1134, 1181, 1212, 1224) and hence judge Hekabe's famous remarks at the news of Polyxena's death concerning nature and nurture, the shameful and the noble (591–602) not only as a eulogy for Polyxena but also, as Reckford (1985, 118–19) puts it, as "a funeral oration for herself . . . eulogizing the nobility that she must lose while still living." Reckford goes on: "What is really tragic is the inner death of the being who was called Hekabe. She suffers what Polyxena escaped, a kind of rape." See also, for example, the conclusions of Tarkow 1984; and Michelini 1987, 141. The semantics of the text warn against such facile moral judgments.

will also never be a future *thēsauros* for Polymestor who should have nurtured him as his own and for whom he would have been a better recompense in time of need than all the golden treasure of Troy. At the same time, Dionysos himself in the role of the stranger god, as many of his myths attest, is the bearer of gifts (viniculture). He gives gifts *(dōra)* to his host but expects to be given *xenia* in turn. Since wine is the acculturating substance of social relations between nonkin, Dionysos's arrival initiates (and enforces) the system of reciprocal exchange on which society is based, which especially includes mutual obligations of hospitality. From this point of view, the two names of Hekabe's children, Poly*xena* and Poly*doros,* complement one another as embodiments of these principles in abundance *(polu* = much). Violation of these norms appropriately earns a typically Dionysiac revenge, as in this play, in the form of retaliation upon one's own. Hekabe may play the part of the avenging Erinys, but she does so, as Polymestor correctly divines, under the name of Dionysos.[74]

These are the various convergent factors that mobilize the response of Hekabe and her collective of women who, although compared to other feminine groups, such as the Danaids and the Lemnian women (886–87), enact a specifically Dionysiac revenge: on the one hand, a return *to* the notion of an unsublimated body as defined in and through its physical parts and its corporeal bonds as a family member and, on the other, an act given in return *for* the refusal to honor the ties of *xenia* that obligate the self to others who are not of its own blood.[75] The Dionysiac effect then

74. On the implications of Dionysos's status in many of his myths as a *xenos* (stranger or guest), see Massenzio 1969, 71–81. and 110–13. In brief, he argues that myths relating the advent of Dionysos among men, whether of positive or negative outcome, belong to a single system of acculturation with three major elements: (1) the acceptance of a new god; (2) the acceptance of a new type of agriculture (the vine), whose product, when used correctly, serves as a "cultural instrument of social relations"; and (3) the acceptance of relations between nonkin, which the correct use of wine requires and indeed facilitates. The logical outcome of the refusal of the god and his gifts is a retaliation that takes the form of some autodestructive action within the family. See further note 75, below.

In this Dionysiac perspective, Polymestor's offense against *xenia* assumes a more profound meaning, as does the mode of retaliation, both in Hekabe's reception of him inside her tent as a form of *xenia* and in the revenge she exacts upon his children in return for his failure to show the *xenia* of *trophē* to hers.

75. Aelian, *Varia Historia* 13.2, recounts an anecdote that perfectly demonstrates Dionysiac mechanisms of cause and effect in the relations between self and other, whereby the violation of *xenia* protocols leads to an autodestructive retaliation upon the self and its own: Makareus, a man of Mytilene, was a priest of Dionysos, gentle and affable in outward respects but in reality the most impious *(anosiōtatos)* of men. A stranger/guest *(xenos)* came to him and gave him a quantity of gold as a deposit entrusted to his care. Makareus dug a hole in the inner recesses of the shrine and buried the gold there. In time the *xenos* returned

becomes fully manifest through the maenadic interchange of Hekabe and
Polymestor. It continues in his subsquent empowerment as a Dionysiac
oracle that challenges the ideal of the self as an autonomous, stable unit
and that turns metaphor of speech into permanent physical fact. By so
doing, the drama thwarts at the end, as it must, any of those cherished
conversions from local to transvalued levels of meaning, which are promoted by divine and civic structures in the service of communal life and
networks of social exchange. Instead, by the logic of its dramatic enactment, the play converts the only figure who supports such ideals into an
avenging Erinys in the guise of a bacchant of Hades, with the violent consequences we have seen. Even the *Bacchae*, the explicitly Dionysiac paradigm of the regressive order of things, will not reach this degree in revealing those darkest of secrets that reside in the exposed and tangible form of
the human body. Dionysos in Thrace goes more than one step beyond
Dionysos in Thebes.

---

and asked for the gold back. Makareus brought him inside as though to give back the deposit
but slaughtered him instead *(katesphaxe)* and having dug up the gold, put the body of the
xenos there in its place. He thought he could escape the god's detection just as he had fooled
the others. But matters turned out otherwise. A short while later, at the trieteric festival,
Makareus offered sacrifices of great magnificence. And while he was busy with the Dionysiac
celebration *(bakcheian)*, his two children were left inside the house. Imitating *(mimoumenoi)*
the father's sacred offices *(hierourgian)*, they came to their father's altar where the offerings
were still burning. The younger child stretched out his throat and the older one, who had
found a sacrificial knife *(sphagida)* that had been overlooked, killed his brother as a sacred
offering *(hiereion)*. The folks in the house raised up a shout, and the mother, hearing their
cries, leaped up *(exepēdōse)*, and seeing the one child a corpse and the other still holding the
bloody knife, snatched up a half-burned piece of wood from the altar and killed this child in
turn. The news came to Makareus who abandoned the rites *(tēn teletēn)* and rushed into the
house *(eisepedēsen)* in haste and anger *(thumōi)* and with the thyrsos he was still carrying
killed his own wife. The story ends with the revelation of the deed, Makareus's confession
under torture, as a result of which he died, and the account of how the one who was slaughtered *(sphageis)* unlawfully was honored publicly with burial at the god's behest. In this way,
Aelian concludes, Makareus paid "a not blameworthy penalty, as the poet [Homer, *Il.*
4.160–61] says, with his own head, that of his wife, and those of his children besides."

PART THREE

Gender and Selfhood:
The Boy's Story

· SIX ·

The Power of Aphrodite: Eros and the Boundaries of the Self in Euripides' *Hippolytos*

The Second Phaedra

The *Hippolytos* of Euripides may be unique in the history of the Greek tragic theater as an example of a second treatment by the same poet of a myth he had earlier represented on stage. Only a few suggestive fragments of the first *Hippolytos* survive as well as the traces it has probably left behind in later works. But our evidence is strong that the play outraged its audience by the shamelessness of its Phaedra, who openly declared her guilty passion to Hippolytos and when rebuffed, just as brazenly confronted her husband face to face and herself accused Hippolytos of sexual assault.[1]

The second *Hippolytos,* according to the hypothesis of the play, corrected the indecencies and improprieties of the first (τὸ ... ἀπρεπὲς καὶ κατηγορίας ἄξιον ... διώρθωται). The changes affected not the terms of the myth itself but rather the depiction of the principal female character. The new Phaedra is the opposite, we might say, of her former self. She is the unwitting victim, the respectable woman whom Aphrodite, as the goddess herself tells us in the prologue, has coldly chosen as her instrument for vengeance against Hippolytos, who has scorned her worship (47–48).

This Phaedra is now the paragon of female virtue, embodying the ideals of *aidōs* (reticence), *sōphrosunē* (chastity), and the *eukleia* of her good reputation. Instead of a well-born Phaedra who asserted her sexual

In the earlier version of this essay I acknowledged the good counsels and generosity of Glenn Most and David Quint and, above all, an unpayable debt of gratitude to Marylin Arthur Katz, Anne Carson, Helene Foley, and the late Jack Winkler.

1. On the relations between the first *Hippolytos (Kaluptomenos)* and the second, called *Stephanephoros,* see especially Barrett 1964, 1–45; Séchan 1911, 105–51; Fauth 1958 and 1959; Zintzen 1960; Tschiedel 1969; Snell 1967, 47–69; Herter 1940, 273–92; Herter 1971, 44–92; and Herter 1975, 119–56 (with full bibliography).

desire, thereby dangerously subverting the norms of feminine behavior in an affront to all respectable women, as Aristophanic comedy several times reminds us,[2] we have a Phaedra who knows all too well the conventions of Greek social life that relegate the woman to a silence that would be her glory.[3] The new Phaedra is acutely aware that women are vulnerable to blame, to the charge of being a hateful thing to all (*misēma*, 406–7), and she reserves her personal hatred (*misō*, 413) for the disgraceful type of wife exemplified by the earlier Phaedra, as if she were responding directly to (and identifying with) the audience's reaction to the previous play.

Unlike the first Phaedra, this one will not seek to justify her love for Hippolytos or scheme to bring about its fulfillment with drugs and potions. Rather, she seeks desperately to repress her desire. She certainly will not address herself directly to Hippolytos, whose name she cannot even mention (352). It must therefore fall to another, the devoted nurse, to adopt all these positions in her pragmatic concern to save the life of the sick and suffering woman whom she loves and tends as her child. It follows that this Phaedra would never confront her husband face to face, once the nurse has extracted her guilty secret and betrayed it to Hippolytos. Phaedra would rather die of shame, and die she does, at her own hand, before the return of Theseus. She thus concludes the resolve she had made at the beginning of the play to save the honor by which she defines herself in her own eyes and in the eyes of others. Deeming that honor more precious than life—both her own and that of Hippolytos (721)—and responding now to the tragic impasse of a self caught hopelessly between innocence and guilt, "desire and honor, conscience and reputation,"[4] inner self and external image,[5] she too, like her wicked counterpart, lays a false charge against Hippolytos. But she chooses now an indirect means in the form of a letter, which together with her lifeless body will serve as silent and concrete testimony to her accusation.

In the end, the honorable Phaedra only seems to corroborate the supposition of woman's essentially duplicitous nature, and her defeat therefore seems even more explicitly to support Hippolytos's indictment of the entire female sex in his memorable outburst against that "counterfeit evil" we call women (616). Yet if the virtuous woman feels herself ruined, the scandal of the first play is averted, and above all, the myth is saved. Hippolytos must meet his fate in order to reconfirm the truth of the cultural dictum that no one may refuse the power of Aphrodite with

2. E.g., *Thesmophoriazousae* 153, 497, 547, 550; *Frogs* 1043–52.

3. On this aspect, see Loraux 1978. On the possible correlation between Phaedra's concern with her *eukleia* and the cult of Artemis Eukleia at Athens to whom prospective brides and bridegrooms sacrificed (Plutarch, *Aristides* 20.5), see Braund 1980, 184–85.

4. Sale 1977, 58.

5. See especially Segal 1970; and Avery 1968.

impunity, not even the Amazon's child and the worshipper of Artemis. Phaedra's reversion to her traditional role in the story (and the earlier play) only reinforces the lesson that the power of Aphrodite is indeed irresistible. It justifies Aphrodite's confidence in the prologue (40–41) that the queen, as the Cretan Pasiphae's daughter (or perhaps like any woman), will eventually become her ally as well as her victim if, like the goddess before her, she is scorned by the other. But in the process—because of the process—the innovations of the plot that are necessitated by the new Phaedra deepen the import of the myth, as the play shifts its focus to consider the discrepancy in the self between character and role, between, we might say, the second and the first Phaedras.[6] Through the twists and turns now required by the plot, the drama must also reach a level of unparalleled complexity. I will argue that this very complexity is essential for our understanding of Aphrodite and the correspondingly more complex part she is seen to play in the theater and the world.

We should consider the significant elements of the new plot for their intrinsic value as well as for their practical use in the structuring of the story. It matters, for example, that the shameless declarations of the earlier play are now replaced by lacunae in the text, communications never made public but only grasped from the reactions of those who hear (Hippolytos), overhear (Phaedra), or read them (Theseus). The ruling theme of eros is expanded if instead of the outrageous confrontations between male and female of the first play (Phaedra and Hippolytos, Phaedra and Theseus), the burden of the plot is now carried by parallel encounters between female and female (Phaedra and the nurse) and male and male (Hippolytos and Theseus). Finally, we should observe that to overcome the queen's initial reticence, the *aidōs* that threatens to block the plot devised by the goddess, the play is obliged to find oblique strategies by which to seduce Phaedra into playing her part so that Hippolytos may be seduced into playing his. As a result, the most striking feature of our drama is that it reaches its expected conclusion only through deviation and detour and above all, by means of one character acting as intermediary for the other.

For one critic, who is concerned only with ends and not means, the play demonstrates Euripides' turning of the tables on his "philistine" audience, with the aim of suggesting that the *aidōs* of the new Phaedra might be as much a source of evil and moral disorder as the shamelessness *(anaischuntia)* of the first.[7] But one might equally argue that the scandal caused by the first play only verifies Phaedra's anguished concern that society will judge her solely by its ruling conventions. The "palinode" therefore seems to incorporate and turn to its own purposes the external

6. See Reckford 1974, especially 314–18.
7. Masarracchia 1972, 1:289–302.

social reality that marked the relationship between the first play and its spectators.

Furthermore, the conventions that the second Phaedra seems to respect too much and that now determine the course of her actions are themselves subject to more suggestive implications for understanding the larger world that the play aims to represent. Conformity to social rules is always open to criticism, insofar as it gives public image precedence over considerations of personal integrity. But on another level, respect for convention acknowledges the realities of social relations in which the self must be responsible for the image it presents to others, an inevitable fact of life that is as true for Phaedra as she (and the structure and events of the play) will prove it to be for Hippolytos.

For the first Phaedra, who would contrive to satisfy her passion, Eros is the *didaskalos,* as she declares, the teacher of boldness and daring *(tolma, thrasos),* the god who is most resourceful *(euporōtatos)* at finding a way where there is no way *(en amēchanois,* 430 N²). This is the first time, as far as we know, that Eros has earned the title of *didaskalos.*[8] The novelty of this attribute is matched by the novelty of the woman who coined it, who in daring to use Eros as the teacher for her own ends, teaches others in turn by her bad example. Thus, in Aristophanes' *Frogs* Aeschylus can reproach Euripides for having put debased women such as this Phaedra on stage, claiming that "the poet" (like Phaedra, it would seem) "ought to conceal *[kruptein]* what is wicked and not produce or teach *[didaskein]* such things (*Frogs,* 1049–56).

For the second Phaedra, however, who would contrive with all her power to conceal *(kruptein)* what is wicked, the notions of teaching and learning recur in the theatrical context but now with different and still more novel connotations. Phaedra means to teach Hippolytos, as she says enigmatically in her last statement before she leaves to write the fateful letter and to take her own life. "He will share in my disease *[koinēi metaschōn]* and he will learn *[mathēsetai]* to practice *sōphrosunē*" (730–31), the quality of modesty/temperance/chastity, which both characters have claimed and which paradoxically belongs to Artemis's domain, not Aphrodite's. Hippolytos has already spoken of a virtue that cannot be taught (79–80, but cf. 667),[9] and his father will later take up the same theme of education in his angry speech against his son (916–20).

Phaedra, whether as victim or agent, is only a means to another end. The true objective of the play (and Aphrodite) might be called the education of Hippolytos. This is the moment for the young man to complete the initiatory scenario that would have him pass from the yoking of horses to

8. On Eros as counselor, see Lasserre 1946, 97.
9. On teaching and learning in the play, see Berns 1973, 165–87.

the yoking of maidens, from the hunting of game to the hunting of a wife.[10] Phaedra may incriminate Hippolytos to save her honor (716–21), while Aphrodite, like all divinities, intends to safeguard her own, and perhaps these are sufficient lessons about the nature of the adult world. But in this matter of passage from one state to another, in which eros is culturally programmed to play an essential part, the second Phaedra has much to learn and in turn to teach Hippolytos. This instruction applies to the larger scheme of things beyond Aphrodite's traditional functions, which the play is compelled to celebrate over and over again;[11] it also goes beyond the stereotyped interplay between the lustful woman and the chaste young man, which emphasizes the dangers to the social system that female sexuality is thought to pose. These other lessons the characters need not, indeed ought not, to express directly because they underlie the surface actions of the plot and are conveyed by the structures and details of the play itself.

Broadly speaking, Hippolytos's refusal of eros can be summarized as the self's radical refusal of the "other." Eros is the most dangerous of all relations. While answering most deeply to human needs of dependency, reciprocity, and empathy, Greek thought typically perceives it as posing a serious threat to the boundaries of the autonomous self by putting it in another's power under the magnetic pull of desire. At the same time, the exercise of eros acknowledges the force of the animal nature within us. It is also necessary, as we will see, for constructing an adequate model of that single self and for defining it in a network of proper social relations.

Hence, to meet Hippolytos's challenge, the entire dramatic structure enacts the irresistible power of Aphrodite. It does so through the development of actions, gestures, and language as it acts upon the structure of the self and puts it, even and especially against its will, into relations with others. We will discover that the self must learn to play its theatrical role in the complex—knotted and reknotted—plot of life itself. It must enter into the necessary but inevitably ambiguous exchanges between self and other, exchanges now confused and misread to the highest degree by reason of that initial refusal to worship the goddess.[12]

10. On rites of passage, see Vidal-Naquet 1986a, "Black Hunter" and "Recipes"; Vidal-Naquet 1986b. On hunting and adolescence, see also Detienne 1979a, 10–52; on horse taming, Calame 1977, especially 385–420; and on such patterns in the play, Segal 1978.

11. The nurse recalls these traditional powers (443–56): her cosmic sway over land, sea, and air; connections with sexuality and generation; irresistible effect on gods, mortals, and animals. Two odes (525–64, 1268–81) can be read as hymns to the goddess. Cf. Sophocles, frag. 841 Radt; and Euripides, 431 N². See also Segal 1965, 118.

12. On Greek notions of exchange, see Kahn 1978, 126–46, especially the close relations between Hermes and Aphrodite. Greek words of "exchange" privilege the idea of an

Thus, although Phaedra's prophetic statement about Hippolytos "sharing in her disease" (723–31) looks to the future events of the drama, the process of education has effectively begun long before we reach this midpoint of the play. From the moment Aphrodite determines to avenge herself on Hippolytos, not directly but through an other (Phaedra), who will act for her in the human domain and yet who, through her own language, gestures, and actions, will prefigure and determine the experience of the other (Hippolytos), the goddess activates a plot remarkable in its construction. Unlike the plot of any other extant play, this one binds all the characters together in an "inextricable nexus of interdependence." [13]

In the last part of this essay, I will call the role of Aphrodite into question, suggesting that Aphrodite's revenge upon Hippolytos through the displacing of desire on to an innocent other (Phaedra) runs counter to her typical mode of intervention in human affairs. As a result, I will argue, there is a latent tension between the familiar narrative patterns of the tale of Potiphar's wife to which the story of Phaedra and Hippolytos belongs and the mythic scenario usually associated with Aphrodite's intrusion into human affairs and the motif of her wrath. But before we can understand just how well this initial deviation also works in the service of Aphrodite's plan, we must trace out the intricate and various ways by which the goddess operates, especially through the significant images of the knot and the mirror. We must examine why she uses the woman as her instrument and agent on the stage, and to what end she deploys all the theatrical means at her disposal to demonstrate the fullness of her power over the self.

Rather than summarizing in detail here, let me simply propose that at its most inclusive level, Aphrodite's power will prove to be consonant with the power of the theater itself: as regards, for example, the structure and functions of plot, the representation of the body and its sensory faculties, relations between inside and outside and between seen and unseen, types and modes of communication, role playing and reversal of roles, the interactions of actors and spectators, and the general mimetic properties of dramatic art. As a way, then, of entering into Aphrodite's world (and that of the theater), let us begin by taking the measure of the phrase, "the inextricable nexus of interdependence," which I earlier invoked to characterize the plot of the play.

---

other (allos), e.g., allassō and its compounds. These terms recur frequently in our text (360, 629, 652, 726, 935, 1181, 1256, 1385).

13. I have borrowed the phrase from Segal 1969, 302. Knox (1952, 40), noting the unusual construction of the play in assigning almost the same number of lines to Phaedra, Theseus, the nurse, and Hippolytos, remarks: "When the action is so equally divided between four characters, the unity of the work cannot depend on any one, but must lie in the nature of the relationships between all four."

The Plot

To Bind and Unbind

The image of a nexus or knot is a leading idea, both literal and metaphorical, in the workings of the drama. Through the idiom of binding and unbinding or loosening (and related terms), this nexus operates on several different levels and embraces a wide variety of references, all organized around Phaedra's despairing cry at the turning point of the play after the betrayal of her secret to Hippolytos: "What devices [technai] or words [logoi] do I have, now that I have been tripped up, to loosen/unbind [luein] the knot [kathamma] of the logos?" (670–71).[14]

The knot of the logos that implicates Phaedra—the logos that includes the speech of the nurse to Hippolytos and his response overheard by the queen—can only be undone with the fastening of another knot. This knot is first of all the noose Phaedra binds around her neck (770–71) from which she will be "loosened" once she is dead (781, 783). It is also the knot of the new logos she fabricates for Hippolytos in the letter, the deltos she suspends from her suspended body (ērtēmenē, 779, 866). That action finds its first echo in Hippolytos's own gesture when he suspends (artēsas) his body back upon the thongs of his reins (1222), as he struggles to steer the stampeding horses that no longer turn in obedience to his guiding hand or to their own "binding harness" (hippodesmōn, 1225). Yet the knot of the new logos will eventually entangle Hippolytos in the reins (emplakeis, 1235), "binding him in a bond that is impossible to unravel" (desmon dusexelikton . . . detheis, 1237). This entanglement results directly from the tablet that Phaedra has wrapped with sealing cords and that Theseus must unravel (exelixas) to read its message. The bonds of Hippolytos, like those of Phaedra, will only be loosened (ek desmōn lutheis, 1244) at the cost of loosening his limbs from the bonds of life.[15] The reversal of his fortunes is now complete, fulfilling perhaps the ominous etymology of his name, since he turns from the "one who binds (or yokes, 111, 1183) and loosens horses" to one who is truly a "Hippolytos," that is, one whose body is "loosened by horses."[16]

---

14. Others have noted some instances of binding and weaving in the play, but not systematically or in light of larger issues. See, e.g., Segal 1965, 133–35; Reckford 1972, 415; and Padel 1974, 229.

15. Cf. Euripides, Iphigenia in Tauris 692, Bacchylides 1.43; Sophocles, Oedipus at Colonus 1270.

16. See Fauth 1959, 428–30; Segal 1965, 147n.48, 166; Burkert 1979, 112–13. Burkert's argument that the etymology refers not to a person but to a "time, place, or occasion of unharnessing horses" is not convincing. In any case, the frequency of luō words in the text suggests that Euripides is exploiting the nomen-omen of Hippolytos's name. On the impor-

The action of loosening corresponds, in turn, to the condition of Phaedra at the outset of the play. Her soul is bound fast *(dedetai)* to her sickbed (160), while at the same time the "fastening" of her limbs is loosened by the afflictions of her disease—eros *(lelummai meleōn sundesma,* 199). Eros, according to his traditional epithet, is the *lusimelēs,* "the one who loosens the limbs," an epithet he shares with both sleep and death [17] and from which Phaedra can liberate herself only by fastening the tightly drawn rope around her neck (769–75).

Binding and loosening, then, both work their destructive effects on the body itself, but the correspondences between the conditions of Phaedra and Hippolytos can come about only through the irreversible movement of the dramatic action itself. One character's repetition or re-enactment of the other's experience is already conveyed by the chorus in the second stasimon immediately before the peripeteia of the drama and just after Phaedra's last exit from the scene (752–63). There the chorus recalls the ship that brought Phaedra from Crete to Athens long ago when she was a bride, and they describe the woven ends of the mooring cables that were bound to dry land *(ekdēsanto,* 761–63). But the word *archai,* which here means "ends" in the sense of "extremities," more usually signifies "beginnings." The end point of the journey that began Phaedra's story long before the opening of the play is recollected at the moment when her story is to end. Yet it inaugurates in turn the beginning of the other's journey that will lead him away as an exile from his father's house to the shores of the sea—neither as a bridegroom in his nuptial procession nor as a young hero following in his father's footsteps on a road that had earlier brought Theseus from Troezen to Athens (977–80, cf. 1208–9) to claim his rightful identity as the son of his own father, Aegeus. Instead, Hippolytos will take the road to destruction, determined in the play from the moment Phaedra succumbs to the nurse's entreaty to "loosen" the "silent road of her thought *[gnomē]*" (290, 391).

At the critical moment of reversal, recorded in this second stasimon, the interlinking of destinies by which the unbinding of one becomes the binding of the other corresponds quite literally to Aristotle's notion of the basic structures of plot. "Every tragedy," he declares, "has a *desis* and a *lusis* . . . I call the *desis,* the knot, the binding, the tragedy from its beginning *[archē]* up to that part which is the last *[eschaton],* from which the

---

tance of yoking/unyoking in the play, see Bushala 1969, 23–29; and Reckford 1972, 415–27. This vocabulary (111, 545, 548, 1131, 1183, 1389, 1425) should be connected with the motif of binding/unbinding.

17. *Lusimelēs* of Eros: Hesiod, *Theogony* 911; Archilochus, 118; Alcman 3.61 PMG Page. Of sleep: *Odyssey* 20.57, 23.343. Of death: Euripides, *Suppliants* 47 (modeled on the Homeric formula of loosening the limbs, *Iliad* 4.469; 22.335; 5.176).

change of fortune proceeds, and the *lusis,* the dénouement, from the beginning of this reversal until the end *[telos]*" (*Poetics* 1455b). This *desis* Aristotle also calls a *plokē,* "a weaving," and this image too has its literal counterparts in the play. The woven *(plekton)* garland (73) Hippolytos plaits for the goddess (the *anadēma,* 83) finds its doublet in the woven garland (807) Theseus casts down from his own head in response to the twisted cords of Phaedra's noose (783). It leads to the last interweaving, that of Hippolytos entangled (*emplakeis,* 1236) in his horses' reins. But how are we to define the intricacy of a plot that from first to last interweaves these two actions of *desis* and *lusis* themselves? The terms shift back and forth from one signifying level to another, from one referent to another, and persist until the end, implicating not only Phaedra and Hippolytos but also Theseus, the third one, in a bond that must be unbound.

For Theseus the process of unbinding begins when he orders the bolts of the doors to be loosened (*eklueth'harmous,* 809; cf. 808). It is completed when, for the second time, he curses his son who in keeping the oath that binds him, does not "loosen" his mouth to tell his father what he knows (*luō,* 1060). Theseus is bound by his own *hamartia,* the error that causes the death of Hippolytos, but Artemis can "loosen" (*ekluei,* 1335) him, as she says, because he acted out of ignorance. Yet at the resolution of the drama, it is Hippolytos, bound and in turn unbound, who has the power to "loosen" or "dissolve" (*luō,* 1442) the quarrel between himself and his father, to free (*eleutherō,* 1449, 1450) Theseus from the guilty pollution of his son's approaching death. In absolving Theseus, however, Hippolytos can be said to have fastened at last a durable social bond, now acknowledged by his noble character *(gennaios)* as the legitimate *(gnēsios)* son of his father (1452, 1455, cf. 309).[18]

Aphrodite is the primal cause. Dionysos is, of course, the lord of the theater who regulates the formal symmetries, reenactments, and reversals of tragic plots. Dionysos Lusios, we might say, is the god who presides over the tragic patterns of binding and loosening that operate reciprocally in the service of necessity, entailing constraint *(desis)* on the one hand and dissolution and death *(lusis)* on the other.[19] Yet this play specifies that all these operations belong to Aphrodite, for whom eros both loosens the limbs and fashions the bonds that bind the self in the nets of desire.[20] Thus

18. See, e.g., Plato, *Politicus* 310a–b, where the extended metaphor of weaving as statecraft refers to fashioning human bonds *(desmoi)* that include marriage and adoption of children. See also Plato, *Republic* 520a, *Laws* 921c.

19. On Dionysos's activities in this sphere, see Ramnoux 1962, 200–202; Kahn 1978, 114–16 ("the unbinding of Dionysos is itself a bond," p. 116); and Segal 1982, 21–22, 88–89, 100–101, especially 92–93n.16.

20. For the latter, cf. the tragic poet, Diakaiogenes, frag. 1.1 N².

in demonstrating the ineluctable necessities that Aphrodite controls, all the mechanisms of the play—structure, action, gesture, and language—enact in their tragic and destructive version the terms that are fully consonant with her sphere of power.

Aphrodite, like Dionysos in the *Bacchae,* demands recognition of her divinity. She too insists that mortals recognize the alien power of passionate forces in the world as also intrinsically their own. But Dionysos's mode of expression is collective: the *thiasos* and initiation into cultic mysteries bind worshippers to one another and to their god, loosening them from the ordinary restrictions of daily life. Aphrodite's desire is directed instead to the mysteries of sexuality and marriage, whereby one self is bound to an other and the bride first binds on the girdle of her virginity and then unbinds it in the first encounter with eros.[21] More generally, however, the goddess's effects extend to the wider network of interdependence and interconnection for which eros provides the patterns, and it is under her influence too that the typical Dionysiac idiom of madness, maenadism, and *sparagmos* may be absorbed into a tragic plot.[22]

The intricate network of *desis* and *lusis* not only replicates the abstract notion of plot, it also serves as the particular structuring device that links the sequence of events and binds them (with the characters) into a series of reciprocal and parallel actions. It is as if the play were demonstrating its own premises and reproducing a message of intersubjectivity in the terms of its own composition. Still further, the spectrum of use suggests that the idea of a nexus reproduces the broader principle of structure itself, whether regulating the bounded structure of the body or defining the forms of social relations between one self and an other.

To refuse the bonds of eros, then, means that binding will operate upon the self as a sign of intolerable emotional and physical pressures—as external contacts made upon the body (in noose or reins) and as internal constraints upon speech and action—so that unbinding, when it comes, will bring disaster to the self (and the other) but joy to offended Aphrodite (725–29). The nurse unwittingly provides the norm, when in

21. E.g., *Od.* 11.245; Euripides, *Alcestis* 177. See Detienne 1979a, 32–33; and Schmitt-Pantel 1977, 1059–73.

22. The process begins with Phaedra's delirious fantasies of hunting on the mountains (215–18). The transfer, the point of no return, is sealed already in the first ode to Eros and its tales of unhappy loves, where Aphrodite is named as the agent of doom both for Iole, who is figuratively compared to "a running naiad and bacchant" (550–51), and for Semele herself, the bride of Zeus and actual mother of Dionysos. See below, note 99; and now Schlesier 1993, 108–12, who rightly points to the mutilation of Hippolytos's body at the end as a kind of *sparagmos* and to the bacchic patterns that affect the figures of both mother and son. More precisely, Dionysos and Aphrodite combine forces, as, for example, in Sophocles' *Antigone,* where the third stasimon (the ode to the power of Aphrodite and Eros) marks the turning point of the plot to its inevitable tragic end. See Zeitlin 1993a, 155–59.

speaking of her own close attachment to Phaedra, she warns that "the loves of the heart [stergēthra phrenōn] should be easily loosened [euluta], both to thrust away and draw in tight" (256–57; cf. frag. 340 N²). Her gnomic wisdom will apply in more concrete (but still figurative) fashion to the noose Phaedra puts around her neck. But the metaphor of horse racing will find its literal referent in Hippolytos who, by refusing the yoke of marriage, must find himself "yoked" instead "to destruction" (1389), unable to loosen the reins that fatally bind him.[23]

To refuse the bonds of eros also means to refuse the bonds of dependence, to attempt to remain alone and aloof from an other—an asyndeton, we might say, in the grammar of life. Once again the play acts out these principles in literal gestures and language. Phaedra can resist the pressure to reveal her secret (which will activate Aphrodite's plot) until the nurse grasps her and de-pends, hangs (exartēmenē, 325), from her hand in a suppliant's appeal. But after this human contact with another has worked its deadly purpose, dependency turns back upon the single self, finding a negative echo in the isolated inanimate deltos (tablet) that conceals the secret and de-pends (ērtēmenē, 857) from the same hand of Phaedra, now dead. We recognize its import for Hippolytos, who so closely identifies with his chariot and horses and from whose harness he finally de-pends (artēsas, 1222) as he leans his body back upon the reins.

The use of the word harmozō in these last two instances further confirms the reversion of both Phaedra and Hippolytos to the status of a now isolated self. In negation of its potential meaning as the "fitting together of a man and a woman in wedlock," it is applied first to the one who "fits" the noose to her neck (katharmozousa, 771) and then to the other who "fits" his feet in the footstalls of his chariot (harmosas, 1189).[24]

At the end of the play Artemis, the other goddess, takes over the stage, but Aphrodite, long vanished, is also present.[25] She had presided at a distance over the main event that unleashed the demonic and destructive energies of eros, which erupted in the confrontation between the bull from the sea and the horses of Hippolytos.[26] Yet we also find her in the final reunion between father and son. Hippolytos's last act, which absolves the other, is granted by Hippolytos in obedience to his goddess's commands

23. See especially Reckford 1972.

24. For harmozō in a matrimonial context, see, e.g., Herodotus, 9.108; Pindar, Pythians 9.13, 177; Euripides, Phoenissae 411. Harmostēs as a betrothed husband: Pollux, Onomasticon 3.35, cf. 3.39. Aphrodite as performing this function in Sparta: ad Lycophron 832 (266f. Scheer). See Carson 1982, 122. I discuss the cognate harmonia in more detail below.

25. If, as has been supposed, the stage decor included the statues of the two deities, the figure of Aphrodite would stand as a silent witness to her rival's intervention.

26. For the sexual connotations of the bull and horse in the play, see Knox 1952, 6n.8; and Segal 1965, 125, 144–48.

(1435, 1442–43). But as a reconciliation of a divided pair, it also attests to Aphrodite's power, as signaled by the benign ode to the charms of Eros that immediately precedes the scene.[27] The direct aim of eros, concealed behind the nurse's delicate suggestion of a love charm to cure her ailing mistress (508–10), had been sexual. To "join together [sunapsai] one charis from two" (515), as she suggests, hints at an erotic union by means of a magical act that is designed to bind the other to oneself. Yet we may interpret her words more broadly, because the two chief encounters in the play (between the nurse and Phaedra, and between Theseus and Hippolytos) also show Aphrodite's influence at work. Love of Phaedra is the primary emotion that produces both outcomes, motivating the nurse's actions on behalf of her charge and leading Theseus in turn to condemn his son without a second thought. Yet beyond this simple and obvious fact, the contents of these two meetings imply that Aphrodite rules over other forms of face-to-face intimacy along the spectrum from erōs to philia, all of which involve reciprocity and exchange in the interests of persuasion (seduction).[28]

In the woman's world, the nurse functions as a maternal figure to Phaedra in a relation corresponding to that in the man's world between father and son, for all of whom the linking power of Aphrodite invokes the more diffused and more ambivalent sides of erōs/philia. When the nurse complains how "grievous a burden it is that one soul suffer pain on behalf of two" (258–60), the self and the other, she is referring to herself and Phaedra. But in her homely complaint, her words can speak for the other characters as well, who in the course of the play will each come to experience this inescapable necessity. Thus, at the end, the goddess Aphrodite is the one (mia) who has brought not two, but three together—the son, the father, and his mate (sunēoron)—out of their isolation into the commonality of their mutual ruin (1403) to constitute a belated if tragic family reunion.[29] More to the point, the one who in his association with the goddess Artemis could neither see nor touch her now enters into the

---

27. This last ode (1268–81) is sung just after the messenger speech and before the entrance of Artemis. Curiously enough, it now celebrates the god's sweet, exalting powers. Hippolytos has fallen and Eros is ascendant, but the praise of Eros also suggests the reconciliation to come. Eros embraces (amphibalōn), enchants (thelgei, 1270, 1274), and is golden-gleaming (chrusophaēs, 1275), attesting to the gentler side of glukupikros (bittersweet) Aphrodite.

28. The goddess, to be sure, shows a different side in each case. Appropriately enough, the nurse's persuasion of her beloved Phaedra succeeds, while Hippolytos's appeals to his angry father are dismissed as empty rhetoric and signs of shameless hypocrisy.

29. Luschnig (1980, 98) suggests that when Hippolytos claims the goddess has destroyed all three (1401, 1403), he refers to Artemis, not Phaedra, as the third figure in question. Artemis's rewording makes it clear that the tragedy affects mortals, not gods.

comfort of a reciprocal and acknowledged exchange. Having earlier refused physical contact with others, abhorring the touch of another's hand
(606, 1086), he finds at the end a loving embrace in the circle of his father's
arms (1431–32, 1445).[30]

Hippolytos had refused to cross the boundary between child and
adult, thereby also transgressing the line of temporality that divides human from divine. As a result, the self is compelled to experience the transgression of its own boundaries in the plot that entangles him in the complexities of human life.[31] Subject to the constraining bonds placed on the
untouched and untouching body, first in speech and then in action, he will
be released only in death. The operations of binding and loosening enacted along the seashore transform the workings of eros, the rhythms of
tension and relaxation, into those of death. At the same time, the entire
process that leads to his destruction delivers him from one state to another
in the modality of birth by which bonds are also loosened.[32] The child

30. Knox (1952) and Segal (1965) both stress the import of the reconciliation scene but
from a different perspective. Neither notes that the goddess commands it. Words of contact,
excluding those of binding, are *psauō* (14), *haptō* and *sunaptō* (187, 515, 606, 1026, 1359),
harpazō (1220), *helkō* and *proselkō* (1084, 1221, 1237, 1362, 1432), *thigganō* (310, 885,
1044, 1086), *athiktos* (652, 1002), and other more general words of handling, touching, and
their negatives.

31. References to boundaries and lines of demarcation are prominent in the play. At the
start of the prologue, Aphrodite claims hegemony over the territory between the Black Sea
and the boundaries of Atlas (the *termōn*), that is, the expanse of the known world beyond
which lie the Hesperides to the west (746) and where Theseus would send Hippolytos, if he
could (1053). As it is, Theseus sends him to the boundaries *(horoi)* of the land (974) and, at
the end, apostrophizes the "renowned boundaries *[horismata]* of Athens and Pallas" (1459).
At first, Phaedra longs for the *terma*, "the boundary of death" (139–40), and she later speaks
of the *pathos* (trouble) that is moving across the boundary of life in an ill-starred crossing
(peran dusekperaton, 678). The shore *(aktē)* is another significant boundary (737, 742, 762,
1173, 1197, 1199, 1205, 1208, 1210), and the position of Troezen itself is precisely fixed in
reference to Athens as the outermost *(eschaton)* point of land (373–74, cf. 30–31).

32. The entire scene mixes images of sexuality and childbirth. The great wave that
swells up and seethes thick foam when the sea was spouting forth (1210–11) suggests a
mighty ejaculation, and the explicit mention of foam *(aphros)* recalls both the birth of
Aphrodite and the semen of Ouranos that created her (Hesiod, *Theogony* 189–98). On the
relation of Poseidon and Aphrodite here, see Segal 1965, 144–45. *Kuma*, "wave" or "swell,"
also means "pregnancy," so the language suggests that the wave is giving birth to the bull,
depositing it on the shore *(exethēke*, 1214; a word commonly used for exposing a newborn
child), and the great roaring that fills up the whole earth (1215) might then recall an infant's
first cries. *Kuma* also means "that which is produced by pregnancy," i.e., the fetus, and this
meaning too seems to subtend the messenger's first line when he speaks of the *aktēs kumo-
degmonos*, the shore that receives the wave/fetus (1173).

On the other hand, the phrase describing Hippolytos's fall to earth, once the thongs
were cut and his bonds loosened (1244), suggests the delivery of an infant, where loosening
of all bonds and knots was thought to facilitate childbirth (e.g., Pliny, *Natural History* 28.42,

comes forth in death, on the one hand, and in filiation, on the other. And this filiation is none other than the birth into a fuller selfhood, socially as the legitimate son of his father, and also in the cognitive experience of a tragic consciousness. This experience, in tracing its signs on and within the body, has now defined the approved boundaries of the self in the world, a self that has moved from the untouched meadow where he had culled the flowers of Artemis's woven garland (73), the wreath that binds (*anadēma*, 83), to the place on the shore where land and sea define each other's boundaries.[33]

Time, Story, and the Self

The untouched meadow, as many have observed, is the spatial analogue of Hippolytos, who in identifying himself with the meadow and its im-

---

59; and see Kahn 1978, 103–4). Furthermore, Hippolytos's cries of anguish when he is brought back on stage (1350–51) suggest himself as a parturient, as I will discuss more fully below.

Finally, Artemis instructs Theseus to take the child into his arms (1432), as though she were now indeed the goddess of childbirth, as a result of which Theseus finally acknowledges his son's legitimacy. Further support for this interpretation can be found in the last antistrophe of the first stasimon (the first ode to Eros and Aphrodite), where Semele is described as both bride and new mother, "wed to the flame-girt thunder and bringing forth in childbirth [*tokada*] the twice born [*digonos*] Bacchos" (555–62). In its myths of women's unhappy loves, the context refers to Phaedra, but both theme and language apply more directly to Hippolytos. Like Semele, he is destined for destruction by a supernatural force, and like Bacchos, he too will be "twice born." It is therefore still more significant that, just before the messenger enters with the terrible news, the chorus should refer to his "poor mother, who bore him to no avail" (1142–46), in echo of Hippolytos's belated mention of grief for his mother and his *pikrai gonai* (bitter begetting, 1082).

33. A last word about the complex of binding and unbinding, which has a vast range of uses, both positive and negative, well treated in Onians 1951, s.v. "bond." See also Eliade 1969, 92–114; Delcourt 1957, 15–28; Detienne and Vernant 1978, 270–326, 330; and Kahn 1978, 75–117 and 119–64. The last two references give special attention to Eros and Aphrodite in this context. See also Schreckenberg 1964, 175, whose study of the word *anankē* (necessity) defines the concept as an allophone of *desmos*.

In addition to the various associations I have recalled concerning Aphrodite's power and the construction of a plot (*desis/lusis* and *plokē*), we should note that knots and bonds are particularly associated with love magic (*katadesmos*). In general, acts of binding and unbinding are signs of *mētis* (cunning intelligence), an attribute equally relevant to erotic activity and hence sharing a semantic field that includes deceit (*apatē*), trickery (*dolos*), contrivance (*mechanē*), and ways and means (*poros*), as well as their opposites (*amēchania, aporia*). All these terms belong to our play, whose plot Aphrodite (and Phaedra) has devised (*mēsato*, 592, 1400).

Reversibility is a key element in the mechanism of binding/unbinding. "To exercise all its powers, the intelligence of *mētis* needs the circular reciprocity between what is bound and what is binding" (Detienne and Vernant 1978, 305), and therefore it also represents a labile and ambiguous reality (Kahn 1978, 93–94). Hence the language of knots is especially appropriate to the actual situation and theme of the play.

mortal mistress defines himself as an unworked territory: all surface and no depth, outside of time that marks the seasonal activities of human culture and the cycles of human generation.[34] *Always (aei), alone (monos),* and *all (panta,* 80, 84) are words that define the self in regard to this edenic enclosure whose perfect circles of time and space exclude the temporal and linear narrative of a human life. "May I turn around the *telos,* the goalpost of life, exactly as I began it" is the fervent wish that concludes Hippolytos's prayer to Artemis (87).

Hippolytos will indeed realize that *telos* in the action of his horses and chariot, which will bind his life to the destiny, the *moira,* appointed for him by Aphrodite (894, 1436). But, in truth, Hippolytos's wish cannot be granted as he would like. How could it be, since the end is separated from the beginning by the entire narrative chain of events in the play? Hippolytos does fall into time, not an eternity but its diametrical opposite: the split second in which he condemned an other (Phaedra) and was condemned in turn, when his father would not wait for time to reveal the necessary proofs of his innocence (1052–53, 1322). As a result, Hippolytos falls into narrative. As a result, he becomes at the end the subject of a story for maidens always to tell (1428). Now the love Phaedra bore him will be made public in a recital whose cultic repetition after his death relegates it appropriately to the duration of abiding time (*di' aiōnos makrou,* 1426).

Hippolytos is to be bound, not without irony, to Aphrodite and Phaedra forever, in the cult of the nubile maidens.[35] Yet given this future commemoration of his story, the mechanics of the new plot the goddess furnishes for the new Phaedra assume a richer significance. Without Phaedra, we might say, Hippolytos cannot be an actor in the drama of life, which the text imitates in all its baffling complexities. Alone in a perpetual cycle of ludic repetition, he can have no story, no *mythos.* The *agones* of athletic competition (1016) promise him a life without the risks (1019) that the Greeks deemed essential for the achievement of a heroic (that is, manly) self (cf. Euripides, frag. 1052 N[2]). Hippolytos's sporting activities are only rehearsals of the real thing, keeping him too long from the serious *praxis* of real life, which, as Aristotle tells us, drama imitates (*Poetics* 1450a12).

Hippolytos's story comes into being because of the lying message Phaedra leaves behind on the writing tablet, which in effect reverses subject and object (I desire him/he desires me). By making him "share in her disease" (730–31), Phaedra has now transferred her story to him, making

---

34. See Bremer 1975, 268–80, for the ambiguities of the meadow; also Segal 1965, 122. On its traits as coextensive with Hippolytos, see Pigeaud 1976, 3–7, although he mistakenly takes the gardener's work as applying only to the little sterile gardens of Adonis in the festival bearing his name. For associations of the meadow with images of the golden age see Turato 1974, 136–51. More generally, see Motte 1973; and Calame 1992, 119–38.

35. On the ironies, see Segal 1978, 138–39.

him the unwitting double of herself. Accused of a deed he did not commit, he will now imitate her *praxis,* so to speak, in an *agōn* for his life and honor, as she had struggled for hers—in both language and action.[36] More precisely, she has now required him to stand in the place of the other (Phaedra), to be identified with her, to hear from the other (his father), what she, the other, had heard from him (Hippolytos). In short, he will have to live through her experience in every respect, sharing the symptoms of her "disease" in the eyes of the world until the condition of his sick and suffering body as seen at the end of the play symmetrically matches her physical state at the beginning. Perhaps most important, by playing the role Phaedra has assigned to him, Hippolytos will be forced into the position of an other in relation to his true self. He will suffer the consequences of his own alterity in an adult social system that requires one to verify the self through the perception of an other.

This means that on the level of the dramatic action, the import of the entire chain of communication in its deviations and detours, whereby everything passes indirectly through the intermediary of an other, can be understood as a dramatic means of bringing into focus the implications of Hippolytos's refusal to allow an other to intrude upon his visual and tactile space. It also means, as far as language is concerned, that the typical proleptic techniques of tragedy, by which the first part of a play prepares for the second and can only be fully apprehended retrospectively in the light of what follows, will now perform a double duty in forecasting through enigmatic images the fates of not just one (Phaedra) but also the other (Hippolytos). The end of the new plot finally insists that this principle of alterity be permanently installed in cult: the male's story will later and for all time serve as the model for the female. Yet this outcome is preceded by its exact reverse: the female and her story will serve throughout the play as the model for the male.

The Feminine Body

Virgin

In the exchange of roles, the play is, in a sense, simply acting out what Hippolytos's claim to the status of *parthenos* (1106, 1302) implies. It therefore arranges his initiation into the world as one resembling the experience of the female body.[37] After all, the image of the *parthenos* pluck-

36. See also Segal 1965, 137–38.
37. On the female body as the model for male suffering, see Loraux 1981b, 37–67, especially 53. She appropriately cites Plato, *Republic* 3.395e, who expressly forbids a man to imitate a woman, especially when she is sick, in love, or in childbirth.

ing flowers in the inviolate meadow (73–80) already invokes its paradigmatic antecedent, the Kore (Persephone) figure, for whom "the doors of Hades will gape open"—just as Aphrodite predicts for Hippolytos in the prologue (56–57) and Hippolytos himself echoes at the end (1447).

Hippolytos's virginity in the service of the goddess Artemis seems to tell us that the untouched body can only be imagined as feminine, but it also suggests that untouchability bears a metaphysical charge transcending the laws of nature and even of gender. Hippolytos sacralizes virginity, and the manner of his exclusive worship of the goddess suggests the cultural values often embedded in the idea of maidenhood. For the self to be alone with the goddess in the pure space of the meadow implies that sexual purity may represent the self as an "image of an original identity: that is, what is objectively untouched symbolizes what is subjectively contained."[38] Yet Kore's well-known story reminds us that the *parthenos* cannot linger forever in the meadow, content to embody a static symbol of external and private wholeness. Rather, the mythic associations of flower, meadow, and maiden align the human maturational cycle with that of the seasons so that the *parthenos* signifies the one who is poised precisely at the place and moment of passage. The virgin is obliged to enter into the temporal flow of life, which is represented by the progress of the drama itself and recollected within it as the retrospective experience of Phaedra, who was once a *parthenos* (429) but now is a mature woman.

The drama is built on the erotic tensions between male and female and on the contrasts between the genders. Therefore, when Hippolytos reenacts and imitates the words, gestures, and actions of the other, we recognize the workings of the dramatic rule of reversal into the opposite as the sign of a peripeteia. Yet Hippolytos's identity as the *parthenos* figure suggests that this *kouros,* this young man, may well be the potential bride as well as the bridegroom, and it is this status that logically leads him into the wider sphere of feminine experience exemplified by his secret double, Phaedra. In other words, the quality of "subjective containment" embodied in the male as virgin *(parthenos)* also necessarily entails an intersubjective relation with the woman *(gunē),* the no-longer-*parthenos,* who is Phaedra, with the result that these same devices of imitation and reenactment attest to the hidden affinities between them.

This relation between the two selves is marked exactly at the turning point of the action, just before Phaedra's posthumous message ensures that Hippolytos will be called upon to play her part. There, in the second stasimon to which I have earlier referred, those *archai,* the ends and

38. Frye 1976, 153. The essential meaning of *parthenos* is not so much physical integrity as the fact that she belongs to no man. See further Fauth 1959, 481–90.

beginnings of the ropes that bound Phaedra's nuptial ship to the shore when she came to Athens as a bride, signify the end for one (Phaedra) and the beginning of the story for the other (Hippolytos) (762–63). Lamenting Phaedra's fate, the chorus begins its song by referring to the maidens who "drip their radiant tears into the purple deep" in mourning for the young Phaethon (735–41), who plunged to his death when he lost control of the fiery steeds of his father, the sun god. Phaethon, as has been observed, is the male doublet of Hippolytos, both as a driver of chariots and as a failed bridegroom, while the maidens' lament reflects the grief of the chorus for Phaedra and also anticipates Hippolytos's future place in the cult for virginal brides.[39] But Phaethon, the "shining" one, who shares his fate with Hippolytos and his name and etymology with Phaedra,[40] is also the figure who mediates this intersubjective relation between the two selves. Phaethon is the mythic other through whom the identities of the two characters are confounded just at the moment of crossing when their paths are to take linked but separate directions to their deaths.[41]

Woman, House, World

Eros provides the focus for confronting the more general experience of relations between two subjects, because rather than effacing all differences, eros calls for a complementary opposition between one self and an other. In dramatizing the implications of Hippolytos's resistance to eros, which extend outward to encompass all the relations between one self and an other, the play appropriately develops and enlarges this intersubjective experience in ways that involve not only Phaedra and himself but all the characters, including the nurse, Theseus, and even Aphrodite and Artemis. Bernard Frischer defines this distinctive characteristic of the play as a *discordia concors*: "while each character stands alone as a unique individual, he/she still shares in and mirrors qualities of his/her opposite."[42] This insight is truer than he may have suspected, because his Latin phrase hap-

39. See Reckford 1972, 414–21.

40. For another outlook on Phaethon's symbolic function, see Padel 1974, 235.

41. For discussions of this passage in addition to Reckford 1972, see Segal 1965, 133–35; and Parry 1966, 317–26, who suggests that the ode reflects Phaedra's own thoughts—another form of intersubjectivity. See also Padel 1974, 228.

42. "*Concordia* is realized by means of three devices: a character is regularly associated with the same images as his [or her] polar opposite; a character consistently repeats the words and deeds of his [or her] opposite; and the values which generate his [or her] actions, the laws which regulate them, and the qualities which they reveal are remarkably similar to the qualities, laws, and values observable in the behavior of the other characters in the play" (Frischer 1970, 86–87). Many others have commented on one or more aspects of this sharing.

pens to have an exact Greek equivalent located in the text itself, with its direct referent as none other than the adult female body.

As the first choral lyric tells us, "woman's nature is a *dustropos harmonia*, a discordant harmony [or *discordia concors*], and there is wont to cohabit with it *[philei . . . sunoikein]* an ill, unhappy helplessness *[amēchania]* that goes together with travail *[odinōn]* and unreasoning thoughts *[aphrosunē]*" (161–64). Through the natural workings of the feminine body, the woman experiences herself as a diversity in unity. Biological constraints subject her to flux and change and put her at odds with herself, creating an internal *dustropos harmonia,* in short, a "natural" oxymoron of conflict and ambiguity.

Woman herself can therefore be construed as a self-reflexive microcosm of the differential relations between the various characters in the play, herself included, and more generically between one self and an other. Still further, she is in a sense the "topocosm" of the world of the here and now upon which can be mapped life's conflicts and ambiguities. Because the play specifically locates these complexities in the sexual domain, the "natural" construct of the woman's body serves as the proper and literal terrain for the work of Aphrodite. At the same time, this feminine body supplies the objective correlative to the broader questions of intersubjective relations that are explored in the course of the play.

Woman is a character in the drama, acting and acted upon; she struggles, in truth, against the facts and desires of the body, but as a generic category she also serves as a sign. An enigmatic sign, like the world itself in which she lives, she is difficult to interpret, requiring the services of a seer or *mantis,* as the nurse and chorus claim when Phaedra stubbornly refuses to speak (236, 269–70, 346; cf. 729, 858, 873). The conjectures in the first choral lyric regarding the aetiology of Phaedra's disease are instructive beyond their explanatory value for Greek medical ideas, as they indicate what general influences are thought to impinge on the representative figure of woman. The symptoms presented by Phaedra are overdetermined; they can be interpreted indifferently according to each of the three cardinal zones of relations in which the self may be involved: the divine domain where she might be possessed by a god (141–50); the personal domain of relations within the family, with either husband or parents, news of whom might have adversely affected her (151–60); and, as we have noted, the body in its conflictual relation with itself (161–69) as the appropriate model for all relations. In other words, the complex organism that is the woman's body supplies the symbolic locus for organizing the entire cultural system—physical, psychological, social, metaphysical, epistemological, and ethical—of which Aphrodite is the cosmic emblem and Phaedra her human instrument and tragic paradigm.

Yet it is significant that the chorus at this moment calls not upon Aphrodite but upon Artemis, who watches over women in childbirth (166–69). It has often been noted that the women's invocation demonstrates the insufficiency of Hippolytos's view of the goddess both in his exclusive claim to her and in his denial of natural procreation through the female body.[43] But I want to emphasize further why Artemis properly belongs in the world of women, whether presiding over their integral state as untouched virgins or overseeing the moment when that "breeze" *(aura)*, as the chorus refers to labor pangs, "darts through the womb" (165–66).[44] The goddess protects the female body, whether closed or open. There is no contradiction in that fact. But in her links with both virginity and childbirth, the intervention of Artemis informs us that for the married woman, society insists that maternity be separated from sexuality and rejoined with chastity, closing and enclosing the body in the inner spaces of the house. This, then, is that other *dustropos harmonia,* the social rather than physiological fact in woman's life, which is the cultural oxymoron of the virtuously chaste wife. Aphrodite, in truth, has little visible place in married life once the bridal period is over and a child is born. In her Homeric hymn, once she has borne a child as a result of her mating with Anchises, she gives him to others to rear. In some contexts, the language of childbirth and sexuality overlap. Both attest to the permeability of the body's boundaries and are often conflated in image and metaphor (e.g., Archilochus, 104D). At the same time they are antitheses, as opposed to one another as Artemis is to Aphrodite.

In defining Phaedra's inner conflict as one between Artemis and Aphrodite within this framing design of self and other, one can further justify the role she plays as model for Hippolytos in both formal and thematic terms. After all, as their figures are represented in this second play, the other is not truly an other. This Phaedra, as often noted, shares many traits with Hippolytos. Despite contrasting genealogies that seem to polarize their sexual attitudes into two representative extremes—the child of the wanton Cretan mother (Phaedra) and the child of the sex-shy Amazon (Hippolytos)—the two characters are not actually incompatible in temperament or values. Both are concerned with purity of body and soul, both would maintain the integrity of their inner selves at all costs, and both adhere to an outlook of aristocratic idealism. It is precisely Phaedra's refusal to abandon these "Artemisian" values that leads the queen to engineer Aphrodite's revenge. Yet it is the power of Aphrodite, above all, that

43. See, e.g., Segal 1965, 160. See also Sale 1977, despite some of his exaggerated claims and his zeal to coopt the play into a modern perspective.
44. On this passage, see Loraux 1981b, especially 53–55. On Artemis's roles in feminine life, see further Vernant 1991, 195–206.

defines the Artemisian through opposition to herself and compels all finally to confront the *dustropos harmonia* of the world in which they must
live. Thus, Phaedra's affinities with Hippolytos are indispensable to the
workings of the plot. Moreover, they are essential because they tell us (and
Hippolytos) that the simple dichotomies of Hippolytos's existence, his division of the world into good and bad individuals, will not be able to
withstand the complexities of Phaedra herself.[45]

This last observation, in the most general terms, constitutes the drama's fundamental lesson, one that is common to the experience of all
tragedy. Only in discovering that the universe is a place of conflict and
that words, values, and humanity itself are ambiguous entities, can one
accept a problematic vision of the world and acquire what might be called
a "tragic" consciousness.[46] Tragic man, like Oedipus, is a riddle to be
solved, and the adolescent Hippolytos, in his anomalous state between
beast and god, male and female, child and adult, is another, if distinctive,
example of this rule.[47] But other cherished Greek ideas tell us that woman
herself is the source of ambiguity and conflict in the world and that she
subverts the simple and untroubled integrity of man's original state. Defined in her nature by the mode of her creation, the first woman is introduced into the world by Hesiod's Zeus to redefine its topography, whose
contours will be mapped on the model of the female body as a division
between outside and inside, surface and depth, seen and unseen. In his

45. For the significance of Phaedra's and Hippolytos's genealogies, see Winnington-
Ingram 1960a, 173–78; Reckford 1974; Rankin 1974, 71–94; Smoot 1976, 37–51; Segal
1970, 295; Segal 1978, 135–39. Both psychoanalytic and mythico-ritual critics agree on
the splitting of the feminine figure between Aphrodite (Phaedra) and Artemis (Amazon). For
the psychoanalysts, splitting is a common defense mechanism against incestuous wishes. The
other group associates the same phenomenon with the pre-Greek Mediterranean figure of
the Great Goddess, who combines both aspects within herself: both benign and destructive,
loving and/or destroying her consort. See further Fauth 1959, 406, who observes that for the
Greeks, the "original homogeneity was split into a polarized tension." Oddly enough, the
conflicts of the new Phaedra of this play seem to express in social and human terms what
already may have existed at a deeper substratum of the myth. At the same time, Euripides
shows a marked fondness for splitting the feminine figure—either between virgin and
mother, as in the *Hekabe* or the *Heracleidae*, or more akin to our play, in the *Helen*, where
Helen is divided between her "bad" side (the phantom) and her "good" one (the "real" one
marooned in Egypt).

46. Paraphrase of Vernant 1981a, 18.

47. Vernant (1981a, 94), in speaking of the "logical schema of reversal, corresponding
to the ambiguous type of thought that is characteristic of tragedy," remarks that it "offers
the spectators a particular kind of lesson: man is not a being that can be described or defined;
he is a problem, a riddle, the double meanings of which are inexhaustible." For Hippolytos's
contradictions, see Segal 1978, 134–39. Parthenopaios, the child of another Amazon-type
mother (Atalanta), reveals these ambiguities by the very fact of his name (maiden/boy), and
in Aeschylus's *Seven against Thebes*, he appropriately carries the emblem of the Sphinx on
his shield. See further Zeitlin 1982a, 98–105.

tirade against Phaedra, Hippolytos will invoke the canonical characterization of this first woman, Pandora, who is both the lovely useless *agalma*
that "husbands will ruin their houses to adorn" and the deceitful conniving bitch, the "counterfeit evil" in whom the power of Aphrodite brings
mischief to birth (616–18, 630–33, 642–44).[48]

One might say that Hippolytos's repetition of the Hesiodic discourse
at the heart of the drama defines him as the nostalgic standard-bearer of
the golden age. Even more, his fall into the "human condition" is predicated on the fateful experience of its deceptions and falsehoods, contrived
according to stereotype through the agency of a woman. The drama indeed builds on the Hesiodic foundations of human culture, which are
based on the imperatives of marriage, procreation, and agriculture, and
which Hippolytos flouts in his mode of life. But the play also transcends
these, as it must on the tragic stage, to attain its proper objective—the
fashioning of a tragic consciousness, experience of which is essential to
the construction of a self that is otherwise imprisoned and isolated in its
world of single, nonproblematic meanings.

Woman, as the other, is the object that embodies the external realities
of the world for men. She therefore constrains and defeats the boundless
desire of the male self to escape these unwelcome necessities. But as a
speaking subject, woman also embodies the prerequisites to bring about
that development of fuller consciousness in herself. Given the social constraints under which she must live and the strains of the multiple roles
assigned to her, she is best constructed to experience this tragic "double
bind." In breaking the silence that propriety demands of her, she necessarily transgresses the social rules that would repress and deny, if they could,
the best kept secret of cultural ideology: the reality of the sexual, even
adulterous wife.[49] Hence the critical role of Aphrodite. In entering into the
woman and into the house as the agent of illegal and unspeakable desire,
the goddess transforms the "natural" dissonant unity of the woman's
body in pregnancy and childbirth into a cognitive dissonance within the
self. In struggling to harmonize its disparate aspects, that feminine self is

48. See Hesiod, *Works and Days* 59–82; for discussion of this version and its counterpart in *Theogony* 535–616, see Vernant 1980, "Prometheus"; Vernant 1979b; and Pucci
1977, 82–126.

49. Tanner's remarks (1979, 13) are instructive here: "From the point of view of . . .
society, adultery introduces a bad multiplicity within the requisite unities of social roles.
From another point of view, we could say that the unfaithful wife is, in social terms, a self-
canceling figure, one from whom society would prefer to withhold recognition so that it
would be possible to say that socially and categorically the adulterous woman does not exist.
Yet physically and creaturely she manifestly does, as she becomes a paradoxical presence of
negativity within the social structures, her virtual non-being offering a constant implicit
threat to the being of society." The offense is compounded here, of course, by the incestuous
element. On the lethal aspects of Phaedra's speaking, see Rabinowitz 1987.

led through the subjective experience of her own ambiguities to an epistemological inquiry into the nature of virtue and the self's identity in a
world (373–430) whose structures she also objectively represents.[50]

There is a paradox here. Woman as body may be relegated in the eyes
of society to the corporeal side of human existence. But men's view of her
mysterious physical nature as marked by a private interior space already
predisposes her to a self-consciousness that replaces the virginal quality of
"self-containment" with a deeper subjectivity, which is capable of furnishing a more adequate model of the self. This self must now confront that
interior, which is made problematic as the subjective container of a secret
that must be hidden within. The text is careful to distinguish between
physical and cognitive dissonance. To the *dustropos harmonia* of the
woman's body, the birth pangs *(ōdinai)* she suffers, she responds with a
passive *aphrosunē*, an *anoia* (164, 398), that is, the surrender of mental
faculties in the face of biological pressures. But the other dissonance, the
anguish of her unwanted erotic desire, demands the exercise of *sōphrosunē*, an active attempt of the intellect to constrain the irresistible forces
of instinct and passion (399), which elicits her cry of pain *(odunāi, 247)*,
as she strives to set her mind aright.[51]

Without Aphrodite, the ambiguities of women's lives pass unnoticed
as they freely come and go in widening circles from the house to the outside spaces described by the chorus of women in the parodos. The idyllic
vignette of women washing clothes in the "dews of the river's stream"
(124–30) contrasts with the preceding scene in which Hippolytos defines
his meadow (tended metaphorically by *aidōs* with its river dews, 78). It
also contrasts with Phaedra's later longings to escape to the landscape of
mountain and seashore, whose language expresses her conflicting desires
for both purity and erotic fulfilment (209–11). In the scene of the women
by the river, the dripping water is said to issue from Okeanos, the primordial source, and it ripples out in a flowing stream. Here all is flow and
flux, surface and depth, as the women dip their pitchers into the water and
wet the crimson cloaks to cleanse them, laying them to dry upon the sunny
rocks. Purity is not original or constant in the cycle of household chores.
It can be restored by washing the clothes that have been subjected to the
ordinary pollutions and dirt of human life. But once Aphrodite takes over,

50. This is her famous soliloquy: "Many a time in night's long empty spaces / I have
pondered on the causes of life's shipwreck. / I think that our lives are worse than the mind's
quality / would warrant. There are many who know virtue. / We know the good, we apprehend it clearly. / But we can't bring it to achievement" (375–81, trans. D. Grene).

51. Pigeaud (1976, 8–9) links knowledge of the self to woman's experience of her body
(cf. Hippocrates, *Diseases of Women* 61 [8:126 Littré]). Our text, however, seems to contrast one kind of knowledge (that of the physical body) with another, cognitive kind that
consciously aims to overrule the body and its instinctual demands.

purity and pollution split into irreconcilable opposites. With the revelation of Phaedra's secret, the simple details of women's work will reveal their deeper affinities with the tragic situation that is taking shape.

The women's action of wetting the garments, described as *teggousa*, will find its analogue in the tears that will flood their eyes in grief over the misfortunes of the house and the bereaved husband (128, 854). But the contact implied by *teggousa* is earlier invoked by the nurse who, reproaching Phaedra's silence, laments that her mistress is not "softened" or persuaded by her words (303). Women are expected to mourn for the sorrows of others and, like the clothing they "soften" in the water, to be pliant and permeable themselves. *Teggousa* already intimates the potential dangers to come, but there are other, even more ambiguous signs. The water that drips from the rock will find its echo in the desire that drips by the agency of eros from the eyes (121, 526). The benign heat of the sun (128–29) suggests the torrid passions of eros itself (cf. 530) and will be recalled later when the chorus invokes another spring, the mouth of Dirce at Thebes—the place that sets the stage for the lethal erotic encounter where "Aphrodite gave Semele as a bride to the flame girt thunder" when she was pregnant with the child Dionysos (554–55).

In the second stasimon sung by the chorus at the midpoint of the drama, when Phaedra has made her final exit from the stage, the language of the opening parodos returns. Fiery sun and water are now transformed into the amber-gleaming radiance of the tears (*dakruōn tas elektrophaeis augas*, 740–41) that the mortal maidens shed for Phaethon as tangible tokens of their grief.[52] The ambrosial springs that pour forth in abundance (748) refer now to the erotic paradise of the Hesperides, site of the bed of the immortal couple, Zeus and Hera, a land that "offers no road to sailors" at the boundaries of the world, beyond mortal limits where heaven and earth meet.[53] This is the point that returns us to the context of the parodos itself and the implicit contrast between purity and pollution. There the chorus shifted immediately from the description of the scene by the river to thoughts of Phaedra, who lies sick within the house with the symptoms of her as yet unidentified disease (eros). The garments the women have exposed upon the sunny rocks (126) give way to the robe Phaedra uses to shade her face, hiding the secret shame that pollutes her (131–32).

---

52. *Electron* (amber) derives from *elektōr* (sun). The description of the tears as *elektrophaeis augas*, "amber-shining rays," distills the action (Phaethon's encounter with the sun) into a product (amber tears) and translates the experience from fire to water. See also Padel 1974, 231, on this passage.

53. See Segal 1965, 133; Padel 1974, 233. Parry (1966, 322) points to the ambiguities inherent in the Garden of the Hesperides, which promises immortality to the gods but is in the "westernmost area where earth, heaven, and death are in closest conjunction."

From this moment on, the women will leave the stage no more and Phaedra, except in her fantasies, will make only the briefest journeys in and out of the house. The world narrows down to the space of the stage and what lies behind it, as Phaedra oscillates between secrecy and revelation in her conflict between the two roles of virtuous wife and desiring subject. The social import of these spaces is therefore intensified. The oscillation between them exerts pressure on the ordinary, unquestioned relations between inside and outside, bringing those tensions and ambiguities into play and thereby also recoding the intimate zones of the woman's body and the isotopic house she inhabits into complex psychological interiors.

Inside and Outside

The drama exploits to the fullest the symbolic potentials of Greek scenic conventions. The action is set on stage before the façade of the house, thus arranging a spatial dialectic between outside and inside, seen and unseen, open and closed, exposed and hidden. In one respect, the secret finds appropriate shelter in the inmost recesses of the house (as it does within the deepest marrow of the soul, 255), the place that harbors other undisclosed secrets of women's lives that the dictates of modesty safeguard. In other respects, of course, the secret of adulterous desire is incompatible with the house and the social values it objectifies, so that the woman is no longer "at home" with herself or in the space that replicates her physical construct. The secret, repressed, confines her to her bed and blocks all the normal forms of domestic exchange and those of the body itself: food cannot enter in and the secret cannot issue forth.[54]

The door is the significant boundary between the two zones. Once Phaedra has crossed its threshold from interior to exterior, her dramatic action informs us that the secret, if not yet revealed, is at least now out of doors. Only outside can she find her voice and utter her first words. And her riddling speech, in which she recodes her erotic passion into passionate longing for the remoter Artemisian spaces of mountain and shore (208–38), signifies how far from domestic territory lies the site assigned to feminine desire. Phaedra's exit from the house indicates in advance the

54. Phaedra's fasting is described as keeping "her body pure [hagnon] of the grain of Demeter by the non-eating of her mouth" (275). The Homeric expression, Damatros aktas (cf. Il. 13.322; 21.76), is especially appropriate, for where adulterous desire is present, Demeter, goddess of legitimate marriage, is not. On the other hand, fasting indeed belongs to the cult of Demeter, whether at the Thesmophoria or the Eleusinian mysteries. The latter was the occasion of Hippolytos's visit to Athens where Phaedra first saw him and fell in love (25–27). We might also, therefore, understand her abstention from Demeter's grain as an indication that other mysteries will take their place (those of Aphrodite). The mysteries will be discussed further below.

homology, later made explicit in the text, between the door and the mouth as apertures of the interior that can be opened or closed. In the idiom of the play, these operations are principally those of *desis* and *lusis,* "binding" and "loosening,"[55] which are to prove the determining factors of the plot. Indeed, only through the first *lusis,* that is, the exit of Phaedra from the house and the ensuing "exit" of the secret from her mouth, does the true *desis,* the binding of the plot, begin, and the door becomes the pivotal point of passage and exchange. This is the same door, we may recall, at which the figure of Aphrodite stands in the prologue, unrecognized and unaddressed by Hippolytos (100–101), just as occurs later in Phaedra's case when he appears again on stage (cf. 575).

Phaedra leaves the house at the beginning and enters it again irrevocably as the place of her death after she has been betrayed by the nurse. Hippolytos, on the other hand, enters the house upon arriving on stage, after he has offered his garland in homage to Artemis and made provision for his horses. He leaves it in indignation at the nurse's proposal made to him within, never to enter it again. Once his father discovers the secret written on Phaedra's tablet, Hippolytos is banished not only from the precinct of the house but also from the land itself. All this happens because Theseus three times performs a significant act of opening: the doors of the house ($\chi \alpha \lambda \hat{\alpha} \tau \epsilon \; \kappa \lambda \hat{\eta} \iota \theta \rho \alpha \; \ldots \; \pi \upsilon \lambda \omega \mu \acute{\alpha} \tau \omega \nu$ / $\epsilon \kappa \lambda \acute{\upsilon} \epsilon \theta$' $\acute{\alpha} \rho \mu o \acute{\upsilon} \varsigma$, 808–9), the wrappers of the tablet (*deltos,* (864–65), and the words he can no longer contain within the "doors of his mouth" ($\sigma \tau \acute{o} \mu \alpha \tau o \varsigma \; \acute{\epsilon} \nu \; \pi \acute{\upsilon} \lambda \alpha \iota \varsigma$, 882).[56]

For both Phaedra and Hippolytos, the house has become the purveyor of death. It reclaims one of them literally for its own and expels the other beyond its limits, until he is brought back at the end, when on his deathbed he beholds, as he says, the "doors of the nether regions" ($\nu \epsilon \rho \tau \acute{\epsilon} \rho \omega \nu \; \ldots \; \pi \acute{\upsilon} \lambda \alpha \varsigma$, 1447; cf. 895). Aphrodite's ominous statement that closed the prologue, "he does not know that the doors of Hades are gaping open for him" (56–57), corresponds to Hippolytos's dying utterance. But Hippolytos's passage in the course of the play has already taken him through the doors of the house itself, whose secret interiors anticipate its sinister analogue as the death-dealing abode.

This relation between inside and outside that correlates the self and the house is continued through an important gesture shared by Phaedra at the beginning of the play and Hippolytos toward the end. This is the act

---

55. The vocabulary includes *anoignumi* (open, 56, 793), *chalaō* (relax, 807), *aphiēmi* (let loose, 991; cf. 418, 1324), *methiēmi* (release, 499, 1202), and *katechō* (keep back, 882; cf. *echō* [hold], 660), as well as *sugkleiō* (lock up, 498) and, of course, *luō* (unbind, 1060).

56. The *deltos* is closed up with seals (*sphragismata*) and requires unfolding (*exelixas*) of its wrappings, but *luō* is also used for opening a *deltos* (Euripides, *Iphigenia in Aulis* 38, 109ff., 307). On the homology of mouth and door, see Artemidorus, *Oneirocritica* 1.31.

of covering the head. In Greek social life, the woman ordinarily veiled her head as a distinctive mark of feminine modesty or *aidōs*. It is the sign of her social invisibility, a gesture whose import is heightened by the action of the play. Before the queen's entrance on stage, the chorus had described her "shading her head with fine garments" on her sickbed, doubly confined in her resignation to silence and to death in the interior of the house (131–40). Once outside, however, Phaedra alternately removes her headdress to speak and then covers her face with her cloak to hide her shame (243–44, 250). This suggests, as Artemidorus's dream book later verifies (*Oneirocritica* 4.30), that house and cloak are equivalent to one another as coverings for the self, the one able to signify for the other in predicting the future. Hippolytos's last act is to call for Theseus to cover his face with his robe (*peploi*, 1458). The gesture is the appropriate sign to greet the darkness of death that is thought to "cover over" the body, but here it is also a final confirmation of the queen's forecast that he "would share in her disease." [57] But in the broader context of the play, Hippolytos's act of self-veiling may also signify a fuller awareness of the body's interior dimensions, now that he has come to recognize the boundaries between outside and inside.

What determines this outcome is another enclosure, the miniature *deltos*. Like a pair of doors, it too must be opened, and in both form and content it mediates the homologous relations between the woman's body and the house. The *deltos* is an inanimate object. Like the house, it cannot actually voice an utterance. But when it is opened, like a woman, it can speak the language of the intimate body in its message of erotic violence. Even closed, the *deltos,* cognate with the shape of the letter *delta,* can be identified as the external sign of the woman's inward parts, exposed yet still concealed.[58] Artemidorus may be invoked again to confirm this obser-

---

57. See Padel 1974, 230n.1; and Avery 1968, 35. The first version of the play was called *Hippolytos Kaluptomenos* because he veiled his head in shame at Phaedra's propositions, a gesture of *aidōs* transferred to Phaedra in this play. Thus his act of veiling alludes to his other self as *Kaluptomenos* and yet in the present context is another sign of his changing places with Phaedra to repeat her experience. Death, like the robe (or veil), covers the self, as if it were a palpable cloud that by its contact effected a change of state in the person. See Onians 1951, 420–25. In addition, the mention of Hippolytos's *peploi* recalls his earlier encounter with the nurse. She had first intended to take a scrap from his *peploi* for use in a love charm (514), but later, when she pleads for his silence, he will not even allow her to touch these robes (606).

58. For *delta* as female genitals, see Scholia *ad* Aristophanes, *Lysistrata* 151; and Hesychius, s.v.; with remarks by Taillardat 1965, 77; and Henderson 1991, 146. Etymologically, *delta* is probably related to *deltos*, both owing their origin to the Semitic word for the fourth letter of the alphabet, which is named as the sign for door *(deleth/daleth)*. Cf. Chantraine, 260; and for explicit mention of the "doors of the *deltos*" (letter), see Euripides,

vation: "To dream of a *deltos* is to dream of a woman because all sorts of imprints *[tupoi]* are left inside her" (2.45).[59] Phaedra effectively rebinds herself to the interior of the house by the noose she attaches to its rafters, and she completes the image of the chaste wife not only through the *tupoi* (presumably the *grammata,* "letters," written inside the *deltos*) but also through the external signs with which she seals it. For Theseus explicitly refers first to the imprint (*tupoi,* 862) of her signet ring as the authenticating mark of her identity and second to the "encircling embrace of the seals *[peribolas sphragismatōn]*" by which she has refastened the double folded tablet. As keeper of her husband's house (cf. 787), the woman protects both the treasures of his house and her own body to which he alone has private access.[60] It is not surprising then that Theseus first surmises that the message in the sealed *deltos* will implore him not to allow another woman into his house and bed (860–61). His actions are equally appropriate: he first opens the doors of the house, then the seal on the *deltos,* and finally his own mouth to utter the curses against the male whom he believes has trespassed upon his domestic space, an offense aggravated by its incestuous nature.

On the level of the action, the *deltos* is Phaedra's ploy to cover up her shame and incriminate Hippolytos instead. Hence it plays a pivotal role in

---

Iphigenia in Tauris 727. Other associations of woman and *deltos:* "door" *(thura, pulai)* is an obscene term for vagina (Aristophanes, *Ecclesiazousae* 962–63, 990, cf. 709; *Wasps* 768–69; *Thesmophoriazousae* 424–25; *Lysistrata* 309, 265, 423, 1163); see further Taillardat 1965, 77; and Henderson 1991, 137. Woman and *deltos* are also related through the metaphor of plowing, where *alox* (furrow) refers both to the woman (Sophocles, *Oedipus Tyrannos;* Euripides, *Phoenissae* 18) and to writing on a *deltos* (Aristophophanes, *Thesmophoriazousae* 782, parodying Euripides' *Palamedes*). On the implications of the *deltos* in Sophocles, *Trachiniae* 47, 156, 683, see duBois 1982, 98–99, and her further discussion of woman as tablet in 1988, 130–66. At the same time, the *phrenes,* or "inmost thinking parts of the self," are imagined as a *deltos* on which one writes, records, and remembers (e.g., Aeschylus, *Suppliants* 179; *Prometheus Bound* 789; *Eumenides* 275; Pindar, *Olympians* 10.1–3; Sophocles, *Philoctetes* 1325; *Trachiniae* 683, frag. 579 N[2]; Aeschylus, frag. 281.21 Radt; and Euripides, frag. 506 N[2]). See also Sansone 1975, 60–63. *Deltos* in this context is also appropriate to the sexual and cognitive aspects of Phaedra's secret.

59. See also the comic fragment of Antiphanes' *Sappho* (196K, Athenaeus, 10.450e–51b), which poses the riddle of a female figure who keeps her children under her bosom, and these cry out, although they have no voice. The answer is an epistle *(epistolē)* and the letters are her children.

60. See, e.g., the famous double entendre of Clytemnestra in Aeschylus, *Agamemnon* 609–10; and Euripides, frags. 1063 and 320 N[2]. The women in Aristophanes' *Thesmophoriazousae* complain that as a result of Euripides' slander against them, their husbands come home from the theater and search for hidden lovers, putting them under seal and iron bars *(sphragidos . . . mochlous,* 415) and taking away the women's secret little keys *(kleidia . . . krupta,* 410–21) to the household storerooms.

the plot as a whole. But it is also the nodal point that gathers all the other acts of opening and closing in the play into a symbolic field of reference. Mouth and genitals, speech and sexuality, exterior and interior, exposed and hidden: all converge in this metonymic condensation of the feminine that is displaced onto the inscribed object. The wrapped *deltos,* therefore, is the most tangible sign of the pervasive conflict between inside and outside that the woman resolves only through death—her own and that of the other.

For Hippolytos (this other), now barred from the house, the effects of Phaedra's message will lead to the projection of these spatial relations on a cosmic scale that seems to convert the entire landscape into a vast interior. The messenger describes how the gigantic wave that was to bring forth the bull from the sea "towered up to heaven so that my eye *[omma]* was deprived of the sight of the Scironian shore and it *hid* the Isthmus and Asclepian rock" (1207–9), and he concludes his report with the words: "the horses and the terrible prodigy of the bull were *hidden* somewhere, I know not where, on earth" (1247–48).

In the interval between the two moments—the first when the engulfing wave confounds the boundary of land and sea and the second when Hippolytos covers his head as he approaches the boundary of Hades, whose doors gape open—Hippolytos comes to an experience of the body that replicates that of the sick and suffering Phaedra seen on stage at the beginning of the play. Her prediction that he would "share in her disease" comes to a violent physical fulfillment here when the combined action of the bull from the sea and the stampede of his own horses have subjected his body to what might be called a "demonic parody" of eros. The congruence is even more striking because Hippolytos goes to meet his fate in terms that act out with uncanny precision the abstract phrase that the chorus used to describe the body of his secret double, the woman.

That *dustropos harmonia,* the *"ill-turned fitting together,"* with which the woman is wont to *dwell* (*sunoikein,* 161–63), supplies the model of a conflicted self, which Hippolytos will parallel in two ways: first, by his close attachment to the ensemble of chariot and horses representing an extension of his masculine self, and second, by the physical ordeal of his own body. Hippolytos first *fits (harmosas)* his feet into the matching footspaces in the chariot (1189),[61] fusing himself, as it were, with its compact solidity (cf. *kollēton,* 1225), while it is with the "ways of

61. The word for "footstalls," *arbulai,* is unique in its semantic use here because, as Barrett (1964, 380) remarks, the term normally means "shoes" or "boots." The *hapax* is perhaps significant in two ways: its use transfers to the chariot what should belong to the person, and it confuses the container (i.e., the space for the shoe) with that which is to be contained (the shoe).

horses" that he is said to *dwell* (*sunoikōn,* 1220). With the advent of the
bull, "the horses do not *turn* with *[metastrephousai]* the bindings of their
harness or with the compact structure of the chariot" (1226) but are
turned back *(anastrephein)* by the bull until the disaster ensues.[62] Then
once Hippolytos is separated from the entangling reins (1244), the chariot
and horses also part. The chariot is broken, like the body of Hippolytos
(1239), and the horses disappear together with the bull (1247–48), leaving only a double wreckage behind.

Brought back on stage in a pitiable state, Hippolytos is brought by
pain to express his bodily suffering in language that recalls the symptoms
of a *dustropos harmonia.* He cries out that "pangs dart through his head"
(1351) as they were said to dart through the belly of a woman in travail
(164–66) and that "a spasm leaps up in his brain" (1352). A little later,
he voices his desire *(eramai)* for a two-edged sword to divide his body in
two and "put his life to bed" (1375–77). In conflating the language of
childbirth and sexuality,[63] Hippolytos reenacts a deadly version of these
two aspects of feminine experience. As a result, he is compelled to acknowledge the permeable boundaries of the physical self, as these pertain
to both head and body. We recognize here the power of Aphrodite that,
when refused, converts rapture to pain and eros to death. But we know,
too, that this physical experience is the culmination of the longer and more
profound process by which her power has affected the self in mind as in
body, in mind through body, as leading to a fuller awareness of interior
space.

Artemis will bid Theseus to take Hippolytos's dying body into his
arms (1431–32). Yet at this moment, when the physical and mental are
still unified in a living organism, the goddess has already separated the
different effects of eros on body and mind. He suffers because of the "passions caused by the will of Aphrodite" *(Kupridos ek prothumias orgai)*
that have violently swooped down upon his body *(demas)* (1417–18). But
in forecasting the founding of prenuptial rites in honor of Aphrodite in
which Hippolytos will have a future share, Artemis grants him spiritual
recompense for that somatic suffering, which his good *phrēn* (mind) has
earned (1419).

The text had earlier intimated Aphrodite's more pervasive effects in
a remarkable phrase uttered by the chorus just after Hippolytos leaves
the stage to begin his exile and last journey. These words significantly
reorganize those topological spaces of wood and meadow where Hip-

---

62. *Trepō, tropos,* and *strephō* are related terms.
63. Loraux (1981b, 58–59) notes only symptoms of *ponos* in childbirth in lines 1351–
53, while Segal (1965, 151) sees only the erotic in 1375–77. But the two sets of symptoms
in fact converge as they do in Archilochus, 104D, and the same goes for Herakles' suffering
in Sophocles' *Trachiniae,* as elsewhere.

polytos is most at home. In the prologue, Aphrodite had spoken of Hippolytos as consorting always with the *parthenos* (Artemis) in the verdant wood (χλωρὰν δ᾽ ἀν᾽ ὕλην, 17). We may recall too the virgin grassy meadow from which Hippolytos culled the flowers for her garland (πλεκτὸν στέφανον ἐξ ἀκηράτου λειμῶνος, 73–74). These two allusions merge just after his exit, when the chorus, lamenting Hippolytos's final departure from these Artemisian spaces, refers to the "*deep* verdure" (βαθεῖαν . . . χλόαν) of the "resting places of the maiden of Leto" (that is, Artemis) that "will no longer receive their customary garlands" (ἀστέφανοι δὲ κόρας ἀνάπαυλαι / Λατοῦς, 1137–38). The word *bathus,* "deep," appears only here in the play, and at this painful moment of leave-taking, it may be a subtle but telling clue that a corresponding shift from surface to depth has taken place in Hippolytos himself.

The context of the phrase is even more interesting when we consider that the chorus now turns to voice regret that by this exile, the maidens have now lost "their nuptial rivalry" for Hippolytos's bed (*numphidia . . . hamilla,* 1142–43). The erotic language of their ode might suggest an "anti-epithalamium," because the chorus of Hippolytos's age-mates seems to divide into male and female parts.[64] In such a context, the reference to "the deep wood" may foreshadow the sexual implications of another setting, when Hippolytos is undone through the bestial violence of the bull and his ensavaged horses on the seashore.

Yet the chorus's words of the preceding stanzas in this "anti-epithalmium" already integrate the overlapping levels of body and mind into a more coherent whole. Reflecting on what has brought Hippolytos to this awful moment of leavetaking, the chorus (the male part) translates his experience into the expression of its own subjective feelings. Here at the moment of Hippolytos's own peripeteia, the chorus is moved to ponder the general peripeteias of the world (1104–10), in terms not unlike those of Phaedra's earlier soliloquy on the limits of human knowledge (373–87). They allude to their own interior perceptions, their *phrenes* (1104), and they speak of a consciousness *(sunesin)* that they hide *(keuthōn)* in their hopes within the self (1105). Praying for a spirit *(thumon)* that is untouched *(akēraton)* by pain (1114), they find when reviewing Hippolytos's story that their own *phrēn* (mind) is no longer pure (*katharan,* 1120) and that, like his, their innocence is stained forever.[65]

64. On the arguments for a divided chorus, see, e.g., Reckford 1972, 417–18n.14.

65. Just as the "escape ode" (second stasimon) can be construed with Parry (1966, 323) as the chorus's expression of Phaedra's most intimate feelings at the moment when she is putting an end to her life, so this "anti-epithalamium" seems to perform a similar function with respect to Hippolytos in the interval between his exit from the stage and the disaster that befalls him. Hippolytos, it has been suggested, has affinities with the figure of Hymenaios, the male who disappears on his wedding night (Reckford 1972, 415), who functions as

The Secret and the Construct of the Self

All the expressions used by the chorus in the "anti-epithalamium"—concerning the depth of the woods and meadow, the language of purity and pollution, and the hidden sense of self—surely recall Hippolytos's preceding initiation into an interior life, which began the moment Phaedra's secret was transmitted to him. Then, through its violation of his sensibilities, he feels the first penetration of the self, and under the burden of the secret, he begins to develop a *sunesis* (consciousness) that must necessarily be hidden within.[66]

The point of entry is the orifice of the ear, whose pollution he would cleanse with purifying streams of water, if he could (653–54). But the wounding effects of the knowledge imparted by the *logos* cannot be undone. Having heard these words, as he declares at the end of his long tirade, he seems no longer pure to himself (654–55). Henceforth he is conscious of a dividing line between being and seeming; he is aware of the body's surface as a boundary between outside and inside. As a result, the edenic harmony the body had enjoyed with its natural environment in a relationship of unquestioned identification is forever disrupted.

By its nature, a secret alienates the self from its exterior space and divides the self in two. For in disjoining that which can be said from that which cannot, a secret creates a distinction between public and private, self and other. It therefore brings into being an interior space to contain what must be hidden. This space, coextensive with the organic interior of the body, is henceforth also a "cognitive mental region" dividing inner thought from outward expression.[67] In Hippolytos's case, Phaedra's secret is doubly divisive because it now reorients the image of the body in quite specific ways. The secret enters the self as an alien intrusion from an other, which in bearing a message of illegal desire is utterly antithetical to its new owner. Its effects therefore pollute the self at its deepest level, alienating the self from what it perceives as its true essence and mobilizing its defenses for resistance.

Still, *despite* his resistance, Hippolytos has already become a sharer

---

both bride and bridegroom, *parthenos* and *kouros*. See further below, note 115. The device of dividing the chorus into male and female parts thus corresponds exactly to Hippolytos's psychological status. The identification of chorus with character just at the time of her or his greatest isolation from society further enhances the theme of intersubjectivity in the play. At the same time, the associative style of choral poetry allows the chorus to imitate the inner processes of subjective thought with remarkable fidelity.

66. The vocabulary of concealment is, of course, prominent in the play, consisting of *kruptō, kruptos, kaluptō, keuthō, keuthmōn, lanthanō, lathra*. These words refer to the secret, to gestures of the body, and to spatial configurations (139, 154, 191, 243, 250–51, 279, 330, 394–95, 403, 414, 416, 594, 674, 712, 732, 915, 1105, 1209, 1277, 1290, 1458).

67. Paraphrase of Starobinski 1975, 10.

in the disturbing circuit of communication by which he now possesses the secret of an other, betrayed to him by yet another. Like its original owner (Phaedra), Hippolytos also must oscillate between the necessity of retaining the secret within (that is, by his oath of silence) and the desire to betray it to still another (his father Theseus). But *because* of that resistance, we perceive the first signs of the duality of the self in Hippolytos's famous cry: my tongue *(glōssa)* has sworn, but my mind *(phrēn)* has not (612). A gap has now opened up between inside and outside, inversely matching Phaedra's earlier confession to the nurse: my hands are clean *(hagnai)* but my mind *(phrēn)* is not *(miasma,* 317).

There are formal resemblances between the two statements, but the paradox is more profound in Hippolytos's words. In confronting the difference between a form of absolute speech (the oath he had sworn in advance not to reveal what the nurse will tell him) and its context (the secret), he momentarily repudiates the oath to protect the integrity of his self. Yet by this lapse he betrays that integrity, because an oath guarantees that the self must be forever bound to its word, no matter what circumstances may later arise. Moreover, taking any oath is in itself a self-validating act. It is an exercise of the self's autonomy because, in default of any possible enforcement in the world of mortals, the pronouncement of an oath to another must be matched by an inner determination to remain true to one's word.[68] Although the nurse initially required Hippolytos's pledge of silence, the man and his word go together, since oath keeping in this instance is a resolve entirely commensurate with that quality of "subjective containment" that virginity can represent. In short, the moral virtue of keeping an oath of silence intact finds its logical equivalent in the virtue of keeping the physical body pure.

Hippolytos's moment of hesitation is irrevocable; his story has now begun. There is a brief pause between his lapse and recovery during which he castigates the other for her duplicity. He reasserts, as he had done before (80–81), the external dichotomy in the world between the virtuous and the wicked. This time, however, he defines the latter pole as exclusively female (616, 629, 632, 642, 649, 651). In this interval, before the tongue that has sworn accepts the limits that the barrier of the oath has imposed on its freedom to speak, a torrent of language spills forth from within. Here Hippolytos defines the self at the furthest remove from the other, denying, if he could, her right of speech altogether (645–48), as he strives to heal the new cleavage he feels in his being. Yet at the same time, the rift between tongue and mind leaves open for the overhearer (Phaedra)

68. The fragile nature of an oath accounts precisely for the terrible sanctions against breaking it, whether in the invocation of those all-seeing gods who are gifted with awesome powers of surveillance (Zeus, Helios, Erinyes) or in the dire nature of the self-imprecations that accompany it.

the possibility of a duality in himself whereby he too might "hide one thing in his heart and say another" (cf. *Iliad* 9.312–13) and his unswerving stance might yield to change and reversal (cf. also 1109–10, 1115–17).[69]

In his immediate response to hearing the secret, Hippolytos confirms for Phaedra what she already knows. The world will judge her as it does all women, reading her divisions not as a conflictual ambiguity between self and role but rather as a generic duplicity characteristic of her sex. When Hippolytos reiterates this position, well known since Hesiod, he prompts her to close up this enigmatic space. To defeat the image of the counterfeit woman, she ends by sustaining it. In order to resolve the "knot of the *logos*," her "double bind" has indeed turned into double dealing. In acceding to the stereotype of feminine nature, the woman reduces complex duality to simple reversal from inside to outside and plots a revenge that comes as close as it can to the general definition of all revenge: "to repeat what was done to you but reversing it on to the other."[70] Both women and young men are open to suspicion because of their ambiguous positions on the margins of masculine society and its prevailing standards. In this case, the correspondence between Phaedra and Hippolytos is even more exact because the charge against her counterfeit feminine nature finds its direct analogy in his social status as bastard (*nothos*, 309, 962, 1083).[71] Phaedra's lying message can therefore persuade Theseus of its veracity because it substitutes one stereotype (adolescent) for the other (woman), and in the switch it subjects Hippolytos to those same conflicting pressures from inside and outside to which she herself had succumbed.

Thus, before the oath of silence resecures the secret within the self on stage, Hippolytos has unknowingly already included himself as a sharer in Phaedra's scheme. In rejecting complicity with the other (Phaedra), he has collaborated in Aphrodite's broader scheme, which when eros is denied, works to confound the identity of one with an other by replacing radical disjunction with hidden identification. Only when he who has judged is judged in turn on the same terms does he discover for himself the misfit between inside and outside. Only then can he subjectively experience the same cognitive dissonance and also acknowledge it for the other.

The sign of that shared cognitive dissonance by Hippolytos is both formal and precise; it is indicated as a purely semantic shift and is appropriately placed at the end of his long speech of self-defense before his father:

69. In his confrontation with his father, Hippolytos is tempted once again to "loosen his mouth," this time to save himself (1060), a point critics persist in overlooking.

70. Kahn 1980, 220.

71. The marginal status of both is intensified by the fact that she is of foreign (Cretan) origin and he is the child of the barbarian Amazon mother.

ἐσωφρόνησε δ' οὐκ ἔχουσα σωφρονεῖν

ἡμεῖς δ' ἔχοντες οὐ καλῶς ἐχρώμεθα

She exercised virtue *[sōphrosunē]* not being able to be virtuous,
while we, who were able, did not exercise it well.

(1034–35)

In the light of Phaedra's own closing words, "he will share in my disease
and will learn to *sōphronein*" (730–31), Hippolytos's statement seems to
fulfill her prediction *to* the letter—and *in* the letter. His words seem to
distill the issues of the play into a semiotic lesson on the potential of the
signifier to include more than one signified and the ability of the speaker
to distinguish between competence in the abstract rule *(langue)* and individual performance in the speech act *(parole)*. This lesson is far from elementary, considering the general relationship between language, thought,
and consciousness, and the particular relationship of language, as a mode
of communication between self and other, to the problems and plot of this
drama.

The syntactical relations of Hippolytos's two verses are therefore especially illuminating. The structure divides (or doubles) for each personage the concept of *sōphrosunē* and then through chiasmus makes one the
inverted double of the other. As the grammatical near asyndeton between
the two parts of the sentence tells us, they are not interlinked but are rather
situated in a relation of identity in difference. In one sense, we can say that
Hippolytos has come to share with Phaedra a recognition of verbal paradox. In her case this revolved around the allied concept of *aidōs,* which
bears two different and opposing meanings (shame, reticence), as she la-
mented, and yet is composed of the same letters (385–87).[72] Hippolytos's
statement advances the issue still further. The play on a single word extends from an observation on one character's experience of conflict (*aidōs*
for Phaedra) to a relational term that refers to the differential experience
of two (*sōphrosunē* for Phaedra and Hippolytos). In this way, his statement also recasts the psychic phenomenon of a divided self as a phe-

72. In her long soliloquy, Phaedra ponders the gap between knowing the good and
accomplishing it. Some fail, she says, "because of laziness *[argia],* some because they put
some other pleasure *[hēdonēn]* ahead of *tou kalou* [the beautiful, i.e., noble, fair]. There are
many pleasures in life, long gossips, and leisure, a delightful vice *[kakon]*—and *aidōs*
[shame/reticence]. They are dual; one is not base *[kakē],* the other is a burden upon the
house. If the *kairos* [proper time/place/level] were clear, they would not have the same letters." This enigmatic passage has long been the subject of debate on two accounts: how can
aidōs be a pleasure, and what is the meaning of a dual *aidōs*? For the most recent and most
convincing reading, see Craik 1993a, 1993b. In brief, she argues that "in context *aidōs* is a
euphemistic metonymy for *erōs,* which is harmless and pleasurable in its proper place (allied
with sexual *sōphrosunē*), but potentially troublesome or painful (bringing sexual *aischunē*),"
when adulterous (Craik 1993b, 45).

nomenon of language (the oxymoron). This figure of speech embodies the contradictory experience that each had expressed earlier in separate but parallel terms: my hands are pure, my mind is not (Phaedra); my tongue has sworn, my mind has not (Hippolytos).

This recognition of verbal paradox is critical for acquiring the "tragic consciousness" that the drama achieves, compelling the self to relinquish the dream of a pure and univocal language. Such a language would correlate what can be spoken with the truth and would eliminate any semantic confusion between signifier and signified that might subvert interpretation, subjecting words to the charge of being *asēmos* (nonsignifying, 269, 369) or *parasēmos* (falsely signifying, 1115). Human nature aspires to live in this utopia of signs. Either these would be reserved as the private property of a single individual and a single point of view, or else, as in Theseus's dream of two voices inhabiting a single individual (one true, the other speaking anything else, 928–29), they would provide a form of communication in which the value of a speaker's words would be immediately transparent to an other.

The painful lessons of language may be viewed as a gain when we consider that "if everything we know is viewed as a transition from something else, every experience must have two sides; and either every name must have a double meaning, or else for every meaning there must be two names."[73] Therefore, we might say, Phaedra is essential to Hippolytos, for only through the exchange of roles with her does he come to acknowledge that *sōphrosunē* indeed has a double meaning—for himself and for her— and that with this expanded and polysemous definition in mind, there are indeed two names, Hippolytos and Phaedra, who are entitled to share it.[74]

73. See Freud 1958, 60, citing the philologist Karl Abel.
74. For the best discussion of *sōphrosunē* in this passage, see North 1966, 81. She would translate 1034–35 as "Phaedra behaved with self control *[esōphronēsen]* though she had not the power to be chaste *[sōphronein]*, while I, who have the power, have not used it well." The statement is still clearer if we recall that the effect of eros is to produce *aphrosunē*, since eros takes away the wits *(phrenes)*: Phaedra was in the grip of eros and therefore did not have the capacity for *sōphrosunē*, while I, untouched by eros, did (and do) have the capacity, but did not use it well (i.e., the angry tirade, which he must now realize she overheard). A fragment of Antiphon (39 D-K) seems especially appropriate in this context: "Whoever has not desired *[epethumēse]* or touched *[hēpsato]* what is shameful *[aischron]* or the base *[kakon]*, is not *sōphrōn*. For there is nothing over which he has gained mastery *[kratēsas]* and proved himself well-ordered *[kosmion]*." Cf. Plato, *Symposium* 196c4–5. In other words, genuine *sōphrosunē* is an active not a passive principle and is won by the self through the experience of resisting and overcoming desire. On questions of inside/outside, Starobinski (1975, 14–15, commenting on Achilles and the Embassy in *Il.* 9) puts it well: "Wisdom . . . dictates a control which is not exercised only over the precious substance of life *(psuchē)*, but over a proud spirit *(megalētora thumon)*. To keep it *(ischein)* in the breast *(stēthessi)* can seem like the image-archetype of 'repression.' To 'keep in the breast' just as to 'hide in the heart,' is made possibly by the reality of a visceral *inside,* which the individual

On the other hand, these lessons also involve loss, if ambiguity can be said to contaminate the ideal of a pure and innocent language and to violate unity of word and meaning either with confusing admixtures or through the fragmentation and dispersal of the "original" signification. In this sense, our drama amplifies the tragic lesson by choosing for wordplay the precise terms for shame and chastity (both *aidōs* and *sōphrosunē*) and adjusting the game to the demands of Aphrodite in the links it makes between speech and sexuality.

In this play, the secret—the knowledge of adulterous desire—that Phaedra and Hippolytos now share and would both deny provides the route to articulating a language, and hence a consciousness, more adequate to the complex geography of the body and world than the shallow surfaces of the untested meadow and the unchallenged language of the self would allow. Double speaking is inevitable in the face of adulterous (let alone incestuous) desire, which indeed contaminates social meanings and confuses the interpretation of social roles. It is unspeakable for Phaedra in terms of the proprieties of the social code that calls it *aischrologia* (shameful talk or obscenity). It is unspeakable now for Hippolytos in another way—through the oath that constrains his speech. Hence language is thickened through the riddling ambiguities to which he must resort in trying to explain himself, and all his logical arguments only incur the charge of duplicity. But what other means does he have to maintain control over language (or eros)? Recourse to another oath, this time to swear his innocence by the gods in the form of juridical proof (1025–31), is worse than useless in persuading his father, as he later realizes. Its value relies on the trustworthiness of the self in the eyes of the other; being dependent on its appeal to the gods (who punish perjurers), his oath has no human context to support it.

Double speaking is perhaps a disease that the bewildered Hippolytos suspects Theseus is attributing to him (933) when his father first enigmatically pronounces his wish for the two voices that would distinguish

---

can make the receptacle of the 'breath' that he actively refuses to exteriorize: in preventing the 'haughty' from finding an external issue, the act which bars the passage requires an organic interior (the breath and its viscera) to make a space for the repressed discourse: thus, in the voluntary economy which rules, evaluates, restrains the quantity of passion which can be displayed outside, a wisdom is born, and it installs an interior dimension, a subjectivity. . . . This mastery such as Peleus had recommended to Achilles, is neither simulating nor lying: it invites him simply to keep his passion quiet, to rein it in, not to hold an *other* discourse in its place: this is the virtue called *'retenue,'* . . . and which consists in having dealings with others, always deferring the gesture or word which would harm them. . . . We find everywhere the same lesson: the mastery exercised at the gates, the surveillance exercised over the lips, the voluntary suppression which proves (which creates) the virtue of prudence (i.e., *sōphrosunē*), and which protects the 'soul.'"

the true from the false word in the self's utterances (927–29). But in the situation of the play, double speaking is an inevitable disease, inflicted first on Phaedra as the secret of Aphrodite, which in arousing conflicting desires for fulfillment and repression, necessarily recodes language into the double entendre. As Aphrodite's secret of desire, owned or disowned by both Phaedra and Hippolytos, the secret, like desire itself, cannot be contained. Instead it finds devious paths of language to entice the one who has refused Aphrodite into the mysteries of worldly communication.

Hippolytos has already been privy to the sacred mysteries of Demeter, as the text tells us when it arranges Phaedra's first glimpse of him coming to Athens for initiation (25). This detail directs our attention to the potential correlation between sacred and profane secrets, both of which are *apporhēta*, unspeakable, in their respective milieux.[75] Aphrodite's mysteries will eventually be revealed in the supernatural epiphany of the bull that the goddess shares with Poseidon, by whose agency the body of Hippolytos will be initiated into a demonic version of eros. But the initiation began far earlier with the "mystery" at Troezen, for the secret desire of the silent Phaedra organizes the entire play around notions of hiding and revealing, speech and silence. "The *mythos* is not *koinos* [shared] in any way" (609, cf. especially 293–96), and Phaedra will be ruined once she has "revealed her woes to the light" (368). The nurse says enigmatically that she will speak only "to those within" (524), a mystic formula that conceals her plan to address Hippolytos in the secret interior of the house, while the chorus, hearing Phaedra's report of Hippolytos's muffled words of indignation uttered from within, exclaims: "he has revealed hidden things" (*ta krupt' ekpephēne*, 594). Theseus continues the theme of unspeakability in another way when he responds with horror to the unutterable sight of his dead wife (*ou rhēton*, 846) and again after he has read the message on the *deltos* (*ou lekton*, 875, *pace* Barrett). But it is Hippolytos, bound by his oath of silence, who must play the initiate in confronting his father, because he may not reveal what is forbidden (*ou themis*) to those who do not know (1033).[76] Hence his enigmatic couplet on *sōphrosunē*, which follows directly.

75. The mysteries are called a *telos, teletē* (cf. 25), as was marriage. For the Eleusinian mysteries, based on the myth of Demeter-Kore, marriage as a *telos* might well bear a double charge. The *mystēs*, "initiate," is one whose eyes and lips are closed. The same will be true of Hippolytos, as discussed further below. His witnessing, his *opsis*, of the mysteries (25) anticipates but does not prepare him for the "mysteries" of Aphrodite.

76. The mystic way of life is represented for Hippolytos in three ways: (1) the reference to the *opsis*, the sacred viewing at Eleusis; (2) his personal cult of Artemis in whose meadow it is *ou themis* for the *kakoi* to pluck its flowers (81); and (3) his father's naming him a votary of the Orphic mysteries (952–54). An important link, however, between Aphrodite's men-

At the outset of the play, the servant inquires of Hippolytos: "Do you know what *nomos*, what social rule is established for mortals? And Hippolytos replies: "I do not know" (*ouk oida*, 90–91). But when all his words have failed and he leaves the stage at the end, he goes as the true initiate—the one who knows but cannot speak. Now his last despairing cry, "I know it but I don't know *how* to say it" (*oida d'oukh hopōs phrasō*, 1091), suggests that Aphrodite has also revealed through her mysteries how Hippolytos's refusal of eros has affected his general status as a speaking subject in a social world.

Eros and *Logos*

From this perspective, let us reexamine the judgment, shared by many critics, that language in the play operates in a "pessimistic and regressive frame as an instrument of seduction and entrapment, of compromise and theft, or as an impotent means and a dismal failure" in human relations.[77] It is true that the play offers a wide spectrum of forms of communication, all of which end in what might be called a "failure" of *logos*. But by not considering relations of cause and effect, this assessment perhaps states the problem in reverse, because the failure of *logos* is directly related to and determined by the prior "failure of eros." To grasp what happens in the domain of the *logos* then, let us first measure the extent and import of this initial failure.

Eros is the representative form of communication, the sign of reciprocity and exchange in the human world. Physical in nature, it is culturally regulated as a communication between proper partners in the social system of marriage. The matrimonial system, like a system of language, articulates its own proper grammatical rules, and in the enforcement of social differentiations, it is designed to produce unambiguous meanings. In this system, "women, like words, are signs to be communicated and exchanged among men," but women too, as persons, says Lévi-Strauss,

---

tion of Hippolytos's initiation into the mysteries at Athens and the events in the play is suggested in the nurse's enigmatic remarks at 191–96: "But if there is something dearer *[philteron]* than this life, the embrace of darkness *[skotos]* hides it in clouds. We seem to be unhappy lovers *[duserōtes . . . phainometha]* of that which glitters upon the earth, through inexperience *[apeirosunē]* of another life and the non-showing *[ouk apodeixin]* of what lies beneath the earth." That "other life" and the showing of things "beneath the earth" evoke the context of the mysteries, but the terms she uses will later be fulfilled in another way, when events will make Hippolytos *seem* to be the one who is *duserōs* of things on earth.

77. Turato 1976, 183. This important study expands Knox's (1952) formalist abstractions of alternating speech and silence among the characters, offering a rich analysis of the various, even competing, systems of communication at work in the play.

"are generators of signs. . . . In the matrimonial dialogue of men, woman is never purely what is spoken about; for if women in general represent a certain category of signs, destined to a certain kind of communication, each woman preserves a particular value arising from her talent, before and after marriage, for taking her part in a duet. In contrast to words, which have become wholly signs, woman has remained at once a sign and a value."[78]

By refusing eros, Hippolytos has refused to enter into the normative system of communication into which the self might be integrated. Instead, he stays with the horses whose ways he shares (1219–20), whom he can both see and touch, and to whom he may speak but who cannot reply in kind. On the other hand, he reserves his language (and only his language) for the ears of the goddess whom, by the rules that govern relations between mortals and immortals, he cannot see and cannot touch (84). In the virginal enclosure of the meadow (or, equally, the spaces of the mountains or shore), he remains outside the circuit of human communication, dissociated from others who are unlike himself. More particularly, he removes himself from contact with that other goddess, Aphrodite, who like all mortals and all gods, as the servant reminds Hippolytos in the prologue, wishes to be addressed by an other (*en d'euprosēgoroisin*, 95). To honor the goddess in this context means to address her image that stands at the doors of his house (99) because, as the servant says, she is *semnē* (august) and *episēmos* (significant, bearing the mark of a distinguishing sign, like a device on a coin). But Hippolytos has no words for her except to wish her a "long goodbye" (113).

This modest dialogue is worth recalling at the moment after the nurse has revealed Phaedra's secret, when Hippolytos utters his long denunciation of all women. Just before he says he wants to cleanse his ears with pure, running water, he utters another, more dramatic wish: no servant should be able to go near a woman. Rather, women should dwell together (*sugkatoikizein*) with savage beasts who have no voice. In this way, Hippolytos would never have to address (*prosphōnein*) any one of them or receive in return any utterance voiced by them (645–48). "As things are," he says, "women sit *within* and in their wickedness contrive wild schemes and these their servants bear to the world *outside*" (649–50). His indictment is generic. Hippolytos, we might say, desires to repress those "speaking signs" that are women. While reserving for himself

78. Lévi-Strauss 1967, 496. For the connections between language, kinship, and sexuality with reference to Eteocles, son of Oedipus, who, like Hippolytos, utters a long tirade against women, see Zeitlin 1982a, 29–36. The similarities between the two figures are reinforced by the fact that both are connected to unlawful sexuality: one is the product of an incestuous marriage, and the other is accused of "shaming his father's bed" (943–94).

the right of speech, he forbids women to communicate in any economy of exchange and reciprocity. Indeed, his opening broadside against that "counterfeit evil" called woman reveals the terms of his own economic system and indicates how intimately his desire for control over the *logos* is linked to his exclusion of eros.

Woman is indeed a sign for Hippolytos, but a false and deceptive one and hence an unworthy source for begetting children. He proposes rather that "mortals deposit in the temples of the gods either bronze or iron or gold in order to buy the seed of children, each man according to the amount appropriate to his assessment. Then one could live in houses that are forever free of the female" (616–24). In wishing to acquire children by purchase in the temples, Hippolytos accomplishes two objectives. He bypasses that shadowy, ambiguous interior of the woman and the house in favor of the domain of the sacred. He also bypasses the ambiguous realm of social relations in favor of a direct and unerring judgment of the gods on a man's true value. Instead of matrimonial exchange between families, he prefers the commercial exchange of coinage—palpable tokens of the self's worth. He thereby indicates his desire for a world without dissonance or dialogue, refusing any resignation to the uncertain mixtures that the Hesiodic view grudgingly accepts as the human condition, after men have been separated from the gods.

Like Hesiod, Hippolytos describes woman in terms recalling the creation of Pandora—a beautiful form, an *agalma,* like a statue one must adorn (631), but concealing a counterfeit evil within (616). In the Hesiodic economy, however, man cannot dispense with that beautiful evil with which he must dwell. Although woman sits in the house, draining his resources, she is essential to him precisely because of her reproductive function, through which he may acquire an heir to inherit his goods and continue his father's lineage. Hesiod grudgingly accedes to the compromise that requires a man to take an other into his house or else forfeit the chance of legitimate offspring he can claim as his own.[79] Hippolytos rejects this limited solution, which is only a fictive fulfillment of the "dream of a purely paternal heredity that continually haunts the Greek imagination."[80] This counterfeit woman cannot bear true children—that is, true and perfect replications of the autonomous masculine self. Instead, Hippolytos fashions another fiction that would guarantee progeny as authentic signs of the self. As objects exchanged for true and durable coins, they would then forever bear the stamp of a single, original identity that can never be lost.

79. See above, chapter 2, 59–72.
80. Vernant 1969, 106.

In Hippolytos's world, then, woman is truly the other who is excluded from dialogue. Alone in this world, he is as free to speak as he is to roam in those external spaces where Phaedra can only wander in her verbal imaginings as a way of escaping from the imprisoning word of the secret. But in the social system of communication, Hippolytos is actually the other. He is the one who in essence is not a "speaking sign": figuratively, because in safeguarding his virginal status, he has excluded himself from the system of exchange and literally, in the fact that, as he will later acknowledge before his father, he is unaccustomed to speak before those who are not the same as himself (986–87). The unspeakable secret is alien to him. Yet paradoxically the silence required by its repression better exemplifies the permanent aspect of "nonspeaking" implied in his virginal status of "subjective containment." Additionally, his sworn oath of silence to the nurse, which formally restrains his speech, corresponds in its inhibition of verbal expression to the condition of physical restraint imposed by the denial of eros. The oath of silence serves the direct needs of the plot, but the second oath of self-imprecation, volunteered by Hippolytos in his own defense, is finally his sole, if unpersuasive, means of convincing his father of his innocence. For in general an oath, construed as a speech act, is an isolating form of utterance that breaks with dialogic exchange. Its value of proof for the other, as noted earlier, depends wholly on the self-representation of the speaker who swears it. Under the present circumstances, how can it do otherwise than serve to condemn Hippolytos still further in his father's eyes? (1025–40, 1054–57, cf. 960–61).

An oath, once separated from a context in which the self is known to its society, might be termed a disembodied voice. It corresponds on a symbolic level to the strategies of the plot, which works its baneful effects through speech detached from the physical presence of its original speaker and destined to circulate without the face-to-face contact that might guarantee its trustworthiness. The text explicitly formulates this principle in Phaedra's statement, which applies to her situation but still better to that of Hippolytos: "For there is nothing trustworthy [piston] in the tongue, which knows how to admonish the thoughts of someone else but which itself by itself [autē d'huph' hautēs] wins a multitude of troubles" (395–97).

Critics who have examined the status of language in this play, whether focusing on the abstract dialectic between speech and silence or taking inventory of the varied forms of communication deployed, have much to teach us about Euripidean attitudes and techniques.[81] But to grasp more fully the mechanics of communication in the Hippolytos, we need to look further and ask how they operate and what purposes they serve in the plot.

81. E.g., Turato 1974; and Knox 1952.

Hippolytos, who gives his name to the play, is the determining factor. He is the figure who, as the precision of tragic justice requires, needs (and gets) a plot made expressly for him. That is, the plot must reply to his first refusal to address the statue of Aphrodite, which he will only greet from afar (102), and to the nature of his relations with Artemis, whose voice *(audē)* he hears but whose eye *(omma)* he cannot see (86). Hippolytos will experience a rift between the tongue and the mind *(phrēn)*, but the fundamental gap in his sensory system is that between the tongue (or the ear) and the eye.

The Tongue, the Ear, and the Eye

Hippolytos fetishizes the ear, as it were, first through his anguish at its penetration by the secret and then again when he inquires of Theseus whether one of his friends has slandered him *(dieballe)* "into" his father's ear (932–33). It is therefore no coincidence that the first sign of the demonic epiphany of the bull is a terrible chthonic echo, a deep-booming roar, terrifying to *hear*, to which the horses are the first to respond, pricking up their ears and raising their heads to heaven (1201–4). But auditory signs play an important role throughout, starting with the desire professed by all present to *hear* Phaedra's secret (270, 344). In the first uttering of the fateful name, Hippolytos's words about Artemis *(kluōn audēs)* return exactly when the nurse inquires, "Do you speak *[audais]* of Hippolytos?" and Phaedra replies, "You hear *[klueis]* it from yourself, not from me" (352–53). The chorus immediately responds with the same emphasis: "you have heard *[aies]*, you have heard *[eklues]* of the wretched passions of our mistress which are unfit to hear *[anēkousta]*" (362–63).

Yet this is what Hippolytos will indeed hear from the nurse inside, and his voice will in turn be overheard by the other, first from within, when Phaedra eavesdrops at the door of the house, and then when she remains unnoticed on stage while he utters his long speech outside. The excited scene at the door in the rapid interchange between the chorus and Phaedra (565–601) is a remarkable *coup de théâtre*, which, let us note, focuses entirely on the voice that can be heard but whose owner cannot be seen.[82]

Phaedra hears the voice first, indistinctly (567). It throws her into a panic, as she strains to catch the words. The chorus, eager to learn the reasons for the commotion, begs her to tell them. "Go stand at the doors and listen yourself to the unholy din," she replies (575). No, "you are there already," they say, "you can tell us best" (577–79). It is "the child

---

82. Taplin (1978, 70–71) notes that "the sustained scene of eavesdropping with its almost grotesque associations of listening at the keyhole, is quite without parallel in surviving Greek tragedy."

of the horse-loving Amazon, who shouts," says Phaedra, identifying only the speaker. He is "uttering [audōn] terrible, ugly words" (584). The chorus now catches the sound of the muffled voice, but only as an audible sound, until Phaedra articulates the words he "speaks forth" (exaudei, 590).[83] These exacting details serve more than a purely theatrical function, as we will recognize if we recall that once Hippolytos exits from the house to speak out loud, his voice sets the tragic action on a path of no return. Now he and Phaedra are both present on stage—but not to each other— so that she hears every terrible word he utters but he does not see her eye to eye. At the end, when the chariot overturns and Hippolytos's head is crushed against the rocks, this fateful scene at the door reechoes in our ears. One last time he will "speak forth" (exaudei), uttering things "terrible to hear" (deina kluein, 1239).

In the interval, Hippolytos will have come back on stage having heard his father's shout of alarm. Not knowing the news, he will desire, as the nurse did in questioning Phaedra, to hear it from the other (904, cf. 344). Theseus, for his part, will end by exclaiming to his servants: "Will you not drag him away? Have you not heard me now for a long time addressing [prounneponta] him for banishment?" (1085). This line repeats almost word for word the servant's admonition to Hippolytos in the prologue to address (prosennepeis) the figure of Aphrodite (99).

Hippolytos will wish at the moment of direst need that the house could take voice and bear witness for him, but it would be a voiceless witness, as his father reminds him, because "it is the deed itself that speaks" (1074–77).[84] What he needs most of all is an eyewitness, since Phaedra no longer lives, no longer "looks upon the light" (1023). Yet even here the witness he desires is not truly an other, but rather one, he says, "just like himself" (1022). By contrast, the nurse can call upon the women of the chorus, as present with her on stage, to "witness her zeal in tending to her mistress' misfortunes" (287). The chorus in turn assumes that Theseus, were he at home, could assess the nature of Phaedra's symptoms just by "looking at her face" (280). Now Phaedra's figure is the "clearest" witness—her corpse that is present on stage before his eyes (972). Theseus may wish that mortals might have a clear token of proof (tekmērion) of those who are their friends and a valid means of discerning their state of mind (diagnōsin phrenōn, 925–26). But without such signs, no oaths, no

83. The variety of words for speech, shout, noise, voice, and utterance in this passage is remarkable. Nouns: audē (571), logos (571), phēma (572), kelados (576), phatis (578), ia (585), boa (587). Verbs: throeō (571), boaō (571, 581), audaō (582), gegōna (586), exaudaō (590).

84. Segal (1965, 146–47) notes the correlation of this wish with Hippolytos's earlier desire to refuse speech to women, but not in the ruling perspective of Hippolytos's preference for hearing over sight.

words, he says, could furnish more powerful proof than this lifeless body (960). Conversely, Hippolytos comes to realize that if he were to "loosen his mouth" (*luō stoma,* 1060) in breaking his previous oath of silence to the nurse, he still could never persuade the other, his father, of the truth.

In this juridical procedure, when Hippolytos must present his face to his father, the division in his life between voice *(audē)* and eye *(omma)* reveals its full implications. At one end of the visual spectrum is the force of eros, which "drips desire from the eyes" (525–26) in the gaze of the other. Phaedra had been struck with a terrible eros in her heart when she saw Hippolytos in Athens. She dedicated a temple to her passion there on the rock of the Acropolis, and now as a silent lookout *(katopsion)* of that love, it can be glimpsed at Troezen across the gulf (26–34). Not to see or be seen means not to be subject to eros; it means standing outside the optical range by which the attractive magnet of desire works its double effects on lover and beloved alike. But in the ordinary sphere of social relations, not to see and be seen also means to lack a reciprocity of regard through which one might accurately judge the face of the other—and conversely, through which one can find an other, an eyewitness, to verify the self, whether to judge it or to pity and mourn. Without such an other, one might well wish, as Hippolytos does, that the house, whose façade is visible on stage, could take voice and speak as a witness (1074–75). Or one might long for the impossible—to divide oneself into two: "Would that I were able to stand opposite and look at myself *[prosblepein],*" he says, "so that I could weep for myself at the woes I suffer" (1078–79).[85]

Let us define more closely this problem of sight and the eye. It is not, of course, that Hippolytos is deprived of vision; rather, what counts is the mode of his seeing. His own words give us the clue: "I do not know the *praxis* of eros, except having heard of it in speech *[kluōn logōi]* and seeing *[leussōn]* it through pictures *[graphēi].* For I am not eager to look upon *[skopein]* these things, since I have a maiden soul *[parthenon psuchēn]*" (1004–6).

His outlook on life takes a distanced view. Appropriately for one who greets Aphrodite from afar, he sees woman only in objectified form. Hip-

---

85. The chorus justifies its presence on stage as having come to mourn (*penthēteria,* 805). Greek ritual customs suggest that mourning is an antiphonal affair, involving both kin and nonkin (or those related by marriage *[kēdestai],* where *kēdos* pertains both to family alliances and to funerals or grief). Cf. the pun in Aeschylus, *Agamemnon* 609, on *kēdos* as both "marriage tie" and "woe," and also the likely semantic connection between *penthos* (grief) and *pentheros* ("father-in-law," afterward just "in-laws"). See Alexiou 1974, 10–14. I further suggest that the antiphonal lament may be a way to formalize the need for an other who is truly an other (outsider) to witness and share in the mourner's grief, while the mourners in turn identify with the one they have lost. For a different point of view, see the discussion of self and other in Pucci 1980, 21–32, 226n.24.

polytos knows the body of the other as a sculpted figure, an *agalma,* like the mute statue of Artemis that stands in for the goddess. If he scornfully speaks of the husband who is forced to adorn his vain *agalma* of a wife, we recall that Hippolytos first enters bearing garlands to adorn Artemis's image and later even names himself as the guardian of all her statues (*phulax agalmatōn,* 1399). Although venting his hatred of the entire feminine sex, Hippolytos would at least prefer the silent *agalma* type, a foolish creature of little sense, to the clever *(phronousa)* kind, who can only use her wits for contriving evils (641–44) and suborning others through deceitful words.

It is in Phaedra's interest, of course, to leave behind these "clearest proofs" (972), the visible, solid evidence of her body and the tangible "speech" of her *deltos.* But Hippolytos too, in his scheme for acquiring children, had wished for a clear proof of identity in the material substance of coinage that would answer to some external and guaranteed standard of value. Even more to the point, Phaedra's action returns against him a caricature of his image of the feminine: an *agalma* that is the lifeless body and the *deltos* that conceals its duplicity. Now, as a "dead letter," she can truly be only a "speaking sign" (cf. 857). For one who only sees second-hand through images in pictures and books, what better means to destroy him than this startling tableau of inanimate figure and lettered inscription?[86] But we are in the theater now, where the spectator too may see from afar. Let us turn then to the "viewing place," the *theatron,* to take the measure of its potential lessons for the self.

The Theater, Identity, and the Self

Phaedra's last appearance on stage is a well-devised act of theater. Theseus has just returned from a mission as a sacred observer, a *theōros* (792). Hearing the news of her death, he flings off the woven garland that was the sign of his happy errand, proclaiming himself an unfortunate viewer (*theōros,* 806–7) in anticipation of the sight he will see when the doors are opened and he gazes at the "bitter spectacle" *(pikra théa)* of his wife. Hippolytos's visual shock is still greater. He had just left her, he says, still "gazing at the light *[phaos tode . . . eisederketo].*" Regarding her face to face for the first time now that she is dead, he expresses the beholder's astonishment *(thauma)* at the sight that meets his eyes (905–8).

---

86. Hippolytos's language betrays his image of the body as a text or book: he opens his hands as one unfolds a scroll (*anaptuchai,* 601, 1190) and urges his father to "unfold" *(diaptussō)* the matter to get at the truth (985). *Anaptussō* for "unfolding to read": Herodotus, 1.125; Euripides, frag. 369.6 N². Also *diaptussō:* Euripides, *Iphigenia in Tauris* 727, 793. And *ptuchai* as "the leaves of the book": Aeschylus, *Suppliants* 947; Sophocles, frag. 144 Radt. Segal 1979, 155, notes the vocabulary for a different purpose.

Reference to theatrical spectacle will recur in a cognate word at the end of the text, when the epiphany of divine power rejoins those two sensory affects of sight and hearing that Hippolytos had earlier sundered: first, hearing alone, then sight and hearing together. At the first subterranean roar, the wave rose up to heaven "so that my eye," says the messenger, "was prevented from seeing the Scironian shores" (1207–8). But once the wave has cast up the bull from the sea, what follows is another terrible sound, which fills up the entire earth. Then a "spectacle appeared *[theama . . . ephaineto]*" to the onlookers' gaze, one "too overwhelming to behold," which terrified the horses into their mad stampede (1215–18). The bull keeps "appearing before" them (*prouphaineto*, 1228), but now in silence it redirects the horses and chariots to ruin until at last, in the manner of such sudden prodigies, it vanishes from the line of vision, together with the horses (1247–48). For the messenger, the apparition had provided a great and terrible spectacle, which he had seen only from afar. But for Hippolytos, the bull from the sea provided the most dramatic moment of his life, when he confronted the combined powers of beasts and gods and was overwhelmed by the forces of nature.

Aphrodite and Poseidon, it is true, arranged this remarkable ordeal for Hippolytos. Theseus was its more immediate cause, but Phaedra was its true agent. Thus to grasp the import of this epiphany within the visual code we have been tracing, let us look back to an earlier moment in the text for another word from the theatrical lexicon, which Hippolytos uses at the end of his long denunciation of womankind. "I will go away and keep silent, but when my father returns, so will I, and I will be a spectator *[theasomai]*, looking at the way that you will look at *[prosopsēi]* him" (661–63).[87]

What happens instead is that she will be the *théa*, "spectacle," that all will behold, while Hippolytos will be obliged to present his *prosōpon* before his father (947, cf. 1458). But what will this *prosōpon* reveal? Accused of an act he did not commit, he is turned into an actor—in both senses of the word. He must now take the leading part in the other's (Phaedra's) drama and assume the *prosōpon* before his father that rightfully belongs to her. Slated to play a role that the other had transferred to him, he will find himself accused of only playing a role; his *prosōpon* will be viewed as a mere mask, offering only a false mirror of the self to the eyes of the other.

87. *Théa* and *theaomai* (and *theatēs*) later become technical terms of the theater. *Théa* as "spectacle": Theophrastus, *Characters* 5.7. *Théa* as "seat in the theater": Aeschines, *De falsa legatione* 2.55; Demosthenes, *De corona* 18.28; *Meidias* 21.178. Also *theaomai*: Aristophanes, *Frogs* 2; *Clouds* 518; and Isocrates, *Panegyric* 4.44. *Prosōpon* is the standard word for mask (*persona*). Unlike the English "face," it is not that which "faces" you, the other, but rather the visage, that which you, the other, look at or regard.

The wish, "would that I could stand opposite and look at myself so that I could weep for my sufferings" (1078), is an *adunaton*, impossible to fulfill, except in the experience of a mirror, which teaches the self the first lesson of perspective on its own alterity. For in regarding oneself in a mirror, one views oneself both as a subject seeing and as an object being seen. Through one's reflection, therefore, one takes the first step toward the recognition that the identity of the self must always include "the representation of its subjectivity in relation to an other."[88] "The mirror," as Vernant observes, "is the means of knowing oneself, losing and again refinding oneself, but only on condition of separating oneself, dividing oneself, taking a distance from oneself, as self to other, in order to attain an objective figure of the subject."[89]

Narcissus finds a mirror in which he misrecognizes the self for the other. Hippolytos, when others misrecognize his self, discovers for the first time that he needs a mirror to return to him an objective acknowledgment of the self's experience. Yet Narcissus and Hippolytos meet at the same point. In the absence of an other, the self can only divide (or double) and can only hopelessly yearn to play both parts, self and other. Narcissus wastes away, caught in the specular fascination of impossible desire, doomed to gaze at the surface of the water but never to fathom its depths. Hippolytos, however, as he mounts the chariot and takes up the reins of the horses that will lead him to disaster, goes on to act out the consequences of having refused to meet the other's eye (or touch) in a human contact. This he does, as we have already seen, through an active reprise of those terms that belong to the woman, his secret double, terms that exemplify the cultural perception of her body—that *dustropos harmonia*, that divided self, which suffers in the pangs of erotic desire and childbirth.

The horses with whom he identified himself prove to be creatures alien to the self, although, as he reproaches them, they were his own, "reared and nurtured by his own hand" (1240, 1356). In the same breath he now calls for an other, a person, who would be present at his side to save him (1243). But these others, his companions, are left far behind (1244–45), no longer even able to witness in full the final spectacle of his ruin.

Upon Hippolytos's return to the stage after the disaster, Artemis is waiting, having bidden Theseus to *hear* the story she will recount (1283, 1296, 1314). Now the final implications of "hearing the goddess's voice, but not seeing her eye" come into play. In response to Artemis's greeting,

---

88. Schwartz and Kahn (1980, xiii): "In the continuity of relation between self and other . . . the process is circular and development is the broadening of the circle of possible representations."

89. Vernant 1981d, 485, and see his entire discussion, 457–65.

Hippolytos recognizes her presence, this time through another of the senses—the perfume of her divine emanation (osmēs pneuma, 1391–92)—but what now concerns him most is the question of vision. Although mortals may not look upon gods, nothing precludes the reversal of the gaze. Accordingly, Hippolytos insists that he be seen, first by Zeus (1363), whose eye (omma) Theseus had accused him of dishonoring (886), and then by Artemis herself: "Do you see me, in my wretched state?" (1395). In other words, he demands that she play the part he could not accomplish alone: that she be the other who stands opposite and looks at him so as to weep for his sufferings (1078–79). "I see," she says, but according to the rules, "it is not themis for a goddess to shed tears from her eyes"; still less is she permitted to pollute an immortal eye with the sight of the dying (1396, 1437–38). Such are the constraints imposed on the relations between mortals and immortals that necessarily limit the value of a divine regard in the human world.

Yet Hippolytos will obtain a version of his earlier wish. Continuing to weep for himself, he goes forth with his comrades to meet his ruin (1178).[90] But once he no longer "looks upon the light," there will be others to weep for him. The chorus in its closing lines will refer to the communal grief (koinon achos) of all the citizens and to the tears of grief that will follow hereafter (1462–64). In the cult that is founded in his honor for the future, the mythos has indeed become koinos (cf. 609), the one, however, that he had shared with Phaedra (cf. koinēi metaschōn, 731). The others, the maidens, will forever mourn for him as the other, mourning in truth for themselves.[91]

Once the drama, the spectacle, is over and the body has gone to the "hiding places of dark earth into the house of Hades, the unseen" (Theognis, 243), then and only then will hearing and the voice come fully into their own. In the oath sworn before his father, Hippolytos had prayed that "if he proved a base man [kakos], he should perish aklees [without kleos, "renown"] and anōnumos [without a name]" (1028, 1031). The oath did not save him from destruction, but Artemis's words, in forecasting his cult, redeem his honor by reversing the terms of his self-imprecation. For as she predicts, "maidens will always take care to make songs for you [mousopoios . . . merimna]," and Phaedra's eros for you will not disappear into silence to vanish "without a name [anōnumos]" (1428–30).

After death, only the name and the story remain for those who come after. This is the meaning of kleos, central to the goals of Greek poetics

90. It is evident throughout that Hippolytos's age-mates do not count in the sociopolitical world of adults. While the text shows him as isolated from others, it also suggests a social life with his peers (cf. 996–1001). These are presumably the ones who are "identical to himself."

91. Reckford 1972, 431. On the rite, Fauth 1959, 389–97.

for rewarding the accomplishment of heroic deeds. Immortal renown depends on the transmission of a story for others to tell and hear *(kluō)* over the long span of time—the *mythos* of Hippolytos and Phaedra, whose own desire to preserve her *eukleia* (good fame)[92] brought all these events to pass.[93] By this traditional means of preserving cultural memory, Hippolytos achieves the immortal status he had longed for in consorting with the goddess, granted to him as a parting gift by the one whose voice he heard but whose eye he did not see. The process has already begun in the grief we witness on stage, and it extends into the future through Theseus's bitter last words, addressed to Aphrodite: "I will remember *[mnēsomai]* the evils you have wrought" (1461).

Theseus's promise is the point of transition from personal experience to collective commemoration, all in the name of Aphrodite. It is a fitting close to this last scene in which Hippolytos, in his final mortal moments, repairs his relationship with the other, his father. That is, he now reverses the otherness his father had assigned to him—at birth by reason of his social status as a bastard and more recently as an alienated *xenos,* forcibly sent into exile (1085).

The previous confrontation between father and son showed what it meant to have no other—whether witness or mourner. But the exchange of roles brought about by Phaedra introduces Hippolytos to the principle of reciprocity. When required for the first time to stand in the place of the other (Phaedra), he is also required, for purposes of persuasion, to invoke a rhetorical identification with the other (Theseus). Hence he attempts to reverse the roles between speaker and listener in order to share the perspective of the other. "If I were the father and you were the son" (1042), he says. This effort does not succeed, but it does prepare him for the future when in their shared suffering, he and his father exchange sentiments of pity for each other. Thus to Hippolytos's statement, "I grieve for you more than for myself," his father replies, "If only I could be the one who dies in

92. On the intricate connotations of Phaedra's *eukleia,* see Loraux 1978; and Gilula 1981.

93. E.g., Theognis, 237–54. The archaic poet's famous address to Cyrnus is remarkably relevant, especially the last lines: "When you go beneath the hiding places of the earth to the much-lamenting house of Hades, never, although dead, will you lose your *kleos* but you will be a concern *[meleseis]* for men, possessing an imperishable name *[aphthiton onoma]* forever. . . . The shining gifts of the violet-crowned Muses will send you off, to all those to whom you are a care, and to those yet to come you will be an *aoidē,* a song, as long as earth and sun endure." See also Plato, *Symposium* 208d, for the link between the self's longing for immortality and the winning of an *athanatos mnēmē* of *aretē* (immortal commemoration of virtue). We might further note that, unlike usual finales in Greek tragedy, there is no mention of burial rites to come, as though the cult foundation obviates this necessity by replacing the other variant ending to Hippolytos's story: attempted resurrection through the skills of Asklepios (e.g., Euripides, *Alcestis,* 3–4).

place of you" (1409–10). On these same terms, the son can forgive his father, because "to forgive" in Greek is *suggignōskein*, "to know something together with" someone else, and through the consciousness of shared knowledge, to grant pardon. In return, then, for those curses, whose verbal power Theseus had released (*ephiēmi*, 1324) to destroy his son, Hippolytos now grants his father release (*aphiēmi*, 1450) from blood guilt, sealing his word with Artemis as his witness (*marturomai*, 1451). Before he could only release (*aphiēmi*) his tongue to speak under duress in his own defense (991), a tongue constrained by the oath he had sworn to the nurse. Now he validates at last the power of his own *logos* through his shared experience with the other.

This scene also repairs the other sensory defect to which his relation with Artemis had consigned him—that is, touch. Having refused the touch of the other (14, 606), he could not himself be touched until he had lived through the sequence of events that followed from his seeming to have "touched" what he was forbidden to touch (652, 885, 1002, 1044, 1086). Given the premises that ruled Hippolytos's existence, his earlier *logos* can only fail, for the one who is not open to eros is also not open to persuasion, and on the same principle, he has no convincing means by which to persuade the other. Instead, when he tries to exercise the verbal skills of *peithō* (persuasion), the other judges his words as deceitful seduction and a species of false rhetoric.[94]

By the same logic, the one who is open to contact with others is also open to eros and finally also to persuasion. After all, the entire chain was set into motion by the touch of another's hand, when the nurse supplicated Phaedra. She held fast to her hand, vowing never to let go (326, cf. 335), insisting that the queen *look* at her directly (300) and *touching* Phaedra first with the simple mention of Hippolytos's name (310). Yet the chain also depended on the one from whose eyes tears flowed and who turned her own eye away in shame (245–46). To protect herself lest she "be *seen* to be among those wicked of mortals" (428, 450), Phaedra became in turn an evil to Hippolytos (729). Accusing him in her letter of "dishonoring the majestic *eye* of Zeus" (886), she gave him that *prosōpon* that mirrored her own.

Time, the Mirror, and the Virgin

The mirror effect is the operative term in the drama that will prove to govern the more general patterns of mimetic action. We have seen the import of Hippolytos's impossible wish "to stand opposite and look at him-

94. See Turato 1976 for the relationship of seduction to rhetoric in the context of the Sophists. More generally, see Detienne 1973; Kahn 1978, 119–64.

self" (1078–79) and how it can be understood in reference to a self-regarding mirror. But in view of an earlier direct mention of a mirror *(katoptron)*, his turn of phrase gains in significance as an oblique reminder to us of that first allusion and its context. Phaedra is the speaker, and the statement that closes her great speech on the mysteries of life is strangely enigmatic: "Only this, they say, competes in life, a good and upright judgment *[gnōmē]* for the one who has it, but for the wicked among men time shows forth *[ekphēn[e]* . . . *chronos]*, as it happens to, when before them as before a young virgin, time sets up its mirror. Among these may I never be seen" (426–30).

The mirror, as W. S. Barrett remarks, is both self-revealing where one sees oneself and other-revealing where one is seen, revealing it to another.[95] But the notion of a mirror here is far more inclusive because it applies not to one character but to two. Further, because Phaedra's expression links together time, the mirror, and the virgin, the mirror concentrates in its optic all the significant problems of the drama. The mirror holds the key to the play's structure and its underlying mythic patterns, making use of all the dazzling complexities that a game of mirrors affords. Unlike Hippolytos, the woman indeed has knowledge of the mirror in all its meanings—for herself and for the other—especially in its ability to double the self in its reflected image. The drama is built on the contrast in access to modes of vision, perception, and knowledge, as it counters Hippolytos's preference for the ear over the eye with Phaedra's heightened awareness of the uses of seeing and being seen. These are exemplified in the contradictory, even antithetical qualities associated with the mirror.

A brief inventory of these properties will suggest why Phaedra's curious remark merits closer inspection and why it is worth looking over the ensemble of the drama from the perspective afforded by this key symbol. The mirror is that which reveals the truth and yet offers a deceptive illusion. It reflects back the image of feminine vanity, but it offers too the means for introspection. It poses at its most problematic conjunction the division between being and seeming, between how one sees oneself for oneself and how one is seen by others.[96] In embracing the whole of the phenomenal world, *ta phainomena,* the mirror encompasses the spectrum of what one sees both with the eye of eros and with the eye of knowledge.

Phaedra's struggle is between an interior self and her external image in the eyes of society. She chooses paradoxically to protect (yet also to

95. Others who have discussed the mirror include Avery 1968, 31n.26; Willink 1968, 16; and more fully, Pigeaud 1976.

96. On the properties of mirrors, see Vernant 1981d.

dishonor) that self by honoring the conventions that regulate a woman's life. Let us not forget that the future of her children is also at stake; they require their parents' *eukleia* (good name) in order to speak freely in the world (421–25). At stake too is the self that will feel a radical dishonor in the words of an other. But in the play's new representation of the figure of Phaedra, it is empowered to probe the dialectic of reality and appearance, being and seeming.[97] Through the mirror that belongs to Aphrodite, it can raise the basic epistemological questions about human life.

Let me clarify what we might infer from the mirror of Aphrodite by contrasting it with another, more typical mode of knowing in tragedy, which belongs to Apollo. In Aeschylus's *Seven against Thebes,* the sixth combatant is the Argive seer Amphiaraos, who alone among the other warriors carries a blank shield that bears no visible sign to the outside world. This is because he would rather *be aristos* (noble) than *seem* so, "reaping the deep furrow in his mind *[phrēn]* from which trustworthy counsels grow" (*Seven* 591–94). In the eyes of the Theban Eteocles, Amphiaraos is acknowledged as possessing the four cardinal virtues: the seer is *dikaios* (just), *agathos* (brave), *eusebēs* (righteous), and above all, *sōphrōn* (prudent, 610), because he knows how to speak the appropriate words (*legein ta kairia,* 619). He maintains the stability of an interior self that knows what to utter and what to keep hidden. But he is also the prophet who mediates between divine and human worlds. As a seer, he has a synoptic vision of past, present, and future, but he also knows his own mortal limits, even prophesying the day of his own death. He knows too the cult that awaits him after he is buried in the earth of that other city, Thebes (*Seven* 587–88). Thus to speak *ta kairia* means that he controls the polysemous values of language. It also attests to his ability to speak the ambiguous language of oracles to an other (Eteocles), whose fate will confirm the truth of Apollo's word that comes from Delphi.[98]

In Aphrodite's play, Eros takes the place of Apollo (and Zeus too), as the chorus seems to tell us after the nurse has taken Phaedra's secret into the house and the women begin their great hymn to this god who "drips desire from the eyes" (525). "In vain," they say, "we offer sacrifice by the river Alpheios [Olympia] and at Delphi, but Eros, the tyrant of men, we do not worship. Rather than give reverence to the inmost shrine at Delphi from which prophecy issues forth, we must honor the keeper of the keys of the inmost chambers of love [*philtatōn thalamōn kleidouchon,* 540]," where the *logos* has no *mantis* (seer), the *kairos* (the opportune time/

97. See Avery 1968; and Segal 1970.
98. See Zeitlin 1982a, 114–35.

place) is not clear, and no one knows how to read the signs without error
(269, 346, 386, 585).[99]

The seer, as the bearer of Apollo's word, needs no other and can see
without being seen (the blank shield). The woman, however, as the agent
of Aphrodite, is at the opposite end of the spectrum. She needs the pol-
ished surface of the mirror because society requires her above all to see
herself through others' eyes. The language of furrow and field (as well as
the seer's contact with time and process) are borrowed from the agricultural world, where the feminine earth sown and reaped by man now supplies the metaphorical field of his mind, a process more usually associated
with the career of the *parthenos*. Like the meadow, she must not lie unworked for too long, but must be transformed from its flowering surface
to a deep furrow. The woman, like Amphiaraos, has a *sōphrosunē*, but,
as the chorus says just after Phaedra's allusion to the mirror, its function
is to reap noble *doxa* (glory/reputation, 431–32), a term that must also
include validation in the public social domain.

In Aphrodite's world, the woman draws insight from her experience
of the social and physical body, because "time has taught her much from
which she can take her counsels" (375–76) and has given her a mirror as
an instrument of double vision:[100] first, as the truth together with the semblance of the true and second, as the eye of the self and the eye of the other.
Time will indeed reveal her to herself. Yet because self and other coincide
in the image of the *parthenos*, reminiscent of an earlier state in Phaedra's

99. I partly quote and partly interpret here on the basis of other statements in the play.
In this hymn to Eros that follows the nurse's entry into the house with Phaedra's secret, the
text gives the play over to the power of Aphrodite. The progress of the ode is significant. First
strophe/antistrophe: there is acknowledgment of the power of Eros and Aphrodite and the
need to substitute their worship for that of Zeus and Apollo. Second strophe/antistrophe: the
Dionysiac now enters the scene under the pressures of Aphrodite and is drawn into her orbit,
so that Iole, compared to a bacchant, is delivered by Aphrodite to a murderous wedding, and
Semele herself, mother of the twice-born Dionysos, is wed to a bloody doom. See above, note
22. Henceforth, Phaedra herself will be the only signifier, the only bird sign to interpret (759,
827; see Segal 1965, 183), and no oath, pledge, or seercraft (1055, 1321) will avail, both
because Theseus's passion is aroused by the erotic insult he suffers and because the "double
speaking" of eros replaces the "double speaking" of oracles. Eros is, as Plutarch says (Stobaeus, *Florilegium* 64.31) an *ainigma dueureton kai dusluton* (an enigma difficult to find a
way through, difficult to unbind/resolve). A study of the epistemological language of the play
(*oida, katoida, sunoida, gignōskō, epistamai* and related *manthanō, ekmanthanō*) would
require too much space here, but the frequency of "I don't know" in one form or another is
remarkable (40, 56, 92, 249, 271, 277, 346, 394, 517, 599, 904, 919, 981, 1033, 1091,
1248, 1335).

100. Pigeaud (1976, 14–15) rightly links time, the mirror, and the virgin, and understands the mirror as indicating a double reflection—*of* the self and *on* the self—as necessary
prerequisites for self-knowledge. But he treats Phaedra without Hippolytos and even so,
views her merely as morally wicked. His aim, in any case, is to use Euripides for comparison
with Plato.

life but corresponding to the present moment of Hippolytos's, Phaedra possesses the only means by which Hippolytos, the current *parthenos,* can see the self and see it in a temporal perspective.[101]

Reversing the Image

The necessary medium is the mirror, and we can only grasp the full extent of its power in the play if we recall that the mirror reflects a *reversed* image that is returned to the one who gazes in it (cf., e.g., Plato, *Timaeus* 46a–b). By invoking the image of the mirror and linking it to time, Phaedra activates the dynamic mechanism of a plot, which works precisely by reversing the image of one for the other. Through the dramatic sequence of events the plot plays out those interrelations of being and seeming to which the mirror naturally lends itself. In the optic of the reversed image that governs the play, what is the peripeteia—that formal reversal of one state into its opposite—if not a turnabout that reverses the image of the self and projects it onto the other? And what is the message on the *deltos* ("he desires me" vs. "I desire him"), if not a species of reversal we might call "mirror writing?" Furthermore, the rhetorical play with the word *sōphrosunē,* which I earlier identified as a chiasmus, might well be recoded in visual terms to suggest that the first sentence is but the mirror image of the second.[102]

More precise still are the words that the servant addresses to the statue of Aphrodite in the prologue after Hippolytos has left the stage. The goddess should pardon *(suggnomēn echein)* the foolishness of the young man, he says, for "one should not imitate *[ou mimēteon]* the young who think in this fashion" (117, 114). Rather, he implores her to be *wiser than mortals* and "to *seem* not to *hear* him" (*mē dokēi toutou kluein,* 119). Aphrodite does not reply, but Phaedra, her substitute, does, as she goes on to play the part of the goddess in the human domain. For the servant's plea proves to be an exact reversal of what will actually occur in the dramatic structure of the play. Phaedra must *seem* to Hippolytos not to have *heard*

101. Frye's (1976, 117) comment on the genre of romance is relevant here: "In ordinary life there are two central data of experience that we cannot see without external assistance: our own faces and our own existence in time. To see the first we have to look in a mirror, and to see the second we have to look at the dial of a clock. . . . The classical romancers had to make do with doubles only, as the clock had not been invented."

102. There are many instances in the play of mirror images. The most striking visual example occurs in the prologue where Aphrodite, in speaking of her temple in Athens founded by Phaedra to commemorate her first erotic glimpse of Hippolytos (27), calls it a *katopsion* of this land (Troezen)—that is, a "lookout" seen now from the opposite or even reverse perspective (cf. 373–74). As the first *Hippolytos* was set in Athens, this early mention of a reversed point of viewing may well remind the audience how much this play functions as a mirror reversal of the first.

the words he speaks at the door. As a result, she can arrange for the young to imitate the adult by giving him the role that reversing the *prosōpa* will require him to play.

Why should this be so? The reason is that Phaedra rejects the nurse's practical morality, which names those as "*wise among mortals* who overlook those things that are not as they should be [not *kala]*" (465–66). After all, says the nurse, "how many do you suppose of those who have good sense, when they see adulterous affairs, *seem* not to see [*mē dokein horan]*?" (463). But among these Phaedra will emphatically refuse to be seen (or even seem to be such a one). That is, the queen refuses to be an actor, masking the self through playing another's part (413–18). She refuses too to imitate the gods by taking their mythological amours for her model, which the nurse's sophistic rhetoric would have her believe it would be *hubris* to reject (474–75). But with the mirror as her instrument, Phaedra does in fact become the *pikra thea,* not only the bitter *spectacle (théa)* but by a mere shift in accent, the *pikra theá,* the bitter *goddess* (cf. 727), who can transform one into the unhappy mimetic double of the other when, like the goddess before her, she feels Hippolytos's scorn. Phaedra may discover that her own image rejoins the reflection of that other self, her double in the first play, which she had been determined to resist. But through her inversion of the mirror's image, Hippolytos will discover, as we have seen, what it means to have no mirror of the self or of an other.

What Phaedra brings about through her concern for society's mirror might seem to provide a premature and ironic commentary on a famous text of Plato in which Eros is shown to provide the route to that knowledge of the self through the metaphor of the mirror. As Socrates observes, "the face [*prosōpon]* of the person who looks into another's eyes [*theōmenos]* is shown forth in the optic confronting him as in a mirror, and this we call the *korē* [pupil], for it is the *eidōlon* or image of the person. . . . Then an eye viewing another eye and looking at its most perfect part [the pupil or *korē]* wherewith it sees, it will thus see itself" (*Alcibiades* 1.132e–33a).[103]

103. Shakespeare, as usual, says it best (*Troilus and Cressida,* III.iii.103ff., Achilles to Ulysses):

> The beauty that is borne here in the face
> The bearer knows not, but commends itself
> To Others' eyes; nor doth the eye itself,
> That most pure spirit of sense, behold itself,
> Not going from itself; but eye to eye oppos'd
> Salutes each other with each other's form;
> For speculation turns not to itself
> Till it hath travell'd and is mirror'd there
> Where it may see itself.

Phaedra, who brings together time, the virgin, and the mirror, would seem to be the first *korē*, the *parthenos* of the past, who sailed from Crete to Athens for her nuptials with Theseus. She provides the *prosōpon* for the other *korē*, the *parthenos* Hippolytos, who will pass through the identity of the first one as through a mirror—a mirror of illusion, however, and not of truth. At the end, time will show her forth, as she says, a *kakon* to him—a prediction that, in Artemis's words, will be shifted from her to Theseus, as the third and final agent of Hippolytos's destruction, precisely because he did not wait for time to bring forth the necessary proofs.[104] But in the temporal span of the drama, when time *seems* to reveal Hippolytos as wicked, Phaedra's mirror suggests that to confront the interplay of truth and illusion is an essential phase of development that teaches the critical lessons of perspective and configures the self as an entity with both internal and external dimensions. This interplay between inside and outside continually subtends the dynamics of daily life in the encounters between one self and an other. It also lies at the heart of the theatrical experience, which involves relations between actors, and uses the resources of the stage as well as the curious status of the theater itself as the frontier between the fictional and the real, the perceived and the true.

Involvement in the theatrical process opens the way for Hippolytos to achieve an objective status as a subject in a world where Aphrodite, as the play declares, rules alone (*mona kratuneis*, 1281), a world of realities that would otherwise lie beyond his ken. The ending of the play, in which Hippolytos is restored to his father and his honor is vindicated on stage by the goddess Artemis (along with her promise of a future cult), suggests that the workings of the plot are both necessary and valid. The tragic experience is required, it would seem, for authenticating the identity of a son

---

104. A crucial point, overlooked by critics, is the fact that after disaster befalls Hippolytos, no one ever says that Phaedra was *kakē*—neither Artemis nor Theseus nor even Hippolytos. Instead, Phaedra's "prophecy" about the mirror revealing *(ekphēn[e])* the wicked is ironically (but justly) transferred by Artemis to Theseus, who was the actual instrument of his son's doom (1403): "In Hippolytos' eyes and in mine you are shown *[phainēi]* wicked *[kakos*, cf. 1316], precisely because you did not wait for pledges or the voice of seers, nor did you conduct any interrogation, nor did you press an inquiry in the length of time *[chronōi makrōi]*, but swifter than was necessary, you cast your curses at your son and killed him" (1320–24). Phaedra's statement had applied to the entire time span of a human life. Theseus, in a sense, erred in the opposite direction. Because he did not wait for time to reveal the truth, he now stands morally condemned. Note, however, the critical difference between Phaedra's language and that of Artemis, which involves a small but telling shift in the use of the prefix *ek-* (connoting full accomplishment of the activity in question). Phaedra speaks of *ek-phainō*, that is, the definitive revelation of a fully base self. Artemis, on the other hand, in judging Theseus, uses only the simple form, *phainō*. She modifies her censure because of his ignorance at the time, and for this reason she can fully absolve (release/unbind, *ek-luei*) him from the charge of evildoing (*kakēs*, 1335). It is Aphrodite, I might add, for whom all reserve their opprobrium.

whose bastard status would have forever cast a long shadow on his claims to nobility in the social domain. More broadly, Hippolytos's entanglement in the demands of this world also gives him the occasion for resisting them and in so doing to prove the virtue, the *sōphrosunē*, of remaining steadfast to the ideal of a self he continues to cherish. Only in this way can Hippolytos's life take on meaning as he makes the transition, once his span of time on earth is ended, from a mortal youth doomed in the here and now to the permanent status of cult hero. His experience of pain will provide the symbolic model for the physical experience of others—nubile maidens on the eve of their marriage. But in weeping for him, as they will when retelling his story of eros refused, the young virgins are acknowledging at the same time that his story is one they themselves must not literally imitate.

If the world of Aphrodite replicates, often with startling fidelity, a version of the real world in all its confusions and contradictions, it also seems to be equivalent to the theater itself, whose manipulations of reality offer the ideal medium for such an imitation. Illusion is what theater aims to achieve through its mimetic conventions in order to deceive the audience with its visual representations of the real. This is its formal function. But in cognitive terms, the question of illusion goes still deeper into the content of this drama, where in the binding and unbinding of its plot, it must stage a two-level "imitation of an action" in order to bring to light what lies behind the façade of the visual spectacle. Only then is the anagnorisis complete, as ignorance gives way to knowledge and illusion to truth.

Yet what is that knowledge and what is that truth if not the admission that illusion and deception are necessary components of reality for the self in the world, without which such a self cannot be constituted? [105] Hippo-

---

105. How can one resist invoking here Gorgias's famous statement on tragedy? "Whereas the tragic poet who deceives is juster than he who does not, the deceived is also wiser than the one who is not deceived" (frag. 23 DK). In another perspective, we might consider the significant features of masculine puberty rites as discussed by Vidal-Naquet (1986a, "Black Hunter," and 1986b), especially those of the Spartan *krupteia*, which promote acts of "cunning, deception, disorder, and irrationality." These features, along with evidence of transvestite garb in related rituals, are explained as obeying the "law of symmetrical inversion" whereby one sex takes on the characteristics of the other just before entry into adult hoplite status will require the adoption of unambiguous masculine norms. In this sense, boys are playing the role of the other—whether of the savage or the female. We might go further. Considering the emphasis on secrecy *(krupteia)* and deceit *(apatē,* one etymology of the Athenian festival, the Apatouria, when fathers presented their sons for admission to their phratry), these same activities perhaps signified more than the temporary assumption of traits associated with femininity. They would also serve the broader function of introducing the ephebes to the more complex world that awaits them, obliging them to practice the very exercises that represent an adult perception of reality. Tragedy, in particular, makes use

lytos was tripped up when the blocking action of the bull from the sea led the horses to overturn his chariot (1232). But this event comes to pass because, as Theseus says to his son at the end, "I was tripped up by an illusion, a *doxa,* that emanated from a divine source" (1214).[106]

The true anagnorisis is, of course, the revelation that Aphrodite was the agent. The prologue had shared this crucial information with the audience, but it is imparted to Hippolytos only at the very end. He is the last of all the characters to attain this knowledge. "I understand *[phronō],*" he says, "the divinity who destroyed me" (1401), thereby acknowledging the power the goddess has wielded, even over himself. Anagnorisis comes late and hard and only with the help of another goddess, Artemis, who will reveal the truth first to Theseus and then to his son. Her appearance is utterly essential. Without Artemis, the human characters in the drama would never know.

The primary obstacle to anagnorisis is Phaedra herself, whose desire to repress and deny her secret ultimately leads her to install the central misanagnorisis at the heart of the play, when she reverses the terms of the message on the tablet and disappears forever from the scene. But the real obstacle, I suggest, lies even deeper, in the structure of the play, which is organized from the outset around a more fundamental reversal, one that the chorus signals to us in the parodos.

In their conjectures about the possible causes of Phaedra's sickness, the women pose a set of questions that are initial examples of the reversing mirror effect that will regulate the drama. They ask whether her husband tends a secret love in the house (151–54), when we know that it is Phaedra who is gripped by eros. Or perhaps it is some news from faraway Crete (155–59), they suggest, when we know that, on the contrary, the cause of her malady, Hippolytos, has just been present before us on stage. But the preceding strophe furnishes the essential clue, where the chorus logically begins its query by speculating on a divine cause to explain the queen's symptoms. There are two possibilities. Is she *entheos,* "possessed by some god or daimon," and if so, is the deity in question Pan, Hecate, the Corybantes, or the Mountain Mother (141–44), all possible agents of erratic behavior? Or, they inquire, is the cause an offense against Dictynna (the Cretan Artemis) occasioned by neglect of her worship (145–47)? This last query, let us note, doubles the reversing mirror effect. The goddess in question is, of course, Aphrodite and not her polar opposite,

---

of its theatrical resources to stage this learning process for such figures as Orestes in Aeschylus's *Choephoroi* and Neoptolemos in Sophocles' *Philoctetes* (both treated by Vidal-Naquet 1981a, 1981b as ephebic exemplars). Euripides' *Ion* is another case in point. See below, chapter 7.

106. On words of tripping and stumbling *(sphallō),* see Knox 1952, 25–26.

Artemis. Even more critical, it is not Phaedra but Hippolytos who has neglected the worship of a divinity. The nurse, when she learns the secret of the queen's amorous passion, reads the situation as anyone might expect: "the wrath of the goddess [Aphrodite] has swooped down upon Phaedra" (438, cf. 476). But as Aphrodite informs us in the prologue, Hippolytos is the target of her wrath, and this *orgē*, she confidently predicts, will "swoop down upon his body" (1418), as Artemis confirms at the end of the play in describing his pitiable condition.

The new Phaedra is remarkable, as I have emphasized throughout, in her resistance to the dictates of desire and therefore to those of the myth itself. Her resistance obscures the truth she alone knows, the secret of the love she bears within her heart. But how could Phaedra know the full truth—the reason why this passion afflicts her? How could anyone else on stage know, since the plot Aphrodite has devised reverses the usual mode of her intervention in human affairs?

The Wrath of Aphrodite

According to the inexorable law of the talion that regulates the logic of Greek myth, any extreme attitude or form of behavior is countered exactly by its equally unacceptable reverse, and the offender is punished exactly according to the nature of the offense. Thus the one who refuses eros or scorns Aphrodite is typically smitten in turn with an immoderate eros— transgressive, illicit, or impossible to fulfill.[107] This retaliation may take the form of a simple reversal, as when Atalanta and Melanion, both of whom had previously resisted marriage, consummate a passionate and sacrilegious union in the temple of the goddess herself.[108] The madness that afflicts the daughters of Proitos and sends them running wildly to the mountains is erotic in nature and results directly from a god's punishment, this time Hera (or Dionysos), for an offense that suggests they too have been loath to marry.[109] In other cases the emphasis may fall on a disastrous choice of love object, the theme that directly concerns us here. Polyphontes, to take an extreme example, is struck by an outrageous passion for a bear.[110] But more subtly and more faithful to our own understanding of

107. On these unhappy loves, see Rohde 1913; Radermacher 1916, 3–5; Trenkner 1958, 26–27n.5; and especially Detienne 1977, 64; and Detienne 1979a, 25–26. Pellizer 1982 treats the topic in greater detail; see too the examples in Rudhardt 1982. The motif of Aphrodite's wrath comes more fully into its own in Hellenistic poetry and romance, but its later use is probably indebted, in part, to Euripides' influence on erotic plots. See Fauth 1958, 572–73.

108. See Detienne 1979a, 26–34.

109. See Calame 1977, 218–21, 416–18.

110. Detienne 1979, 26; Pellizer 1982, 22.

psychological drives, the refusal to desire an other will mean that when desire comes, it will turn not outward but rather within: to the self as an unattainable object of love, as was the case for Narcissus, or to those intimately connected with the self in the family. Myrrha falls in love with her father, Leukippos with his sister, *kata mēnin Aphroditēs*,[111] and by this logic we might expect Hippolytos to be struck with incestuous desire for his father's wife. Indeed, to the best of my knowledge, nowhere else except in this play, the second *Hippolytos*, does Aphrodite punish the one who has rejected desire by inspiring an illicit passion in an innocent other.[112]

The manner in which Hippolytos meets his end, as a driver of horses done to death by his own mares, is a fitting retribution for one who, in refusing the yoke of marriage, finds himself instead bound to the yoke of destruction in accordance with the familiar analogy between conjugal relations and the taming of horses. The myth of Glaukos Potnieus, son of Poseidon, who was devoured by his own horses, supplies a significant parallel, as tradition reports that he too had offended Aphrodite.[113] As in the

111. On Myrrha, see Detienne 1977, 63–64, 80–83, 90–91. On Leukippos (Parthenius, *Erotika Pathemata* 5), see Pellizer 1982, 66–69. Rudhardt 1982 gives further examples.

112. Pellizer (1982, e.g., 23–24, 29–30) elides this distinction and includes Hippolytos among the other transgressive hunters by saying that he "becomes the victim of a passion contrary to the rules of the family and of kinship." Another story he cites, that of the hunter Tanais, fulfills the pattern exactly (Ps.-Plutarch, *De fluviis* 14.1). "Tanais was the exceedingly chaste son of Berossos and Lysippe (an Amazon). He hated the female race, honoring only Ares, the god of war, and naturally, he held the idea of marriage in great contempt. Aphrodite therefore inspired in him a desire for his own mother. At first, Tanais succeeded in resisting such an insane passion. Still bound by these torments of love and wanting to remain righteous *[eusebēs]*, he leaped into the river Amazonios, which henceforth was called the Tanais." Fontenrose (1981, 160–61) also avoids the problem, since his aim is to fit Hippolytos into his model of the mythic hunter: "Hippolytos . . . is wholly chaste . . . and so cannot be guilty of assault, as Orion and Aktaion were. Hence an accusation of assault must be substituted, and the Potiphar's wife theme supplies this feature; furthermore, it is not the huntress (i.e., Artemis) but her rival (i.e., Aphrodite/Phaedra) who is the supposed victim." Note that Fontenrose must resort to a double inversion in order to retain his pattern. I omit here those myths of reluctant virgin girls (such as Daphne) that end in metamorphosis, as these supply another solution to the problem of maintaining chastity.

113. The case of Glaukos, son of Poseidon, is especially relevant here (for further discussion, see Radermacher 1916, 8–13). The mythic tradition of Glaukos is complex and is attached to several sites. I therefore select a few significant details. According to Pausanias, 6.20.19, Glaukos drives along the Isthmus of Corinth as a *daimōn* who terrifies horses, exactly like the god Poseidon Taraxippos. Servius, commenting on Vergil, *Georgics* 3.268, tells us that since Glaukos had spurned the rites of Aphrodite, she maddened his racing mares and they tore him apart with their teeth. A slightly different version, he continues, attributes the wrath of Aphrodite to another cause: Glaukos was torn apart by his mares who were goaded into a frenzy by an excess of lust, since he had prevented them from coupling in order to increase their swiftness. The logic relating these two variants should be obvious.

case we are considering, Poseidon can even make common cause with Aphrodite, when at the appeal of his son, Theseus, he intervenes in his role as Taraxippos, "frightener of horses." [114]

Scholars have long pondered the strange anomalies of Hippolytos's story in which several divergent motifs oddly converge: the familiar theme of Potiphar's wife, found in Near Eastern sources and elsewhere in Greek myth; the relations of the pre-Greek mother goddess with a young consort; and the combined effect of the bull from the sea and the stampeding horses. Little of the tradition, however, is known before Euripides, although the cult of Hippolytos at Troezen is attested from other sources (e.g., Pausanias 2.32.1–3). The quest for sources is useful for tracing the historical development of mythic traditions and for considering how variants of a given myth or motifs shared with other myths can be integrated into a larger signifying system. [115] Our interest lies elsewhere. What may be implied by the particular shape of Euripides' version, and how do his innovations pertain to typically tragic concerns? To this end, I want to reopen the question of Aphrodite's intervention in the drama as a character on stage, along with the explicitly stated motif of her wrath. Given what we know about the first *Hippolytos,* there was no need to introduce this motif. The first Phaedra, in her role as the "bad woman," was determined to satisfy her desire at any cost. In this earlier drama, it is agreed, Phaedra and the nurse must have exchanged roles, so that the queen herself invoked the power of Aphrodite, using sophistic arguments to justify her transgressive actions, while it was the nurse who demurred. [116]

114. Burkert (1979, 112) sums up the problem: "One may wonder . . . about the curiously complicated method Aphrodite uses to take her revenge: she has Phaedra cause Theseus to pronounce a curse, which moves Poseidon to send a bull from the sea, who in turn causes Hippolytos' horses to go wild, which finally kills the hero. If I were Aphrodite, I would not trust this assassination machine to work properly. At any rate, Aphrodite could have driven the horses mad herself, as she did in the case of Glaucus Potnieus." On the function of Poseidon as Taraxippos and Damasippos (tamer of horses), see especially Detienne and Vernant 1978, 190–206, whose discussion illuminates many details of the messenger's narrative.

115. Hippolytos himself has certain affinities with many other figures, including Phaethon, who is specifically named in our text, and even more Hymenaios, of whom it is told that he disappeared on his wedding night. On these various elements, see, for example, Radermacher 1916; Séchan 1911; Tschiedel 1969; Herter 1940 and 1971; Burkert 1979; and Fauth 1959. On Hymenaios, see especially Muth 1954; the discussion in Sissa 1987, 128–31; and Zeitlin 1986b.

116. If Seneca's *Phaedra* is a reliable guide, the first play would have invoked the excuse of Aphrodite's wrath against Phaedra as a female descendant of the Sun because it was Helios who had exposed the adultery of Ares and Aphrodite (Seneca, *Phaedra* 124–28). If this were the case, then the nurse's general reference to the "wrath of Aphrodite" (438, cf. 476) along with Phaedra's own allusion to the unhappy erotic history of the women in her family (337–41) might remind the audience more directly that Phaedra's passion in the earlier play had followed a more typical aetiology of cause and effect, this time on hereditary grounds.

But in light of the new Phaedra, Aphrodite's appearance in the prologue is indispensable to the plot. At the simplest level, we need her to
reveal what Phaedra will not reveal as the reason for her mysterious ail-
ment. More broadly, we need her to reveal what Phaedra does not know—
that she is an innocent victim of Aphrodite in the goddess's plot to punish
Hippolytos. Without the framing device of the two omniscient goddesses,
Aphrodite and Artemis, the play, as has often been observed, makes ample
sense on the psychological level in treating Phaedra's false accusation as
the revenge of a woman scorned and love turned to hate. The motif of
Potiphar's wife contains all the ingredients needed for a suspenseful and
engrossing plot, pitting lust against virtue and falsehood against truth in
ways that explain in part its continuing popularity as a recurrent episode
in later Greek novels. The flirtation with Oedipal themes involving an
older woman, a young man, and an angry paternal figure is also a factor
that assures the perennial appeal of such a tale. But I argue that the wrath
of Aphrodite, which obeys the logic of its own rules, works as a significant
counter-current against the predictable structures of the original motif,
with the result that the drama may now profit from the unusual interplay
between the two themes.[117]
    On the one hand, the shape of the play reveals with unblinking clarity
the tragic gulf between human and divine domains, and Aphrodite's care-
less dismissal of the plight of her innocent intermediary has been construed, not without reason, as evidence of Euripides' characteristic attitude toward traditional Olympian theology. In formal terms, however, the

117. On the motif of Potiphar's wife in myth and story, see Brelich 1958, 302–3; Radermacher 1916, 4:51; Rohde 1913, 33–34; Trenkner 1958, 64–66; and Fauth 1958, 565–
67. No other example of this type, we might add, includes the wrath of Aphrodite as its
motivating cause. In our case, it might be argued that Phaedra is only a stand-in for the
goddess: first her victim and later her agent and substitute (as I have emphasized throughout). After all, Phaedra herself claims origins as a child of Zeus (683) through her descent
from Europa, and she may perhaps be identified with Cretan goddess figures. The doubling
of woman and goddess may therefore represent a secondary stage of the myth's development,
in which a shift from divine to human personage has taken place. Likewise, Hippolytos's
relationship to both Artemis and Aphrodite (in cult) may recall a prior story type involving
a young male consort in the power of the Great Goddess, whose ambivalent quality is maintained by the splitting of her figure into antithetical opposites (cf. note 45 above). Theseus,
for his part, can bring about Hippolytos's destruction because of his own divine ancestry
from Poseidon. For fullest discussion, see Fauth 1959. Nevertheless, the figure of Hippolytos
is too complex to be reduced to this schema. He is both hunter and horseman, and the variety
of his attributes suggests his affinities with such disparate types as Actaeon, Bellerophon,
Glaukos, Atalanta, and Hymenaios (cf. note 115 above). Hence, we need to approach this
new elaboration of the myth (probably due in large part to Euripides) on its own terms
without diminishing its complexities, so as to uncover the logic of its operations on the level
of its dramatic representation. Certainly, Euripides is playing off divine against human domains and is interweaving the two with greater emphasis on the secular and human intrigue.

explicit mention of the *mēnis* of Aphrodite ensures that Phaedra's accusation, *if taken at face value,* strictly fulfills the terms of Aphrodite's typical mode of intervention. That is, Hippolytos's refusal of the role of *erastēs* (lover) is reversed into its logical opposite—or rather, the *semblance* of that opposite—when he is compelled to play the part of an *erastēs* who has acted out an illicit and "unjust" passion.[118] Thus, he can symbolically undergo the punishment that fits his original offense against Aphrodite, which as a result of the combined action of the bull and the horses, inflicts a tragic rending of the body that has refused union with an other.

The mirror of illusion Phaedra provides for the male *parthenos* is therefore, according to the latent mythic pattern, the proper optical medium through which to view the entire network of associations that cluster around the organ of sight in its social, sexual, and cognitive aspects. Hippolytos must *seem* to have "dishonored the *eye* of Zeus" and to have gazed at the feminine mysteries of his father's wife, which are unlawful *(ou themis)* to view. In the *Bacchae,* Pentheus's secret wish, brought out of hiding by the cunning of Dionysos, is none other than the desire to see his mother's body, and Pentheus goes off, literally dressed in the costume of the female other, to play the voyeur at the secret rites. The standard transgression for a hunter, such as Hippolytos, who remains in Artemis's company would have been to come upon the naked goddess bathing and to suffer the consequences of an illicit gaze. Actaeon, Pentheus's cousin and mythic counterpart, invoked as a warning example

---

118. Society would obviously judge any sexual relationship between Phaedra and Hippolytos as transgressive and hence unjust by its standards (614, 672, 676, 942, 1081, 1171). But Greek norms identify another kind of "injustice" between erotic partners that is highly relevant to the issue at hand. This "erotic injustice" consists in the refusal of the beloved to reciprocate the lover's affections, even though by the very fact of that love the beloved is placed under an obligation to return it. The typical penalty for such a refusal obeys the law of the talion in prescribing a future exchange of roles. According to this rule, the *erōmenos* will in time become the *erastēs* (often of still another) and will experience the same rejection and anguish as his/her former *erastēs*. Phaedra's actions in contriving to reverse the roles of *erastēs* and *erōmenos* between herself and Hippolytos then seem *on the surface* to fullfill this law of reciprocity. We might therefore judge the pattern we earlier identified (the affliction of an illicit eros as the penalty for eros refused) as an extreme example of this kind of "erotic justice." Now the *erōmenos* may change or seem to change into the *erastēs* (i.e., Hippolytos), but it is too late to enter into the game. This exchange of roles can only come to a tragic end, because its initiation (let alone its consummation) constitutes a moral injustice as well against the entire social system.

The notion of "erotic justice" is articulated in the archaic period, especially in lyric poetry, in accordance with a more general set of reflections on alternating cycles of exchange in the world (cf. Anaximander, frag. 1 DK), and it applies to both heterosexual and homosexual relations (cf. especially Sappho, frag. 1 LP; and Theognis, 1283–93). For further discussion, see Privitera 1967 and 1974; Gentili 1972; Bonnano 1973; and Giacomelli [Carson] 1980.

(*Bacchae* 230, 336–40, 1227, 1291), is punished by Artemis herself, who turns his hounds against their master to destroy him, a fate that closely resembles Hippolytos's own.[119] But the nature of Hippolytos's relation with Artemis (not seeing her eye) precludes him from replicating Actaeon's offense, which would have compelled Artemis, we might say, to join forces with Aphrodite.[120] As a spectator who only sees from afar, Hippolytos is no voyeur. Hence he cannot be tempted to enter into the sequence that leads from sight to desire and from desire to physical contact with the other. Hence the indispensable role assigned to Phaedra. From the perspective of the mythic pattern we have been exploring, she might be viewed (in yet another turn of the mirror) as the one conscripted by Aphrodite into playing the part that should rightfully be that of Hippolytos, which, in this sense, she is perfectly justified in returning to him.

We may assess this whirl of mimetic reflections by examining one last instance of mimesis, which occurs in the beginning of the play. Phaedra exits from the house *after* Hippolytos has made his first appearance on stage. Does she not then express her desire to imitate Hippolytos? That is, to recline on grassy slopes and drink the pure spring waters, to follow the hunt and the hounds with spear and javelin in hand, and finally to race Venetian horses on Artemis's terrain (208–12, 215–22, 228–31)? But the context of Phaedra's words surpasses any simple or single mimetic identification. In its impossible ambiguities, her speech makes abundantly clear the confusions introduced into the social (and poetic) system when the *kouros* (youth) has appropriated the role of the *parthenos* (maiden) and, through Aphrodite, attracts the eye of the *gunē* (woman). Hippolytos has, in effect, reversed the typical patterns of courtship, so that when he is com-

119. The evidence for Actaeon as voyeur of Artemis is late (Callimachus, *Hymn* 5.110–16), but he is always a sexual transgressor. In Stesichorus, 236P (Pausanias, 9.2.3), for example, he seems to have incurred the wrath of Zeus for attempting to seduce Semele, his aunt. On voyeurs in general and their connections with sexual transgression, see Buxton 1980.

120. Aphrodite and Artemis do, of course, meet up (along with Dionysos, Pan, and other deities) in connection with assaults against the self as a punishment for too much or too little desire. In this category I also include such agents as those who are driven by madness to attack the god's victims, whether animals (e.g., the hounds of Actaeon and the horses of Hippolytos and Glaukos) or a human collective. Orpheus refuses eros (or, at least, heterosexual eros) after his loss of Eurydice and is consequently torn apart by maenads (Vergil, *Georgics* 4.516–22; Ovid, *Metamorphoses* 10.78–83, 11.7; cf. Phanocles, frag. 1 [Powell]; and Hyginus, *Poetica astronomica* 2.7). The nymph Echo wishes to remain a virgin forever and at Pan's instigation is torn apart by maddened shepherds and goatherds who "fall upon the poor girl like enraged wolves or dogs" (Longus, *Daphnis and Chloe* 3.23). In the *Bacchae*, Pentheus is subject to his mother's Dionysiac violence, but both initially had refused the god's worship. For further discussion of some of these themes, see Borgeaud's splendid study (1979, especially 124–34, 165–75). Even in this grouping, Hippolytos occupies an odd position, as his punishment requires another catalytic force of violence (the bull).

pelled later to depart his land, the maidens of the chorus lament that they will no longer be able to compete for his hand in marriage (114–41). Phaedra's fantasies express the mixture of masculine and feminine, active and passive, subject and object, even mortal and immortal. Moreover, they attest to the slippage of the boundary between the chaste and the erotic. Who does she want to be? In desiring and desiring to be desired in turn, yet also desiring not to desire, she plays all the roles at once— herself (now woman, once virgin), Aphrodite, Hippolytos, and Artemis (the eternal *parthenos*).

But such a mimetism lies only in the theater of the imagination as projections of the mind's eye. Thus, while Phaedra sets the stage for those far-off places where she desires to cast the javelin (*eramai . . . rhipsai*, 220), the nurse recodes her image as text, interpreting the *epos* (words) that Phaedra has "cast" (*erripsas*, 232) as evidence only of her wandering wits *(paraphrōn)*, until the actions of the nurse herself lead the queen to reinterpret—to find a new *logos* in order to unbind the knot of a still more complex *logos*. This is what Phaedra accomplishes by recourse to the mimetic devices of theater in order to stage a plot for the other: an "imitation of an action," which is none other than the drama itself whose events we witness through eye and ear. In this she proves indeed to be the *didaskalos*—the teacher *and* the producer—who binds Hippolytos into her *mythos* and who, through her insistence that "he share in her disease," reminds us of the fundamental role mimesis plays in the making of the self. As Aristotle tells us, this is the source of "the first learning for all" (*tas mathēseis . . . prōtas, Poetics* 4.1448b).

·SEVEN·

Mysteries of Identity and Designs of the Self in Euripides' *Ion*

The *Ion* is one of Euripides' most dazzling plays. Poised on the boundary between the sacred and the skeptical, the mysterious and the mundane, the mythic and the realistic, and, as so many have noted, between the tragic and the comic,[1] the drama dips and twists and turns and turns again in a series of theatrical tours de force. The birds that swoop down at Apollo's shrine in Delphi in the opening scene and intervene again in the most important moment of the plot at Ion's farewell banquet might well exemplify these paradoxes. Defilers of the sacred temple dedications with unwanted offerings of their own (106–7, 176) and nesting in the eaves of the roof, no doubt, crudely "making offspring," as Ion suspects (172–75), they are at the same time bearers of sacred messages *(phēmas)* to mortals from the gods (180–81).[2] These oracular portents *(oiōnoi)*, both generic and particular (377, 1191, 1333,) will prove their worth later at the banquet, precisely when one of the birds drinks the poisoned wine meant for Ion and by its own lifeless form reveals the lethal plot to its interpreter (1196–1211).

The birds link the different scenes of the play by their cameo appearances. They also lend themselves for metaphorical use by the human

A shorter version of this essay was originally presented as the Corbett lecture at Cambridge in May 1988 and, in somewhat different form, at Oxford and at a conference on Greek drama at Ohio State University, also in May 1988. It was also delivered in a French translation at the Ecole Normale Supérieure and at the Ecole des Hautes Etudes in Paris in spring 1989. The text has been revised for this publication. For further discussion of some of the issues raised here, see my later essays: Zeitlin 1993a, on Dionysos in Athens; and Zeitlin 1993b, on the iconography of the artworks.

1. Knox (1979, 264) goes so far as to characterize the play as the "prototype of comedy in the modern sense of the word."

2. Citations, unless otherwise noted, are from the Oxford Classical Text, ed. Diggle (*Euripidis fabulae*, vol. 2 [Oxford, 1981]).

actors, especially the unknown mother, Creousa, who, once her intrigue has been uncovered, cowers like a bird as a suppliant at the altar (1280; cf. 796, 1238). Above all, the birds exemplify the themes of the play—pollution and purity, violation and salvation—which are played out in the critical interchange between the roles of victims and victimizers.[3] As intruders in the Delphic precinct where they are reluctantly allowed to reside, the birds, it is true, disturb the peaceful purity of Ion's life with the mess and turbulence they represent. But they also mediate between the spatial contradictions of the play, moving on the horizontal plane between zones of interior and exterior space, and on the vertical axis, wheeling down from the sky and circulating between the temple roof and the floor of Ion's tent where the banquet takes place.

Still further, these birds configure the dilemmas of Ion himself, the nameless temple servant and orphan child. First, like him, they are both outsiders and insiders to the different spaces in which they dwell. Second, in communicating, as they do, between heaven and earth, they cover the distance between the two extreme antitheses of Ion's genealogical status: as the child of heaven on the side of his father, the luminous Olympian Apollo, and on his mother's side the last descendant of the earth-borns, the Erechtheid *gēgeneis* (autochthons) of Athens's ruling house.

We will meet these birds again briefly in the scene of Ion's tent, but I invoke them here once more as harbingers of my own interpretive strategies, by which I hope to decipher some of the signs, secrets, and riddles that abound in this complex and enigmatic play, which is set at Delphi, the locus of the enigmatic word. To complicate matters further, Delphi is the home of the god who authors the oracle's voice and who is at the same time (or so it is said) the author of the hero, Ion himself. My strategies are aimed at tracing out a still larger circuit of exchange that takes in the entire world of the drama, in which the archaic energies of myth and ritual meet up with the theatrical resources of staging, spectacle, role playing, reenactment, and reversal that this late Euripidean piece so cunningly and self-consciously deploys.[4]

---

3. On the significance of birds in the play, see especially Barlow 1971, 48; Hanson 1975, 31–32, 37; and Wolff 1963, 190n.4.

4. A word about this complicated plot. Creousa, last descendant of the royal line of Erechtheus, and her husband Xouthos, former military ally of her father, have come from Athens to Delphi to inquire of Apollo's oracle about their childlessness. Long before, Apollo had raped Creousa, and in shame and fear of her parents, she exposed the newborn child. Apollo had Hermes bring the boy to Delphi where, reared by the Pythian priestess, he is now a temple servant. Creousa, in advance of Xouthos's arrival, has determined to ask the oracle in secret about the fate of her abandoned child. She first meets Ion and tells him her quest (claiming it is a friend's story). In the meantime, Apollo's oracle has declared to Xouthos that

Identity and the Performing Self

The global compass to which I alluded above is so extensive in this play because the circumstances of the plot address in liveliest and most intricate form the project that subtends the entire theatrical enterprise and lends the greatest excitement to tragic plots. This project is none other than the status of the self's identity in the world and the modes of its revelation, or anagnorisis, to itself and to others—especially when, as Aristotle says, it is "combined with surprising reversal," and when, as in our play, "the recognition [between persons] will be on both sides" (*Poetics* 1452a–b).

On the most matter-of-fact level (the one to which Aristotle, no doubt, refers), the self is constructed in its social network with others. It is endowed at the outset with an identity involving a name, a family and parentage, a place of origin, and social status, whether high or low, legitimate or bastard, of royal or of ordinary birth. Anagnorisis is the usual means in tragedy for establishing these coordinates of the self, in the transformation both from ignorance to knowledge and from enmity to *philia* (or vice versa). By Aristotle's standards, then, the case of our anonymous temple waif might embody these essential dramatic principles to their highest degree. Here is a character in urgent need of the basic accouterments of an identity: a mother, a father, a name, and a home of his own. He has none of these in the world he inhabits at Delphi, the sacred shrine where strangers come and go. But Ion's identity and the process that leads

---

he would find a son in the first person to cross his path after leaving the shrine. This is Ion, whom Xouthos with difficulty persuades of his paternity. He bids Ion make a birthday feast at Delphi before leaving with his father for Athens. He himself goes off to Mount Parnassus to make birth offerings to Dionysos to celebrate the news, under the assumption that he had engendered his son with some unknown girl at a Dionysiac revel at Delphi long ago. He never returns to the stage. The chorus of Athenian women is indignant at this betrayal of their mistress and her Athenian royalty. Although enjoined by Xouthos to silence, they tell the secret to Creousa, who in turn tells her secret to the faithful old *paidagōgos*, her late father's trusted servant. He convinces her to plot against this foreign intruder upon Athenian soil. Creousa gives the servant a poisonous drop of the Gorgon's blood, which Athena had given into the family's keeping (there are two drops, one poisonous, one beneficent). He goes to Ion's banquet and puts it in the boy's winecup. The plot is discovered by chance when the wine spills and a bird laps it up and dies. Ion and the armed Delphians pursue Creousa, who takes refuge at the god's altar. The Pythia now enters with news of the basket and the tokens that she has hidden in the shrine all these years. Revelations follow: Ion is the son of Apollo and Creousa. A joyous reunion takes place (contrary to Apollo's plan, as outlined by Hermes in the prologue, which would postpone any such meeting at Delphi). Athena appears as *dea ex machina*. She verifies Ion's identity, but for purposes of a legal standing in the city, Xouthos will continue to think he is Ion's father. Athena forecasts Athens's glory through Ion's descendants and those of Creousa and Xouthos, and they leave Delphi for home, with the goddess as guide.

to its recognition prove far more intricate than Aristotle's prescriptions might imply. The complexities exceed too the typical scenarios of heroic myths, even those that follow the pattern of Ion's story: a child born of a maiden raped by a god, exposed by his mother and brought up by others elsewhere, whose true parentage is discovered when he comes of age.[5]

At his crossing from childhood to adulthood, Ion will be endowed with a surplus—even a conflict—of paternal identifications. Eventually his paternity will be divided between two fathers. The first is his true (or biological) father, the god Apollo; the other his social (fictive or adoptive) father, his mother's foreign husband, Xouthos, to whom Apollo's oracle "gives" the boy for his own (775, 781, 788, 1532, 1561). Additionally, Ion will be shown to incarnate aspects of the previous male ascendants of his mother's autochthonous line: the late king, his maternal grandfather, Erechtheus, and the more distant forebear, the earth-born Erichthonios, another mysterious baby in a basket given over first to the care of the Cecropid maidens and and then taken up by none other than Athena herself.[6]

Ion's destiny is, after all, to be the hero of a foundation myth, the last in the genealogical series of his maternal *oikos* (household). He is the missing male heir necessary to the continuance of the royal family and of the city of Athens it governs. As successor in the Erechtheid line, he will become in his turn the eponymous founder of the Ionians, but at the same time his lineage will guarantee the "racial purity," as one critic puts it, demanded by the contemporary ideology of this particular polis,[7] before whose audience this drama is being performed. Current political preoccupations, especially concerning the status of citizenship and relations with strangers, are kept in the foreground of the play. Yet, to be installed in this city, Ion must leave Delphi (and childhood) behind him. He must also give up his identity as the son of Apollo and Creousa, a fact that Xouthos must never know. Although Ion is acknowledged at Delphi as his mother's true child (and the child of her heritage) and verified as the son of Apollo by the goddess Athena at the end, he must assume another identity in Athens—one that is false but also truer to real life. As his mother tells him plainly, "If you were said to be born of the god, you could never have secured a house to inherit or the name of a father" (1541–43).

5. On this pattern, see, e.g., Burnett 1970, 2–3; and Loraux 1981a, "Créuse," 198–99, with relevant bibliography. The pattern is applicable, as Murray (1943) argues, to many lost plays of Euripides as well as to New Comedy and is pressed into service even for historical personages, such as Cyrus.

6. Burnett (1971, 105) marks the parallels between Erichthonios and Ion, noted by many others. See further Loraux 1981a, "Créuse," 207–9, 224–25, on the double role of Ion as another Erichthonios and another Erechtheus, discussed further below.

7. Walsh 1978, 303.

It may be true that Euripides is using the mythic theme of heroes with dual parentage to its most ironic effect.[8] It is also true that gods and mortals do not mix as readily as they did in the mythic past. Ion, after all, takes his mother aside at the end to ask whether the story of Apollo as her ravisher might just be a cover-up for a more mundane tale (1521–27), in which it was not a god—as Verrall, that most skeptical of Euripidean critics, insists—but some lusty blond-haired delinquent.[9] Similarly, myths about autochthonous ancestors (Erichthonios and Erechtheus) don't sit very well with more plausible versions of the "facts of life," such as Xouthos's conjecture that he had engendered the child at Delphi with a local girl while in his cups during the revels of Dionysiac rites (549–55).

Paternity may always be a vexed question, as Telemachos's famous statement at the beginning of the *Odyssey* acutely confirms: "my mother says indeed I am the son of Odysseus. I for my part do not know. Nobody really knows his own father—his own begetting *[gonos]*" (*Od.* 1.215–16). A perennial uneasiness attaches itself to the disquieting social fact of "Mama's baby, Papa's maybe,"[10] which so engages the Greek imagination in its dramatization of family relations. Once again, the *Ion* takes this issue much further.

First, Ion's mother herself is unknown to him, and she in turn does not know her child, having exposed him in a cave on the slopes of the Acropolis at Athens (the same site where she was raped by Apollo). She does not even know whether he survived or whether, more likely, the infant perished there alone. Moreover, contrary to the ordinary Greek rules of filiation, it is Ion's link with the Erechtheid mother that assures him of his Athenian legitimacy,[11] while Xouthos is charged with the "feminine" offense of smuggling a supposititious child into the spouse's household (1090–1105).[12]

Second, in direct proportion to the blank cipher of this little temple servant who has no story of his own, the drama proliferates an encyclopedic array of myths, figures, and paradigms as though providing a full (even too full) repertory of possible elements and roles that might be inscribed upon the screen of an unknown self. I have already mentioned those that pertain directly to the genealogy of the orphan child. Others include the great Panhellenic heroes (Herakles and Bellerophon) and myths

8. As, e.g., the tension in Euripides' *Herakles* between the hero's two fathers, Zeus and Amphitryon, and to a lesser extent in *Hippolytus* in Theseus's dual status as son of Poseidon and of Aegeus.

9. Barlow 1971, 49, on Verrall's rationalist hypothesis about the play (1895).

10. I have borrowed this expression from Hortense Spillers.

11. Loraux 1981a, "Créuse," 203–7, 223–29.

12. E.g., Lysias, 1.32–34 (on the murder of Eratosthenes); and Aristophanes, *Thesmophoriazousae* 502–19.

of exemplary battles (such as those against the Giants, Centaurs, and Amazons), which, as connected to the works of art represented in the play, remind us that any project of "self-fashioning" must also finally replay the wider Greek cultural patterns of the "world-making" struggles between civilization and savagery, so dear to Athenian iconography and ideology.[13] But there are still other dramatic and cultural paradigms that implicitly regulate what I have called the "mysteries and designs" of the self that unfold in the theatrical process of its recognition to itself and to others. The result is a bewildering array of possibilities and strategies for engendering children, with or without partners, of which the "true" versions here belong to the world of the myth and the "false" to the world of reality; even more to the point, there are too many fathers, and also potentially too many mothers. The play thus problematizes all the issues relating to identity and selfhood and what these categories might entail.

For identity to be accredited—to be believed by both characters and audience—requires more than bare information or the simple assertion of "facts" that may or may not be true. We are brought to realize the scope of this problem in Ion's case, when in Xouthos's first claims to the boy, the attribution of identity actually starts off as a false one. As a result of this fundamental and potentially fatal misconception that henceforth guides the actions (and reactions) of the characters within the play, the crucial questions about personhood inevitably come to the fore: How is one to stabilize a "self" that may continually be drifting into uncertainty and contradiction? How may this self identify itself and be identified with others to whom it belongs? What are the authenticating mechanisms for its legitimation, which can verify those elusive truths that the act of naming itself cannot accomplish? Furthermore, how are we to judge what nature *(physis)* and nurture *(trophē)* each contribute to the constitution of a self, when Ion's upbringing as a foster child in his true father's residence unknowingly combines the two?

In the theater, especially, where terms like "self" and "identity" are made present before us as living figures set in relation to other figures, the action and the ongoing experience on stage heighten these mysteries surrounding identity. "The self," as one critic puts it, "takes up roles. Although hypothesized, it cannot be perceived or defined except as represented through its actions, gestures, and speech." All these "provide evidence from which motives, intentions, and a central core of selfhood can . . . be inferred." In other words, the self on stage is a "performed

---

13. For the theme of civilization vs. savagery (especially of earth-born monsters), see Immerwahr 1972; Mastronarde 1976; Müller 1975; Rosivach 1977; and Goff 1988. For another perspective, see Wolff 1963, 177, 179–82.

character."[14] If Aristotle judges anagnorisis to be the defining theatrical moment, we can extend his insight further to suggest that the "covert theme of all drama is identification," that is, "the art of finding oneself out." In the pursuit of "that most elusive of all entities," the goal is finally "the establishment of a self that in some way transcends confusions of self."[15] This enterprise is even more compelling in the case of a self searching for the rudiments of an identity and who in the course of the search also grows into maturity. This process entails passage from innocence to experience. It also requires a return, by mythic necessity, to the primordial time of origins—in this instance, to Ion's own birth and to the history of his family—which culminates in the discovery of the basket with the birth tokens that identify the child as a member of the Erechtheid house.

The consideration of identity, therefore, as represented on the Athenian stage, requires the deployment of certain theatrical conventions and strategies that contribute to the sense of this performed self. The most important of these is consistency as a character throughout the course of a play. In the economy of the drama, this means that a character is identified with (and by) a particular nexus of ongoing preoccupations, images, actions, and attributes. These are engaged from first to last, especially in the character's interaction with other characters. The performed self is a self under pressure, always at risk. It has a set of vested interests to which the character would remain "true," and during the course of the play it will experience certain disclosures and recognitions, both small and great. For Ion, this nexus consists of his concern with the defining questions of purity and pollution, as befits his vocation of temple servant; his intelligent questioning of others, which is closely linked to his pressing interest in who he himself may be; and, less prominent but dramatically essential, a certain masculine aptitude for violence in defense of his youthful ideals. As a hunter of birds in the beginning of the play, he is tested on a grander scale when the "bird" is transformed into his unknown mother Creousa

14. Burns 1972, 129–30.
15. I combine Whitman (1974, 70) and Goldman (1975, 123). Gouldner's (1969, 99, 100) remarks about "modal elements in the Greek self-image" are even more pertinent. Relying on Homer, Plato, and tragedy, he observes: "The nature of the self, one's own as well as that of others, is of strong and salient *interest* to the Greeks. The self has become an object to itself, and the importance attached to it is matched by a sense of ignorance concerning its character. The self is felt to contain a mystery that invites a quest to 'know thyself.' It is not only that the Greeks feel that they do not (but should) know themselves; they also have a nagging feeling—or a fantasy—of being other than what they seem. . . . The Hellenic fascination with the problem of identity and the sense of the precariousness of the self are closely related. The more precarious the sense of self, the more problematic it becomes, the more aware may one become of the difficulties of self-maintenance and of the self's varying, elusive character."

at the altar. Above all, as we shall see, is his construction of the tent, made of tapestries taken from the temple treasury, and the fateful part he plays there that will motivate all the subsequent events.

Yet, however this "character" performs his identity according to conventions of theatrical verisimilitude, the seemingly independent choices he makes are predicated on deeper and more extensive associations. Being "oneself" also necessarily entails an identification—whether positive or negative, repeated or reversed—with those significant others who, although unknown to the character, share traits and experiences that underlie his own. Ion bears a notable resemblance to his sire Apollo, even on the visual level, when he first enters equipped for his temple tasks carrying a lowly broom and also the archer instruments of the god himself.[16] The likeness to his father is further revealed in Ion's intelligent (Apollonian) reasoning and still more in his concern with riddling speech and omens, which he interprets in mantic style at the decisive moment in the tent (1209, 1218). Even his later physical threat against his as yet unknown mother at the altar also in a sense recalls Apollo's earlier assault on her person.[17]

The question of family resemblance on his maternal side is, of course, more complex and more central to the plot. Creousa herself is a more complex figure with a tangled story of her own. Her situation encompasses not only her ambivalent relationship with a lost child but also her own earlier story and its place in the more extended chronicles of the ruling family in Athens. Erechtheus's daughter is a figure with a troubled history in her father's house. Before Creousa's traumatic encounter with Apollo and the subsequent exposure of her child, Erechtheus had sacrificed her sisters when the city was in peril; she alone was saved because she was still a babe in arms. As has justly been observed, she is "perhaps the only figure of ancient tragedy whose unconscious motives are a matter of legitimate concern."[18] At the same time, as the last representative of the autochthonous line, she holds the political future of Athens in her hands. For all these reasons, both private and public, she is, as Nicole Loraux notes, the figure in whom "all the threads of this complicated plot are bound up together."[19] Most obviously, Creousa and Ion are linked in the present by their mutual preoccupation with finding the missing other and with resolving (or at least working through) the circumstances surrounding Ion's birth that affect them both so profoundly—in substantive, political, and also psychological ways.

16. Wasserman 1940, 601; Wolff 1963, 172; Hanson 1975, 31.
17. Wolff 1963, 172; Hanson 1975, 32.
18. Burnett 1970, 12–13.
19. Loraux 1981a, "Créuse," 197–98.

The psychology of recognition in this play follows the conventions of anagnorisis, already established in epic, in which evidence of likemindedness *(homophrosunē)* between apparent strangers seems to be a prerequisite to formal recognition. Ion and Creousa share this affective sympathy from the scene of their first meeting, when the young temple servant encounters the aristocratic woman from Athens and they confide in one another.[20] Their reciprocal attraction is an authenticating device that gains in power by its reverse in the mismatch between Ion and his false father, Xouthos, whose clumsy and ill-timed embraces in the scene that ensues soon after produce the opposite reaction. Affinity and affiliation go together. Hence this first encounter between Creousa and Ion, which develops with such apparent spontaneous ease, serves in retrospect as the convincing rehearsal (and preview) of their joyful reunion at the end.

The success of a theatrical plot depends on such structuring devices that persuade the audience "to experience each event, while recalling previous events and anticipating those to come." Narrative structure consists, in fact, of "many kinds of interconnected relationships which generate motifs that hold the play together. Characters reflect other characters, scenes reflect other scenes, verbal images reflect other verbal images, etc.," to create the illusion of an enclosed but dynamic world that unfolds in dramatic time.[21] In the *Ion* especially, where the path to recognition depends on a mutual recovery of what was originally lost, the play further requires continuous and subtle interaction between the events of the past and those in the present, between those performed on stage and those that preceded the dramatic action.

Repetition and Reenactment

Family Resemblances

Reenactment, repetition, doubling, and reversal are, as many have noted,[22] the theatrical mechanisms that govern this play on all its levels. Generating each time new versions of preceding events, often with simultaneous com-

---

20. Cf. the first encounter between Iphigenia and Orestes (also between male and female kin) in the *Iphigenia in Tauris*. The major antecedent of such exhibitions of *homophrōsunē* is, of course, the meetings between Penelope and Odysseus in Homer, especially in Book 19, although Odysseus knows her identity and is testing her through his disguise. See above, chapter 1. The interchange between Creousa and Ion goes still further, because it is essential to the latter's maturation during the play. Here, as later at the altar, Creousa's revelations about Apollo challenge Ion's simpler notions of purity and pollution and introduce the theme of sexuality in the sacred place. On the mutual sympathy in the scene, see, e.g., Wolff 1963, 171; Hanson 1975, 33.

21. Hornby 1986, 20.

22. See especially Wolff 1963; and Loraux 1981a, "Créuse," 193–95.

posite, even conflicting, cross-references to different figures, motifs, and gestures, these operations are centrally related to the dominant themes of birth, rebirth, and death, which are relevant not only to this child's history but also to a more general concern with mythic beginnings and origins.

Creousa tells and retells in various forms the story of the birth of the child whom she abandoned to probable death, yet went on hoping was still alive.[23] The ambivalence she reveals about what happened to her and what she in turn did to the other returns in her plot against the stranger child, appropriately at the birthday celebration that Ion is bidden by the happy Xouthos to prepare in the tent. When she unwittingly repeats her first attempt against his life when he was newly born, he dies, as it were, only to be reborn once again in the ensuing recognition scene—this time as her own child.[24] "Discovery I despaired of," she exclaims, "you the child whom I thought lived underground with Persephone." He replies, "But here I am in your arms again, a living apparition, who died and did not die" (ὁ κατθανών τε κοὐ θανὼν φαντάζομαι, 1441–44).

The basket with its tokens, which the Pythia brings forth from the inmost shrine of Apollo, is the material proof of his identity. Miraculously preserved in its pristine state, the basket recalls the moment of his birth and forecasts his new life as Creousa's son and the true heir to the Erechtheid line. "My house has its hearth," declares Creousa, "my land its king—Erechtheus has grown young again (anēbāi), and the line that sprang from earth no longer shrouds itself in night but looks upon the sun" (1464). Even more, as Loraux convincingly demonstrates, Ion is proven a child of autochthonous ancestry because the circumstances of his story "imitate," whether in replay or inversion, elements that recall the stories of both Erechtheus and Erichthonios.

Briefly put, Loraux argues that Ion reincarnates and even resurrects the figure of his grandfather, King Erechtheus, whom the earth had swallowed up, in that the boy was also dedicated to death and yet "returned" from the world below. The same interplay between hiding and exposing, above and below, however, as well as the ambiguous role of earth as the site of both birth and death, may refer equally, in the opposite sense, to the earlier story of the child Erichthonios. The latter, born from the depths of the earth, was taken up and reared by Athena, while Ion's mother, who laid him on the earth and concealed him in the hollow of a cave, destined her child not for life but for extinction. Ion, the child of a union between a mortal and a god, becomes an autochthon at the last, when his basket,

---

23. On Creousa's vacillations, see Burnett 1971, 124–25.

24. The ambiguity in Greek between the indicative statement of action fulfilled and the conative of attempted action blurs the boundary between "killing" and "trying to kill," so as to suggest an actual death (1221, 1224–25, 1286, 1291, 1300, 1308; cf. 1499–1500).

so long concealed at the *omphalos,* the navel of the Delphic shrine, is produced by the Pythia at the critical moment to disclose its identifying birth
tokens.[25] Ion's basket is already an imitation of the original that had belonged to Erichthonios, in accordance with the ancestral tradition decreed
for a child of the royal house. So too are the tokens of the golden serpents,
replicas *(mimēmata)* of the real ones that had guarded the first infant and
are now a family heirloom (22–23, 1427–29).[26]

As was the case for Erichthonios, Ion's early nurture *(trophē)* is at
risk. In each case, a failure is followed by a success through the offices of
a foster mother. Athena had originally entrusted the basket with the child
to the daughters of Cecrops. But when they failed in their task by disobey-
ing Athena's injunction not to open it, the goddess "raised him up from
the earth, although she did not bear him *[ou tekousa]*" (270). Creousa
kept the custom of her ancestors by placing the infant Ion in the basket
(20), but, like the daughters of Cecrops, she did not save him and did not
give him his *trophē.*[27] Athena's counterpart is the Pythia, who assumes
both these functions: she picked him up from the threshold of the shrine
where Hermes had deposited him and has tended him all these years. Ion
calls her "my dear mother, although not in birth" (*ou tekousa,* 1324; cf.
320), and at their last farewell, she embraces him "just like the one who
bore you" (*ison hōs tekousa,* 1363). She is the mediating figure, therefore,
between Creousa and Athena, between Erichthonios and Ion.[28] In this
role, she is also the sacred functionary, who in her sudden fortuitous appearance on stage plays the intermediate part of the *dea ex machina,* just
preceding the epiphany of the goddess Athena herself.

The Pythia, however, is always careful to attribute her benevolence to
the god's inspiration (1346–47, 1357–60; cf. 47–48), and Apollo too is
credited with having bestowed *trophē* upon the child (357, 531, 1531,

25. The infant Ion had been laid in his basket and left in a cave until brought to Delphi
where he lived a life outside. The basket, however, had been hidden all this time in a cavelike
enclosure at Delphi, the inmost shrine from which Ion has been barred. Thus there is an important distinction between the two. In this respect, I differ from Loraux (1981a, "Créuse,"
251), who claims that "the Delphic *omphalos* has received Ion, who can at last be born an
Athenian—not from the earth, like his model, Erichthonios, but because he has come, metaphorically speaking, from death." The omphalos and basket are discussed further below in
another context.

26. Loraux 1981a, "Créuse," 207–9.

27. In the dazzling play of sound and sense surrounding the key word *trophēs,* the text
(1376–78) emphasizes the significance of maternal nurture, first, through alliterating the
letter *tau* (e.g., in the repeated *mētros,* in *ti, philtatēs, tlēmōn, tekousa, tauton),* and second,
by the verbal puns in *truphōsai* (coddling) and *terphthēnai* (taking pleasure), which are more
extensive indications of a mother's love.

28. Loraux (1981a, "Créuse," 207–9) elides this analogy in her otherwise excellent
analysis.

1600).[29] In Ion's eyes, when he determines to open the basket, it was Apollo who had saved for him the tokens *(sumbola)* of his lineage (1385–86). But the god has a broader soteriological function of granting safety and salvation, phrased mostly in the negative. "You did not save the one you ought to have saved," says Creousa after explaining her errand to Ion as a favor for a friend (386). She later justifies to the old servant her exposure of her newborn child because she expected that "the god would save his own offspring" (965). But once her plot against the boy is discovered, Creousa too will be in need of salvation, which only the god can bestow upon her, this time as a suppliant at his altar. Ion is indignant: "Neither the altar nor the shrine of Apollo will save you" (1275). He is wrong. The chorus knows better. They had urged her to take refuge there, "giving her body as a sacred object into the god's possession" (1285). These are the rules. It is forbidden to kill a suppliant (1256, cf. 1259–60), precisely because contact with a god's altar is equivalent to an act of sacralization. Earlier I suggested that Ion's violent attempt against Creousa threatens to repeat the violence of his father, Apollo, who had taken her by force (11, 939–41). Yet the ritual protection afforded by his altar now reverses (or in some sense repairs) the god's previous sexual assault on Creousa and renders her body sacred *(hieron)* or untouchable (1285). Given the metaphorical links between virgins and suppliants and between defloration and sacrifice, it is significant that if the god has harmed her sexually before, he (or the sanctity of his shrine) now will "save" her.[30]

But sacrifice has a more literal and more local reference. The scene at the altar answers to Creousa's own attempted violence against the boy. He is also under the god's protection, and in the scene in the tent, he too is called *hieros* (1224–25). References to sacrifices *(thusiai, sphagia,* and *sphagai)* are abundant throughout the play. They refer to the ordinary mantic sacrifices necessary for consultation of the shrine (226, 376–77) and to those birth offerings Xouthos intends to dedicate on Mount Parnassus for his new-found son (653, 805, 1124–27, 1130).[31] But the

29. *Trophē* includes both actual nurture (food and drink) and child rearing. Ion often is fed from leavings at the altars *(bōmious trophas,* 52, 322–23), and he in turn serves those who "nurture" the shrine of Apollo (110). He knows about omens because he was raised *(trapheis)* in the temple and the god's mantic seat (1190). The text consistently hesitates between masculine and feminine roles in this regard (e.g., 322, 821, 826), and presumably both parents are included when the chorus praises legitimate children in the house (475, 487).

30. On the correlation between the suppliant and the virgin, see Zeitlin 1986b, 139; and above, chapter 4, 127–36. On that between sacrifice and defloration, see Loraux 1987, 31–48, 61; between sacrifice and marriage, Foley 1985, 68–102; and in general, Burkert 1983, 58–71.

31. *Sphagē* and *sphazō* need not refer to sacrificial killing, but in tragedy they generally are attracted into the vocabulary of the sacred: sacrifices are twice called *sphagai* (377, 1126). These terms are also used for the intrigue against Ion (616) and the pursuit of Creousa that will end in her seeking sanctuary (1250, 1309).

sacrificial theme also refers to a troubling event of the more distant past—that is, Erechtheus's sacrifice of his daughters (ἔθυσε συγγόνους, 277), when "he dared to immolate the maidens on the earth's behalf" (ἔτλη πρὸ γαίας σφάγια παρθένους κτανεῖν, 278). Although Creousa's sisters perished, she was saved, being a newborn in her mother's arms (279–80). Autochthony may be used to represent the mysterious continuum of birth, death, and rebirth, but the fate of the other Erechtheid girls implies the heavier charge of a patriotic sacrifice for the earth.[32]

Two opposing story patterns seem to be relevant to children of the Erechtheid house: "to save" (or "to keep") and "to lose" (or "to sacrifice"). True, Erechtheus, the adult king, also "returns to the earth," when he is swallowed up in the aftermath of the same battle that saw the death of the maidens. At the same time, it was he, the father, who "dared to sacrifice his daughters," although Creousa herself was fortuitously saved.

Others have pointed to the parallel in reverse between Creousa, the baby who was saved, and Ion, the infant left out to die, even though his life is preserved by others not once but twice.[33] Creousa exposes her baby in secret to escape her father's notice (14, 340),[34] but in this second attempt on Ion's life, it is the old servant, a father figure (and stand-in for Erechtheus, as we shall see), who instigates and carries out Creousa's plot to kill this stranger child, and under sacrificial auspices. In their conspiracy, Creousa, and the old man too, in a sense, can claim to be acting on the earth's behalf *(pro gaias)*—but this time, to save the Erechtheid autochthons from an imposter usurping power in their land. Likewise, Creousa's scene at the altar also gains in resonance by recalling the traumatic family history. If Ion is successful in laying hands on her, she might well meet the fate of her sisters (in being made to leap from the rocks, 1266–68),[35] and the sacrificial implications of her suppliant status bring her back to her own childhood when, as now, she was saved. As offspring of an autochthonous lineage, both son and mother, who are playing themselves and the roles of others, seem equally vulnerable to the scenario of potential sacrifice, exactly as an important passage in the text seems to suggest.

Just after the messenger describes what happened in the tent and an-

32. Autochthony, *pro gaias*, and the idea that sacrifice will save the city recur in Praxithea's speech in the *Erechtheus* where she offers to sacrifice her daughter: frag. 50 A = 10 C (frag. 360 N²).

33. As Loraux (1981a, "Créuse," 225) or Wolff (1963, 171) remarks, one might say both are also miraculously saved.

34. Her fear of her mother also motivates her action (898, 1489), as Loraux (1981a, "Créuse," 234) points out.

35. This mode of death also recalls the daughters of Cecrops (cf. 272–74), who leaped to their death in the wake of their disobedience to Athens. The two sets of maidens differ, however: the fate of Cecrops's daughters is a punishment, while that of the Erechtheids is a noble self-sacrifice. On Creousa and the Cecropids, see Loraux 1981a, "Créuse," 243n.194.

nounces the imminent pursuit of Creousa, the chorus speaks of "sacrifices of/to the underworld that are now made manifest *[phanera thumata nerterōn]*" (1235). The referent is ambiguous: does it look back to the just reported attempt on Ion's life or ahead to the misfortune and destruction awaiting both Creousa and the women of the chorus? The answer must be that the sacrificial image applies to both son and mother: in the first instance to Ion, but in context also to Creousa (agent and victim), a sign of the heritage they share.

In Ion's first meeting with his unknown mother, he had originally asked three questions concerning the history of her house. These relate to (1) Erichthonios (and the Cecropids); (2) Erechtheus's sacrifice of his daughters; and (3) the fate of Erechtheus himself, swallowed up by the earth. We have already seen how Ion is to be revealed as both a second Erichthonios (1) and a reincarnation of Erechtheus himself (3). The addition of the middle term completes—or rather, inaugurates—the dramatic series of events. Indeed, the potential "sacrifice" of Creousa serves as the motivation for the revelation of the other two events, once her own "sacrificial" plot against Ion has been revealed. The moment is perfectly timed: Just before the Pythia's entrance and the showing of the basket, Creousa, now grown, finds herself in exactly the same position as her sisters long ago, replaying both her own story in the rape and violence of Apollo, and her family's sacrificial history. Between the scene in Ion's tent, meant to serve as a belated birthday celebration for the boy, now grown, and the subsequent confrontation at the altar, where Creousa also reenacts a version of her childhood experience, the interchange between Ion and Creousa recapitulates all the earlier stages related to autochthony as well as those of their own relationship. The latter will yet be redeemed by the contrary outcome: the saving of the child and the basket, on the one hand, and the miraculous renewal of the family lineage on the other. By the end, the negative elements recede into what has become the past history of the completed drama.

Ion's story is a success. What had threatened to become a typical tragic scenario, in which misrecognition between kin leads to a mother's destruction of her child (as in the *Bacchae*), has been turned into a series of happy reversals centering on the miracle of the basket, untouched by age through all these years and brought forth as in a mystic revelation to initiate those present into the forecast of a propitious future. This is an Athenian play, after all, representing its own city on stage, and leading not to destructive negation (as in Thebes) but to a joyful if complicated ending about parents and children, lost and safely found.[36] The conclusion also

36. On Ion and Oedipus as questers of their origins and of knowledge, see, e.g., Knox 1979, 257–58; Whitman 1974, 78–79; Hanson 1975, 28–29; Bushnell 1988, 109–10, 117–19. On the representation of Thebes on stage, see Zeitlin 1986a; and now Zeitlin 1993a.

releases generative power for the future: in the genealogies to come and in the finding of pragmatic ways of treating various forms of kinship. This will have powerful implications for politics in the city and later for the idea of empire. The play, therefore, indoctrinates us not only into the complexities of ideological mythmaking but also into the sources and resources of the theater that stages the myth, especially as they revolve around the key questions of identity and recognition, mobilizing the dense network of signs and designs required for "matching" the unknown self to the identity it is asked to claim.

It is Athena, finally, who ratifies Ion's status as an authentic child of autochthonous lineage and as a true son of Apollo, in keeping with both her function as poliadic goddess of Athens and her association with the maternal fosterage of earth-borns. Her victory in the Gigantomachy, as significantly depicted early in the play on the temple facade, had shown her opposition to those other Gegeneis, the primordial foes of the Olympian gods. Now she can reclaim for Athens the positive valences of civic autochthony, which had been compromised by Creousa's reenactment of the earth-born Gorgon's role against the Erechtheid child in the drops of the monster's blood used for the poisoned drink.[37] At the same time, she reconfirms her own initial victory against the negative forces of Earth, which is replayed in the course of the drama. Both events—victory in the Gigantomachy and the birth of Erichthonios—were jointly celebrated in fact at the Panathenaea, the goddess's own festival, whose founding was attributed by tradition to none other than Erichthonios himself.[38]

Dramatically speaking, however, Athena stands in for Apollo as *dea ex machina*, and she does so on his own home ground. Nevertheless, her arrival in Delphi also has a practical function: to escort the rightful heir back to his native land. In this respect, Athena matches up with Hermes, who as speaker of the prologue is her dramatic counterpart. His original role in the story, as he tells us, involved traversing the same road but in the opposite direction, when he had come from Athens to Delphi, bringing with him the newborn child. In both structure and substance, then, the

37. On the negative aspects of autochthony, see Wolff 1963, 182; Whitman 1974, 97–99; Immerwahr 1972, 286; Mastronarde 1975, 164–65; Rosivach 1977; and Loraux 1981a, "Créuse," 239–40.

38. Loraux 1981a, "Autochtonie," 46–47 and n. 45; Parker 1987, 192–93. Vian (1952, 249–53) even suggests reenactment of the Gigantomachy at several stages of the festival. The Panathenaic milieu is also evoked by the reference to Athena's birth (452–57), the representation of which occupied the place of honor on the Parthenon and was probably itself celebrated at the festival, while the prominence of weaving and woven materials together with the theme of Gigantomachy might recall Athena's peplos. While it is true that our evidence for Erichthonios's connection with the Panathenaea comes later from fourth-century Atthidographers, this play may reflect a tradition already in place or may adumbrate its future creation.

conclusion to this drama of comings and goings completes the round-trip journey and ties the end to the beginning.

Athena's arrival may be unexpected, given the frame of reference in which she appears. But her figure is always present, one could say: it was openly portrayed on the sculptured reliefs of the Gigantomachy, which the chorus first sees when it enters, identifying her figure as "my goddess" (211). It recurs too, and in riddling form, as I shall later suggest when surveying the iconography of the tent. There are other explicit allusions as well, whether recalling her gifts to the Erechtheid house and her role in the rearing of Erichthonios or directly invoking her name and her powers. Above all, as already noted, she provides an implicit paradigm for the roles of both Creousa and the Pythia, having been herself an integral part of the myth—also from the beginning.

Another divine figure, however, is represented alongside the goddess on that same sculpted façade. Strictly speaking, this divinity, unlike Athena, bears no relation to the history of the Erechtheid house and, unlike Apollo, has no obvious role to play in this, the last act of the story. The god in question is Dionysos, whom we might even view as the antithesis of Apollo. But if Dionysos has nothing to do with the Athenian tale, he has everything to do with the conduct of the play itself—both the regulation of its tragic rhythms and the central quest for identity. Apollo may intervene providentially from behind the scenes, and Athena may speak for him at the end. Yet, as we shall see, Dionysos, the lord of the theater, is more powerfully at work in the drama under his multiple aspects than is the lord of Delphi whose precinct this other god also shares.

Mysteries of Dionysos

Dionysos is viewed by the choral spectators who identify him on the sculpted façade (along with Athena) near the start of the play (216–18). They also invoke him twice more in ritual, or more precisely in mystic, contexts, one pertaining to rites at Delphi on Mount Parnassus (714–17), the other to those at Eleusis (1074–86). Aside from brief mentions of preliminary sacrificial practice in mantic ritual, Dionysos is the only one to whom special sacrifices are to be made. This is Xouthos's idea, as a belated thank-offering for Ion's birth (653), since he supposes that he engendered this unknown child at a nocturnal Dionysiac festival in Delphi, when he was besotted with "the pleasures of Bacchios" (553). While Xouthos is tending to these ritual chores on Mount Parnassus, Ion in his tent is also involved in what I shall argue is represented as a Dionysiac scene. In this way, Dionysos and his rites become an essential part of the plot.

The first invocation of Dionysos thus introduces us to a wider frame of reference that leads beyond the intricacies of the Erechtheid patterns we

have been retracing so as to venture into the region where ritual and theater cross, where mysteries of identity meet up with patterns and echoes
of actual cultic mysteries. As the "fathering" agent, Dionysos supplies the
auspices under which reenactments of Erechtheid history may take place.
But Dionysos also, in his own person and story, provides the appropriate
paradigms for mimetic replay, with their dual potential for disaster or success. His ambiguous figure exemplifies the questioning and confusions of
identities that are such integral traits of his theater. His is the story that
most closely corresponds to the mythic patterns entwined in this plot:
the lot of the child *(neos)*—his birth and early rearing—and the outcome
of the youth's *(neanias)* quest for identity when on the threshold of
adulthood.[39]

To start with, is not Dionysos the most conspicuous "prototype of the
divinely engendered child,"[40] born of a union between a god and a mortal? Even more, is he not the child whose circumstances of entry into the
world designate him as the "twice born?" The epithet refers to the fact of
his having been taken from his mother's womb at her death and placed in
Zeus's thigh from which he was born a second time. Figuratively, the analogy between Dionysos and Ion is sustained in two ways. First, Ion too was
separated at birth from a mother he presumes may have died. Left for dead
by his mother, he was miraculously transferred to his father's domain to
remain among the living. Second, Ion is the twice-born because the secret
of his birth (the basket with its tokens) was kept hidden in the inmost
shrine of Apollo—a space forbidden to women (222–32)[41] and equipped
with an omphalos, the navel stone of the earth (6, 223, 933), which bears
a striking structural resemblance to the "male womb" from which Dionysos issued forth as the son of Zeus.[42]

The theme of the "twice born" is also reenacted on stage as the climax
of the dramatic action. When the basket is brought out for the recognition

---

39. On the alternating terms *pais* and *neanias*, see Loraux 1981a, "Créuse," 200n.8.
At 316, where the distinction is factually important, it is asked whether Ion came to Delphi
as a *pais* or as *neanias* (cf. 780). The specific term for "baby" is *brephos* (16, 31, 280, 317,
503, 1339, 1399, 1454, 1599). It is combined with *pais* (16) and often qualified by *neognos*
(newborn, 31, 280, 1339).

40. Burnett 1970, 4. See below, note 47.

41. Creousa must ask her husband and the *Paidagogos* to make inquiries for her. Cf.
Plutarch, *On the E at Delphi* 385c–d; and the discussion of Kerényi 1976, 226.

42. Loraux (1981a, "Créuse," 248–50), followed by Daraki (1985, 177), understands
both the basket and the omphalos (flanked by Gorgons, 224–25) as representations of the
"chthonic womb," whose symbolism she refers to autochthonous birth. But the basket and
Ion are independent entities at Delphi until "reunited" in the recognition scene (see above,
note 25). Even more, it is precisely the fact that the omphalos, the "chthonic womb," belongs
to the shrine of the masculine god that suggests the male appropriation of what is properly
female anatomy and function.

scene, it evokes the triumphant assertion of the first "double birth": he died but did not die. The motif of the "twice born" may be extended even further if we consider that the natural father, Apollo, issuing oracles from his shrine, bestows his son upon yet another father, Xouthos. This action redoubles, as it were, the insistence on the primal role of paternity so central to the Dionysiac myth (despite the prominence of women in his cult). Dramatically speaking, it is the pivotal event that triggers the rest of the plot.

Even more obvious than the principle of the "twice born" is the literal detail of the child in the basket. Ion's placement in his basket, we are specifically told, was meant to imitate the family custom that began with Erichthonios (19–21). But Erichthonios, in turn, follows the pattern of Dionysos Liknites, who as an infant was placed in a basket (or winnowing fan: *liknon*); both of them were given over to female nurses for fosterage. The ritual of Dionysos Liknites took place on the heights of Mount Parnassus at Delphi during the trieteric festival, the same occasion on which Xouthos was supposed to have engendered his child from the unknown maenad when the women were dancing on the mountain. Our knowledge about this ritual is scanty and derived from late sources. Some scholars have argued that the rite was added only during the Hellenistic era.[43] But I believe that our text alludes indirectly to the activity surrounding Dionysos Liknites, when the Thyiades on the mountain would have wakened the infant Dionysos (probably in the Corycian cave) with a mystic torchlit ceremony[44] that may have celebrated the god's "death and disappearance, revival and rebirth."[45]

Just after the chorus of Athenian women learn of Xouthos's good fortune in finding his child, they sing of their disappointment and dismay on behalf of their queen and their city. They have already uttered their wish that this "new" child of a "new" father might perish (711–12).[46] Now they close their song by invoking "the ridges of Mount Parnassus where Bacchios lifts up his fiery torches and leaps to lead the night-wandering bacchants in the dance," and they pray that "this child never come" to

43. This is primarily the influential view of Nilsson (1957, 42), who relies mainly on later iconographical evidence. For further discussion of the trieteric rituals, the Thyiades, and Dionysos Liknites, see Harrison 1922, 401–3, 517–34; Jeanmaire 1951, 196–97; Kerényi 1976, 212–26; Daraki 1985, 20–21, 127–29, 260n.49; Burkert 1983, 124–25; and Villanueva-Puig 1986.

44. Waken the infant: Plutarch, *Isis et Osiris* 35 = *Moralia* 365a; cf. *Orphica* frag. 214 Kern. Torchlit mystic ceremony; Scholiast *ad* Lycophron, *Alexandra* 212.

45. Φθοράς τινας καὶ ἀφανισμοὺς εἶτα δ' ἀναβιώσεις καὶ παλινγενεσίας (Plutarch, *On the E at Delphi* 389a). Burnett (1970, 3–5) notes the parallels between Dionysos Liknites and Ion, but pushes the analogy too far in comparing Creousa to Ino or Semele and Xouthos to Silenos (as though this were a satyr play).

46. I accept Diggle's emendation, following Hartung.

their city. "Let him die," they say, "as infants do, at the moment when he celebrates his birth" (714–21).[47]

In context, the allusion to the nocturnal Dionysiac rites may refer merely to the supposed place and time of Ion's engendering and to Xouthos's intention, as he tells them, to make belated birth sacrifices *(genethlia)* in that same spot (653). But the passage takes on added resonance if we interpret the women's prayer as a precise reversal of the Thyiadic women's ritual gestures at the close of their maenadic activity on the mountain, when they woke the sleeping child in the basket *(liknon)* and brought him back to life.[48]

In the next phase of development, from child to youth, Dionysos is again the paradigm for the figure born of a god and a mortal, who returns to his city to claim his rightful place and identity. Like Ion, he embodies the paradox of a stranger who is also native born (cf. 805). And Dionysos also meets with resistance from those of his kin who resent his intrusion and, as in the *Bacchae,* do not believe his father was a god.

Nevertheless, as is generally the case in doublet relations, the two figures are both complements and antitheses of each other. As an immortal's offspring, Dionysos comes to claim his divinity, while Ion leaves behind his identity as the child of the god to take up an all too mortal status. Ion's true genealogy (born from a god, born from the earth), however, accommodates without strain the tensions that opposed Dionysos, son of Olympian Zeus, in the *Bacchae* to his adversary, Pentheus, son of the autochthonous Echion. Yet Ion, as the drama unfolds, bears a significant resemblance to Pentheus, for he is also the doomed Dionysiac child in the potentially tragic scenario by which he almost played Pentheus to his mother's Agave. But again this relation is reversed, since Pentheus owes his autochthonous status to his father Echion, while Ion derives his from his mother, who gave the old servant the poisoned drop of the earth-born Gorgon's blood to use in the wine at the Dionysiac banquet in the tent.[49]

---

47. Burnett's translation here captures the ambiguity of νέαν δ᾽ ἁμέραν ἀπολιπὼν θάνοι, which can mean leaving "his young life," or "the day on which he celebrates his birth." See Owen 1939, *ad loc.* Burnett wisely keeps both, understanding the coincidence of death and rebirth in the context of a birthday feast.

48. Or if, as Daraki (1985, 63) suggests, the women in the trieteric rites engaged in both hostile and nurturant behavior toward the young god, then the chorus's negative prayer would emphasize only one aspect of the ritual to the neglect of the second and climactic one.

Xouthos's rites are an irregular form of Greek family rituals on the occasion of birth (see Immerwahr 1972, 294–95; Loraux 1981c, 222n.99), but their place and nature might also suggest he is about to conduct a kind of private *trieteris,* his own *dithyrambos* for the "twice born."

49. On this analogy, Creousa, bearer of the autochthonous line, is the one who plays the part of Pentheus in a struggle between earth-born and Olympian forces, suggested already from the sculpted iconography. However, to name her a *theomachos*—as do, for ex-

The two elements intermingle quite literally, when the chorus sings of "the libation of [from] Dionysos, the mixture of the grape with the murderous venom of the Gorgon" (1231–35).[50]

In this interplay between the roles of Dionysos and Pentheus, what might be called a Dionysiac tragedy is only narrowly averted. It might and does take place in Thebes, but not in Athens. The crucial difference between the two scenarios resides first in the goddess Athena herself, who "stabilizes" Dionysos and engages his energies as a positive force within the Athenian context. Their alliance has already been depicted on the façade of the Delphic temple, where in the archetypal battle against the Giants, Dionysos is placed in the company of the Olympians, Athena and Zeus.[51] Again, at the end, Athena puts the seal of approval on the recognition of the twice-born and officially ratifies Ion's dual identity as child of the autochthon and child of the god. But the Athenian milieu is not limited to the poliadic goddess alone or to her feminine presence and prestige. Other goddess figures by their implicit paradigms promote the soteriological outcome and are also linked to a "positive" Dionysos.

Mysteries of Eleusis

The mysteries of the "twice born" were represented as a return from the dead, that is, a return from the domain of Persephone (1441–42) and the house of Hades where Ion was "reared" (*paideuetai*, 953). These words belong to Creousa; her reference to Persephone follows the lyrics in which she describes her rape in the meadow while gathering flowers (881–906). These and other significant details make clear, as Loraux suggests, that the model for Creousa's experience is that of the Kore figure who was ravished by an Apollo-Hades.[52] In keeping with her focus on autochthony, Loraux emphasizes the interchangeability of earth and Hades as the way

---

ample, Burnett (1962) and Rosivach (1977)—is to oversimplify the tensions between role and character.

50. Σπονδὰς ἐκ Διονύσου, βοτρύων θοᾶς ἐχίδνας σταγόσι μειγνυμένας φόνωι. The syntax is complex and may be understood in several ways (see Owen 1939, *ad loc.*), but the meaning seems quite clear. Diggle obelizes.

51. The allusion to Dionysos's role in this exemplary battle is ambiguous. The other two gods' adversaries are named, but for Dionysos we are only told that he slays one of the children of Earth (Gaia). While a name may be supplied from the mythic tradition (see Owen 1939, *ad loc.*), the vagueness of the reference leaves the dramatic situation still open in which Dionysos might be responsible for slaying another earth-born (i.e., Ion).

52. Loraux 1981a, "Créuse," 245–47. She also stresses the double aspects of maiden (Kore) and queen of the dead (Persephone) as corresponding to the duality of Creousa, herself a victim of sexual violence and yet one who delivers her child to the realm of death (i.e., to Persephone).

in which Ion's story may be read as replaying those of his forebears. But taken on its own terms, the paradigm of Kore/Persephone has a closer relevance to the present action of the drama and a broader import for Ion's identity as an Athenian child. This motif aligns Ion with the redemptive elements of Athenian myth and ritual that are exemplified in the mysteries celebrated at Eleusis and justifies the explicit references these rites receive in the text.

The pattern of the "twice born," once joined to the other motif of "lost ones reunited after a long separation," identifies Creousa with both goddesses of Eleusis: the maiden raped (Kore) and the grieving mother who searches for her lost child (Demeter).[53] The mythic motif of descent and ascent, it is true, belongs to the male members of the Erechtheid family. Ion too may be viewed as imitating the Kore figure, who is sent off, presumably to reside in Hades, and returns at last to a mother's embrace. We may recall as well that Erechtheus, whom Ion reincarnates, was also swallowed up by the earth in a direct parallel to Kore's experience as described in the *Homeric Hymn to Demeter*.[54]

Erechtheus's connection with the mysteries is still more insistent, if we consider what we know of Euripides' earlier play of the same name. In that drama, Erechtheus was at war with the Eleusinians and their ally, the Thracian Eumolpos. This crisis occasioned the sacrifice of his daughters and his own mysterious demise, and in its aftermath Athena also appeared as *dea ex machina,* this time not only to decree cult honors for Erechtheus and his family, but also to assign hieratic roles at Eleusis for the mysteries.[55] The allusions in the text of the *Ion* to Eleusinian elements of myth and ritual are therefore even more pertinent to the Athenian strategies of

53. Loraux (1981a, "Créuse," 246) recognizes the "tragic overdetermination" that marks the "figure of Creousa, sterile like Persephone, goddess of the Underworld, and nevertheless a mother in quest of a lost child." But the Demetrian side is not strictly relevant to her analysis, which focuses rather on the mythic paradigm of the "*parthenos* who has given birth."

54. Cf. *chasma chthonos* (281); and *chane . . . chthōn* (*Homeric Hymn to Demeter* 16). Male figures, such as Amphiaraos, were also said to have been swallowed by the earth, but the Eleusinian context recalls this central feature of the Kore's myth, which is often represented in both narrative and image. See Richardson 1974, *ad loc.*

55. On the *Erechtheus,* produced probably in 422 or 423, see Austin 1967 and 1968; and Cararra 1977. For Athena's cultic pronouncements, clear with regard to the family of Erechtheus but unfortunately fragmentary regarding the mysteries, see frag. 65A, 109–14 (= 18C). Some later traditions, attempting to bring order to genealogical confusion, assign the foundation of the mysteries to Eumolpos himself (e.g., Scholiast *ad* Sophocles, *Oedipus at Colonus* 1035 = Andron, *FGrH* 10 F 13) or to a descendant of his name in the fifth generation. In many respects the *Ion* looks like the sequel to the *Erechtheus,* but the two are also incompatible in some significant details. For discussion, see Cararra 1977, 18–36; and Parker 1987, 202–3, especially n. 64.

the play, especially as the reference to Erechtheus follows directly the earlier choral appeal to Dionysos on Mount Parnassus (721–24).[56]

In mythic terms, Ion may be said to take the place of Kore, as suggested above, but he also has a ritual part to play on his own. The rites at
Eleusis, we may note, concluded with the celebration of the birth of a mystic child,[57] a motif even more appropriate to the context of our drama.
Several scholars have noted more generally the correspondences in both
myth and iconography between the birth and fosterage of Erichthonios
and that of this unidentified child of Eleusis,[58] who are both given over to
the care of female deities. The most obvious parallel between the two is
the basket *(kistē)* used as a container first for the child and then for certain
sacred and secret talismans that were displayed when it was opened.[59] The
happy unveiling of the basket in the *Ion* may contrast with the Cecropids'
disaster when they disobeyed Athena's injunction *not* to open the parallel
basket of Erichthonios, but it matches up with the Eleusinian display of
mystic secrets, which turned grief to joy and brought the initiates out of
darkness into a great light.

There are many hints, I think, of a certain mystic quality in this scene
in the *Ion,* which sacralizes the typical features associated with theatrical
recognitions of this kind. The basket itself has been kept within a sacred
mysterious place to which only a single religious official was allowed access ("no one of mortals knew we had these things nor where they were
hidden," 1361–62), while the tokens are not only maternal emblems but
also, first and foremost, sacred talismans of hallowed origins. The basket
is merely a material object, it is true, the existence of which is kept secret
and in which certain familial articles are hidden. But hiding, secrets, and
silence are especially insistent features of this play and cover a wide se-

56. The passage referring to Erechtheus is unfortunately obscure and may well be la-
cunose. Many solutions have been offered (see Owen 1939; also Burnett 1970, *ad loc.*). But
however the text is read, there is a likely correlation between Ion's entry into Athens as a
"foreign invasion" *(xenikon esbolan)* and Erechtheus's military intervention on behalf of
Athens against Eleusis.

57. On the birth of a mystic child at Eleusis, see, e.g., Burkert 1983, 288–89; and
Lévêque 1982a, 188–90. The identity of the child is disputed (he is called Brimos in mystic
terminology) and may refer to Ploutos, Iacchos, or Dionysos as well as to other candidates.

58. See, e.g., Burkert 1966; and Richardson 1974, 25 and 234–35, who speaks of De-
mophon and Erichthonios. Picard (1931) also notes the resemblances between Erichthonios
and Ion, but advances a more speculative argument to account for the numerous Athenian
mythic, ritual, and iconographical parallels to the "mystic child" as Athens's conscious political attempt to rival the traditions of Eleusis. Metzger (1951, 255–56) observes that the
iconography of the birth of a divine child takes three different forms, relating to the myths
of Erichthonios, Ploutos, or Dionysos.

59. On the *kistē* and its contents, see, e.g., Burkert 1983, 269–73.

mantic field.[60] These elements are appropriate, of course, to the intrigue, deceptions, and counter-deceptions that comprise the action of the drama[61] and that depend in turn on earlier acts of secrecy and concealment (the rape, the childbirth, the exposure of the infant, the hiding of the basket). Nevertheless, the combined effect of the general concern in the play with keeping or revealing secrets is to generate a pervasive sense of mystery that will culminate in disclosures of a more specifically mystic cast, addressed only to those who may know and always to remain secret outside of the Delphic precinct (1601–3). In context, this means that Xouthos is to remain forever in the dark about the identity of his "son." Fictive paternity serves practical social needs and preserves the image of masculine honor, even at the price of compromising the truth. But from a cultic perspective, the fact that Xouthos never returns to the stage once he has departed implies that he is one who is not to be "initiated" into the secret mysteries of the maid, the mother, and the child.

In the stichomythic exchange of the recognition scene, the Pythia's language may be ordinary enough. The general business of tragedy is, after all, epideictic—to show and reveal. But the repeated references to speaking (1325, 1335–36), hearing (1326–27), seeing (1337–38), and showing (1341) might also suggest a formal procedure not unlike the instruction of initiates, who will hear a new *mythos* (sacred story, 1340), learn secrets they had not previously known (1341–42), and behold a container of sacred objects that has been miraculously exempted from the ravages of time (1391–94). In a similar vein, when mother and son use the word *phasma* to refer to their vision of one another (1395, 1444, cf. 1354), the primary sense is that of a ghostly apparition: the vanished one has now returned. But *phasmata* may also recall the "blessed phantoms" of the visionary experience at Eleusis, which the initiates witnessed among other sights and sounds during the mystic night.[62]

---

60. The operative terms are *kruptō* (and its derivatives), *lanthanō*, and *lathra*, as well as language relating to silence *(sigō, siōpē)*. The occurrences are too numerous to list.

61. Creousa desires to learn a secret prophecy (*krupton*, 334) and warns Ion not to tell the secret she related about her friend (*krupta*, 396, cf. 430; *siga*, 395, 432). The plot to kill the boy is secret (*krupt-*, 1114, 1116; *lathra*, 1408). Xouthos engendered a child secretly (*lathra*, 816, 819) and bids the chorus keep silent about the identity of Ion as his son (666–67, cf. 656–60).

62. We know virtually nothing about the nature and identity of these Eleusinian *phasmata* (figures? statues? apparitions?), which seem to belong to the *epopteia* (the highest level of initiation). In addition, almost all our evidence uses the mysteries as metaphor, beginning with the most famous and influential passage of Plato (*Phaedrus* 250b–c); cf. Aristides, *Eleusinia* (Dindorf, 1.416); Plutarch, frag. 168 Sandbach = Stobaeus, *Anthologia* 4.52.49; and Seneca, *Epistulae* 90.28 *(vera simulacra verasque facies cernendas)*. See further Kerényi 1967, 98–99, 203–4.

The rapturous joy that pervades the emotional scene of reunion is precisely the response one would expect in the unexpected turning of fortune
from misery to happiness (1447–49, 1456–57, 1468–69).[63] Yet again we
might think of the peripeties of the mystic experience, which culminates in
a pleasure *(hēdonē)* that bestows the grace of a permanent *makarismos*
(blessing) on those who have seen the rites. Creousa's expression (*maka-
riōtatas . . . hēdonēs,* 1461) is therefore especially appropriate to the scene
in which the child she thought "was dwelling with Persephone beneath
the earth" now "appears as one who died but did not die" (1440–44).[64]
It is even more suggestive that Creousa caps her joy with the exclamation
that "the earth-born house no longer looks upon the night" but "gazes
upward at the gleaming rays of the sun" (οὐκέτι νύκτα δέρκεται / ἀελίου
δ' ἀναβλέπει λαμπάσιν, 1466–67; cf. 1445). It is true that the child, the
life-giving hope of the family, is often called the light *(phōs)* of the house
(476, 1439; cf. Aeschylus, *Choephoroi* 961–63). But our sources unanimously agree that the climax of the mysteries always entailed the experience of a dazzling light *(mega phōs)* that broke through the dark night of
despair and confusion, bringing the initiates into a state of illumination

63. See McDonald 1978, 195–210, on the frequent terms for happiness in the play
(*eutuchēs/dustuchēs, olbos, makar,* and *eudaimōn*), which refer to wealth or power and
more often to the possession of children. *Makar* in particular expresses "the godlike bliss
which follows the event of finding a son," 201. On the relation to mystic terminology, see
Lévêque 1982b.

64. Ion is thus an amalgam of the Kore figure and the divine child. On mystic joy and
the *makarismos,* see Richardson 1974, 310–14; Lévêque 1982a, 200; and Burkert 1987, 93
and n. 17. The most important texts are *Homeric Hymn to Demeter* 480–82; Pindar, frag.
137a Snell; and Sophocles, frag. 837 Radt. The passage in Plato, *Phaedrus* 250b–c, is again
invaluable for its references to the *makarian opsin te thean* of the mysteries and is cited
further below.

Ion himself seems to echo the *makarismos* formula in reverse, when in his reply to
Xouthos's promise of prosperity and wealth to the future ruler in Athens, he says: "Who is
makarios, who *eutuchēs* [fortunate], if in a state of fear and looking askance at life, he lives
out his allotted span *[aiōna teinei]*?" (623–25). The context is appropriate (and see the rest
of the passage, 625–32): Xouthos emphasizes the secular and material sides of *ploutos* and
olbos, which are blessings also promised to the mystic initiates along with spiritual happiness
(*Homeric Hymn to Demeter* 488–89).

Mystic terminology recurs at the end of the play, just after Athena enjoins that the secret
be kept from Xouthos. The goddess announces to Creousa and Ion the promise of a
eudaimona . . . potmon (fortunate destiny) after their respite from troubles (*anapsychēs
ponōn,* 1604–5). Cf. Euripides, *Suppliants* 615, where the latter phrase recurs, immediately
followed by a reference to Eleusis.

"Release from troubles" recurs in many mystic contexts (e.g., Aristides, *Orationes*
19.259; Aristophanes, *Frogs* 185–86; Alciphron, *Letters* 4.17.8; Plato, *Republic* 365a). In
the *Oresteia,* which, as Thomson (1935) and Tierney (1937) argued, is pervaded with allusions to the mysteries, "release" *(apallagē)* already occurs in the opening line of the *Agamemnon,* again in a nocturnal cosmic setting. See Headlam-Thomson 1966, *ad Agamemnon*
1 and 336, index s.v. "Eleusinian Mysteries," and introduction, 42–43.

that was thereafter to be perpetually theirs, even after death. The references to sun and radiant light that preface and conclude the joyous exchange between mother and son in this scene (cf. 1439) also recall, of course, the influence of Apollo, who from the start of the play has been associated with the sun and the break of day.[65] Yet there is also a wider mystical sense of a solar radiance (1445, cf. 1516)[66] that is finally transferred to the epiphany of Athena (1550) who is to take Apollo's place at the critical moment of divine intervention.

As the play draws to its close, all the various figures overlap and converge: Demeter and Kore, the autochthonous child, the "twice born," the mystic infant, and the rejuvenated Erechtheus in the person of Ion—Erechtheus who, as we have seen, has his own decisive links with Eleusis. The final scene performs a double function: on the father's side, the twiceborn issues forth from the "male womb" of Apollo's shrine in a Dionysiac affirmation of paternity, while Eleusinian echoes also situate the twiceborn in the domain of the mother.[67]

Dionysos, however, had his place at the mysteries in the figure of Iacchos, to whom he is closely assimilated. According to some authorities, Iacchos was a version of that same mystic child, but he performed his most important ritual role in the preliminary phases of the rites. As the young *daimōn* who embodied the mystic cry *"iacchos"* of the initiates and was identified with the torches he carried, Iacchos led (or accompanied) the procession along the Sacred Way from Athens to Eleusis. Upon arrival, he was welcomed at the outer court of the Sanctuary where the women sang and danced around the well of the Kallichoron in nocturnal celebration of the two goddesses.[68] This is the Iacchos to whom the chorus directly al-

65. See Burnett 1970, 125, on Helios and Apollo in the play; also Barlow 1971, 45–51 and passim, on the imagery of Ion and Creousa.

66. On mystic illumination and the interplay of light and dark in the mysteries, see, e.g., Richardson 1974, 26; and Kerényi 1967, 96–100. Plato, *Phaedrus* 250c, speaks of a pure light *(en augēi katharai)*; Plutarch mentions a *mega phōs* (*De profectu in virtute* 81d–e; cf. frag. 168 Sandbach = Stobaeus, *Anthologia* 4.52.49); and Dio Chrysostom, 12.33, speaks of the alternation of light and dark. Even more to the point is the assimilation of the light of the mysteries to that of the sun: shining in the dark, it symbolizes both enlightenment and the concept of life in death. "Only for us is the sun and the holy light," sings the chorus of initiates in Aristophanes' *Frogs* (454–55), and Pindar speaks of the power of the sun, which illuminates the night of the netherworld (frag. 129, 1–2).

Immerwahr (1972, 290–92) notes the temporal framing of the play as a passage through an entire day from daybreak to sunset (cf. 1516–17). Athena's radiant appearance at the end thus runs directly counter to a logical progression that would correlate the play's end with nightfall, a point that further supports the idea of a mystical light, especially as analyzed below.

67. On the shift between maternal and paternal identity, see Loraux 1981a, "Créuse," 232–36.

68. On Iacchos and Dionysos, see Burkert 1983, 279; Graf 1974, 51–66; Jeanmaire 1951, 437–39; Metzger 1951, 257–58; Bérard 1974, 94; and Sfameni-Gasparro 1986, 114–

ludes when introducing the Eleusinian mysteries into the text of the play, along with references to the maiden and her mother (1085–86), whose mention alerts us to the potential relevance of these rites.

The ode in question takes place between the departure of the old man on his murderous errand to Ion's feast and the entrance of the messenger, who comes to report what happened there. In this dramatic moment of transition, the first strophe prays that the lethal potion will arrive success-fully at its destination here at Delphi, while the second and corresponding strophe shifts the scene to Eleusis and the arrival there of the celebrants. Each strophe ends with a similar objection to the stranger, who in the first instance would come to rule over the city, and in the second would assume a kingly role of priest at Eleusis. The chorus would be ashamed, the women say, if in the presence of Iacchos, "the much hymned god," the newcomer would witness (theōros . . . opsetai) the nocturnal torches when all of nature (starry ether, moon, and Nereid maidens)[69] danced to the two goddesses by the springs of the Kallichoron (1074–86).[70] The accomplish-ment of the first journey (that of the old servant) would prevent the sacri-lege, as it were, of the second. But an allusion to the preliminaries of the mysteries is already present in the first strophic pair, and it invests the old servant's errand with the air of a sacred mission whose aim, paradoxically, is to invert Eleusinian values and traditional concepts of piety.

At the opening of the ode, the chorus invokes Einodia, daughter of Demeter, to guide the servant's way at Delphi, and the transition is com-pleted in the reference to Iacchos, whose presence signifies the journey's end at Eleusis. This Einodia (or Enodia) is called upon as the one "who rules [anasseis] over nocturnal assaults [nuktipolōn ephodōn] to guide [hodōson] the lethal cup with the Gorgon's poisoned drops to its destina-tion in the daylight hours [methameriōn]" (1048–55). Persephone, the mother's child, merges here with Hekate who as Enodia, goddess of the

---

22. "They give the name 'Iacchos' not only to Dionysos but to the leader of the mysteries, the *daimōn* of Demeter" (Strabo, 10.3.10). See also Sophocles, *Antigone* 1152; and above all, Aristophanes, *Frogs* 325–36, 340–53, 395–408: Iacchos "comes as the *phōsphoros astēr* [light-bringing star] of the nocturnal rite to waken the fiery torches" (340–42).

69. In one of the Orphic hymns (24), the Nereids, who "play the bacchant" among the waves, are invoked to bring prosperity to the initiates because they were the "first to reveal the holy mystic rite [teletōn semnōn] of sacred Bacchos and pure Persephone." See also Kerényi 1967, 25.

70. The text is difficult here: some have thought that the viewer is Iacchos himself (or even Apollo) rather than Ion. The syntactical ambiguity may well be significant, as implying a reciprocal relation between Ion and Iacchos. I accept Diggle's version, reading *theōros* for *theōron* and *ennuchion* for *ennuchios*. *Theōros* has a ritual connotation as an observer at a festival and fits well too with Xouthos's earlier proposal that he first bring Ion to the city as a *theatēs* or spectator (656).

road, is summoned in her own name under her dual aspects. Hekate is the sinister goddess of nocturnal magic, associated with the moon, the dangerous crossroads, and mysterious feasts *(deipna)*; she is also the divine guide of the mysteries, who accompanies Persephone on her descent and return.[71] In this case, Enodia is to lead the way not to Eleusis but to the banquet in the tent, and not to the secret life-giving rites of restoration and joy but to the secret plot of violent death.[72] Hekate and Iacchos: behind the first is screened the figure of Creousa, behind the second, that of Ion.

The ode promotes a further aberration in representing the mysteries as exclusively Athenian, even female-centered, rites that bar all strangers. Despite some traditions that outsiders were not admitted to the proceedings in earlier times,[73] the distinctive claim of the mysteries was that they were open to all *(pankoinoi)*—men, women, slaves, and foreigners.[74] As the text obliquely suggests (1087–88), the chorus fears the interloper will take an official Athenian role at the mysteries,[75] but the homicidal intent of the plot against Ion reminds us that the one explicit disqualification for admission to the rites (providing one could understand Greek) was the ineradicable taint of blood guilt.[76]

71. The strophe puns on the name of Einodia, which refers both to her position at the crossroads, the site of dangerous magical assaults *(ephodoi)*, and to her function as guide *(hodōson)*, appropriate to the mysteries. For Hekate at Eleusis, see Richardson 1974, 294–95 *ad* 440; Burkert 1985, 171, 222. On the famous Niinnion pinax tablet of the late fifth century (National Museum, Athens, 11036 [CC 1698]) that depicts the preliminary rites, Hekate and Iacchos may be represented together. See, e.g., Metzger 1951, 236–37; Mylonas 1961, 213–21; and Kerényi 1967, 64. Like our choral ode, the pinax also represents the women dancing at the close of these ceremonies.

72. The antistrophe continues to invert the Eleusinian promise of life out of death in quasi-mystic language. The chorus claims that "if Ion's death is unaccomplished *[atelēs]*, Creousa will meet her own death, completing her suffering with suffering *[pathesi pathea]* and will go down into other forms of life" (1061–68). Death is to be Ion's end *(teletē*, also the formal name for "mysteries"), and if not successful, Creousa herself, like a Kore in reverse, will undergo not a mystic ascent *(anodos)* but a descent *(kathodos)*, and instead of joy that follows *pathos*, as the initiates experience it, she will find only another *pathos*.

73. Our evidence names only the mythic heroes, Herakles and the Dioskouroi, who required a preliminary adoption or even, as for Herakles, the institution of the lesser mysteries. Scholiast, *ad* Aristophanes, *Plutus* 1014; Plutarch, *Theseus* 33; Ps.-Apollodorus, 2.5.12; and cf. Xenophon, *Hellenica* 6.3.6.

74. E.g., Sophocles, *Antigone* 1119–21; Herodotus, 8.65; and cf. *Homeric Hymn to Demeter* 480–82.

75. The reference to kingship *(basileuein)* recalls the Athenian magistrate called the *archōn basileus;* for his role in the mysteries, see Aristotle, *Athenian Constitution* 57.1.

76. Scholiast, *ad* Aristophanes, *Frogs* 369; Isocrates, *Panegyric* 157; Origen, *Against Celsus* 3.59; Theon of Smyrna, 14.23 (Hiller); Suetonius, *Nero* 34; Libanius, *Declamationes* 13.19.52.

One claim of sacred values competes with another. If the women re-verse the norms of the mysteries to call for deadly retaliation against the outsider and to imagine a version of mystical death for Creousa, were the mission to fail,[77] they do so to protect the city's political and ritual integrity and to keep it "pure."[78] But in celebrating their own piety *(eusebeia)*, as they do in the ode's conclusion, the women claim that it is men who have already reversed the sacred norms, this time in the domestic sphere. The same charges that men often level against women in accusing them of making "unholy and unlawful sexual unions" (ἁμέτερα λέχεα καὶ γάμους / Κύπριδος ἀθέμιτος ἀνοσίους) can now, in the chorus's words, be turned against a male (Xouthos) for his act of an "unjust sowing" of seed (*adikon aroton*, 1090–95).[79]

Such is the prelude to the messenger's account, framed as a choral song of ritual initiates celebrating the opening ceremonies of the mysteries that will end when Iacchos and the dancing women arrive at the precinct of Demeter. All that Ion will see *(opsetai)* is the fire of the torches blazing in the nocturnal festivities that precede the mysteries proper. What takes place in the tent, therefore, can be construed as the continuation of the mystic scenario, conducted in a secluded interior space, shut off from the rays of the sun. This space too will be violated, and in two ways: by the intrusion of an outsider (the old man and through him, Creousa) and by the sacrilege he commits in a sacred place,[80] designed to bring death instead of (re)birth.

The result is that Creousa must seek refuge from her angry Delphian pursuers as a sacred suppliant at Apollo's altar. Her act of supplication leads eventually to the revelations that I have suggested are Eleusinian in character and to the conclusion in which Creousa and Ion set off for Athens in the company of the goddess Athena as their "guide upon the road" (*hoduros*, 1617).

Through his identification with Iacchos, Dionysos is the transitional figure who links Athens and Delphi by way of Eleusis, so that the twice-born may return home as a full participant in the political and ritual life of the city. In this sense, Dionysos, flanked by Athena on one side and by Demeter on the other, deflects the play from a premature and tragic closure. But Dionysos is also the figure of ambivalence, whose invocation

77. See note 72 above.

78. On the different values of *katharos,* see Whitman 1974, 90–93, although his equation of purity and "authenticity" is too modern a concept. See also Walsh 1978, 305–6.

79. The referent is Xouthos, but the same charge may be laid against Apollo. Loraux (1981a, "Créuse," 246n.211) notes that in contrast to the dances and torches of the sacred night of the mysteries (1075–76), Creousa's "bridal" was conducted without such celebration.

80. Hanson 1975, 31.

may lead to the success of the servant's "journey to the tent" that would forever prevent Ion from making that other journey to Athens.[81] We might say that the "mysteries" inside the tent are more Dionysiac than Eleusinian in nature. They correspond exactly in time and intent to Xouthos's parallel rites on Mount Parnassus, "where the god's Bacchic fire leaps up" and where, as the messenger reports, Xouthos will "moisten the double rocks of Dionysos with [the blood of] sacrifices *ant' optērion*" (1127)— that is, instead of the customary gifts offered at the first sight of the new-born child or, in our context, perhaps, "instead of the *opsis*" (the revelations and divine epiphany Creousa's husband is never to share).[82]

The domain of Dionysos and not that of Apollo. Located on the slopes of Mount Parnassus, Dionysos's space contrasts with Apollo's shrine. Indeed, as the imagery of the play suggests, the contrast between the two gods is represented in cosmic terms: Apollo is associated with the sun and the light of day, Dionysos with the starry nocturnal sky. Night is the time for dance and ritual celebration, and the place of darkness, hidden secrets, and death. It is the time of the Thyiadic rites on the mountain and the procession with Iacchos to Eleusis. A Dionysiac play in an Apollonian setting, an Apollonian child in a Dionysiac setting who would, as the chorus imagines, intrude upon an Athenian-Eleusinian rite.

The entire plot takes place under Dionysos's auspices. For with Xouthos as Ion's putative father, Dionysos is associated with the engendering gods *(Genetai Theoi),* to whom Xouthos will make sacrifices on Mount Parnassus, the site of Ion's supposed conception at the Dionysiac rites (1130). Moreover, the tent Ion erects for his celebratory banquet where the poisoned wine is served is constructed as a Dionysiac space, where a convivial scene threatens to turn into a tragedy of misrecognition, to change from a consecrated moment into a drama of perverted sacrifice. This outcome is averted only by a substitute victim, the bird that, as the language of the text suggests, dies a violent bacchic death (1203–5).[83]

81. Müller 1975 sees only a positive Dionysos.

82. The *optēria* would then correspond to the chorus's insistence that Ion not come as viewer *(theōros . . . opsetai)* to the mysteries (1076–77). The choice of *optēria* is a marked substitute for Xouthos's term, *genethlia,* "birth sacrifices" (654, cf. 805), and the choice is still more curious in that *optēria* are gifts to the child, not offerings to the gods, presumably given by others and not by the father (cf. Callimachus, *Hymn to Artemis* 74). Bachofen (1948 [1861]) also construes the tent as a Dionysiac scene for his own reasons. See below, note 136.

83. Given the split between Dionysiac rites on Mount Parnassus and the scene in the tent, both concerned with birth, we might even think here of Plutarch's assertion (*Isis and Osiris* 365a) that when the Thyiades wake the Liknites on the mountain, men called Hosioi (the sacred ones) offer an "unspeakable sacrifice" *(thusian aporrhēton)* in the shrine of Apollo. On the other hand, the Eleusinian context might suggest the Plemochoai. At this the closing ritual of the mysteries, two vessels, one set up in the east and the other in the west,

Dionysos and the Theater

Apollo had in mind another plot, one that might have succeeded had not the chorus of women breached one of the ironclad rules of tragic convention by betraying a secret they had been forbidden to reveal. When the women determine to tell Creousa her husband's news about Ion being his son, even if they "might have to die twice over" (760), they activate a plot involving the excitement and dangers of kin misrecognition—the very one, if we believe Aristotle, that best conforms to the conventions of the tragic stage.

Yet what Aristotle ignores in his discussion of plot and what Apollo, the "author," seems not to know is how the theatrical game is played between the genders. It is the woman's part to occupy the center stage, when faced with male transgression of social norms, and she is the agent called upon to challenge men's monopoly over power or knowledge. In so doing, she reverses the normal social rules, but the mode of that reversal equally follows a typical tragic pattern in mobilizing what men view as women's transgressive capacity for violence and deception. Thus when Apollo hands on a son from one father to another and defers the anagnorisis of mother and son to a date beyond the frame of the play, the god would do more than bypass the essential role of the mother in biological, social, and emotional terms.[84] He also bypasses the rules of dramatic enactment on which Dionysiac tragedy thrives. Hence the unusual intervention of the chorus. And also for this reason, in accordance with standard mechanisms of tragic operation, the women are provoked to turn the tables and "take over" the plot, playing true to form.[85] What is more, they do so in response to the reversal of roles they perceive in the deception that males have practiced on them. At the end of the ode discussed above, the chorus refers to a "palinodic song" *(palimphamos aoida)*, a song of reversal (1096) in which women now claim the right, in the name of piety *(eusebeia)*, to

---

were filled and the contents overturned "into a cleft in the earth," while people exclaimed *hue* (rain) to the sky and *kue* (conceive) to the earth. Athenaeus, 496b, cites Euripides, frag. 592N², for the *chthonion chasma* and speaks of a *rhēsis mystikē*. Cf. Hippolytus, *Refutation of All Heresies* 5.7.34; Proclus, *In Timaeum* III 176.28 Diehl. See the discussion in Kerényi 1967, 141–42; Burkert 1985, 289; and Burkert 1983, 293. A cosmic setting on the tapestries (could the mention of the watery Hyades [1156] be relevant?), a careful spatial orientation (horizontal and vertical), filling and overturning of vessels, and concern with birth are all relevant to the scene described in the *Ion*.

Euripides, of course, is well known for his syncretism and inventive reuse of ritual and mythic elements. It is entirely possible that the ensemble of actions in the tent combines allusions to different moments in different mystic rituals.

84. See Saxenhouse 1986, 267–71.

85. On conventions of women's actions in tragic plots, see below, chapter 8, 356–61.

redress those same misdoings that men have always attributed to them. This maneuver transforms Creousa, the Kore maiden, into a terrifying Hekate-Persephone. In the name of outraged femininity, it also turns her into a form of the maenadic mother, a *theomanēs*, as ironically Ion later calls her (1402), armed with the deadly poison from that female earth-born creature, the Gorgon, who in Euripides' version, was produced by Earth herself as an ally in the Gigantomachy.[86] Her offerings, in fact, are termed "infernal sacrifices" *(thumata nerterōn)*, which mix the "Dionysiac libation" with drops of the serpent's blood (1232–34).

We are thus plunged into the heart of the tragic drama along with the lord of the theater himself, the god Dionysos, who presides over those theatrical activities of role playing, reenactment, doubling, repetition, and reversal, and who sets the stage for probing the mysteries of identity and designs of the self. In Dionysos's theater, where epistemological concerns about truth and illusion, the fictive and the real, are played out in all their paradoxical confusions, Apollo again furthered these designs, unwittingly, it seems. Violating the expectations of tragic convention, he issued a false oracle from his precinct that leads to the remarkable feature of a first, equally false, anagnorisis. This event paves the way for the Dionysiac "takeover" in the tent scene, where the "other" plot will be enacted. The "takeover" is precipitated, it is true, by Apollo's rule-breaking fictions, and it will require that Apollo himself intervene to save the situation. According to the messenger, the god found a way to avoid the pollution of bloodshed in the name of justice (1118). Athena, at the end, is even more direct: "Once the business got out, and afraid that Ion might die through the plots of his mother and she by his, Apollo rescued them through his own 'devices' or 'plots' *[mēchanais]*" (1563–65; i.e., the birds, the Pythia). Yet even so, we should recall that the birds' true home is on Mount Parnassus (155), as if to suggest that the Dionysiac realm remains the point of departure for those winged agents of the other god.

Be that as it may, this "other plot" meanwhile opens up the theater to improvisation and the freedom to play. In the absence of the "other" father, Xouthos, who has gone off to the real Dionysiac locale, Ion is able to create his own little "theater" offstage—in both explicit and implicit terms. With the *skēnēmata* he selects and assembles for his banquet tent (1129–34) and the authority he asserts over the proceedings, Ion is finally an actor on his own. He is being tested to his limits as the Delphic child educated in the temple precinct, but in the process he also recapitulates significant elements from his past in condensed and symbolic form. These

86. For the Gorgon myth and its variants, see Mastronarde 1976, 174n.33; Rosivach 1977, 287; and Loraux 1981a, "Créuse," 239.

will give proof of his authentic identity in advance and prepare him for his future position in Athens.

Designs and Mysteries: The Performed Self

Ion's banquet tent is the iconographic counterpart to the temple sculptures of Herakles, Bellerophon, and the Gigantomachy that the chorus describes in the parodos. The tapestries used to construct it are covered with important depictions that look back to the first set of sculpted images, especially as these relate to scenes of contest and struggle. The explicit link between the temple and the tent is the figure of Herakles. He was shown on the sacred façade along with his helper Iolaos, in combat with the Hydra, and another of his feats is now recalled in the fact that the woven materials that cover the roof were taken by the hero as spoils from his expedition against the Amazons and deposited in the Delphic shrine (1143–45). But while the temple is an architectural structure with images sculpted on the outside for all, even strangers, to view, Ion himself constructs the tent as a private space. Selecting sacred tapestries from the treasuries, the *thēsauros* at Delphi (1141), he makes an enclosure that is reserved for his Delphic friends to celebrate his supposed new-found identity. The occasion is both a belated birthday fête and a farewell to Delphi, which also takes the form of a civic repast, a *sussition* (1165).[87]

It is both important and ironic that at the moment of leavetaking, Ion makes a home for himself, even if a temporary one, within the temple precinct. Exposed at birth on the slopes of the Acropolis and barred at Delphi from the inmost recesses of the sacred shrine, his place has always been outside—at the entrance and on the steps of the temple (104, 415). In constructing the tent, Ion is also "constructing" an identity, just at the point when he has accepted a false one. Hence all the events that happen in the tent are signposts along the road to finding, authenticating, and fashioning himself.[88] In this improvised space, Ion may continue inside what he had performed outside in his purifying rites. He can demonstrate who he is and what he knows, using his ritual expertise in judging the rules for well-omened libations and drawing on his mantic heritage to "divine"

87. See Schmitt-Pantel 1992, 209–21, for the hybrid and ambivalent nature of the banquet, and the reasons for the stranger Xouthos's exclusion from it, although it was he who initiated it.

88. Schmitt-Pantel (1992, 218–21) observes that while tents were set up in Greek sanctuaries for different purposes, including banquets, the unusual size might remind the spectators of an actual building on the Acropolis: the Hekatompedon (hundred feet), a temple of Athena constructed in the sixth century, rebuilt by Peisistratus, destroyed by the Persians, then restored, and finally destroyed by fire in 406. For the allusion to Persian tents, see note 93 below.

the perpetrator of the plot against his life (1190, 1218). These are his Apollonian traits. But this performance contains more than meets the eye: in it lie two further "mysteries" that, when deciphered, prove to associate Ion in advance with his other heritage as the child of Erechtheus and descendant of Erichthonios.

Ion fabricates his tent from offerings deposited by others (Herakles, some unknown Athenian, victors in recent battles). He has selected them from the repertory of pictorial images through which he has acquired his knowledge of the traditional lore—images that he had previously mentioned, in addition to the myths represented on the temple façade, as the source of his information about the birth of Erichthonios (271). For the moment, let us say that this fabrication is a kind of *bricolage* whose subjects and provenances align him with the common store of cultural myths and ideologies, already adumbrated in the sculptural representations on the temple façade and augmented by reference to more recent events in Athenian history. Emblematic of both Panhellenic (Herakles) and Athenian (in Cecrops and his daughters whose images frame the entry) identity, the tapestries have a composite nature that suggests the necessary interrelation of Athenian and world-making myths. In drawing upon the distant and not so distant past, they re-create a text or texture in the dramatic present, yet with enigmatic resonance for the immediate future. As such, the tapestries, like all such pictorial descriptions, are visual texts to be deciphered.

Framed in space and narrated in sequence, the tapestries possess a symbolic value that places them at a higher level of representation than the dramatic actions of the play to which they relate on a different plane of coded, even oracular, signification. This relation involves past, present, and future, because the depictions on the tapestries recall the past (both the dramatic events and what preceded them) while supplying the decor, the theatrical backdrop, for the coming scene. They also prefigure what follows just afterward. Their riddling nature, which invites the interpretive efforts of the audience,[89] exemplifies the general atmosphere in our Delphic play concerning riddles, oracles, and mysteries that will reach maximum intensity in the aftermath of this narrated scene.

Several factors contribute to the particular complexity and ambiguity of these representations. First, the iconography is spatially organized not on a single plane, but at three different levels (roof, sides, entrance), which are separated but also juxtaposed in suggestive ways. They form a composite ensemble, yet they retain discrete iconographical identities.[90] Sec-

89. On the iconography, see Wolff 1963; Immerwahr 1972; Müller 1975; Mastronarde 1976; Dufner 1983; Chalkia 1986. See also Goff 1988, without reference to the foregoing.
90. On the spatial organization of the tent and the relation of its parts, see, in particular, Chalkia 1986, 105–9.

ond, while all the tapestries are dedications to the Delphic treasury, each one draws on a different source. Still further, because the coverings of the roof and sides of the tent are examples of foreign, even barbarian, handiwork, a tension is established between their original provenance and their current status as possessions of the Panhellenic shrine. The sides of the tent show naval battles between Greeks and barbarians, combats with beasts of hybrid nature, and two hunting scenes. These are indeed themes of oriental iconography, though they are also popular pictorial motifs of contemporary Greek art that, like the decoration of the temple facade, represent forms of combat between opposing forces of civilization and savagery.[91] They may therefore be assimilated into a Hellenic context, whose ownership already signifies the victory of Greek culture, most especially in the Persian wars. Although not identified as such, the images may be attached to exploits of Greek heroes (e.g., Centauromachy, Labors of Herakles),[92] which served as allegories of that historical victory.[93] Finally, as others have observed, the portrayal of Cecrops as a hybrid mixture of man and beast implies that the line between civilization and savagery may be less solid than one might have supposed.[94] The stability of figures frozen in stone yields to the fluidity of those woven into fabric, and the easy legibility of a coherent ensemble passes into zones of ambiguity and dense networks of allusion. Moreover, like every moment that restages primordial events in the present, the outcome of the original contest is not necessarily assured but is once again placed in the balance. This is the principle that will guide the more detailed analysis of these images, which must be deferred until we have grasped the deeper implications of the dramatic action and can better consider the meaning of the auspices that the images provide.

91. Immerwahr (1972, 293) suggests that the naval battle would remind the Athenian audience of Salamis.

92. See, e.g., Mastronarde 1976, 175n.42.

93. Myth meets up with history even more closely in that the construction of the tent seems to follow Persian rather than Greek custom. Additionally, the audience may well have been reminded of Xerxes' famous tent, taken from Mardonius probably after the battle of Plataea and brought from Boeotia to Athens (Herodotus, 9.82). The dramatic tension between ownership and appropriation is heightened by the fact that Xerxes' tent figured in the construction of theatrical buildings, whether in its shape as the model for the Odeion, probably built by Themistocles (Vitruvius, *On Architecture* 5.9.1, although Plutarch, *Pericles* 9, names Pericles; see Davison 1958, 33–36), or, according to another theory, in its actual reuse as the first *skēnē* of the theater of Dionysos (Broneer 1944). See Immerwahr 1972, 291–93.

The sculptures on the temple façade may be allegories of contemporary history, but the barbarian tapestries both represent a historical scene (i.e., a naval battle) and are themselves presumably spoils of the recent war. The reference to *skēnēmata* (1133) correlates the material to both form and function in two ways: their oriental provenance fits their oriental use, while, if Broneer is correct, the tent, as I have earlier proposed, is also a miniature stage.

94. Mastronarde 1976, 169.

Let us begin with an overview of the dramatic functions of the tent, which is highly overdetermined as a symbolic space. First of all, it reverses Ion's relation to exterior and interior space at Delphi, where, as he says, his task is to tend the things outside *(ta exō)* and to leave the care of what is inside to others (414). More concretely, it serves as the house *(dōma)* that had always been denied him (52–53, 314–15); it is a place where the orphan child, who owes his nurture *(trophē)* to Delphic largesse (323, 852–53), may reciprocate with hospitality *(xenia)* in kind (e.g., 805). In light of the divinatory acts that take place there, it is also the alternate to Apollo's oracular shrine *(aduton)*. As a dark interior space from which the rays of the sun are explicitly excluded, it also recalls the hidden "sunless" cave of Ion's conception and birth (500), a repository of secrets and forbidden knowledge.[95] Even more, it is a miniature cosmos because the covering of the roof represents a nocturnal sky, a "textile planetarium," as one critic has put it.[96] Beginning as it does with Ouranos and the starry heavens, it suggests a primordial cosmogony, a first moment of "world making." Yet, because its representation includes the whole array of cosmic symbols that pass from dusk through night to the glimmer of dawn, it also suggests the temporal cycle, renewed each day and night. The cyclical nature of this scene (1147, 1154–55) also returns us to the opening of the play: the darkness of the tent with its star-studded ceiling contrasts with the opening scenes of a sunny morning and the description of the temple façade.[97]

In its more local context, the cosmic covering responds directly to the preceding ode, in which the chorus evoked the starry ether of Zeus and the dance of the moon and the Nereid maidens in the scene of the mystic Eleusinian procession (1078–84).[98] In this way, the relationship between the two sacred settings is represented in graphic form. These in turn are further linked to the nocturnal setting of the still earlier choral ode that had summoned Dionysos in the evocation of the Thyiadic rites on Mount Parnassus (714–17).[99]

In another sense, the depiction of an external scene on the interior of the tent signifies more than a crossing of the boundary between the real and the fictive. The inversion also confuses the usual relations between

95. See Chalkia 1986, 113–39, for the enclosed spaces in the play. Note that *aduta* refers alike to the inner shrine of Apollo at Delphi and to the cave of Pan on the Acropolis (662, 938, 1309). See also Loraux 1981a, "Créuse," 250–51.

96. Shapiro 1980, 268.

97. See especially Immerwahr 1972, 288.

98. Müller 1975, 42–43.

99. Creousa too is obliquely drawn into the domain of night: cf. her anguished wish to fly across the sea to the "western stars" *(asteras hesperous, 797)* and her invocation of the "star-spangled abode of Zeus" *(Dios poluastron hedos, 870).*

outside and inside, as though reiterating the underlying thematic intersection, essential to Ion's history and identity, that is poised both spatially and socially between inside and outside. Situated then between birth and leavetaking, between beginnings and ends, and between inside and outside, the tent becomes the theatrical site of enigmatic reenactment and reversal under the vault of a "textile planetarium," which, let us not forget, once belonged to the Amazons, who themselves exemplify reversals of gender roles.

This is then the stage upon which the temple child, nourished by others and fed from the altars, would reciprocate in kind to the Delphic community with a feast of his own. This is the moment when Ion, exposed as an infant to be a feast *(thoinē)*, a banquet *(daïs)* for the birds, and deprived of the nurture *(trophē)* of his mother's milk (as he reiterates several times), receives her deadly poison in its place and is saved by the bird whose *thoinē* it becomes instead.[100]

The drops of Gorgon blood belong to the mother, but it is the old man who acts as Creousa's emissary. He is ready to carry out the intrigue he has instigated against the perceived intruder, and he is the one who takes the leading role. This ancient Paidagogos, finally, is the figure whose dramatic relationship to Ion marks him as the overt enemy and also as a hidden double. Through certain symmetries at the level of the plot and certain textual echoes, he authenticates Ion's autochthonous ancestry long before it is officially revealed and justifies the special link between Ion and Erechtheus.

The Father I

The correspondences between Ion and the old man, to which I have just alluded, come about in two ways. First, the Paidagogos and Ion are both represented as servants to their respective masters. One servant is treated as a father, the other will be discovered to be a son.[101] Second, both conduct an extended dialogue with Creousa concerning the history of the Erechtheid house: Ion inquires about its myths and genealogies (260–84), while the old servant upholds the pedigree and entitlements of the noble house (735–37, 808–16, 836–41).

100. *Thoinē* and/or *daïs* for the birds: 504–5, 903, 1495; in the tent: 652, 807, 852, 982, 1131, 1140, 1168, 1206, 1217.
101. The vocabulary includes *douleuō, therapeuō, latreuō,* and their cognates: Ion of himself as a temple servant (111, 123, 129, 132, 152, 182–83, 309, 327, 556; but cf. 675), confirmed by the Pythia (1343); as the possible child of a slave mother (819, 837, 1382); the Paidagogos (854, 856, 983). The chorus too are servants (748, cf. 1109). See also Walsh 1978, 304–5, who on this basis notes "a superficial similarity between the old man and his intended victim that underscores their utter disparity," but Ion too is prepared to retaliate with violence if not restrained by the Pythia.

Next, both are engaged in similar types of activities, although directed to exactly opposite ends. The Paidagogos has come with the Gorgon's poison, and under the guise of dispensing wine at the feast, he fills the cups for all the banqueters, reserving the baneful drops for Ion's alone (1050–57, 1173–85). Ion, dedicated to his purificatory tasks in the temple, is concerned from the first with flowing liquids and acts of pouring, and he diligently sets about filling and emptying vessels (95–97, 104–6, 146–49). Although the respective containers differ in type and function and accordingly are variously named, each is also generically called a vessel (*teuchos*, 146, 1179, 1184), and each is made of gold (146, 1175, 1182). Ion's liquid is water used for cleaning and purification, and the Paidagogos also begins his convivial task by drawing water to wash the hands of the guests (1173–74). When one of the feasters accidentally utters an ill-omened word, Ion too reverts to his own practiced gestures by giving orders to pour out the wine and fill the cups again (1191–92, 1194–95).[102] At the banquet, however, temporality is reversed, for Ion follows and thus may be said to repeat the old man's prior actions.

The loyalty of an old household retainer is sufficient to explain the role of the Paidagogos in representing the paternal interests of the Erechtheids, and his low social status can be made to account for the crime he is prepared to commit in patriotic defense of Athens.[103] But the text also plainly encourages us to think that he is meant to stand in for Erechtheus himself. Entering as though on cue just after the chorus ends its song with reference to the former ruler, "the lord Erechtheus" (724), Creousa recalls the old man's affiliation to her father ("when he was still living [*ontos*] and was yet in the light") and tenderly greets him with an ambiguous phrase, *antikēdeuō patros* (734). This may mean, as A. S. Owen suggests, "I care for you as for a father," but it could also mean "I care for you in my father's place (since he is dead)" or even "I care for you as my father did." The old man sustains the ambiguity by consistently calling Creousa "daughter" *(thugatēr)*, either as a sign of affection or, more properly, as the address to a true offspring (735, 763, 925, 942, 970, 998). The unusual intimacy between servant and mistress continues throughout this extensive scene (e.g., 925–26) in the course of which all the essential details are recounted in the old man's presence: Apollo's oracle to Xouthos, Creousa's confessional monody, the repetition of her story under the old man's gentle prodding, and, of course, the plot to kill the spurious child.

Age is a heavy burden for the old man, emphasized again and again. Creousa had first intended to send him to the mantic shrine to find out

102. *Drosos* (dew) is the poetical term used several times for the water Ion pours (96, 117, 436), and it recurs in the present scene (1194).
103. Walsh 1978, 303–8, 313.

what the god had prophesied about her childless condition. The way up to the shrine is a steep ascent for a pair of old legs, and much is made of this fact in his request to Creousa for assistance (738–43). The motif recurs again with the change in destination from the shrine to Ion's tent, but now he goes alone, addressing "his aged foot" *(o geraie pous)* with the exhortation, "be thou youthful once more" *(neanias, 1041).*[104]

Old men on stage are typically presented in this way, sometimes accompanied by a daughter or helper. But given that the later discovery of Ion's identity will mean that Erechtheus has indeed been "restored to youth" *(anēbāi),* we might understand these earlier homely gestures as both signaling the miracle to come and sharpening the irony of the attempt against Ion's life.[105] At the same time, in preparing a "sacrificial" death for the Erechtheid child, the stand-in for Erechtheus is only repeating the king's earlier action against his children, when "he dared to sacrifice his kin" (277–78).

The Father II

Behind the old man is screened yet another figure in disguise and another more mysterious reenactment that directly pertains to the setting of a birthday celebration and leads us back to the origins of the primordial autochthon. The mention of the Gorgon's blood already recalls Erichthonios, who was its first recipient. Athena gave it as a protective talisman to her nursling, "the first ancestor whom the earth sent forth" (999–1000), and from him it passed down in the family line until it came into the safekeeping of Creousa.

The earth brought forth Erichthonios, and Athena picked him up (267–69). This is all we are told. But how and under what circumstances did this event come about? Before recounting the story, let us pause for a moment and review the range of reproductive strategies that are mentioned in the course of the play.

The first, the ordinary, the "natural" way, assures us that children are begotten from the sexual union of two: a mother and a father. In the social and civic order, the norm is the ordinary marriage of husband and wife, which produces legitimate children as future citizens of the city and heirs

---

104. By contrast, the messenger comes in haste, with a *prothumia podōn* (eagerness of foot, 1109–10), which also contrasts with the old man's *prothumia* in filling the cups (1173, 1211).

105. Old men and difficulty of walking: e.g., the chorus in Aeschylus, *Agamemnon* 73–83; and in Euripides, *Herakles* 108–29; Oedipus and Antigone in Sophocles, *Oedipus at Colonus* 188–201; and Euripides, *Phoenissae* 1710–21; and the old man in Euripides, *Elektra* 489–92, the closest analogue to our scene. Conversely, Teiresias and Cadmus in *Bacchae* 181–90, 363–65, are miraculously rejuvenated under the god's influence.

to the familial household. But children may also be bastards, "of impure birth," born out of wedlock and belonging to one or the other partner.[106]

The mythic modes are far more unusual. Two of them we already know as constituting Ion's heritage: born of a union between mortal and god, born of autochthonous ancestry. Framing these two possibilities and restricted only to gods are two other reproductive means: born from the male alone without a mother, like Athena from her father's head (452–57), or else, like Dionysos, born twice, first of a mother, then of a father. In addition to these, matching autochthony in the human sphere, there is a true parthenogenesis, that of the Gorgon, whom Gaia herself produced on her own to be her ally in the Giants' war against the Olympians (988–90).

But there is yet another strategy, one that constitutes an intriguing compromise between autochthony and sexual union in a way that accommodates both. How Erichthonios entered upon the scene is an unusual and widely popular tale, one version of which was used elsewhere by Euripides, perhaps even in his play, the *Erechtheus:* "Hephaistos lusted after Athena and wanted to possess her. She rebuffed him, preferring to keep her virginity. . . . but he made a surprise assault on her, thinking he could overpower her. She then struck him with her spear and as a result of the blow he ejaculated his semen which fell instead to the earth. In this way, they say, a child was born, who for this reason was called Erichthonios [Eri-, "truly"; -chthonios, "of the earth"]."[107] As John Peradotto has astutely observed, the myth of Erichthonios functions as a middle term that mediates between the two alternatives: birth from two parents, birth from the earth. Athena retains her virginity yet participates in motherhood; the child is engendered by an immortal couple but is still of autochthonous birth.[108]

106. Pericles' decree of 451, refusing citizenship to those not born of two Athenian parents (whose *genos* was therefore not *katharos;* Aristotle, *Athenian Constitution* 13, 5; 26, 3) is a topical political issue that underlies the emphasis on mythic autochthony. Questions of bastardy and low birth (by contrast to *eugeneia*) are also involved. See Walsh 1978; and Loraux 1981a, "Créuse," 213–19, who, in addition, stresses Creousa's status as an heiress or *epiklēros.*

107. Eratosthenes, *Catasterisms* 13, specifically ascribes this story to Euripides; and cf. Hyginus, *Astronomica* 2, 13, p. 446, cited as Euripides, frag. 925 Nauck²; as well as Hyginus, *Fabulae* 166, which says that "Athena defended herself with arms and in the struggle the semen fell on the earth." Ps.-Apollodorus, *Bibliotheca* 3.14.6, includes the alternate version that Hephaistos ejaculated on Athena's thigh, and wiping the semen away with some wool, she threw it on the ground. The myth was already current in the sixth century (Pausanias, 3.18.13, on the throne of Amyclae, cited from the epic *Danais:* Frag. 2 Kinkel = Harpokration, s.v. *autochthones;* Pindar, frag. 180 Turyn); and see Robertson 1985, 272, with further bibliography; also Loraux 1981a, "Autochtonie," 57–58; Loraux 1981a, "Nom," 132–46; Cook 1940, 3:218–23 (with full dossier); and Parker 1987, 193–95.

108. Peradotto 1977, 92–98.

Let us now look again at the representation of the old man in the light of this myth. First, the old man was actually the Paidagogos of Erechtheus and hence belongs to a still earlier generation than the king (725). His extreme old age is demonstrated in his complaints about walking, as we have seen, but it is emphasized further in his request to Creousa to "help him work his leg" and be the healer *(iatros)* of his infirmity (740).

Next, when we hear of the old man at the banquet, we are told how his officious bustling about in preparing both the water for washing and the wine for the cups arouses laughter from the other feasters (1171–73). If we search for a model of just such a scene, the figure that comes to mind is Hephaistos himself in *Iliad* 1.595–600, who at the banquet of the gods had provoked their laughter in just the same way.[109]

The setting in the text is also suggestive. The use of tapestries to represent a cosmos might be echoing a mythic tradition that the world was created as a woven textile.[110] But more to the point is the earliest example we know that describes the fabrication of a nocturnal sky. That description is also the first ekphrasis of a work of art: the Iliadic shield of Achilles made by the hands of the master craftsman, Hephaistos. Although the Homeric description is less detailed and follows a somewhat different arrangement, the enumeration of the heavenly bodies is almost identical (sky, sun, moon, Pleiades, Orion, Hyades, Arktos; *Il.* 18.483–89).[111]

Still further, we note that Ion's reaction to the unlucky omen at the feast is to shun the liquid the old man had distributed and have it spilled on the ground—as the text says, to "give it to the earth" (1193). Like the seed of Hephaistos, the liquid is rejected as a polluted substance. At the same time, the result of this action reverses the first primordial gesture: it brings death, not life, to the bird who laps it from the earth, and its intended victim was this last autochthonous child.

Lameness of foot, laughter at the feast, fabrication of a nocturnal sky, and causing liquid to be spilled on the ground: all these details seem to point to Hephaistos even as other elements, more directly, invoke the figure of Erechtheus. Two fathers, therefore, can be condensed into a single

109. Burnett 1971, 117, mentions the similarity. In both scenes, the laughter arises in part from the incongruity of such a figure as cupbearer, a task usually assigned to a beautiful boy (e.g., Ganymede). Ion observes this norm when he replaces the old man with a youth to refill the wine vessels (1192–93), yet another sign of the substitution of young for old at this important juncture.

110. E.g., Pherecydes of Syros on the robe of Chthoniē (or Gē), woven by Zeus as his wedding gift to her (frag. 2 D-K), although the heavens do not figure explicitly on the design.

111. Curiously enough, a later commentator on Homer (third century B.C.E.), a learned Corcyran woman named Agalli[a]s, argued that because Hephaistos was the father of Erichthonios, the scenes on his Iliadic shield were drawn from the early history of Attica, and insisted that the two cities depicted were Athens and Eleusis (Scholiast, *ad Il.* 18.490 Dindorf). See also Cook 1940, 3:596; and Hardie 1986, 343–46.

substitute figure: first, Erechtheus, and behind him, the shadow of the absent "progenitor" himself, Hephaistos.[112]

This apparent memory trace of Hephaistos's pollution of the earth with his offerings is only a subdued motif, to be sure, but it prompts us to review the significance of Ion's purificatory tasks at the temple. First, he assiduously sweeps and cleans the entrance to the god's shrines with a broom of laurel leaves and pours drops of water on the ground to settle the dust (102–7). He repeats the action, this time naming the water as drawn from the spring of Gaia (146–47). Then, as soon as he hears Creousa's shocking story about Apollo's sexual violence against her "friend," his first thought is to attend to his other sacred task of transferring water from the golden jars into the purificatory basins needed for visitors to the shrine (434–36). Later, in the tent, upon divining "Erechtheus's daughter" as the author of the plot against him, his first response is an indignant appeal to "revered [semnē] Gaia" (1220).

The initial concentration on earth (and cf. 582) may hint at Ion's affinity to the autochthons of his mother's line. He had already shown his curiosity about the myth of Erichthonios and, to Xouthos's scorn, had suggested that he, Ion, was perhaps also engendered from "mother earth" (542). But the fact that the boy tends to "sacralize" the earth may also color that affinity with the idea that autochthonous birth is—or ought to be—pure of sexuality. He resents the birds "making children" in the temple precinct (172–75). The pourer of pure water is himself "pure of sex" (hosios ap' eunēs, 150).[113] As an infant in the basket, Ion was laid at the entrance (eisodoi) of the shrine (34), the spot he now sweeps with such diligence (104). When making his tent, he drapes the tapestry depicting the true earth-born, Cecrops, over its entrance (1163).

To be the son of Apollo is to claim descent from a god, but it is also to find a father who, unlike Hephaistos, has had sex with his mother. This is the knowledge Ion finally attains—and accepts—after having contem-

---

112. The text neither refers directly to this myth nor mentions the name of Hephaistos in other contexts. The chorus at 455–57 oddly substitutes Prometheus for Hephaistos as the traditional male midwife who assisted at Athena's birth from Zeus's head (our earliest extant example, we may add, of this secondary tradition; cf. Ps.-Apollodorus, Bibliotheca 1.3.6). I agree with Loraux (1981a, "Créuse," 229–30) that the reason for suppressing the story of Erichthonios's birth lies in the fact that "the tragic tension in the play lies elsewhere, in the distinction between birth from the earth and birth from human beings." This fact also accounts for the innovative genealogy of the Gorgon, presented only here as the offspring of Gaia. To invoke Hephaistos in connection with the birth of Athena would also recall his other function. Or perhaps if Euripides was indeed the first to assign Prometheus this role, the audience might well have recalled Hephaistos by the inverse fact of his unexpected absence, especially if frag. 925 Nauck[2] (see above, note 107) belongs to the Erechtheus.

113. Might the ambiguous phrase hosios ap' eunas also refer to his mother's marriage bed rather than his own, thus implying his own "immaculate" engendering?

plated the far worse possibility of being both a bastard child and of servile birth. The recognition scene and the discovery of the basket also align him with the circumstances of Erichthonios's engendering, which is reenacted, albeit as a shadow play, at his birthday feast. Yet the introduction of Hephaistos into this tent scene of death and rebirth now also aligns Athena with Creousa in the motif of the *parthenos* who is threatened with sexual pursuit against her will.

If the phantom Hephaistos is indeed present and active in this first Erichthonian scene in the tent, the woven figures of Cecrops and his daughters may serve not only as emblems of Athenian heritage but also, more specifically, as iconographic replicas, such as are represented on the works of art that illustrate the birth of Erichthonios, to which Ion has specifically alluded (271). There are many examples of this type (in which Cecrops and his daughters, often with Hephaistos, are shown as witnesses to the scene) that show the passing over of Erichthonios from the arms of Gaia to the waiting embrace of Athena.[114] This composite arrangement is not what we are given to view in the tent; rather, as I have argued, the preceding moment of the myth (Hephaistos vs. Athena) prepares the way for the successful sequel (one also represented, though far more rarely, in art).[115] There are allusions to earth, as we have seen, though not in personified form, and Hephaistos is displaced to another plane of representation. But, we may ask, where in this scene in the tent is the major feminine personage to be found? Is she not conspicuously absent from this wholly masculine world of the Delphian banquet? Not entirely, I propose, if we know how to read the signs.

Signs and Wonders

Everything is previewed here in the oracular setting of the tent, displaced once again, this time to a higher and more distant level. Let us therefore look again at the visual texts, the *grammata,* that cover the roof of the tent (1143–58). Can we find any trace of Athena and of the intervening events in the myth that precede her full appearance? If, as I suggested earlier, works of art are enigmatic visual emblems that invite interpretation, they are even more so when these represent celestial signs, which are in themselves legitimate objects for divination.

The Amazons were the first owners of this tapestry, a detail that provides an essential clue to deciphering these heavens, given the nature of the

114. For the representations, see Loraux 1981b, 145–46; and Parker 1987, 193n.28 (with bibliography).

115. Represented, e.g., on the sixth-century Amyclaean throne (Pausanias, 3.18.13) and probably on an early red-figured amphora (Bologna 158) ARV² 636, 19.

plot to take place in the tent. The combat between Herakles and the Amazons stands as the exemplary myth of Greek struggle against the barbarian. It also represents the archetypal struggle of male against female. The recollection of this myth extends and more clearly identifies what the chorus of women adumbrated at the conclusion of the preceding ode, when they framed the scene to come as a contest for power between the genders in which the usual roles would be reversed. The point is perhaps subtly underlined by the fact that these tapestries are woven work. Juxtaposed with the stone architecture of the façade, the textiles also look back to the numerous other references to weaving in the text. Weaving is the artistic medium of women's mythmaking (196–97, 506–7, 747–48), including the specimen of Creousa's virginal handiwork that she placed in the infant's basket (1417–19, 1421, 1425; cf. 1489–91).[116] The paradoxical fact that the tapestries belonged to the warlike Amazons, who on principle refused to perform traditional women's work, only intensifies the ambiguity of the feminine in both its "normal" and "abnormal" aspects.

For most critics, the cosmic tableau with its orderly progression of the heavenly bodies represents a stable guarantee of world order.[117] Yet the dynamic energy of the description suggests a dramatic progress amid opposing forces that takes place before the night is over and the dawn is seen to rise. At this moment when all is in doubt, the sense of a cyclical turning that heralds the peripeteia is anticipated (and confirmed) in the great arc of movement across the heavens that is centered on the Bear in her rotation around the pole.[118] Moreover, although tradition governs the choice and arrangement of the celestial signs, their depiction is deeply colored with violent images of warfare and hunting,[119] as if to suggest an epic contest between the sexes for control of the heavens, in which the female predominates and emerges victorious.[120]

The first two figures are male: Ouranos initiates the proceedings, his task to gather or muster *(athroizōn)* the stars. Helios is shown next leaving the scene, driving his horses into the last rays of light and dragging off with him *(ephelkōn)* the "shining light of Hesperos," the evening star. Night now takes over the scene. Dressed in a black robe, she drives her

116. On women and weaving, see Loraux 1981a, "Créuse," 241–42 and n. 188. The women suspect Ion of "weaving a trick or plot" (692).

117. E.g., Mastronarde 1976, 109; and Chalkia 1986, 107.

118. *Kuklos:* 1147, 1155; *strephei:* 1154; midpoint: 1152. As the world turns, so turns the plot. For a similar type of rotation (this time with a shield), see Aeschylus, *Seven against Thebes* 486–99; and Zeitlin 1982a, 94–95.

119. Immerwahr (1972, 290) notes the dynamic nature of the scene and its verbs of movement.

120. I am indebted here to the prior suggestion of Christina Dufner who, in an unpublished paper (1983), notes the martial aspects as appropriate to an Amazonian context and the conflictual relations between the sexes. We differ, however, in interpretation.

yoked chariot vigorously *(epallen)* across the sky, with the stars following in her train. We next see Arktos (the Bear), another feminine figure, as she turns her golden tail about the pole, and after her the full circle of the moon *(kuklos . . . panselēnos),* who casts her beams like a javelin to "cleave through the month" in the lunar cycle. The movement pauses with the Hyades, the "clearest sign to sailors," but behind these sisters, as the night begins to wane, comes Eos, the dawn, the light-bearer *(phōsphoros),* who completes the journey through the skies by pursuing *(diōkei)* the stars and putting them to flight (1146–58).

There is, however, another pair of celestial luminaries, who seem to compromise the theme of female dominance. What is more, this couple occupies the center of the textured vault, above which the Bear revolves, as always, in the nocturnal sky. Here is the Pleias who crosses the skies at the midpoint of her journey, and after her comes Orion in eternal pursuit, his sword forever drawn (1152–53). Each night this lustful hero repeats a violent assault against the feminine, repeating the characteristic activity of his entire mythic career. His usual quarry, however, is not a single Pleias but the collective band of Pleiades.[121] Why is the plural reduced to the singular, and why is this one situated at the midpoint of both the sky and the narrative sequence?

Rape and violence lie at the heart of the drama. This is the obsessively reiterated tale from which everything else follows. The cycle continues in Creousa's sense of betrayal at the introduction of the spurious child who, it is imagined, will himself do violence to the Erechtheid house. The threat of this intrusion, after all, motivates the more global battle the women would undertake against men in defense of their rights and in reversal of gender roles.

Is this, then, the reason for reminding us visually of the original offense, just at the moment of reversal when a woman will attack the male (not with a sword, to be sure, but in the "feminine" way, with the poisoned drop)? Or should we look for a more literal correspondence to this celestial sign? Who, as the drama proceeds, will be armed with a sword and pursue a feminine figure with furious intent? Who, if not Ion himself, together with the sword-bearing Delphians? After the discovery of the plot against him, he bursts violently on the scene in pursuit of the fugitive (1250, 1253–54, 1257–58). As we have seen, this is the act that will

---

121. Orion the great hunter, son of sea and earth (hence called "earth-born" or *gēgenēs*), made sexual assaults on Merope (daughter of Oinopion), Opis (companion of Artemis), and in some versions, Artemis herself, in addition to his five-year pursuit of the Pleiades, daughters of Pleione. For fuller discussion and for the ancient sources, see Fontenrose 1981. 5–32. Orion's connections with Artemis, Eos, and Helios, as well as Dionysos, are significant but are not strictly relevant here.

threaten to repeat the original masculine violence against Creousa. If this reading is correct, then the Bear's revolution reinstalls the original act of male domination in the past at the pivot of the scene. It also forecasts the second attempt, in Ion's retaliation against his mother, which will lead through another peripeteia until the surprising advent of Athena.

This reading, however, does not account for the shift between the female pursued (Pleias) and the javelin-bearing goddess of the full moon who "cleaves the month in two." Are they merely juxtaposed in sequence? Or might there be a thematic relation between the two, as though the second were reacting or responding to the first? The allusion to the moon and the previous reference to Orion recalls Artemis, who is especially appropriate to an Amazonian tapestry. Artemis has already been invoked by the chorus in tandem with Athena when they prayed to the "two goddesses, two *parthenoi,* august sisters of Phoibos" for the birth of Erechtheid children (452–71). But the Erechtheid context also tempts us to look for another thematic relation between the Pleias and this unnamed goddess. This armed virgin is more than an appropriate Artemisian figure. She also reminds us of the other goddess, Athena, who successfully resisted her attacker (Hephaistos) with arms. As the anagrammatic play of letters might well indicate, she may indeed have first been a *Pleias* but turned out to be a *Pallas.*[122]

This proposition might seem too obscure, were it not for other subtle clues that in retrospect have already predicted the cosmic role Athena is to play at the end of the drama, when Ion, learning of his parentage, determines to rush into Apollo's shrine to demand secure knowledge of his paternity. At this moment a brilliant light appears over the temple as though Apollo were going to show at last the immortal face the boy has never seen and to bestow upon the scene the solar radiance associated with him since the opening action of the play. If the god had indeed chosen this moment for an epiphany, the end would have circled back upon the beginning to join up with Ion's invocation of the chariot of Helios in his worshipful monody to Apollo. The luminous gleam does show a visage, but not that of the sun. Instead, it is the countenance of one "bright as the sun" *(antēlion prosōpon),* or even better, "instead of the sun"—and Athena takes the place of Apollo.[123]

122. Immerwahr (1972, 291) also suggests the relationship between Athena and the moon, but he misplaces his emphasis by stressing only iconographical renderings of sun and moon. One tradition, attributed to Pherecydes, associates Athena with the moon (Plutarch, *On the Appearance of the Face on the Moon* 938b = Frag. 13a D-K; cf. 922a). See also Rorscher, *Lexikon* 2:3188–89.

123. Immerwahr (1972, 291) construes *antēlion* as "viewing the sun" or "reflecting the sun." If Athena's appearance were indeed "reflecting the sun" (130) and took place on the

Athena has been invoked several times (452–58, 1528–29) and is present in sculptural form on the temple decor (209–11). Yet her sudden epiphany still seems a mysterious theatrical surprise, except perhaps to the scanner of textured nocturnal skies, who will recall that once Ouranos has mustered the stars, Helios (that is, Apollo) makes his exit into the dying light of day, dragging after him the shining light of Hesperos (1147–49). Then Night takes over. Garbed in her black peplos, she "shakes" *(epallen)* her chariot as she rides, accompanied by stars (1150–51) and passing through the circuit of the nocturnal sky, until Eos, the *phōsphoros,* comes to pursue *(diōkei)* the stars at dawn (1157–58).

Night accompanied by stars, Dawn causing the stars to flee: both are encompassed in Pallas Athena, when Helios has been banished from the scene.[124] *Pallas* derives her name from the verb *pallō,* as the etymological play had described her on the sculpted façade, when half the chorus exclaims, "Do you see *[leusseis]* her shaking *[pallousan]* her shield with the Gorgon face?" The other half replies, "I see Pallas *[leussō Pallad(a)],* my goddess" (209–11). Night is therefore a stand-in for Pallas Athena, the martial goddess of the Gigantomachy, who "shook" *(epallen)* the chariot in her dark nocturnal aspect, who gave the drops of Gorgon blood to the Erechtheid house. But here she is preceded by the Hyades, "the surest sign"—those who, according to Euripides in the *Erechtheus,* were transformations of the daughters of Erechtheus.[125] Pallas Athena is also equivalent to the goddess of the dawn, who chases away the stars and before whose radiance Ion now shrinks back. "Let us flee," he cries to his mother, "lest we see the gods—unless it is the right moment for us to see" (φεύγωμεν, ὦ τεκοῦσα, μὴ τὰ δαιμόνων ὁρῶμεν—εἰ μὴ καιρός ἐσθ' ἡμᾶς ὁρᾶν, 1550–51).[126] And it is. For Athena arrests them with her

---

theologeion of the stage building, it would correspond to Ion's description of the peaks of Mount Parnassus at daybreak "reflecting back" *(katalampomenai)* the first light (86–88).

124. The correspondence is precise: in Ion's monody, Helios puts the stars to flight *(pheugei,* 84); here Eos pursues them *(diōkei,* 1158).

125. Scholiast, *ad* Aratus, *Phainomena* 172. See Owen 1939, *ad loc.;* and Austin 1967, frag. 65, 107–8. For other genealogies, Rorscher, *Lexikon,* s.v. As "signs to sailors," the Athenian Hyades are one of the links to the other tapestries where the naval battle is depicted, as the moon with javelin and the pursuing dawn are relevant to the hunting scenes. See Chalkia 1986, 106.

126. The reference to *antēlion prosōpon* may also refer back to *didumōn prosōpōn kalliblepharon phōs* (188–89) in the parodos, a puzzling phrase whose precise meaning has baffled critics (the two façades of the temple? the façades of two temples? pillars of the colonnade? herms with two faces? statues of the gods?). Whatever the reference, the chorus links the phrase to the sculpted Athena, when they turn their attention to the façade, "roving [literally, "pursuing"] with their eyes" *(blepharon diōkō,* 205), just before they stress the act of beholding. The language of Athena's epiphany at the end thus recalls the references to sunrise in Ion's monody as well as the chorus's description of the temple scene.

command: "do not flee from me: for you are not fleeing me as an enemy [polemian], one who is kindly [eumenē] both in Athens and here" (1553–54). She has come as pacifier and pacified, with no need to brandish a Gorgon against the earth-born. In her peaceful aspect, Athena now resembles her sculpted companion, Dionysos, whose bacchic insignia of ivy were unwarlike weapons (apolemioi, 216–18) that nevertheless could slay (or threaten) a descendant of the children of Gaia (216–18).

Dawn putting the stars to flight is a stand-in for Athena, and Athena, in turn, bathed in a borrowed light and equipped with a diurnal chariot (1571), is a stand-in for Apollo: a last flourish of this theatrical tour de force that describes yet a wider circle, one that begins in the first line of the play's prologue. There Hermes—like Athena, an offspring of mightiest Zeus (4, 1606)—declares his genealogy from Atlas who holds up the sky (ouranos) on his brazen shoulders. This is the model, it seems, for the cosmic roof of the tent that Ion himself constructed and whose theatrical and cultic properties we have explored in the interests of the self's identity and of Athenian ideological mythmaking.[127]

Athena stands in for Apollo to confirm his paternity, and Apollo, in turn, has Xouthos stand in for him as the father of his son. Ion goes off to Athens, secure in his mother's lineage, destined to play his political and genealogical role in the history of the city. Having "constructed" his true identity and aligned himself with the mystic figures of Athenian and Delphic cult, Ion has a public self that is also a "false" one, as we know, by which claims of social status take partial precedence over ties of blood. The native-born child is to be in name the stranger's offspring. The mother's line may secure the privileges of autochthony, but the system, it seems, also tolerates the role of the outsider and accepts the expedient of a legal fiction that finally suppresses the mother's part.

The Discourse of the Other

Viewed in terms of truth and falsehood, the compromise of a legal fiction, according to some critics, compromises the integrity of the drama (as well as that of the gods). But in the context of Athenian ideology, the solution balances the two sources of national pride: autochthony, which justifies the successful defense of territory in the name of a closed circle of citizenship, and philoxenia, which assures a receptivity to admitting outsiders. These are two divergent ideals, which may, as in this case, come into con-

---

127. Hermes completes his functions once the play has begun, including that of preliminary model for Ion. Like Ion, Hermes traces his ancestry to the third generation through his mother's father, but his role as latris, "servant to the gods," will no longer, of course, apply to Ion at the drama's end.

flict with one another.[128] Although the myth of autochthony retains its power, much has happened in the play, as others have observed, to question its implications and to subject the policy of a closed city to closer scrutiny.[129] Autochthony intensifies the primacy of blood kin as the dominant principle of relatedness, excluding or denigrating other modes of association as foreign and potentially hostile. But, as the semantics of *xenos* tell us, the encounter with the outsider covers a wide spectrum of possibilities, ranging from dangerous enemy alien to cherished guest friend. Thus the term refers as well to alliances between nonkin, to the relations of convivial hospitality, and, in the family, to the two institutions of fosterage and adoption.

"The scene is Delphi but in a sense it is Athens," observes Owen, and one can only agree that in principle Delphi is topographically "a one-dimensional image, while the reality of civic space is at Athens."[130] But Delphi is also an elsewhere, and "the shape of things," says Ion, "does not appear the same when viewed from far away and when seen up close" (585–86). Distance supplies perspective. Even more, given the issues at stake in the play, the choice of another locale sets the stage for an inevitable reversal of roles, in which the xenophobic figures of Athens themselves become *xenoi*.[131] In fear that Ion will "invade" the "pure" land of Athens, they violate an other's territory (1220–21) and abuse both the *xenia* of the banquet and the special purity of this sacred place. As a result, Creousa and her entourage are put at risk. Isolated and helpless strangers, they are saved only because of the extrapolitical status of the god's altar and a fortuitous revelation by his representative, the Pythia.

Delphi is not just any other place. It has its own integral community, to be sure, but apart from (and because of) its oracular function, it also constitutes a meeting ground for everyone. The sacred tripod belongs to all of Hellas (*koinon Hellados*, 366), a common sacrifice is offered on behalf of all the foreigners (*chrēstērion . . . koinon*, 419–20), and all comers require the services of a Delphian host (*proxenos*, 335, 551). Delphi is the place of comings and goings, of chance encounters between strangers, whether for a casual affair with a Delphian maenad or for the discovery

---

128. Walsh 1978, 308–9 and n. 33; Parker 1987, 201–2 and n. 63. The two major examples of defense against the foreign intruder were Erechtheus's battle against Eumolpos and Eleusis (with the addition of the Thracian element) and Theseus's repelling of the Amazons' invasion. Herakles was responsible for the Amazonian tapestries of the tent, but the Erechtheid context also assimilates the Amazonian reference into the Athenians' political program. Examples of *philoxenia:* the wars on behalf of the Heracleidae and of the kinfolk of the Argives who perished in their expedition against Thebes; the welcoming of Oedipus, Herakles, and Orestes.

129. In particular, Walsh 1978; and Saxenhouse 1986.

130. Owen 1939, xxii; Loraux 1981a, "Créuse," 211; Immerwahr 1972, 281.

131. Walsh 1978.

of one's child in the first person one meets (naming him as Ion for that very encounter). In Ion's speech describing Athenian xenophobia, he praises the random life of Delphi, where some are always leaving and others continue to arrive: "Sweet it is to be a new face among other new ones" (*kainos en kainoisin*, 641). His is entirely the world of strangers or at least of the local folk who have looked after the nameless child and to whom he would now offer a banquet of *xenia* (805) at the moment of his farewell.

The chance encounter may be the result of the providential power of Tuche (Fortune), while the almost fatal misrecognition of mother and child may exemplify the highest standard of the Aristotelian plot. But the special focus of the play integrates the generic tragic conventions with a thematic content that revolves around autochthony and the question of what and who is truly one's own, and it stages these concerns in maximum contrast to the open circulation at Delphi.

We should note first that the solidarity of kin is not always the single criterion for making common cause. Xouthos is intent on "sharing a common mind" *(koinophrōn)* with his new-found son (577) and wants to celebrate the bond in a feast at a "common table" (652, cf. 807). Likewise, Creousa's reunion with Ion is a joy that is "common" to the two of them (1462). Yet kinship may also be the basis for divisiveness, when one parent does not share the child with the other (358, 772, 1101). This situation will be rectified only at the end of the play in the prediction of a common stock *(koinon genos)* that Creousa and Xouthos will share in their future progeny (1589). But the allegiance of others, of nonkin, is far more essential to the plot. Household servants are bound by loyalty to the family of their masters, especially in tragic drama, but Creousa's maidservants will go so far as to share the fortunes of the house (566), even if it means they might die for it (858, cf. 1235–43). The old Paidagogos on his own recognizance volunteers "to labor along with" Creousa (*sunekponein*, 850; cf. 851, 1040, 1044) in a common task, and she in turn uses the same word to express the matching of her step to his (740).

The old man first suggests slaying the stranger child through the agency of sword-bearing attendants (980) in order to wage a battle against the intruder he brands as enemy (998, 1043), a view of Ion that Creousa has come to share (1290–91). The Delphians, for their part, come to the defense of Ion as his allies (1271). The whole city takes up the pursuit of the woman, who flees her enemies as they rush upon her, armed with their swords (1222–23, 1254, 1257–58).

In this miniature war, which is previewed, as we have seen, in the tapestry of the nocturnal sky, we are brought still further back to the scene of the Gigantomachy displayed on the façade of the temple, especially through the figure of the Gorgon, whom Athena slew but whom Earth had borne to be the ally *(summachos)* of her children in battle (987–97). But we also recall the first scene of that temple façade where Herakles does combat with the Hydra, and Iolaos, with his fiery torch, takes up "common labors" *(koinous . . . ponous)* to share the ordeal *(sunantlei)* with the son of Zeus (194–200)—the only labor in the traditional canon of twelve whose success requires the assistance of an other.[132]

Above all, Xouthos owes his position to the fact that he was Erechtheus's ally. He toiled valiantly along with the king in war (*sumponēsas,* 61) and received Creousa as his reward, having sacked the enemy city with a "common sword" (*koinōi dori,* 296). He can never achieve full status, being only an ally *(epikouros)* and not a legitimate inhabitant of Athenian land (*oikētōr,* 1299; cf. 297). Hence, according to Creousa, he is entitled only to his shield and sword (1305). Yet Xouthos's example proves that the chorus is in error in attributing only to legitimate children the task of defending their native land (483).[133]

Xouthos, the stranger, marries into the Erechtheid house. In turn he meets a stranger child who is given to him as his own. The stranger child, for his part, owes his *trophē* to others who, as far as he can tell, stand in for his parents. But the discrepancy between Ion's perception of Apollo the father as the source of his nurture and our knowledge that sire and nurturer are really one contributes more than a fine note of irony. In Ion's lyric address to Phoibos Apollo as his *genetōr patēr*—because, as he explains, the god's sustenance entitles him to the name of father-begetter (136–40, cf. 1530–31)—the boy confuses the clear dividing line between nature and nurture. Yet the effect is also to establish a double and valid principle: parentage itself may be a fictive category, an "as if," and ties of blood, although essential to one's genetic identity, are not the only relations that count. We recall the consistent references to Creousa as his "daughter" made by the Paidagogos: intimacy may easily pass into kinship. But more significant still is the idea of autochthony, which requires that a nurse take over the care of the newborn child: a *kourotrophos,* one like a mother (a *hōs tekousa*), but not a true one. This is the exact role Athena fulfills for Erichthonios and the Pythia for Ion.[134] Dionysos, the

---

132. By contrast, when Creousa accuses Ion of being an enemy and equates his intrusion into her house with setting it on fire, he points out that "he was not coming to her land, either with arms, or with torches or flame of fire" (1291–94).

133. Once again echoes of the earlier *Erechtheus* may resonate in this debate. Eumolpos the Thracian had come to the aid of the Eleusinian king against Athens. Erechtheus, we think, gives advice to some adopted son (frag. 53 A, cf. frag. 49 A). A possible reading of the corrupted passage about Erechtheus in the *Ion* (see above, note 56) is one that justifies the intrusion of the stranger *(xenikon esbolan)* if the city is in danger (723–24).

134. See Saxenhouse 1986, 267, on the priestess who is able to "love something [one] other than what is her own."

other baby in the basket, also was separated from his mother at birth and reared by *kourotrophoi*. His displacement from his natal terrain is another feature in child-rearing practices and provides the model for the paradox that one can be both an insider and outsider, both at home and not at home. Meanwhile, the god Apollo, who intervenes in the pure heritage of the autochthonous line by his union with Creousa, also introduces the element of exogamy embodied in Xouthos, his human doublet in the play.

The mythic exemplars are far removed from the realities of everyday life. They may be imitated, as we know, but never replicated. Yet as the mortal Xouthos takes the place of Apollo, still another principle is established that goes beyond the practical benefits for Ion expounded by both Creousa and Athena (1532–43, 1560–62). Apollo gave his son as a gift to one who did not beget him, "as sometimes happens when a friend gives another friend his son, that he may be master of a house" (1532–36). The reference is to the institution of adoption, the legal mechanism by which one may "make" another man's child one's own, and thus definitively and for all time convert a stranger to kin.[135]

J. J. Bachofen long ago noticed the innovative nature of this solution. According to his theory of cultural evolution, fictive fatherhood under the sunlit sponsorship of Apollo is the highest achievement of civilization. Adoption is as far removed as possible from the biological and hence tellurian aspects of life, which he attributes to the first and earliest stage of "Mother Right." In fact, Bachofen uses Euripides' play as the incontrovertible proof of his threefold evolutionary schema. The first stage is embodied in the mother Creousa and her connection to the autochthonous, earthbound race of Erechtheids. In the second, there is a shift to the Dionysiac as the middle term, identified by Bachofen as the phallic power of generation in union with a woman (in this case, Xouthos). In the third stage, we finally ascend to the solar world of an unmixed masculine nature. For Bachofen, the luminous and spiritual Apollo is the purest emblem of this exalted level, and "in place of mortality and the past which rules over the law of Earth," the god bestows "immortality that connects fatherhood with light."[136] Athena, not of woman born, is Apollo's

---

135. The technical term for "adoption" is *poiēsis* or *eispoiēsis* (LSJ, s.v.). As Owen (1939, *ad loc.*) points out, Apollo's oracle had to say that Ion was begotten of Xouthos because the name of the real father, which Athenian law required for the record of transfer, could not, of course, be given in this case. In practice, adoption most often involved relatives rather than strangers, but in principle, there was no such limit to eligibility. See further Harrison 1968, 82–96.

136. Bachofen 1948 [1861], 623, and see the entire discussion, 606–47. In his reading, the tent is a Dionysiac space, a nocturnal scene, illuminated by the moon, as befits the "Bacchic erotic fire of tellurian vulcanic nature." The construction and dimensions are sig-

messenger, who confirms the truth of this metaphysical principle in the idea of adoption, the *naturae imitatio,* which leaves nature behind (and below).[137]

For Saxenhouse, a recent critic, precisely the opposite holds true: autochthony is a system of reproduction that "serves to denigrate the female, to deny the origins of cities in heterosexual relations, and in turn to emphasize male potency without the female as intermediary."[138] In claiming to produce its children from the earth, such a system promotes the idea of the social unity of the body politic, which accounts for its appeal to political and military discourse. By bypassing the mother's role, as Apollo had intended to do for the duration of the play, the god in effect joins up with the ideological basis of autochthony. Creousa too subscribes to this doctrine in her "refusal to accept what is not her own," which "leads to the heart of the action of the play." She also, however, foils Apollo's plan to give a son to a father without taking account of her necessary role in procreation.[139]

Bachofen elides, of course, several fundamental facts: Apollo's all too physical rape of Creousa and the indispensable role of the father(s) in autochthonous lineage, as well as the psychological impact of the child's relationship with his mother, which, as the play shows, is not to be dismissed with impunity. Most of all, Bachofen reads Athens's dramatic representation of itself as a true historical account, not only of Athens, but also of all cultural evolution. Yet Saxenhouse's analysis is also deficient in certain significant details: on the one hand, Creousa exposed the child she had borne and did not nurture him as mothers are expected to do, and on the other, she is needed as the *epiklēros,* her father's daughter, who, in default of a male heir, is indispensable for producing children to maintain the paternal lineage.[140] It may fairly be argued that all of Creousa's actions and roles are predicated on the structure of gender relations imposed by a masculine society to which she can only react. But in the conflicting claims of the two sides that generate the dramatic action, it is not such a simple

---

nificant: e.g., the uprights (*orthostatai,* 1133) recall the phallic image of Dionysos *orthos;* the quadrated shape, its *eugōnia* (1137), according to Proclus, is the image of "Ge who receives the forces of procreation." The measurement of 10,000 feet as obeying a decimal system is inconsistent with the Apollonian number 12. The two drops of Gorgon's blood correspond to Dionysiac dualism, etc. For other details, see 615–21.

137. Bachofen 1948 [1861], 625–26.

138. Saxenhouse 1986, 258.

139. Saxenhouse 1986, 268–69, who does not, however, know Loraux 1981a, "Créuse," 197–253, on the *Ion.* In this and other more general considerations of Athenian autochthony, Loraux anticipates Saxenhouse's readings. Loraux replies in the afterword of the second edition (1981a = 1990), 265–66.

140. Loraux 1981a, "Créuse," 223–29.

matter to separate masculine rights from feminine ones, as Loraux shows throughout her discussion.

Yet each of these two lines of argument contains a partial truth. Teleologically speaking, the law of the father is maintained on both sides and even advanced through adoption. At the same time, the play dramatizes the role of maternity and the bond between mother and child, insisting on the reunion of the pair just at the moment when Ion's age should dictate their separation.

Theatrically speaking, in resorting to all these compromises that insist on the sharing of privilege in constructing both Ion's identity and that of the Athenian polis, the drama exemplifies the ways in which Athens represents itself as "escaping" a tragic dénouement. In observing the grounds of comparison between Athens and Thebes on stage, as we did earlier, the approach to the problem of "know thyself" takes a far different turn in Athens than it does for Oedipus or Pentheus in Thebes. There characters are constrained by the limits of kinship that dominate their modes of action, and they remain forever trapped in the dilemmas (or tragedies) of identity. Who is the self and who is the other? Who is the outsider and who the insider? The past replayed in the present can only serve to conspire against the potentiality of the future. Thebes, as we know it from the tragic theater, the home of autochthonous Spartoi, cannot seem to make use of substitutions. It cannot resort to fictions of "as if" or, at another symbolic level, create new institutions in the face of new problems. Athens, however, does precisely this in using the mythic idea of fosterage to arrive at the civic idea of legal adoption. In this play Athens may flirt with the possibilities of a Theban disaster; it may also run the risk of conflating the tragic with the comic and go so far as to jeopardize the idea of "truth" in its subversion of the norms of *anagnōrisis,* but the city seems to get what it wants in the end.

The result is that Athens may have it all ways: a child of divine parentage, a certified product of autochthonous lineage, a legitimized son of the proper social standing. Imported from Delphi, Ion brings his "purity" of upbringing to merge with the other sort of "purity," which Athens claims. His act of "founding," or setting up the tent as a central point of assembly for all the people *(laos)* of Delphi,[141] prefigures his role as the one who will consolidate the organization of the polis, in that his fourfold progeny from a "single root" will constitute the Athenian people (*laos,* 1575–78). At the same time, his actions at home will be matched abroad in future generations. Through the sons of his sons, Ion will export Ath-

---

141. Xouthos had spoken of the multitude of friends *(tōn philōn plērōma)* Ion is to muster *(athroisas)* for the feast (663–64); Ion, however, summons *all* the people of Delphi *(panta . . . laon,* 1140).

enian ancestry far and wide to Europe and Asia, the islands and the mainland. Thus he is made to account in advance for the Ionians-to-be. Brought up elsewhere and negotiating a successful transition to the place he now can call home, Ion sets an example to colonists, who will also make their home elsewhere (*epoikēsousi,* 1583; *katoikēsousin,* 1586), and he opens the way to visions (and even justifications) of Athenian empire. Ion becomes the principle of unity in diversity, the central point of an expanding periphery. Moreover, once the Ionian world is settled, Athena goes one step further when she forecasts that the common progeny *(koinon genos)* of Xouthos and Creousa will be eponymous founders—the first Dorian and the first Achaean in Greece. Through Athena's prophecies the city of Athens virtually displaces Delphi as the seat of Panhellenic identity, and this with the full approval of Apollo (1595), the god most closely associated with foundations and colonies. In this way, Ion can prove his true identity away from Delphi as his father's son—to perform Apollonian tasks in the name of Athens.

The destiny of the nameless orphan child, who receives his name in the course of the play from what seems to be the most trivial of reasons (a chance encounter), engenders in Athena's prophecy a veritable flood of proper names, all appropriated for Athens's designs. But if Athena, standing in for Delphic Apollo, validates the transitive role of Ion and his mediation between stranger and kin, family and polis, city and empire, we detect also the constructive role that Dionysos is sometimes asked to play in the Dionysiac tragic theater of Athens.

PART FOUR

Gender and Mimesis:
Theater and Identity

·EIGHT·

Playing the Other: Theater, Theatricality, and the Feminine in Greek Drama

For a specimen of sheer theatrical power, it would be difficult to match the climactic scene of Euripides' *Bacchae* (788–861), in which Pentheus at last comes under the spell of his adversary, the god Dionysos, and acknowledges his secret desire to spy upon the women of Thebes who have left the city to go as maenads to the mountain. His violent antagonism toward the women, who in abandoning their homes, children, and domestic tasks have challenged the civic, masculine authority of the king, gives way to a sudden softening of will—a yielding to the cunning wiles of the god disguised on stage as the Asiatic stranger, the leader of his own troops of maenads. This first surrender is followed by another. Giving up now his original intention to marshal his forces for an open combat of men against women, Pentheus also relinquishes his stubborn claim to an unequivocally masculine identity. To see what the women are doing without himself being seen, Pentheus must trade his hoplite military tactics for an undercover operation that involves adopting a devious stratagem and assuming a remarkable disguise. He must let the god take him inside the

This essay was originally published in *Representations* 11 (1985): 63–94; it was reprinted (with some small differences) in Winkler and Zeitlin 1990, 63–96, through the kind permission of the University of California Press. In this version I have made a few further additions, particularly in the notes and at the end. An earlier, shorter version of this essay was presented at a conference, "After *The Second Sex*," held at the University of Pennsylvania, and at a symposium honoring Helen Bacon, held at Barnard College, New York, both in April 1984. I wish to thank the commentators on these two occasions, Carolyn Heilbrun and Marylin Arthur [Katz], respectively, as well as others who participated in the discussion. Thanks also to the members of the Women's Studies Colloquium at Princeton University who offered acute and thoughtful comments at the presentation of this paper, in particular, Natalie Davis, Suzanne Keller, and Elaine Showalter. Jean Rudhardt and Philippe Borgeaud also made useful remarks at the University of Geneva, and Claude Calame at the University of Lausanne. I am especially grateful to Jack Winkler, Simon Goldhill, and Jean-Pierre Vernant, who read the manuscript and from whose incisive and valuable criticism I have, as always, greatly profited.

palace and dress him as a woman in a flowing wig and headdress, and a long pleated robe and belt, to which he adds the typical insignia of the maenads—the dappled fawnskin and ritual thyrsus. When the god completes this elaborate toilette, Pentheus will also resemble Dionysos himself, whose effeminate appearance the king had earlier mocked.[1] But as much as they might seem doublets of one another, the power relations between them have been decisively reversed. Now Dionysos will turn Pentheus from the one who acts to the one who is acted upon, from the one who would inflict pain and suffering, even death, on another, to the one who will undergo those experiences himself. For now, however, the preliminary sign of Pentheus's total defeat, at the hands first of Dionysos and then of the women, is given to us on stage in the visual feminization of Pentheus when he is induced against all inhibitions of shame to adopt the costume and gestures of the woman.

But if Pentheus's feminization is the emblem of his defeat, Dionysos's effeminacy is a sign of his hidden power. Here are two males, cousins through their genealogical ties, both engaged in a masculine contest for supremacy. One, however, gains mastery by manipulating a feminized identity, while the other is vanquished when he finally succumbs to it. At the moment when the two males appear together on stage in similar dress, we might perceive an instructive spectacle of the inclusive functions of the feminine in the drama—one on the side of power and the other on the side of weakness.

Pentheus, at first ashamed of wearing women's clothing and terrified lest he make a spectacle of himself for all the city to see, now has a fleeting intimation of the new force he has acquired. He exults in the surge of unnatural physical strength that suffuses him and dreams of uprooting mountains with his bare hands. But under the god's gentle prodding, he just as eagerly abandons his desire for violence to acquiesce with pleasure in the contrary tactics of hiding and deception by which he will confront the women on their own terms (*Bacchae* 945–56). The moment of triumph and confidence, however, is brief. We know in advance what the fate of Pentheus will be once the feminized god Dionysos, who plays his role to perfection, delivers over his disguised victim, his man clumsily concealed in women's dress, to the "real" women. They will tear the impostor apart in a terrible ritual *sparagmos,* while the god reverts to his function of divine spectator at the drama he himself has arranged on stage.

I have chosen to begin with the robing of Pentheus because, beyond its dramatic impact within the context of the play, the mechanics of this scene suggest a wider and more emblematic set of significations. These

---

1. E.g., *Bacchae* 451–59; Dionysos is called *thēlumorphos,* 351 (cf. Pentheus's description as *gunaikomorphos* [his costume as imitating a woman's, *gunaikomimoi,* 981]).

refer both to the conditions of Dionysiac ritual itself as a deadly version of initiation into the mysteries of the god's worship and to the conditions of the theater of Dionysos and the conventions of its artistic representations.[2] For the first, Pentheus must be dressed as a woman for consecration to the god as the surrogate beast-victim he will become in the ritual on the mountain; for the second, the costuming of Pentheus reminds us that the theater requires mimetic disguise, by which it creates and maintains its status as dramatic festival.[3] Through this scene we arrive at the dynamic basis of Greek drama, catching a momentary glimpse of the secrets of its ritual prehistory as it merges with and is imitated by the techniques of the theater. In particular, the fact that Pentheus dons a feminine costume and rehearses in it before our eyes exposes one of the most marked features of Greek theatrical mimesis: that men are the only actors in this civic theater. In order to represent women on stage, men must always put on a feminine costume and mask.[4] No woman speaks or acts for herself and in herself on stage; it is always a man who impersonates her.[5]

If we consider that in order to direct the proceedings of the drama, to manipulate its theatrical effects, contrive its plots, set its stage, and control its mimetic play of illusion and reality, Dionysos, the god of the theater, must also take on womanish traits, then perhaps we may venture yet further. Might some intrinsic affinities link the phenomenon of Athenian tragedy, invented and developed as a civic art form, to what the society culturally defines as feminine in its sex/gender system?[6]

There is nothing new in stressing the associations of Dionysos and the feminine for the Greek theater. After all, madness, the irrational, and the

2. For the fullest account of this hypothesis, see Seaford 1981.

3. For the metatheatrical aspects of this scene in particular, and of the play as a whole, see Foley 1980; Foley 1985, 205–58; and Segal 1982, 215–71.

4. See further chapter 9 below.

5. It should be noted that unlike other public Dionysiac festivals in Attica (and elsewhere) in which both men and women participated, the City Dionysia seems to belong to men only (with the sole exception of a girl assigned to carry the ritual basket in the preliminary procession). I omit here the recently renewed discussion of the vexed problem as to whether women were included as spectators. If they were, their presence (unlike that of the Athenian citizen body) could only have been optional, in my opinion, and the dramatic productions were certainly not addressed to them.

6. The question I raise here about the development of drama in Athens and its political and social motivations is obviously too complex for this limited discussion. I suggest merely that the historical conditions of drama, interestingly enough, coincide with a period that sharply polarizes definitions and distinctions of masculine and feminine roles. Drama, like the woman, we might say, is useful for its society and at the same time potentially subversive and destructive. It is also worth remarking that as theater reaches its full flowering in the fifth century (c. 425), the iconography of Dionysos undergoes a shift in the vase paintings from a masculine, bearded figure to a more youthful one who displays effeminate and more androgynous features. See Carpenter 1986, 124–26; Carpenter 1994.

emotional aspects of life are associated in the culture more with women than with men. The boundaries of women's bodies are perceived as more fluid, more permeable, more open to affect and entry from the outside, less easily controlled by intellectual and rational means. This perceived physical and cultural instability renders women weaker than men; it is also all the more a source of disturbing power over men, as reflected in the fact that in the divine world it is feminine agents for the most part (in addition to Dionysos) who inflict men with madness: Hera, Aphrodite, the Erinyes, or even Athena as in Sophocles' *Ajax*.

Taking a different approach, we might want to see the androgyny of Dionysos—already in Aeschylus (frag. 61 N[2]) called a *gunnis* (womanish man) and *pseudanōr* (counterfeit man)—as a true mixture of masculine and feminine. This mixture, it can be argued, is one of the emblems of his paradoxical role as disrupter of the normal social categories. In his own person he attests to the *coincidentia oppositorum* that challenges the hierarchies and rules of the public masculine world, reintroducing into it confusions, conflicts, tensions, and ambiguities, insisting always that life is more complex than masculine aspirations would allow.[7] Such a view would stress male and female aspects alike; it would regard the god as embodying a dynamic process or as configuring in his person an alternate mode of reality. Convincing as this approach may be, it runs the risk of underrating the importance of Dionysos's identification with the feminine in giving him and his theater their power.

Along the same lines, in the quest for equivalence between the genders, one could fairly remark that although all the actors in tragedy are men, within the plays feminized males are countered by masculinized women: for example, Aeschylus's Clytemnestra of the "man-counseling mind" *(Agamemnon)*, Euripides' Medea, and, of course, the maenadic Agave herself, who in the *Bacchae* boasts of her warrior prowess over the body of Pentheus, her yet unrecognized son whom she has killed (*Ba.* 1202–10). This notion of a balanced, symmetrical inversion finds support in Greek festivals outside Athens where men and women change their costumes for a day, each imitating the appearance and behavior of the other.[8] Better yet, there is evidence that in initiation rites at puberty or sometimes in nuptial arrangements, young men and women in their own spheres tem-

7. For the bisexual consciousness of Dionysos, see especially Hillman 1972, 258–66. For the more general paradoxes of Dionysos's role, see the synthesis of Segal 1982, 10–19.

8. These festivals are occasions for riotous carnival (e.g., the Cretan Ekdysia, the Argive Hybristika). Dionysiac merriment also lends itself to such behavior, at least as Philostratus, a late source, describes a painting of a Dionysiac revel: "Dionysos is accompanied by a numerous train in which girls mingle with men, for the revel *[kōmos]* allows women to act the part of men, and men to put on women's clothing and play the woman" (*Imagines* 1.2).

porarily adopt the dress and behavior of the other sex.[9] Such reversals
are usually explained according to a ritual logic that insists that each gender must for the last time, as it were, act the part of the other before assuming the unequivocal masculine and feminine identities that cultural
rules require.[10]

As a theoretical concept, this proposition makes eminent sense. On
the level of practice, however, these symmetries are often more apparent
than real; the notion conforms better to our habits of binary thinking than
to recorded evidence. First, such rites for men are far better attested and
more numerous than similar rites for women, not least because their performance, aimed at creating men for the public life of the city, is of greater
concern to the culture at large.

Second, and more to the point, critics tend to treat inversion of roles
as a sufficient explanation in itself—that is, a temporary reversal before a
decisive correction. They do not extend their analysis to consider what the
various aspects of the actual experience might imply for achieving male
identity. What might these actions and attitudes teach a man? How might
the processes of imitating the feminine prepare him for access to adult
status, other than to teach him the behaviors he must later scrupulously
avoid? Unless there were something to learn and something necessary to
repeat, the Athenian polis would not have needed the genre of tragedy at
all to call these different roles into question and, most of all, to challenge
the masculine civic and rationalized view of the universe.

Finally, the pairing of feminized men and masculinized women, though
a useful notion in many respects, runs the risk of assuming mutually inverted categories without looking to the internal dynamics of tragic conventions that shape and predict the conditions of this exchange. Even
more, such a concept tends to reduce the scope of the feminine in the
drama. It is too limited to encompass her double dimensions as a model
of both weakness and strength, endowed with traits and capacities that
bear negative and positive messages for self and society.

Thus my emphasis falls not upon the equal interchange or reversal of

9. On the various forms of transvestism in Greek rite and myth, see Delcourt 1961, 1–
16; Gallini 1968, 211–18, especially 215n.6; and Burkert 1979, 29–30.

10. "For both sexes the initiation through which a young man or woman is confirmed
in his or her specific nature may entail, through a ritual exchange of clothing, temporary
participation in the nature of the opposite sex whose complement he or she will become by
being separated from it" (Vernant 1980, "Warfare," 24). Cf. also Jeanmaire 1939, 153, 321.
See further Vidal-Naquet 1986a, "Black Hunter" and "Recipes"; and Vidal-Naquet 1986b.
I borrow his term, "law of symmetrical inversion." On initiations of the young, see further
Jeanmaire 1939; Brelich 1969; Chirassi-Colombo 1979; Vernant 1991, 207–19, 220–43.
Girls' initiations are currently of much interest: see, in addition to the above, Calame 1977;
Sourvinou-Inwood 1988; and Brulé 1987.

male and female roles but upon the predominance of the feminine in the theater, a phenomenon that used to (and may still) puzzle some commentators, who perceived a serious discrepancy between the mutedness of women in Athenian social and political life and their expressive claims to be heard and seen on stage.[11] My focus on imbalances rather than on equivalences between the genders is aimed primarily at understanding the implications of theater and theatricality as these are integrally related to and reflective of the thematic preoccupations of drama. I am less concerned with the content and themes of the various dramas in their political and social dimensions. If tragedy can be viewed as a species of recurrent masculine initiations, for adults as well as for the young,[12] and if drama, more broadly, is designed as an education for male citizens in the democratic city, then the aspects of the play world I wish to bring into sharper relief may well merit the speculations I am about to offer on theater, representation, plot and action, experience and identity—all linked in some radical way with the feminine.

From the outset, it is essential to understand that in the Greek theater, as in Shakespearean theater, the self that is really at stake is to be identified with the male, while the woman is assigned the role of the radical other.[13] Given the numbers and importance of female protagonists in Greek tragedy (in contrast to those of Shakespeare),[14] it may seem unfair that theoretical critics from Aristotle on never consider anyone but the male hero as the central feature of the genre; they devote their attention to outlining *his*

11. For judicious discussion, see Foley 1981b.

12. On tragedy as initiation, related both to the mysteries and to puberty rites, see the discussion of Seaford 1981, drawing upon the pioneering work of Thomson (1946). For aspects of puberty ritual reflected imaginatively in the various dramas, see, for Aeschylus's *Oresteia*, Vidal-Naquet 1981a, 150; and above, chapter 3, 98–107. For Sophocles' *Philoctetes*, Vidal-Naquet 1981b. For Euripides' *Hippolytos*, Segal 1978; and above, chapter 6. For the *Bacchae*, Seaford 1981; Segal 1982, 158–214. See also Winkler 1990. Also relevant to these speculations is Montrose 1980, who discusses the public functions of Shakespearean theater as a secularized means of confronting the transitions of life that had earlier been framed in the milieu of Catholic ritual.

13. I am indebted here to the stimulating discussion of Bamber 1982, as much for its provocative arguments as for its use in confronting some fundamental differences between the feminine in Greek and Elizabethan tragedy. There are other "others," to be sure, on the Athenian stage (e.g., barbarians, servants, enemy antagonists, and even gods), but the dialectic of self and other is consistently and insistently predicated on the distinctions between masculine and feminine, far more than in Shakespeare. Even the plays with more strictly military and political themes (excepting only Sophocles' *Philoctetes*) arrange their plots around critical confrontations between masculine and feminine actors.

14. No Shakespearean tragedy has a woman as its main character, though sometimes she shares double billing (Juliet, Cleopatra). By contrast, in extant Greek drama women often lend their individual names or collective functions to the titles (*Antigone, Electra, Medea; Choephoroi, Trachiniae, Bacchae*). Moreover, women play far more extensive roles in Greek tragedy, which increase in subtlety and variety as the genre develops.

traits, configurations, and dilemmas. Yet despite Clytemnestra, Antigone, Phaedra, Medea, and many others, it must be acknowledged that this critical blindness is also insight. Even when female characters struggle with the conflicts generated by the particularities of their subordinate social position, their demands for identity and self-esteem are still designed primarily for exploring the male project of selfhood in the larger world. These demands impinge upon men's claims to knowledge, power, freedom, and self-sufficiency—not, as some have thought, for woman's gaining some greater entitlement or privilege for herself and not even for revising notions of what femininity might be or mean. Women as individuals or chorus may give their names as titles to plays; female characters may occupy the center stage and leave a far more indelible emotional impression on their spectators than their male counterparts (Antigone, for example, with respect to Creon). But *functionally* women are never an end in themselves, and nothing changes for them once they have lived out their drama on stage. Rather, they play the roles of catalysts, agents, instruments, blockers, spoilers, destroyers, and sometimes helpers or saviors for the male characters. When prominently represented, they may serve as antimodels as well as hidden models for that masculine self and concomitantly, their experience of suffering or their acts that lead them to disaster regularly occur before and precipitate those of men.[15]

An excellent case in point is Sophocles' *Trachiniae,* a play that will serve us well throughout this essay. The distress and despair of Deianeira, the innocent, virtuous wife, commands our attention for most of the play. She loses none of our sympathy when she unwittingly destroys her husband Herakles for love of him. Yet we come to realize that her entire experience, her actions and reactions, are in truth a route for achieving another goal, the real *telos* of the drama. She is the agent designated to fulfill the deceptive, riddling oracles that predict, as it turns out, not the well-earned respite from his labors here on earth, but the tragic destiny of Herakles. Deianeira kills herself offstage in remorse, but his are the sufferings we witness publicly on stage, and it is he who, in his first and last appearance before us, provides the climax and resolution of the drama.

Moreover, if we consider more generally that the tragic universe is one that the specifically male self (actor, spectator, or both) must discover for himself as other than he originally imagined it to be, then the example of Deianeira is particularly instructive for articulating the complex position

---

15. The functional argument is even more obviously true in the case of those plays— which I will not discuss in this essay—in which the plot revolves around the demand made upon an army for a virgin sacrifice (such as Iphigenia and Polyxena) and where female heroic nobility in dying is used most often to offer an ironic counterpoint to masculine *Realpolitik.* See, for example, Foley's (1985) analysis of the *Iphigenia in Aulis;* on the *Hekabe,* see above, chapter 5.

occupied by that feminine other. For in the course of the action, Deianeira does indeed make that discovery for herself, realizing too late that she has been duped. The love charm the centaur had bequeathed to her was in fact a deadly poison, whose fiery potential was concealed within the recesses of the house until exposed to the warming heat of the sun. But her education into the treacherous opacity of the tragic world holds no interest for Herakles, preoccupied as he is with unraveling the riddle of his own story. The ensemble of Deianeira's life and death seems to have nothing to teach Herakles that he can acknowledge openly on his deathbed. Even more telling, he will not allow it to have meaning for their son Hyllos when he prescribes for the boy's future in terms that define him only as his father's son.

Medea in Euripides' play comes closest to the demand for an equivalence of that feminine self to the male, preferring, as she says, to stand three times in the van of battle than to bear one child (*Medea* 250–51). Yet although she has a defined geographical destination to which she will go once she leaves Corinth in exile, having obtained in advance from its king the promise of sanctuary in Athens, her spectacular departure from the city on the dragon chariot of her cosmic ancestor, Helios, suggests that there can be no place for her in the social structure down here on earth. A woman who insists on the binding nature of the compact she made on her own with a man, a woman who defends her right to honor and self-esteem in terms suspiciously resembling those of the male heroic code, and finally a woman who would reverse the cultural flow in founding a new genre of poetry that celebrates the exploits of women rather than those of men (as the chorus sings, 410–45): such a woman is meant only for superhuman status.[16] Accordingly, it is only logical that she disappear once the drama is over—upward and out of sight. Yet even in this revolutionary play the typology still holds. Medea's formal function in the plot is to punish Jason for breaking his sacred oath to her, through an exacting retribution of tragic justice, and she is the predictable and appropriate agent, even if embodied in exotic form, for accomplishing that crucial end.

Let us return now to the central topic: to identify those features that are most particular to drama, serving to differentiate it from all other art forms that precede it, such as narrative (epic), choral lyric and dance, solo songs, and stylized exchanges of dialogue. Though profoundly indebted to ritual representations and reenactments, to ritual costumes and masks, drama develops along the deeper lines of character and plot and establishes its own conventions and entitlements in the more secular sphere.[17]

---

16. See especially Knox 1977, for discussion of Medea's "imitation" of male heroic traits.

17. It should be emphasized that I equate drama here with serious drama rather than with comic types, such as the satyr play and comedy itself, whose primitive elements may

At the risk of drastic oversimplification, I propose four principal elements as indispensable traits of the theatrical experience, all linked in various ways to one another and to the sum total of the tragic spectacle. And I will assume another, more dangerous risk by boldly proposing in advance that each of these traits can find its more radical (though not its only) cultural referent in the traits and aspects that the society most associates with the feminine domain.

The first of these elements is the representation of the body itself on stage as such, including its somatic dimensions and the sense of its physical reality. The second is the arrangement of architectural space on stage, which continually suggests a relational tension between inside and outside. The third is the plot itself, that is, the strategies by which theater best represents a tragic story on stage and contrives to bring that story through often surprising means to the conclusion that the terms of its traditional myth demand. In this sense, plot as the shape of the story often coincides in fact with the other connotation of plot as intrigue and deception. The fourth and final element is the most extensive: the condition of theatrical mimesis itself or more generally, the representation of a self as other than it seems or knows itself to be, a self with inner and outer dimensions. For the purposes of this discussion, this defining feature is limited to the question of role playing, impersonation, and disguise.

The Body

The emphasis in theater must inevitably fall upon the body—the performing body of the actor as it embodies its role, figures its actions, and is shown to us in stylized poses, gestures, and attitudes. We see this body before us in the *theatron*, "the viewing place," in rest and in movement. We observe how it occupies different areas at different times on stage, how it makes its entrances and exits, how it is situated at times alone or more often in relation to others. This performing body engages at every moment its sensory faculties: it hears, sees, touches, and moves. Above all, it is the actor as body or body as actor who projects the human voice in all its inflections.

Theater has been defined as the "adventure of the human body," [18] but for Greek tragedy it could more accurately be called the "misadventure of

---

well have preceded the growth of the strange mutant that is tragedy. For even if we renounce any hopes of reconstructing a plausible story of origins, there seems no doubt that the tragic play is the first to achieve the status of art and that the other forms only follow in its wake and under its influence. To speak of theater, in the full sense of the word, then, is to speak first of tragedy.

18. Belaval 1965, 3–16, especially 8.

the human body." What interests the audience most in the somatics of the stage is the body in an unnatural state of *pathos* (suffering), when it falls away furthest from its ideal of strength and integrity. We notice it most when it is reduced to a helpless or passive condition (seated, bound, or constrained in some other way), when it is in the grip of madness or disease, undergoing intermittent and spasmodic pain, alternating between spells of dangerous calm and violent storm. Tragedy insists most often on exhibiting this body, even typically bringing offstage corpses back onstage so as to expose them to public view. When characters are still alive, some demand us to witness the spectacle of their suffering so we may pity them. Others call for a covering to hide their shame or wish to be hidden inside the house or in some supernatural way to vanish from the eyes of the beholders. More to the point, at those moments when the male finds himself in a condition of weakness, he too becomes acutely aware that he has a body. Then, at the limits of pain, is when he perceives himself to be most like a woman.

Herakles, at the end of Sophocles' *Trachiniae,* when his flesh is being devoured by the poison of the fateful robe, appeals to his son:

> . . . Pity me
> For I seem pitiful to many others, crying
> and sobbing like a girl, and no one could ever say
> that he had seen this man act like that before.
> Always without a groan I followed a painful course.
> Now in my misery I am discovered a woman.
> (*Trach.* 1070–75)[19]

Sophocles' Ajax, in despair after the madness that the goddess Athena had sent upon him has abated and determined now to die a manly death that will restore his heroic image to himself, considers the temptation to yield through pity to his wife's entreaties. If he tempers his will, his tongue that is hard and firm like a sword, he will have blunted its sharp edge; he will have, in effect, feminized it, as he says *(ethēlunthēn),* for the sake of a woman (*Ajax* 650–52). A warrior man often likens himself to a sword; his mind is obdurate, his will and words are whetted like iron (cf. Parthenopaiosin Aeschylus, *Seven against Thebes* 529–30, 715). His is the instrument of power that wounds others, while his body remains impenetrable to outside forces. Ajax will harden his will; he will have his heroic death by the sword of iron. But how? By burying that sword in the earth and falling upon it, breaking through the flesh of his side (*pleuran diarrēx-*

---

19. The translation is that of Michael Jameson. Cf. Euripides, *Herakles* 1353–56.

anta, 834). As he violates the boundaries of his body, he also violates tragic convention by staging his death as a public act. Yet paradoxically, there is another anomaly in the method he chooses. Suicide is a solution in tragedy normally reserved for women—and what we are given to witness is this convention borrowed for a man's version of it. A heroic death, then, in the woman's way, a whetted will penetrated by a whetted weapon, befitting the curious ambiguities of this most masculine hero.[20]

My last example in this context is Hippolytos in Euripides' play. Refusing eros, refusing the touch and even the sight of a woman, he is brought back on stage in mortal agony after his horses stampeded in fright before the apparition of the bull from the sea. Then he cries out that pains dart through his head and spasms leap up in his brain, while his desire is now all for a sword to cleave himself in two and "put his life at last to bed" (*Hipp.* 1351–52, 1371–77). His symptoms are those of a woman, racked with the pain of childbirth or the torment of sexual desire.[21] We remember then Phaedra's last words, which prophesied that he would "share in her disease" (*Hipp.* 730–31): the deadly pangs of unrequited eros that earlier had reduced her to a sick and suffering body. Yet in that first scene, when no one on stage knows the cause of her malady, the chorus speaks in generic terms about the body of a woman, calling it a *dustropos harmonia,* an ill-tuned harmony. The female body suffers the misery of helplessness *(amēchania),* and is open to the breeze that darts through the womb in pregnancy as well as to the torments of eros.[22] This body is permanently at odds with itself, subject to a congenital dissonance between inside and outside. Woman can never forget her body as she experiences its inward pain, and she is not permitted to ignore its outward appearance in that finely tuned consciousness she acquires with respect to how she might seem to the eyes of others. Bodiliness defines her in the cultural system that associates her with physical processes of birth and death and emphasizes the material dimensions of her existence, as exempli-

20. Loraux (1987, 12) views Ajax's suicide as an unequivocal warrior's death. "Even suicide in tragedy obeys this firm rule that a man must die at a man's hands by the sword and with blood spilled. . . . Ajax kills himself by the sword, faithful to the end to his status as a hero who lives and dies in war where wounds are given and received." It is true, of course, that the sword is a man's weapon and that if women resort to it, they are violating the rules of gender. Yet it is also true that Ajax's death, by whatever means and in whatever mood, is still a suicide, an act the culture regards in itself as inherently shameful and therefore imagined far more as a feminine solution.

21. On the general question of the female body as the model of male suffering, see the superb study of Loraux 1981b. For these symptoms in the *Hippolytos,* see respectively Loraux 1981b, 58–59; Segal 1965, especially 122; and above, chapter 6.

22. See the discussion of this remarkable passage and its key function in the play in chapter 6 above, 237, 247–48.

fied, above all, in Hesiod's canonical myth of how the first woman, Pandora, was created.[23] Men too have bodies, of course, but in a system defined by gender the role of representing the corporeal side of life in its helplessness and submission to constraints is primarily assigned to women.

Thus, it is women who most often tend the bodies of others, washing the surface of the body or laying it out for its funeral. Theirs is the task to supply the clothing that covers the body, and they have a storehouse of robes that may encircle the male victim in textured folds. When men suffer or die in the theatrical space, the female is typically the cause. She seems to know, whether consciously or not, how vulnerable, how open—how mortal, in fact—is the human body. These figures may be goddesses like Aphrodite and Hera or, above all, the Erinyes, avenging ministers of retributive justice, but they may also be women, such as Clytemnestra, Deianeira, Hekabe, and, of course, Agave, the mother of Pentheus.[24]

In contrast, it is Pentheus, dressed as a woman, who makes the first discovery of his corporeal self. Before this he has defended himself militantly against any touch of the other. Now he allows Dionysos to make contact with his body and, in a grotesque parody of female coquetry, is eager for the god to adjust the details of his costume and to arrange the stray locks of hair peeping out from beneath the snood (*Bacchae* 925–38). With this laying on of hands, Dionysos breaches that physical integrity so prized by the male and prepares Pentheus for the terrible sequel, when the voyeur, coming as a spectator to see what he imagines are the women's illicit physical contacts with others, is himself exposed to view, his body becoming instead the focus of their ministering hands. Then they indeed touch his body, and in the strength induced by their maenadic state they easily tear it apart in the literal act of *sparagmos*.

In this primitive regression, women undo the body; its structures cannot hold, its limbs are unbound, and the masculine self, originally so intent on opposing himself to anything feminine, is fragmented and flies apart. Female violence may be viewed through the lens of role reversal, but in the Greek imagination the maenadic woman is regularly endowed with this power, especially over the masculine body. She herself is the model for the male who, when he too is seized like Euripides' Herakles in the grip of this madness, can only be described as "playing the bacchant" and imitating the part of the woman (*Herakles* 1119).[25]

23. On Pandora in the Hesiodic text, see especially the fine analyses by Vernant 1980, "Prometheus"; Vernant 1979b; and Loraux 1981a, "Race." See also above, chapter 2.
24. It is worth noting too that the details of the sacrifice of the virgin's body hold particular fascination for the messenger speeches of the relevant tragedies. See further chapter 5 above.
25. See further Padel 1983. It is remarkable that in Euripides' *Herakles,* where the great Herakles goes mad and kills his wife and children, the chorus in response compares

Theatrical Space

The second indispensable element of the theatrical experience is the space itself onstage in the Greek theater, where the human actors situate themselves and the theatrical action takes place before the spectator. By convention, this space is constructed as an outside in front of a façade of a building, usually a house or palace, with a door that leads to an inside, which is hidden from view. What happens inside must always in some way be brought outside—for example, through use of the wheeled platform called the *ekkuklēma*. This device is most often used to display the corpses of those bodies who have met their fatal doom within the house—visual proof of the violence that must also by convention take place offstage.[26] The ordinary business of entrances and exits, of comings and goings through the door of the house, maintains a symbolic dialectic between public and private, seen and unseen, open and secret, even known and unknown.[27]

In this simple mapping of spatial relations, the stage conventions chart the bounded areas of social relations between the genders, which assign men to the outside and women to the inside.[28] They also suggest an analogy to the tragic world itself, which in the course of its plot and actions inevitably comes to reveal its hidden and unknown dimensions.

Earlier I defined the tragic universe as one that is other than the self originally imagined it to be. Going one step further, we may add that tragedy is the epistemological form par excellence. What it does best, through the resources of the theater, is to chart a path from ignorance to knowledge, deception to revelation, misunderstanding to recognition. The characters act out and live through the consequences of having clung to a partial single view of the world and themselves.[29] In the process, in the conflicts and tensions that mark the relations between the opposing characters, all come in some way to experience the complexities of the world— its multiple dimensions, its deceptions and illusions. Inside and outside

---

him only with women (1016–27): the Danaids, who slew their husbands on their wedding night, and Procne, who slew her child in revenge for her husband's rape and mutilation of her sister, Philomela.

26. For discussion of this apparatus and the controversies over its use, see Padel 1990. The apparent parodies in Aristophanes of this device convince me of its use on the Attic stage of this time.

27. On the uses of these stage conventions and their relations of the inside/outside, see especially Dale 1969; Padel 1990; and chapter 6 above, 243–47.

28. The *locus classicus* is Xenophon's *Oikonomikos*. The best discussion is Vernant 1969.

29. See, for example, Vernant 1981a. This epistemological emphasis, therefore, both exploits and is conditioned by the special capacity of theater to represent and embody the interaction between other points of view, attitudes, gestures, and values.

organize the dramatic action of the drama, and these concepts refer not only to the shifting planes of reality (the known and the unknown) but also to the tragic self—both mind and body. They find their material referent in the house and the façade it presents to the outside world.

The house, let us now observe, is the property of the male and his family line. The *oikos* is the visual symbol of paternal heredity that entitles sons to succeed their fathers as proprietor of its wealth and movable goods and as ruler over its inhabitants. As the male in tragedy is often conflated with king, the house extends further as a locus of masculine power to include the sign of sovereignty over the city as a whole, and the solidity of its architectural structure symbolically guarantees the enduring stability of the social order. Yet the house, as we know, is primarily the proper domain of the woman, to which the social rules of the culture assign her, while its men go forth into the outside world to pursue manly accomplishments in war and politics.

Thus, in conflicts between house and city or between domestic and political concerns that are the recurrent preoccupations of tragic plots, the woman, whether wife or daughter, is shown as best representing the positive values and structures of the house, and she typically defends its interests in response to some masculine violation of its integrity. As a result of the stand she takes, however, the woman also represents a dangerous threat to male authority as an adversary in a power struggle that resonates throughout the entire social and political system, raising the terrifying specter of rule by women. Here we may note how disruptive is the presence of this feminine other, who in asserting legitimate values most associated with her social role is also perceived as illegitimately asserting the entitlements reserved for the masculine project of self. She never achieves these privileges in any permanent way. But in the contest over rights to control domestic space that the stage conventions exploit, the woman and not the man, by reason of her close identification with the house as her intimate scene, consistently rules the relations between inside and outside and shows herself as standing on the threshold betwixt and between.

Men find out in tragedy that they are likely to enter that interior domain mostly at their peril. Consider Agamemnon, as he walks upon the crimson carpets his wife has spread to lead him to his death at her hands within the house; or Hippolytos, confronted inside with the nurse's revelation to him of Phaedra's guilty secret, which is the beginning of his doom; or Polymestor, the Thracian king in Euripides' *Hekabe,* whom the Trojan queen lures into the tent so she may take a woman's revenge on him for killing her child, who had been entrusted to him for safekeeping.

As a general principle, the absent hero returns to his house either never to enter through its doors again, as in the extreme case of Herakles in the *Trachiniae,* or to meet with his own destruction within, as in the cases cited above, or finally, like Herakles in Euripides' play, to go mad once inside the house, slaying his wife and children and literally ensuring the fall of the house by toppling its supporting columns. On the other hand, if the male would successfully penetrate the interior of the house and reclaim it for his own, he typically requires feminine assistance, best exemplified in the pairing of Orestes with his sister Electra, in all the extant versions of Orestes' story.

Men imagine they can control that interior space by attempting to control the women within it. The men object—often violently, as Pentheus does in the *Bacchae*—when in the most dramatic reversal the women leave the stifling environment of the house to venture forth to the open (although equally uncivic) world of forest and mountains. But the king's authority lapses on all fronts. He is unable to bring back his Theban women from the mountains to put them in their rightful place and is compelled finally to meet them on their new terrain, with the results we already know. He fails, too, on domestic territory when he aims to lock up the other maenads (and their leader Dionysos) and imprison them in the house. Binding them with fetters, he discovers all too soon the futility of applying coercive force as they easily—magically—loosen themselves from his restraints. His larger demands for mastery over the house literally collapse when Dionysos sends the earthquake to shake the *oikos* to its foundations.

The situation of Pentheus leads to a further point. The king erects barriers around himself (and his psyche) against the invasion of Dionysos, even as he struggles to maintain the integrity of the house and the walled city of Thebes.[30] If tragedy, as I have suggested, can be defined as the epistemological genre, which continually calls into question what we know and how we think we know it, it often does so by confronting the assumptions of rational thought with those psychological exigencies that cannot be denied.

The master example of Pentheus gives another turn to the dialectic of inside and outside that focuses on the woman and the house as containers for the emotional energies of the self and the society. The house has many kinds of secrets that men do not know, and the challenge to male authority over it takes place on several levels—social, cognitive, and psychological. If men enter this domain, assuming their legitimate rights to its custody, only to meet with a welcome they had not foreseen, at the same time they also inevitably fail to lock up, to repress those powerful forces hidden in the recesses of the house. Quite the contrary: tragic process, for the most part, conveyed through the catalyzing person and actions of the feminine,

---

30. On the symbolic value of the house, see Wohlberg 1968; and the amplified discussion in Segal 1982, 86–94 and *passim*.

puts insistent pressure on the façade of the masculine self in order to bring
outside that which resides unacknowledged and unrecognized within.
Here in the *Bacchae,* where the inversion of roles is expressly posed in
spatial terms that send the women outside and situate the man within, the
stage conventions are used to their best effect as Pentheus leaves the interior space for the last time—for his liberation and for his destruction—
dressed, as we might now expect, like a woman.

The Plot

Third, we come to the plot itself, that which brings about the recognition,
the *anagnōrisis.* Aristotle describes its process as a combination of *desis*
(binding) and *lusis* (unbinding or dénouement). In its complex form he
calls it by the corresponding Greek term *sumplokē,* "interweaving," as
that which describes the fabric or texture of the play (*Poetics* 1455b).

At a higher level, these terms are even more suggestive, reminding us
how the tragic world works its ruinous effects through modes of entrapment and entanglement that cause its characters first to "stumble"
through ignorance and error and then to "fall" to their doom. In the elaborate tragic game, the metaphoric patterns of binding and unbinding continually exhibit reciprocal tension; as signs of constraint and necessity, on
the one hand, and of dissolution and death, on the other, they define the
parameters between which characters are caught in the "double bind."[31]

In the cognitive psychology of tragic man, inner choice and external
necessity (or *ēthos,* "character," and *daimōn,* "divine power") finally converge to sanction whatever form of tragic justice the plot demands for its
logical fulfillment. Thus the "nature of tragic action appears to be defined
by the simultaneous presence of a 'self' and something greater at work
that is divine."[32] In this sense, the gods finally may be said to direct the
energy of the action and may be understood retrospectively as supporting
and advancing the outcome of the myth.

Gods (frequently goddesses, as previously noted) sometimes appear
"in person" on stage, although most often they operate from afar as inhabiting that other, unknown dimension of existence that mortals may
only grasp dimly and generally too late. But it is remarkable how often
that energy is channeled through the feminine other, who serves as the
instrument of the gods even when she acts or seems to act on her own
terrain and for her own reasons, and even when she acts out of ignorance

---

31. For fuller discussion of these terms and their relation to the structures and structuring capacities of plots, see chapter 6 above, esp. 225–32.

32. Vernant 1981b, 51. His is the most nuanced discussion of the psychology of the
double determination that is often misperceived as a conflict between fate and free will.

or from partial knowledge of the tragic world she inhabits. Women frequently control the plot and the activity of plotting and manipulate the duplicities and illusions of the tragic world.

On the one hand, women's exclusion from the central area of masculine public life seems to be matched by their special access to those powers beyond men's control, to those outside forces that make sudden forays into human lives, unsettling all their normal assumptions. On the other hand, the same exclusion that relegates them to the inside as mistresses of the interior space equips them for deviousness and duplicity, gives them a talent, or at least a reputation, for weaving wiles and fabricating plots, marks of their double consciousness with regard to the world of men.

Tragedy is above all the art form that makes the most of what is called discrepant awareness—what one character knows and the other doesn't, or what all the characters don't know but the audience does. Thus, irony is tragedy's characteristic trope; several levels of meaning operate at the same time. Characters speak without realizing what they say or what their words might mean, and misreading is the typical and predictable response to the various cues that others give.

This pervasive irony may manifest itself in many ways, and it owes its effectiveness to a strong conviction about the ambiguous, even opaque nature of verbal communication that is reflected in the belief in oracles. These riddling, divine utterances invite their hearers to feats of interpretation or evasion and at the same time suggest, when disaster (or near disaster) is the outcome, how misguided and ignorant these human attempts are likely to be. Apollo and his oracle often serve as the primary source for this demonstration, as Oedipus, his most famous client, confirms. But other factors make for dramatic irony, particularly in connection with the deceptive powers of the feminine and the special verbal skills that accompany these.

Clytemnestra in Aeschylus's *Agamemnon* is the most powerful paradigm of the woman who plots, who through the riddling doubleness of her language builds the play to its climax in the murder of her husband within the house when she entangles him in the murderous web of the robe. Only Cassandra, another woman of second sight, perceives but cannot convince her listeners of what lies behind the guileful persuasion. The case of Phaedra, the virtuous wife in Euripides' *Hippolytos,* is also instructive. Caught in the conflict between desire and honor and determined to preserve her integrity at any cost, Theseus's queen, despite herself or rather in defense of that apparently indefensible feminine self, fabricates the lying message that will implicate Hippolytos as the cause of her death and lead to his entanglement in the reins of his own chariot.

The pattern holds even at the other end of the dramatic spectrum, in the late romantic plays of Euripides that shift to exotic locales, where the feminine other takes on a different configuration as the remote object of a mythic quest. Now men are sent forth, albeit unknowing, in search of the absent, forgotten woman who longs to return to the home and loved ones she has lost. In the process of rescuing the feminine, the men find out they have redeemed and refound a version of male heroic identity. But still it is the woman who plots and now openly devises a plan on stage before us, this time for the best of reasons: her own rescue and that of her menfolk. Consider Iphigenia in the *Iphigenia in Tauris* or Helen in the play of the same name. The men here are only adjuncts of the women; they propose escape schemes of their own but inevitably yield to and cooperate in the women's superior plans that all involve elaborate dramas of deception.

If we take a rapid inventory of the plot as intrigue in the extant plays of the tragic corpus, some interesting principles emerge.[33] First, the women's plots are more generally successful.[34] If men succeed, they do so precisely because they have allied themselves with women—for example, in the Euripidean plays just cited and more broadly in the various treatments of the Orestes story where Orestes succeeds in avenging his father through the murder of his mother because he has joined forces with his sister Electra. Thus, the recognition between the siblings must necessarily precede the *praxis* of vengeance, however and at what moment of the action the poet chooses to stage their reunion. In the *Choephoroi* of Aeschylus (the second play of the *Oresteia*), for example, only after the long interchange between himself, Electra, and the female chorus of libation-bearers is Orestes able at last to interpret Clytemnestra's dream. Thus psychologically armed, he is empowered to assume a stranger's disguise that will gain him successful entry into the feminine domain of the house.[35]

Second, although deceit and intrigue are condemned in woman, they are also seen as natural to her sphere of operations and the dictates of her nature.[36] For the man, however, resort to *dolos* (trickery) undermines masculine integrity and places his honor under the gravest of suspicions.

33. For discussions of intrigue plots in general, see especially Solmsen 1932; and Strohm 1949–50. See also the broader discussion of Muecke 1982a.

34. The *Ion* of Euripides, a play that is in many ways a precursor of New Comedy, foils the woman's plot against her unrecognized son (not without some fancy help from the gods) in order to bring about the joyful reunion. The play, I might add, is careful not to credit the woman Creousa as the one who first initiates the intrigue. See further chapter 7 above.

35. Euripides' *Electra* is still more complex, as the play separates the two acts of vengeance against Clytemnestra and her lover Aegisthus, and the venue has changed from the palace in Argos to the countryside where Electra lives with her farmer "husband." The old servant suggests the plot against Aegisthus (to take place outside in a sacred precinct), while Electra contrives the elaborate and doubly deceitful intrigue against Clytemnestra to lure her to her peasant dwelling.

36. This is a commonplace in tragic texts (as elsewhere): e.g., *Iphigenia in Tauris* 1032; *Medea* 834–35; *Andromache* 85; *Hippolytos* 480–81; *Ion* 483.

This deficit is best mitigated when the one to be deceived is a cruel barbarian king of another land (as in the late Euripidean plays), a ruler whose adversary status comes closer to the role of melodramatic villain.[37] The case of Orestes at home in Argos is even more informative in this regard. His success, it is true, depends on reunion with his sister, but the resort to trickery and disguise *(dolos, mēchanē)* entails a further risk to his masculine stature, no matter how urgent and obligatory his task of vengeance. Appeal to the higher authority of a god is an excellent and irrefutable way to justify this mode of action. Even so, Apollo (in both Aeschylus and Sophocles) further specifies the retribution as one that must exactly match the original crime: as she (Clytemnestra) killed, so must she be killed in turn—inside the house and by guile (Aeschylus, *Choephoroi* 556–59; Sophocles, *Electra* 32–37).

Sophocles' *Trachiniae,* that schematic paradigm of gender relations, again supplies an excellent version of the norm. Herakles too practices deception, first to conquer the girl Iole, the current object of his erotic desire and the immediate cause of all his woe, and afterward to introduce her secretly into the house. But in his case, deception returns quite literally (and most dramatically) against him. His deception, revealed by others to his wife, activates the Centaur's ruse, plotted long ago when he entrusted the deadly poison in the guise of a secret love charm to Deianeira's safe-keeping inside the house. The point is that, innocent as Deianeira may be of conscious intent to harm her husband, she still proves a far better and more successful plotter than he. Masculine guile is repaid in full—even when retaliation does not openly bear the name of revenge.

If this Herakles conforms so well to the normative pattern, Ajax, that other great hero, does not. His is a curious case, but one whose anomaly may prove the point. At the crucial moment of Sophocles' play, having determined to die an honorable death, he delivers a deceptive speech that suggests he has changed his mind and has learned to bend with the vicissitudes of time and change (Sophocles, *Ajax* 644–718). With this speech he puts off those who would guard him and gains the solitude he needs to stage the elaborate suicide to which I have earlier referred. Critics have energetically contested the status of this speech as truth or lie. For while the outcome of the plot tells us that Ajax has not undergone any radical conversion of spirit, his words also seem to indicate that he has arrived at the kind of tragic knowledge we recognize as intrinsically true to the genre. How then can we read the enigma of this speech? Better still, how

---

37. Even in these plays, masculine honor is protected, as it were, in that each man (Orestes, Menelaus) first proposes force before he accedes to the woman's practical, clever schemes (Iphigenia, Helen), and each, just before the end, is permitted a display of manly strength against the forces of the barbarian king in question.

can we read Ajax himself, the traditional epic hero, who would resort to a deceptive plot that goes against the grain of strict masculine values in which he has put too much store? This is the man, after all, who could not, would not endure, as the belated oracle now riddlingly suggests for his salvation, to remain *inside* the tent even for the space of one single day (792–802). But the ambiguities of this hero who in his madness has not acted a hero's part and the question of a dishonor finally converted to honor together account for the interesting ambiguities of his later actions, which rewrite the theatrical conventions associated with gender. Thus, the deceptive speech makes sense as a feminine strategy enlisted in the service of restoring an unequivocal manliness he can only achieve, as I suggested before, by dying the manly death—heroically and publicly on stage—in the woman's way.

When other male characters—those not designated as tragic figures in the dramatic action—seek to deceive, their devices generally flounder, and such men as these are dismissed out of hand. Agamemnon, so easily duped by his wife in Aeschylus's play, miserably fails, for his part, when in Euripides' *Iphigenia in Aulis* he and Menelaos plot to bring Iphigenia as a sacrifice for the expedition to Troy under the pretext of a marriage with Achilles. Clytemnestra finds them out by a fortuitous accident, and the sacrifice takes place only through Iphigenia's voluntary and open choice of the role assigned to her by her father and the myth. Most telling of all, Odysseus, the master plotter on his own epic territory (and a familiar trickster figure in the plots of mischievous satyr plays), only sees his plans go awry on the tragic stage—in Sophocles' *Philoctetes* when Neoptolemos, son of Achilles, rejects finally the man and his plans, the man of whom his father had said in the *Iliad,* "I hate like the gates of Hades a man who hides one thing in his heart and speaks another" (9.312–13).[38]

The *Bacchae,* as we might expect, furnishes the most striking example of the uses of plotting and exposes the conventions of its theatrical deployment as the pivotal point around which the entire play revolves and on which the peripeteia depends. All the operative terms come into play—secrecy, guile, entrapment, and femininity—as Dionysos and Pentheus en-

---

38. A man's plots are often associated with villainy. Orestes, in Euripides' *Andromache,* shamefully engineers a murderous plot offstage against Neoptolemos at Delphi. As for Odysseus, with the exception of his sympathetic role in the *Ajax,* he is most often portrayed as a man of evil counsel or an archdeceiver. He would have been at his worst in Euripides' lost play, the *Palamedes,* where through false testimony he brings about the downfall of his rival in inventive skills. At best, he is called a crafty and sophistic demagogue, whose persuasive powers are used in the service of political expediency. He comes to epitomize the moral callousness of the Greek victors in the aftermath of Troy's defeat (e.g., *Hekabe, Troades*). On the interesting function of Odysseus in the *Hekabe,* see chapter 5.

gage in their power struggle over one other, the city, the women, and ultimately the plot itself. Pentheus aligns himself with physical force as the masculine means to victory, trying and failing to bind his adversary (and his followers) and ready to dress as a soldier and deploy an army for a military battle against the women. Dionysos retaliates against threats of force at this critical moment with a devious plot: to entice Pentheus to go alone to the mountains in secrecy.

Dionysos persuades Pentheus to trade his ready reliance on physical combat for that other, diametrically opposite mode of action, resort to a deceptive ploy of self-concealment. In other words, Dionysos's strategy for victory over his opponent involves first luring him into embracing the same kind of strategy. They are co-conspirators now, plotting together but for ultimately divergent results; for one the intrigue will succeed in every respect, and for the other it will disastrously fail.

But the first victory over Pentheus already lies in his agreeing to shift his tactics from open force to secret spying; the second, which follows directly upon the first, is the change in dress from male to female, which, as Dionysos argues, is essential for the success of the expedition. These two steps, however, imply each other: a woman is adept at contriving devious plots, the charge Pentheus has laid against both Dionysos and the maenads (e.g., 475, 487, 805–6), while the costume Pentheus dons matches and visually represents the feminine nature of the strategy he has already chosen. But in the ways of women Pentheus is only an impostor, easily betrayed by the other, superior plotter. Hence his venture into female territory is truly a trespass and can only recoil against him for his own doom.

Mimesis

I come now, very briefly, to my fourth and most inclusive element: mimesis itself, the art of imitation through which characters are rendered lifelike, and through which plot and action offer some adequate representation of reality. Yet mimesis also focuses attention on the status of theater as illusion, disguise, double dealing, and pretense. There is a serious and wonderful paradox here. For while theater resorts continually, as it must, to artifice, to techniques of make-believe that can only resemble the real, this allows it to better represent the larger world outside, subject to the deceptions, the gaps in knowledge, the tangled necessities, and all the tensions and conflicts of a complex existence.

Role playing is what actors must literally do in the theater as they don their costumes and masks to impersonate an other—whether king or servant, mortal or god, Greek or barbarian, man or woman. But the reverse side of the coin is to be dubbed an actor, a *hypokritēs,* one who is *only* playing a role, offering the other only a persona *(prosōpon)* that does not match what lies behind the mask.

Recognition *(anagnōrisis)* of persons whose identities were unknown or mistaken is a typical and even focal device of tragic action. But this literal type of recognition is the overtly theatrical event that condenses the epistemological bias of the entire phenomenon of drama. Thus, recognition extends along a far wider spectrum, embracing the world, the other, and the self. The problem of accurately reading the other is a continuing, obsessive concern in Greek tragedy that increases in urgency as the genre displays a greater self-consciousness with regard to its own theatrical resources. But recognition of the unknown self, as for Oedipus, or of the hidden self, as for Pentheus or even Deianeira, is perhaps the most elusive but also the most psychologically significant innovation of the tragic stage. This feature, above all, suggests what the invention of theater for and in the city might imply about an emerging image of the private individual and the growing pains of masculine identity.[39]

This double dimension of role playing is a feature that Greek society would perceive as not exclusively but yet fundamentally feminine.[40] Woman is the mimetic creature par excellence, ever since Hesiod's Zeus created her as an imitation with the aid of the other artisan gods and adorned her with a deceptive allure.[41] Woman is perennially under suspicion as the one who acts a part—that of the virtuous wife—but hides other thoughts and feelings, dangerous to men, within her heart and within the house. "Counterfeit evil" is the charge that Hippolytos is not alone in bringing against the *genos gunaikōn,* "the race of women," for woman has the best capacity, by her nature and origin, to say one thing and hide another in her heart, to sow the doubt in her husband's mind, to cite perhaps the radical cause, that the child she bears may or may not be his.[42]

Woman speaks on the tragic stage, transgressing the social rules if she speaks on her own behalf. In this role, her speech and action involve her

39. "The covert theme of all drama," Goldman (1975, 123) suggests, "is identification, the establishment of a self that in some way transcends the confusions of self."

40. Odysseus is the exemplar in the masculine sphere, but he does not generically represent "the race of men," and this adaptable survivor (with strong affinities to the feminine) is not a candidate for tragedy in the dramatic milieu. See note 38 above.

41. Earlier I alluded to the creation of Pandora as exemplifying the physical, "creaturely" side of life. I emphasize now the other aspect of woman's creation as an object cunningly wrought; she is a deceptive gift in return for Prometheus's deception of Zeus, herself endowed with a crafty intelligence. Woman, therefore, embodies both extremes of nature and culture that together conspire to waste a man's substance and dry him up before his time.

42. For a similar idea, see Bergren 1983, 74, 77.

in the ensemble of tragic experience and thereby earn her the right to tragic suffering. But by virtue of the conflicts generated by her social position and ambiguously defined between inside and outside, interior self and exterior identity, the woman is already more of a "character" than the man, who as an actor is far more limited to his public social and political roles. Woman comes equipped with a "natural" awareness of the complexities that men would resist, if they could. Situated in her more restrictive and sedentary position in the world, she is permitted, even asked, to reflect more deeply, like Phaedra, on the paradoxes of herself. Through these she can come closer to understanding the paradoxes of the world that she, much better than men, seems to know is subject to irreconcilable conflict, subject as well to time, flux, and change (the very themes, I might add, of Ajax's great deceptive speech). Hence the final paradox may be that theater uses the feminine for the purposes of imagining a fuller model for the masculine self, and "playing the other" opens that self to those often banned emotions of fear and pity.

Woman may be thought to speak double, and sometimes she does. But she also sees double; the culture has taught her that too, and it is perhaps no accident that only when Pentheus dresses as a woman does he see double for the first time—two suns, two Thebeses (Euripides, *Bacch.* 918–19). This is a symptom of madness, to be sure, attributed by the ancient commentators to inebriation, but madness is the emblem of the feminine, and seeing double is also the emblem of a double consciousness that a man acquires by dressing like a woman and entering into the theatrical illusion. The fact of that dressing up already demonstrates the premise in unequivocal and theatrical terms.

The feminine figure onstage is tragic; she is also the mistress of mimesis, the heart and soul of the theater. The feminine instructs the other through her own example—that is, in her own name and under her own experience—but also through her ability to teach the other, whether Pentheus or Dionysos, to impersonate her.

This brief discussion can only suggest how closely the tragic genre in its theatrical form, representation, and content is linked to Greek notions of gender, and how for the most part man is undone (or at times redeemed) by feminine forces or himself undergoes some type of "feminine" experience. On the simplest level, this experience involves a shift, at the crucial moment of the peripeteia, from active to passive, from mastery over the self and others to surrender and grief. Sometimes there is madness, always suffering and pathos, and this in turn leads to expressions of lamentation and pity from the chorus or the characters. In a more complex view, tragedy, understood as the worship of Dionysos, expands an awareness of the world and the self through the drama of "playing the other," whose mythic and cultic affinities with the god logically connect the god of women to the lord of the theater.

If drama tests masculine values only to find that these alone are inadequate to the complexity of the new situation, it also, as Linda Bamber remarks (with respect to Shakespeare), "does not dismiss them"; rather, it most often shows that manliness and self-assertion need no longer compete with pity and even forgiveness.[43] Moreover, the male characters whose sufferings are the most stringent and most reductive of self, like Herakles, are also allowed to discover the internal strength for transcending them.[44] In the end, tragedy arrives at closures that generally reassert male, often paternal (or civic), structures of authority, but before that the work of the drama is to open up the masculine view of the universe. It typically does so, as we have seen, through energizing the theatrical resources of the female and concomitantly enervating the male as the price of initiating actor and spectator into new and unsettling modes of feeling, seeing, and knowing.

We can trace the persistence of this "initiatory" process from the work of the first tragic poet to that of the third.[45] History has cunningly arranged it that Euripides' last play, the *Bacchae,* should also refer back to the archaic scenario that underlies the ritual conditions of the theater.[46] Yet viewed in its metatheatrical aspects, the *Bacchae* also makes claims to be considered in a diachronic perspective as a belated examplar of the genre that by now has developed a keen awareness of its own properties and conventions. As a result, the play is in a position to exemplify and reflect what was always implicit in the theater, and at the same time, by the admission of that theatrical awareness, to transform its object of reflection and reorient it in new directions.

If my basic hypothesis is valid, then the distinctive features of Euripidean theater (which are more obvious in plays other than the *Bacchae*) may lend support to my suggestion about the intimate relations between the feminine and the theater. Thus, I see the distinctive traits of Euripidean drama as various and interlocking functions of one another: his greater interest in and skill at subtly portraying the psychology of female characters and his general emphasis on interior states of mind as well as on the private emotional life of the individual, most often located in the feminine

43. This is a combined quotation and paraphrase (with one small alteration) of Bamber 1982, 15.

44. In this respect, there are strong continuities with the earlier epic tradition. See the interesting conclusions of Monsacré 1984, 199–204.

45. We might note that initiation into the "real" Eleusinian mysteries involved some forms of imitating the specifically feminine experiences of Demeter and Kore.

46. More accurately, it is one of the last, produced posthumously in Athens, as was the *Iphigenia in Aulis.*

situation. We may add to these his particular fondness for plots of complex intrigue (usually suggested by women) that use strategies of trickery,
deceit, contrivance, and devising *(dolos, apatē, technē, mēchanē)* and that,
with their resort to disguise and role playing, are an explicit sign of an
enhanced theatricality. Finally, we may include more generally Euripides'
thematic concern with metaphysical questions of reality and illusion in the
world.

The *Helen* is the most splendid example, because it is a drama that
allows itself the fullest play with the resources of theater and uses these to
direct the most elaborate inquiry into the complexities of being and seeming and the paradoxical crossings of illusion and reality.[47] The source of
the confusion is the ontological status of the feminine itself. There are two
Helens: the real, chaste version who was left in Egypt and never went to
Troy, and the more traditional adulterous wife whom Menelaos thinks he
has recovered at Troy but who is really a phantom, an *eidōlon,* imperson-
ating Helen's true self. I alluded earlier to the symbolic inferences we might
draw from Pentheus dressing as a woman and seeing double for the first
time. Here in the *Helen,* where double vision rules the play in every respect, the woman is both a character, who to her irremediable sorrow
learns firsthand about the fundamental problems of the self's identity, and
at the same time an objective referent through which the man must question all his previous perceptions of the world. What is more, the essential
strategy for ensuring the success of the intrigue she invents for their rescue
requires that he too adopt a disguise and pretend to be another than himself, allowing her to recount the most potentially dangerous fiction that
the real Menelaos has died.

The uses of the play have their deadly serious side for all concerned,
and the unhappy residue of spoiled lives persists behind the successful outcome of the play. But for desire of this woman, whether in her imagined
or real persona, the man willingly enters into the theatrical game and
shows a capacity now to act a part and enter into a stage illusion. The
Helen is a rare play; it pushes its original improbable (and theatrical)
premises as far as they can go, but the uxorious Menelaos is also a novelty,
and the erotic element already diverts the play from the more typical tragic
mode to that of romance. In this new kind of play-world Euripides invents,
the uses to which he puts the feminine and the theater may be seen as the
logical result of the premises of tragedy. On the other hand, by disclosing
those premises too well, he also revises them and subverts the genre that
was so firmly bound up with the context of the masculine civic world.

47. For the interplay of illusion and reality, see Solmsen 1934; Pippin [Burnett] 1960;
Segal 1971; and Walsh 1984, 96–106. On the connections with theater and femininity in the
context of comic parody, see below, chapter 9, 392–95.

Thus, in this sense, Euripides may be said to have "feminized" tragedy and, like his Dionysos in the *Bacchae,* to have laid himself open to the scorn that accrues to those men who consort with women. Aristophanic comedy, which loves to lampoon Euripides and all his newfangled ideas, continually presses the scandal of his erotic dramas, especially those that let women speak more boldly (and hence more shamefully) upon the stage, until Aristophanes, in his own late play the *Frogs,* evaluates the development of the tragic genre by staging an open contest between the old poet, Aeschylus, and the new, Euripides (755–1853).

At stake is the choice of which poet Dionysos should bring back from the underworld to the city and theater of Athens. Who is more worthy to save the city, which seems to link its loss of political potency to the absence of a fertile, potent poet in the tragic theater? Broadly stated, the contest develops into one between masculine and feminine sides, with Aeschylus espousing a manly, virile art that exhorts its citizens to military valor and Euripides representing a feminine, slender Muse who is weaker and more insubstantial, leaning toward the sensual and the pathetic. Not surprisingly, when these two are tested in the scales, Aeschylean tragedy outweighs the Euripidean by its superior mass and weight. Dionysos therefore abandons his original desire for Euripides, to whose seductive allure he had earlier succumbed, in favor of resurrecting the heroic warrior energies of the earlier poet and, by extension, of the glorious past.[48] Aristophanes, as is typical, assumes that when things go badly for men and masculine interests, the cause lies in a decay of moral and aesthetic values, from which he slides easily into hints of effeminacy and all that that charge implies.

In any case, the solution of the *Frogs* in bringing back the archaic spirit of Aeschylus as a solution to the city's problems is also a formal, generic one. It is predicated on the controlling convention of Old Comedy that fulfills its festive function of social renewal by consistently choosing the idealized past over the distressing, chaotic present, even as it prefers to rejuvenate the old (father) rather than, as in New Comedy, to promote the young (son). Moreover, the comic poet paints with a broad, satirical brush, and whatever the justice or truth of the cause he thinks he is advancing (and *his* play, of course, is what he imagines will save the city), he has the generic right to misrepresent, and how he does it here affects Aeschylus even more than Euripides.

Leaving aside the fact that Euripides too has his military and patriotic plays (e.g., *Heracleidae, Suppliants, Erechtheus*), Aristophanes would have us believe that the essence of the *Seven against Thebes,* that drama "full

---

48. I simplify here the terms of the debate. Both sides are thoroughly satirized in this brilliant parody. For an excellent discussion, see Walsh 1984, 80–97.

of Ares" invoked to support Aeschylus's case, was some conventional treatment of military prowess. It was rather a tragedy concerning the sons of Oedipus and the dangers they posed to the safety of the city by their resort to armed combat in the style of the old heroic duel, while the function of the avenging Erinys returning to fulfill the father's curse conforms precisely, even schematically, to the rules of the feminine in the theater as I have earlier outlined them.[49]

Nevertheless, Aristophanes is a witness we cannot afford to ignore. He speaks about the theater from within. Skewed as his caricature of Euripides (and his comic genre) may be, his strategy of clustering the poet's theatrical, psychological, and noetic innovations around a particular affinity for the feminine is valuable testimony to a popular contemporary perception of Euripidean theater, even if it is bought at the price of suppressing the strong continuities with earlier drama.

Along the same lines, we may even be able to swallow Aristophanes' parting shot, which implies that Euripides' loss of the tragic art is due to "sitting at the feet of Socrates" (1491–95), another favorite target for comic misrepresentation. Aristophanic comedy may be justified in singling out Euripides and Socrates as spokesmen for the new intellectual trends that confuse and unsettle the older, simpler (and hence more manly) values of the city. But philosophy would never consort with tragedy, which it comes to see as its implacable rival in laying claim to teach the truth, to impart knowledge, to improve its fellow citizens—and without doubt to save the city.

Socrates—as Plato in the next generation has him argue—makes no distinction whatsoever among any of the tragic poets when he comes to discuss the theatrical arts. Indeed, he founds his critique of drama on Homer, whom he characterizes as the first teacher and guide of tragedy.[50] The same Aeschylean play *(Seven against Thebes)* is invoked again when Socrates's interlocutor in the *Republic* first quotes one of its famous verses in an appropriate context, only at the next moment to invert the meaning of the lines that follow it by applying them to the unjust man rather than to the just.[51] The argument in Plato between tragedy and philosophy is well known, and it is not my intention to air all the usual questions or to

49. See Zeitlin 1982a, for fuller discussion; on gender in the play, see Zeitlin 1990. Cornford (1914, 162–63) takes Aristophanes' two adversaries as representative of contrasting stock types of impostors: Euripides the Learned Doctor (or professor) and Aeschylus the Miles Gloriosus.

50. See especially *Republic* 595c, 598d, 605c–d, 607a, 602b.

51. *Republic* 2.366a–b, cf. 361b–c. Significantly, the verse in question (referring to the Argive seer, Amphiaraos) reads: "I would rather be noble *[aristos]* than seem so." The Aeschylean quotations precede the discussion of the mimetic arts in Book 3; their misuse may not be fortuitous.

resolve the time-worn dilemmas. But I do suggest that Plato, standing out-side the drama, can be called in as a last witness to support my claims about the intrinsic links between femininity and theater, viewed now from a wholly negative perspective. Plato's insistence on banishing tragedy from his ideal state and his consistent distaste throughout his writings for the tragic poets, whom he sometimes associates quite closely with sophists and rhetoricians, are based on several complex and disparate factors. But in addition to the explicitly philosophical issues, I argue that Plato's posi-tion on theater can also be illuminated by considering its relationship to his notions of gender and his attitudes toward the feminine.[52]

Strange as it may seem, Plato's aim is not all that remote from what Aris-tophanes wants in the *Frogs*. The project is more far reaching in every respect, and the means will forever change the shape of Western thought. But like Aristophanes, Plato is concerned with restoring men and their morals in the city, and again like the comic poet, he insists on the relevance of aesthetic style and form. Briefly put, for the purposes of this discussion, Plato's larger concerns may also be translated into his general desire to remake man in a masculine society and through philosophical training to purify and enhance traditional heroic notions of manliness *(andreia)* in a new, revised version in which courage, vigilance, self-sufficiency, and strength may be better directed toward the improvement of self and society.

Certainly, Plato comes closest to codifying under the name of philoso-phy the dream of the Greek male for a world that is constituted as his alone, where he might give birth to himself and aspire finally to an im-mortal status he has always craved. In tragedy, this desire leads to disaster, most often, as we have seen, through the resistance of the gods—and of the women. Philosophy, on the other hand, offers the promise of success in this endeavor, provided one follows the patterns that are carefully de-signed to retrain the masculine self.

It may be objected that Plato breaks with the old stereotypes of gender when he insists that women may be just like men with the exception of a natural inferiority in physical strength, which does not disqualify them from participating as guardians (and even warriors) in his vision of the ideal city in the *Republic*. This is a revolutionary proposal whose signifi-cance we ought not to minimize.[53]

But we should note that this reevaluation of women's capacities does not really upgrade the feminine in its differences from the masculine. On

---

52. I include in the discussion the relevant portions of *Republic, Gorgias,* and *Laws,* to be followed by the *Symposium.*
53. This issue deserves far more attention than space permits here.

the contrary, Plato defuses the distinctive power of the feminine when he would abolish the family and the domestic sphere in which that influence operated. If he includes the participation of certain women who may prove to possess masculine abilities, it is precisely because in the *Republic* he believes that they may be successfully taught to imitate the masculine model. Even here, the principle of equality falters when Plato would reward men who have distinguished themselves in battle with special breeding privileges but does not suggest granting the same or any other special opportunities to their female counterparts. This may or may not be a trivial slip (or finally, too impractical to consider, given the differences in male and female biological roles in procreation). It is striking, however, that elsewhere in Plato's work femininity generally plays its usual role of negative foil to the masculine as it heads the long list of undesirable models for men that descends to the servile, the buffoonish, the bestial, and the nonhuman (*Rep.* 3.395d–96b).

Plato's attack on tragedy and its traditional repertory operates on several fronts: he objects to the deceptive nature of theatricality as a misleading and deficient imitation of reality, deplores the often unworthy quality of what or who is being imitated, and insists on the damaging effects such imitations are liable to produce on the actors and spectators in the theater.[54]

For the first item, I would not go so far as to claim that Plato explicitly refers the art of making illusions to the feminine per se, even if women, like children, are most susceptible to its charms (e.g., *Laws* 658d, 817c) and most likely to tell those lying stories about the gods to their young (*Rep.* 377c). But Plato's interest never focuses for long on women as such. Rather, his concern is with the inferior type of man, who deceptively passes off appearances for truth and who appeals to the inferior parts of the self (and the citizenry) that are likely to yield to the emotions and pleasures (not lessons) of make-believe. Plato confirms the conventional dictum that woman is inclined by nature to be secretive *(lathraiōteron)* and crafty *(epiklopōteron)* because of her intrinsic weakness or lack of strength *(to asthenes)* and concomitantly that her natural potential for virtue is inferior to a man's (*Laws* 781a–b). He hardly sees her (or her representation), however, as a powerful acting force in the world of men.[55]

---

54. Tragedy is the real target, despite the remarks about epic poetry and comedy. See especially *Laws* 816d–e, 935d–36b, for comedy, and 817a–d for tragedy, where Plato expressly sets up the legislators as authors of their own true tragedies as "rivals . . . artists and actors of the fairest drama."

55. One single exception is the woman (wife and mother) who by her nagging and greed instigates in her son the slide toward timocratic behavior (*Republic* 549c–e). We will shortly consider the function of Plato's most famous woman, the priestess Diotima in the *Symposium*.

But by a whole series of innuendos and juxtapositions, poets (and artists) are enrolled in the ranks of male trickster figures who fall furthest from the ideal of manliness and seek only to cajole, seduce, and pander to the tastes of their audience. Imitators (artists and musicians) and poets and their entourage of actors, dancers, and producers join the multitude of callings that are signs of the luxury that corrupts the primitive city. These figures directly precede those "makers of all sorts of goods, especially those that have to do with women's adornment," to be followed in the list by those servants like "beauty-shop ladies, barbers, cooks, and confectioners" (Rep. 373b–c).

Once assimilated to the broader category of sophistics, dramatic art, reduced finally to prose rhetoric on a par with oratory, shares in the same field of reference that likens their false imitations of justice to those activities practiced by and for women: cookery (especially confectionery), which "puts on the mask of medicine and pretends to know what foods are best for the body" (Gorgias 464c–d), and beauty culture, "the counterfeit to physical training . . . a mischievous, swindling, base, servile trade, which creates an illusion by the use of artificial adjuncts and make-up and depilatories and costume" (Gorgias 465b–c). All these arts traffic in deceptive appearances, and their effect on others is to pander to the appetites and to the pleasures of gratification.

The Gorgias stresses a certain sensual, effeminate roster of pleasures. But the Republic, in which Plato directly addresses the emotional power of the tragic, emphasizes the experience of pain and suffering, and evaluates its effects on those who act in and attend the tragic spectacles. Here the association with the feminine is clear and explicit, reiterated each time Plato returns to the topic. When heroes are shown to weep and lament their misfortunes, they are not only endorsing a false theology about the justice of the gods but are weakening themselves and others by their indulgence in womanish grief (Rep. 387e–88a, 605d–e). Such a man does not remain steadfast to himself, exercising self-control and rationally pondering the meaning of the events that have happened to him. Rather he gives way to cowardice, terror, and a host of conflicting, changeful emotions that ill suit the model of a brave and noble manliness that the state (and the soul) requires. Worst of all, he entices the spectators into the pleasures of vicariously identifying with his pitiable state and ends by setting them the example they unfortunately will learn to imitate for themselves.[56]

56. The ostensible motive for banning poets in Book 3 is the education of the young guardians to protect the city. Courage in battle is the model for control over warring forces within the self, as is emphasized in the second discussion of imitation in Book 10. Cowardice is the radically feminine trait, despite Plato's willingness to train selected women as guard-

For Plato, who so often strives to efface or remove all mixture, confusion, and changeability, the theory of drama is simple because, stripped down to essences, his categories are also simple. The mobility of temporary reversals and dialectical play with opposites already introduces a cognitive complexity that is the sign itself of a dangerous indeterminacy; it undermines the principle of like to like that governs much of his thinking and that is designed, by its literalness, to reinforce a simple stability. At the most inclusive level is the dictum that no man can play more than one part, in life or in the theater (e.g., *Republic* 3.394e–95b).

The other is always weaker than and inferior to the self, whose idealization requires that once perfectly established, it cannot change and still be itself. That lack of strength (attributable to the lack of mastery by the rational faculty and hence equatable finally to a lack of wisdom) can be most easily codified according to the conventional terms of the society under the name of the feminine other, to include the cognate negative traits of cowardice, fearfulness, and emotional lability. Hence, in Plato's reductive view of drama and of gender, playing the other is a species of wrongful imitation that threatens to infect reality and degrade the aspiring, virile self. It is therefore forbidden, above all, "for a man, being a man—in training, in fact, to become a good/brave man"—to imitate a woman in any way whatsoever: "whether old or young, whether railing against her husband, or boasting of a happiness which she imagines can rival the gods, or overwhelmed with grief and misfortune; much less a woman in love, or sick, or in labor" (*Rep.* 3.395d–e). Men are neither permitted to impersonate a woman nor to show themselves in a male persona as undergoing the experiences of a woman—precisely the routes I have proposed as leading to masculine initiation into the lessons (and benefits) of the tragic world.

Limited as his discussion of theater may be, Plato, as a spectator who fails to come under the spell of tragic mimesis (or who perhaps once did and was cured), nonetheless darkly confirms the inextricable relationship between theater and the feminine. Tragedy cannot control the ambiguities of role playing, most particularly when the male actor is called upon to

---

ians. (The *locus classicus* is *Timaeus* 90e–91a, in which Plato describes the first creation of women as due to "creatures generated as men who proved themselves cowardly and spent their lives in wrongdoing and were transformed at their second incarnation into women.") I simplify Plato's intricate argument, as he further sees this lack of control over the emotions, engendered by tragedy, as leading to an unruliness and violence he does not specify as feminine. Yet the tyrannical man, the most "theatrical" in Plato's view, whose exterior pomp and costume does not at all match his inner self (*Republic* 577b), is seen ultimately as a slave to his passions who becomes so fearful that he "lives for the most part cowering in the house like a woman" (*Republic* 579b–c).

represent the woman who herself is not under control, either because she is actively unruly or because she succumbs to the pressures of her bodily nature. More generally, tragedy by its nature and intention can make no solid provision for controlling the ambiguities of a world view that theater is expressly designed to represent. Thus Plato, from his point of view, is entitled to deny to "the solemn and marvelous *poiēsis* of tragedy" the very task we might agree it is well equipped to accomplish, that of imparting "beneficial if unpleasing truths," and to claim instead that it gives its credulous and vulgar audience what it desires to see and hear (*Gorgias* 502b).

Plato goes still further into the matter of gender and drama in the playful contest he stages between theater and philosophy in the *Symposium*, where the party to celebrate the recent victory of the tragic poet Agathon at the City Dionysia ends with the crowning of Socrates instead of Agathon. In mounting his own rival drama to explore the subject of *erōs*, Plato excludes the presence of the feminine at the banquet but subtly and significantly uses the categories of effeminacy and femininity to enhance the philosophical outlook that is meant to include and supersede the appeal of the theater.

The *Symposium* is one of Plato's most artful and complex dialogues and deserves, of course, much fuller discussion than can be undertaken here.[57] It is established early on that love of women is an inferior sort of *erōs* (181a–d). This is not the crucial point. But we may note in our context the persuasive if unfair value of using Agathon as the representative of all tragic art. Agathon speaks second to last, just before Socrates, and in his flowery speech on *erōs*, which parodies perhaps the play that earned him the tragic victory (*Anthos* [or *Antheus*], "flower"), he demonstrates the soft and effeminate nature for which he was known and which Aristophanes wickedly lampoons in his comic drama (e.g., *Thesmophoriazousae*).[58] Although at the end of the dialogue Aristophanes is made to fall asleep before Agathon, thus establishing his rank in a hierarchy that leads upward from comedy to tragedy and then to philosophy, the comic poet is represented as a far more robust character than the tragic poet, and his

57. In particular, the discussion would benefit from including the important contribution made by Alcibiades, the disruptive latecomer and party crasher, but this would not in any case substantially alter my basic argument.

58. In this comedy, which satirizes Euripidean tragedy through the women's indignation at the poet for his unflattering (and oversexed) portraits of them, Agathon comes off as the truly effeminate male by contrast to the trickster (but more manly) figure of Euripides. Agathon appears in feminine accessories, claiming that to write female parts for the theater one must dress as a woman. He refuses to infiltrate the women's festival on the grounds that he would provide unfair competition for the "real" women and finally supplies the feminine costume for Euripides' kinsman, who has been persuaded to go instead. See further chapter 9 below, esp. 383–86.

well-known contribution to the theme of *erōs* is more memorable and more substantial.[59] The contrast is even more striking between the love-lorn Agathon and Socrates, whose physical endurance and resistance to pederastic temptation attest to the remarkable self-control on the part of this soldier/philosopher/lover/hero.

Philosophy, however, appropriates for its own use the one kind of feminine authority the culture acknowledges as legitimate when Socrates names the prophetic priestess Diotima as the source of his initiation long ago into the sacred mysteries of Eros and as the author of the inspiring discourse on *erōs* he now is about to deliver. The feminine retains here her more "instinctive" alliance with the erotic as well as her mysterious connection with that other world and its secrets whose power we have come to recognize when manifested in the theater. Armed with the prestige of her sacred vocation, the woman is called upon to instruct men as to how they might transcend feminine influence (paradoxically, by imitating to some degree the feminine roles in sex and procreation) and, through the sublimations of pederastic love, even give birth to themselves.[60]

In Plato's counter-drama, the female as benevolent priestess has no cause of her own to protect and no conflictual interests to distract her. She is then free to lend wholehearted support to the cause of men and to transmit to them a wisdom without tragic pain that may become entirely theirs. She imparts a myth about the genealogy of Eros that makes the erotic principle a male child and explains his nature by assigning potency and presence to his father, Poros (Ways and Means), and a famished emptiness to his mother, Penia (Poverty), who deceitfully (and characteristically) tricks the one who is endowed to consort with the one who is not.

In suborning theater as well as the feminine, Plato's drama puts the former to sleep in the presence of the wakeful philosopher and transfers feminine oracular power to Socrates—the midwife—who also incorporates the Dionysiac into his satyrlike image of Silenos, appropriately imagined as a form of statue, which when opened reveals the hidden figure of a god. Socrates, in a sense, finally rewrites the feminine under the name of a phallus that is both sublimated and restored: the midwife figure is transferred to a male for men's self-reproduction, and the Silenos figure, notorious for his large member (and attendant sexuality) as well as for his trickster habits, plays the woman's part in the hypermasculine way. Additionally, this particular Silenos, as an *agalma* (sculpted figure concealed

59. Aristophanes presents the famous myth of the spherical human beings who, separated by Zeus for their hubris toward the gods, are forever searching for reunion with their other halves. These may be of the same or opposite sex, depending on the original composition of each entity.

60. See now Halperin 1990, on the *Symposium;* and duBois 1988, 169–83, on the *Phaedrus,* another, equally instructive dialogue.

within another one), transfers that quality of interiority to the male, as well as the idea of a molded objet d'art. By these various means, Plato obviates twice over the tragic necessity that requires the feminine presence upon the stage—the tragic necessity whose complicated and essential functions in the theater of Dionysos we have followed throughout the course of this essay.

· NINE ·

Travesties of Gender and Genre
in Aristophanes' *Thesmophoriazousae*

*Equal of opposites, evolved by a onesame power of nature or
of spirit . . . as the sole condition and means of its himundher
manifestation and polarized for reunion by the symphysis of
their antipathies.* JAMES JOYCE

*The sexes were not two as they are now, but originally three
in number; there was man, woman, and the union of the two,
having a name corresponding to this double nature, which had
once a real existence but now lost, and the word "androgynous"
is only preserved as a term of reproach.*
ARISTOPHANES IN PLATO'S *SYMPOSIUM*

Three of Aristophanes's eleven extant comedies use the typical comic device of role inversion to imagine topsy-turvy worlds in which women are
"on top." [1] Freed from the social constraints that keep them enclosed
within the house and silent in the public realms of discourse and action,
women are given a field and context on the comic stage. They issue forth
to lay their plans, concoct their plots, and exercise their power over men.

The *Lysistrata* and the *Ecclesiazousae* stage the intrusion of women
into the public spaces of Athens—the Acropolis and Agora, respectively—
as an intrusion into the political and economic life of the city. The *Thesmophoriazousae*, however, resituates the battle of the sexes in another
domain: that of aesthetics and, more specifically, that of the theater itself.
Instead of the collective confrontation of men and women, the play directs

My general thanks go to the Aristophanes seminar at Princeton University, spring 1980, who
contributed more to this essay than can be acknowledged. The current version has undergone numerous stylistic revisions and some additions and clarifications, along with some
updated bibliography, where appropriate.
1. For this phrase, see Davis 1975.

the women's actions against a single male target—the tragic poet, Euripi-des. Like the better known *Lysistrata,* performed the same year (411 B.C.E.), the *Thesmophoriazousae* (Women at the Festival of the Thesmo-phoria) is set on the sacred hill of Athens. This time the location is not appropriated by the women as a crucial and outrageous strategy to further their plans; instead it is granted to them in accordance with the rules of their annual festival, which reserved this hallowed space for the ex-clusive use of women in their fertility rites, dedicated to Demeter and Persephone.[2]

Past criticism was not generous to this play. Studies of role inversion generally focused on the other two plays because of their implications for the political and economic spheres that are the city's dominant interests.[3] In respect to literary questions, the *Frogs* claimed almost exclusive atten-tion, both because of its formal contest between Aeschylus and Euripides and because of its emphasis on the role of the poet as teacher and "savior" of the city in its time of need.[4] Judgments about the *Thesmophoriazousae,* on the other hand, while admiring its ingenuity and wit, once dismissed it as a "parody play," a trifling interlude in the comic poet's more significant and enduring dialogue with the city and its institutions. Some critics looked for simplistic equivalences between transvestism, effeminacy, and Euripides' newer forms of tragedy, and all used to find difficulties with the plot, especially with Euripides' apparently sudden reconciliation with the women at the end.[5]

2. The Thesmophorion, a sacred building, was located on the Pnyx, just below the Acropolis. The festival, one of the most archaic and widespread in Greece, took place in the autumn at the time of the fall sowing. Consisting of three days (named respectively the An-odos [the way up], Nesteia [fasting], and Kalligeneia [fair birth]), the festival was open only to women (and was probably restricted to citizens' wives). Among other activities, it in-cluded special fertility sacrifices, ritual obscenity, and a final feast, presumably to celebrate Persephone's return and to assure the prosperity of the crops and the birth of children. On the Thesmophoria, best known in its Athenian form, see especially Deubner 1932, 50–60; Farnell 1896–1909, 3:83–112; Nilsson 1906, 313–25; Nilsson 1955, 1:461–66; Fehrle 1910, 137–54; Harrison 1922, 120–34; Arbesmann, s.v. *Thesmophoria, RE* 1937 c. 15–28; Burkert 1985, 242–46; Detienne 1977, 78–83, 129–30, and *passim;* Detienne 1979b; Sfameni-Gasparro 1986, 223–83; Scarpi 1976, 151–59 and *passim.* Dahl 1976 collects all the ancient sources.

3. On the *Lysistrata* and/or the *Ecclesiazousae,* see Rosellini 1979; Saïd 1979; Loraux 1981a, "Acropole"; Foley 1982a; and now Taaffe 1993. For a historian's view, see Lévy 1976. See further note 5 below.

4. E.g., Harriott 1969 devotes half a page to one passage from the *Thesmophoriazou-sae,* and Snell 1953 makes no mention of the play at all in his chapter "Aristophanes and Aesthetic Criticism," 113–35.

5. At the time of the original writing of this essay in 1981, there was virtually no ex-tended treatment of this play as a play. Whitman (1964, 216–17) devoted half a chapter to

But the *Thesmophoriazousae* is a far more complex and better integrated play than it might appear at first. It is located at the intersection of several relations: between male and female, between tragedy and comedy, between theater (tragedy and comedy) and festival (ritual and myth), between festival (the Thesmophoria) and festival (the Dionysiac, which provides the occasion for its performance and determines its comic essence), and finally between bounded forms (myth, ritual, and drama) and the more fluid "realities" of everyday life. All these relations are unstable and reversible; they cross boundaries and invade each other's territories, erase and reinstate hierarchical distances, reflecting ironically upon each other and themselves.

In this essay I take another look at this play from two conjoined perspectives: the theme of "women on top" and the self-reflexiveness of art concerned with the status of its own mimetic representation. However satirically the play may represent Euripides' "unnatural" and "unmanly" concern with *erōs* and with women, with female sexuality and female psyche, it poses a more necessary and intrinsic connection between the ambiguities of the feminine and those of art, linked in various ways in Greek notions about poetics from the archaic period on. The setting of the play and the progress of the plot are constructed to make the most of the perennial comic value of female impersonation, but they also use the notion of gender as a way of posing questions about genre, drawing attention to the problematics of imitation and representation that connect transvestism of costume with mimetic parody of texts. Transvestism works on the visual level; parody, on the verbal. Together they expose the interrelations of a crossing of genres and a crossing of genders; together they exemplify the equivalence between intertextuality and intersexuality.

My aim is to examine these different issues in the play—transvestism, parody, myth, ritual, and literary tradition—under the rubric of mimesis, first to uncover the "secret" logic of the text that works through a fusion of festival, theater, and gender, and second to offer some speculations on the relation of the feminine itself to some general principles of imitation.

---

it and generally took a negative view: "The parody here is without venom, and the plot, or fantasy, is without reference to very much beyond its own inconsequential proposition. . . . The art of tragedy is shown to be on the wane, but any deeper implications that might have been involved in that fact are saved for the *Frogs*" (217). For him the play had "little of the theme of fertility or life" (216). Even more, he added, "Somehow . . . femininity, whether real or assumed, is under a somewhat morbid cloud; by contrast, there is something genuinely refreshing about the masculinity of Mnesilochos, however coarse, and of the Scythian archer, whose main male attribute plays an unblushing role in the solution of the play" (224). Hansen (1976) followed Whitman's interpretation, but focused on theatrical presentation. See now, e.g., Moulton 1981; Saïd 1987 (on comic transvestism); and Taaffe 1993.

Mimesis: Gender and Genre

There are those who want a text (an art, a painting) without a
shadow, without the dominant "ideology" but this is to want a
text without fecundity, without productivity, a sterile text.

ROLAND BARTHES

In the brilliant and ingenious play that is the *Thesmophoriazousae,* the
contest between the genders must share the spotlight with the contest between the genres, comedy and tragedy. Along with the parody of other
serious forms of discourse within the city (judicial, ritual, political, poetic), *paratragōdia,* or the parody of tragedy, is a consistent feature of Aristophanic comedy.[6] Figures of poets, philosophers, and other intellectuals
are often also found on the comic stage, along with politicians and other
prominent figures that comedy, in its license for abuse, delights in bringing
down from high to low. But the effect of placing a tragic poet as the comic
protagonist in a comic plot and of elevating parody to the dominant discourse of the play modulates the contest between the sexes into another
key, one that not only reflects the tensions between the social roles of men
and women, but also focuses on their theatrical representation as tragic
and comic personae on the stage.

In the privacy of their ritual precinct, the women have determined to
act in their own defense—to exact vengeance from the tragic poet Euripides, whom they charge with having slandered the female sex with misogynistic abuse in his dramatic representation of women. He has made
their lives intolerable, they complain, for thanks to him they can no longer
have the freedom at home that they once enjoyed. Their husbands come
home from the theater all fired up with suspicion at every gesture and
every movement the women make and keep them locked up inside the
house. Euripides himself, forewarned of their plan, appears at the opening
of the play to devise his counter-plot and to rescue himself from this clear
and present danger that will determine his fate this day, whether he will
live or die.

Euripides tries to persuade the effeminate tragic poet, Agathon, to go
in woman's dress in order to infiltrate the women's rites and to argue in
the poet's defense, but failing in the attempt, he turns to his old kinsman
instead. Coerced now into dressing as a woman with costumes borrowed
from Agathon's wardrobe and shaved and depilated on stage to enhance
his disguise, the kinsman, Mnesilochos, makes his way up the sacred hill
to mingle unnoticed with the other women on the Pnyx and to carry out
the mandates of the master plotter. He is ultimately unmasked and his true

6. On *paratragōdia,* see Rau 1967 with appropriate bibliography. For other forms of
parody, see Horn 1970; and Komornicka 1967.

sex revealed both by the nature of his defense of Euripides and by the information of Cleisthenes, the effeminate politician and friend of women, who comes to warn them of the interloper in their midst. While Cleisthenes goes off to bring back the Scythian policeman to remove the malefactor, the poor kinsman has recourse to elaborate parodies of Euripidean drama. In increasing desperation, he tries now one tragic role and now another in his efforts to save himself, bringing Euripides finally on stage, not once but twice, to impersonate characters in his own plays who might rescue the kinsman. When this strategy fails, Euripides at last reconciles himself with the women, and dressed now as an old procuress, he succeeds in diverting the Scythian policeman with a comic, not a tragic, ploy (the perennial dancing girl) so that he and the kinsman can make their happy escape.

The meeting of the poet and the women complicates both the typical topos of "women in charge" and the role and stance of the comic hero himself. The launching of the great comic idea, which is the heart and soul of the comic plot, is divided between the women, whose decision to prosecute Euripides is taken before the play actually begins, and the poet hero, who under the circumstances cannot initiate action, as other Aristophanic figures do, in the free exercise of his own imaginative vision of the world. Instead, as comic protagonist he must employ all his professional techniques to extricate himself from a situation in which he is also a potential victim.

Similarly, the device of staging the women's presence on the Pnyx has a double edge. On one level, by occupying civic space, they maintain the same transgression that their exposure to public gaze on stage implies, and the ritual regulations that put women in charge offer, as in the other cases of role inversion, rich comic possibilities for women's use and misuse of male language when they imitate the procedures of those typically male institutions of tribunal and assembly. Moreover, this same topos of changing places gives the women, as always, an opportunity to redress the social imbalances between male and female in an open comic competition with men for superior status, here especially in the parabasis (the section of the comic play reserved for the chorus to address the spectators in its own voice).[7] But on another level, the women's legitimate presence at their own private ritual also reverses the direction of the transgression; now it is men

7. The parabasis is a peculiar and distinctive feature of Old Comedy in which the chorus can break the dramatic illusion and address the audience directly on topical matters of the day. In the *Thesmophoriazousae*, the parabasis is actually integrated into the action insofar as the members of the chorus keep their identity as women at the festival and respond to the themes of the play. The parabasis is discussed in more detail below. For a brief summary of the complex formal structure of the parabasis, see Dover 1972, 49–53; and now Hubbard 1991.

who trespass on forbidden space and men who penetrate the private world of women for the purpose of spying on them and disclosing their secrets in public.

Another paradox is evident as a result of the confrontation between the poet and the women. In their eyes, the scandal of Euripides' theater lies in his exhibition upon the tragic stage of erotic heroines who openly solicit men, like the first unhappy Phaedra with her Hippolytos and the wanton Sthenoboia who like Potiphar's wife shamelessly tempted the young Bellerophon. But the kinsman's defense brazenly claims that Euripides, in fact, exercised restraint: the tragic poet could have told other stories, far worse than these, about errant wives (473–75).[8] Mnesilochos's charges of misdoing against the entire female sex arouse the women's anger at their supposed betrayal by one of their own within their very midst, a betrayal that will serve, in part, to unmask the female impersonator. Yet the anecdotes he tells of adultery and supposititious babies come straight out of the typical male discourse of the comic theater, and the women he depicts as overly fond of wine and sex conform to the portrait of the comic woman, who displays her unruly Dionysiac self (even in this play) in the spirit of carnival and misrule. As the comic male character in the comic play, the kinsman then is only playing true to form. If he defends the tragic poet in the comic way, he makes "unspeakable" what comedy has always claimed as its right to speak. Is tragedy taking the fall for comedy? Is the kinsman's defense in fact the defense mounted by comedy against the trespass on its ground by Euripidean tragedy?

The speech in which the kinsman corroborates Euripides' intimate familiarity with women's domestic secrets repeats and replicates Euripides' transgression of tragic decorum, a transgression that is now also spatialized in dramatic form as the violation of the sacred precinct reserved for women at their ritual. Having penetrated earlier into a feminine world that he was forbidden to enter, the poet now penetrates it again through the kinsman's infiltration of the Thesmophoria, an act that profanes the pieties of deportment again, and twice over. In comedy, revelations about women's promiscuous "nature" raise no indignation among the spectators; they are intended to provoke laughter. It is rather in the tragic theater that the mimetic effects of representation work with such persuasive realism that drama overtakes and invades the real world, sending the husbands away, wild with anxiety, to look to their womenfolk at home.

At the heart of this repeated violation is the transgression of the distance that normally maintains the fiction of theater with relation to the "real" world to which it refers and in which it registers its effects of pity and fear. Tragedy is "the imitation of a serious action," as Aristotle tells

8. The text of the *Thesmophoriazousae* is cited from the Budé edition (Coulon 1973).

us. Designated as the genre that holds up a more heroic and more mythic mirror to the society of its spectators, who come to learn its lessons and to participate in its imaginative *mise en scène*, tragedy must depend upon the integrity of its fictions in the light of its own theatrical conventions and generic norms. To make a comic point, the violation of that dramatic integrity is focused on the issue that bears the greatest psychological charge for the society of men: the integrity of their households and above all of their women.[9] The encroachment on women's sexual secrets, therefore, not only stands as the actual topical reason for complaint but also metaphorically represents in social terms the poet's trespass of aesthetic modes.

At stake in this theatrical tug of war between tragedy and comedy is the nature of mimesis itself. The *Thesmophoriazousae* wants it all ways— dramatizing and exploiting to the extreme the confusions that the notion of imitation suggests—as to whether art is a mimesis of *reality* or a *mimesis* of reality, whether it conceals its art by verisimilitude or exposes its fictions in the staging and testing of its own illusions.

Consider the ascending complications of the mimetic process when, first, comic character and tragic poet are conflated in the person of Euripides. Add to this the fact that the comic character (the kinsman) is designated as the actor who is to carry out the plot that Euripides has devised within the comic play. Finally, once the kinsman's "true" identity has been revealed, he must transform himself into the theatrical actor of the Euripidean parodies whose lines he now self-consciously and incongruously renders with reference to his comic role.

Moreover, the play as a whole takes its cue from and sets as the condition of its plot the offense of Euripides in having tilted his dramas too far in the direction of a mimesis that exceeds the boundaries of the theater. For given the comic stage as the ground of "reality" in the play, the "real" women, who resent being "characters" in his drama, put him in a "real" situation in which he himself must live out for himself the mimetic consequences of his own mimetic plots. As others have noted, Euripides is not a character in a typical comic scenario. Rather, he plays the hero/victim in a parodic version of his favorite type of tragic drama, the intrigue-rescue play, in which the hero/heroine faces overwhelming danger. Often a rec-

9. Cf. the interchange between Aeschylus and Euripides in the *Frogs*, where Aeschylus reproaches Euripides for having put on stage Phaedras and Sthenoboias who behaved like whores (*pornai*, 1043). "And how did my Sthenoboias harm the city?" inquires Euripides. "By persuading noble wives of noble men to drink hemlock because they were so ashamed by your Bellerophons," replies Aeschylus. "But," asks Euripides, "didn't I tell a true story about Phaedra?" "Yes, indeed, but the poet must conceal what is wicked and not introduce or *didaskein* [teach/produce] such things . . . but only the virtuous" (1049–56). This Phaedra, it should be added, refers to Euripides's first version, called *Hippolytos Kaluptomenos*. It is known to us from fragments and testimonia. See further chapter 6.

ognition takes place with a lost loved one, and the reunited pair attains the desired salvation through a series of clever intrigues.[10] What better comic version of tragic justice than to turn the tables on Euripides and put him precisely in the place of his own characters? Yet for this man of a thousand plots (927), what better stage than that of his comic host, which allows him to exhibit the full range of his ingenious *mēchanai* (tricks) and enables him to turn at last from potential victim to savior of himself and his kinsman? Euripides plays first in the tragic mode and then, finally, in the comic one, when Aristophanes, cleverer than he, puts him squarely on the "real" ground of the comic play.

From the beginning, Euripides must act the part of the playwright within the play to devise his own plot. He does so first by choosing and then by directing the actor to play an appointed part. Next, he furnishes him with the texts from which to read, and eventually he intervenes as an actor himself in the parodies of two plays he has already composed. The comedy, therefore, can never escape the metatheatrical implications of a play within a play, with all the variations and permutations of such a device. As the comedy progresses, as the kinsman's own improvisations founder and he is "unmasked," the temple and the altar of the Thesmophorion conveniently serve as the "theatrical" space within the play on which to stage those parodies of Euripidean theater.[11] But by the last paratragic scene, the comedy draws upon all its theatrical resources, from within and without. The Scythian policeman's cruel fastening of the kinsman to the punishment plank suggests the cast, the setting, and the prop for Euripides' poor Andromeda, bound to the rock in far-off Ethiopia, awaiting her fate from the sea monster who is to devour her. But then Euripides himself as Perseus flies by on the "real" theatrical device of the *mechanē* and cues the kinsman as to the role he intends to play in this little farce. Thus, as the play moves on to the end and as Euripides assumes not one but two parts in the *Andromeda*, the *Thesmophoriazousae* exposes more and more the obvious inconcinnities between theater and "reality," to the apparent detriment of the former, even as it implicitly conspires to validate those same dramatic fictions.

Mimesis: Transvestism

Everyday, precious, . . . m'm'ry's leaves are falling deeply on my
Jungfraud's Messongebook.   JAMES JOYCE

---

10. On connections of the comic plot with Euripidean patterns, see Russo 1962, 297; Rau 1967, 50; and Rau 1975, 349. See further Hall 1989. On the motif of salvation in Euripidean drama, see Garzya 1962.

11. See Russo 1962, 297.

The feat is to sustain the mimesis of language (language imitat-
ing itself), the source of immense pleasures, in a fashion so radi-
cally ambiguous (ambiguous to the root) that the text never suc-
cumbs to the good conscience (and bad faith) of parody (of
castrating laughter, of the "comical that makes us laugh").

ROLAND BARTHES

The theme of mimesis is specifically set in the prologue of the play, the first attested technical use of the word *mimēsis* and the first demonstration, albeit absurd, of the mimetic theory of art that will later figure so largely in Plato's and Aristotle's aesthetic theories.[12] Agathon, the tragic poet for whom Euripides is searching, is wheeled out of the house on the *ekku-klēma* (the stage device used in the theater to bring an interior scene out-side), while singing sensual hymns that send the kinsman into an erotic swoon (130–33). Androgynous in appearance, Agathon wears women's clothing and an incongruous assortment of male and female accessories (134–40).[13] In reply to the kinsman's questions as to his identity and his gender, Agathon now replies:

I wear my garb according to my thought.
The poet, you see, must shape his ways
In accordance with the plays to be composed.
If someone is composing women's plays,
His body must needs share in women's ways
If plays of men, he has already what it takes.
Whatever we don't have, we must capture by mimesis.

(146–52)[14]

So far, so good. The poet is a versatile fellow who must dress for the dra-matic roles he creates. But Agathon then seems to shift ground and declare the contrary: a beautiful poet wears beautiful clothes and writes beautiful dramas—and vice versa for an ugly one. One must compose in accordance with one's nature (159–72). The clue to this apparent confusion between mimesis as impersonation or investiture and mimesis as a congruence of body, soul, and poetic talent lies in the comic fact that Agathon was well known in Athens for his effeminate "nature," just the type of male whom

12. For a general discussion of mimesis in antiquity, with bibliography, see Sörböm 1966. See also Vernant 1979a. For useful surveys of aesthetic theory and criticism before Plato, see Lanata 1963; Harriott 1969; and Webster 1939.

13. "A lute *[barbitos]* and saffron gown *[krokotos]*, an animal skin and hair net, an athlete's oil flask and a brassiere, a sword and a mirror. . . . If you were raised as a man, where is your cock? If a woman, where are your tits?" On Agathon's costume, see further Muecke 1982b.

14. Hansen's (1976) translation.

Aristophanic comedy likes to mock.[15] Hence, what Agathon imitates (female appearance) turns out indeed to be all too much in harmony with his nature and his ways. And if he refuses to go as a spy among the women, it is precisely because he fits the role too well. As a poet, he is second only to Euripides (187), but as a "woman," he can pass to such an extent that he can claim that the women at the Thesmophoria would resent him for unfair competition in stealing away their nocturnal lovers (204–5). The sample of his poesy, the choral hymns he sings, beginning with an invocation to the two goddesses, Demeter and Persephone, and ending with an appeal to Leto, the mother of Apollo and Artemis, are all too much in tune. In short, he is the unnatural "natural" for the part, the pathic well adapted for tragic pathos, as the kinsman wryly observes (199–201). How could Agathon defend Euripides against the charges that are leveled against him? He is as much their kindred spirit as is the effeminate politician Cleisthenes, who identifies himself as "woman crazy" (gynaikomanēs) when he later enters the precinct of the women's festival to denounce the male impostor in their midst (574–76).

No, it is Mnesilochos, the bushy kinsman, male from top to toe, who must go instead; he is the one to be dressed on stage in a woman's costume; he must be shaved of his beard and raise his rump in full view of the audience to have it singed with a flame, as women do, when depilating their pubic hair in accordance with Greek standards of female beauty. In this interchange between Agathon and Mnesilochos in the prologue scene, Aristophanes has accomplished a real coup de théâtre. With artful economy, he has managed to introduce his topos of "women on top" so as to expose its implications to the naked eye right from the start. Transforming Mnesilochos into a woman exactly reproduces in advance the inevitable result of the inversion of gender roles: when women are in a position to rule men, men must become women.[16] In the miniature reversal played out between the kinsman and Agathon, Mnesilochos, as the comic character, first indulges in all the witty obscenities to which he is entitled at the expense of the effeminate poet. But the transfer of Agathon's persona to him returns against the kinsman the full measure of that social shame which the

15. Critics miss the point of this confusion, especially Cantarella (1967, 7–15), who imagines that since Agathon is effeminate, he is somehow no longer a male. It should be noted that poets, beginning with Thespis, did, in fact, act in their own plays in the earlier years of the Greek theater before acting became a more professional specialty. Aeschylus most probably did so and Sophocles also in the beginning of his career. See Pickard-Cambridge 1968, 93–94; and on the rise of the actor, see Slater 1990.

16. "Feminine power is by nature abnormal . . . but this abnormality can take two forms which are rigorously opposed to each other and involve either a virilization of women, if women are adapting themselves to the nature of power, or, on the contrary, a feminization of power, if the women adapt power to their own nature and put the domestic domain over the political one" (Saïd 1979, 36).

breach of gender norms poses to identity, manhood, and hierarchies of power. Comedy's scandalous privilege to expose those parts and functions of the body that decorum keeps hidden—physically, in the padded leather phallos that the comic actor wears, and verbally, in the obscenities and sexual jokes that are licensed by the Dionysiac festival—takes on a double twist here. For in exposing Mnesilochos, the lusty comic male, only in the process of his becoming a woman, the comedy is playing with the extreme limit of its own promiscuous premises where all can converge in the ambiguities of intersexuality.

But transvestism in the theater, and especially in this scene, has another function in addition to exposing the natural facts of the body that the social conventions keep off stage[17] and away from public notice. This is the exposing of the secret artifices that theatrical conventions keep off stage to maintain the fictions of theatrical mimesis. Mnesilochos, after all, is dressing as a woman because he is to play the part of a woman in order to carry out Euripides' clever stratagem of self-defense.

From a theatrical perspective, to take the role of the opposite sex is not simply a question of loss. Rather, it invests the wearer with the power of appropriation, of a supplement to what one already has. Androgynous myths and transvestite rites speak to this increased symbolic charge even as, socially speaking, the same androgyny and cross-dressing incur the shameful label of deviance. Thus the depilation of Mnesilochos is balanced by the donning of women's clothing, for in this ambivalent game of genders, the female is far more than a "not," she is also an "other."[18] When the women in the parabasis examine the comic contradictions of misogyny and put the superiority of men to the test, they joke in terms of attributes common to each, transferring the names for women's articles to their masculine counterparts: we women have still kept safe at home our weaving rod *(kanōn)* and sunshade *(skiadeion),* while you men have lost your "rod" and spearhead *(kanōn)* along with your shield *(skiadeion)* (821–29). The teasing play with castration is appropriate enough to the inversion of roles, but the ambiguities of role playing involve both this and that, even for Mnesilochos who plays so ill and who by his misplaying exposes, when the women expose him, the outer limits of mimesis.

Since all female roles in the Greek theater were played by men, the exhibitionist donning of female costume focuses the problem of mimesis at its most ambiguous and most sensitive spot, where social and artistic rules are most in conflict with each other. Impersonation affects the whole

17. We may remember that obscene, *ob-scaenum,* in its usual etymology, means "off stage," i.e., off the "serious" stage.

18. See the excellent distinction made by Gilbert 1980. For the ancient evidence, see Delcourt 1961, 1–16.

creative process from the poet to the actor and determines its aesthetic success, but feminization attracts to itself all the scorn and abuse that the culture—and comedy—can muster. To reverse the terms, feminization first unmans those whom the culture would scorn and abuse, the ones it would lay open to aggressive violence, and finds this sexual slander the convenient point of entry through which to exercise mastery over the other. Just so in this play, Aristophanes at the end completes his ridicule of Euripides by finally putting him in female dress (as the old procuress) but also grants him the stage on which to display with ultimate impunity the repertory of his mimetic tricks.

The contradictions inherent in the mimetic process, as adumbrated by Agathon, between what you play and what you are, are tested again and again from within the play itself, as it uncovers the dissonances between the fictive theatrical device and the comic ground of "reality." Twice Mnesilochos is put up against a "true" effeminate, once in the case of Agathon and once with Cleisthenes, as if to pose a theatrical distance between one actor in women's clothes and another. A third layering is the fact that the women of the Thesmophoria are played by men. Mnesilochos himself, in the instability of his dual roles and his all too male discomfort with his female role, is best suited to reflect ironically on his current situation during the course of the play. Still in feminine disguise, he indignantly asks Cleisthenes, the "true" impersonator, "What man would be such a fool as to allow himself to be depilated?" (592–94). Yet when his first two theatrical parodies of Euripides fail, parodies in which he plays male roles in female costume (another reversal), he has a new and happy idea: "Why, I'll play Helen, the new version—I've got the feminine dress I need" (850–51). In the next stage, when the magistrate whom Cleisthenes has summoned comes and orders the poor Mnesilochos to be bound to the punishment plank for breaking the city's laws and invading the secret rites of women, he begs: "At least, undress me and bind me naked to the plank; I'm an old man, sir; please don't leave me dressed up in feminine fripperies! I don't want to give the crows a good laugh as well as a good dinner" (939–42). Now that the masculine world of authority has intruded into the play, Mnesilochos can express in full the reversal from mastery to subjugation that his masculine identity has undergone. When the magistrate reports the council's decree that the precise point of his punishment is to be bound to the plank in a woman's costume in order to exhibit to all the villainy of his imposture, he has reached the point at which he most conforms to the role of the pitiful Andromeda that he now is about to play. Yet, at the same time, he offers the last and best mismatch between his masculine identity as a lusty old man and the feminine persona of a beautiful young maiden.

Mimesis: Parody

*Parodic writing can be defined as triangular desire—the desire of
a subject (parodist) only projected into a text (parodying) by the
detour of another text (parodied).*   CLAUDE LEROY

Just as the comic actor's discrepancies between character and costume
threaten his mimetic integrity, so does parody, in more complex and more
extended fashion, address the critical questions of mimesis in the service
of a fictive reality. The transvestite actor might succeed in concealing the
tell-tale sign that marks him as an imitation with a difference, but parody,
by its nature and its definition, is the literary device that openly declares
its status as an imitation with a difference. In the rhetorical logic of the
play, the exposure of the kinsman's intersexual game appropriately brings
parody fully out of hiding to play its intertextual games with comedy and
tragedy. Given the thematic logic of the play, however, the first defense of
Euripides, misconducted by the kinsman in the comic mode, is properly
transferred to the parodies of the plays that will eventually bring Euripides
on stage to play the tragic roles he has composed. It is also consonant with
the narrative logic of the plot that the kinsman should have recourse to
Euripidean parodies. For with the peripeteia in his comic situation, he is
now truly imitating the typical Euripidean plot of danger–recognition–
intrigue–rescue. The sequence of the four plays might read in fact as a
brief chronological survey of Euripidean drama—the *Telephos* of 438,
already parodied in Aristophanes' earlier *Acharnians* in 425, the *Palamedes* of 415, and the *Helen* and the *Andromeda,* both presented the year
before in 412.

The parodies themselves function as the new intrigues of the kinsman
(and later of Euripides), invoked in suitable response to each new exigency
of his plight. But these are also intrigues now carried out fully on the theatrical plane, whose comic success depends upon their failure as specimens of tragic art to deceive the comic audience inside the play with their
mimetic credibility. Read as successive intrusions into the text, the parodies work as metatheatrical variants of the series of different impostors
(alazones) who normally intrude to threaten the comic hero's imaginative
world and who, like those presumptuous figures, must be deflated and
driven out. If we read the parodies as a sequence, however, we see that the
kinsman must move further and further into the high art of mimesis with
increasing complications and confusions, while the comic spectators on
stage, whom he would entice into performing in his parodies, move further and further down the scale of comprehension, ending with the barbarian Scythian policeman, who speaks only a pidgin Greek. In the course
of their development, the parodies play again with notions of gender and

genre, with costume and character, with comic and tragic modes. Together, they orchestrate a medley of variations on the theme of mimesis
itself.

Some critics have judged these parodies as opportunistic displays of
Aristophanic skill, which take over the play and relegate the conflict of the
women and Euripides to the sidelines. Others see the discontinuous leaps
from one text to another as signs of the failure of Euripidean tragedy in
each case to maintain the necessary mimetic illusion that would effect the
rescue of the kinsman. The success of Euripides' last plot, a comic and
not a tragic strategy, only confirms the opinion that Aristophanic parody
is remaining true to its usual vocation as a critique of the aesthetic values
of another poet's work. Certainly, Euripides' scandalous novelties in the
theater lend themselves as ideal targets for the satirist's barbs. It is also
true that, on the surface, comedy seems to be indulging its license for dispensing with strict dramatic coherence. But such judgments overlook the
fundamental ambiguities of parody itself. These arise from "the taking in
and taking over"[19] of another's text to generate what has been called "a
poetics of contradiction," always double edged and double voiced, poised
uncertainly between mockery and homage, contempt and envy, appropriation (even theft) and critical distance.[20] These same critics of the play
overlook the fact that comedy can profit from its looser requirements of
structure, using paratactic techniques as a subtle and sophisticated means
to imply rather than state. In the artful composition of the second part of
the play, the parodies, I suggest, serve double and discrepant purposes:
both as framed disruptions of its narrative continuity *and* as integral and
integrating elements of the entire plot. The outer and inner surfaces of the
texts play off one another, with and against each other, as sequence and/
or juxtaposition. Furthermore, each parody has a double allegiance, the
comic context in which it now is situated and the tragic context of the play
from which it is drawn. Thus each parodic scene conveys a series of multiple messages, including each time some significant reflection of its status
as a theatrical artifact.

Telephos

In the *Telephos* of Euripides, Telephos, the Mysian king, who has been
wounded by Achilles on a Greek expedition that went to Mysia instead of
Troy, is advised by an oracle that he can only be cured by the one who
wounded him. Accordingly, he dresses as a beggar and comes to Agamem-

19. I am indebted to Stewart (1979, 20) for this formulation. I have profited from her
work more than I can indicate in this essay.

20. I have borrowed this definition of parody from Rose 1979, 185. See also Rose and
Stewart 1979; Abastado 1976; and Hutcheon 1985.

non's court. In the safety of his disguise, the Mysian king argues in his own defense, but fails to persuade the Greeks. Identified finally by Achilles, who makes a late entry upon the scene, Telephos snatches up the baby Orestes and takes refuge at an altar, threatening to slay the infant if he does not attain his cure and precipitating the crisis that will ultimately bring about the play's satisfactory conclusion in fulfillment of his wish.[21]

In the comic parody, the kinsman, once unmasked by Cleisthenes, snatches up the baby of a woman nearby and threatens it with Orestes' fate. The woman and the kinsman play the paratragic scene up to the hilt, but with a crucial difference: the child is named as a daughter, not a son, and once undressed by the kinsman, it turns out to be a wineskin, four or five pints old, conceived at the last Dionysiac festival, whom the "mother" will go to any lengths to save. Unlike Telephos, the kinsman makes good his threat. He slays the Dionysiac "child" with a knife, placing a sacrificial bowl beneath to catch every last drop of "blood" and eliciting the mother's pitiful cry that now she has lost her *kore,* her "maiden" *and* her "maidenhead" (689–761).[22]

The kinsman, we should recall, is playing a male role in female costume. But viewing the terms of the women's earlier confrontation with the kinsman in the light of the dramatic details of the *Telephos* (disguise, infiltration, speech of defense), we realize retrospectively that from the beginning of the scene, Mnesilochos has already been playing a tragic part in a scenario whose underlying plot the open parody of Euripides' play has now at last explicitly exposed.[23] Now that the kinsman's identity has been revealed, he turns from verbal insults against the women into an open show of masculine force, even though the wine-happy women seem to confirm all the charges he has already made about them in his earlier defense of Euripides. Nevertheless, we should note that the exposure of the male (Mnesilochos) is exactly matched by the exposure of the "female child" (the *korē* wineskin), so that the mimesis of the transvestite male is exactly symmetrical with the mimesis of the "transvestite female." The genders of the roles are reversed between the comic and the tragic versions, but the twin unmaskings of comic character and tragic persona also turn out to be fully consonant with one another.

21. The *Telephos* has survived only in fragments. For an extensive treatment, see Handley and Rea 1957; also Webster 1967, 43–48.

22. The Euripidean scene of Telephos at the altar with the baby Orestes is represented in both Attic and Italiot vase paintings, attesting to the popularity of the play. But a lucky find in a recently discovered Apulian bell krater (Würzburg H 5697) represents the Aristophanic parody itself. See Kossatz-Deissmann 1980; Csapo 1986; Taplin 1987; Taplin 1993, 36–41; and Keuls 1990.

23. On the *Telephos* in this play, see Miller 1948; Rau 1967, 42–50; Rau 1975, 344–46; and Muecke 1982a, 21.

Palamedes

The *Palamedes,* which is set in the Greek camp at Troy, has as its plot the treachery of Odysseus against Palamedes, the wisest of the Greeks, who is credited with inventing the art of writing and many other skills beside. Odysseus, probably envious of the higher prestige of Palamedes in cunning intelligence, contrives the conviction of Palamedes on a charge of treason with fabricated evidence—a forged letter from King Priam and Trojan gold planted in his tent. In the trial that intervenes between the discovery of the letter and the search for the gold, the innocent Palamedes eloquently defends himself as the noble man unjustly accused, but he is condemned on the basis of the false evidence and subsequently put to death. In the aftermath, his brother Oiax cleverly contrives to send news of Palamedes's fate to their father Nauplios across the sea by novel means, and this is the scene that is parodied here. For the kinsman, in despair at the comic-tragic end of his "Telephic" scheme, resolves in his isolation and despair to send a message to Euripides, but how can he do it? "Why, I'll find a way from the *Palamedes,*" he thinks, and determines, like Oiax, to transmit word of his misfortunes by writing a message on oars and casting them into the sea. No oars are available, but wooden votive tablets from the altar will do. On these Mnesilochos carves out the letters of Euripides' name to the accompaniment of a lyric apostrophe to his hands[24] which "are tracing the furrows of the letters with slow and painful toil" (765– 84). In rewriting this text in parodic form, the kinsman is playing the proper role from the proper play with the right gender, but still in the wrong costume.[25]

Parabasis

This section of the play is closed by the parabasis, the formal convention of comedy that allows the chorus to step forward and speak directly to the spectators. They defend themselves against the slanders heaped upon women, speaking first to the illogic of misogyny that condemns the entire race of women as a bane to humankind and the source of all ills (quarrels, strife, sedition, suffering, and war). But if we are such a bane, they con-

24. In etymological reference to his name: *palamē* (palm of the hand).

25. For an attempted reconstruction and interpretation of the *Palamedes,* which, like the *Telephos,* we know only from fragments and other testimonia, see Scodel 1980. On the parody of the play in Aristophanes, see Rau 1967, 51–53; and Rau 1975, 347–48. The figure of Palamedes appears in the cyclic epic, the *Cypria,* which recounts the origins of the Trojan War down to the *Iliad.* In addition to his military innovations at Troy (army emplacements, organization of night watches), Palamedes invents two games of chance (draughts, knucklebones) along with the alphabet, numeration, and a system of weights and measures. See Detienne 1989c, 105–10.

tinue with mischievous logic, why marry us? Why refuse to let us leave the house, if we are such a plague? And if a woman happens to look out of the window, why are the rest of you so eager to catch a glimpse of this pest? Women, they argue, are in any case superior to men in both worth and value (785–99). As they later claim in a comic bid for parity between the sexes, both have the same accessories *(kanōn* and *skiadeion)* in their respective spheres, but the women keep their utensils safe in the house, while the men have lost theirs in war (821–29).

But first the women make their case by appealing, in their own way, to the theme of mimesis that rules the entire play. In reduced and absurd form, they introduce a theory of imitation that Cratylus will make famous in Plato's dialogue according to which proper names "imitate" the nature of those who bear them. In this eponymous game, the women intend to meet the men on their own ground of war and politics and to go one better: No man can compete with Nausimache (battle at sea), Aristomache (best in battle), Stratonike (victory of the army), and Euboule (good counsel)—or, they add, forgetting theory in favor of sex, with Salabaccho (the name of a famous courtesan). Yet, in pointed contrast to their comic literalism, the women revert to their roles as mothers and vaunt their prowess in producing useful citizen sons who excel in military affairs. These mothers, they propose, should be rewarded with seats of honor at the women's own festivals. Conversely, mothers of bad sons should be demoted, like Hyperbolos's usurious mother, who is equally at fault in her double progeny: the interest *(tokos)* she begets from money and the demagogic son *(tokos)* she has begotten in turn (830–45).

I will return to the women's claims. For the moment, let us note that the parabasis serves as a specific closure to the theme of defense that has dominated the play from its beginning in the premises of the plot. The theme was extended in the comic confrontation between the disguised kinsman and the women, with its latent parody of the *Telephos,* and was continued in yet another key in the *Palamedes.* While this last play is represented on stage in Oiax's ingenious graphic stratagem, the reference, I suggest, also evokes the most famous scene of that drama—Palamedes's trial during which the inventor of writing gave a speech in his own defense.

On the other hand, the women's defense of the feminine sex opens up the drama to its next developments. The parabasis marks the turning point from male roles in the tragic theater to those of women—Helen and Andromeda—and from the kinsman's solo performances to a final duet with Euripides. It also marks the shift from explicit to implicit defense, because from now on the kinsman must fully enter into his female role in order to "earn" his rescue. Dressed in the theatrical costume he donned so long ago, he must live through the consequences of his impersonation in subjection to female experience.

Helen

The *Helen* holds the center of the play. It is framed on one side by the parabasis and on the other by the women's renewal of their festive dance and song during the brief interval when the transvestite impostor has been temporarily removed from the stage. The parody of the *Helen* is the last direct appeal to the women of the Thesmophoria, since the *Andromeda*, the final parodic scene in the series, is addressed to a new audience—the barbarian Scythian archer.

The "new Helen" whose part the kinsman will play refers not only to the recent production of the play the year before but also to the new representation of Helen in a new role as the chaste and virtuous wife. In this version (which has precedents in the mythological tradition), the true Helen never went to Troy, but was transported to Egypt, and an *eidōlon*, a cloudlike imitation of herself, was sent in her stead to Troy. This Helen has remained for ten years in isolation, faithful to her husband and her ideals of purity, while her phantom double was present at the center of hostilities at Troy, where Greeks and Trojans fought with each other and fell in battle—for her sake. In Euripides' play, the old king Proteus, her former protector, has died, and his impious son and heir, Theoclymenos, who is smitten by her beauty, is determined to impose a forcible marriage upon her. This new king has vowed to slay all Greeks who come to his shores in order to keep Helen safe for himself.

Menelaos, now that the war is over, is returning home with his crew along with the phantom Helen he imagines is his real wife whom he has rescued from Troy. Storm and shipwreck drive him to Egypt where he confronts the "real" Helen. Once their complicated recognition has been accomplished, the reunited couple plan their escape with a false story of Menelaos's death and a false promise by Helen to marry Theoclymenos if she can first perform funeral rites by the sea for her "dead" husband. The success of their fictions depends upon the cooperation of the prophetess Theonoe, the virgin sister of the king, whose purity of mind stands in radical opposition to the mood of her violent brother. No synopsis can do justice to the brilliant energy of this romantic play, which combines the themes of *erōs* and *thanatos* with a philosophical testing of the categories of illusion and reality, of name *(onoma)* and fact *(pragma),* name *(onoma)* and body *(sōma),* mind and body, truth and falsehood.[26] For our purposes, however, Aristophanes' parody is significant in two respects.

First, the audience in the comic parody is Critylla, the woman designated to guard Mnesilochos, before whom the kinsman and Euripides enact the dramatic fiction of their happy reunion as husband and wife

26. On Euripides' *Helen,* see Solmsen 1934; Pippin [Burnett] 1960; Zuntz 1960; Kannicht 1969; Wolff 1973; and Segal 1971.

with the aim of effecting Euripides' rescue of Mnesilochos from his/her plight. But Critylla doesn't know how to play, either as spectator or as Theonoe, the daughter of Proteus whose part the kinsman eventually assigns to her ("By the gods, if I am not Critylla, the daughter of Antitheos from Gargettos and you are a villain," 897–99). She knows exactly where she is, not in Egypt but in the Thesmophorion (877–80). This can't be the house of Proteus, for the only Proteus she knows has been dead for ten years (874–76, 881–84). As for the kinsman's insistence that his name is Helen, Critylla rightly replies: "Have you become a woman again, before you have paid the penalty for that other 'womanization' *[gynaikēsis]* of yours?" (863–64). She is so little convinced by his impersonation that when the kinsman claims to Euripides/Menelaos that he is being forced into a marriage with Proteus's son, she scolds the kinsman for deceiving the poor stranger with this and other lies (890–94).[27]

To Critylla, whose comic realism insists on literal readings, there is no Helen, only the scoundrel kinsman. The stranger (Euripides/Menelaos) who has entered the scene is the innocent outsider whom she must enlighten, until she recognizes the Egyptian intrigue for the fakery it is and identifies the stranger/Menelaos as a co-conspirator who must be driven off. Only once does she make a concession to the theatrical mimesis, but she gets it wrong. In correcting the kinsman's tale of a forced marriage, she replies that his real motive for coming on stage was to steal the women's gold (893–94), a claim that draws upon the plot of the *Palamedes,* which furnishes the text for the parody that has just been performed.[28]

On the level of the comic plot, the parody of the *Helen* functions explicitly as the kinsman's lure to bring Euripides on stage to bring about his rescue (846–51). But in this brief and absurd scene, all the issues that characterized the novelty of the original play are present, but they are wonderfully deflected through the comic travesty as a dissonance between the two levels of reference: the circumstances of the plot and the paratragic rendition. In the counterpoint of the text that sets the *recognition* scene from the *Helen* against Critylla's *misrecognition* of the identity of the parody, the questions of illusion and reality, of truth and falsehood, of mimesis and deception, are reframed in metatheatrical terms.

In this new key, the problem of the name as a guide to identity is transposed exactly in reverse to its Euripidean model. In the *Helen* the epistemological confusion lay in the possibility that the same name may be distributed to more than one person (two Helens), but in the parody

27. On the parody of the *Helen* in Aristophanes, see the technical analysis of Rau 1967, 53–65; and Rau 1975, 348–50. See also the useful discussion of Muecke 1977, 64–67.

28. Critylla also gets it partly right: her false accusation of the kinsman matches the fact that Palamedes was *falsely* accused of stealing the gold.

the theatrical confusion lies in the refusal to allow the same character/
actor to bear more than one name, to say nothing of more than one gender. Crytilla seems to have learned all too well the lessons about nomenclature in the parabasis. In this case, the costume can never conceal what
the naked truth has exposed and serves here as the focal point to test the
mimetic premises of the theater in general and the premises of Euripides'
romantic play in particular. The *eidōlon* of Helen is neither visible nor
even mentioned in the parody. Nevertheless, as the personification of illusion itself, the phantom figure hovers over the entire scene.[29]

In the split perspective in which the incongruities of the comic and
tragic fictions are made most evident, the failure of the tragic parody to
persuade lies as much with the comic spectator, who entertains no illusions, as it does with those characters who are trying to create them. I
believe there is more. In the relationship of the parody to its larger comic
matrix, another set of reversals comes into play through the silent juxtaposition of different texts, reversals that pertain to thematic and theatrical
concerns alike. We may recall that the original basis of the women's complaint was the hyperrealism of Euripidean drama, its failure to create the
proper distance between fiction and life with its all too believable portraits
of Athenian wives. Now we regard exactly the opposite: a play whose plot
places it directly in the mode of the fabulous, the unbelievable, the "un-
real," and whose illusionistic *eidōlon* serves as a mimesis in the service of
the theater itself. Thematically speaking, however, instead of the "bad"
women whom Euripides had shamelessly put upon the stage, he has given
us one who against all odds (and credence) remained true to her husband,
waiting for him all these years in true fidelity. When the women earlier
asked the kinsman why Euripides had never put any Penelopes on stage,
he retorted that "there aren't any women like Penelope nowadays, only
Phaedras" (547–50). Yet here he stages the myth of another Penelope,
who like the first was besieged with importunate suitor(s) yet resisted all
efforts to make her remarry. Best of all, in the normative tradition, Helen
is no Penelope, but rather her opposite: the woman who ran off with another man and whose beauty (and perfidy) caused the Trojan war. Helen
is the worst of her sex, who through the poet's art is re-created in the
image of the best of wives, whose fidelity in the *Odyssey* counteracts the
blame that, in Agamemnon's censure, accrues to all women, even the virtuous kind (*Od.* 24.191–202).

By reversing the myth of Helen, Euripides has indeed reversed the
terms, and in playing the part of Menelaos, he has turned from the ma-

29. Rau (1967, 1975) assumes that all these significant motifs have dropped out of the
parody and concludes that Aristophanes is just playing for laughs at the lowest level of
humor.

ligner of women to their potential redeemer, a role he will play once again, in even better form, as the hero Perseus to the kinsman's Andromeda.

Andromeda

The *Helen* and the *Andromeda* are doublets of each other, both presented by Euripides at the City Dionysia in the preceding year. Both imagine similar situations: an exotic locale (Egypt/Ethiopia), a woman in captivity and in danger of erotic predation, a dramatic rescue. But in the *Andromeda* the situation is more extreme. Andromeda is immobilized, bound to a rock. She does not have to outwit a lustful suitor but can only await death from a monster of the deep. No reunions or recognitions for her, but rather a handsome stranger, Perseus, who, flying by with the Gorgon's head tucked in his pouch, falls in love with her at first sight. This play, unfortunately lost to us except for fragments, was famous in antiquity for the seductiveness of its erotic theme.[30] In the *Frogs* Dionysos, who has descended to the underworld to bring Euripides back to Athens, claims as the reason for his mission the sudden desire *(pothos)*, the overwhelming passion *(himeros)* that struck at his heart while he was reading the *Andromeda*—a passion not for a woman but for the clever *(dexios)* poet who created her (*Frogs* 51–56, 59). Euripides' Helen, rehabilitated and "revirginized," can stand, therefore, as the middle term between the wanton whores who were the Phaedras and Sthenoboias of his earlier plays and this purest of all pure virgins, Andromeda. If the *Thesmophoriazousae,* in a sense, traces out the career of Euripides as it moves from one extreme to another, from hyperrealism to seductive fantasy, the woman in her two faces—carnal sexuality and romantic eroticism—serves not only as the subject but also as the essential metaphor for the art of mimesis as it is represented in two modes.

The parody of the *Andromeda* is addressed to two different audiences and provokes two different reactions. On the theatrical level, the *Andromeda* is not a critical success. The policeman spectator, far from being enraptured by its performance, can hardly understand a word of what is going on and therefore unwittingly and fittingly plays the role of the sea monster. Perhaps more reasonably, he is a "comic travesty of the parts played by duped barbarians in Euripides' escape-dramas."[31] But the par-

30. On Euripides' *Andromeda,* see Webster 1967, 192–99; and the references in Rau 1967, 66n.111. For the parody itself, see Rau 1967, 66–89; and Rau 1975, 353–56. Rau sees this parody as redundant of the *Helen,* motivated solely by comic opportunism, not by dramaturgical need.

31. See now Hall 1989, 41. The extant escape dramas are *Helen* and *Iphigenia in Tauris,* the latter also a recent play. Hall (42–43) argues for the possibility of a barbarian presence in the *Andromeda* (the princess's guards or perhaps her own father). Bobrick (1991)

ody might well have been an unspoken thematic success with the women. The ensuing choral song, which begins with the invocation to the virgin Pallas Athena of the city and ends with the two goddesses of the Thesmophoria (1136–59), might only refer to the chorus's joy at the policeman's triumph over the violator of their ritual, a point to which I will return. But it cannot be coincidence that immediately afterward Euripides offers terms of peace to the women: "Never again will I slander women, this I promise" (1160–64). He adds, "If I can take away this kinsman of mine who is bound to the plank, never again will I speak ill of you." He threatens, however, in a comic disavowal, "If you don't give in, I'll reveal everything you do at home to your husbands when they come back from the army" (1166–69). The women accept the offer, since it's the best they can get, but the male world has already taken matters out of their hands; Euripides must persuade the barbarian too (1170–71).

The appearance of the Scythian policeman who ties the kinsman to the punishment plank sets the stage for the performance of the *Andromeda*. At the same time, his entry creates the maximum distance between the romantic nature of the play itself and the would-be spectator/actor who is meant to fall under its spell. For the Scythian policeman belongs fully to the conventions of the comic theater, as do all barbarians and others whose outlandish language, gestures, and costumes offer a dependable source of ethnic laughter. The first scene of the *Telephos*, played between the kinsman and the mother of the "child," was played "straight," according to paratragic rules, which encourage comic characters in dire comic circumstances to resort to mock-tragic expressions of their plight. In the *Helen* the comic already intrudes more directly in the intervention of Critylla. In the *Andromeda* the parody takes on a double focus by playing both to the tragic and the comic: it exploits the props and scenery for its tragic setting along with the intrinsic comic properties of the Scythian archer.

"Double exposure" rules this last and grandest finale, and the perplexities of gender and genre reach their extremes. Once Euripides, flying by on the machine, has given him the cue, the kinsman plays two roles (himself and Andromeda) and in two modes (as solo and duet), both with increasing skill and independence. His opening monody of lament wonderfully combines the details of his own comic predicament with the tragic

---

suggests a more direct parody of the *Iphigenia in Tauris*. Linking the names of Artemisia (the procuress) and the dancing girl (Elaphion, "little deer") to the circumstances of Iphigenia's rescue from sacrifice by the goddess's (Artemis) substitution of a deer, Bobrick finds an analogy in Euripides' rescue of his kinsman (Artemis/Iphigenia) by the substitution of the dancing girl (Little Deer). The Scythian policeman would then be taking the part of Thoas, king of the Taurians.

plight of Andromeda. Now he shifts from one voice to the other; now he merges the two together (1015–55). Euripides also plays two roles and likewise alternates between female (Echo) and male (Perseus). What is more, in taking the part of Echo, Euripides divides his attention between two characters, first tormenting the kinsman with his abusive repetitions and then turning the same technique on the Scythian policeman.

Echo itself is the doubling of another's voice; it also represents the purest form of mimesis. In retrospect, all three formal parodies bear a metarepresentational stamp: the *Palamedes,* in the art of writing, which imitates words in visible signs; the *Helen,* in its intimations of the *eidōlon,* which imitates the human form; and now Echo as the direct mimesis of voice. To these we may also add the parabasis with its etymological theory of names as comic mimetic guarantors of true identity.

What distinguishes Echo from the other phenomena is its paradoxical status as both nature and artifice. As the one example of a mimesis in nature itself, the mimetic reproduction of an echo in personified form translates the imitation of nature into an artificial theatrical effect. In turning his parodic skills on Echo, who appeared as a figure in a cave at the opening of the *Andromeda,* Aristophanes has singled out a radical innovation in Euripidean art. By giving it a run in all its possibilities, the comic poet succeeds in exposing the figure of Echo as the prime example of conscious mimetic illusion. But it is also significant for the general theme of mimesis that Echo is not an "it," but a "she." Always a female voice that imitates, and always situated in an erotic milieu, she is connected in myth to Narcissus in Ovid's *Metamorphoses* (3.356–401) and in Longus's *Daphnis and Chloe* to Pan (3.23). Euripides, the male, must dress as a female to imitate Echo who herself is the principle of imitation. Echo as the embodiment (more properly, disembodiment) of mimesis is also the focal point for the concept of the feminine that can never be grasped as primary and original, but only as the one who is imitated or the one who imitates; yet as such she is also empowered as the mistress of imitation.

I will return to this link between the feminine and mimesis. Here it is important to note that the exposure of Echo as played by Euripides, who brings her into view from behind the scene, turns the tragic to comic or better still mixes up the two modes. Echo might stand as the mediating figure between tragedy and comedy, divided between them and yet bringing the genres together, as the artful device of the original model and the slapstick cliché of the comic theater. No longer framed as a contest between Euripides and the women, the encounter is one between the comic poet and his tragic rival whom the comic poet parodically imitates.[32] Imi-

32. This rivalry is attested in ancient texts. A fragment of Aristophanes' older contemporary Kratinos reads: "'And who are you?' Some clever theater-goer may ask: 'some subtle

tation in the form of parody retains to the end its ambivalent status as a "poetics of contradiction," for in his last theatrical act, Euripides is compelled to turn finally and fully to the comic stage. Dressed as an old procuress (Artemisia), he offers the Scythian policeman a dancing girl to distract his attention while he hustles both the kinsman and himself off stage.

The play began with one tragic poet in drag, and it ends the same way—or does it? Does Euripides' having to dress as a woman (not once, but twice) unman him or empower him? Is Euripides brought down now to the comic level, his true affinity for the other genre revealed at last? Or given this plot—the expert ending to a comic play—is Euripides led to imitate his imitator, and by that imitation is he allowed to take over the comic stage? This is a comedy, after all, and comedy ends with signs of unimpeded libido, most typically in the pairing of a lusty man and a dancing girl. Euripides is the rival poet, but he is also Aristophanes' "creature." The comic playwright controls the plot and activity of his characters. Yet the distinctive feature of comic protagonists is precisely their seeming ability to improvise their own scripts, just as Euripides does here. Aristophanes has already purloined Euripides' type of tragic plot to stage his own play, for the ostensible purpose of punishing Euripides' transgression of social (and aesthetic) norms. Yet this purloined plot has allowed the tragic poet to repair that transgression—on the condition that he conform to the conventions of comedy. In this interplay between norm and transgression, relevant for both genres, Aristophanes' solution to Euripides' plight finally escapes any stable decision as to who is the victor in the game. This inextricable nexus of reciprocal trespass on each other's terrain is perhaps the point. But by the same token, the resort to a bawdy comic finale in the dancing girl also signifies that the women's victory over Euripides has concluded with the return of the comic female to her proper place as the one whose function is to provide satisfaction for male desires.

Yet the motif of "women on top" has not altogether disappeared; it is distilled and defused in the name Euripides adopts for his role as the old procuress. Artemisia was the Carian queen who "manned" a ship during the Persian Wars and put up a brilliant fight, to the Greeks' undying shame in that, as they note again and again, they had to do battle with a woman who was an equal of a man.[33] In his accommodation to a comic ending

---

quibbler, an idea-chaser, a euripidaristophanizer?' " (frag. 307 K). The scholiast to Plato's *Apology*, who quotes these lines, observes: "Aristophanes was satirized for imitating Euripides through his mockery of him." He continues with a quotation from Aristophanes himself: "I use his rounded elegance of style, but make the thoughts less vulgar than his" (frag. 471 K = schol. *Plato* Clack. 330 Bekker).

33. For the Persian side, Herodotus, 8.88.3, reports Xerxes' reaction to Artemisia's skills: "My men have become women, my women men."

that brings about the dual salvation of himself and his kinsman, Euripides has reverted to a purely sexual mode. The barbarian had already dispelled the erotic enchantment of the *Andromeda* with his crude and explicit jokes about the sexual identity (and vulnerability) of the kinsman. Euripides may have no choice but to meet him now on his own terms. But the poet has kept his promise to the women, displacing as far as possible from the world of the respectable married women of the Thesmophoria the open sexual obscenity that promotes the life-enhancing program of the comic world. Yet the Thesmophoria is a sacred festival. Like the comic performance, and more directly, it leads to a renewal of vital energies. Thus, as the play draws to a close, comedy, tragedy, and festival all converge for a common purpose of celebration.

Euripides, by his cunning inventions and his myriad schemes for salvation, has rescued the kinsman and has redeemed himself of his impiety. He has done so, I will argue, more directly than has previously been recognized. For despite his creative innovations both on this comic stage and on his own terrain, Euripides has not invented everything himself. Rather, he has realigned his plots with more traditional paradigms. Two "secrets" lie at the heart of the text, serving to integrate the ritual and aesthetic elements of the play and to explain with greater cogency why the women were willing to accept Euripides' tender of peace. At one level, the parodies display their status as "mere" fictions that can only pretend to represent "reality" to a lesser or greater degree. Yet these same fictions are also essential to sustain the mystifying properties of myth and poetry that underlie the effects of tragic and comic genres alike. The sottish Scythian policeman mistakes the name of the Gorgon that Perseus/Euripides carries as that of Gorgias, the fifth-century sophist, for whom the value of tragedy resides precisely in its capacity to deceive (frag. 23 D-K).[34] "Tragedy deceives by myths and the display of various passions; and whereas the tragic poet who deceives is juster than he who does not, the deceived is also wiser than the one who is not deceived."

Mimesis: Festival: Dionysos/Demeter

It is not the earth that imitates the woman in the matter of conception and birth, but it is the woman who imitates the earth.

PLATO

34. The reference to "Gorgo the scribe" may refer to another contemporary and not to the famous sophist, but Aristophanes mentions Gorgias several times in his comedies, and Plato's *Symposium*, 198c, contains a wordplay between *Gorgias* and *Gorgon*. See further Rogers 1904, 119, commenting on l. 1102.

Myth is speech stolen and restored. Only, speech which is re-
stored is no longer quite that which was stolen; when it was
brought back, it was not put exactly in its place.

ROLAND BARTHES

The *Thesmophoriazousae*, organized as a dialogue between comedy and
tragedy, draws attention to and explores the inconstant relations between
the realities of everyday life and the fictive arrangements of the theater.
But a third term needs to be considered here: cult, which is integrated into
the play as its scene and its context, yet stands outside the structures of
make-believe by its marked form as sacred ritual.

At one level, the ritual center of the play serves as the intermediate
and mediating borderland between the events of everyday life and those
of the theater. The ritual space of the Thesmophorion, as suggested earlier,
is analogous to the domestic space of the women at home, so that the
kinsman's intrusion into their ritual enclosure replicates the impious intrusion of Euripides' theater into the other forbidden female domain.[35] But
on another level, the literal fact of that ritual identity invites us to reverse
these terms to consider the import of the underlying *mythos* of the Thesmophoria in its dialectical relationship to that other *mythos* that always
and everywhere presides over the theater. More generally still, the focus
on cult reminds us that the theater is, after all, an "imitation with a difference" of mythic and ritual forms. These provide the latent structuring
patterns over which and with which drama plays out its variations and
deviations in new and different keys.

Rereading the play in cultic terms brings to center stage a dialogue
between Demeter and Dionysos, each representing a mode that defines the
feminine and each furnishing a mythic scenario that can be related to both
genres, comedy and tragedy. The ritual space sacred to women evokes
Dionysiac as well as Demetrian associations. Its trespass by men, therefore, also recalls the founding plot of the theater itself, best known from
Euripides' late play, the *Bacchae*. The Dionysiac has a tragic and a comic
side. The tragic side is seen in the serious consequences of violating ritual
taboos, when the male, who comes to spy on women's secrets, arouses
their bacchant madness and suffers *sparagmos* at their hands. The comic

---

35. The text further supports this link between invasion of domestic privacy and trespass upon ritual piety in the charges that two women bring against Euripides for adversely
affecting their lives. The first speaker, as we have seen, blames the poet's "bad" women for
making their husbands suspicious about the sexual misconduct of their own wives, which
leads to a curtailment of their freedom at home. The second woman, however, alleges economic rather than domestic hardship, in that she has lost her poor widow's livelihood (selling
garlands to the faithful) because of Euripides' well-known fondness for characters who claim
the gods do not exist (443–58).

side has as its carnivalesque license, even its duty, to transgress all taboos. It therefore delights in sacrilege and in violating ritual solemnity so it can deflect a potential Dionysiac tragedy into comic farce.

On social grounds, the occasion of the Thesmophoria legitimates the women's intrusion into public space. But in ritual terms, the festival is, in a sense, an intrusion onto the comic stage. For the three days of its duration, the women must abstain from sex. Even more, we are specifically told that the play is set on the second and most solemn day, the Nesteia, when the women also abstain from food in imitation of Demeter's mourning for her lost daughter (80, 983). The Thesmophoria thus answers to the role of antifestival, as Lent is opposed to Carnival, for fast rules instead of feast and chastity replaces sexual indulgence. The women's intention, which generates the comic plot, is thus entirely consonant with the spirit of their ritual day: the trial and punishment of one who has inappropriately exposed their sexual selves and with serious tragic intent. The kinsman, therefore, performs a double function. As Euripides' representative, he goes to defend the integrity of tragic art, but as the comic character, he rightly disrupts the solemn proceedings by means of his defense—the further exposure of women's sexual secrets. This same duality means that the women must also play a double role as followers of Demeter *and* as bacchants of Dionysos.

Theater encompasses both modes of drama and both modes of cult. It can use one to test the other, as it already does in the prologue scene with Agathon. For Agathon is more than a tragic poet. His mimetic theory, which attributes his transvestite dress both to art (mimesis) and nature (effeminacy), is itself a mixture of manner and modes. His ritual entrance, which sacralizes the calling of his art through invocation and prayer, also offers in advance a private version of the Thesmophoria.[36] Yet his costume evokes from the kinsman a quotation from Aeschylus's *Edonians* that was addressed to Dionysos himself in his indeterminate sexual status, thus suggesting that this man-woman *(gynnis)* represents the god of the theater (or a mimesis of him, which amounts to the same thing, according to Agathon's theories).

In the dramatic plot, Agathon refuses to infiltrate the Thesmophoria because he would play the woman's part too well. In the Dionysiac scenario, he refuses to go because as the sacral figure in transvestite garb, he may stand outside the action as the spirit of theater itself. The one who "plays at playing and visibly reduplicates the act of acting"[37] has the

36. On this point, see Kleinknecht 1937, 101; and Horn 1970, 101–2.

37. Salingar 1974, 94. On the notion that Dionysos in the *Bacchae* himself stages and directs the proceedings, functioning both as a character within the drama and as the god of the theater, see Foley 1980; and Segal 1982, 215–71. The *Thesmophoriazousae*, we might note, antedates the *Bacchae* by about seven years.

power to transform others—to provide them with their costumes and their roles for the play that is about to begin.

The robing of the kinsman on stage with articles from Agathon's wardrobe functions within the mythic plot exactly like the robing of Pentheus in the *Bacchae*, for precisely the same purpose—the infiltration of women's mysteries—and with precisely the same voyeuristic expectation of spying on women's sexual secrets.[38] What the kinsman brings out of hiding, once his own identity has been exposed, is the Dionysiac, which lurks beneath the women's Demetrian façade: the wineskin that masquerades as a baby was "conceived" at the last Dionysia and its "mother," Mika, calls upon another woman, Mania (Madness) for help (728, 739).

By slaying the wineskin, the kinsman indeed turns tragedy into farce, but he also puts an end, so to speak, to the bacchic plot. The situation now no longer conforms to the Dionysiac pattern in which the women would themselves overpower the male and do him violence. Instead, Mnesilochos becomes again the violator of women, and given the nature of his act, he furnishes the transition to the Demetrian plot.[39] The abduction of the baby follows the *Telephos* but, as noted previously, although the scene fits the gender of the infant is reversed. Now let us note that the "baby" whom the kinsman abducts from the woman and consigns to "death" is a girl named Kore, whose abduction and violation have deprived the "mother" of her daughter (Kore) and her daughter of her virginity *(korē)*. This episode, I suggest, reactivates the scenario of the Thesmophoria, which begins with the abduction of the maiden Kore-Persephone that takes her down to the underworld. The Nesteia is located temporally at the midpoint of the Thesmophoria and at the midpoint of the myth, in the liminal time after the loss of Kore and before her rescue and return. Now that the kinsman himself will require rescue, he begins to reenact stages of Euripides' escape dramas that can and should be correlated with the ruling *mythos* of rescue in Persephone's story. In broadest terms, the *mythos* of Dionysos gives the pattern for transgression, while the Demetrian provides the pattern for redemption—both linked in their own way to the larger theme of deliverance.

The Dionysiac impulse is synchronic, divided in the same action between tragic and comic moods, like Dionysos Lusios himself, who de-

---

38. The doublet of Pentheus in Aeschylus's *Edonians* is Lycurgus, another defier of Dionysos's power who undergoes a similar fate. See above, chapter 5.

39. This opposition between Dionysiac and Demetrian modes is not as stable as I suggest for the purposes of this analysis, because any situation that places women "on top," even for legitimate cultic purposes, invokes the anxiety that women will do violence to men in the bacchant or the Amazonian way. Two historical anecdotes tell such a tale of men who infiltrated the mysteries of the Thesmophoria, one in Cyrene (Aelian frag. 44 Hercher) and the other in Laconia (Pausanias, 4.17.1). See further Detienne 1979b, 183–214.

stroys or redeems. But the Demetrian mode is diachronic: its scenario passes through the spectrum from tragedy to comedy—from death, captivity, and mourning to return, recovery, and joy. The Demetrian plot exemplifies the salvational motif, not only for the Thesmophoria in its invocation of fertility and renewal but also, above all, in the Eleusinian mysteries, which are open to men and women alike. In this play, the Thesmophoria provides the ritual background for Euripides' rescue dramas. In the *Frogs,* however, where Dionysos descends into Hades to rescue the poet who will save the city, his quest is properly accompanied by the songs of mystic initiates from Eleusis. The Demetrian plot mixing with the Dionysiac can thus bring together the genres of tragedy and comedy, and it joins up with the comic theater in mutual celebration of joy.

Once the kinsman is made captive, the parodies seem to meet with failure in their immediate reception. At the same time, they are increasingly invested with the unspoken power of mimesis, which "insists on the reality of the moment, even while practicing its own form of 'deceit.'"[40] This mimesis exposes theater as "mere" illusion, but reinstates it under the name of a higher mimesis. The kinsman moves *down* the scale of male potency to assume his last humiliating role as a woman. But the theatrical experience itself moves *upward* through the mythic plot as it converts the male who has abducted the Kore into the Kore herself, whose *mythos* promises that she will be redeemed.

In this double perspective, the parodies stand out in high relief against the choral background of ritual songs, a contrast that places ritual and theater at opposite ends of the spectrum. In one sense, the increasing validation of the festival mood (which combines the fast with celebration) can be correlated with the deteriorating situation of the male intruder: first, after his temporary removal from the stage by the policeman and then after the parody of the *Andromeda* scene, which leaves the Scythian still in charge of his captive. But a closer look at the content of these songs shows a subtle series of responses on the part of the chorus to the underlying mythic tenor of the parodic scenes.

The *Helen* episode, framed by the parabasis on one side and the choral song on the other, is the focal point for this conversion both of the kinsman and the chorus. The last part of the parabasis, which extols for the first time, though in comic terms, the role of the chorus as worthy mothers in the city rather than as errant wives, ushers in this turn from their Dionysiac to their Demetrian personae. The *Helen* scene itself, with its conversion of Helen from the adulterous wife into the faithful spouse or in larger terms from the whore to the virgin, is followed by a choral dance that turns around in a circle and then around again (*kuklos, tropos,*

40. Salingar 1974, 104.

ana-strephō, torneuō, 959–1000). For the first time, the motif of legitimate marriage connected with Hera Teleia appears in their song (973–
76), as if in response to the evocation of marriage in the parody of the
Helen. In this festive mood, the chorus proclaims the sanctity of the rites,
at which it would now be inappropriate to slander men (962–64), and
offers a long invocation to the gods—the Olympians, Artemis, Apollo,
Hera, Pan, and the Nymphs—inviting them all to join in the dance.
Now the chorus includes Dionysos himself in his idyllic setting on the
mountain as he sports in lovely song and dance among his nymphs (987–
1000).

That the *Helen* earns this response is consonant with Euripides' portrait of his heroine, but the Demetrian connection is still more intrinsic to
his play. For in that drama itself, the motif of Persephone is evoked again
and again, shaping the mythic frame of the plot,[41] and several times Helen
even explicitly likens herself to Persephone (*Hel.* 175, 244ff.). Egypt is
envisioned as the underworld, the place that threatens death to Greek sailors who touch upon its shores, while the lustful king who keeps Helen
captive in anticipation of a forced marriage takes on the role of Hades. At
the critical moment of the play, when Helen and Menelaos have devised
their rescue plot, the chorus sings an elaborate ode to the Great Mother,
charting her shift from grief to laughter in response to the consoling effects
of dance and song (*Hel.* 1301–68). The laughter of the mourning mother
in both the *Helen* and the *Homeric Hymn to Demeter* (occasioned in the
latter by Iambe's obscene joking) is the first sign of her recovery into life,
the same laughter whose echoes we hear in the comic choral song of the
Thesmophoriazousae (979).

But with the figure of the pure virgin Andromeda, the Persephone
theme of the maiden finally comes to the fore. The choral song that follows expands the context to include the city's goddess in the circle of the
Thesmophoric divinities. The women begin by invoking Pallas Athena,
the "unyoked virgin maiden" (*parthenon azuga kourēn,* 1139), and celebrate her civic power as the one who "holds the keys of the city" (1142),
thereby replacing Hera Teleia in the previous ode, who was named in her
domestic function as "keeper of the keys of marriage" (976). The "people
of women" (*dēmos gunaikōn*) call upon their city goddess in her joyful
aspects as "a lover of choral song and dance," the divinity who, when she
comes, brings "festival-loving peace" (1136–47).[42] Appropriately for this

41. For Helen as the Kore, see Guépin 1968, 120–22, 128–33, 137–42. The motif is
also treated by Wolff 1973 and Segal 1971, but especially now by Foley 1992.
42. Strictly speaking, Pallas Athena has no place in the rites of the Thesmophoria, but
it is entirely in keeping with the political orientation of Old Comedy that she have the pride

choral song that addresses only female deities, the women end by inviting
the two goddesses of the Thesmophoria "to come with kindness to these
sacred rites, forbidden for men to see, so that with their torches they might
make manifest an immortal vision *[ambroton opsin]*" (1136–59). The
women themselves whom "Andromeda" now addresses as her maiden
chorus (1015) are virgins again, and "Andromeda" herself, repeatedly
called *korē* and *parthenos,* laments the fate that binds her to death instead
of to her marriage couch (1034–36, cf. 1122).

In the division of the actor's roles between the kinsman and Euripides,
the kinsman stands in for the poet and speaks in his name. But Mnesilochos plays the transgressive role in both Dionysiac and Demetrian plots
until he takes the part of the maiden who needs to be saved. Euripides
himself, however, is reserved for the role of potential rescuer, introduced
on stage to bring liberation to the captive Dionysiac figure of comedy and
salvation to the imprisoned "Kore" heroine of his plays. At the comic end,
Euripides himself assumes at last the female role, and with it he finally
achieves the role of redeemer. As the old woman, who brings relief with
laughter, he joins Demeter and Dionysos together in discrepant harmony.
Two men in women's dress continue the transvestite sport of Dionysos,
but in their female masquerade of old and young, they also comically
mime the reunion of the mother and the maid, leaving the stage together
and the comic denizens of the underworld behind.[43]

This harmony, however, is not as incongruous as it might seem. The
Nesteia, the day of the fast at which the women imitated the mourning of
Demeter, ended with *aischrologia,* or obscene ritual banter, in commemoration of the woman, Iambe, who met Demeter at the crossroads and with
her scurrilous jokes made Demeter laugh and so broke through her death-
like grief. Thus in the Thesmophoric ritual, *aischrologia* has its place, as
it does in the cult of Dionysos, elsewhere and in the comic theater.[44] The
Andromeda parody, played out as a mixture of erotic lyrical pathos and
obscene sexual jests, belongs as much to the cult of Demeter as to that of
Dionysos, and it brings the play back full circle to its beginning with its
other tragic poet, Agathon, and the theme of mimesis it sets in both ritual
modes.

---

of place as the virgin figure in the city. Similarly, the myth of the Thesmophoria involves a
relationship between a mother and daughter (Demeter-Kore), but the women in the parabasis, when they boast of their maternal function, refer to the hoplite sons they have borne
for the city. I am indebted to Nicole Loraux for raising this issue.

43. The restoration of the rites also signals the rehabilitation of Euripides over the wom-
en's second charge of impiety. See note 35 above.

44. On the nature and types of *aischrologia,* see Fluck 1931. On the use of ritual obscenity within the social and cultural parameters of women's lives, see Zeitlin 1982b.

Mimesis: Art and the Literary Tradition

Language is the universal whore whom I have to make into a
virgin.   KARL KRAUS

The *Helen* is the ritual "secret" within the text; it is also the stage for the
discovery of another "secret," one that belongs to the domain of art and
literary tradition. The kinsman's impersonation of the "new" Helen, I
have suggested, introduces a new role for women in Euripides' plays that
serves implicitly to counteract the charges of slander that the women of
the Thesmophoria have brought against the poet. A new, positive version
of the feminine is offered in place of the old, and its representation forecasts Euripides's renunciation of his earlier errant ways. In this respect, the
Helen functions in the play as Euripides' palinode, the song that reverses
itself to "run backward" *(palin-ōdē)*. More precisely, that reversal is located within the *Helen* itself, since the play offers a revised version of the
traditional errant wife whom we know from epic and elsewhere. Euripides
is not, however, the inventor of the "new" plot of the *Helen*. He follows a
sixth-century poet, Stesichorus, who, as tradition has it, was the first to
compose a palinode. The subject of Stesichorus's palinode was Helen herself, and his version introduced the motif of the *eidōlon*. The story goes
that Stesichorus, having slandered Helen, was blinded for his blasphemy.
But being a wise poet, he recognized the cause of his blindness and composed another song that began: "That story was not true; you did not go
within the well-oared ships, nor did you come to the walls of Troy." As a
result, he regained his sight (Plato, *Phaedrus* 243b).[45]

The story has been interpreted as a reflection on the double and contradictory role of Helen—as goddess, daughter of Zeus, and as woman,
the adulterous wife of Menelaos. The case of Stesichorus has been referred
to the violation of the cultic norms in Sparta, where Helen was actually
worshipped in a cult role as a goddess. By creating the *eidōlon* who remained pure from any taint, the palinode unequivocally confirmed her
divine status.[46] We may compare the tale of another *eidōlon* or cloud-
image, this one appropriately created by Zeus, the "cloud gatherer," again
in an erotic setting and with the purpose of foiling an attempt at unlawful
possession. This time the *eidōlon* was made as a substitute for Zeus's own

45. Stesichorus, *PMG* 193. Other sources: Isocrates, *Helen* 64; Conon, *FGrH* 26 F
1.18; and Pausanias, 3.19.11.
46. On Stesichorus (especially in relation to Euripides' *Helen*), see the discussion with
bibliography in Kannicht 1969, 26–41. Some recently discovered papyrus fragments suggest
the possibility of a second palinode, but Kannicht persuasively argues for one, although the
issue does not affect my argument. More recently, see Bassi 1993 with extensive bibliography.

consort, Hera, whom the mortal Ixion had tried to ravish. When grasping at the goddess, he found only Nephele (cloud) instead.[47]

The *Thesmophoriazousae*, as it proceeds, suggests a model of the female who veers between the impious (bad woman) and the sacred (pure virgin), but Stesichorus's diptych of ode and palinode seems to propose a more radical division between the two categories of the female, separated by the fine but firm line that divides mortal from immortal. But if we look back at Stesichorus in the light of the *Thesmophoriazousae*, the question of the two Helens may be posed differently. The fault for Stesichorus may lie not with the received *mythos* of Helen itself (that Helen went to Troy) but with its mode of poetic representation, which violated Helen by violating the norms of poetic decorum.[48]

Having revealed too much of the mortal Helen (her wanton sexuality),[49] Stesichorus turns in repentance to the other extreme: untainted erotic beauty, which is preserved in the split between the figure of the pure Helen who never went to Troy and the look-alike imitation, who played her traditional part. By this device, Stesichorus avoids altogether the problem of the woman as morally "good" (respectable) or "bad" (shameless), but in so doing he raises another question with regard to femininity. This new eros that Helen incarnates divides itself from within to establish another set of opposites—the false *eidōlon* and the true figure of the divine—which are now equally unattainable. One is a false imitation of

47. On the myth of Ixion and Nephele, see especially Detienne 1977, 83–87.

48. Nagy (1990, 422) interprets Stesichorus's palinode as "a local version in the process of making a bid for Panhellenic status."

49. We learn from ancient testimony that in Stesichorus's version, Tyndareus, the father of Helen and Clytemnestra, had forgotten to sacrifice to Aphrodite while giving worship to other gods. The goddess, angered by his neglect, predicted that his daughters would be twice-wedded *(digamoi)* and thrice-wedded *(trigamoi)*, i.e., they would suffer an excess of Aphrodite to match their father's undervaluation of the goddess. (Note the punishment is on his daughters and not his wife.) The slander of Helen, then, perhaps lay in the charge of lubricious sexuality, a trait belonging to her by "nature," as it were, rather than to the circumstantial facts of the myth itself. See further Kannicht 1969, 39–41.

Euripides himself may be said to have composed a "palinode" when he offered a second version of the *Hippolytos* in circumstances that resembled those of Stesichorus. The first *Hippolytos* (known to us from fragments and other evidence) caused a scandal in Athens because of its shameless Phaedra, to whom Aristophanes refers in the *Thesmophoriazousae* and in the *Frogs* (see above, note 9). In response, Euripides revised his representation of Phaedra to the figure of a noble woman who struggles heroically to suppress the fatal passion inflicted on her by Aphrodite. See further chapter 6 above.

The reason given for Stesichorus's blindness may be a "sacralized" version of Euripides' violation of literary decorum. Blindness is a punishment for mortal men who mingle with goddesses or who view them naked at their bath, but it is also an attribute of poets and prophets. See the data in Buxton 1980.

the other, which itself (as divine) can never be grasped by mortals in a
"real" state, but only in the empty form that is inevitably substituted for
the original. Helen, as the darling of Aphrodite in any form and for all
time, incarnates the irresistible principle of eros, perpetually desirable and
desired by all. But Stesichorus's story also suggests that eros is not divided
from poetics. The poet slandered Helen, and to atone he fabricated a fictive *eidōlon* in her place and openly declared the original version as a
fiction *(ouk etumōs)*. Helen, whose "true" (traditional) *mythos* may be
denied as a fiction, may thereby also personify poetics even as she embodies eros. For as fictive *eidōlon*, Stesichorus's Helen acquires the capacity
to impersonate herself and to draw attention to the notion of imitation as
a conscious poetic creation.

Stesichorus uses Helen, as it were, to assert his role as a poet. Working
within a received tradition that he alters in two different ways (the "blasphemy" in the first version and the recantation in the second), he raises
the notion of fictionality as a possible attribute of mythic texts in order to
account for his own innovations. In the process, he invents a new literary
genre—the palinode. He also inaugurates a new tradition, establishes a
new paradigm, which Aristophanes uses to construct his own piece by
which Euripides' *Helen* can serve to exonerate the tragic poet from the
charge of blaspheming against women. This paradigm, reproduced in the
Euripidean play itself, can serve at the same time to raise similar questions
about fictionality and imitation. Other critics have noted that Euripides'
play itself shows a consciousness of its status as a piece of theater, particularly when Helen and Menelaos, in contriving their fictive devices for escape, also indicate their desire *not* to imitate the clichés of other tragic
plots (e.g., *Hel.* 1056). In satirizing Euripides' theatrical innovations in
the *Helen* and in presenting a parody with metatheatrical dimensions, Aristophanes reaffirms, as it were, through the tradition that goes back to
Stesichorus, the perennial utility of Helen as the figure upon whom can be
focused the poetic problems of imitation itself.

One might call Stesichorus's *eidōlon* a proto-theatrical and proto-
mimetic representation insofar as the poet precedes the fifth-century developments of the theater and of theories of mimesis. Yet although Stesichorus invented the *eidōlon* of Helen, he is not the first to associate Helen
with questions of imitation. A longer tradition stands behind her that begins with her first appearance in Greek epic. It is worth exploring this
tradition briefly in order to understand better Helen's paradigmatic value
for the particular aesthetic problems that are raised in the time of Aristophanes and Euripides. This exploration will serve in turn to shift the
discussion to my final area of concern: the categories of Greek thought
that associate the feminine with mimesis, whether figural or poetic.

Mimesis: Eros and Art

*In dreams, a writing tablet signifies a woman, since it receives
the imprint of all kinds of letters.* ARTEMIDORUS, ONEIROCRITICA

Already in the *Iliad*, Helen, as the erotic center of the poem, is connected
with the art of poetry when she weaves a tapestry of double fold, depicting on it "many contests of horse-taming Trojans and bronze-mailed
Achaeans, which they suffered on account of her" (*Il.* 3.125–28), as if she
were "weaving the very fabric of heroic epic."[50] Better still, in the fourth
book of the *Odyssey*, when Telemachos visits Sparta and finds Helen and
Menelaos reunited as a married pair, they each tell a tale of Helen and
Odysseus from the days when she was still at Troy. In her story, Odysseus,
disguised as a beggar, comes secretly into the city as a spy. She alone recognizes him and does not betray him, but cares for him and rejoices that
her homecoming will soon be at hand (*Od.* 4.240–64). Menelaos, on the
other hand, tells another story of Helen that puts her in a very different
light. On the night in which the Trojan horse stood inside the gates of the
city, he says, Helen, now the wife of Deiphobos, the brother of Paris, came
down, and by imitating all the different voices of their wives, tempted the
Greeks who were hidden inside to betray their presence, a ruse that would
have succeeded had it not been for Odysseus's discerning prudence (*Od.*
4.266–89). Two stories are juxtaposed, each offering the same characterization of a clever Odysseus but a different version of Helen. She is the
mistress of many voices, the mistress of mimesis, linked in both stories to
secrecy, disguise, and deception.[51]

Even more, Helen is the mistress of ceremonies, who stages the mood
and setting of the tales, when to counteract the grief stirred up by their sad
memories of Odysseus, she casts a drug into their wine, a *pharmakon*,
which takes away pain and brings forgetfulness of sorrows. And she bids
them to delight themselves with stories *(mythoi)*, which she herself will
initiate, narrating "a plausible (appropriate) tale" (*Od.* 4.220–39). These
pharmaka belong to the poetics of enchantment, seducing the hearer with
tales of deception, tales of impersonation in costume and voice. They sum-
mon up the best memories of Odysseus for an evening's recollection. As

50. Clader 1976, 8.
51. Helen's skill may be compared to the extraordinary talents of the Delian maidens,
in the service of Apollo, who sing sacred hymns and epic deeds. "They also can imitate the
tongues of all humankind *[anthrōpoi]* and their chattering speech. Each one would say that
he himself were uttering the sound, so well is the beautiful song fitted to them" (*Homeric
Hymn to Apollo* 156–64). Cf. the myth of Echo, especially the version of her relationship to
Pan in Longus, *Daphnis and Chloe* 3.23. See further the feminist discussion of Echo in
Greenberg 1980; and Loewenstein's (1984) discussion of the tradition.

tales of Helen, they are told without comment, as tales from a past that
seems to have been forgiven, transmuted into a play of symmetrical reversals that charm instead of dismay.[52]

Yet the ordering of the two stories also makes clear that the second
tale of Helen is meant as an implicit comment on the first one, which may
function like a proto-palinode (but in reverse). Menelaos's tale operates
on two levels. On the first, it undermines Helen's earlier version, which
represented her fidelity to the Greeks, in favor of one that shows she can
imitate many different voices, each time with the intention to seduce and
betray. On the second level, his story, in this setting ruled by the enchantment of the *pharmakon,* functions as a self-reflective comment on the nature of fiction and mimesis, which Helen embodies. Menelaos's story thus
intimates that Helen's previous story may be a fiction and suggests in the
process that Helen and storytelling may be one and the same: the imitation
of many voices in the service of seduction and enchantment. Helen is the
figure who by her imitation of the voices of different men's wives, links
eros and poetics under the rubric of mimesis. Only Odysseus, the master
storyteller himself, is capable of unmasking her disguise.

Menelaos's story can only hint at the difference between fiction and
truth. But another story is more precise in this regard, the one Menelaos
recalls the next day when he recounts his experience with Proteus, the old
man of the sea, after he left Troy and came with Helen to Egypt. Proteus
is the master of lies and truth; better still, he is the figure of the shifting
nature of truth, which Menelaos can grasp as one and true only if he
grasps Proteus himself. But Proteus will change his shape from one creature to another until, under Menelaos's unremitting grip, he will return to
his single original form. Menelaos's success depends upon the advice of a
female, Proteus's daughter, who perfectly fulfills her feminine role. She
betrays the existence of Proteus, the secrets of his powers, and the means
of overcoming him (a mimetic disguise of sealskins and a secret ambush,
Od. 4.351–570). The story of mimesis practiced by Helen can never escape the ambiguities of its telling, but the mimetic repertory of Proteus has
a limit that will result in the revelation of an absolute truth. Here that
truth is the future of Menelaos, his homecoming and his ultimate fate: not
a mortal death, but eternal sojourn in the Elysian Fields, the paradisiac
islands to the west, "because Helen is yours and you are son-in-law therefore to Zeus" (*Od.* 4.561–70). Helen in the end rules both tales of mimesis—as a divinity, connected through her lineage to truth (and immortality), beyond the reaches of fiction (or perhaps the supreme fiction), and
just previously, as a mortal, skilled in the arts of mimesis and seduction.

---

52. For two excellent but different treatments of these stories, see Dupont-Roc and Le
Boulluec 1976; and Bergren 1981.

For the *Odyssey,* this ultimate "truth"—whether the translation of Menelaos to the permanence of the Elysian Fields or the "truth" of the recognition between Odysseus and Penelope, grounded on the fact that Penelope has truly been "true" to him—suggests the alternatives to the ambiguities of poetics and erotics that the pairing of the two stories of Helen and Menelaos represents. In the light of the marital reunion on Ithaca, these ambiguities are not only recollections of a past that belongs to Helen and Menelaos but also potential alternatives for Penelope herself. This future depends upon Penelope's choice of one of the two possible roles that the two stories offer her: that of the faithful woman who receives the beggar in disguise and welcomes him or that of the woman who, surrounded by men (read suitors for Greeks), practices the wiles of seduction, although another man's wife.[53] Penelope is no teller of stories; quite the contrary. She is worn out by hearing false tales of Odysseus that travelers have brought to her over the years or by encountering impostors of Odysseus himself. She has become skilled at testing the fictions of another's words, which have no power to seduce her with falsehoods. Yet she is the mistress of one guileful deception—and that to preserve her "true" self for Odysseus—in the weaving and secret unweaving of the fabric of Laertes' shroud. This is the one story she tells again and again, until she can claim Helen's, not Menelaos's, story as her own.

The *Odyssey,* by virtue of its Penelope, can afford its Circes, Calypsos, Sirens, and Helens whom Odysseus encounters at various stages on his journeys or in his visit to Troy. But as the repertory of all stories, all fictions, the *Odyssey* adumbrates, even in the ambiguities of Odysseus himself, the ambivalence that Greek thought will manifest with increasing insistence toward the verbal and visual arts with their mimetic powers to persuade with the truths of their fictions. This ambivalence is not incongruent, at some level, with the increasing ambivalence with which the city's male ideology views its other gender, an attitude that serves to connect the feminine still more closely with art and artifice.[54] Thus the two Helens, the daughter of Zeus and the fictive *eidōlon,* may exemplify in the erotic sphere the hesitation in the aesthetic domain between an art that is divinely inspired and a craft that makes counterfeits of the real.[55] But

53. See also Anderson 1977, 5–13. Katz (1991, 79–80) suggests that the Helen paradigm for Penelope is operative from Book 18 (Penelope's appearance before the suitors) to the reunion in Book 23.

54. Space does not allow a more detailed discussion of the ambiguities of persuasion and the *logos* in connection with the feminine and with eros. See further Laín Entralgo 1970, 51–69; Detienne 1973, 51–80; and Kahn 1978, 119–64. For art and literature, see also Svenbro 1976; and Petre 1979.

55. The more pejorative notion of art as a counterfeit imitation of the real owes more to Platonic aesthetic theories. Craft includes and even gives first priority to artisanal skill.

while the *eidōlon* can be separated from the real Helen as an insubstantial likeness of herself, a mere figment, the *eidōlon* as a seductive objet d'art cannot be separated from the generic image of the feminine. For the "real" woman could be defined as a "real" *eidōlon*, created as such from the beginning in the person of the first woman, Pandora.

Instead of the ambiguity maintained in the dual genealogy of Helen as mortal and divine, Pandora is from the outset, in Hesiod's text of the *Theogony*, a fictive object, a copy, not an original. Fashioned at the orders of Zeus as punishment for Prometheus's deceptive theft of celestial fire for men, the female is the first imitation and the living counterpart to that original deception. She is endowed by the gods with the divine traits of beauty and adornment that conceal the bestial and thievish nature of her interior (*Theogony* 571–84). Artifact and artifice herself, Pandora installs the woman as *eidōlon* in the frame of human culture, equipped by her "unnatural" nature to seduce and enchant, to delight and deceive. More specifically, as Pietro Pucci has argued, the origin of Pandora coincides in the text with the origin of language:

> Because of her symbolic function and, literally, because of her ornaments and flowers, her glamor and her scheming mind, Pandora emblematizes the beginning of rhetoric; but at the same time she also stands for the rhetoric of the beginning. For she is both the "figure" of the origin and the origin of the "figure"—the first being invested with symbolic, referential elements. The text implies both the human dawn unmarked by imitation and rhetoric and a turning point that initiates the beautiful, imitative rhetorical process. In this way, the text reproduces the split between a language identical to reality and a language imitative of reality.[56]

This reading of Pandora is suggested by the implicit terms of the text, for rhetoric in Hesiod's time (c. 700 B.C.E.) had not yet been invented. But his negative view of Pandora, which arises naturally from his farmer's instrumental view of nature and culture, can still serve as a preview of the later philosophical thought, which in testing the world of physical appearances,

---

But this category also has its ambiguities for Greek thought in which the artistic product is far more admired than the artist who produces it. Poetry claimed a higher status than representational art, but greater consciousness of the poet as *poiētēs* (maker) introduces comparisons with artisanal activity. The *Thesmophoriazousae* itself reproduces the two opposing notions of poetic composition in the presentation of Agathon's poetry, where the sacred aspects, as discussed above, are comically juxtaposed with technical terms drawn from the more homely métiers (52–57).

56. Pucci 1977, 100–101. See chapter 2 above.

finds it deceptive precisely in the two spheres of carnal eros and artistic mimesis, specifically in the art of rhetoric itself.

It should therefore come as no surprise that Gorgias, the historical figure most closely identified with the development of rhetorical theory in fifth-century Athens, composed an encomium on Helen that is as much a defense of his art of the *logos* as a defense of Helen. I invoke this last example to return, after this long detour, to the text and context of Aristophanes, because I suspect that Gorgias is very much present in the *Thesmophoriazousae,* and not only as the possible garbled reference to him by the barbarian policeman who confuses Gorgon with Gorgias. The *Palamedes* and the *Helen* serve as parodies of Euripides' plays, but these are also titles of the two specimens of Gorgias's epideictic oratory in which the rhetorician himself speaks for Helen and Palamedes speaks in his own defense. More broadly, Gorgias's theories owe much to the theater—in the psychological effects it produces in the spectators and in the aesthetic effects it employs.

Gorgias, having accepted the premise that the phenomenal world cannot be grasped as real, is free to embrace the shifting world of appearances, of *doxa* (opinion), in its deceptions and its fictions. Hence he is also in a position to embrace Helen. The control of that world can come about only through the installation of the *logos* as its master *(dynastēs).* Through the techniques of persuasion, *logos* manipulates the sense impressions and emotions of those who hear it. For Plato, who is to stand directly on the other side of the divide, Gorgias (along with the other sophists) will, like a painter, "make imitations which have the same names as the real things and which can deceive . . . at a distance." The sophists, who practice not the plastic arts but those of the *logos,* can exhibit "spoken images *[eidōla]* of all things, so as to make it seem that they are true and that the speaker is the wisest of all men in all things" (Plato, *Sophist* 234b–c).

For Gorgias, the *logos* possesses a reality akin to a physical substance that resembles the magico-medical quality of a *pharmakon.* Hence its power *(dynamis),* like that "of the incantation, mingles together with the *doxa* [opinion] of the *psychē* and charms it and persuades it and changes it by enchantment." The force of persuasion, when attached to the *psychē,* can leave an impression, a stamp *(tupos)* in the *psychē,* which in turn responds to these stimuli with whatever emotions they are meant to arouse. The persuasive quality of the *logos* affects the *psychē* of the one who hears. Similarly, sight *(opsis)* affects the *psychē* of the one who sees, "stamping *[tupos]* it with its sensations of objects." It "engraves in the mind the images of the things one sees." If these are fearful, it instills fear, if they are beautiful, it brings pleasure, "like the sculpting of statues and the production of images which afford the eyes divine delight. Thus some things naturally please or pain the sight, and many things produce in many men love and desire for many actions or bodies."[57]

Gorgias's defense of Helen reverses the image of the seductive and deceitful woman by portraying a Helen overmastered by irresistible forces, whether as a result of the gods' intervention, physical violence, the persuasion of the *logos,* or the power of eros. It is here that *opsis* (sight) enters into the discourse as the key to an erotic theory, leading Gorgias to inquire: "If Helen's eye was so entranced by Alexander's [Paris's] body, and she delivered up her soul to an eager contest of love, what is so strange in that?" Since the entire discourse is a *logos* that is designed to persuade the listener, the internal argument for the persuasive power of the *logos* over Helen reinforces the dominant role it is given in the piece. As the *megas dynastēs,* the *logos* even proves to overmaster the other categories of coercion, whose indisputable claims to power it appropriates for itself.

Stesichorus's and Euripides' excuse of the *eidōlon* has no place in Gorgias's argument. But the aesthetics of the image remain, now interiorized within the body as the *psychē* that *logos* or *opsis* molds, a process analogous to that of the artist, who shapes and molds his crafted product. The *psychē,* in turn, responds to the physical body whose visual impressions it receives as a spectator who gazes upon an objet d'art. By treating the *psychē* as a corporeal entity and endowing *opsis* and *logos* with physical properties, Gorgias emphasizes a set of tactile relations that somatizes psychology as it psychologizes aesthetics. *Opsis* is already invoked in the cause of eros, but *logos* behaves like eros, which takes possession of another's body to penetrate it to the core and to work its effects within. The relation between rhetor and auditor, therefore, is not unlike that between a man and a woman, even as the writing tablet, as Artemidorus tells us, signifies a woman to the dreamer, "since it receives the imprints *[tupoi]* of all kinds of letters" (*Oneirocritica* 2.45). Thus, if Helen is the subject of the discourse, she is also its object. She is the auditor who, seduced and persuaded by the deceptive rhetoric of Paris, is seduced again (and therefore exonerated) by the rhetoric of Gorgias, who claims as the *truth* of his discourse the demonstration of the power of rhetoric to *seduce* and *deceive.* For the external auditor, the artful beauty of the text, with its persuasive *logos* about persuasion, operates as the rhetorical equivalent of the godlike beauty of Helen, which Gorgias mentions at the beginning of

57. Citations from Gorgias, *Encomium of Helen* frag. 11 in D-K, 288–94. Relevant work on Gorgias includes Untersteiner 1954, 101–201; Rosenmeyer 1955, 225–60; Segal 1962; de Romilly 1973; and relevant sections in Lain Entralgo 1970; and Detienne 1973. Much has been written recently on this piece. I single out Worman 1994 for sophisticated and original analysis.

the text, to describe its irresistible erotic effect upon the suitors who came to her from all parts of Greece.

Moreover, the seduction of this *logos* works a double pleasure of the text: for the auditors it masters within and without the discourse and for Gorgias himself. This he acknowledges when he concludes, "This speech is a plaything *[paignion]* for me, but an encomium for Helen," who by the terms of his argument is worthy not just of defense but also of praise. This ending best explains the choice of Helen for his discourse, beyond her being an unpopular case that he aims to win by his rhetorical skill. Helen, as the paradigm of the feminine, is the ideal subject/object of the discourse: first in sexual terms, as the passive partner to be mastered by masculine rhetorical persuasion, and second in aesthetic terms. Helen, as the mistress and object of mimesis, is a fitting participant in the world of make-believe, the antiworld that reverses the terms in a display of mimetic art and reserves the right, under the name of playful experiment, to take everything back. Seduction, like rhetoric, is a game, a *paignion,* and both eros and *logos* are now invested with a new power that is precisely the ludic power of play, a delight in the aesthetic capacity to seduce and deceive. This point of view, I believe, must inevitably invoke and rehabilitate the feminine whom Greek thought represents as the subject/object of eros (nature) and artifice (culture). In her corporeal essence, she functions both as the psychological subject and as the aesthetic object, and the artist needs her to substantiate his own conception of his art.

Thus, for both Gorgias and Euripides, the woman has a place, one that the end of the fifth century increasingly reserves for her, to Aristophanes' comic chagrin. Her place is gained from two points of view. First, it comes from the domain of art itself, which is discovering a sense of its capacities for mimesis as an explicit category of the fictive, of the make-believe. This discovery takes place in the various verbal arts, which in turn are influenced by the earlier advances in illusionist painting. In this development, which includes the other plastic arts, theater played no small role, as Aristophanes' play itself attests. Second, there is the social world. As the war dragged on to its unhappy close, attention began to shift away from the masculine values of politics and toward the private sphere—the domestic milieu, the internal workings of the psyche—and a new validation of eros, all of which the cultural category of the feminine can best exemplify. This new focus will receive further emphasis in the next century with the emergence in sculpture of the female nude as an art form and in the privately directed literary genres of New Comedy, mime, romance, and pastoral. It is worth remarking here that Old Comedy comes to an end with Aristophanes, whose last productions already make the transition to Middle Comedy, while Euripides, who scandalized his Athenian audiences again and again, winning only four first prizes in his lifetime, will become the theatrical favorite of the next era and thereafter.

In this "feminization" of Greek culture, Euripides was above all a pioneer, and so Aristophanes perhaps correctly perceived that Euripides' place was indeed with the women (as that of Socrates in the *Clouds* was with the men). In a second *Thesmophoriazousae,* which is lost to us except for a few fragments and testimonia, the same cast of characters, more or less, seems to have been involved (Agathon, Euripides, Mnesilochos). This time, our information (from an ancient life of Euripides, which seems to refer to this piece) states explicitly that the women, provoked by the censures he passed on them in his plays, attacked him at the Thesmophoria with murderous intent. They spared him, however, first because of the (his) Muses, and next, on his undertaking never to abuse them again. These Muses are perhaps still to be found in the play we have, hidden behind the noisy laughter of Aristophanic parody.

BIBLIOGRAPHY

Abastado, C. 1976. "Situation de la parodie." *Cahiers du 20e siècle* 6:9–37.

Adkins, A. A. 1966. "Basic Greek Values in Euripides' *Hecuba* and *Hercules Furens*." *CQ* 16:193–219.

Alexiou, M. 1974. *The Ritual Lament in Greek Tradition*. Cambridge.

Anderson, Ø. 1977. "Odysseus and the Wooden Horse." *SO* 52:5–18.

Arbesmann, P. 1937. "Thesmophoria." In *RE*, 2d ser., 6 (1937), c. 15–28.

Arrowsmith, W. 1973. "Aristophanes' *Birds*: The Fantasy Politics of Eros." *Arion* n.s. 1:119–67.

Arthur [Katz], M. 1976. "Review Essay: Classics." *Signs* 2:382–403.

———. 1977. "Politics and Pomegranates: An Interpretation of the Homeric Hymn to Demeter." *Arethusa* 10:7–48.

———. 1982. "Cultural Strategies in Hesiod's *Theogony*: Law, Family, Society." *Arethusa* 15:63–82.

———. 1983. "The Dream of a World without Women: Poetics and the Circles of Order in the *Theogony* Prooemium." *Arethusa* 16:97–116.

Atchity, K. J. 1978. *Homer's "Iliad": The Shield of Memory*. Carbondale and Edwardsville, Ill.

Auerbach, E. 1953. *Mimesis: The Representation of Reality in Western Literature*. Trans. W. R. Trask. Princeton.

Auger, D. 1979. "Le théâtre d'Aristophane: Le mythe, l'utopie et les femmes." In Auger, Rosellini, and Saïd 1979, 71–101.

Auger, D., Rosellini, M., and S. Saïd. 1979. *Aristophane, les femmes et la cité*. Fontenay-aux-Roses.

Austin, C. 1967. *De nouveaux fragments de l'*Erecthée *d'Euripide*. Recherches de papyrologie 4. Paris.

———. 1968. *Nova fragmenta Euripidea in papyris reperta*. Berlin.

Austin, N. 1975. *Archery at the Dark of the Moon*. Berkeley.

Avery, H. 1968. "'My Tongue Swore, But My Mind Is Unsworn.'" *TAPA* 99:19–35.

Bachofen, J. J. 1948 [1861]. *Das Mutterrecht.* Ed. K. Meuli. 3d ed. 3 vols. Basel.

———. 1967 [1954]. *Myth, Religion, and Mother Right: Selected Writings of J. J. Bachofen.* Trans. R. Manheim. Princeton.

Bal, M. 1983. "Sexuality, Semiosis and Binarism: A Narratological Comment on Bergren and Arthur." *Arethusa* 16:117–35.

Bamber, L. 1982. *Comic Women, Tragic Men: A Study of Gender and Genre in Shakespeare.* Stanford.

Bamberger, J. 1974. "The Myth of Matriarchy." In Rosaldo and Lamphere 1974, 263–80.

Barlow, S. 1971. *The Imagery of Euripides.* London. Rpt. Bristol, 1986.

Barnes, J. A. 1973. "Genetrix: Genitor :: Nature: Culture?" In *The Character of Kinship,* 61–73. Ed. J. Goody. Cambridge.

Barrett, W. S., ed. 1964. *Euripides:* Hippolytos. Oxford.

Baslez, M. F. 1984. *L'étranger dans la Grèce antique.* Paris.

Bassi, K. 1993. "Helen and the Discourse of Denial in Stesichorus' Palinode." *Arethusa* 26:51–76.

Belaval, Y. 1965. "Ouverture sur le spectacle." In *Histoire des spectacles,* 2–19. Ed. R. Queneau. Paris.

Bérard, C. 1974. *Anodoi: Essai sur l'imagerie des passages chthoniens.* Neuchâtel.

Bergren, A. 1981. "Helen's 'Good Drug', *Odyssey* iv 1–305." In *Contemporary Literary Hermeneutics and the Interpretation of Classical Texts,* 201–14. Ed. S. Kresic. Ottawa.

———. 1983. "Language and the Female in Early Greek Thought." *Arethusa* 16:69–95.

Berns, G. 1973. "Nomos and Physis: An Interpretation of Euripides' *Hippolytus.*" *Hermes* 101:165–87.

Besslich, S. 1966. *Schweigen-Verschweigen-Übergehen: Die Darstellung des Unausgesprochenen in der Odyssee.* Heidelberg.

Bettelheim, B. 1954. *Symbolic Wounds, Puberty Rites and the Envious Male.* New York.

Beye, C. R. 1968. *The "Iliad," the "Odyssey" and the Epic.* London.

Blaise, F. 1992. "L'épisode de Typhée dans la *Théogonie* d'Hésiode (v. 820–85): La stabilisation du monde." *REG* 105:349–70.

Blaise, F., P. Judet de la Combe, and P. Rousseau, eds. 1995. *Les métiers du mythe: Hésiode et ses vérités.* Paris.

Bliss, F. R. 1968. "Homer and the Critics: The Structural Unity of *Odyssey* 8." *Bucknell Review* 16/3:53–73.

Blok, J. 1995. *The Early Amazons: Modern and Ancient Perspectives on a Persistent Myth.* Leiden and New York.

Bobrick, E. 1991. "Iphigeneia Revisited: *Thesmophoriazousae* 1160–1225." *Arethusa* 24:67–76.

Boedeker, D. 1983. "Hecate: A Transfunctional Goddess in the *Theogony*?" *TAPA* 113:79–93.

Bogner, H. 1947. *Der tragische Gegensatz.* Heidelberg.

Bollack, J. 1971. "Mythische Deutung und Deutung des Mythos." In *Terror und Spiel: Probleme der Mythenrezeption,* 111–18. Ed. M. Fuhrmann. Munich.

Bonnafé, A. 1985. "L'olivier dans l'*Odyssée* et le fourré du Parnasse: Reprises de termes et reprises de thèmes." *QS* 21:101–36.

Bonnano, M. G. 1973. "Osservazioni sul tema della 'giusta' reciprocità da Saffo ai comici." *QUCC* 16:110–20.

Booth, N. 1955. "Aeschylus' *Supplices* 86–95." *CP* 50:21–25.

Borgeaud, P. 1979. *Recherches sur le dieu Pan.* Geneva. = *The Cult of Pan in Ancient Greece.* Trans. K. Atlass and J. Redfield. Chicago, 1988.

Boyancé, P. 1962. "Sur les mystères d'Eleusis." *REG* 75:460–82.

Boyarin, D. 1993. *Carnal Israel: Reading Sex in Talmudic Culture.* Berkeley.

Braswell, K. 1982. "The Song of Ares and Aphrodite: Theme and Relevance to *Odyssey* 8." *Hermes* 110:129–37.

Braund, D. C. 1980. "Artemis Eukleia and Euripides' *Hippolytus*." *JHS* 100:184–85.

Brelich, A. 1958. *Gli eroi greci.* Rome.

———. 1969. *Paides e Parthenoi.* Rome.

Bremer, D. 1976. *Licht und Dunkel in der frühgriechischen Dichtung. Archiv für Begriffsgeschichte,* Supplementheft 1. Bonn.

Bremer, J. M. 1975. "The Meadow of Love and Two Passages in Euripides' *Hippolytus*." *Mnemosyne* 28:268–80.

Broadbent, M. 1968. *Studies in Greek Genealogy.* Leiden.

Broneer, O. 1929–44. "The Tent of Xerxes and the Greek Theater." *University of California Publications in Classical Archeology* 1:305–11.

Brown, N. O. 1953. *Hesiod's "Theogony."* Indianapolis and New York.

Buddenhagen, F. 1919. *Peri Gamou: Antiquorum poetarum philosophorumque graecorum de matrimonio sententiae, etc.* Zurich.

Burian, P., ed. 1985. *Directions in Euripidean Criticism: A Collection of Essays.* Durham, N.C.

Burke, K. 1966. "Form and Persecution in the *Oresteia*." In *Language as Symbolic Action,* 125–38. Berkeley.

———. 1969. *A Rhetoric of Motives.* 2d ed. Berkeley.

Burkert, W. 1960. "Das Lied von Ares und Aphrodite zum Verhältnis von *Odyssee* und *Iliad*." *RhM* 103:130–44.

————. 1966. "Kekropidensage und Arrhephoria." *Hermes* 94:1–25.

————. 1970. "Jason, Hypsipyle, and New Fire at Lemnos: A Study in Myth and Ritual." *CQ* n.s. 20:1–16.

————. 1979. *Structure and History in Greek Mythology and Ritual.* Berkeley.

————. 1983. *Homo Necans: The Anthropology of Ancient Greek Sacrificial Ritual and Myth.* Trans. Peter Bing. Berkeley.

————. 1985. *Greek Religion, Archaic and Classical.* Trans. J. Raffan. Cambridge, Mass.

————. 1987. *Ancient Mystery Cults.* Cambridge, Mass.

Burnett, A. P. 1960. "Euripides' *Helen:* A Comedy of Ideas." *CP* 55:151–63.

————. 1962. "Human Resistance and Divine Persuasion in Euripides' *Ion.*" *CP* 57:89–103.

————. 1970. *Ion by Euripides.* Trans. and comm. Englewood Cliffs, N.J.

————. 1971. *Catastrophe Survived: Euripides' Plays of Mixed Reversal.* Oxford.

————. 1973. "Medea and the Tragedy of Revenge." *CP* 58:1–24.

Burns, E. 1972. *Theatricality.* New York.

Bushala, E. W. 1969. "*Suzugiai Charites: Hippolytus* 1147." *TAPA* 100:23–29.

Bushnell, R. 1988. *Prophesying Tragedy: Sign and Voice in Sophocles' Theban Plays.* Ithaca, N.Y.

Buxton, R. G. A. 1980. "Blindness and Limits: Sophocles and the Logic of Myth." *JHS* 100:22–37.

Calame, C. 1977. *Les choeurs de jeunes filles en Grèce archaïque.* 2 vols. Rome.

————. 1992. *I Greci e l'eros: Symboli, pratiche e luoghi.* Rome and Bari.

Caldwell, R. 1974. "The Psychology of Aeschylus' *Supplices.*" *Arethusa* 7:45–70.

Cantarella, R. 1967. "Agatone e il prologo della 'Tesmoforiazuse.' " In *Komoidotragemata,* 7–15. Ed. R. E. M. Westendorp Boerma. Amsterdam.

Cararra, P. 1977. *Euripide, Eretteo. Papyrologica florentina,* vol. 3. Florence.

Carpenter, T. 1986. *Dionysian Imagery in Archaic Greek Art: Its Development in Black-Figure Vase Painting.* Oxford.

————. 1993. "On the Beardless Dionysus." In Carpenter and Faraone 1993, 185–206.

Carpenter, T., and C. Faraone, eds. 1993. *Masks of Dionysus.* Ithaca, N.Y.

Carson, A. 1982. "Wedding at Noon in Pindar's *Ninth Pythian.*" *GRBS* 23:121–28.

———. 1990. "Putting Her in Her Place: Woman, Dirt, and Desire." In Halperin, Winkler, and Zeitlin 1990, 135–69.

Cave, T. 1988. *Recognitions: A Study in Poetics.* Oxford.

Chalkia, I. 1986. *Lieux et espace dans la tragédie d'Euripide.* Thessalonika.

Chantraine, P. 1968–80. *Dictionnaire étymologique de la langue grecque.* Paris.

Chirassi-Colombo, I. 1975. "I doni di Demeter: Mito e ideologia nella Grecia arcaica." In *Studi triestini di antichità in onore di L. Stella,* 183–213. Trieste.

———. 1979. "Paides e Gynaikes: Note per una tassonomia del comportamento rituale nella cultura attica." *QUCC* n.s. 1 (30):25–58.

Clader, L. L. 1976. *Helen: The Evolution from Divine to Heroic in Greek Epic Tradition.* Leiden.

Clarke, H. W. 1967. *The Art of the* Odyssey. Englewood Cliffs, N.J.

Clay, D. 1969. "Aeschylus' *Trigeron Mythos.*" *Hermes* 97:1–9.

Clay, J. S. 1984. "The Hecate of the *Theogony.*" *GRBS* 25:27–38.

Cohen, J. 1989. *"Be Fertile and Increase, Fill the Earth and Master It":* The Ancient and Medieval Career of a Biblical Text. Ithaca.

Collard, C. 1991. *Euripides, Hecuba.* Warminster.

Conacher, D. 1967. *Euripidean Drama: Myth, Theme and Structure.* Toronto.

Cook, A. B. 1940. *Zeus: A Study in Ancient Religion.* Vol. 3. Cambridge.

Cornford, F. 1914. *The Origin of Attic Comedy.* London.

Coulon, V., ed. 1973. *Aristophane.* Vol. 4. [Budé.] Paris.

Craik, E. 1993a. "Tragic Love, Comic Sex." In *Tragedy, Comedy, and the Polis,* 253–62. Ed. A. Sommerstein, R. Halliwell, J. Henderson, and B. Zimmermann. Bari.

———. 1993b. *"Aidōs* in Euripides' *Hippolytos* 373–430: Review and Reinterpretation." *JHS* 113:45–59.

Csapo, E. 1986. "A Note on the Würzburg Bell-Crater H5697 ('Telephus Transvestitus')." *Phoenix* 40:379–92.

Dahl, K. 1976. *Thesmophoria: En graesk Kvindefest.* Copenhagen.

Daitz, S. 1971. "Concepts of Freedom and Slavery in Euripides' *Hecuba.*" *Hermes* 99:217–26.

Dale, A. M. 1969. "Seen and Unseen on the Greek Stage." In *Collected Papers,* 119–29. Cambridge.

Daraki, M. 1985. *Dionysos.* Paris.

Davis, N. 1975. *Society and Culture in Early Modern France.* Stanford.

Davison, J. A. 1958. "Notes on the Panathenaea." *JHS* 78:23–42.

De Angeli, S. 1988. "Mimesis e Techne." *QUCC* 57:27–45.

Delcourt, M. 1957. *Héphaistos ou la légende du magicien.* Bibliothèque de la Faculté de Philosophie et Lettres de l'Université de Liège 146. Paris.

———. 1959. *Oreste et Alcméon.* Paris.

————. 1961. *Hermaphrodite: Myths and Rites of the Bisexual Figure in Classical Antiquity.* Trans. J. Nicholson. London.

Detienne, M. 1973. *Les maîtres de vérité en Grèce archaïque.* 2d ed. Paris.

————. 1977. *The Gardens of Adonis.* Trans. J. Lloyd. Atlantic Highlands, N.J. Rpt. Princeton, 1994.

————. 1979a. *Dionysos Slain.* Trans. L. and M. Muellner. Baltimore.

————. 1979b. "Violentes 'eugenies': En pleines Thesmophories: Des femmes couvertes de sang." In Detienne and Vernant 1979, 183–214. = Detienne and Vernant 1989, 129–47.

————. 1989a. "*L'écriture d'Orphée.* Paris.

————. 1989b. "Les Danaïdes entre elles ou la violence fondatrice du mariage." In Detienne 1989a, 41–57.

————. 1989c. "Une écriture inventive, la voix d'Orphée, les jeux de Palamède. In Detienne 1989a, 101–15.

Detienne, M., and J.-P. Vernant. 1978. *Cunning Intelligence among the Greeks.* Trans. J. Lloyd. Atlantic Highlands, N.J.

————, eds. 1979. *La cuisine de sacrifice chez les grecs.* Paris. = *The Cuisine of Sacrifice among the Greeks.* Trans. P. Wissing. Chicago, 1989.

Deubner, L. 1932. *Attische Feste.* Berlin.

Diamantopoulos, A. 1957. "The Danaid Tetralogy of Aeschylus." *JHS* 77:221–29.

Dietz, G. 1971. "Das Bett des Odysseus." *Symbolon* 7:9–32.

Dover, K. J. 1972. *Aristophanic Comedy.* Berkeley.

duBois, P. 1982. *Centaurs and Amazons: Women in the Prehistory of the Great Chain of Being.* Ann Arbor.

————. 1988. *Sowing the Body: Psychoanalysis and Ancient Representations of Women.* Chicago.

Dumézil, G. 1924. *Le crime des Lemniennes.* Paris.

Dupont-Roc, R., and A. Le Boulluec. 1976. "Le charme du récit (*Odyssée,* IV, 219–89)." In *Ecriture et théorie poétiques: Lectures d'Homère, Eschyle, Platon, Aristote,* 30–39. Ed. J. Lallot and A. Le Boulluec. Paris.

Edinger, H. G. 1980. "The Lay of Demodocus in Context." *The Humanitarian Association Review* 31:45–52.

Edwards, A. T. 1985. *Achilles in the "Odyssey": Ideologies of Heroism in the Homeric Epic.* Beiträge zur klassischen Philologie 171. Königstein.

Eilberg-Schwartz, H. 1990. *The Savage in Judaism: An Anthropology of Israelite Religion and Ancient Judaism.* Bloomington, Ind.

Eisenberger, H. 1973. *Studien zur* Odyssee. Weisbaden.

Eisler, R. 1910. *Weltmantel und Himmelszelt.* 2 vols. Munich.

Eliade, M. 1958. *Rites and Symbols of Initiation.* Trans. W. R. Trask. New York.

————. 1963. *Myth and Reality*. Trans. W. R. Trask. New York.

————. 1969. *Images and Symbols*. Trans. W. R. Trask. New York.

Ellis, R. 1893. "On Some Fragments of Aeschylus and on the *Suppliants*." *Journal of Philology* 21:25–36.

Emlyn-Jones, C. 1984. "The Reunion of Penelope and Odysseus." *Greece and Rome* 31:1–18.

Erffa, C. E. F. von. 1937. *Aidos. Phil. Supp.* 30/2.

Euben, J. P., ed. 1986. *Greek Tragedy and Political Theory*. Berkeley.

Faraone, C. 1985. "Aeschylus' *humnos desmios (Eum.* 306) and Attic Judicial Curse Tablets." *JHS* 105:150–54.

Farnell, L. 1896–1909. *Cults of the Greek States*. 5 vols. Oxford.

Fauth, W. 1958. *Hippolytos und Phaidra: Bemerkungen zum religiösen Hintergrund eines tragischen Konflikts*. Part 1. Akademie der Wissenschaften und der Literatur in Mainz, Abhandlungen der Geistes- und Sozialwissenschaftlichen Klasse 9, 517–88. Wiesbaden.

————. 1959. *Hippolytos und Phaidra: Bemerkungen zum religiösen Hintergrund eines tragischen Konflikts*. Part 2. Akademie der Wissenschaften und der Literatur in Mainz, Abhandlungen der Geistes- und Sozialwissenschaftlichen Klasse 8, 387–516. Wiesbaden.

Fehrle, E. 1910. *Die kultische Keuschheit im Altertum. RGVV* 6. Giessen.

Finley, J. H. 1955. *Pindar and Aeschylus*. Cambridge, Mass.

Finley, M. I. 1978. *The World of Odysseus*. 2d rev. ed. London.

Fischer, U. 1965. *Der Telosgedanke in den Dramen des Aischylos*. Hildesheim.

Flaumenhaft, M. J. 1982. "The Undercover Hero: Odysseus from Dark to Daylight." *Interpretation* 10:9–41.

Fluck, H. 1931. *Skurrile Riten in griechischen kulten*. Endingen.

Foley, H. 1978. "'Reverse Similes' and Sex Roles in the *Odyssey*." *Arethusa* 11:7–26.

————. 1980. "The Masque of Dionysus." *TAPA* 110:107–33.

————, ed. 1981. *Reflections of Women in Antiquity*. London and New York.

————. 1982a. "The 'Female Intruder' Reconsidered: Women in Aristophanes' *Lysistrata* and *Ecclesiazousae*." *CP* 77:1–21.

————. 1982b. "The Conception of Women in Athenian Drama." In Foley 1981, 127–67.

————. 1985. *Ritual Irony: Poetry and Sacrifice in Euripides*. Ithaca, N.Y.

————. 1992. "*Anodos* Dramas: Euripides' *Alcestis* and *Helen*." In *Innovations in Antiquity*, 133–60. Ed. R. Hexter and D. Selden. London and New York.

Fontenrose, J. 1959. *Python: A Study of Delphic Myth and Its Origins*. Berkeley.

————. 1981. *Orion: The Myth of the Hunter and the Huntress.* Berkeley.

Fortes, M. 1959. *Oedipus and Job in Western African Religion.* Cambridge.

Foucault, M. 1985. *The Use of Pleasure.* Trans. R. Hurley. New York.

Fowler, B. H. 1967 [1970]. "Aeschylus' Imagery." *C&M* 28:1–74.

Fraenkel, E. 1962. *Aeschylus,* Agamemnon. Oxford.

Freud, S. 1958 [1939]. *Moses and Monotheism.* Trans. K. Jones. New York.

————. 1961 [1930]. *Civilization and Its Discontents.* Trans. J. Strachey. New York.

Friis Johansen, H. 1966. "Progymnasmata." *C&M* 27:40–43.

Friis Johansen, H., and E. H. Whittle. 1980. *Aeschylus:* The Suppliants. 3 vols. Copenhagen.

Frischer, B. 1970. "*Concordia Discors* and Characterization in Euripides' *Hippolytos.*" *GRBS* 11:85–100.

Froidefond, C. 1971. *Le mirage égyptien dans la littérature grecque d'Homère à Aristote.* Aix-en-Provence.

Frye, N. 1976. *The Secular Scripture: A Study of the Structure of Romance.* Cambridge, Mass.

Gallini, C. 1968. "Il travestismo rituale di Penteo." *SMSR* 34:211–18.

Gantz, T. 1978. "Love and Death in the *Suppliants* of Aeschylus." *Phoenix* 32:279–87.

Garvie, A. F. 1969. *Aeschylus' Supplices: Play and Trilogy.* Cambridge.

Garzya, A. 1962. *Pensiero e tecnica drammatica in Euripide: Saggio sul motivo della salvazione.* Naples.

Gaster, Theodore. 1961. *Thespis.* 2d ed. New York.

Gauthier, P. 1972. *Symbola: Les étrangers et la justice dans les cités grecques.* Nancy.

Gellie, G. 1980. "*Hecuba* and Tragedy." *Antichthon* 14:30–44.

Gennep, A. L. Van. 1960 [1909]. *The Rites of Passage.* Trans. M. B. Vizedom and G. L. Caffee. Chicago.

Gentili, B. 1972. "Il 'letto insaziato' di Medea e il tema dell' Adikia a livello amoroso nei lirici Saffo, Teognide e nella *Medea* di Euripide." *SCO* 21:60–72.

————. 1988. *Poetry and Its Public in Ancient Greece from Homer to the Fifth Century.* Trans. A. T. Cole. Baltimore.

Germain, G. 1954. *Genèse de "l'Odyssée."* Paris.

Gernet, L. 1981. "The Mythical Idea of Value in Greece." In *The Anthropology of Ancient Greece,* 73–111. Ed. J.-P. Vernant. Trans. J. Hamilton and B. Nagy. Baltimore.

Giacomelli [Carson], A. 1980. "The Justice of Aphrodite in Sappho Fr. 1." *TAPA* 110:135–42.

Gilbert, S. 1980. "Costumes of the Mind: Transvestism as Metaphor in Modern Literature." *Critical Inquiry* 7:391–418.

Gilula, D. 1981. "A Consideration of Phaedra's *Eukleia.*" *Sileno* 7:121–33.

Girard, R. 1977. *Violence and the Sacred.* Trans. P. Gregory. Baltimore.

Goff, Barbara. 1988. "Euripides' *Ion* 1132–65: The Tent." *PCPS* 34:42–54.

Golden, M. P., and Golden, N. H. 1975. "Population Policy in Plato and Aristotle: Some Value Issues." *Arethusa* 8:345–58.

Goldhill, S. 1991. *The Poet's Voice: Essays on Poetics and Greek Literature.* Cambridge.

Goldman, M. 1975. *The Actor's Freedom: Toward a Theory of Drama.* New York.

Gould, John. 1973. "*Hiketeia.*" *JHS* 93:74–103.

Gouldner, A. 1969. *Enter Plato.* Part 1. *The Hellenic World.* New York.

Graf, F. 1974. *Eleusis und die orphische Dichtung Athens in vorhellenistischer Zeit.* Berlin.

Green, A. 1969. *Un oeil en trop: Le complexe d'Oedipe dans la tragédie.* Paris. = *The Tragic Effect: The Oedipus Complex in Tragedy.* Trans. A. Sheridan. Cambridge, 1979.

Greenberg, C. 1980. "Reading Reading: Echo's Abduction of Language." In *Women and Language in Literature and Society,* 300–309. Ed. S. McConnell-Ginet, R. Borker, and N. Furman. New York.

Griffin, J. 1980. *Homer on Life and Death.* Oxford.

Griffith, M. 1983. "Personality in Hesiod." *CA* 2:37–65.

Grossmann, G. 1970. *Promethie und Orestie.* Heidelberg.

Guarducci, M. 1927. "Leggende dell'antica Grecia relative all'origine dell'umanità e analoghe tradizioni di altri paesi." *Atti della Reale Accademia Nazionale dei Lincei:* 379–458.

Guépin, J.-P. 1968. *The Ritual Paradox.* Amsterdam.

Hadley, W. S., ed. 1904. *The* Hecuba *of Euripides.* Cambridge.

Hall, E. 1989. "The Archer Scene in Aristophanes' *Thesmophoriazousae.*" *Phil.* 133:38–54.

Halperin, D. 1990. "Why Is Diotima a Woman? Platonic *Erôs* and the Figuration of Gender." In Halperin, Winkler, and Zeitlin 1990, 257–308.

Halperin, D., Winkler, J. J., and F. I. Zeitlin., eds. 1990. *Before Sexuality: The Construction of Erotic Experience in the Ancient Greek World.* Princeton.

Hamilton, R. 1989. *The Architecture of Hesiodic Poetry.* Baltimore.

Handley, E. W., and Rea, J. 1957. *The* Telephus *of Euripides.* BICS *Supplement 5.* London.

Hansen, H. 1976. "Aristophanes' *Thesmophoriazousae:* Theme, Structure, and Production." *Phil.* 120:165–85.

Hanson, A. 1990. "The Medical Writer's Woman." In Halperin, Winkler, and Zeitlin 1990, 309–38.

————. 1992. "Conception, Gestation, and the Origin of Female Nature." *Helios* 19:31–71.

Hanson, J. O. de Graft. 1975. "Euripides' *Ion*: Tragic Awakening and Disillusionment." *Museum Africum* 4:27–42.

Hardie, P. 1986. *Vergil's* Aeneid: *Cosmos and Imperium.* Oxford.

Harriott, R. 1969. *Poetry and Criticism before Plato.* London.

Harris, G. 1973. "Furies, Witches, and Mothers." In *The Character of Kinship,* 149–59. Ed. J. Goody. Cambridge.

Harrison, A. R. W. 1968. *The Law of Athens: The Family and Property.* Oxford.

Harrison, J. E. 1922. *Prolegomena to the Study of Greek Religion.* 3d ed. Cambridge.

Heath, M. 1987. "'Iure Principem Locum Tenet': Euripides' *Hecuba*." *BICS* 34:40–68.

Henderson, J. 1991. *The Maculate Muse: Obscene Language in Attic Comedy.* 2d ed. Oxford.

Herter, H. 1940. "Theseus und Hippolytus." *RhM* 89:273–92.

————. 1971. "Phaidra in griechischer und römischer Gestalt." *RhM* 114:44–77.

————. 1975. "Hippolytus und Phaidra." In *Kleine Schriften,* 119–56. Munich.

Heubeck, A., and A. Hoekstra, eds. 1989. *A Commentary on Homer's "Odyssey."* Vol. 2. Oxford.

Heubeck, A., S. West, and J. B. Hainsworth, eds. 1988. *A Commentary on Homer's "Odyssey."* Vol. 1. Oxford.

Hillman, J. 1972. *The Myth of Analysis.* Evanston, Ill.

Hiltbrunner, O. 1950. *Widerholungs- und Motivtechnik bei Aischylos.* Bern.

Hoffmann, G. 1986. "Pandora, la jarre et l'espoir." *QS* 24:55–89.

Horn, W. 1970. *Gebet und Gebetsparodie in den Komödien des Aristophane.* Nuremberg.

Hornby, R. 1986. *Drama, Metadrama, and Perception.* Lewisburg, Pa.

Hubbard, T. 1991. *The Mask of Comedy: Aristophanes and the Intertextual Parabasis.* Ithaca, N.Y.

Humphreys, S. C., [and A. Momigliano]. 1978. "The Social Structure of the Ancient City." In S. Humphreys, *Anthropology and the Greeks,* 177–92. London.

Hutcheon, L. 1985. *A Theory of Parody.* New York and London.

Immerwahr, H. 1972. "Athenaikes Eikones ston 'Iona' tou Euripide." *Hellenika* 25:277–97.

Ireland, S. 1974. "The Problem of Motivation in the *Supplices* of Aeschylus." *RhM* 117:14–29.

Jeanmaire, H. 1939. *Couroi et Courètes.* Lille.

————. 1951. *Dionysos: Histoire du culte du Bacchus.* Paris.

Jones, J. 1962. *On Aristotle and Greek Tragedy.* New York.

Jouanna, J. 1982. "Réalité et théâtralité du rêve: Le rêve dans l'*Hécube* d'Euripide." *Ktèma* 7:43–52.

Judet de la Combe, P. 1995. "'Pandore' dans la *Théogonie.* In Blaise, Judet de la Combe, and Rousseau 1995.

Kahn, C. 1980. "The Providential Tempest and the Shakespearean Family." In Schwartz and Kahn 1980, 217–43.

Kahn, L. 1978. *Hermès passe ou les ambiguïtés de la communication.* Paris.

Kakdridis, J. 1971. "The Recognition of Odysseus." In *Homer Revisited,* 151–63. Lund.

Kannicht, R. 1969. *Euripides,* Helena. 2 vols. Heidelberg.

Katz, M. Arthur. 1991. *Penelope's Renown: Meaning and Indeterminacy in the "Odyssey."* Princeton.

Kerényi, K. 1963. "Kore." In C. G. Jung and C. Kerényi, *Essays on a Science of Mythology,* 101–55. Trans. R. F. C. Hull. Princeton.

————. 1967. *Eleusis: Archetypal Image of Mother and Daughter.* Trans. R. Manheim. Princeton.

————. 1976. *Dionysos: Archetypal Image of Indestructible Life.* Trans. R. Manheim. Princeton.

Keuls, E. 1990. "Clytemnestra and Telephus in Greek Vase-Painting." In *EUMOUSIA: Ceramic and Iconographic Studies in Honour of Alexander Cambitoglou,* 87–94, plates 19–22. Ed. J.-P. Descoeudres. Sydney.

Kiefner, W. 1965. *Der religiöse Allbegriff des Aischylos.* Hildesheim.

King, H. 1983. "Bound to Bleed: Artemis and Greek Women." In Cameron and Kuhrt 1983, 109–27.

King, K. 1985. "The Politics of Imitation: Euripides' *Hekabe* and the Homeric Achilles." *Arethusa* 18:47–66.

Kleinknecht, H. 1937. *Die Gebetsparodie in der Antike.* Stuttgart and Berlin.

Knox, B. M. W. 1952. "The *Hippolytus* of Euripides." *YCS* 13:1–31.

————. 1977. "The *Medea* of Euripides." *YCS* 25:193–225.

————. 1979. "Euripidean Comedy." In *Word and Action: Essays on the Ancient Theater,* 250–74. Baltimore.

Komornicka, A. M. 1967. "Quelques remarques sur la parodie dans les comédies d'Aristophane." *QUCC* 3:51–74.

Kopperschmidt, J. 1967. *Die Hikesie als dramatische Form zur motivischen Interpretationen des griechischen Drama.* Tübingen.

Kossatz-Deissmann. 1980. "Telephus transvetitus." In *Tainia: Festschrift für Roland Hampe,* 281–90. Ed. H. A. Cahn and E. Simon. Mainz.

Kranz, W. 1933. *Stasimon.* Berlin.

Kraus, T. 1960. *Hekate: Studien zu Wesen und Bild der Göttin in Kleinasien und Griechenland.* Heidelberg.

Kraus, W. 1948. *Die Schutzsuchunden.* Frankfurt am Main.

Kuhns, R. 1962. *The House, the City and the Judge.* Indianapolis.

Lain Entralgo, P. 1970. *The Therapy of the Word in Classical Antiquity.* Ed. and trans. L. J. Rather and J. M. Sharp. New Haven.

Lanata, G. 1963. *Poetica preplatonica.* Florence.

Lasserre, F. 1946. *La figure d'Eros dans la poésie grecque.* Paris.

Lattimore, R., trans. 1953. *Aeschylus:* Oresteia. Chicago.

———., trans. 1965. *The* Odyssey *of Homer.* New York.

Leach, E. 1966. *Rethinking Anthropology.* London.

Legrand, P. 1927. *Bucoliques grecs.* 2 vols. [Budé.] Paris.

Lembke, J. 1975. *Aeschylus:* Suppliants. New York and London.

Lesky, E. 1951. *Die Zeugung- und Vererbungslehren der Antike und ihr Nachwirken.* Wiesbaden.

Lévêque, P. 1982a. "Structures imaginaires et fonctionnement des mystères grecs." *Studi storico-religiosi* 6 : 185–208.

———. 1982b. "*Olbios* et la félicité des initiés." In *Rayonnement grec: Hommages à Charles Delvoye,* 113–26. Ed. L. Hadermann-Misguich and G. Raepsaet. Brussels.

Lévi-Strauss, C. 1967. *The Elementary Structures of Kinship.* Trans. J. H. Bell, J. R. von Sturmer, and R. Needham. Boston.

———. 1969. *The Raw and the Cooked.* Trans. J. and D. Weightman. New York.

Lévy, E. 1976. "Les femmes chez Aristophane." *Ktèma* 1 : 99–112.

———. 1985. "Inceste, mariage, et sexualité dans les *Suppliantes* d'Eschyle." In *La Femme dans le monde méditerranéen,* 29–45. Ed. A. M. Verilhac. Lyons.

Lindsay, J. 1965. *The Clashing Rocks.* London.

Lloyd, G. E. R. 1983. *Science, Folklore, and Ideology.* Cambridge.

Loewenstein, J. 1984. *Responsive Readings: Versions of Echo in Pastoral, Epic, and the Jonsonian Masque.* New Haven.

Loraux, N. 1973. "L'interférence tragique." *Critique* 317 : 908–25.

———. 1975. "*Hêbê* et *Andreia:* Deux versions de la mort du combattant athénien." *Ancient Society* 6 : 1–31.

———. 1978. "La gloire et la mort d'une femme." *Sorcière* 18 : 51–57.

———. 1981a. *Les enfants d'Athéna: Idées athéniennes sur la citoyenneté et la division des sexes.* Paris. = *The Children of Athena: Athenian Ideas about Citizenship and the Division between the Sexes.* Trans. C. Levine. 2d ed. Princeton, 1993.

"L'autochtonie: Une topique athénienne," 35–74. = Loraux 1993, 37–71. Referred to as 1981a, "Autochtonie."

"Sur la race des femmes et quelques-unes de ses tribus," 75–117. = Loraux 1993, 72–110. Referred to as 1981a, "Race."

"Le nom athénien: Structures imaginaires de la parenté à Athènes," 119–53. = Loraux 1993, 111–43. Referred to as 1981a, "Nom."

"L'Acropole comique," 157–96. = Loraux 1993, 147–83. Referred to as 1981a, "Acropole."

"Créuse autochtone," 197–253. = Loraux 1993, 174–236 [also in Winkler and Zeitlin 1990, 184–236]. Referred to as 1981a, "Créuse."

———. 1981b. "Le lit, la guerre." *L'Homme* 21:37–67. = Loraux 1989, 29–53.

———. 1981c. "Origine des hommes: Les mythes grecs: Naître enfin mortel." In *Dictionnaire des mythologies*, 2:197–202. Ed. Y. Bonnefoy. 2 vols. Paris.

———. 1982. "*Ponos*. (Sur quelques difficultés de la peine comme nom du travail)." *Annali dell'Istituto Orientale di Napoli. Archeologia e storia antica* 4:171–92. = Loraux 1989, 54–72, 318–25.

———. 1984. "Le corps étranglé." In *Le châtiment dans la cité*, 195–218. Ed. Y. Thomas. Rome and Paris. = Loraux 1989, 124–41, 336–43.

———. 1987. *Tragic Ways of Killing a Woman*. Trans. A. Forster. Cambridge, Mass. = *Façons tragiques de tuer une femme*. Paris, 1985.

———. 1989. *Les expériences de Tirésias: Le féminin et l'homme grec*. Paris.

———. 1990. *Les mères en deuil*. Paris.

Luca, R. 1981. "Il lessico d'amore nei poemi omerici." *SIFC* 53:170–98.

Luschnig, C. A. E. 1976. "Euripides' *Hecabe*: The Time Is Out of Joint." *CJ* 71:227–341.

———. 1980. "Men and Gods in Euripides' *Hippolytus*." *Ramus* 9:89–100.

Marg, W. 1956. "Das erste Lied des Demodokos." In *Navicula chiloniensis: Festschrift für Felix Jacoby*, 16–29. Leiden.

Marquardt, P. 1981. "A Portrait of Hecate." *AJP* 102:243–60.

Masaracchia, A. 1972. "Una polemica di Euripide con il suo pubblico: *Ippolito* 373–402." In *Studi classici in onore di Quintino Cataudella*, 289–301. Catania.

Massenzio, M. 1969. *Cultura e crisi permanente: La "xenia" dionisiaca*. *SMSR* 40:27–113.

Mastronarde, D. 1976. "Iconography and Imagery in Euripides' *Ion*." *California Studies in Classical Antiquity* 8:163–76.

McDonald, M. 1978. *Terms for Happiness in Euripides*. Göttingen.

Méridier, L., ed. 1965. *Euripide*: Hippolyte, Andromaque, Hécube. Vol. 2. [Budé.]. Paris.

Meridor, R. 1978. "Hecuba's Revenge: Some Observations on Euripides' *Hecuba*." *AJP* 99:28–35.

———. 1983. "The Function of Polymestor's Crime in the *Hecuba* of Euripides." *Eranos* 81:13–20.

Metzger, H. 1951. *Les représentations dans la céramique attique du IVe siècle*. Paris.

Mezzadri, B. 1987. "La pierre et le foyer: Notes sur les v. 453–506 de la *Théogonie* hésiodique." *Mètis* 2:215–20.

Michelini, A. 1987. *Euripides and the Tragic Tradition*. Madison, Wis.

Miller, H. W. 1948. "Euripides' *Telephus* and the *Thesmophoriazousae* of Aristophanes." *CP* 43:174–83.

Monsacré, H. 1984. *Les larmes d'Achille: Le héros, la femme et la souffrance dans la poésie d'Homère*. Paris.

Montrose, L. 1980. "The Purpose of Playing: Reflections on a Shakespearean Anthropology." *Helios* n.s. 7:51–74.

Morgan, K. 1991. "*Odyssey* 23.218–24: Adultery, Shame, and Marriage." *AJP* 112:1–3.

Motte, A. 1973. *Prairies et jardins de la Grèce antique: De la religion à la philosophie*. Brussels.

Moulton, C. 1981. *Aristophanic Comedy*. Göttingen.

Muecke, F. 1977. "Playing with the Play: Theatrical Self-Consciousness in Aristophanes." *Antichthon* 11:52–67.

———. 1982a. "I Know You—by Your Rags: Costume and Design in Fifth-Century Drama." *Antichthon* 16:17–34.

———. 1982b. "A Portrait of the Artist as a Young Woman." *CQ* 32:41–55.

Müller, G. 1975. "Beschreibung von Kunstwerken im *Ion* des Euripides." *Hermes* 103:25–44.

Murnaghan, S. 1986. "Penelope's *Agnoia*: Knowledge, Power, and Gender in the *Odyssey*." In *Rescuing Creusa: New Methodological Approaches to Women in Antiquity*, 103–15. Ed. M. Skinner. *Helios* 13, special issue.

———. 1987. *Disguise and Recognition in the "Odyssey."* Princeton.

Murray, G. 1943. "Ritual Elements in the New Comedy." *CQ* 37–38:46–54.

Murray, R. D. 1958. *The Motif of Io in Aeschylus' Suppliants*. Princeton.

Muth, R. 1954. "Hymenaios und Epithalamion." *WS* 47:5–54.

Mylonas, G. 1961. *Eleusis and the Eleusinian Mysteries*. Princeton.

Nagy, G. 1973. "Phaethon, Sappho's Phaon, and the White Rock of Leucas." *HSCP* 7:137–77.

———. 1979. *The Best of the Achaeans: Concepts of the Hero in Archaic Greek Poetry*. Baltimore.

———. 1982. "Hesiod." In *Ancient Writers: Greece and Rome,* 1:43–
73. Ed. T. J. Luce. 2 vols. New York.

———. 1983. "*Sêma* and *Nóēsis:* Some Illustrations." *Arethusa* 16:
35–55.

———. 1990. *Pindar's Homer.* Baltimore.

Néraudau, J.-P. 1981. "La métamorphose d'Hécube en Ovide, *Métamor-
phoses,* XIII, 538–75." *BAGB:* 35–51.

Neumann, E. 1954. *The Origins of Human Consciousness.* Trans. R. F. C.
Hull. Princeton.

Newton, R. 1987. "Odysseus and Hephaestus in the *Odyssey.*" *CJ* 83:
12–20.

Nilsson, M. 1906. *Griechische Feste.* Leipzig.

———. 1955. *Geschichte der griechischen Religion.* 2 vols. Munich.

———. 1957. *The Dionysiac Mysteries of the Hellenistic Age.* Lund.

Noica, S. 1984. "La boîte de Pandore et 'L'ambiguïté' de l'Elpis." *Platon*
36:100–124.

Norden, E. 1924. *Die Geburt des Kinds.* Leipzig.

North, H. 1966. *Sophrosyne.* Ithaca, N.Y.

Nussbaum, M. 1986. "The Betrayal of Convention: A Reading of Euripides' *Hecuba.*" In *The Fragility of Goodness,* 397–412. Cambridge.

Oliver, J. H. 1960. *Demokratia, the Gods, and the Free World.* Baltimore.

Olson, S. D. 1989. "*Odyssey* 8: Guile, Force, and the Subversive Poetics
of Desire." *Arethusa* 22:135–45.

———. 1990. "The Stories of Agamemnon in Homer's *Odyssey.*" *TAPA*
120:57–72.

Onians, R. B. 1954. *The Origins of European Thought.* 2d ed. Cambridge.

Ortner, S. 1974. "Is Female to Male as Nature Is to Culture?" In Rosaldo
and Lamphere 1974, 67–87.

Owen, A. S., ed. 1939. *Euripides, Ion.* Oxford.

Padel, R. 1974. "Imagery of the Elsewhere: Two Choral Odes of Euripides." *CQ* 24:227–42.

———. 1983. "Women: Model for Possession by Greek Daemons." In
Images of Women in Antiquity, 3–19. Ed. A. Cameron and A. Kuhrt.
London.

———. 1990. "Making Space Speak." In Winkler and Zeitlin 1990,
336–65.

Parker, R. 1983. *Miasma: Pollution and Purification in Early Greek
Religion.*

———. 1987. "Myths of Early Athens." In *Interpretations of Greek Mythology,* 187–214. Ed. J. Bremmer. London.

Parmentier, L., and H. W. Grégoire, eds. 1965. *Euripide.* Vol. 3. [Budé.]
Paris.

Parry, H. 1966. "The Second Stasimon of Euripides' *Hippolytus* 732–75." *TAPA* 97:317–26.

Peek, W. 1955. *Griechische Vers-Inscriften*. Vol. 1. *Grab-Epigramme*. Berlin.

Pellizer, E. 1982. *Favole d'identità, favole di paura: Storie di caccia e altri racconti della Grecia antica*. Rome.

Pembroke, S. 1965. "The Last of the Matriarchs: A Study in the Inscriptions of Lycia." *Journal of Economic and Social History of the Orient* 8/3:217–47.

———. 1967. "Women in Charge: The Functions of Alternatives in Early Greek Tradition and the Ancient Idea of Matriarchy." *Journal of the Warburg and Courtauld Institutes* 30:1–35.

———. 1970. "Locres et Tarente: Le rôle des femmes dans la fondation de deux colonies grecques." *Annales ESC* 25:1240–70.

Peradotto, J. J. 1977. "Oedipus and Erichthonius: Some Observations on Paradigmatic and Syntagmatic Order." *Arethusa* 10:85–102.

———. 1993. "The Social Control of Sexuality: Odyssean Dialogics." *Arethusa* 26:173–82.

Peretti, A. 1956. "La teoria della generazione patrilinea in Eschilo." *PP* 49:241–62.

Pestalozza, U. 1964. "Generationi e rinascite umane nell' Egitto e nell' Ellade." In *Nuovi saggi di religione mediterranea*, 567–78. Florence.

Petre, Z. 1979. "Un âge de la représentation—artifice et image dans la pensée grecque du VIe Av. N. E." *Revue roumaine d'histoire* 2:245–57.

———. 1980. Astoxenoi: À propos du statut des femmes dans la cité d'Eschyle." *Revue roumaine d'histoire* 19:173–81.

———. 1986. "Le décret des *Suppliantes* d'Eschyle." *Studi clasice* 24:25–32.

Philippson, P. 1936. *Genealogie als mythische Form*. Oslo.

Picard, C. 1931. "Les luttes primitives d'Athènes et d'Eleusis." *Revue historique* 165:1–76.

Pickard-Cambridge, A. 1988 [1927]. *The Dramatic Festivals of Athens*. 2d ed. Revised by J. Gould and D. M. Lewis. Oxford.

Pigeaud, J. 1976. "Euripide et la connaissance de soi: Quelques réflexions sur *Hippolyte* 73 à 82 et 373 à 430." *LEC* 44:3–24.

Podlecki, A. 1975. "Reconstructing an Aeschylean Trilogy." *BICS* 22:2–8.

Porzig, W. 1926. *Aischylos: Die attische Tragödie*. Leipzig.

Prier, R. A. 1976. *Archaic Logic: Symbol and Structure in Heraclitus, Parmenides, and Empedocles*. The Hague and Paris.

———. 1989. *Thauma Idesthai: The Phenomenology of Sight and Appearance in Archaic Greek*. Tallahassee.

Privitera, G. A. 1967. "La rete di Afrodite: Ricerche sulla prima ode di Saffo." *QUCC* 4:11–41.

———. 1970. *Dioniso in Omero e nella poesia greca arcaica.* Rome.

———. 1974. *La rete di Afrodite: Studi su Saffo.* Palermo.

Pucci, P. 1977. *Hesiod and the Language of Poetry.* Baltimore.

———. 1980. *The Violence of Pity in Euripides "Medea."* Ithaca, N.Y.

———. 1987. *Odysseus Polutropos: Intertextual Readings in the "Odyssey" and the "Iliad."* Ithaca.

Rabinowitz, N. S. 1981. "From Force to Persuasion: Aeschylus' *Oresteia* as Cosmogonic Myth." *Ramus* 10:159–91.

———. 1987. "Female Speech and Female Sexuality: Euripides' *Hippolytos* as Model." *Helios* n.s 13:127–40.

Radermacher, L. 1916. *Hippolytus und Thekla. Sitzungsberichte der Akademie der Wissenschaft in Wien* 182.3.

Ramnoux, C. 1959. *La Nuit et les enfants de la Nuit dans la tradition grecque.* Paris.

———. 1962. *Mythologie ou la famille olympienne.* Paris.

Rankin, A. V. 1974. "Euripides' Hippolytus: A Psychopathological Hero." *Arethusa* 7:71–94.

Rau, P. 1967. *Paratragodia: Untersuchung einer komischen Form des Aristophanes.* Munich.

———. 1975. "Das Tragödienspiel in den 'Thesmophoriazusen.'" In *Aristophanes und die alte Komödie,* 339–56. Ed. H.-J. Newiger. Wege der Forschung 265. Darmstadt.

Reckford, K. J. 1972. "Phaethon, Hippolytus, and Aphrodite." *TAPA* 103:405–32.

———. 1974. "Phaedra and Pasiphae: The Pull Backward." *TAPA* 104:307–28.

———. 1985. "Concepts of Demoralization in the *Hecuba.*" In Burian 1985, 112–28.

Reece, S. 1993. *The Stranger's Welcome: Oral Theory and the Aesthetics of the Homeric Hospitality Scene.* Ann Arbor.

Reik, T. 1960. *The Creation of Woman.* New York.

Richardson, N. J. 1974. *The Homeric Hymn to Demeter.* Oxford.

Robertson, D. S. 1924. "The End of the *Supplices* Trilogy of Aeschylus." *CR* 38:51–53.

Robertson, N. 1985. "The Origin of the Panathenaea." *RhM* 128:231–95.

Rode, J. 1965. *Untersuchungen zur Form des aischyleischen Chorlieds.* Tübingen.

Rösler, W. 1992. "Danaos à propos des dangers de l'amour: Eschyle, *Suppliantes,* 991–1013." *Pallas* 38:173–78.

Rogers, B. 1904. *The* Thesmophoriazousae *of Aristophanes.* London.

Rohde, E. 1913. *Der griechische Roman und seine Vorlaüfer.* 3d ed. Leipzig.

———. 1925. *Psyche.* 8th ed. Trans. W. B. Hillis. New York.

Romilly, J. de. 1973. "Gorgias et le pouvoir de la poésie." *JHS* 93: 155–62.

Rorscher, W. H. 1897–1909. *Ausführliches Lexikon der griechischen und römischen Mythologie.* 5 vols. Leipzig.

Rosaldo, M. Z., and L. Lamphere, eds. 1974. *Women, Culture, and Society.* Stanford.

Roscalla, Fabio. 1988. "La descrizione del sé e dell'altro: Api ed alveare da Esiodo a Semonide." *QUCC* 29:23–47.

Rose, M. A. 1979. *Parody/Metafiction.* London.

Rosellini, M. 1979. "Lysistrata: Une mise en scène de la féminité." In Auger, Rosellini, and Saïd 1979, 11–32.

Rosenmeyer, T. 1955. "Gorgias, Aeschylus, and *Apate.*" *AJP* 76:225–60.

Rosivach, V. 1977. "Earthborn and Olympians: The Parodos of the *Ion.*" *CQ* 27:284–94.

Rudhardt, J. 1958. *Notions fondamentales de la pensée religieuse et actes constitutifs du culte dans la Grèce classique.* Geneva.

———. 1982. "De l'inceste dans la mythologie grecque." *Revue française de psychanalyse* 46:731–63.

———. 1986. "Pandora: Hésiode et les femmes." *MH* 43:231–46.

Russo, C. 1962. *Aristofane, autore di teatro.* Florence.

Russo, J., M. Fernandez-Galliano, and A. Heubeck. 1992. *A Commentary on Homer's "Odyssey."* Vol. 3. Oxford.

Sabbatucci, D. 1965. *Saggio sul misticismo greco.* Rome.

Saïd, S. 1979. "L'Assemblée des Femmes": Les femmes, l'économie et la politique." In Auger, Rosellini, and Saïd 1979, 33–69.

———. 1985. *Sophiste et tyran ou le problème du Prométhée enchaîné.* Paris.

———. 1987. "Travestis et travestissements dans les comédies d'Aristophane." *CGITA* 3:217–46.

Saintillan, D. 1987. "Le discours tragique sur la vengeance: Remarques sur la complémentarité des Charites et des Erinyes dans le mythe et la tragédie." *CGITA* 3:179–96.

———. 1995. *Du festin à l'échange: Les grâces de Pandore.* In Blaise, Judet de la Combe, and Rousseau 1995.

Sale, W. 1977. *Existentialism and Euripides: Sickness, Tragedy and Divinity in the* Medea, *the* Hippolytus, *and the* Bacchae. *Ramus* monographs. Victoria, Australia.

Salingar, L. 1974. *Shakespeare and the Traditions of Comedy.* Cambridge.

Sansone, D. 1975. *Aeschylean Metaphors for Intellectual Activities.* Wiesbaden.

Saxenhouse, A. 1986. "Myths and the Origins of Cities: Reflections on the Autochthony Theme in Euripides' *Ion*." In Euben 1986, 252–73.

Scarpi, P. 1976. *Letture sulla religione classica: L'inno omerico a Demeter: Elementi per una tipologia del mito*. Florence.

Schäfer, G. 1974. "Zum Typ *Anax Anakton* bei Aischylos *Hiket*. 524, *Pers*. 666, 675, 681: König der Könige, Lied der Lieder." In *Wege zur Aischylos*, 390–402. Ed. H. Hommel. Darmstadt.

Schlesier, R. 1989. "Die Bakchen des Hades: Dionysische Aspekte von Euripides' *Hekabe*." *Mètis* 3:111–35.

———. 1993. "Mixtures of Masks: Maenads as Tragic Models." In Carpenter and Faraone 1993, 89–114.

Schlesinger, E. 1933. *Die griechische Asylie*. Giessen.

Schmiel, R. 1972. "Telemachus in Sparta." *TAPA* 103:463–72.

Schmitt-Pantel, P. 1977. "Athéna Apatouria et la ceinture: Les aspects féminins des Apatouries à Athènes." *Annales ESC* 32:1059–73.

———. 1992. *La cité au banquet: Histoire des repas publics dans les cités grecques*. Collection de L'Ecole Française de Rome 157. Rome.

Schreckenberg, H. 1964. *Ananke*. Munich.

Schwabl, H. 1966. *Hesiods Theogonie: Eine unitarische Analyse*. Vienna.

Schwartz, M., and C. Kahn, eds. 1980. *Representing Shakespeare*. Baltimore.

Schwinge, E.-R., ed. 1968. *Euripides*. Wege der Forschung 89. Darmstadt.

Scodel, R. 1980. *The Trojan Trilogy of Euripides. Hypomnemata*. Vol. 60. Göttingen.

Seaford, R. 1981. "Dionysiac Drama and the Dionysiac Mysteries." *CQ* 31:252–75.

———. 1982. "The Date of Euripides' *Cyclops*." *JHS* 102:161–72.

———. 1987. "The Tragic Wedding." *JHS* 107:106–30.

Séchan, L. 1911. "La légende d'Hippolyte dans l'antiquité." *REG* 24:105–51.

Segal, C. 1962. "Gorgias and the Psychology of the Logos." *HSCP* 66:99–155.

———. 1965. "The Tragedy of the *Hippolytus:* The Waters of Ocean and the Untouched Meadow." *HSCP* 70:117–69. Rpt. in Segal 1986, 165–221.

———. 1969. "Euripides, *Hippolytus* 108–12: Tragic Irony and Tragic Justice." *Hermes* 97:297–305.

———. 1970. "Shame and Purity in Euripides' *Hippolytus*." *Hermes* 98:278–99.

———. 1971. "The Two Worlds of Euripides' *Helen*." *TAPA* 102:553–614. Rpt. in Segal 1986, 222–67.

———. 1978. "Pentheus and Hippolytus on the Couch and on the Grid:

Psychoanalytic and Structural Readings of Greek Tragedy." *CW* 72:
129–48. Rpt. in Segal 1986, 268–93.

———. 1979. "Solar Imagery and Tragic Heroism in Euripides' *Hippolytus.*" In *Arktouros: Hellenic Studies Presented to B. M. W. Knox,*
151–61. Ed. G. Bowersock, W. Burkert, and M. Putnam. Berlin and
New York.

———. 1982. *Dionysiac Poetics and Euripides'* Bacchae. Princeton.

———. 1983. "*Kleos* and Its Ironies in the *Odyssey.*" *L'antiquité classique* 52:2–47.

———. 1986. *Interpreting Greek Tragedy: Myth, Poetry, Text.* Ithaca,
N.Y.

Sfameni-Gasparro, G. 1986. *Misteri e culti mistici di Demetra.* Rome.

Shapiro, H. A. 1980. "Jason's Cloak." *TAPA* 110:263–86.

———. 1993. *Personification: The Representations of Abstract Concepts
600–400* B.C. Kilchberg and Zurich.

Shaw, M. 1975. "The Female Intruder: Women in Fifth-Century Drama."
CP 70:255–66.

Sicherl, M. 1986. "Die Tragik der Danaiden." *MH* 43:81–110.

Simon, G. 1988. *Le regard, l'être et l'apparence.* Paris.

Sissa, G. 1987. *Le corps virginal.* Paris. = *Greek Virginity.* Trans.
A. Goldhammer. Cambridge, Mass., 1990.

Slater, N. 1990. "The Idea of the Actor." In Winkler and Zeitlin 1990,
385–96.

Slater, P. 1968. *The Glory of Hera: Greek Mythology and the Greek
Family.* Boston.

Smoot, J. J. 1976. "Hippolytus as Narcissus: An Amplification." *Arethusa*
9:35–51.

Snell, B. 1928. *Aischylos und das Handeln im Drama. Phil. Supp.* 20–21.

———. 1953. "Aristophanes and Aesthetic Criticism." In *The Discovery
of the Mind: The Greek Origins of European Thought,* 113–35.
Trans. T. Rosenmeyer. Cambridge, Mass.

———. 1967. *Scenes from Greek Drama.* Berkeley.

Solmsen, F. 1932. "Zur Gestaltung des Intriguenmotivs in den Tragödien
des Sophokles und Euripides." *Phil.* 84:1–17. Also in Schwinge
1968, 326–44.

———. 1934. "*Onoma* and *Pragma* in Euripides' *Helen.*" *CR* 48:
119–21.

———. 1949. *Hesiod and Aeschylus.* Ithaca, N.Y.

Sommerstein, A. H. 1977. "Notes on Aeschylus' *Suppliants.*" *BICS* 24:
67–82.

———., ed. 1989. *Aeschylus,* Eumenides. Cambridge.

Sorböm, G. 1966. *Mimesis and Art.* Uppsala.

Sourvinou-Inwood, C. 1988. *Studies in Girls' Transitions: Aspects of the Arkteia and Age Representation in Attic Iconography.* Athens.

Stanford, W. B., ed. 1961. *The "Odyssey" of Homer.* 2d ed. 2 vols. London.

Starobinski, J. 1975. "Inside and Outside." *Hudson Review* 28:333–51. = "'Je haïs comme les portes d'Hadès.'" *Nouvelle revue de psychanalyse* 9 (1974): 7–22.

Stewart, S. 1979. *Nonsense: Aspects of Intertextuality in Folklore and Literature.* Baltimore.

Strohm, H. 1949–50. "Trug und Täuschung in der euripideischen Dramatik." *Würzburger Jahrbücher für die Altertumswissenschaft* 4: 140–56. Also in Schwinge 1968, 345–72.

Sussman, L. 1984. "Workers and Drones: Labor, Idleness and Gender Definition in Hesiod's Beehive." In *Women in the Ancient World: The Arethusa Papers,* 79–94. Ed. J. Peradotto and J. P. Sullivan. Albany.

Sutton, D. F. 1980. *The Greek Satyr Play.* Meisenheim am Glan.

Suzuki, M. 1989. *Metamorphoses of Helen: Authority, Difference, and the Epic.* Ithaca, N.Y.

Svenbro, J. 1976. *La parole et le marbre: Aux origines de la poétique grecque.* Lund.

Taaffe, L. 1993. *Aristophanes and Women.* London.

Taillardat, J. 1965. *Les images d'Aristophane.* Paris.

Tanner, T. 1979. *Adultery in the Novel: Contract and Transgression.* Baltimore.

Taplin, O. 1978. *Greek Tragedy in Action.* Berkeley.

———. 1987. "Classical Phallology, Iconographic Parody and Potted Aristophanes." *PCPS* 33:92–104.

———. 1993. *Comic Angels and Other Approaches to Greek Drama through Vase Paintings.* Oxford.

Tarkow, T. 1984. "Tragedy and Transformation: Parent and Child in Euripides' *Hecuba.*" *Maia* 36:123–36.

Thomson, G. 1935. "Mystical Allusions in the *Oresteia.*" *JHS* 55: 20–34.

———. 1946. *Aeschylus and Athens.* 2d ed. London.

———. 1965. *Studies in Ancient Greek Society.* New York.

———. 1966. *Aeschylus and Athens.* 3d ed. London.

Thomson, George, [and Walter Headlam], eds. 1966. *The* Oresteia *of Aeschylus.* 2d ed. 2 vols. Amsterdam.

Thornton, A. 1970. *People and Themes in Homer's "Odyssey."* London.

Tierney, M. 1937. "The Mysteries and the *Oresteia.*" *JHS* 57:11–21.

———, ed. 1946. *Euripides:* Hecuba. Dublin.

Trenkner, S. 1958. *The Greek Novella in the Classical Period.* Cambridge.

Tschiedel, H. J. 1969. *Phaedra und Hippolytus: Variationen eines tragischen Konflicts.* Warnsdorf.

Turato, F. 1974. "L'*Ippolito* di Euripide tra realtà e suggestioni di fuga." *BIFG* 1:136–63.

———. 1976. "Seduzioni della parola e dramma dei segni nell' *Ippolito* di Euripide." *BIFG* 3:159–83.

Turner, V. 1962. "Three Symbols of Passage in Ndembu Circumcision Ritual: An Interpretation." In *Essays on the Ritual of Social Relations.* Ed. Max Gluckman. Manchester.

———. 1967. *The Forest of Symbols.* Ithaca, N.Y., and London.

———. 1969. *The Ritual Process: Structure and Anti-Structure.* Chicago.

———. 1974. *Drama, Fields, and Metaphors.* Ithaca, N.Y.

Tyrrell, W. 1984. *Amazons: A Study in Athenian Mythmaking.* Baltimore.

Untersteiner, M. 1954. *The Sophists.* Trans. K. Freeman. Oxford.

Verdenius, W. J. 1985. *A Commentary on Hesiod:* Works and Days, *vv. 1–382.* Leiden.

Vernant, J.-P. 1969. "Hestia-Hermès: Sur l'expression religieuse de l'espace and du mouvement chez les Grecs." In *Mythe et pensée chez les Grecs: Etude de psychologie historique,* 97–143. 2d ed. Paris. Rev. and enlarged ed., 1971, rpt. 1985. = "Hestia-Hermes: The Religious Expression of Space and Movement among the Greeks." Trans. H. Piat. *Social Sciences Information* 8/4 (1969): 131–68.

———. 1979a. "Naissances d'images." In J.-P. Vernant, *Religions, histoires, raisons,* 105–37. Paris. = "The Birth of Images," in Vernant 1991, 164–85.

———. 1979b. "A la table des hommes: Mythe de fondation du sacrifice chez Hésiode." In Detienne and Vernant 1979, 37–132. = Detienne and Vernant 1989, 21–86, 224–37.

———. 1980. *Myth and Society in Ancient Greece.* Trans. J. Lloyd. Atlantic Highlands, N.J. = *Mythe et société en Grèce ancienne.* Paris, 1974.

"City-State Warfare," 19–44. Referred to as 1980, "Warfare."

"Marriage," 45–70. Referred to as 1980, "Marriage."

"Between the Beasts and the Gods," 130–67. Referred to as 1980, "Beasts and Gods."

"The Myth of Prometheus," 168–85. Referred to as 1980, "Prometheus."

———. 1981a. "Tensions and Ambiguities in Greek Tragedy." In Vernant and Vidal-Naquet 1981, 6–27.

———. 1981b. "Intimations of the Will in Greek Tragedy." In Vernant and Vidal-Naquet 1981, 28–62.

———. 1981c. "Ambiguity and Reversal: On the Enigmatic Structure of *Oedipus Rex.*" In Vernant and Vidal-Naquet 1981, 87–119.

———. 1981d. *Annuaire du Collège de France, 1979–80: Résumé des cours et travaux*, 453–66. Paris. = Vernant 1990, 118–36.

———. 1990. *Figures, idoles, masques*. Paris.

———. 1991. *Mortals and Immortals: Collected Essays*. Ed. F. I. Zeitlin. Princeton.

———. 1995. "Les semblances de Pandora." In Blaise, Judet de la Combe, and Rousseau 1995.

Vernant, J.-P., and P. Vidal-Naquet. 1981. *Tragedy and Myth in Ancient Greece*. Trans. J. Lloyd. Atlantic Highlands, N.J. Rpt. with vol. 2 (1986). New York, 1988. = *Mythe et tragédie en Grèce ancienne*. Paris, 1972.

Verrall, A. W. 1895. *Euripides the Rationalist*. Cambridge.

Versnel, H. 1994. "What Is Sauce for the Goose Is Sauce for the Gander: Myth and Ritual, Old and New." In *Inconsistencies in Greek and Roman Religion II: Transition and Reversal in Myth and Ritual*, 15–88. Leiden and New York.

Vian, Francis. 1952. *La guerre des Géants: Le mythe avant l'époque hellénistique*. Paris.

Vickers, Brian. 1973. *Towards Greek Tragedy*. London.

Vidal-Naquet, P. 1981a. "Hunting and Sacrifice in Aeschylus' *Oresteia*." In Vernant and Vidal-Naquet 1981, 150–74.

———. 1981b. "Sophocles' *Philoctetes* and the *Ephebeia*." In Vernant and Vidal-Naquet 1981, 175–91.

———. 1986a. *The Black Hunter: Forms of Thought and Forms of Society in the Greek World*. Trans. A. Szegedy-Maszak. Baltimore and London. = *Le chasseur noir: Formes de pensée et formes de société dans le monde grec*. Paris, 1981.

"The Black Hunter and the Origin of the Athenian *Ephebia*," 106–28. Referred to as 1986a, "Black Hunter."

"Land and Sacrifice in the *Odyssey*," 15–38. Referred to as 1986a, "Land and Sacrifice."

"Recipes for Greek Adolescence," 129–56. Referred to as 1986a, "Recipes."

"Slavery and the Rule of Women in Tradition, Myth, and Utopia," 205–23. Referred to as 1986a, "Slavery."

———. 1986b. "The Black Hunter Revisited." *PCPS* 212:126–44.

Villanueva Puig, M.-C. 1986. "A propos des Thyiades de Delphes." In Ecole de Rome, *L'association dionysiaque dans les sociétés anciennes: Actes de la table ronde organisée par l'Ecole Française de Rome, Rome 24–25 Mai 1984*, 31–51. Rome.

Vogel, C. J. de. 1966. *Pythagoras and Early Pythagoreanism*. Assen.

Vries, J. D. de. 1956. *Altgermanische Religionsgeschichte*. 2 vols. Berlin.

Vürtheim, J. 1928. *Aischylos: Schutzflehende.* Amsterdam.

Walcot, P. 1958. "Hesiod's Hymns to the Muses, Aphrodite, Styx and Hecate." *SO* 34:5–14.

Walsh, G. 1978. "The Rhetoric of Birthright and Race in Euripides' *Ion.*" *Hermes* 106:301–15.

———. 1984. *The Varieties of Enchantment: Early Greek Views on the Nature and Function of Poetry.* Chapel Hill, N.C.

Wasserman, F. 1940. "Divine Violence and Providence in Euripides' *Ion.*" *TAPA* 71:587–604.

Webster, T. B. L. 1939. "Greek Theories of Art and Literature Down to 400 B.C." *CQ* 33:166–79.

———. 1967. *The Tragedies of Euripides.* London.

Wehrli, F. 1969. *Klearchos.* 2d ed. Basel and Stuttgart.

West, M. L., ed. 1966. *Hesiod's* Theogony. Oxford.

Whitman, C. 1964. *Aristophanes and the Comic Hero.* Cambridge, Mass.

———. 1974. *Euripides and the Full Circle of Myth.* Cambridge, Mass.

Whittle, E. W. 1964a. "Two Notes on Aeschylus' *Supplices.*" *CQ* n.s. 14: 24–31.

———. 1964b. "An Ambiguity in Aeschylus, *Supplices* 315." *C&M* 25: 1–7.

Wilkens, K. 1974. *Die Interdependenz zwischen Tragödienstruktur und Theologie bei Aischylos.* Munich.

Willink, C. W. 1968. "Some Problems of Text and Interpretation in the *Hippolytus,* 373–432." *CQ* 18:11–43.

Wilson, J. A. 1946. "Egypt." In *Before Philosophy: The Intellectual Adventure of Ancient Man,* 39–136. Ed. H. Frankfort, H. A. Frankfort, J. A. Wilson, and T. Jacobsen. Chicago.

Winkler, J. J. 1990. "The Ephebes' Song: *Tragōdia* and *Polis.*" In Winkler and Zeitlin 1990, 20–62.

Winkler, J. J., and F. I. Zeitlin, eds. 1990. *Nothing to Do with Dionysos? Athenian Drama in Its Social Context.* Princeton.

Winnington-Ingram, R. P. 1948. "Clytemnestra and the Vote of Athena." *JHS* 68:130–47. Rev. version in Winnington-Ingram 1983, 101–31.

———. 1960a. "Hippolytus: A Study in Causation." *Euripide: Entretiens sur l'antiquité classique* 6:169–97.

———. 1960b. "The Danaid Trilogy of Aeschylus." *JHS* 81:141–72. Revised version in Winnington-Ingram 1983, 55–72.

———. 1983. *Studies in Aeschylus.* Cambridge.

Wohlberg, J. 1968. "The Palace-Hero Equation in Euripides." *AAntHung* 16:149–55.

Wolff, C. 1963. "The Design and Myth in Euripides' *Ion.*" *HSCP* 69: 169–94.

———. 1973. "On Euripides' *Helen.*" *HSCP* 77:61–84.

Woodhouse, W. J. 1930. *The Composition of Homer's "Odyssey."* Oxford.

Worman, N. 1994. "The Persuasion of Style: Helen and Odysseus in Court and Theater." Diss. Princeton.

Zeitlin, F. I. 1966. "Postscript to Sacrificial Imagery in the *Oresteia, Ag.* 1235–37." *TAPA* 97:645–53.

———. 1982a. *Under the Sign of the Shield: Semiotics and Aeschylus' Seven against Thebes.* Rome.

———. 1982b. "Cultic Models of the Female: Rites of Dionysus and Demeter." *Arethusa* 15:129–58.

———. 1986a. "Thebes: Theater of Self and Society." In Euben 1986, 101–41. Also in Winkler and Zeitlin 1990, 130–67.

———. 1986b. "Configurations of Rape in Greek Myth." In *Rape*, 122–151, 261–64. Ed. S. Tomaselli and R. Porter. Oxford.

———. 1988. "La politique d'Eros: Féminin et masculin dans les *Suppliantes* d'Eschyle," *Mètis* 3:230–59.

———. 1990. "Patterns of Gender in Aeschylean Drama: The *Seven against Thebes* and the Danaid Trilogy." In *Cabinet of the Muses: Essays on Classical and Comparative Literature in Honor of Thomas G. Rosenmeyer,* 103–15. Ed. M. Griffith and D. J. Mastronarde. Atlanta.

———. 1993a. "Staging Dionysus between Thebes and Athens." In Carpenter and Faraone 1993, 147–82.

———. 1993b. "The Artful Eye: Vision, Ekphrasis, and Spectacle in Euripidean Theatre." In *Art and Text in Ancient Greek Culture,* 138–96, 295–305. Ed. S. Goldhill and R. Osborne. Cambridge.

Zintzen, C. 1960. *Analytisches Hypomnema zu Senecas Phaedra.* Meisenheim am Glan.

Zuntz, G. 1960. "On Euripides' *Helena*: Theology and Irony." *Euripide: Entretiens sur l'antiquité classique* 6:201–27.

INDEX OF KEY PASSAGES

GENERAL INDEX

Acharnians (Aristophanes), 387
Achilles, 20, 29n.26, 179n.19; ghost's demand for Polyxena's sacrifice, 175, 206; quarrel with Odysseus, 36n.41; shield of, 324; tomb of, 174, 175
Actaeon, 282–83, 283n.11
Adam and Eve, 53, 57, 60–61, 70, 71
adoption, 335, 335n.135, 337
Adrestos, 179
adultery: of Aphrodite and Ares, 33–41; *moicheia,* 32n.31; in *Odyssey,* 32–34; of wife, 240, 241n.49
Aegisthus, 92, 150
Aelian, 215n.75
Aeschylus, 12, 87, 384n.15; *Agamemnon,* 63n.18, 91–93, 201, 263n; *Amymone,* 163, 163n.108; appearance in Aristophanes' *Frogs,* 366–67, 381n; *Choephoroi,* 93, 94–97, 98–100, 358; Danaid trilogy, 12–13, 123–71; *Eumenides,* 87, 93–94, 100, 101–2, 116–17; *Lykourgeia,* 178; *Oresteia,* 8, 87–119, 162, 164, 168–71; *Prometheus Bound,* 156, 157; *Seven against Thebes,* 271, 366–67; *Suppliants,* 124, 168. *See also individual titles*
aetiologies. *See* origins, myths of
agalma (statue, adornment), 57n.5, 240, 259, 264, 373. *See also* statue

Agamemnon, 92, 174, 179, 183, 192n.45, 200, 360; and Cassandra, 92, 174, 175, 192n.45, 201, 202, 203, 204–5, 211, 212n.70; and Clytemnestra, 12, 92, 212n.70; Hekabe supplicating, 192, 192n.45, 195, 201, 202, 203, 204–5, 206, 211; Polymestor on death of, 194; views Polydoros's body, 188, 189–90; on women as untrustworthy, 29, 48. *See also Hekabe; Odyssey; Oresteia*
Agamemnon (Aeschylus), 63n.18, 201, 263n; carpet scene, 92–93; Clytemnestra in, 91–92. *See also Oresteia*
Agathon (tragic poet), 372–73, 378, 383–84, 384n.15, 386, 401–2
Agave, 344, 352
aidōs (shame, reticence): dual meaning of, 253, 253n; Hekabe's appeal to, 206; lack of as reason for blinding, 191, 191n.42; of Phaedra, 219, 221; as tending Hippolytos's meadow, 241; and veiling the head, 245, 245n.57
aischrologia (shameful talk, obscenity), 405
Ajax (Sophocles), 350–51, 351.n.20, 359–60
akoitis (bedmate, wife), 28n.26

funerary rites, 211–12
Furies. *See* Erinyes

Gaia: and the castration of Kronos,
72; emergence after Chaos, 82, 83;
as giver of gifts, 60; Gorgon produced by, 323, 325n.112, 333–34;
as primordial principle of earth, 79;
Zeus's relation to, 73, 78, 79n.51
Gegeneis (the Earthborn), 299. *See
also* autochthony
gender: and abstract categories, 9; and
the body, 171–216; creation of, 83;
and divinities, 9; and genre, 378–
86; Greek system of, 3; and mimesis, 339–416; and paradigm, 17–
119; reversal of, 344–45, 363,
371; and selfhood, 217–338; as
standing for more abstract categories, 9; stage conventions regarding,
353–56; in *Thesmophoriazousae*
(Aristophanes), 375–416; and
tragedy, 363–74; transvestism, 377,
382–86. *See also* femininity;
masculinity
genealogy, 82–83, 102
Genesis (Bible), 53, 57, 57n.6, 60–61,
70, 71–72
genethlē (race, progeny), 63, 63n.18
Gennep, A. L. van, 99n.24
genos (race, clan, kinship), 61, 125,
155, 163. *See also* kinship
gērokomos (caretaker in old age), 58,
63n.18
Gigantomachy, 299, 299n.38, 300
Glaukos, 179
Glaukos Potnieus, 279, 279n.113
goddesses, 356; Charites, 55, 60n.12;
Great Goddess, 239n.45, 281n;
Hestia, 80n.56, 131n.22; split between mortal women and, 9, 83–
84. *See also individual names*
gods (immortals), 175, 211, 356; as
gendered, 9; Hades, 10, 172; Helios,
327, 329, 330, 348; mating with
mortals, 160–61; Pandora and, 62,
71, 72–74, 83, 83n.63, 86; pan-

theon in Homer and Hesiod, 110.
See also individual names
Goldman, M., 291n.15
Gorgias (sophist), 137n.37, 276n,
399, 413–15
Gorgias (Plato), 370
Gorgon: Gaia's production of, 323,
325n.112, 333–34; poison of, 299,
303, 310, 320–22
Gould, J., 141n.48
Gouldner, A., 291n.15
Graces (Charites), 55, 60n.12
Great Goddess, 239n.45, 281n
Griffin, J., 19

Hades, 10, 172
hagneia/hagnos (purity), 128,
128n.13, 129–30, 241–42. *See also*
purity and pollution
Hall, E., 395n.31
Hanson, A., 65n.21
harmozō (fit together), 229, 229n.24
Harris, Grace, 114
hearing, 261–64
Heath, M., 178
Hekabe, 6, 177, 183–84, 190, 198,
201, 202, 207, 214: cenotaph of,
174; choice of revenge, 188–89;
Danaids and Lemnian women compared to, 215; as daughter of Kisseus, 177, 177n.12, 180n.21; as
Erinys, 215, 216; Euripides on,
13, 172–216; and Hekate, 185,
185n.35; in Iliad, 179, 180; justice
for, 177–78, 206; killing Polymestor's children, 180–81, 199–200,
208; metamorphosis into a dog,
183–86; mother-daughter relationship, 200, 204–5, 207; mother-
son relationship, 193–94; Odysseus
supplicates in Troy, 196–97, 206;
Polydoros's body discovered by,
173, 187–88, 191, 203, 205;
Polymestor blinded by, 188–89,
191n.41, 196, 200, 208; Polymestor's prophecy regarding, 184–85,
189, 194; on Polyxena's sacrifice,